The Perception of the Environment

In this work Tim Ingold offers a persuasive new approach to understanding how human beings perceive their surroundings. He argues that what we are used to calling cultural variation consists, in the first place, of variations in skill. Neither innate nor acquired, skills are *grown*, incorporated into the human organism through practice and training in an environment. They are thus as much biological as cultural. To account for the generation of skills we have therefore to understand the dynamics of development. And this in turn calls for an ecological approach that situates practitioners in the context of an active engagement with the constituents of their surroundings.

The twenty-three essays comprising this book focus in turn on the procurement of livelihood, on what it means to 'dwell', and on the nature of skill, weaving together approaches from social anthropology, ecological psychology, developmental biology and phenomenology in a way that has never been attempted before. The book is set to revolutionise the way we think about what is 'biological' and 'cultural' in humans, about evolution and history, and indeed about what it means for human beings – at once organisms and persons – to *inhabit* an environment. *The Perception of the Environment* will be essential reading not only for anthropologists but also for biologists, psychologists, archaeologists, geographers and philosophers.

Tim Ingold is Professor of Social Anthropology at the University of Aberdeen.

The Perception of the Environment

Essays on livelihood, dwelling and skill

Tim Ingold

Routledge
Taylor & Francis Group

LONDON AND NEW YORK

For Anna and Susanna,
in memory of my mother,
L. M. Ingold (1910–1998)

First published 2000
by Routledge
Reissued with a new preface 2011
by Routledge
2 Park Square, Milton Park, Abingdon, Oxon OX14 4RN

Simultaneously published in the USA and Canada
by Routledge
711 Third Avenue, New York, NY 10017

Routledge is an imprint of the Taylor & Francis Group, an informa business

© 2000, 2011 Tim Ingold

Typeset in Garamond by Florence Production Ltd, Stoodleigh, Devon
Printed and bound in Great Britain by
CPI Antony Rowe, Chippenham, Wiltshire

British Library Cataloguing in Publication Data
A catalogue record for this book is available from the British Library

Library of Congress Cataloging in Publication Data
A catalogue record for this book has been requested.

ISBN13: 978–0–415–61747–5 (pbk)

Contents

Chapter Twenty-three
**The poetics of tool-use: from technology, language and intelligence
to craft, song and imagination** 406

Figures

Acknowledgements

I am a perpetual student of anthropology, taught largely by those whom I am supposed to have been teaching. And no-one could have had a more inspiring set of teachers than the group of research students with whom I have had the privilege to work over the last ten years or so in the Department of Social Anthropology at Manchester University. This book is, in many ways, a summation of all I have learned from them, and with them. So here they are, with my thanks to each and every one: Stephanie Bunn, Sveinn Eggertsson, Ramsey Elkholy, James Leach, Claudia Gross, Wendy Gunn, Kawori Iguchi, Axel Köhler, Nuccio Mazzullo, Martin Ortlieb, Antonia Phinnemore, Amanda Ravetz, Javier Taks, Paul Towell, Nikolai Zhoukov.

Everyone who has ever visited Manchester University's Social Anthropology Department has the same thing to say about it. There is an extraordinary buzz about the place: a sense of intellectual adventure, of radical thinking, bold innovation, crackling debate, and above all, collegiality. Like everywhere else, the department has had its fair share of the ups and downs of British academic life. But all things considered, it has been a wonderful environment in which to work. I would like to take this opportunity to thank all my erstwhile colleagues in the department – over a period spanning a quarter of a century, from 1974 to 1999 – for their support, encouragement and criticism.

The book would never have been completed, however, had it not been for the award of a two-year Research Readership from the British Academy (1997–99). After a stint of over four years as head of department, which left me with little time or energy to put pen to paper, this award came as a godsend. It gave me that extra space I needed to think, read and write. At a time when genuine scholarship has been squeezed into the margins of academic life, the kind of support offered by the British Academy is more vital than ever. I would particularly like to thank the Academy's ever-helpful Assistant Secretary for Research, Ken Emond.

In September 1999, only months before completing this book, I left Manchester to take up a newly-established Chair of Social Anthropology at the University of Aberdeen. Thus the book was finished amidst the chaos of moving house and offices. For me, however, its completion marks not an ending but a new beginning, and I would like to extend my gratitude to Steve Bruce and his staff in the Department of Sociology at Aberdeen, and to the University's Principal, Duncan Rice, for making this possible.

Two scholars to whom I am particularly indebted for their inspiration and guidance are sadly no longer with us. They are Edward Reed and Alfred Gell. I offer this work as a tribute to them both. Many, many more friends and colleagues have, over the years, been generous with their ideas, and have done their best to educate me, point me in the right directions and suggest works I should read. They include: Barbara Adam, David

Anderson, Michael Bravo, Nurit Bird-David, Bjorn Bjerkli, Mary Bouquet, Ben Campbell, Juliet Clutton-Brock, Denis Cosgrove, Alan Costall, Akira Deguchi, Philippe Descola, Marcia-Anne Dobres, Robin Dunbar, Roy Ellen, Gillian Feeley-Harnik, Harvey Feit, Raymond Firth, Katsuyoshi Fukui, Maurice Godelier, Brian Goodwin, Peter Gow, Paul Graves-Brown, Robin Grove-White, Steven Gudeman, Mark Harris, John Haworth, Harry Heft, Mae-Wan Ho, Alf Hornborg, Mitsuo Ichikawa, Charles Keller, Heonik Kwon, Jean Lave, Ivan Leudar, David Lowenthal, Lye Tuck-Po, Bill McGrew, Kathleen Gibson, Mary Midgley, Kay Milton, Howard Morphy, Brian Morris, John Morton, Emiko Ohnuki-Tierney, Susan Oyama, Gisli Palsson, Bryan Pfaffenberger, Rik Pinxten, Alan Rayner, Paul Richards, Laura Rival, Sidsel Saugestad, Colin Scott, John Shotter, François Sigaut, Marilyn Strathern, Yutaka Tani, Luke Taylor, Christina Toren, David Turnbull, Eduardo Viveiros de Castro, Gerry Webster, James Weiner, Harvey Whitehouse, Peter Wilson, James Woodburn and Tom Wynn. My thanks to all.

I dedicate this book to three remarkable women: to my mother, Nora Ingold; to my wife, Anna Ingold; and to my daughter, Susanna Ingold. They have given me life, love and happiness. Who could ask for more?

The majority of the essays making up the book have been previously published. All have been more or less extensively revised for the present volume.

Chapter One was originally presented in the series of Linacre Lectures at the University of Oxford, and I thank Sir Bryan Cartledge for the invitation to deliver the lecture. It was first published in *Mind, brain and environment: the Linacre Lectures 1995–96*, edited by Bryan Cartledge (Oxford: Oxford University Press, 1998, pp. 158–80).

Chapter Two has evolved from a paper presented to the session on 'Nature and society: a contested interface', at the Third Conference of the European Association of Social Anthropologists, University of Oslo, June 1994. It was first published in *Nature and society: anthropological perspectives*, edited by Philippe Descola and Gisli Palsson (London: Routledge, 1996, pp. 25–44).

Chapter Three has its origins in a paper presented at the MOA International Symposium, 'Beyond nature and culture: cognition, ecology and domestication', held in Kyoto and Atami, Japan, in March 1992. I am grateful to Katsuyoshi Fukui for the invitation to attend the symposium. The paper was first published in *Redefining nature: ecology, culture and domestication*, edited by Roy Ellen and Katsuyoshi Fukui (Oxford: Berg, 1996, pp. 117–55), and is reproduced by permission.

The essay included here as Chapter Four was first presented to a conference organised by the Royal Society of Edinburgh on 'Animals and society: changing perspectives', in October 1991. It was published in the resulting volume, *Animals and human society: changing perspectives*, edited by Aubrey Manning and James Serpell (London: Routledge, 1994, pp. 1–22).

Chapter Five started life as a presentation to a conference of the Prehistoric Society on 'The origins and spread of agriculture and pastoralism in Eurasia', held at the Institute of Archaeology, University of London, in September 1993. It was first published in this form under the title 'Growing plants and raising animals: an anthropological perspective on domestication', in the conference volume, *The origins and spread of agriculture and pastoralism*, edited by David Harris (London: UCL Press, 1996, pp. 12–24). The essay was subsequently revised for presentation to the colloquium on 'cognitive aspects of early food production', organised by the Italian Institute for Philosophical Studies and the

Anthropological Museum of Naples, and held in Naples in March 1996. I am most grateful to Francesca Giusti for the invitation to contribute to the symposium.

Chapter Six actually began as an undergraduate lecture, and was subsequently presented (in Finnish) as a guest lecture to the Anthropological Society of Finland, Helsinki, in March 1995. It has however been completely rewritten for the present volume, and is published here for the first time.

A preliminary sketch for the essay that appears as Chapter Seven was presented to the Seventh International Conference on Hunting and Gathering Societies, held in Moscow in August 1993. I did not find time to write it up properly, however, until 1998, in response to a commission to contribute to a volume, entitled *Animal. Anima. Animus*, accompanying a highly innovative exhibition of the same name mounted by Pori Art Museum, Finland. The volume, edited by Marketta Seppälä, Jari-Pekka Vanhala and Linda Weintraub, was published by the Museum in 1998, and the essay (pp. 181–207) is reproduced here by permission.

Chapter Eight has evolved from a paper first presented to the session on 'Images of self and other' at the Eighth International Conference on Hunting and Gathering Societies, held at the National Museum of Ethnology, Osaka, Japan, in October 1998. It has not been published previously.

Chapter Nine began as one of a series of lectures presented to postgraduate students in psychology at the University of Manchester. It was subsequently published as a chapter in a book based on the series, entitled *Psychological research: innovative methods and strategies*, and edited by the series co-ordinator, John Howarth (London: Routledge, 1996, pp. 99–119).

The essay included here as Chapter Ten has a long history, and has gone through many versions. A rough sketch was presented to the workshop 'Constructing Environments', organised by the Biological and Social Anthropology Committee of the Royal Anthropological Institute, and held in London in January 1991. Later versions were presented to the graduate seminar of the Department of Social Anthropology at the University of Bergen, and to the seminars of the International Centre for Contemporary Cultural Research and the Department of Architecture at the University of Manchester. I then rewrote it once more for the opening session, entitled 'Shifting contexts', of the Fourth Decennial Conference of the Association of Social Anthropologists held at St Catherine's College, Oxford, in July 1993. The essay was first published in a volume of papers from the session, entitled *Shifting contexts: transformations in anthropological knowledge*, edited by Marilyn Strathern (London: Routledge, 1995, pp. 57–80).

Chapter Eleven was originally presented to the session 'Place, time and experience: interpreting prehistoric landscapes', at the Conference of the Theoretical Archaeology Group held at the University of Leicester in December 1991. I later rewrote it for a special issue of the journal *World Archaeology* on 'Conceptions of time and ancient society', under the editorship of Richard Bradley (Volume 25, 1993, pp. 152–74).

An early version of Chapter Twelve was presented to the Association of Social Anthropologists Conference on 'Environmentalism', held at the University of Durham in April 1992. It was published in the resulting volume, *Environmentalism: the view from anthropology*, edited by Kay Milton (London: Routledge, 1993, pp. 31–42).

The essays comprising Chapters Thirteen and Fourteen have been written especially for this volume.

Chapter Fifteen was originally written for presentation to the symposium on 'Doing things with tools', co-organised by Ed Reed and myself, and held as part of the Fourth

International Conference on Event Perception and Action, Trieste, Italy, in August 1987. It was subsequently published in the journal *Techniques et Culture* (Volume 12, 1988, pp. 151–76), and is reproduced here, in a substantially revised form, by permission of the Editor, Jean-Luc Jamard.

Chapter Sixteen is based on a paper originally presented to a comparative workshop on tool technology held at the University of Cambridge in November 1989, and first published in *Archaeological Review from Cambridge* (Volume 9, 1990, pp. 5–17). I later revised the paper for presentation to the Wenner-Gren International Symposium on 'Tools, language and intelligence: evolutionary implications', held in Cascais, Portugal, in March 1990. In this form it appeared under the title 'Tool-use, sociality and intelligence', in the symposium volume *Tools, language and cognition in human evolution*, edited by Kathleen Gibson and myself (Cambridge University Press, 1993, pp. 429–45). It has since been further revised, and is reproduced here by permission of Cambridge University Press.

Chapter Seventeen started life as an undergraduate lecture, and was subsequently rewritten for presentation to the Eleventh Annual Conference of the Association for Social Studies of Time, on 'Time and work', held at Dartington Hall, Devon, in July 1994. As it turned out, I was unable to attend the conference; however, I subsequently revised the paper for publication in the journal *Time and Society* (Volume 4, 1995, pp. 5–28). It is reprinted here by permission of Sage Publications Ltd.

I was encouraged to write the essay that now appears as Chapter Eighteen by Mary Butcher, in response to the superb exhibition on basketry and textiles, entitled 'Beyond the bounds', that she had assembled in the Righton Gallery of Manchester Metropolitan University, in March and April 1996. A much revised version of that original essay was recently published in a volume entitled *Mind, materiality and modern culture*, edited by Paul Graves-Brown (London: Routledge, 2000, pp. 50–71). It has been further revised for the present volume.

Chapter Nineteen overlaps, in part, with a paper presented to a seminar on 'The Anthropology of Technology', sponsored by the Amerind Foundation and held in Dragoon, Arizona, in October 1998. I am grateful to the Foundation and to Michael B. Schiffer for the invitation to contribute.

Much of the material for Chapter Twenty is drawn from a longer paper, 'Eight themes in the anthropology of technology', published in a special issue of the journal *Social Analysis* (Volume 4, 1997, pp. 106–38). This issue, edited by Penny Harvey, resulted from a series of seminars on 'Technology as skilled practice' held during 1995 and 1996 at the University of Manchester, and funded by the Economic and Social Research Council. I am grateful to the Council, and to Penny Harvey, for the opportunity to contribute to this exciting series, and to the editors of *Social Analysis* for permission to reproduce the material here.

Chapter Twenty-one started out as a paper presented to the symposium 'Man, ape, apeman: changing views since 1600', held as part of the Pithecanthropus Centennial (1893–1993) Congress on 'Human Evolution in its Ecological Context' at Leiden University, The Netherlands, in June 1993. It was first published in the conference publication, *Man, ape, apeman: changing views since 1600*, edited by Raymond Corbey and Bert Theunissen (Evaluative Proceedings of the Pithecanthropus Centennial congress, Volume IV, Leiden, 1995, pp. 241–62). A somewhat revised version was subsequently published in the journal *Cultural Dynamics* (Volume 7, 1995, pp. 187–214). It has been further revised here, and is reproduced by permission of Sage Publications Ltd.

The essay that appears as Chapter Twenty-two was first presented as the Jan Wind Memorial Lecture, at the Thirteenth Annual Meeting of the Language Origins Society, held in Pilsen, the Czech Republic, in July 1997. It was subsequently published in the journal *LOS Forum* (Number 25, 1997, pp. 21–38). I am grateful to the Society, and to its President, Bernard H. Bichakjian, for permission to publish a much revised version of the essay in this book.

Finally, Chapter Twenty-three was originally written as a final epilogue to the book *Tools, language and cognition in human evolution*, edited by Kathleen Gibson and myself (Cambridge University Press, 1993, pp. 449–72). I am grateful to Cambridge University Press for permission to reproduce it here in a revised form.

Tim Ingold
Aberdeen
March 2000

Preface to 2011 Reissue

It usually happens with books that by the time they are published and embark on a life of their own, their authors have already tired of them. For the writer, a book demands completion, yet thought carries on regardless. No sooner is one book finished, then, than another is on the way. With *The Perception of the Environment*, however, my experience did not quite follow the usual pattern. Perhaps because it was the culmination of over a decade's work, and perhaps because I felt that in writing it, I had at last found my own voice, the book has stayed with me. I have never forgotten the advice of the great sociologist, C. Wright Mills, that the good intellectual craftsman 'forms his own self in the perfection of his craft' (Mills 1959: 216). Although perfection is a horizon of attainment that no mortal can practically reach, I could nevertheless look back on *Perception* with the satisfaction of knowing that its author was myself, and not some academic persona that I had assumed for the sake of enacting the elaborate charade – with all its posturing and name-calling – that nowadays so commonly passes for scholarship. For all these reasons, I found it more difficult than usual to draw a line under the book and move on. Wherever I would try to go, it came along with me. And the more I tried, the more it seemed to me that I was merely repeating or footnoting what I had written already.

I had however embarked on a new stage in my academic career, having recently moved from the University of Manchester – my base for the previous quarter of a century – to take up a newly created post at the University of Aberdeen. My task there was to create a programme of teaching and research in anthropology, more or less from scratch. For the first few years this kept me so busy that I had little time to worry about where to go next with my own work. Gradually, however, a future began to take shape. Looking back, a key moment was a major international conference on hunting and gathering societies that I and my colleague, Alan Barnard, organised in Edinburgh in September 2002. The conference itself was a success, but it also forced me to admit what I already knew in my heart, that I was finished with hunter-gatherer studies. After more than two decades of comparative work, much of which is gathered together in the first part of *Perception* as well as in an earlier collection of essays on *The Appropriation of Nature* (Ingold 1986a), I realised that I had nothing more to contribute on the topic. I resolved, there and then, to turn my back on the anthropology of hunters and gatherers – a decision I have never regretted. At last I could move on, unfettered by expectations from the past. To anyone who asked me to give a lecture or write a book chapter on a subject relating to hunters and gatherers, I had my response. I was not working in that area any more! Instead, new opportunities for collaboration that had opened up with my move to Scotland drew me increasingly to three themes, all of which were derived from perhaps the most fundamental postulate of *Perception*, namely that 'the growth and development of the person … is to be understood relationally as a *movement along a way of life*' (p. 146). These themes were, first, the dynamics of pedestrian movement; secondly, the linearity of threads and traces; and thirdly, the creativity of practice.

When Hayden Lorimer, a cultural geographer then based at the University of Aberdeen, asked me to join with him in a project on hillwalking, I was more than happy to do so, and with the assistance of Katrin Anna Lund and Jo Vergunst, this developed into a much more wide-ranging and still continuing investigation of the ways in which human beings move around on foot (Ingold 2004, Ingold and Vergunst 2008). In walking, pedestrians thread their trails through the landscape, leaving traces as they go, but this is just one of many ways in which people make and work with lines of various sorts, including both traces and threads. Among the other ways are such activities as weaving, storytelling, drawing and writing. An invitation to present the 2003 Rhind Lectures of the Society of Antiquaries of Scotland gave me the opportunity to adumbrate a kind of anthropological archaeology of the line (Ingold 2007a). Artists and architects, of course, also work with lines. As my contribution to a three-year (2002–5) collaborative project with the School of Fine Art at the University of Dundee, and with the assistance of Wendy Gunn and Raymond Lucas, I began to explore a series of issues on which the interests of anthropology, archaeology, art and architecture converge – issues of design and making, materials and movements, sense and gesture, description and notation. For the last several years I have been teaching a course to advanced undergraduate students at the University of Aberdeen, entitled *The 4 As*, on precisely these issues (Ingold 2007b). Common to them all, however, is the nexus of perception, creativity and skill. How, I wondered, can we understand the creativity of skilled practices of line-making, such as walking, storytelling and drawing, which do not begin here or end there but keep on going, always overshooting whatever destinations might be thrown up in their paths? This question was at the top of our agenda when, in 2005, we hosted the annual conference of the Association of Social Anthropologists of the UK and the Commonwealth at the University of Aberdeen, on the theme of *Creativity and Cultural Improvisation* (Hallam and Ingold 2007). It remains at the core of my current work.

How have the arguments originally set out in *Perception* fared in the wake of these past ten years? Naturally, I have had my critics. One of the most outspoken was Derek Brereton. In a lengthy, two-part article in the *Journal of Critical Realism*, Brereton (2004) rebukes me for a host of sins, of which the most serious and pervasive is 'conflationism'. I am charged with refusing any distinction between self and other, person and environment, consciousness and the world, or more generally, between any one thing and another. This kind of criticism very often comes from those who can understand distinction and difference only in categorical terms, in a world of being in which everything that exists is given in its essential nature by intrinsic attributes, independently and in advance of its relations with anything else. My whole approach in *Perception*, of course, is against this. My claim is that persons and things do not exist as bounded entities, set aside from their surroundings, but rather arise, each as a nexus of creative growth and development within an unbounded and continually unfolding field of relations. This is not to say that they are undifferentiated, or that they all merge into a kind of blur. It is rather to argue that their differentiation is a function of their placement within the relational manifold – that is, of *positionality*. Whether we are speaking of the self, the person, mind or consciousness, its immersion in the manifold is precisely the source of its own differentiation (Ingold 2005a: 114–15). Eduardo Viveiros de Castro, a more friendly critic, similarly misrepresents my argument when, in a lecture delivered at the University of Cambridge, he took me to task for assuming 'that the fundamental or prototypical mode of relation is identity or sameness' (Viveiros de Castro 1998). Nowhere do I make such an assumption. To the contrary, I hold – as indeed does Viveiros de Castro – that things and persons are joined by their differences, whereas judgements of sameness or identity are founded upon the opposite premise of separation.

From a quite different angle, David Howes has launched a stinging critique of my approach to understanding the role of the senses in perception. In his recent book *Sensual Relations*, Howes declares that the very worst thing that anthropologists could do is base their analyses on the models of 'perceptual systems' proposed by psychologists such as James Gibson or philosophers such as Maurice Merleau-Ponty (Howes 2003: 49–50). It is obvious whom he has in his sights here! For Howes, anyone interested in vision and how it works, myself included, is automatically guilty of 'epistemological imperialism' (2003: 239–40, fn. 8). The accusation is bizarre, to say the least. Eyesight is obviously important to most human beings everywhere, and to accuse anyone who chooses to write about it of having succumbed to visualism is about as absurd as banning research on human toolmaking and tool-use on the grounds that it amounts to collusion in the modernist project of technological world-domination! The real issue at stake is about the understanding of perception itself. In my book, I sought to refute the founding axiom of the kind of relativism to which Howes subscribes – namely that perception consists in the cultural modelling of received bodily experience – and to replace it with an understanding of perception as an active and exploratory engagement of the whole person, indissolubly body and mind, in a richly structured environment. It still seems to me that this engagement is precisely what is missing from an anthropology of the senses that has nothing to say about how people practically see, hear and touch as they go about their business, and everything to say about how their experiences of seeing, hearing and touching feed the imagination and infuse its discursive and literary expressions. For Howes, people inhabit worlds of sense. I want to know how people sense the world.

Perhaps the most telling critique of *Perception* comes from a reviewer in the *Journal of the Royal Anthropological Institute*, Yasushi Uchimayada (2004). The 'blind spot' of the book, Uchimayada asserts, lies in the virtual absence of the political. I have been troubled by this lacuna, and it is one that I have attempted to remedy, albeit sketchily, elsewhere (Ingold 2005b). There are a number of possible responses. One, admittedly rather lame excuse might be to ask why a book devoted to the question of how people perceive the world around them should necessarily incorporate a political dimension in the first place. Traditionally, the study of perception has been the preserve of psychologists. In the shelf-loads of psychological treatises on the subject, you will find no mention of the political at all. And how many books on politics and the power of the state, I wonder, have anything to say about environmental perception? Another, more forthright response would be to argue that although I do not explicitly write *about* the political in the book, it is nevertheless highly charged politically. For in it, I take up arms – quite explicitly and directly – against the hierarchies of knowledge and the foreclosure of other people's lives entailed in mainstream ways of thinking, for example in cognitive science and evolutionary biology, which are heavily backed by existing structures of political and financial power. To challenge these ways of thinking head on is to engage in a form of political intervention far more direct than anything fomented by the legions of political analysts who prefer to comment from the sidelines. This argument, however, is unlikely to satisfy readers who baulk at my apparently unqualified appeal to the Heideggerian notion of 'dwelling', without regard to its repugnant political overtones. To this I would answer that just as you can find much inspiration from the writings of Marx without having to be a committed Marxist, so you can find inspiration from Heidegger without having to be a Heideggerian. I am neither a Marxist nor a Hedeggerian, but I have been greatly inspired by the writings of both thinkers. In fact it was Marx who led me to the idea of dwelling before I had even begun to read Heidegger! I came to the idea through my attempt to understand what Marx, in his early work, meant by production as a process of life (Ingold 1986b: 321–24).

In retrospect, however, I regret having coined the expression 'the dwelling perspective' as a hook on which to hang my arguments. It is too facile. Moreover, despite my insistence both that dwelling goes on along paths of movement rather than in bounded places, and that such movement may involve pain and discomfort, there seemed to be no way of avoiding the connotations of snug, well-wrapped localism that come to mind whenever the word 'dwelling' is used. For this reason, I have opted in more recent work for the more neutral notion of 'habitation', and prefer to speak of 'inhabiting' rather than 'dwelling'. Another word that figures prominently in *Perception*, but with which I am no longer entirely comfortable, is 'taskscape'. It is curious how this word, which I coined as long ago as 1991, has taken on a life of its own. My initial purpose in introducing the term was really to do away with it, by showing that in the current of time, landscape and taskscape are one. In recent years, however, I have begun to question the idea of landscape in a more fundamental sense, particularly through a focus on wind and weather (Ingold 2007c, 2010). The world we inhabit, I would now argue, is not a landscape but a world of earth and sky – a weather-world. In the weather-world there are movements, occurrences, growths, swellings and protuberances. But there are no objects. The inhabited world, I contend, is an *environment without objects*. This conclusion has, in turn, led me to take a much more critical view of the ecological approach to perception proposed by Gibson, and which was so central to my arguments in *The Perception of the Environment*. For Gibson's view was precisely that every habitable environment must be furnished with objects, and that these objects are what we perceive. In essays I have written since *Perception* was published, I have begun to think through what it means to inhabit a world without objects – a world in which every thing or being is a certain gathering together of the threads of life. These essays, written over the last ten years, are assembled in my new book of essays, *Being Alive* (2011). There is, however, plenty more to thinking along these lines to be done!

Tim Ingold
Aberdeen
December 2010

References

Brereton, D. P. 2004. Preface for a critical realist ethnology, Part I: The schism and a realist restorative; Part II: Some principles applied. *Journal of Critical Realism* 3(1): 77–102; 3(2): 270–304.
Hallam, E. and T. Ingold (eds) 2007. *Creativity and cultural improvisation.* Oxford: Berg.

Howes, D. 2003. *Sensual relations: engaging the senses in culture and social theory*. Ann Arbor: University of Michigan Press.

Ingold, T. 1986a. *The appropriation of nature: essays on human ecology and social relations*. Manchester: Manchester University Press.

——1986b. *Evolution and social life*. Cambridge: Cambridge University Press.

——2004. Culture on the ground: the world perceived through the feet. *Journal of Material Culture* 9(3): 315–40.

——2005a. Brereton's brandishments. *Journal of Critical Realism* 4(1): 112–27.

——2005b. Epilogue: towards a politics of dwelling. *Conservation and Society* 3(2): 501–8.

——2007a. *Lines: a brief history*. London: Routledge.

——2007b. The 4 As (anthropology, archaeology, art and architecture): reflections on a teaching and learning experience. In *Ways of knowing: new approaches to the anthropology of knowledge and learning*. Oxford: Berghahn, pp. 287–305.

——2007c. Earth, sky, wind and weather. *Journal of the Royal Anthropological Institute* N.S. (2007 special issue): S19-S38.

——2010. Footprints through the weather-world: walking, breathing, knowing. *Journal of the Royal Anthropological Institute* N.S. (2010 special issue): S121-S139.

——2011. *Being alive: essays on movement, knowledge and description*. London: Routledge.

Ingold, T. and J. Vergunst 2008. *Ways of walking: ethnography and practice on foot*. Aldershot: Ashgate.

Mills, C. W. 1959. *The sociological imagination*. New York: Oxford University Press.

Uchimayada, T. 2004. Review of Tim Ingold, *The Perception of the Environment*. *Journal of the Royal Anthropological Institute* (N.S.) 10(3): 723–24.

Viveiros de Castro, E. 1998. Cosmological perspectivism in Amazonia and elsewhere. Lectures delivered at the Department of Social Anthropology, University of Cambridge, 17 February to 10 March 1998. Unpublished.

General introduction

This book has grown from the same concerns as those that, over thirty years ago, led me to embark upon the study of anthropology. At school I had done well in mathematics and, thanks to a wonderful teacher, I had been fired by a passion for physics. It was assumed that I should go to university to read natural science. But my initial enthusiasm soon gave way to disillusionment. Like so many of my contemporaries I was appalled by the extent to which science had reneged both on its sense of democratic responsibility and on its original commitment to enlarge the scope of human knowledge, and had allowed itself to become subservient to the demands of the military-industrial complex. The scientific establishment, it seemed to me, was so massively institutionalised, internally specialised and oppressively hierarchical that as a professional scientist one could never be more than a small cog in a huge juggernaut of an enterprise. Towards the end of my first year at university I went to see my tutor, and politely informed him over a glass of sherry (this was Cambridge!) that natural science was not for me, and that I was seeking a discipline where there was more room to breathe. It would be exciting, I thought, to join in a subject still on the make – one, perhaps, that was in the same formative stage that physics was in at the time of Galileo.

My tutor, whose considerable percipience was laced with a hint of mischief, suggested anthropology. I, of course, with that callow conceit of the Cambridge undergraduate who thinks himself too clever by half, wanted to be the Galileo of anthropology – provided that I did not have to suffer as Galileo did. Though I have long since abandoned these adolescent fantasies, the real intellectual reasons why I took up anthropology then (it was 1967) are still the reasons why I study it now. Concerned about the widening gap between the arts and the humanities on the one hand, and the natural sciences on the other, I was looking for a discipline that would somehow close the gap, or enable us to rise above it, while still remaining close to the realities of lived experience. Anthropology, for me, has been that discipline, and since embarking on it I have never looked back. I have, however, often looked from side to side, observing with mounting despair how it has been fractured along the very lines of fission that I thought it existed to overcome. These fractures ultimately seem to derive from a single, underlying fault upon which the entire edifice of Western thought and science has been built – namely that which separates the 'two worlds' of humanity and nature. For this is what has given us the overriding academic division of labour between the disciplines that deal, on the one hand, with the human mind and its manifold linguistic, social and cultural products, and on the other, with the structures and composition of the material world. And it also cleaves anthropology itself into its sociocultural and biophysical divisions, whose respective practitioners have less to say to one another than they do to colleagues in other disciplines on the same side of the academic fence. Social or cultural anthropologists would rather read the work of historians, linguists, philosophers and literary critics; biological or physical anthropologists prefer to talk to colleagues in other fields of biology or biomedicine.

My aim has always been to bring these two sides of anthropology together. There must be something wrong, I reasoned, with a social or cultural anthropology that cannot countenance the fact that human beings are biological organisms that have evolved, and that undergo processes of growth and development, as other organisms do. But there must be something equally wrong with a biological anthropology that denies anything but a proximate role for agency, intentionality or imagination in the direction of human affairs. Advocates of both extreme positions are not hard to find, from those who insist, on the one hand, that there is nothing that is not socially or culturally constructed to those, on the other, who hold that all there is to know about human beings is written into our genetic constitution, and therefore that by deciphering the genome we would discover the key to our humanity. In steering a course between these extremes, my first inclination was to argue for the essential complementarity of the biogenetic and sociocultural dimensions of human existence. The fact that human beings are organisms whose life and reproduction depends upon their interaction with organisms of other species, as well as with abiotic components of the environment, does not rule out the possibility that they are also aware of themselves as beings who can relate to one another as subjects, and who can therefore – on this intersubjective level – enjoy a distinctively social life. Likewise, the fact that human beings are the bearers of genes whose specific combination is a product of variation under natural selection does not mean that they cannot also be the bearers of cultural traditions that may be passed on by a process of learning in some ways analogous to, but by the same token fundamentally distinct from, the process of genetic replication.

In 1986 I brought out a book, entitled *Evolution and social life*, in which I attempted, among other things, to establish this complementarity thesis. But as several critics pointed out, the argument of the book did not really cohere, since the connection between the human being as a biological *organism*, and as a social subject or *person*, could not be substantiated save by way of a third term, namely the human mind. The discipline that exists to study the mind is, of course, psychology. In my book I had virtually ignored psychology, largely because I had had my work cut out simply in finding my way through the extensive literatures in anthropology and biology. But the criticism was just: there would seem to be no way of piecing together the two halves of anthropology, the biophysical and sociocultural, without taking a loop through psychology. Clearly, I would have to read up on the subject. I was introduced to it, however, from a rather unorthodox angle. On the recommendation of several friends and colleagues, I turned to the writings of James Gibson and, in particular, to his masterpiece of 1979, *The ecological approach to visual perception*. Reading this book was a revelation: indeed I cannot think of any other work that has exerted a greater influence on my thinking over the last ten years or so. This influence is evident in everything I have written since, including the essays that make up this volume.

Gibson wanted to know how people come to perceive the environment around them. The majority of psychologists, at least at the time when Gibson was writing, assumed that they did so by constructing representations of the world inside their heads. It was supposed that the mind got to work on the raw material of experience, consisting of sensations of light, sound, pressure on the skin, and so on, organising it into an internal model which, in turn, could serve as a guide to subsequent action. The mind, then, was conceived as a kind of data-processing device, akin to a digital computer, and the problem for the psychologist was to figure out how it worked. But Gibson's approach was quite different. It was to throw out the idea, that has been with us since the time of Descartes, of the mind as a distinct organ that is capable of operating upon the bodily data of sense. Perception, Gibson argued, is not the achievement of a mind in a body, but of the organism as a whole in its environment, and is tantamount to the organism's own exploratory movement through the world. If mind is anywhere, then, it is not 'inside the head' rather than 'out there' in the world. To the contrary, it is immanent in the network of sensory pathways that are set up by virtue of the perceiver's immersion in his or her environment. Reading Gibson, I was reminded of the teaching of that notorious maverick of anthropology, Gregory Bateson. The mind, Bateson had always insisted, is not limited by the skin. Could not an ecological approach to perception provide the link I was looking for, between the biological life of the organism in its environment and the cultural life of the mind in society?

The issue for me, at the time, was to find a way of formulating this link that could also resolve what I felt to be a deep-rooted problem in my own work. Setting out from the complementarity thesis, I had argued that human beings must simultaneously be constituted both as organisms within systems of ecological relations, and as persons within systems of social relations. The critical task for anthropology, it seemed, was to understand the reciprocal interplay between the two kinds of system, social and ecological. In 1986, alongside *Evolution and social life*, I had brought out a book of essays under the title *The appropriation of nature*, all of which sought to explore this interplay in one way or another. But I had continued to be troubled by the inherent dualism of this approach, with its implied dichotomies between person and organism, society and nature. I vividly remember one Saturday morning in April 1988 – an entirely ordinary one for Manchester at that time of year, with grey skies and a little rain – when, on my way to catch a bus, it suddenly dawned on me that the organism and the person could be one and the same. Instead of trying to reconstruct the complete human being from two separate but complementary components, respectively biophysical and sociocultural, held together with a film of psychological cement, it struck me that we should be trying to find a way of talking about human life that eliminates the need to slice it up into these different layers. Everything I have written since has been driven by this agenda.

Why had this view, that the person *is* the organism, and not something added on top, eluded me for so long? In retrospect it seems so obvious as almost to 'go without saying'. I now realise that the obstacle that had prevented me from seeing it was a certain conception of the organism, one that is built into mainstream theory in both evolutionary and environmental biology. According to this conception, every organism is a discrete, bounded entity, a 'living thing', one of a population of such things, and relating to other organisms in its environment along lines of external contact that leave its basic, internally specified nature unaffected. I had assumed that my task was not to challenge accepted biological wisdom but to reconcile it with what contemporary anthropology has to teach us about the constitution of human beings as persons. This is that the identities and characteristics of persons are not bestowed upon them in advance of their involvement with others but are the condensations of histories of growth and maturation within fields of social relationships. Thus every person emerges as a locus of development within such a field, which is in turn carried forward and transformed through their own actions.

Understanding persons in this way, however, calls for a kind of 'relational thinking' that goes right against the grain of the 'population thinking' that has been *de rigueur* in biological science ever since the establishment of the so-called modern synthesis of Darwinian theory and population genetics. Now so long as the organism and the person are conceived as separate components of the human being, one could perhaps think about the former in populational terms and the latter in relational terms, without fear of contradiction. Whereas the population, it might be said, is of individual objects (organisms), relationships exist between social or cultural subjects (persons). But if persons *are* organisms, then the principles of relational thinking, far from being restricted to the domain of human sociality, must be applicable right across the continuum of organic life. What I glimpsed, on that fateful day in 1988, was that this would require nothing less than a radically alternative biology. For if every organism is not so much a discrete entity as a node in a field of relationships, then we have to think in a new way not only about the interdependence of organisms and their environments but also about their evolution.

Of course, like all good ideas, others had had it before. On further inquiry I discovered that there already existed a considerable literature taking up what I would call a relational view of the organism, and that sets out expressly to break the stranglehold that neo-Darwinian theory has tended to exert, up to now, on mainstream biological thought. Significantly, most of the contributors to this literature work in the field of developmental biology. They have been concerned to unravel the dynamics of those processes of growth and maturation that actually give rise to the forms and capacities of organisms. And they have shown, quite convincingly, that it is not enough to regard these forms and capacities as the mere expressions of designs or blueprints that have already been established by natural selection, and that are imparted to every organism-to-be – along with its complement of genes – at the moment of conception. The characteristics of organisms, they argue, are not so much expressed as *generated* in the course of development, arising as emergent properties of the fields of relationship set up through their presence and activity within a particular environment. Here, then, was the biology that would help to substantiate my view of the organism-person, undergoing growth and development in an environment furnished by the work and presence of others.

It is a biology, however, that also resonates very closely with the principles of Gibsonian ecological psychology. Both approaches take as their point of departure the developing organism-in-its-environment, as opposed to the self-contained individual confronting a world 'out there'. The approaches are linked, too, in terms of their opposition to established positions in biology and psychology. Indeed there is a striking parallel between the 'developmentalist' critique of neo-Darwinian biology and the 'ecological' critique of mainstream cognitive psychology. In both cases the objection is to the idea that what an organism does, or what it perceives, is the calculated output of an intelligent design, whether that intelligence be equated with the mind or with natural selection (which is, after all, but the reflection of scientific reason in the mirror of nature). Moreover, a very similar objection can be raised against those versions of culture theory, in anthropology, that would attribute human behaviour to designs that are passed from one generation to the next as the content of acquired tradition. These parallels led me to suggest that a combination of 'relational' thinking in anthropology, 'ecological' thinking in psychology and 'developmental systems' thinking in biology would yield a synthesis infinitely more powerful than any of the 'biosocial', 'psychocultural' or 'biopsychocultural' alternatives currently on offer, all of which invoke some version of the complementarity thesis.

Crucially, such a synthesis would start from a conception of the human being not as a composite entity made up of separable but complementary parts, such as body, mind and culture, but rather as a singular locus of creative growth within a continually unfolding field of relationships. In the following chapters I pursue three implications of this approach. The first is that much if not all of what we are accustomed to call cultural variation in fact consists of variations of *skills*. By skills I do not mean techniques of the body, but the capabilities of action and perception of the whole organic being (indissolubly mind and body) situated in a richly structured environment. As properties of human organisms, skills are thus as much biological as cultural. Secondly, and stemming from the above, becoming skilled in the practice of a certain form of life is not a matter of furnishing a set of generalised capacities, given from the start as compartments of a universal human nature, with specific cultural content. Skills are not transmitted from generation to generation but are regrown in each, incorporated into the *modus operandi* of the developing human organism through training and experience in the performance of particular tasks. Hence, thirdly, the study of skill demands a perspective which situates the practitioner, right from the start, in the context of an active engagement with the constituents of his or her surroundings. I call this the 'dwelling perspective'. Humans, I argue, are brought into existence as organism-persons within a world that is inhabited by beings of manifold kinds, both human and non-human. Therefore relations among humans, which we are accustomed to calling 'social', are but a sub-set of ecological relations.

The essays collected together here comprise a series of attempts to establish this relational-ecological-developmental synthesis. I have come to the project from a background in ecological anthropology, in the anthropology of technology, and in the history of anthropological theory. In my ecological work I have concentrated on the comparative study of hunter-gatherer and pastoral societies, an interest that has its roots in my earlier research on northern circumpolar reindeer hunting and herding peoples. This accounts for my particular concern with human-animal relations, and with the conceptualisation of the humanity-animality interface. It is also the reason why, in selecting ethnographic material to substantiate my arguments, I have tended to go for studies of northern circumpolar societies. My interest in technology developed in part from a reconsideration of the significance of toolmaking as an index of human distinctiveness, and in part from a growing interest in the connection, in human evolution, between technology and language. More recently, I have tried to find ways of bringing together the anthropologies of technology and of art, and it is this, above all, that has led me to my present view of the centrality of skilled practice. In my work on the history of theory I focused on the way in which the notion of evolution has figured in the writings of anthropologists, biologists and historians from the late nineteenth century to the present. The key question to which I sought an answer was how, if at all, the concept of evolution was to be separated from that of history. I did not resolve this question to my satisfaction, and it has remained at the top of my agenda. I believe now that the proposed synthesis of relational, ecological and developmental approaches offers a solution.

The volume is divided into three parts. In the first, on 'livelihood', my concern is to find a way of comprehending how human beings relate to their environments, in the tasks of making a living, that does not set up a polarity between the ecological domain of their relations with non-human 'nature' and the cognitive domain of its cultural construction. The second part, on 'dwelling', explores the implications of the position that awareness and activity are rooted in the engagement between persons and environment for our understanding of perception and cognition, architecture and the built environment, local and global conceptions of environmental change, landscape and temporality, mapping and wayfinding, and the differentiation of the senses. In the third part, on 'skill', I show how a focus on practical enskilment, conceived as the embodiment of capacities of awareness and response by environmentally situated agents, can help us to overcome both an overly rigid division between the works of human beings and those of non-human animals and, in the human case, the opposition between the fields of 'art' and 'technology'. This tripartite division is, however, largely a matter of convenience. The parts themselves are anything but watertight. All I can say is that there is a rather greater density of thematic interconnectedness among the chapters making up each part than there is between them.

As for the individual chapters, they are of diverse origin. Most were initially written for presentation at conferences, and have been extensively revised since. Earlier versions of many of these have already appeared in conference publications. Naturally, the form and substance of each essay have to some extent been dictated by the needs of the occasion for which it was originally prepared. All were written, however, with the ultimate intention of bringing them together into one coherent work. With one exception, none dates back more than a decade: thus they all represent my post-1988 thinking. The exception is Chapter 15, which I first drafted for a conference in 1987. I have included it here since it marks the beginnings of my reconsideration of the concept of technology. Four chapters (Six, Eight, Thirteen and Fourteen) have been written specially for this volume. Chapter Fourteen is by far and away the longest, and it was undoubtedly, for me, the most challenging to write. Surveying the book in its entirety, I see it somewhat in the shape of a mountain, with a steady climb through the first part, a brief plateau at the start of the second followed by an ascent to the summit in Chapters Thirteen and Fourteen. Having reached that far, the third part affords a relatively easy descent. But like a mountain, one could just as well proceed in the other direction, starting with the third part and ending with the first. Indeed there is no fixed order in which the chapters should be tackled. Each can be read and understood on its own, or as one of the set of explorations of closely connected themes comprising each part, which in turn can be read as one aspect of the total intellectual project comprised by the book as a whole.

Before closing this general introduction, I should insert a note about my use of the concepts of 'the Western' and 'the modern'. These concepts have been the source of no end of trouble for anthropologists, and I am no exception. Every time I find myself using them I bite my lip with frustration, and wish that I could avoid it. The objections to the concepts are well known: that in most anthropological accounts they serve as a largely implicit foil against which to contrast a 'native point of view'; that much of the philosophical ammunition for the critique of so-called Western or modern thought comes straight out of the Western tradition itself (thus we find such figures as the young Karl Marx, Martin Heidegger and Maurice Merleau-Ponty enlisted in the enterprise of showing how the understandings of North American Indians, New Guinea Highlanders or Australian Aborigines differ from those of 'Euro-Americans'); that once we get to know people well – even the inhabitants of nominally Western countries – not one of them turns out to be a full-blooded Westerner, or even to be particularly modern in their approach to life; and that the Western tradition of thought, closely examined, is as richly various, multivocal, historically changeable and contest-riven as any other.

For those of us who call ourselves academics and intellectuals, however, there is a good reason why we cannot escape 'the West', or avoid the anxieties of modernity. It is that our very activity, in thinking and writing, is underpinned by a belief in the absolute worth of disciplined, rational inquiry. In this book, it is to this belief that the terms 'Western' and 'modern' refer. And however much we may object to the dichotomies to which it gives rise, between humanity and nature, intelligence and instinct, the mental and the material, and so on, the art of critical disputation on these matters is precisely what 'the West' is all about. For when all is said and done, there can be nothing more 'Western', or more 'modern', than to write an academic book such as this. Nor can I be anything less than profoundly grateful for the freedom, education and institutional facilities that have allowed me to do so.

Part I

Livelihood

INTRODUCTION

My focus, in the essays making up this part, is on the ways in which human beings relate to components of their environment in the activities of subsistence procurement. I draw, in particular, on ethnographic studies of people who make their living primarily by hunting and gathering. In the existing anthropological literature on hunting and gathering societies, questions of how people interact, practically and technically, with the resources of their environment in obtaining a livelihood tend to be treated separately from questions of how their lifeworld is imaginatively 'constructed', in myth, religion and ceremony. The former are typically addressed in naturalistic terms, often by way of comparison with the foraging behaviour of non-human animals, and drawing on the same frameworks of concepts and theory as have been employed by animal ecologists. The latter, by contrast, are considered suitable topics for cultural analysis, concerned as it is with the ways in which the environment, and people's relations with it, are represented in consciousness. I believe that this division between naturalistic and 'culturalogical' accounts is unfortunate, in that it takes for granted precisely the separation, of the naturally real from the culturally imagined, that needs to be put into question if we are to get to the bottom of people's own perceptions of the world. Starting from the premise that ways of acting in the environment are also ways of perceiving it, these essays suggest how the division might be overcome.

I set the scene, in Chapter One, by comparing the accounts that Western biologists and indigenous hunters give of the behaviour of caribou during episodes of predation. I show that the scientific authority of the former account, as well as the anthropological understanding of the latter as fitting within a culturally specific cosmology, depend on a two-step movement of disengagement that cuts out first nature, then culture, as objects of attention. I then set out to retrace these steps in the reverse direction, in an attempt to replace the dichotomy of nature and culture with the synergy of organism and environment, and thereby to regain a genuine ecology of life. The inspiration for this move comes from the work of Gregory Bateson, whose ideas are introduced through a contrast with those of Claude Lévi-Strauss. Both authors set out to demolish the distinction between mind and nature, but whereas for Lévi-Strauss the mind recovers information from the world through a process of decoding, for Bateson it is opened out to the world in a process of revelation. This contrast is linked to two senses in which it might be said that novices, in learning to perceive the world around them, are furnished with 'keys to meaning'. The key could be a cipher or a clue. I argue that sensory education consists in the acquisition of clues, not ciphers, and that songs and stories – including stories of how animals respond to the presence of the hunter – give shape to a perception of the world guided by this education. The knowledge grounded in such perception, I conclude, amounts to what may be regarded as a 'sentient ecology'.

In the following two chapters I argue, first, against the naturalisation of the hunter-gatherer economy under the rubric of 'foraging', and secondly, against the complementary claim that in the eyes of the people themselves, the environment they inhabit is culturally constructed. Chapter Two is a critique of attempts, under the guise of 'human evolutionary ecology', to apply models designed for the study of non-human foraging behaviour to the analysis of human hunting and gathering. This application results from a conflation of rational choice theory, drawn from classical microeconomics, with the theory of natural selection, drawn from evolutionary biology. In the one case hunter-gatherers are likened to 'economic men' who can work out their strategies for themselves. In the other they are seen as 'optimal foragers' whose strategies have been worked out for them by natural selection. These two characters fall on opposite sides of an overriding opposition between reason and nature, or freedom and necessity. A properly ecological account of hunting and gathering requires however that we dissolve this opposition, showing how people develop their skills and sensitivities through histories of continuing involvement with human and non-human constituents of their environments. For it is by engaging with these manifold constituents that the world comes to be known by its inhabitants.

In Chapter Three, I contrast this view, that hunter-gatherers' perception of the environment is embedded in practices of engagement, with the more conventional alternative that such perception results from the reconstruction of naturally given realities in terms of metaphors drawn from the ideal realm of culture. I develop this contrast through a review, first, of how certain tropical hunter-gatherer peoples perceive their forest environment. Secondly, I look at the way northern hunters, particularly the Cree of northeastern Canada, understand their relations with the animals they hunt. Thirdly, drawing on ethnographic material from Aboriginal Australia and subarctic Alaska, I consider how hunters and gatherers perceive the landscape. I conclude that anthropological attempts to depict the mode of practical engagement of hunter-gatherers with the world as a mode of cultural construction of it have had the effect of perpetuating a naturalistic vision of the hunter-gatherer economy. This vision of hunters and gatherers as 'living in nature' is closely tied to a certain notion of history, as a process in which human beings have gradually risen above, and brought under control, both their own nature, in the process of civilisation, and the nature around them, in the domestication of animals and plants. In Chapters Four and Five, I revisit this Western historical narrative of the human conquest of nature, and seek to replace it with an alternative more in keeping with indigenous understandings.

Chapter Four focuses on the history of human–animal relations, and on the transformation of these relations entailed in the shift from hunting to pastoralism. I argue that relationships between hunters and prey are based on a principle of trust, constituted by a combination of autonomy and dependency. The human–animal relationship under pastoralism, by contrast, is based on a principle of domination. The transition from hunting to pastoralism, therefore, is marked not by the replacement of wild by domesticated animals, but by the movement from trust to domination in the principles of human beings' relations with them. Chapter five continues the critique of the notion of domestication, and with it the dichotomy between collection and production, entailed in the notion of history as the human transformation of nature. In terms of this dichotomy, growing crops and raising animals are viewed as instances of production in the same way as is the manufacture of artefacts. In every case, things are 'made'. Drawing on ethnographic studies of how people who actually live by tilling the soil or keeping livestock understand the nature of their activity, I show that the work people do does not make plants and animals, but rather establishes the conditions for their growth and development. The distinctions between gathering and cultivation, and between hunting and animal husbandry, thus hinge on the scope of human involvement in establishing these conditions. Moreover, growing plants and raising animals are not so different, in principle, from bringing up children. Contrary to the conventional wisdom that not only animals and plants but also children are 'made', through domestication and socialisation, I conclude that children, animals, plants and even – in a sense – artefacts as well, are 'grown'.

I return, in Chapter Six, to the theme of engagement, and to the different approaches to environmental understanding of indigenous hunters and modern science. There is, as I show, a paradox at the heart of science. For while, on the one hand, it asserts that human beings are biological organisms, composed of the same stuff and having evolved according to the same principles as organisms of every other kind, on the other hand the very possibility of a scientific account rests on the separation of humanity from organic nature. To resolve the paradox I suggest an alternative mode of understanding based on the premise of our engagement with the world, rather than our detachment from it. I do this by drawing on one anthropological study of how people in a non-Western society perceive themselves and the world around them. This is A. Irving Hallowell's classic study of the Ojibwa, indigenous hunters and trappers of the Canadian boreal forest. For the Ojibwa, knowledge is grounded in experience, understood as a coupling of the movement of one's awareness to the movement of aspects of the world. Experience, in this sense, does not mediate between mind and nature, since these are not separated in the first place. It is rather intrinsic to the process of being alive to the world. This is linked to a view of personhood in which the self is seen to inhere in the unfolding of the relations set up by virtue of its positioning in an environment. The essay explores the implications of this view of the self and experience for our understanding of animacy, metamorphosis, dreaming and speech. I conclude that what the Ojibwa have arrived at is not an alternative science of nature but a poetics of dwelling. Far from having been superseded, in the West, by the rise of modern science, such poetics is the necessary ground for all scientific activity.

In Chapter Seven I turn from science to art. Whereas science is often supposed to be a specific historical achievement of the Western world, art is commonly regarded as one of the hallmarks of humanity, revealing a universal capacity to represent experience in symbolic media. I argue against this view. Focusing on the ways in which hunters and gatherers depict animals, in painting, drawing and sculpture, I show that activities leading to the production of what we in the West would call 'art' should be understood not as ways of representing the world of experience on a higher, more symbolic plane, but of probing more deeply into it and discovering the significance that lies there. The argument is developed by way of a comparison between two distinct traditions, of 'painting the ancestors' among Australian Aboriginal peoples and of 'carving the spirits' among the peoples of the circumpolar North. The differences between these traditions reflect contrasting understandings of the relationships between human beings, animals and the land, which I call respectively totemic and animic. The fundamental difference between the totemic and animic depiction of animals is that the former focuses on morphology and anatomy, whereas the latter focuses on posture, movement and behaviour. But while hunters and gatherers have been painting and carving figures of one kind or another for thousands of years, only recently have they begun to engage in the production of 'art'.

To understand the original significance of what they were doing, I argue, we have to cease thinking of painting and carving as modalities of the production of art, and view art instead as a historically specific objectification of painting and carving.

Now it is conventional to describe hunters and gatherers as indigenous inhabitants of the lands in which they live. But precisely what it means to be 'indigenous' is a matter of some controversy. According to one definition, indigenous peoples are the descendants of those who inhabited a country when colonists arrived from elsewhere. Yet while habitation of the land is taken to be the source of indigenous identity, the claim that this identity can be passed on by descent implies that it is no longer drawn from the land at all, but from one's genealogical ancestors. I take up this paradox in Chapter Eight. It hinges, as I show, on the interpretation of five key terms: ancestry, generation, substance, memory and land. I show that the conventional meanings of these terms are linked through their common grounding in what I call the 'genealogical model'. After spelling out the elements of this model, and the assumptions it entails, I argue that it fundamentally misrepresents the ways in which peoples whom *we* class as indigenous constitute their identity, knowledgeability, and the environments in which they live. I suggest an alternative, relational approach to interpreting the key terms which is more consonant with these people's lived experience of inhabiting the land. In this approach, which ties together many of the key arguments of the preceding chapters while laying the groundwork for the ecological and developmental perspectives to be elaborated in Parts II and III, both cultural knowledge and bodily substance are seen to undergo continuous generation in the context of an ongoing engagement with the land and with the beings that dwell therein. I conclude that it is in articulating their experience in a way that is compatible with the discourses of the state that people are led to lay claim to indigenous status, in terms that nevertheless invert their own understandings.

Chapter One

Culture, nature, environment

Steps to an ecology of life

As a social anthropologist whose ethnographic interests lie in the northern circumpolar regions, I should like to begin with an observation drawn from my own field experience of mustering reindeer in Finnish Lapland. When pursuing reindeer, there often comes a critical point when a particular animal becomes immediately aware of your presence. It then does a strange thing. Instead of running away it stands stock still, turns its head and stares you squarely in the face. Biologists have explained this behaviour as an adaptation to predation by wolves. When the reindeer stops, the pursuing wolf stops too, both of them getting their breath back for the final, decisive phase of the episode when the deer turns to flight and the wolf rushes to overtake it. Since it is the deer that takes the initiative in breaking the stalemate, it has a slight head start, and indeed a healthy adult deer can generally outrun a wolf (Mech 1970: 200–3). But the deer's tactic, that gives it such an advantage against wolves, renders it peculiarly vulnerable when encountering human hunters equipped with projectile weapons or even firearms. When the animal turns to face the hunter, it provides the latter with a perfect opportunity to take aim and shoot. For wolves, deer are easy to find, since they travel with the herd, but hard to kill; for humans, to the contrary, deer may be hard to find, but once you have established contact, they are rather easy to kill (Ingold 1980: 53, 67).

Now the Cree people, native hunters of northeastern Canada, have a different explanation for why reindeer – or caribou as they are called in North America – are so easy to kill. They say that the animal offers itself up, quite intentionally and in a spirit of goodwill or even love towards the hunter. The bodily substance of the caribou is not taken, it is *received*. And it is at the moment of encounter, when the animal stands its ground and looks the hunter in the eye, that the offering is made. As with many other hunting people around the world, the Cree draw a parallel between the pursuit of animals and the seduction of young women, and liken killing to sexual intercourse. In this light, killing appears not as a termination of life but as an act that is critical to its regeneration.[1]

SCIENCE AND INDIGENOUS KNOWLEDGE

Here, then, we have two accounts – one coming from biological science, the other from indigenous people – of what happens when humans encounter reindeer or caribou. My initial question is: how are we to understand the relation between them? Wildlife biologists are liable to react to native stories about animals presenting themselves of their own accord with a mixture of cynicism and incredulity. The cynical view would be that such stories provide a very handy way of dodging the ethical issues surrounding hunting and killing that cause such anxiety for many people in Western societies. For hunters, it is most convenient to be able to transfer responsibility for the death of animals onto the animals themselves. What the Western scientist finds hard to believe is that anybody should be taken in by patently fanciful excuses of this kind. The fact of the matter, surely, is that caribou are being tracked down and killed. Could any intelligent person seriously think that animals *actually* offer themselves to hunters as recounted in the stories of the Cree? Are the folk who tell these stories mad, lost in a fog of irrational superstition, talking in allegories, or simply having us on? Whatever the answer may be, science insists that stories are stories, and as such have no purchase on what really goes on in the natural world.

Anthropologists are inclined to take a rather different approach. On being told that the success of hunting depends upon the bestowal of favour by animals, the anthropologist's first concern is not to judge the truth of the proposition but to understand what it means, given the context in which it is advanced. Thus it can readily be shown that the idea of animals offering themselves to hunters, however bizarre it might seem from the viewpoint of Western science, makes perfectly good sense if we start from the assumption (as the Cree evidently do) that the entire world – and not just the world of human persons – is saturated with powers of agency and intentionality. In Cree cosmology, the anthropologist concludes, relations with animals are modelled on those that obtain within the human community, such that hunting is conceived as a moment in an ongoing interpersonal dialogue (Tanner 1979: 137–8, see Gudeman 1986: 148–9, and Chapter Three, pp. 48–52). This is not to say that the biological explanation of the stand-off between hunter and caribou at the point of encounter, as part of an innate response mechanism designed to combat predation by wolves, is without interest. For anthropologists, however, explaining the behaviour of caribou is none of their business. Their concern is rather to show how hunters' direct experience of encounters with animals is given form and meaning within those received patterns of interconnected images and propositions that, in anthropological parlance, go by the name of 'culture'.

Though from what I have just said, the perspectives of the wildlife biologist and the cultural anthropologist might seem incompatible, they are nevertheless perfectly complementary, and indeed disclose a common, albeit practically unattainable, point of observation.[2] Whereas the biologist claims to study organic nature 'as it really is', the anthropologist studies the diverse ways in which the constituents of the natural world figure in the imagined, or so-called 'cognised' worlds of cultural subjects. There are any number of ways of marking this distinction, but of these the most notorious, at least in anthropological literature, is that between so-called 'etic' and 'emic' accounts. Derived from the contrast in linguistics between phonetics and phonemics, the former purports to offer a wholly neutral, value-free description of the physical world, while the latter spells out the specific cultural meanings that people place upon it.

There are two points I want to make about this distinction. First, to suggest that human beings inhabit discursive worlds of culturally constructed significance is to imply that they have already taken a step out of the world of nature within which the lives of all other creatures are confined. The Cree hunter, it is supposed, narrates and interprets his experiences of encounters with animals in terms of a system of cosmological beliefs, the caribou does not. But, secondly, to perceive this system *as* a cosmology requires that we observers take a further step, this time out of the worlds of culture in which the lives of all other *humans* are said to be confined. What the anthropologist calls a cosmology is, for the people themselves, a lifeworld. Only from a point of observation beyond culture is it possible to regard the Cree understanding of the relation between hunters and caribou as but one possible construction, or 'modelling', of an independently given reality. But by the very same token, only from such a vantage point is it possible to apprehend the given reality for what it is, independently of any kind of cultural bias.

It should now be clear why natural science and cultural anthropology converge on a common vertex. The anthropological claim of perceptual relativism – that people from different cultural backgrounds perceive reality in different ways since they process the same data of experience in terms of alternative frameworks of belief or representational schemata – does not undermine but actually reinforces the claim of natural science to deliver an authoritative account of how nature really works. Both claims are founded upon a double disengagement of the observer from the world. The first sets up a division between humanity and nature; the second establishes a division, within humanity, between 'native' or 'indigenous' people, who live in cultures, and enlightened Westerners, who do not. Both claims, too, are underwritten by a commitment that lies at the heart of Western thought and science, to the extent of being its defining feature. This is the commitment to the ascendancy of abstract or universal reason. If it is by the capacity to reason that humanity, in this Western discourse, is distinguished from nature, then it is by the fullest development of this capacity that modern science distinguishes itself from the knowledge practices of people in 'other cultures' whose thought is supposed to remain somewhat bound by the constraints and conventions of tradition. In effect, the sovereign perspective of abstract reason is a product of the compounding of two dichotomies: between humanity and nature, and between modernity and tradition.

The result is not unlike that produced by perspective painting, in which a scene is depicted from a point of view which itself is given independently of that of the spectator who contemplates the finished work. Likewise abstract reason can treat, as objects of contemplation, diverse worldviews, each of which is a specific construction of an external reality (Figure 1.1). The anthropologist, surveying the tapestry of human cultural variation, is like the visitor to the art gallery – a 'viewer of views'. Perhaps it is no accident that both perspective painting and anthropology are products of the same trajectory of Western thought (Ingold 1993a: 223–4).

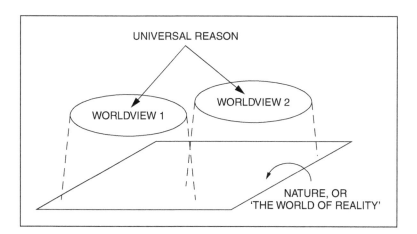

Figure 1.1 The sovereign perspective of abstract or universal reason, which treats the lifeworlds of people of different cultures as alternative constructions, cosmologies or 'worldviews', superimposed upon the 'real' reality of nature. From this perspective, anthropology embarks on the comparative study of cultural world-views, while science investigates the workings of nature.

MIND AND NATURE: GREGORY BATESON AND CLAUDE LÉVI-STRAUSS

We have now reached the stage at which I can introduce the terms comprising the title of this chapter. I have observed that the possibility of an objective account of such natural phenomena as the behaviour of caribou, as well as the recognition of an indigenous account, such as that of the Cree, as fitting within a particular culture-specific cosmology, depend on a two-step movement of disengagement that cuts out first nature, then culture, as discrete objects of attention. Whereas the scientific account is attributed to disinterested observation and rational analysis, the indigenous account is put down to the accommodation of subjective experience within 'beliefs' of questionable rationality. What I wish to do now is to retrace the two steps in the reverse direction. Only by doing so, I maintain, can we level the ranking, implicit in what has been said up to now, of scientific over indigenous accounts. Moreover I believe it is necessary that we take these steps, that we descend from the imaginary heights of abstract reason and resituate ourselves in an active and ongoing engagement with our environments, if we are ever to arrive at an ecology that is capable of recovering the reality of the life process itself. In short, my aim is to replace the stale dichotomy of nature and culture with the dynamic synergy of organism and environment, in order to regain a genuine ecology of life. This ecology, however, will look very different from the kind that has become familiar to us from scientific textbooks. For it comprises a kind of knowledge that is fundamentally resistant to transmission in an authorised textual form, independently of the contexts of its instantiation in the world.

The subtitle of this chapter, 'steps to an ecology of life', is borrowed from the work of Gregory Bateson (1973). I have, however, substituted 'life' for 'mind' as it appears in the title of Bateson's famous collection of essays. This substitution is deliberate. Bateson was a great dismantler of oppositions – between reason and emotion, inner and outer, mind and body. Yet curiously, he seemed unable to shake off the most fundamental opposition of all, between form and substance. His objection to mainstream natural science lay in its reduction of 'real' reality to pure substance, thus relegating form to the illusory or epiphenomenal world of appearances. This he saw as the inevitable consequence of the false separation of mind and nature. Bateson thought that mind should be seen as immanent in the whole system of organism–environment relations in which we humans are necessarily enmeshed, rather than confined within our individual bodies *as against* a world of nature 'out there'. As he declared, in a lecture delivered in 1970,[3] 'the mental world – the mind – the world of information processing – is not limited by the skin' (Bateson 1973: 429). Yet the ecosystem, taken in its totality, was nevertheless envisaged as two-faced. One face presents a field of matter and energy, the other presents a field of pattern and information; the first is all substance without form, the second is all form detached from substance. Bateson likened the contrast to one which Carl Jung, in his *Seven Sermons to the Dead*, had drawn between the two worlds of the *pleroma* and the *creatura*. In the former there are forces and impacts but no differences; in the latter there are only differences, and it is these differences that have effects (Bateson 1973: 430–1). Corresponding to this duality Bateson recognised two ecologies: an ecology of material and energy exchanges, and an ecology of ideas. And it was this second ecology that he christened the 'ecology of mind'.

To bring out the full significance of Bateson's position, it is instructive to set it alongside that of another giant of twentieth-century anthropology, Claude Lévi-Strauss. In a lecture on 'structuralism and ecology' – delivered in 1972, just two years after the Bateson

Figure 1.2 'Day and night' (1938), a woodcut by the Dutch artist M. C. Escher, aptly illustrates, in visual form, the way in which the mind – according to Lévi-Strauss – works upon the data of perception. Drawing upon a selection of recognisable and familiar features of the environment, such as houses, fields, a river, flying swans, the mind casts them into a symmetrical structure of oppositions and contrasts: day/night, left/right, city/country, water/land.

lecture to which I have just referred – Lévi-Strauss likewise set out to demolish the classical dichotomy between mind and nature.[4] Although neither of the two figures made any reference to the other's work, there are some superficial resemblances between their respective arguments. For Lévi-Strauss, too, the mind is a processor of information, and information consists in patterns of significant difference. Unlike Bateson, however, Lévi-Strauss anchors the mind very firmly in the workings of the human brain. Fastening in a more or less arbitrary fashion upon certain elements or distinctive features that are presented to it in the surrounding environment, the mind acts rather like a kaleidoscope, casting them into patterns whose oppositions and symmetries reflect underlying universals of human cognition (Figure 1.2). It is by these interior patterns that the mind possesses knowledge of the world outside. If, in the final analysis, the distinction between mind and nature is dissolved, it is because the neurological mechanisms that underwrite the mind's apprehension of the world are part of the very world that is apprehended. And this world, according to Lévi-Strauss, is structured through and through, from the lowest level of atoms and molecules, through the intermediate levels of sensory perception, to the highest levels of intellectual functioning. 'When the mind processes the empirical data which it receives previously processed by the sense organs', Lévi-Strauss concluded, 'it goes on working out structurally what at the outset was already structural. And it can only do so in as much as the mind, the body to which the mind belongs, and the things which body and mind perceive, are part and parcel of one and the same reality' (1974: 21).

In all these respects, Bateson's position could not have been more different. For Lévi-Strauss ecology meant 'the world outside', mind meant 'the brain'; for Bateson both

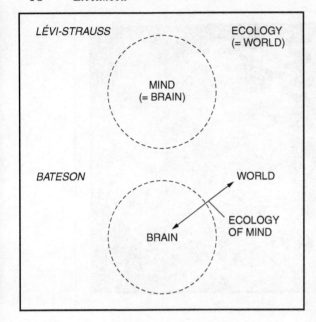

Figure 1.3 Schematic comparison of Lévi-Strauss's and Bateson's views on mind and ecology.

mind and ecology were situated in the *relations between* the brain and the surrounding environment (Figure 1.3). For Lévi-Strauss, the perceiver could only have knowledge of the world by virtue of a passage of information across the boundary between outside and inside, involving successive steps of encoding and decoding by the sense organs and the brain, and resulting in an inner mental representation. For Bateson the idea of such a boundary was absurd, a point he illustrated with the example of the blind man's cane (1973: 434). Do we draw a boundary around his head, at the handle of the cane, at its tip, or halfway down the pavement? If we ask where the mind is, the answer would not be 'in the head rather than out there in the world'. It would be more appropriate to envisage mind as extending outwards into the environment along multiple sensory pathways of which the cane, in the hands of the blind man, is just one. Thus while Bateson shared with Lévi-Strauss the notion of mind as a processor of information, he did not regard processing as a step-by-step refinement or repackaging of sensory data already received, but rather as the unfolding of the whole system of relations constituted by the multi-sensory involvement of the perceiver in his or her environment.

To continue with the example of the blind man, it is as though his processing of information were tantamount to his own movement – that is, to his own *processing* through the world. The point about movement is critical. For Lévi-Strauss, both the mind and the world remain fixed and immutable, while information passes across the interface between them. In Bateson's account, by contrast, information only exists thanks to the movement of the perceiver relative to his or her surroundings. Bateson constantly emphasised that stable features of the world remain imperceptible unless we move in relation to them: if the blind man picks up surface features of the road ahead by sweeping his cane from side to side, people with normal vision do the same with their eyes. Through this scanning movement we *draw* distinctions, in the sense not of representing them graphically, but of 'pulling them out'.[5] Whereas Lévi-Strauss often writes as though the world were sending coded messages to the brain, which it then recovers through an operation of decoding, for Bateson the world opens out to the mind through a process of revelation. This distinction, between decoding and revelation, is critical to my argument, and I shall return to it shortly. First, however, a few words are needed on the subject of *life*.

THE ECOLOGY OF LIFE

My leading question is one from which Bateson also set out. 'What sort of thing is this', he asked, 'which we call "organism plus environment"?' (Bateson 1973: 423). But the answer at which I have arrived is different. I do not think we need a separate ecology of mind, distinct from the ecology of energy flows and material exchanges. We *do* however need to rethink our understanding of life. And at the most fundamental level of all, we need to think again about the relation between form and process. Biology is – or at least is supposed to be – the science of living organisms. Yet as biologists gaze into the mirror of nature, what they see – reflected back in the morphology and behaviour of organisms – is their own reason. Accordingly, they are inclined to impute the principles of their science to the organisms themselves, as though each embodied a formal specification, programme or building plan, a *bio-logos*, given independently and in advance of its development in the world. Indeed the possibility of such a context-independent specification is an essential condition for Darwinian theory, according to which it is this specification – technically known as the genotype – that is said to undergo evolution through changes in the frequency of its information-bearing elements, the genes.

But if the underlying architecture of the organism were thus pre-specified, then its life-history could be nothing more than the realisation or 'writing out' of a programme of construction, under given environmental conditions. Life, in short, would be purely consequential, an effect of the injection of prior form into material substance. I take a different view (Ingold 1990: 215). Organic life, as I envisage it, is active rather than reactive, the creative unfolding of an entire field of relations within which beings emerge and take on the particular forms they do, each in relation to the others. Life, in this view, is not the realisation of pre-specified forms but the very process wherein forms are generated and held in place. Every being, as it is caught up in the process and carries it forward, arises as a singular centre of awareness and agency: an enfoldment, at some particular nexus within it, of the generative potential that is life itself. (This argument is further developed in Chapter Twenty-one, pp. 383–5.)

I can now spell out more precisely what I mean by an 'ecology of life'. It all hinges on a particular answer to Bateson's question: what is this 'organism plus environment'? For conventional ecology, the 'plus' signifies a simple addition of one thing to another, both of which have their own integrity, quite independently of their mutual relations. Thus the organism is specified genotypically, prior to its entry into the environment; the environment is specified as a set of physical constraints, in advance of the organisms that arrive to fill it. Indeed the ecology of the textbooks could be regarded as profoundly *anti*-ecological, insofar as it sets up organism and environment as mutually exclusive entities (or collections of entities) which are only subsequently brought together and caused to interact. A properly ecological approach, to the contrary, is one that would take, as its point of departure, the whole-organism-in-its-environment. In other words, 'organism plus environment' should denote not a compound of two things, but one indivisible totality. That totality is, in effect, a developmental system (cf. Oyama 1985), and an ecology of life – in my terms – is one that would deal with the dynamics of such systems. Now if this view is accepted – if, that is, we are prepared to treat form as *emergent* within the life-process – then, I contend, we have no need to appeal to a distinct domain of mind, to *creatura* rather than *pleroma*, to account for pattern and meaning in the world. We do not, in other words, have to think of mind or consciousness as a layer of being over and above that of the life of organisms, in order to account for their creative involvement in the world. Rather, what we may call mind is the cutting edge of the life process itself, the ever-moving front of what Alfred North Whitehead (1929: 314) called a 'creative advance into novelty'.

A NOTE ON THE CONCEPT OF ENVIRONMENT

Armed with this approach to the ecology of life, I shall now return to the question of how human beings perceive the world around them, and to see how we might begin to build an alternative to the standard anthropological account of environmental perception as a cultural construction of nature, or as the superimposition of layers of 'emic' significance upon an independently given, 'etic' reality. Before we begin, however, I want to make three preliminary points about the notion of environment. First, 'environment' is a relative term – relative, that is, to the being whose environment it is. Just as there can be no organism without an environment, so also there can be no environment without an organism (Gibson 1979: 8, Lewontin 1982: 160). Thus *my* environment is the world as it exists and takes on meaning in relation to me, and in that sense it came into existence and undergoes development with me and around me. Secondly, the environment is never complete. If environments are forged through the activities of living beings, then so long as life goes on, they are continually under construction. So too, of course, are organisms themselves. Thus when I spoke above of 'organism plus environment' as an indivisible totality, I should have said that this totality is not a bounded entity but a *process* in real time: a process, that is, of growth or development.

The third point about the notion of environment stems from the two I have just made. This is that it should on no account be confused with the concept of nature. For the world can exist as nature only for a being that does not belong there, and that can look upon it, in the manner of the detached scientist, from such a safe distance that it is easy to connive in the illusion that it is unaffected by his presence. Thus the distinction between environment and nature corresponds to the difference in perspective between seeing ourselves as beings *within* a world and as beings *without* it. Moreover we tend to think of nature as external not only to humanity, as I have already observed, but also to history, as though the natural world provided an enduring backdrop to the conduct of human affairs. Yet environments, since they continually come into being in the process of our lives – since we shape them as they shape us – are themselves fundamentally historical. We have, then, to be wary of such a simple expression as 'the natural environment', for in thus conflating the two terms we already imagine ourselves to be somehow *beyond* the world, and therefore in a position to intervene in its processes (Ingold 1992a).

COMMUNICATION AND REVELATION

When I was a child my father, who is a botanist, used to take me for walks in the countryside, pointing out on the way all the plants and fungi – especially the fungi – that grew here and there. Sometimes he would get me to smell them, or to try out their distinctive tastes. His manner of teaching was to show me things, literally to point them out. If I would but notice the things to which he directed my attention, and recognise the sights, smells and tastes that he wanted me to experience because they were so dear to him, then I would discover for myself much of what he already knew. Now, many years later, as an anthropologist, I read about how people in Australian Aboriginal societies pass their knowledge across the generations. And I find that the principle is just the same!

In his classic study of the Walbiri of Central Australia, Mervyn Meggitt describes how a boy being prepared for initiation would be taken on a 'grand tour', lasting two or three months. Accompanied by a guardian (a sister's husband) and an elder brother, the boy was taken from place to place, learning as he went about the flora, fauna and topography of the country, while being told (by the elder brother) of the totemic significance of the various localities visited (Meggitt 1962: 285). Every locality has its story, telling of how it was created through the earth-shaping activities of ancestral beings as they roamed the country during the formative era known as the Dreaming. Observing the waterhole while the story of its formation is related or enacted, the novice witnesses the ancestor coming out of the ground; likewise, casting his eyes over the distinctive outline of a hill or rocky outcrop, he recognises in it the congealed form of the ancestor as it lies down to rest. Thus are truths immanent in the landscape, the truths of the Dreaming, gradually revealed to him, as he proceeds from the most superficial, 'outside' level of knowledge to deeper, 'inside' understanding.[6]

Did my father's knowledge of plants and fungi, or the Aboriginal elder's knowledge of the Dreaming, take the form of a set of interconnected beliefs and propositions inside his head? Is it through the transfer of such beliefs and propositions from one generation to the next that we learn to perceive the world in the way we do? If so – if all knowledge is cradled within the mind – why should so much importance be placed on ensuring that novices should see or otherwise experience for themselves the objects or features of the physical world?

One answer might be to suggest that it is through its inscription in such objects or features – plants and fungi, waterholes and hills – that cultural knowledge is transmitted. These objects would accordingly figure as vehicles, or carriers, for meanings that are, so to speak, 'pinned on', and that together constitute a specific cultural worldview or cosmology (Wilson 1988: 50). In other words, cultural forms would be encoded in the landscape just as, according to the standard semiological approach to linguistic significa-tion, conceptual representations are encoded in the medium of sound. The great Swiss linguist Ferdinand de Saussure, who laid the foundation for this approach, argued that a sign is essentially the union of two things, a signifier and a signified, and that the rela-tion between them is established through the mapping of one system of differences on the plane of ideas onto another system of differences on the plane of physical substance (Saussure 1959: 102–22). As sounds stand for concepts, so – by the same logic – fungi (for my father) or waterholes (for the Aboriginal elder) would stand as signifiers for elements of a comprehensive system of mental representations. Was my father, then, communi-cating his knowledge to me by encoding it in the fungi? Do Aboriginal elders transmit ancestral wisdom by encoding it in hills and waterholes?

Strange as it may seem, much anthropological analysis of the cultural construction of the environment proceeds from this assumption. Yet if the idea of encoding beliefs in fungi sounds bizarre, as indeed it is, the idea of the Dreaming as a cosmology encoded in the landscape is no less so. My father's purpose, of course, was to introduce me to the fungi, not to communicate by way of them, and the same is true of the purpose of Aboriginal elders in introducing novices to significant sites. This is not to deny that infor-mation may be communicated, in propositional or semi-propositional form, from generation to generation. But information, in itself, is not knowledge, nor do we become any more knowledgeable through its accumulation. Our knowledgeability consists, rather, in the capacity to situate such information, and understand its meaning, within the context of a direct perceptual engagement with our environments. And we develop this capacity, I contend, by having things *shown* to us.

The idea of showing is an important one. To show something to somebody is to cause it to be seen or otherwise experienced – whether by touch, taste, smell or hearing – by that other person. It is, as it were, to lift a veil off some aspect or component of the environment so that it can be apprehended directly. In that way, truths that are inherent in the world are, bit by bit, revealed or disclosed to the novice. What each generation contributes to the next, in this process, is an *education of attention* (Gibson 1979: 254). Placed in specific situations, novices are instructed to feel this, taste that, or watch out for the other thing. Through this fine-tuning of perceptual skills, meanings immanent in the environment – that is in the relational contexts of the perceiver's involvement in the world – are not so much constructed as discovered.

It could be said that novices, through their sensory education, are furnished with keys to meaning. But the metaphor of the key has to be used with some care. I do not have in mind the kind of key – analogous to a cipher – that might enable me to translate from physical signifiers to mental ideas and thereby to come into possession of the cultural knowledge of my forefathers through a reverse decoding of what they, in their turn, had encoded in the landscape. There is, indeed, a rather fundamental circularity in the notion that cultural knowledge is transmitted across generations by means of its encoding in material symbols. For without the key it is impossible for the novice to read off the cultural message from salient features of the physical world. Yet unless the message has already been thoroughly understood, it is impossible to extract the key. How can features of the landscape figure as elements of a communicative code if, in order to crack the code, you must already know what is to be communicated thereby?

When the novice is brought into the presence of some component of the environment and called upon to attend to it in a certain way, his task, then, is not to decode it. It is rather to discover for himself the meaning that lies within it. To aid him in this task he is provided with a set of keys in another sense, not as ciphers but as *clues* (see Chapter Eleven, p. 208). Whereas the cipher is centrifugal, allowing the novice to access meanings that are attached ('pinned on') by the mind to the outer surface of the world, the clue is centripetal, guiding him towards meanings that lie at the heart of the world itself, but which are normally hidden behind the facade of superficial appearances. The contrast between the key as cipher and the key as clue corresponds to the critical distinction, to which I have already drawn attention, between decoding and revelation. A clue, in short, is a landmark that condenses otherwise disparate strands of experience into a unifying orientation which, in turn, opens up the world to perception of greater depth and clarity.[7] In this sense, clues are keys that unlock the doors of perception, and the more keys you hold, the more doors you can unlock, and the more the world opens up to you. My contention is that it is through the progressive acquisition of such keys that people learn to perceive the world around them.

FORM AND FEELING

When Susanne Langer gave the title *Philosophy in a New Key* to her influential book on art and aesthetics (Langer 1957), she was of course using the metaphor of the key in yet another sense, here referring to a kind of register of understanding, akin to the key of musical notation. In the book, Langer contends that the meaning of art should be found in the art object itself, as it is *presented* to our awareness, rather than in what it might be supposed to *represent* or signify. If people in Western societies find this hard to grasp, it is because they are so used to treating art as somehow representative of something else – for we expect every picture to have a title – that the ways in which we respond to objects or performances themselves are forever getting confused with our responses to whatever they are supposed to stand for. One way around this difficulty, Langer suggests, is to concentrate on the kind of art that – at least for Westerners – is apparently *least* representational, namely music. Music, surely, can stand for nothing but itself, so that an investigation of musical meaning should be able to show how meaning can reside in art as such. 'If the meaning of art belongs to the sensuous percept itself apart from what it ostensibly represents', writes Langer, 'then such purely artistic meaning should be most accessible through musical works' (1957: 209). Pursuing this line of argument, Langer suggests that 'what music can actually reflect is . . . the morphology of feeling' (p. 238).

I believe this idea can be generalised, so long as we recognise that feeling is a mode of active, perceptual engagement, a way of being literally 'in touch' with the world. The craftsman feels his raw material, as the potter feels clay or the turner feels wood, and out of that process of feeling there emerges the form of the vessel. Likewise, the orchestral musician feels – or rather watches – the gestures of the conductor, and out of that feeling comes a phrase shaped in sound. Or more generally, *art gives form to human feeling*; it is the shape that is taken by our perception of the world, guided as it is by the specific orientations, dispositions and sensibilities that we have acquired through having had things pointed out or shown to us in the course of our sensory education.

While on the subject of music, let me give you one example of what I mean, taken from an essay by my favourite composer, Leoš Janáček. Here, Janáček writes of how, on one occasion, he stood on the seashore and notated the sounds of the waves. The waves 'shout', 'bubble', and 'yell' (Janáček 1989: 232). Figure 1.4 is a reproduction of what he

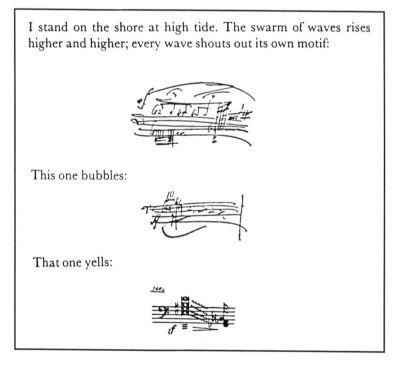

Figure 1.4 Janáček's sketches of the sounds of the waves, as he stood on the shore at the Dutch port of Flushing in 1926 (taken from his essay 'The sea, the land', in Janáček 1989: 229–34).

From *Janáček's Uncollected Essays on Music*, Selected, Edited and Translated by Mirka Zemanová, published by Marion Boyars Publishers of London and New York, 1989, p. 232.

put in his notebook. Now these musical sketches are no mere mechanical record of the sounds as they impinged on his ears. For Janáček is not just hearing, he is *listening*. That is to say, his perception is grounded in an act of attention. Like watching and feeling, listening is something people *do* (see Chapter Fourteen, p. 277). In his act of attention, the movement of the composer's consciousness resonates with the sounds of the waves, and each sketch gives form to that movement.

But Janáček teaches us something more. Throughout his career, he was a compulsive collector of what he called 'speech-melodies'. He scribbled down the melodic form of snippets of speech heard from all kinds of people in all manner of activities: a house-keeper calling to her chickens as she scatters grain, an old man grumbling as he goes to work, children at play, and so on. But these jottings were not confined to human sounds. Speech, for Janáček, was a kind of song, and so were all the other sounds that resonate with our consciousness, from the noises of the waves, through the tolling of an old rusty bell or the ominous sound of a burst water-pipe, to the clucking of hens in the farmyard and the 'bloodthirsty nocturne' of a mosquito.[8] Are we to suppose, then, that in these melodies, nature is trying to communicate with us, to send us messages encoded in patterns of sound? Janáček's point was quite the opposite. It was that we should cease thinking of the sounds of speech merely as vehicles of symbolic communication, as serving to give outward expression to inner states such as beliefs, propositions or emotions. For sound, as Janáček wrote, 'grows out of our entire being ... *There is no sound that is broken away from the tree of life*' (1989: 88, 99, original emphasis).

Let me put this another way. The waves, says Janáček, shout and yell. So, sometimes, do people. When you yell in anger, the yell *is* your anger, it is not a vehicle that *carries* your anger. The sound is not broken off from your mental state and despatched like a message in a bottle cast upon the ocean of sound in the hope that someone might pick it up. The echoes of the yell are the reverberations of your own being as it pours forth into the environment. Maurice Merleau-Ponty, in his *Phenomenology of Perception*, caught the point precisely in his observation that your yell '*does not make me think of anger*, it is anger itself' (1962: 184, original emphasis). And if people pour out their being in the melodies of speech, so the waves pour out theirs in the sounds we describe as foaming and crashing, and the hens pour out theirs in their endless clucking. Thus to take one more hint from Janáček, song – any song, any singing – 'is something from which we are to learn the truth of life' (1989: 89). This is why Aboriginal people sing their songs of the Dreaming, songs which give form to their feeling for the country around them.

CONCLUSION: TOWARDS A SENTIENT ECOLOGY

I have not forgotten the Cree hunter and the caribou, and to wrap up my argument, I now want to return to them. The hunter, let us say, can *tell*. He can do so in two ways. First, he is a perceptually skilled agent, who can detect those subtle clues in the environment that reveal the movements and presence of animals: thus he can 'tell' where the animals are. Secondly, he is able to narrate stories of his hunting journeys, and of his encounters with animals. But in doing so, in telling in this other sense, he is no more aiming to produce a record or transcription of what happened than was Janáček, when he wrote down the sounds of the waves. When the hunter speaks of how the caribou presented itself to him, he does not mean to portray the animal as a self-contained, rational agent whose action in giving itself up served to give outward expression to some inner resolution. Like music, the hunter's story is a performance; and again like music, its aim is to give form to human feeling – in this case the feeling of the caribou's vivid prox-imity as another living, sentient being. At that crucial moment of eye-to-eye contact, the hunter *felt* the overwhelming presence of the animal; he felt as if his own being were somehow bound up or intermingled with that of the animal – a feeling tantamount to love and one that, in the domain of human relations, is experienced in sexual intercourse. In telling of the hunt he gives shape to that feeling in the idioms of speech.

In his recent study of reindeer herders and hunters of the Taimyr region of northern Siberia, David Anderson (2000: 116–17) writes that in their relations with animals and other components of the environment, these people operate with a *sentient ecology*. This notion perfectly captures the kind of knowledge people have of their environments that I have been trying to convey. It is knowledge not of a formal, authorised kind, trans-missible in contexts outside those of its practical application. On the contrary, it is based in feeling, consisting in the skills, sensitivities and orientations that have developed through long experience of conducting one's life in a particular environment. This is the kind of knowledge that Janáček claimed to draw from attending to the melodic inflections of speech; hunters draw it from similarly close attention to the movements, sounds and gestures of animals.

Another word for this kind of sensitivity and responsiveness is *intuition*. In the tradi-tion of Western thought and science, intuition has had a pretty bad press: compared with the products of the rational intellect, it has been widely regarded as knowledge of an inferior kind. Yet it is knowledge we all have; indeed we use it all the time as we go about our everyday tasks (Dreyfus and Dreyfus 1986: 29). What is more, it constitutes a necessary foundation for any system of science or ethics. Simply to exist as sentient beings, people must already be situated in a certain environment and committed to the relation-ships this entails. These relationships, and the sensibilities built up in the course of their unfolding, underwrite our capacities of judgement and skills of discrimination, and scien-tists – who are human too – depend on these capacities and skills as much as do the rest of us. That is why the sovereign perspective of abstract reason, upon which Western science lays its claim to authority, is practically unattainable: an intelligence that was completely detached from the conditions of life in the world could not think the thoughts it does. It is also why reasoning logically from first principles will not suffice to design an ethical system that actually works. For any judgement that had no basis in intuition, however justified it might be on grounds of 'cold' logic, would carry no practical or motivational force whatever. Where the logic of ethical reasoning, setting out from first principles, leads to results that are counter-intuitive, we do not reject our intuitions but rather change the principles, so that they will generate results which conform more closely to what we *feel* is right.

Intuitive understanding, in short, is not contrary to science or ethics, nor does it appeal to instinct rather than reason, or to supposedly 'hardwired' imperatives of human nature. On the contrary, it rests in perceptual skills that emerge, for each and every being, through a process of development in a historically specific environment. These skills, I maintain, provide a necessary grounding for any system of science or ethics that would treat the environment as an *object* of its concern. The sentient ecology is thus both pre-objective and pre-ethical. I have no wish to devalue the projects of either natural science or environ-mental ethics, indeed both are probably more needed now than ever before. My plea is simply that we should not lose sight of their pre-objective, pre-ethical foundations. My overriding aim has been to bring these foundations to light. And what these excavations into the formation of knowledge have revealed is not an alternative science, 'indigenous' rather than Western, but something more akin to a *poetics of dwelling*. It is within the framework of such a poetics, I contend, that Cree tales of animals offering themselves to humans, Aboriginal stories of ancestors emerging from waterholes, Janáček's attempts to notate the sounds of nature and my father's efforts to introduce me to the plants and fungi of the countryside, can best be understood.

Chapter Two

The optimal forager and economic man

INTRODUCTION

Enlightenment thought has proclaimed the triumph of human reason over a recalcitrant nature. As a child of the Enlightenment, neoclassical economics developed as a science of human decision-making and its aggregate consequences, based on the premise that every individual acts in the pursuit of rational self-interest. Whether the postulates of micro-economic theory are applicable to humanity at large, or only to those societies characterised as Western, has been much debated: classic anthropological statements include those of Malinowski – who dismissed as 'preposterous' the assumption that 'man, and especially man on a low level of culture, should be actuated by pure economic motives of enlight-ened self-interest', and Firth – who argued, to the contrary, that 'in some of the most primitive societies known . . . there is the keenest discussion of alternatives in any proposal for the use of resources, of the relative economic advantages of exchange with one party as against another, and the closest scrutiny of the quality of goods which change hands . . . and taking a profit thereby' (Malinowski 1922: 60; Firth 1964: 22, see Schneider 1974: 11–12).

My concern here is not to revisit this old debate. Instead, I want to address the paradox presented by the emergence of an approach within contemporary anthropology which seeks to understand the behaviour of so-called primitive people – or more specifically, hunters and gatherers – not through a direct extension of the principles of formal economics, but through a rather more indirect route. This is to extend to human beings principles already applied in analysing the behaviour of non-human animals, principles that are nevertheless closely modelled on – even to the extent of being identified with – those of economics. The approach in question is known to its practitioners as 'human evolutionary ecology', and it is currently one of the most vigorous areas of research in ecological anthropology.

I aim to show that evolutionary ecology is the precise inverse of microeconomics, just as natural selection is the mirror-image of rational choice. As such, it reproduces in an inverted form the dichotomy between reason and nature that lies at the heart of post-Enlightenment science. But in seeking to account for behaviour in terms of pre-specified and heritable properties of discrete individuals, evolutionary ecology is prevented – despite its claims to the contrary – from developing a truly *ecological* perspective. By this I do not simply mean a perspective that would incorporate external environmental variables as part of the explanation for behaviour. An approach that is genuinely ecological, in my view, is one that would ground human intention and action within the context of an ongoing and mutually constitutive engagement between people and their environments.

Yet such an approach, I argue, calls into question the very foundations of the neo-Darwinian explanatory paradigm.

Suppose you were an advocate of economic formalism in anthropology, and that you were concerned to explain why a particular group of hunters and gatherers should choose to concentrate their efforts on harvesting a certain mix of plant and animal resources. By attaching a utility value to each unit of resource, measured in terms of the satisfaction it yields, you would calculate an optimal strategy of resource procurement, that would yield the highest overall utility relative to time and energy expended. You would then compare this strategy with what the people actually do and, finding a nice fit, you would declare that your model has passed the test of empirical confirmation. Anticipating the 'so what?' challenge of the sceptic, you would conclude that what this proves is that hunters and gatherers are just as capable of making informed choices in their own best interests as anyone else. Reason, you would point out, is a faculty common to all humans, not just 'modern Western' or 'civilised' ones, and it is ethnocentric to imagine that while *we* decide what to do in any given situation on the basis of rational deliberation, *they* are bound in their actions by blind conformity to the received wisdom of cultural convention.

What, then, of non-human animals? They, too, seem to come out with strategies of resource procurement which would look eminently rational, had they worked these strategies out for themselves. But of course, you say, they have not. The animals have had their strategies worked out for them in advance, by the evolutionary force of natural selection. The logic of natural selection is simply as follows: individuals with more efficient resource procurement or foraging strategies will have a reproductive advantage over individuals with less efficient strategies, and since these strategies – or more precisely, the rules or programmes for generating them – are encoded in the materials of heredity, the more efficient strategies will automatically tend to become more firmly established in each generation as their carriers bear proportionally more offspring. Now the point of departure for human evolutionary ecology is that the foraging behaviour of human hunter-gatherers, just like that of their non-human counterparts, can be understood as the application, in specific environmental contexts, of decision rules or 'cognitive algorithms' that have been shaped up through a Darwinian process of variation under natural selection. From this premise has been derived a body of theory, known in the trade as 'optimal foraging theory', consisting of formal models which predict how, under given external conditions, a forager should behave, assuming that the overriding objective is to maximise the balance between the energy intake from harvested resources and the energy costs of procurement.

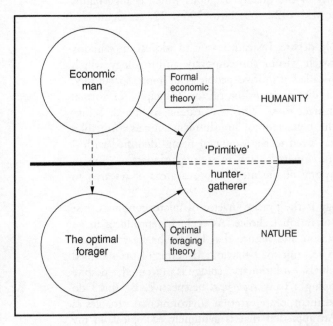

Figure 2.1 The 'primitive' hunter-gatherer conceived as a version of economic man and as a species of optimal forager.

Is the human hunter-gatherer, then, a version of economic man or a species of optimal forager? On the face of it these two figures – both of them, of course, ideal constructs of the analytic imagination – appear diametrically opposed, and their conflation in the archetypal figure of the 'primitive' hunter-gatherer seems to reflect the ambivalent status of this figure, within the discourse of Western science, as transitional between the conditions of nature and humanity (see Figure 2.1). Economic man, surely, exercises his reason in the sphere of social interaction, and in so doing advances in culture or civilisation, against the background of an intrinsically resistant nature. The rationality of the optimal forager, by contrast, is installed at the very heart of nature, while the specifically human domain of society and culture is seen as a source of external normative bias that may cause behaviour to deviate from the optimum. Here, then, is the paradox to which I referred at the outset, of an approach which, while explicitly modelling itself on classical microeconomics, is nevertheless considered applicable to human beings only insofar as their behaviour is in some sense comparable to that of non-human animals. How can we hold, at one and the same time, that the faculty of reason is the distinctive mark of humanity, and that the rationality of human hunter-gatherers, by comparison with that of their non-human counterparts, is compromised by social and cultural constraints? I take this question as my point of departure.

CULTURE AND CHOICE

> Hunters-gatherers, or foragers, live in environments characterised by diverse and heterogeneously distributed resources. From the array of potential food species, foraging locations and pathways, the forager can choose combinations which more or less effectively and efficiently procure subsistence. The forager's choices make up a strategy of adjustment to ecological conditions, an adaptive pattern resulting from evolutionary processes and the constraints of situation, time, and chance.
>
> (Winterhalder 1981a: 66)

This lucid statement, by one of the foremost exponents of optimal foraging theory, takes us directly to the core of the problem. It lies in the contradiction between the notions, on the one hand, that the forager's 'strategy of adjustment' is the result of a series of choices about where to go and what to procure, and on the other hand, that as an 'adaptive pattern' it is the product of an evolutionary process. In explicating this contradiction it helps to have an empirical example in mind, and for this purpose I turn briefly to ethnographic material that Winterhalder himself presents, gathered through fieldwork among Cree people of Muskrat Dam Lake in northern Ontario.

The Cree draw for their subsistence on a variety of large and small mammals, waterfowl and fish, distributed rather sparsely and patchily in an environment which consists of a fine-grained mosaic of different types of dominant vegetation. Not only does the abundance of resource species fluctuate markedly and irregularly from year to year, but the vegetational mosaic also changes in response to climatic variations. The result is that the Cree hunter is unlikely ever to encounter the same conditions from one year to the next (Winterhalder 1981a: 80–1). He has, therefore, to work out his tactics as he goes along. One hunting trip described by Winterhalder exemplifies this point very well. In this trip, ostensibly for beaver trapping, he and his Cree companion came across signs of grouse, moose, wolf, hare, beaver, mink, otter and muskrat. At each sign his companion had to make up his mind whether to pursue the animal in question. In the event, the grouse was shot, the moose and wolf were ignored, snares were set for the hare and beaver, and traps for the muskrat and otter.

But this hunt, Winterhalder tells us, was an example of an older style of doing things: although the journey from the village to the start of the trail was made by snowmobile, during the hunt itself the companions proceeded on snowshoes. Hunters of the younger generation are making greater use of the snowmobile, not just for getting to the trail but in the course of seeking out animals. The consequent reduction in search times allows them to be far more selective, and to concentrate on taking high-priority species. In the past, the mark of a good hunter was supposed to lie in his ability to handle almost any kind of animal; nowadays, by contrast, younger hunters are said to specialise in hunting just one or two species, and to lack competence in dealing with the others (Winterhalder 1981a: 86–9).

It is clear from this account that hunters are faced with choices, that the choices they make add up to a pattern, and that this pattern changes in response to alterations in the parameters of hunting brought about, for example, by the introduction of new technologies. It is not so clear, however, that the pattern has 'evolved' in the Darwinian sense, or that its emergence has anything to do with the process of natural selection. For the sake of argument let us suppose that in the hunting trip described above, taking account of the expected calorific yield of different resource species and of the energy costs of search and pursuit (or of setting and visiting traps), the hunter's decisions conformed closely to what might be modelled as the optimal strategy for a forager seeking to maximise the net rate of energy gain. And let it also be supposed – rather more problematically – that the households of tactically skilled hunters, being relatively securely provisioned, are also prosperous in terms of the production of healthy offspring: in other words that the hunter's success in the woods is matched by reproductive success at home. There would still be no reason to believe that the successful hunting strategy was the result of an evolutionary process.

It is commonly argued, even by biologists who should know better (e.g. Dunbar 1987), that to show how behaviour of a certain kind has evolved by natural selection, one has only to demonstrate that it contributes positively to the reproductive fitness of those individuals who execute it. This argument is critically incomplete. It misses out the essential link that closes the loop of Darwinian explanation. Behaviour will only evolve by natural selection if, through its effects on reproduction, it contributes to the representation, in successor generations, of a set of instructions or a 'programme' for generating it. In other words, the behaviour must not only have consequences *for* reproduction but also be a consequence *of* the elements that are reproduced (Ingold 1990: 226 fn.9). So far as non-human animals are concerned, the replicated programme elements are usually assumed to be genes. Whatever the merits of this assumption, once our attention turns to human beings it looks decidedly unrealistic. I know of no recent author who has seriously suggested that the behavioural variability apparent from ethnographic studies of human hunter-gatherers might be attributed to inter-populational genetic differences. Instead it is proposed that the instructions underwriting human foraging behaviour are cultural rather than genetic, encoded in words or other symbolic media rather than the 'language' of DNA. As Winterhalder himself has noted (1981b: 17), in the case of human foragers 'information passed from generation to generation by culture provides much of the strategic framework within which specific choices and options are exercised by individuals and groups'.

Does this enculturation model take us any closer to understanding the behaviour of the Cree hunter in the above example? Although in the account the hunter is described as having made a number of decisions – to shoot this animal, pass up another, lay a trap for a third, and so on – the model would imply that in reality, the scope of his autonomy in decision-making is extremely restricted. He is, after all, merely applying a set of decision rules acquired more or less unselfconsciously from his seniors, and whose prevalence in the society is due not to their perceived efficacy but to the fact that they served his predecessors well, enabling them to bring in the food to support numerous offspring who – following in their fathers' footsteps – reproduced the same strategic steps in their own hunting activities (Boone and Smith 1998: S146). To put the point in more general terms, if a particular strategy of hunting is inscribed within a cultural tradition, and if that tradition has evolved through a process of natural selection, then all the hunter can do is to carry on in the same way, even if changes in environment or technology have had the effect of wiping out its earlier advantages. This is not to say that behaviour is completely prescribed, and genuine choices may still have to be made. But they are made *within* a received strategic framework, they are not about what framework to adopt.

NEO-DARWINIAN BIOLOGY AND NEO-CLASSICAL MICROECONOMICS

Strangely, however, this view of the human forager as the bearer of evolved cultural propensities that cause behaviour to strain towards the optimum coexists, in the writings of evolutionary ecologists, side by side with a quite different picture. Observing that human behaviour often seems far from optimal, the blame for the discrepancy is placed squarely upon culture itself! Thus Winterhalder explicitly singles out 'cultural goals', situated within systems of belief and meaning, as one of the possible reasons for the disjunction, in the human case, 'between modeled optima and observed behaviors' (1981b: 16). Likewise, Foley (1985: 237) lists, as among the consequences of the human capacity for culture, a number of characteristics that 'may inhibit the achievement of optimality'. Nowhere, however, is the contradiction more blatant than in a recent review of optimal foraging theory in its archaeological and anthropological application to human hunter-gatherers, by Robert Bettinger (1991).

Referring back to the classic debate in economic anthropology between advocates of so-called 'formalism' and 'substantivism', Bettinger reminds us that the terms of the debate have their source in Max Weber's (1947: 184–5) distinction between the formal and substantive aspects of human rationality, the first consisting in the element of quantitative calculation or accounting involved in economic decision-making, the second in the subservience of economic activity to ultimate ends or standards of value of a qualitative nature. Without denying the salience of the latter in human affairs, Bettinger argues that formal models have the great advantage of providing a 'yardstick of objective economic rationality', against which it is possible to gauge how far actual behaviour is governed by 'rational, self-interested incentives' as opposed to 'cultural norms and ideas' (Bettinger 1991: 106). And this, he maintains, is precisely what the models of optimal foraging theorists enable one to achieve. The ideal-typical forager of these models is a creature entirely free from cultural constraint to act out of pure, calculated self-interest. Insofar as real human beings are biased by their commitment to 'cultural norms', it is expected that their behaviour will diverge from the optimum.

This puts the Cree hunter in an entirely different light. The received wisdom of his cultural heritage, far from underwriting his ability to come up with an effective strategy, is actually liable to *prevent* him from recognising the best course of action judged in terms of an objective reckoning of costs and benefits. For example, older hunters, strongly committed to the traditional ideal of spreading their effort across a range of species, continue to practise a broad spectrum style of hunting even when the availability of the snowmobile makes it much more profitable to concentrate on a few preferred, high-yield game animals. By contrast, men of the younger generation, whose commitment to traditional cultural values (at least in the eyes of their seniors) is weak, readily opt for a more specialised strategy. It seems perfectly reasonable to suppose that this strategy is a result of the quite conscious and deliberate decision, on the part of these younger men, *not* to imitate the style of their forefathers. But by the same token, it makes no sense at all to regard it as the outcome of a process of variation under natural selection (Boone and Smith 1998: S146–7).

One cannot avoid the impression that optimal foraging theorists are trying to have it both ways, taking their cue, as it suits them, either from neo-Darwinian evolutionary biology or from neoclassical microeconomics. Indeed in Bettinger's view the fact that optimal foraging theory came to anthropology via biology is more or less incidental – 'it might just as easily have been borrowed from economics' (1991: 83). If that were really so, then the theorems of economics should be as applicable to non-human as to human behaviour, and economic man would have his counterpart among the animals. The 'economic muskrat', for example, would place its own self-preservation before the promptings of its genes, and would choose not to visit the traps laid by the Cree hunter. The following passage, however, gives the game away:

> In Darwinian theories, . . . individuals are essential to explanation: their interests cannot be ignored. It is the self-interested individual that must make *real and metaphorical choices* about reproduction and the selective risks associated with different courses of action
>
> (Bettinger 1991: 152, my emphasis)

Crucially, Bettinger fails to explain what he means by 'metaphorical choices'. We can only surmise that he has in mind the common habit that neo-Darwinian biologists have of speaking *as if* the individual had selected what in fact is built into its *modus operandi* by countless generations of natural selection of which its own constitution is the latest product. The metaphor may have its uses, affording a kind of shorthand, but when reality and metaphor are fused as they are here, the consequences are disastrous.

Are the Cree hunter's choices real or metaphorical? If they are real, then they have not been 'passed on' as part of any inherited schema, whether genetic or cultural, and appeals to natural selection are irrelevant. If, on the other hand, the hunter's behaviour follows a strategy that has evolved through a process of natural selection, albeit working on culturally rather than genetically transmitted characteristics, then strictly speaking, he exercises no more choice in the matter of where to go or what species to pursue than do non-human creatures whose behaviour is presumed to be under genetic control. 'Why', asks Ernst Mayr (1976: 362), 'did the warbler on my summer place in New Hampshire start its southward migration on the night of the 25th August?': his answer is that the bird has an evolved genetic constitution, shaped up 'through many thousands of generations of natural selection', which induces it to respond in this particular way to a specific conjunction of environmental conditions (a reduction in daylight hours coupled with a sudden drop in temperature). Likewise, the muskrat is drawn compulsively into the hunter's trap. And likewise too, according to this selectionist account, the hunter is predisposed to respond appropriately to signs of the presence of animals, as revealed by their tracks, by pursuing some, laying traps for others, and passing yet others by. He could not have chosen to do other than what he actually does, any more than the muskrat could have chosen not to enter the trap, or the warbler not to migrate. For as a product of 'enculturation', the hunter is as stuck with his heritage as are the muskrat and the bird with their respective sets of genes.

In short, to have recourse to neo-Darwinian theory is to show not how individuals design strategies, but how natural selection designs strategies for individuals to follow. Equipped by virtue of its evolutionary past with a programme for generating more or less optimal behaviour, within an appropriate environmental context, the individual is predestined to execute that behaviour; thus its entire life, judged by its reproductive outcome, becomes just one trial in that protracted and ongoing decision process that is natural selection itself. Stephen Toulmin (1981) refers to this as a process of *populational* adaptation, by contrast to the *calculative* adaptation that results from rational decision making. But as he points out, explanations of adaptive behaviour based on rational choice and on natural selection are not incompatible. Indeed it may be argued that the former actually depend on the latter – in other words, that a prerequisite for any theory of calculative adaptation is an account of human nature which must necessarily be couched in populational terms. I present this argument below.

REASON AND NATURE AS AGENTS OF SELECTION

A formal theory of rational choice, as elaborated in classical microeconomics, predicts what people will do, assuming that their deliberate aim is to obtain the greatest benefit from their actions. The relative benefit to be derived from alternative courses of action can, however, only be evaluated in terms of people's own subjective beliefs and preferences. It may, of course, be possible to derive certain 'lower order' beliefs and preferences from 'higher order' ones. But this process of derivation cannot go on indefinitely. Ultimately, if we want to explain where these beliefs and preferences came from in the first place – if, that is, we seek the source of human intentions – then we have to show how they may have emerged through a history of natural selection. Appeal to human intentionality and rational choice, it is argued, reveals only the *proximate* causes of behaviour, while the *ultimate* cause lies in those selective forces that have furnished individuals both with the fundamental motivations underwriting their choices and with the cognitive mechanisms that allow them to be made. As Boone and Smith observe, 'past genetic (and perhaps cultural) evolution has shaped the human psyche to be very effective at solving adaptive problems, and one important element of the psyche is what we commonly label "intentions" or "goals" or "preferences"' (1998: S152, see also Smith and Winterhalder 1992: 41–50). Thus even if strategies are taken to be products of human reasoning, we have still to resort to natural selection to account for the rationality of the strategists.

Does human evolutionary ecology offer such an account? It does not – indeed it *cannot*, so long as it remains committed to its principal tactic of analysing behaviour in terms of its potential reproductive consequences rather than focusing on the effects of differential reproductive success in establishing the psychological mechanisms that give rise to it. As Symons (1992: 148) has put it, evolutionary ecology is concerned with the *adaptiveness* of behaviour, whereas a properly Darwinian account should be concerned with *adaptation*. That is, it should attempt to show how the most basic goals that human beings seek to achieve, and that motivate their behaviour, have been designed by natural selection under the kinds of environmental conditions experienced by ancestral populations in the course of the evolution of our species. Such goals, Symons argues, are both species-specific and inflexible, such that their contemporary pursuit, under environments very different from those of the 'environment of evolutionary adaptedness', can lead to behaviour whose consequences are profoundly maladaptive. A taste for sweet things, for example, may have served our hunter-gatherer ancestors well, in establishing a preference for fruit when it is at its most nutritious. But for the more affluent inhabitants of a modern industrial society it can have the less benign consequences of obesity and tooth decay (Symons 1992: 139).

In recent years a new field of study, styling itself as evolutionary psychology, has grown up around the attempt to identify those capacities and dispositions conventionally gathered under the rubric of 'human nature', and to explain how and why they evolved (Barkow, Cosmides and Tooby 1992). This is not the place for a critique of evolutionary psychology, however it is worth noting that its protagonists find themselves at loggerheads with the advocates of evolutionary ecology, despite their common allegiance to the neo-Darwinian paradigm. The difference between them is this: evolutionary ecology seeks to show how behaviour is sensitively responsive to variations in the environment, but lacks a coherent account of human nature; evolutionary psychology seeks to construct just such an account, but in doing so is insensitive to the fine-tuning of human behaviour to environmental conditions. This is not just a difference of emphasis: on behavioural differences as against cognitive universals. The issue is more profound, for behaviour that evolutionary psychology interprets as the product of evolved problem-solving mechanisms in the human mind/brain, is interpreted by evolutionary ecology as the expression of solutions already reached through the mechanism of natural selection, and impressed upon the mind through a process of enculturation.[1] As I intend to argue, neither alternative offers an adequate, ecologically grounded account of how the subsistence skills of hunters and gatherers are acquired and deployed. The problem lies at the heart of the Darwinian paradigm itself.

COGNITIVE ALGORITHMS AND RULES OF THUMB

Let me return for a moment to Winterhalder's ethnography of the Cree of Muskrat Dam Lake. It will be recalled that the environment presents a heterogeneous mosaic of habitat types, which differ in terms of the kinds and relative abundance of the prey species they support. Optimal foraging theory predicts that under these circumstances, hunters will move from patch to patch, sampling what each has to offer, but will drop low-quality patches from their itinerary once it is clear that more is to be gained from concentrating their efforts in high-quality patches despite the extra costs of between-patch travel (MacArthur and Pianka 1966). Where travel costs are high, hunters will tend to be patch-generalists, where they are low they will be patch-specialists. Winterhalder found that the adoption by the Cree of snowmobiles and outboard motors, which greatly reduced the time spent on travel, did indeed favour specialisation. Yet even in the days when everyone moved about on snowshoes, it appears that their itineraries took in relatively few patch types.

To account for this discrepancy, Winterhalder (1981a: 90) proposes that the Cree employ an 'interstice' rather than a 'patch-to-patch' strategy of foraging (see Figure 2.2). It is a strategy that makes good sense when one is hunting animals, such as moose and caribou, which themselves move frequently from one patch to another, which are not particularly abundant in proportion to the number of patches they are associated with, and which leave tracks or trails that may be used by hunters as evidence for their recent movements and present whereabouts. Moving in the interstices between patches – mainly,

that is, on the hard-packed snow of
frozen lakes and creeks which in any
case makes travel easier – the hunter
can expect to intercept the tracks
left by animals as they move from
patch to patch, and will visit a patch
only when the tracks indicate
that favoured prey are present there.
'Cree foragers', Winterhalder remarks, 'have developed this technique to a high level of skill' (1981a:
91).

There is no reason to doubt the
truth of this remark. My concern is
rather with the significance to be
attached to the notion of *skill* in
this context. For Winterhalder, skill
evidently means an ability to produce rapid solutions to ostensibly
rather complex problems posed by

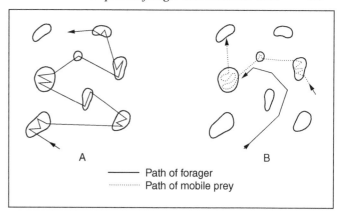

Figure 2.2 Alternative foraging strategies in a patchy environment:
(A) patch-to-patch foraging; (B) interstice foraging (Winterhalder
1981a: 91).

From Winterhalder and Smith (eds) *Hunter-Gatherer Foraging Strategies*,
published by University of Chicago Press 1981.

specific conjunctions of environmental circumstances. Elsewhere, Smith and Winterhalder
(1992: 57) suggest that this is done by means of 'rules of thumb'. Clearly, as they point
out, the formal mathematical techniques (including geometric tangents, partial derivatives,
algebraic inequalities and the like) used in the construction of optimal foraging models
are not replicated in the 'everyday decision processes of actors'. Nevertheless, 'simple rules
of thumb *or cognitive algorithms* provided by natural or cultural selection may allow them
to approach the solution [to a particular foraging problem] quite closely under conditions
approximating the environments in which these "short-cuts" evolved' (1992: 58, my
emphasis). One such rule, for the Cree hunter, might be stated as follows: 'Proceed along
the creek bed until you intercept a track; then, if the track is fresh, search the upland
patch to which it leads'. To become skilled, then, the hunter must be equipped with such
rules through a process of enculturation.

Now I do not wish to deny that Cree hunters have resort to rules of thumb. I believe,
however, that to describe these rules as 'cognitive algorithms' is fundamentally to distort
their nature. The notion of cognitive algorithm comes from planning theory, and posits
a series of linked decision rules, internal to the actor, which operate on received information to generate plans for subsequent action. As a 'solution' to a perceived 'problem',
the plan is supposed to contain a precise and complete specification of the action that is
predicated upon it, so that the latter is fully accounted for by the former: to explain what
foragers do it is enough to have explained how they decide what to do. The power and
utility of rules of thumb, by contrast, rest on the fact that they are inherently vague, specifying little or nothing about the concrete details of action. Invoked against the background
of involvement in a real world of persons, objects and relations, rules of thumb may
furnish practitioners with a way of talking about what they have done, or about what
they mean to do next, but once launched into the action itself they must necessarily fall
back on abilities of a quite different kind – namely, on developmentally embodied and
environmentally attuned capacities of movement and perception. Rules of thumb, as
Suchman (1987: 52) puts it, serve 'to orient you in such a way that you can obtain the

best possible position from which to use those embodied skills on which, in the final analysis, your success depends'. In no sense, however, do they substitute for these skills. Nor, as I shall now show, can we understand the acquisition of technical skills, in successive generations, as a process of enculturation.

ENCULTURATION AND ENSKILMENT

If, as evolutionary ecology would claim, the interstice pattern of foraging has evolved by natural selection as an optimal strategy of resource procurement for hunters and trappers in the boreal forest environment, then it must be expressible in the form of rules and representations that can be transmitted across generations. Let me emphasise once again that there is no question of these rules and representations being encoded genetically. The suggestion is rather that the 'formula' for interstice foraging is contained within a body of cultural information that is passed on, in a manner analogous to genetic transmission, from one generation to the next. According to this analogy, the transmission of cultural information must be distinguished from the experience of its application in particular settings of use, just as the transmission of the constituent elements of the genotype must be distinguished from the latter's realisation, within a particular environment, in the manifest form of the phenotype. This distinction is commonly made by means of a contrast between two forms of learning: social and individual (e.g. Richerson and Boyd 1992: 64, see also Chapter Twenty-one, pp. 386–7). Thus in social learning, the novice absorbs the underlying rules and principles of hunting from already knowledgeable members of the community; in individual learning he puts them to use in the course of his activities in the environment.

Given that social learning occupies such a central place in their theory – as central, indeed, as genetic replication – it is rather surprising that evolutionary ecologists have devoted almost no attention to how it occurs. Consequently, as Hillard Kaplan and Kim Hill are honest enough to admit, 'we know virtually nothing about . . . the developmental processes by which children become adult foragers' (1992: 197). Most often, cultural transmission is viewed as a simple process of imprinting, in which a whole inventory of rules and representations is miraculously downloaded into the passively receptive mind of the novice. It is to precisely this notion of enculturation that evolutionary psychologists have taken exception. Nothing can be acquired, they claim, unless innate processing mechanisms are already in place that serve to decode the signals received from the social environment, and to extract the information contained therein. Thus the traditional model of enculturation, they argue, rests upon an impossible psychology. Not only do innate information-processing mechanisms make the transmission of variable cultural forms possible; they also impose their own structure on what can be learned and how. And it is the evolution of these mechanisms under natural selection, according to evolutionary psychologists, that has to be explained (Tooby and Cosmides 1992: 91–2).

Does this offer an account that is any more convincing? I do not believe that it does, for a simple reason. Human beings are not born with a ready-made architecture of specialised acquisition mechanisms; to the extent that such mechanisms *do* exist, they could only emerge within a process of ontogenetic development. Thus, even if there were such a thing as a 'technology acquisition device' (analogous to the 'language acquisition device' posited by many psycholinguists), it would still have to undergo formation within the very same developmental context in which the child learns the particular skills of his or her community. And if both are aspects of the same developmental process, it is difficult to see how the learning of the 'acquired' skills can be distinguished from the formation of the 'innate' device (this point is argued at greater length in Chapter Twenty-one). However there is no reason to suppose that anything like a 'technology acquisition device' exists at all. Rather, the learning of technical skills appears to depend on what might be called 'technology acquisition support systems' (Wynn 1994: 153). These systems, as Wynn argues, are not even partly innate. They are rather *systems of apprenticeship*, constituted by the relationships between more and less experienced practitioners in hands-on contexts of activity. And it is on the reproduction of these relationships, not on genetic replication – or the transmission of some analogous code of cultural instructions – that the continuity of a technical tradition depends.

Considering how novice hunters actually learn their trade, two points should be made right away. First, there is no explicit code of procedure, specifying the exact movements to be executed under any given circumstances: indeed practical skills of this kind, as I show in Chapter Nineteen, are just not amenable to codification in terms of any formal system of rules and representations. Secondly, it is not possible, in practice, to separate the sphere of the novice's involvement with other persons from that of his involvement with the non-human environment. The novice hunter learns by accompanying more experienced hands in the woods. As he goes about, he is instructed in what to look out for, and his attention is drawn to subtle clues that he might otherwise fail to notice: in other words, he is led to develop a sophisticated perceptual awareness of the properties of his surroundings and of the possibilities they afford for action. For example, he learns to register those qualities of surface texture that enable one to tell, merely from touch, how long ago an animal left its imprint in the snow, and how fast it was travelling.

We could say that he acquires such know-how by observation and imitation, but not, however, in the sense in which these terms are generally employed by enculturation theorists. Observation is no more a matter of having information copied into one's head, than is imitation a matter of mechanically executing the received intructions. Rather, to observe is actively to attend to the movements of others; to imitate is to align that attention to the movement of one's own practical orientation towards the environment. The fine-tuning of perception and action that is going on here is better understood as a process of enskilment than as one of enculturation (I return to this distinction in Chapter Twenty-three, p. 416; see also Pálsson 1994). For what is involved, as I showed in the last chapter, is not a transmission of representations, as the enculturation model implies, but an education of attention. Indeed, the instructions the novice hunter receives – to watch out for this, attend to that, and so on – only take on meaning in the context of his engagement with the environment. Hence it makes no sense to speak of 'culture' as an independent body of context-free knowledge, that is available for transmission prior to the situations of its application (Lave 1990: 310). And if culture, in this form, exists nowhere save in the heads of anthropological theorists, then the very idea of its evolution is a chimera.

CONCLUSION

In short, a technique such as interstice foraging is not passed on as part of any systematic body of cultural representations; it is rather inculcated in each successive generation through a process of development, in the course of novices' practical involvement with the constituents of their environment – under the guidance of more experienced mentors – in the conduct of their everyday tasks. The accomplished hunter consults the world, not representations inside his head. The implications of this conclusion cannot be overemphasised, since they strike at the very core of neo-Darwinian theory itself. It is a fundamental premise of this theory that the morphological attributes and behavioural propensities of individual organisms must be specifiable, in some sense, independently and in advance of their entry into relations with their environments, and that the components of these specifications – whether genes or (in humans) their cultural analogues – must be transmissible across generations. It is my contention, to the contrary, that such context-independent specifications are, at best, analytic abstractions, and that in reality the forms and capacities of organisms are the emergent properties of developmental systems (Oyama 1985: 22–3).

We can now see why the attempt to produce a neo-Darwinian evolutionary *ecology* inevitably runs into difficulties. For if morphology and behaviour truly emerge through a history of organism–environment relations, as a properly ecological perspective requires, then they cannot be attributed to a prior design specification that is imported into the environmental context of development. Yet just such an attribution is entailed in the theory of adaptation under natural selection. As we have seen, evolutionary ecologists have tended to evade the problem by focusing on the reproductive consequences of behaviour while remaining agnostic about its developmental causes, thereby substituting the study of adaptiveness for that of adaptation. On the other hand, evolutionary psychologists, adhering more strictly to the neo-Darwinian logic of adaptation, have come up with an account of human nature that is fundamentally *anti*-ecological in its appeal to an 'evolved architecture' that is fixed and universal to the species, regardless of the environmental circumstances in which people happen to grow up.

Let me conclude by returning to the opposition with which I began, between the optimal forager and economic man. Whereas the latter is credited with the capacity to work out his strategies for himself, the former has to have them worked out for him by natural selection. They appear to stand, thus, on opposite sides of an overriding division between reason and nature, freedom and necessity, subjectivity and objectivity. But this is also a dichotomy on which the project of modern natural science depends, and it underwrites the distinction, as it has appeared in the literature of Western anthropology, between the scientist, whose humanity is not in doubt, and the hunter-gatherer who, it would appear, is only contingently human. The scientist – in this case the evolutionary ecologist – constructs an abstract model on the basis of which he can calculate what it would be best for the hunter-gatherer to do; this prediction is then 'tested' against what the hunter-gatherer actually does. If observed practice conforms to the prediction, the model is said to provide an ultimate explanation for the hunter-gatherer's behaviour. Natural selection features, in this account, not as a real-world process but as the reflection of scientific reason in the mirror of nature, providing the theorist with the excuse to parade models *of* behaviour as though they were explanations *for* behaviour.

No amount of appeal, however, to 'methodological individualism', the 'hypothetico-deductive method', or other such contrivances in the analyst's bag of tricks (Smith and Winterhalder 1992, Winterhalder and Smith 1992), will get around the fact that the individuals whose behaviour evolutionary ecologists purport to explain are creatures of their own imagination. The scientific image of hunting and gathering, as a naturally prescribed course of fitness-maximisation, is as illusory as the image that science has of its own enterprise, as a monument to the freedom and pre-eminence of human reason. Far from confronting one another across the boundary of nature, both the people who call themselves scientists and the people whom scientists call hunter-gatherers are fellow passengers in this world of ours, who carry on the business of life and, in so doing, develop their capacities and aspirations, within a continuing history of involvement with both human and non-human components of their environments. If we are to develop a thoroughgoing ecological understanding of how real people relate to these environments, and of the sensitivity and skill with which they do so, it is imperative to take this condition of involvement as our point of departure. Yet to achieve this, as I have shown, will require nothing less than a fundamental overhaul of evolutionary theory itself.

Chapter Three

Hunting and gathering as ways of perceiving the environment

That nature is a cultural construction is an easy claim to make, and it is one that figures prominently in recent anthropological literature. It is not so easy, however, to ascertain what might be meant by it. One of my principal objectives in this chapter is to demonstrate that this claim is incoherent. To illustrate my argument I shall consider the anthropological treatment of those peoples classically regarded as operating within a natural economy, namely societies of hunters and gatherers. Comparing this treatment with the understandings that people who actually live by hunting and gathering have of themselves and their environments, I shall show that the latter systematically reject the ontological dualism of that tradition of thought and science which – as a kind of shorthand – we call 'Western', and of which the dichotomy between nature and culture is the prototypical instance. I propose that we take these hunter-gatherer understandings seriously, and this means that far from regarding them as diverse cultural constructions of reality, alternative to the Western one, we need to think again about our *own* ways of comprehending human action, perception and cognition, and indeed about our very understanding of the environment and of our relations and responsibilities towards it. Above all, we cannot rest content with the facile identification of the environment – or at least its non-human component – with 'nature'. For as we saw in Chapter One, the world can only be 'nature' for a being that does not inhabit it, yet only through inhabiting can the world be constituted, in *relation* to a being, as its environment.

NATURE, CULTURE AND THE LOGIC OF CONSTRUCTION

Let me begin by outlining what I take to be a commonly adopted position within social and cultural anthropology. I admit that this has something of the character of a 'straw man', and I am indeed setting it up in order to knock it down. Nevertheless, it is one that has proved remarkably resilient, for reasons that will become clear as we proceed.

Of all species of animals, the argument goes, humans are unique in that they occupy what Richard Shweder (1990: 2) calls 'intentional worlds'. For the inhabitants of such a world, things do not exist 'in themselves', as indifferent objects, but only as they are given form or meaning within systems of mental representations. Thus to individuals who belong to different intentional worlds, the same objects in the same physical surroundings may mean quite different things. And when people act towards these objects, or with them in mind, their actions respond to the ways they are already appropriated, categorised or valorised in terms of a particular, pre-existent design. That design, transmitted across the generations in the form of received conceptual schemata, and manifested physically in the artificial products of their implementation, is what is commonly known as 'culture'.

The environments of human beings, therefore, are culturally constituted. And when we refer to an environment – or more specifically to that part of it consisting of animate and inanimate things – as 'nature', then this too has to be understood as an artefact of cultural construction. 'Nature is to culture', writes Marshall Sahlins, 'as the constituted is to the constituting' (1976: 209). Culture provides the building plan, nature is the building; but whence come the raw materials?

There must indeed be a physical world 'out there', beyond the multiple, intentional worlds of cultural subjects, otherwise there would be nothing to build with nor anyone, for that matter, to do the building. Minds cannot subsist without bodies to house them, and bodies cannot subsist unless continually engaged in material and energetic exchanges with components of the environment. Biological and ecological scientists routinely describe these exchanges as going on within a world of nature. It is apparently necessary, there-fore, to distinguish between two kinds or versions of nature: 'really natural' nature (the object of study for natural scientists) and 'culturally perceived' nature (the object of study for social and cultural anthropologists). Such distinctions are indeed commonplace in anthropological literature: examples are Rappaport's between the 'operational' models of ecological science, purportedly describing nature as it really is, and the 'cognized' models of native people; and, perhaps most notoriously, the much used and abused distinction between 'etic' and 'emic' accounts (Rappaport 1968: 237–41, Ellen 1982, Chapter 9, cf. Ingold 1992a: 47–8).

In the formula 'nature is culturally constructed', nature thus appears on two sides: on one as the product of a constructional process, on the other as its precondition. Herein, however, lies a paradox. Many anthropologists are well aware that the basic contrast between physical substance and conceptual form, of which the dichotomy between nature and culture is one expression, is deeply embedded within the tradition of Western thought. It is recognized that the concept of nature, insofar as it denotes an external world of matter and substance 'waiting to be given meaningful shape and content by the mind of man' (Sahlins 1976: 210), is part of that very intentional world within which is situ-ated the project of Western science as the 'objective' study of natural phenomena (Shweder 1990: 24). And yet the notion that there are intentional worlds, and that human realities are culturally constructed, rests on precisely the same ontological foundation. The paradox may be represented as follows:

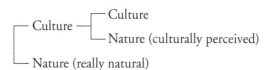

If the concept of nature is given within the intentional world of the Western scientist, then the concept of culture must – by the same token – be given within the intentional world of the Western humanist. Each, indeed, presupposes the other. Not only, then, must the concept of nature be regarded as a cultural construct, but so also must that of culture. As Carol MacCormack puts it: 'Neither the concept of nature nor that of culture is "given", and they cannot be free from the biases of the [European] culture in which the concepts were constructed' (1980: 6). The fact that 'culture' appears twice in this statement at once alerts us to a basic contradiction. For the references, in the second part of the statement, to culture and to the logic of construction take as 'given' the very concepts that, in the first part of the statement, are said to be historically relative.

Nor can the problem be contrived to disappear by trying to have it both ways, as Kirsten Hastrup does when she suggests that instead of regarding nature as 'either a relative cultural category or an objective physical framework around culture', it might better be seen as 'both-and' (1989: 7). For then culture, too, must be both-and, both an objective categorical constructor and a relative category constructed. To attempt to apply this logic is at once to be caught in the vortex of an infinite regress: if the opposed categories of 'nature' and 'culture' are themselves cultural constructs, then so must be the culture that constructs them, and the culture that constructs *that*, and so on *ad infinitum*. And since, at every stage in this regress, the reality of nature reappears as its representation, 'real' reality recedes as fast as it is approached.

In what follows I shall argue that hunter-gatherers do *not*, as a rule, approach their environment as an external world of nature that has to be 'grasped' conceptually and appropriated symbolically within the terms of an imposed cultural design, as a precondition for effective action. They do not see themselves as mindful subjects having to contend with an alien world of physical objects; indeed the separation of mind and nature has no place in their thought and practice. I should add that they are not peculiar in this regard: my purpose is certainly not to argue for some distinctive hunter-gatherer worldview or to suggest that they are somehow 'at one' with their environments in a way that other peoples are not. Nor am I concerned to set up a comparison between the 'intentional worlds' of hunter-gatherers and Western scientists or humanists. It is of course an illusion to suppose that such a comparison could be made on level terms, since the primacy of Western ontology, the 'givenness' of nature and culture, is implicit in the very premises on which the comparative project is itself established (see Figure 3.1).

What I wish to suggest is that we reverse this order of primacy, and follow the lead of hunter-gatherers in taking the human condition to be that of a being immersed from the start, like other creatures, in an active, practical and perceptual engagement with constituents of the dwelt-in world. This ontology of dwelling, I contend, provides us with a better way of coming to grips with the nature of human existence than does the alternative, Western ontology whose point of departure is that of a mind detached from the world, and that has literally to formulate it – to build an intentional world in consciousness – prior to any attempt at engagement. The contrast, I repeat, is not between alternative views of the world; it is rather between two ways of apprehending it, only one of which (the Western) may be characterised as the construction of a view, that is, as a process of mental representation. As for the other, apprehending the world is not a matter of construction but of engagement, not of building but of dwelling, not of making a view *of* the world but of taking up a view *in* it (Ingold 1996a: 117).

In the following three sections I shall move on to examine, in more detail, how this

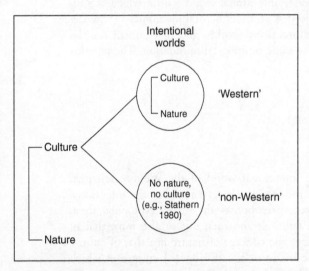

Figure 3.1 A comparison between 'non-Western' and 'Western' intentional worlds assumes the primacy of the Western ontology, with its dichotomy between nature and culture, or between physical substance and conceptual form.

contrast has been played out in the context of Western anthropological studies of hunters and gatherers. First, I shall consider how certain tropical hunter-gatherer peoples perceive their relations to their forest environment. Secondly, I shall look at the way northern hunters, in particular the Cree of northeastern Canada, understand their relations to the animals they hunt. Thirdly, drawing on ethnographic material from Aboriginal Australia and subarctic Alaska, I shall consider the way hunters and gatherers perceive the landscape. I conclude by showing how anthropological attempts to depict the mode of practical engagement of hunter-gatherers with the world as a mode of cultural construction of it have had the effect, quite contrary to stated intentions, of perpetuating a naturalistic vision of the hunter-gatherer economy.

CHILDREN OF THE FOREST

In his classic study of the Mbuti Pygmies of the Ituri Forest, Colin Turnbull observes that the people recognise their dependence on the forest that surrounds them by referring to it as 'Father' or 'Mother'. They do so 'because, as they say, it gives them food, warmth, shelter and clothing, just like their parents', and moreover, 'like their parents, [it] gives them affection' (Turnbull 1965: 19). This form of reference, and the analogy it establishes between the most intimate relations of human kinship and the equally intimate relations between human persons and the non-human environment, is by no means unique to the Mbuti.[1] Precisely similar observations have been made among other hunter-gatherers of the tropical forest, in widely separate regions of the world. For example, among the Batek Negritos of Malaysia, according to Kirk Endicott, the forest environment 'is not just the physical setting in which they live, but a world made for them in which they have a well-defined part to play. They see themselves as involved in an intimate relationship of interdependence with the plants, animals and *hala'* (including the deities) that inhabit their world' (Endicott 1979: 82). The *hala'* are the creator beings who brought the forest world into existence for the people, who protect and care for it, and provide its human dwellers with nourishment. And again, among the Nayaka, forest-dwelling hunter-gatherers of Tamil Nadu, South India, Nurit Bird-David found a similar attitude: 'Nayaka look on the forest as they do on a mother or father. For them, it is not something "out there" that responds mechanically or passively but like a parent, it provides food unconditionally to its children' (Bird-David 1990: 190). Nayaka refer to both the spirits that inhabit the landscape and the spirits of their own predecessors by terms that translate as 'big father' and 'big mother', and to themselves in relation to these spirits as sons and daughters.

What are we to make of this? Drawing an explicit parallel between her own Nayaka material and the ethnography of the Batek and Mbuti, Bird-David argues that hunter-gatherer perceptions of the environment are typically oriented by the primary metaphor 'forest is as parent', or more generally by the notion that the environment *gives* the wherewithal of life to people – not in return for appropriate conduct, but unconditionally. Among neighbouring populations of cultivators, by contrast, the environment is likened to an ancestor rather than a parent, which yields its bounty only reciprocally, *in return* for favours rendered. It is this difference in orientation to the environment, she suggests, that most fundamentally distinguishes hunter-gatherers from cultivators, and it is upheld even when the former draw (as they often do) on cultivated resources and when the latter, conversely, draw on the 'wild' resources of the forest (Bird-David 1990). In a subsequent extension of the argument, and drawing once again on Mbuti, Batek and Nayaka ethnography, Bird-David (1992a) proposes that hunter-gatherers liken the unconditional way in which the forest transacts with people to the similarly unconditional transactions that take place among the people of a community, which in anthropological accounts come under the rubric of sharing. Thus the environment shares its bounty with humans just as humans share with one another, thereby integrating both human and non-human components of the world into one, all-embracing 'cosmic economy of sharing'.

But when the hunter-gatherer addresses the forest as his or her parent, or speaks of accepting what it has to offer as one would from other people, on what grounds can we claim that the usage is metaphorical? This is evidently not an interpretation that the people would make themselves; nevertheless – taking her cue from Lakoff and Johnson (1980) – Bird-David argues that these key metaphors enable them to make sense of their environment, and guide their actions within it, even though '*people may not be normally aware of them*' (1992a: 31; 1990: 190, my emphasis). There is a troublesome inconsistency here. On the one hand, Bird-David is anxious to offer a culture-sensitive account of the hunter-gatherer economy, as a counterpoint to the prevailing ecologism of most anthropological work in this field. On the other hand, she can do so only by imposing a division of her own, which forms no part of local conceptions, between actuality and metaphor. Underwriting this division is an assumed separation between two domains: the domain of human persons and social relations, wherein parenting and sharing are matters of everyday, commonsense reality; and the domain of the non-human environment, the forest with its plants and animals, relations with which are understood by drawing, for analogy, on those intrinsic to the first domain. In short, hunter-gatherers are supposed to call upon their experience of relations in the human world in order to model their relations with the non-human one.

The theoretical inspiration for this analytical tactic comes from Stephen Gudeman (1986), so let us turn to look at how he approaches the matter. Starting from the assumption that 'humans are modelers', Gudeman proposes that 'securing a livelihood, meaning the domain of material "production", "distribution" and "consumption", is culturally modeled in all societies' (1986: 37). Entailed in the notion of modeling is a distinction between a 'schema' which provides a programme, plan or script, and an 'object' to which it is applied: thus 'the model is a projection from the domain of the schema to the domain of the object' (p. 38). Comparing Western and non-Western (or 'local') models of livelihood, Gudeman suggests that in the former, schemas taken from the 'domain of material objects' are typically applied to 'the domain of human life', whereas in the latter the direction of application is reversed, such that 'material processes are modeled as being intentional' (pp. 43–4). But notice how the entire argument is predicated upon an initial ontological dualism between the intentional worlds of human subjects and the object world of material things, or in brief, between society and nature. It is only by virtue of holding these to be separate that the one can be said to furnish the model for the other. The implication, however, is that the claim of the people themselves to inhabit but one world, encompassing relations with both human and non-human components of the environment on a similar footing, is founded upon an illusion – one that stems from their inability to recognise where the reality ends and its schematic representation begins. It is left to the anthropological observer to draw the dividing line, on one side of which lies the social world of human modelers of nature, and on the other, the natural world modeled as human society.

In the specific case with which we are concerned, hunter-gatherers' material interactions with the forest environment are said to be modeled on the interpersonal relations of parenting and sharing: the former, assigned to the domain of nature, establish the object; the latter, assigned to the domain of society, provide the schema. But this means that actions and events that are constitutive of the social domain must be representative of the natural. When, for example, the child begs its mother for a morsel of food, that communicative gesture is itself a constitutive moment in the development of the mother–child relationship, and the same is true for the action of the mother in fulfilling the request. Parenting is not a construction that is projected *onto* acts of this kind, it rather subsists *in* them, in the nurture and affection bestowed by adults on their offspring. Likewise, the give and take of food beyond the narrow context of parent–child ties is constitutive of relations of sharing, relations that subsist in the mutuality and companionship of persons in intimate social groups (cf. Price 1975, Ingold 1986a: 116–17). Yet according to the logic of the argument outlined above, as soon as we turn to consider exchange with the non-human environment, the situation is quite otherwise. For far from subsisting in people's practical involvement with the forest and its fauna and flora in their activities of food-getting, parenting and sharing belong instead to a construction that is projected onto that involvement from a separate, social source. Hence, when the hunter-gatherer begs the forest to provide food, as one would a human parent, the gesture is not a moment in the unfolding of relations between humans and non-human agencies and entities in the environment, it is rather an act that says something about these relationships, a representative evaluation or commentary.[2]

In short, actions that in the sphere of human relations would be regarded as instances of practical involvement with the world come to be seen, in the sphere of relations with the non-human environment, as instances of its metaphorical construction. Yet those who would construct the world, who would be 'modelers' in Gudeman's sense, must already live in it, and life presupposes an engagement with components not only of the human but also of the non-human environment. People need the support and affection of one another, but they also need to eat. How then, to stay with the same argument, do hunter-gatherers deal, actually rather than metaphorically, with non-human beings in the practical business of gaining a livelihood? They cannot do so in their capacity as persons, since non-human agencies and entities are supposed to have no business in the world of persons save as figures of the anthropomorphic imagination. Hence the domain of their actual interaction with the non-human environment in the procurement of subsistence must lie beyond that of their existence as persons, in a separate domain wherein they figure as biological objects rather than cultural subjects, that is as organisms rather than persons. This is the *natural* domain of organism-environment interactions, as distinct from the *social* domain of interpersonal relations. In Figure 3.2 (upper diagram) this result is indicated schematically.

There is a profound irony here. Was not the principal objective to counteract that 'naturalisation of the hunter-gatherer economy' which, as Sahlins comments (1976: 100), has formed the received anthropological wisdom, in favour of an account sensitive to the nuances of local culture? Yet what we find is that such naturalisation is entailed in the very stance that treats the perception of the environment as a matter of reconstructing the data of experience within intentional worlds. The sphere of human engagement with the environment, in the practical activities of hunting and gathering, is disembedded from the sphere within which humans are constituted as social beings or persons, as a precondition for letting the latter stand to the former as schema to object. The consequences are all too apparent from the conclusion towards which Gudeman moves, in bringing his argument to a close:

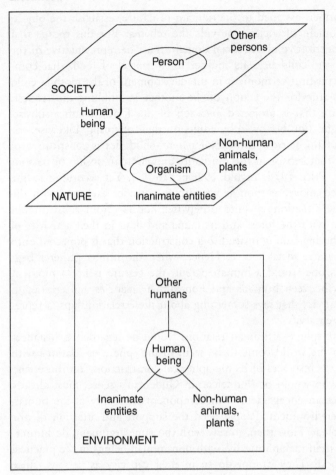

Figure 3.2 Western anthropological (above) and hunter-gatherer (below) economies of knowledge.

In all living societies humans must maintain themselves by securing energy from the environment. Although this life-sustaining process amounts only to a rearranging of nature, a transforming of materials from one state or appearance to another, humans make something of this activity.

(1986: 154)

By his own account, then, the life-process of human beings, shorn of the diverse constructions that are placed upon it, and that 'make something' of it, is nothing more than *a rearranging of nature*.

In this connection, we may recall Sahlins's attempt to treat 'economy' as a 'component of culture', which led him to contrast 'the material life process of society' to 'a need satisfying process of individual behaviour' (1972: 186 fn.1). Hunting and gathering, by this account, are operations that take place in nature, consisting of interactions between human organisms with 'needs', and environmental resources with the potential to satisfy them. Only after having been extracted is the food transferred to the domain of society, wherein its distribution is governed by a schema for sharing, a schema inscribed in the social relations which the economic practices of sharing serve to reproduce (see Ingold 1988a: 275). In the economy of knowledge, as conceived in general by Gudeman and specifically for hunter-gatherers by Bird-David, what applies to food applies also to sensory experience. That experience, gained through human organism–environment interactions, provides the raw material of sensation that – along with food – hunters and gatherers 'take home' with them. Carried over to the domain of interpersonal relations, it too is assimilated to a social schema, to yield a cultural construction of nature such as 'the forest is as parent'.

In Figure 3.2 this anthropological conception of the economy of knowledge is contrasted with that of the people themselves. In their account (lower diagram) there are not two worlds, of nature and society, but just one, saturated with personal powers, and embracing both humans, the animals and plants on which they depend, and the features of the landscape in which they live and move. Within this one world, humans figure not as composites of body and mind but as undivided beings, 'organism-persons', relating as such both to other humans and to non-human agencies and entities in their environment. Between these spheres of involvement there is no *absolute* separation, they are but contextually delimited segments of a single field. As Bird-David observes, hunter-gatherers 'do not inscribe into the nature of things a division between the natural agencies and themselves, as we [Westerners] do with our "nature:culture" dichotomy. They view their world as an integrated entity' (1992a: 29–30). And so one gets to know the forest, and the plants and animals that dwell therein, in just the same way that one becomes familiar with other people, by spending time with them, investing in one's relations with them the same qualities of care, feeling and attention. This explains why hunters and gatherers consider time devoted to forays in the forest to be well spent, even if it yields little or nothing by way of useful return: there is, as Bird-David puts it, 'a concern with the activity itself' (1992a: 30), since it allows people to 'keep in touch' with the non-human environment. And because of this, people know the environment 'intimately, in the way one "knows" close relatives with whom one shares intimate day-to-day life' (Bird-David 1992b: 39).

That the perception of the social world is grounded in the direct, mutually attentive involvement of self and other in shared contexts of experience, prior to its representation in terms of received conceptual schemata, is now well established. But in Western anthropological and psychological discourse such involvement continues to be apprehended within the terms of the orthodox dualisms of subject and object, persons and things. Rendered as 'intersubjectivity', it is taken to be the constitutive quality of the social domain *as against* the object world of nature, a domain open to human beings but not to non-human kinds (Willis 1990: 11–12). Thus according to Trevarthen and Logotheti, 'human cultural intelligence is seen to be founded on a level of engagement of minds, or intersubjectivity, such as no other species has or can acquire' (1989: 167). In the hunter-gatherer economy of knowledge, by contrast, it is as entire persons, not as disembodied minds, that human beings engage with one another and, moreover, with non-human beings as well. They do so as beings *in* a world, not as minds which, excluded from a given reality, find themselves in the common predicament of having to make sense of it. To coin a term, the constitutive quality of their world is not intersubjectivity but *interagentivity*. To speak of the forest as a parent is not, then, to model object relations in terms of primary intersubjectivity, but to recognize that at root, the constitutive quality of intimate relations with non-human and human components of the environment is one and the same.

HUMANS AND ANIMALS

The Waswanipi Cree of northeastern Canada, according to Harvey Feit, 'say that they only catch an animal when the animal is given to them. They say that in winter the north wind, *chuetenshu*, and the animals themselves give them what they need to live' (Feit 1973: 116). This idea, that the nourishing substance of animals is received by humans as a gift, is widely reported among northern hunting peoples, but in what follows I shall confine my remarks to studies of two other Cree groups. Among the Wemindji Cree, 'respectful activity towards the animals enhances the readiness with which they give themselves, or are given by God, to hunters' (Scott 1989: 204). And for the Mistassini Cree, Adrian Tanner reports that the events and activities of the hunt, though they have an obvious 'commonsense' significance insofar as they entail the deployment of technical knowledge and skill in the service of providing for the material needs of the human population, are also 'reinterpreted' on another, magico-religious level:

> The facts about particular animals are reinterpreted as if they had social relationships between themselves, and between them and anthropomorphized natural forces, and furthermore the animals are thought of as if they had personal relations with the hunters. The idealized form of these latter relations is often that the hunter pays respect to an animal; that is, he acknowledges the animal's superior position, and following this the animal 'gives itself' to the hunter, that is, allows itself to assume a position of equality, or even inferiority, with respect to the hunter.
>
> (Tanner 1979: 136)

In short, the animals figure for these northern hunters very much as the forest figures for such tropical hunter-gatherers as the Mbuti, Batek and Nayaka: they are partners with humans in an encompassing 'cosmic economy of sharing'.

Now Western thought, as is well known, drives an absolute division between the contrary conditions of humanity and animality, a division that is aligned with a series of others such as between subjects and objects, persons and things, morality and physicality, reason and instinct, and, above all, society and nature. Underwriting the Western view of the uniqueness of the human species is the fundamental axiom that *personhood as a state of being is not open to non-human animal kinds*. It is for this reason that we are able to conflate both the moral condition and the biological taxon (*Homo sapiens*) under the single rubric of 'humanity'. And for this reason, too, we can countenance an enquiry into the animal nature of human beings whilst rejecting out of hand the possibility of an enquiry into the humanity of non-human animals (Ingold 1988b: 6). Human existence is conceived to be conducted simultaneously on two levels, the social level of interpersonal, intersubjective relations and the natural ecological level of organism–environment interactions, whereas animal existence is wholly confined within the natural domain. Humans are both persons *and* organisms, animals are all organism.

This is a view, however, that Cree and other northern hunters categorically reject. Personhood, for them, *is* open equally to human and non-human animal (and even non-animal) kinds. Here, once again, is Feit on the Waswanipi:

> In the culturally constructed world of the Waswanipi the animals, the winds and many other phenomena are thought of as being 'like persons' in that they act intelligently and have wills and idiosyncracies, and understand and are understood by men. Causality,

therefore, is personal not mechanical or biological, and it is . . . always appropriate to ask 'who did it?' and 'why?' rather than 'how does that work?'

(1973: 116)

This rendering of the Cree perspective is echoed by Tanner, who points to the significant implication of the idea that game animals live in social groups or communities akin to those of human beings, namely 'that social interaction between humans and animals is made possible' (1979: 137–8). Hunting itself comes to be regarded not as a technical manipulation of the natural world but as a kind of interpersonal dialogue, integral to the total process of social life wherein both human and animal persons are constituted with their particular identities and purposes. Among the Wemindji Cree, qualities of personhood are likewise assigned to humans, animals, spirits and certain geophysical agents. As Colin Scott writes: 'human persons are not set over and against a material context of inert nature, but rather are one species of person in a network of reciprocating persons' (1989: 195).

Though the ethnographic accounts offered by Tanner and Scott are in striking agreement, their interpretations are not, and it is revealing to explore the contrast between them. The problem hinges on the question of whether, when the Cree hunter refers to animals or to the wind as he would to human persons, he does so within the compass of what Feit, in the passage cited above, calls a 'culturally constructed world'. Tanner is in no doubt that they do. Thus he asserts that 'game animals participate simultaneously in two levels of reality, one "natural" and the other "cultural"' (1979: 137). On the natural level they are encountered simply as material entities, organic constituents of the object world to be killed and consumed. On the cultural level, by contrast, they are 'reinterpreted' as anthropomorphic beings participating in a domain 'modelled on conventional Cree patterns of social and cultural organization' (*ibid.*). In terms of this analysis, then, animals are constructed as persons through their assimilation to a schema drawn from the domain of human relations. This is entirely in accord with Gudeman's theory of the cultural modeling of livelihood, which I discussed in the previous section. Indeed, Gudeman draws for ethnographic support, *inter alia*, on Tanner's study. 'The Mistassini Cree', he writes, 'construct their hunting and trapping activities as an exchange between themselves and animal spirits . . . and the exchange itself is patterned after ordinary human relationships, such as friendship, coercion and love' (Gudeman 1986: 148–9, citing Tanner 1979: 138, 148–50).

I have already shown, in the case of hunter-gatherer relations with the forest environment, how the constructionist argument is founded on an ontological dualism between society and nature, which in this instance reappears as one between humanity and animality. On one side, then, we have the world of human modelers of animals, on the other the animal world modeled as human. If the people themselves profess to be aware of but one world, of persons and their relationships, it is because, seeing their own social ambience reflected in the mirror of nature, they cannot distinguish the reflection from reality. Now by all accounts, as we have seen, the dualism of humanity and animality, and the entailed restriction of personhood to human beings, is not endorsed by the Cree. This does not mean, of course, that they fail to differentiate between humans and animals. To the contrary, they are acutely concerned about such differences. For example, while humans may have sexual relations with certain other humans, and may kill and consume certain non-human animals, the consequences of categorical confusion – of sex with non-humans or killing fellow human beings – would be disastrous (Scott 1989: 197).

The point is that the difference between (say) a goose and a man is not between an organism and a person, but between one kind of organism-person and another. From the Cree perspective, personhood is not the manifest form of humanity; rather the human is one of many outward forms of personhood. And so when Cree hunters claim that a goose is in some sense like a man, far from drawing a figurative parallel across two fundamentally separate domains, they are rather pointing to the real unity that underwrites their differentiation. Whereas Western thought sets out from an assumed dichotomy between the human and the animal and then searches about for possible analogies or homologies, the Cree trajectory – as Scott explains – 'seems rather the opposite: to assume fundamental similarity while exploring the differences between humans and animals' (1989: 195). To posit a 'metaphorical' equivalence between goose and man is not, then, to render 'one kind of thing in terms of another' (Lakoff and Johnson 1980: 5), as Western – including Western anthropological – convention would have it. A more promising perspective is offered by Michael Jackson, who argues that metaphor should be apprehended as a way of drawing attention to real relational unities rather than of figuratively papering over dualities. Metaphor, Jackson writes, 'reveals, not the "thisness of a that" but rather that "this *is* that"' (1983: 132).[3]

It follows that the equivalence can work both ways. It is not 'anthropomorphic', as Tanner suggests (1979: 136), to compare the animal to the human, any more than it is 'naturalistic' to compare the human to the animal, since in both cases the comparison points to a level on which human and animal share a common existential status, namely as living beings or persons. The move, if you will, is not from the literal to the figurative, but from the actual to the potential – for personhood, at root, is the potential to become a man, a goose, or any other of the innumerable forms of animate being. From this perspective, it makes no significant difference whether one renders animal actions in human terms or human actions in animal terms. As Scott puts it:

> One might observe that a consequence of the sort of analogical thinking that I have been describing would be to anthropomorphize animals, but that would be to assume the primacy of the human term. The animal term reacts with perhaps equal force on the human term, so that animal behaviour can become a model for human relations.
>
> (1989: 198)

This same argument can be applied, *pari passu*, to the metaphor 'forest is as parent', considered in the last section. One could just as well say that 'parent is as forest', for the force of the metaphor is to reveal the underlying ontological equivalence of human and non-human components of the environment as agencies of nurturance.

What humans and non-humans have in common, for Cree as for other hunter-gatherers, is that they are *alive*. Ostensibly, and barring certain geophysical phenomena that Cree would regard as animate but that we might not, this is a conclusion with which Western thinkers would not disagree. Yet in Western biology, as we saw in Chapter One (p. 19), life tends to be understood as a passive process, as the reaction of organisms, bound by their separate natures, to the given conditions of their respective environments. This carries the implication that every organism is pre-specified, with regard to its essential nature, *prior* to its entry into the life process – an implication that in modern biology appears in the guise of the doctrine of genetic preformation. With this view, personal powers – of awareness, agency and intentionality – can form no part of the organism *as such*, but must necessarily be 'added on' as capacities not of body but of mind, capacities that Western thought has traditionally reserved for humans. Even today, now that the possibility of non-human animal awareness has arisen as a legitimate topic of scientific speculation, the basic dualism of mind and body is retained – for the question is phrased as one about the existence of animal *minds* (Griffin 1976, 1984, see Ingold 1988c). Consciousness, then, is the life of the mind.

For the Cree, life has a different meaning. Scott tells us that 'the term *pimaatisiiwin*, "life", was translated by one Cree man as "continuous birth"' (1989: 195). To be alive is to be situated within a field of relations which, as it unfolds, actively and ceaselessly brings forms into being: humans as humans, geese as geese, and so on. Far from revealing forms that are already specified, life is the process of their ongoing generation. Every living being, then, emerges as a particular, positioned embodiment of this generative potential. Hence personhood, far from being 'added on' to the living organism, is implicated in the very condition of being alive: the Cree word for 'persons', according to Scott, 'can itself be glossed as "he lives"' (1989: 195). Organisms are not just *like* persons, they *are* persons. Likewise, consciousness is not supplementary to organic life but is, so to speak, its advancing front – 'on the verge of unfolding events, of continuous birth', as Scott (*ibid.*) renders the Cree conception.

Now the ontological equivalence of humans and animals, as organism-persons and as fellow participants in a life process, carries a corollary of capital importance. It is that both can have points of view. In other words, for both the world exists as a meaningful place, constituted in relation to the purposes and capabilities of action of the being in question. Western ontology, as we have seen, denies this, asserting that meaning does not lie in the relational contexts of the perceiver's involvement in the world, but is rather laid over the world by the mind. Humans alone, it is said, are capable of representing an external reality in this way, organising the data of experience according to their diverse cultural schemata. So when the Cree claim, as indeed they do, that the same events surrounding a hunt afford two possible interpretations, from the points of view, respectively, of the human hunter and of the animal hunted, the Western observer is inclined to regard the former as literal and the latter as figurative, 'as if' the animal were human and so could participate with 'real' humans in a common world of meanings. And this is precisely what Tanner does (1979: 136–7) when he re-presents to us – his readers – as a 'cultural' reality (as opposed to a 'natural' one) what the Cree originally presented to him as a 'bear reality' or 'caribou reality' (as opposed to a 'human' one). Note that the distinction between natural and cultural levels of participation is not one that the Cree make themselves. According to Scott, Cree has 'no word corresponding to our term "nature"', nor does it have any 'equivalent of "culture" that would make it a special province of humans' (1989: 195).

A creature can have a point of view because its action in the world is, at the same time, a process of *attending* to it. Different creatures have different points of view because, given their capabilities of action and perception, they attend to the world in different ways. Cree hunters, for example, notice things about the environment that geese do not, yet by the hunters' own admission (Scott 1989: 202), geese also notice things that humans do not. What is certain, however, is that humans figure in the perceptual world of geese just as geese figure in that of humans. It is clearly of vital importance to geese that they should be as attentive to the human presence as to the presence of any other potential predator. On the basis of past experience, they learn to pick up the relevant warning signs, and continually adjust their behaviour accordingly. And human hunters, for their part, attend to the presence of geese *in the knowledge that geese are attending to them*. 'The perceptions and interpretations of Cree hunters', Scott observes, 'suggest that geese are quite apt at learning in what contexts to expect predation, at learning to distinguish predatory from non-predatory humans, and at communicating appropriate behavioural adaptations to other geese' (1989: 199).

In short, animals do not participate with humans *qua* persons only in a domain of virtual reality, as represented within culturally constructed, intentional worlds, superimposed upon the naturally given substratum of organism–environment interactions. They participate as real-world creatures, endowed with powers of feeling and autonomous action, whose characteristic behaviours, temperaments and sensibilities one gets to know in the very course of one's everyday practical dealings with them. In this regard, dealing with non-human animals is not fundamentally different from dealing with fellow humans. Indeed the following definition of sociality, originally proposed by Alfred Schutz, could – with the insertions indicated in brackets – apply with equal force to the encounter between human hunters and their prey: 'Sociality is constituted by communicative acts in which the I [the hunter] turns to the others [animals], apprehending them as persons who turn to him, and both know of this fact' (Schutz 1970: 163). Humans may of course be unique in their capacity to *narrate* such encounters, but no-one can construct a narrative, any more than they could build a model, who is not already situated in the world and thus already caught up in a nexus of relations with both human and non-human constituents of the environment. The relations that Cree have with the latter are what we, outside observers, call hunting.

PERCEIVING THE LANDSCAPE

Life, of course, is an historical process, embodied in organic forms that are fragile and impermanent. Yet this process is carried on, for terrestrial species, upon the surface of the earth, a surface whose contours, textures and features, sculpted by geological forces over immense periods of time, appear permanent and immutable relative to the life-cycles of even the most long-lived of organisms (Ingold 1989: 504). This surface is what geology textbooks call the 'physical landscape'. How do hunters and gatherers perceive this aspect of their environment?

Among the Pintupi of the Gibson Desert of Western Australia, people say that the landscape was formed, once and for all time, through the activities of theriomorphic beings, ancestral to humans as well as to all other living things, who roamed the earth's surface in an era known conventionally as the Dreaming. The same idea is, in fact, current throughout Aboriginal Australia, but in what follows I shall confine my illustrative remarks to the Pintupi. According to Fred Myers, Pintupi say that, as ancestral beings travelled from place to place,

> [they] hunted, performed ceremonies, fought, and finally turned to stone or 'went into the ground', where they remain. The actions of these powerful beings – animal, human and monster – created the world as it now exists. They gave it outward form, identity (a name), and internal structure. The desert is crisscrossed with their lines of travel and, just as an animal's tracks leave a record of what has happened, the geography and special features of the land – hills, creeks, salt lakes, trees – are marks of the ancestors' activities.
>
> (1986: 49–50)

Such features are more than mere marks, however, for in their activities the ancestors did not leave a trail of impressions behind them, like footprints in the sand, while they themselves moved on. They rather metamorphosed *into* the forms of the landscape as they went along. Ever present in these forms, their movements are congealed in perpetuity.

On the land travelled by the ancestors in the Dreaming, people make their way in the temporal domain of ordinary life, pursuing their own everyday activities. Though the paths they take are not constrained to the lines of ancestral travel, in following tracks (as in hunting) and in making tracks themselves they replicate the original, creative movement of the ancestral beings, inscribing their own identities into the land as they go. As Roy Wagner has put it, with reference to the neighbouring Walbiri people, 'the life of a person is the sum of his tracks, the total inscription of his movements, something that can be traced out along the ground' (Wagner 1986: 21, see also Chapter Eight, pp. 144–6). And for the Pintupi, Myers writes that 'for each individual, the landscape becomes a history of significant social events . . . previous events become attached to places and are recited as one moves across the country' (Myers 1986: 68). There is thus a second level in the constitution of the landscape, one tied to the historical actions of ordinary human beings, as opposed to the 'transhistorical' actions of the ancestors (1986: 55). On the first level, named places were created by the ancestral beings at the sites of their activities, or at points where they entered or emerged from the ground, and, connected by the paths of ancestral travel, these places make up what Myers calls a 'country' – a term he offers as one possible rendering of the Pintupi word *ngurra*. But *ngurra* can also mean 'camp' – that is, the place temporarily constituted by virtue of the everyday activities of a group of people who happen to set up there. Such places, unlike the named places envisioned as the camps of the ancestors in the Dreaming, do not endure for ever. Each is identified with the particular people who live there, and will be avoided for many years after someone thus connected to the place has died. But 'despite these identifications, . . . camps are impermanent. Eventually they are overgrown and their associations forgotten, while significant new spaces are constantly being established' (Myers 1986: 56–7).

If persons inscribe their identities into the landscape as historically constituted, it is from the transhistorical level of the Dreaming that these identities are initially derived. Thus each person takes his or her primary identity from a particular named place, and is regarded as the incarnation of the ancestor whose activity made that place. That is why, as Myers notes (1986: 50), 'it is not unusual . . . to hear people describe actions of the Dreaming in the first person'. For in speaking about my ancestor, I am speaking about myself. Throughout life, additional components of identity accrue through association with other named places, such as where one was initiated or where one has long resided, so that who one is becomes a kind of record of where one has come from and where one has been. It follows that the network of places, linked by paths of ancestral travel, is at the same time a network of relations between persons. When social relations are spoken of, as they often are, in terms of relations between places, the comparison does not draw a parallel across separate domains of society and the physical world, but rather reveals that – at a more fundamental ontological level – these relations are equivalent. That level is the Dreaming. It is a level, however, that is not directly given to experience, but rather revealed in the actions and events of the phenomenal world that are its visible signs (Myers 1986: 49).

We might sum up this Pintupi understanding of the landscape in the following four precepts. First, it is not a given substrate, awaiting the imprint of activities that may be conducted upon it, but is itself the congelation of past activity – on the phenomenal level, of human predecessors, but more fundamentally of ancestral beings. Secondly, it is not so much a continuous surface as a topologically ordered network of places, each marked by some physical feature, and the paths connecting them. Thirdly, the landscape furnishes its human inhabitants with all the lineaments of personal and social identity, providing each with a specific point of origin and a specific destiny. And therefore, fourthly, the movement of social life is itself a movement *in* (not *on*) a landscape, and its fixed reference points are physically marked localities or 'sites'. In short, the landscape is not an external background or platform for life, either as lived by the ancestors in the Dreaming or as relived by their ordinary human incarnations in the temporal domain. It is rather life's enduring monument.

What can we learn from the Pintupi? It could be argued, of course, that their ideas of the Dreaming – though not unique to themselves – are specifically Aboriginal ones, and afford no grounds for generalisation beyond the Australian continent. Indeed, comparisons between Australia and other continents of hunter-gatherers are fraught with difficulty. Nevertheless, in order to indicate that there are genuine similarities in the ways that hunters and gatherers apprehend the landscape and their own position in it, I should like to refer briefly to another study from a quite different region of the world – Richard Nelson's 1983 study of the Koyukon of Alaska.

The Koyukon say that the earth and all the beings that flourish in it were created in an era known as the 'Distant Time'. Stories of the Distant Time include accounts of the formation of prominent features of the landscape such as hills and mountains (1983: 16, 34). An elaborate code of rules, brought down from the Distant Time, establishes forms of proper conduct that people are bound to follow; thus 'the Koyukon must move *with* the forces of their surroundings, not attempting to control, master or fundamentally alter them' (p. 240). As people move around in the landscape, in hunting and trapping, in setting up camp in one locality after another, their own life histories are woven into the country:

> The Koyukon homeland is filled with places … invested with significance in personal or family history. Drawing back to view the landscape as a whole, we can see it completely interwoven with these meanings. Each living individual is bound into this pattern of land and people that extends throughout the terrain and far back across time.
>
> (Nelson 1983: 243)

Places, however, can possess meaning at different levels. Some have a fundamental spiritual potency connected with the Distant Time story of their creation. Some, where people have died, are avoided for as long as the memory persists. Others, again, are known for particular hunting events or other personal experiences of encounters with animals. On all these levels – spiritual, historical, personal – the landscape is inscribed with the lives of all who have dwelt therein, from Distant Time human-animal ancestors to contemporary humans, and the landscape itself, rather than anything erected upon it, stands in memory of these persons and their activities (Nelson 1983: 242–6).

Now let me turn to the anthropological interpretation of these ways of apprehending the landscape. Astonishingly, we find a complete inversion, such that meanings that the people claim to discover *in* the landscape are attributed to the minds of the people themselves, and are said to be mapped *onto* the landscape. And the latter, drained of all significance as a prelude to its cultural construction, is reduced to *space*, a vacuum to the plenum of culture. Thus Myers can write, of the Pintupi, that they have 'truly culturalized space and made out of impersonal geography a home, a *ngurra*' (1986: 54). A moment later, however, the Pintupi achievement reappears as an artefact of anthropological analysis: 'we will consider country *as if it were* simply culturalized space' (p. 57, my emphases). The ontological foundation for this interpretative strategy is an initial separation between human persons, as meaning-makers, and the physical environment as raw material for construction; the 'culturalisation of space' is then what happens when the two are brought into juxtaposition, such that social relations are mapped onto spatial relations. The Pintupi are said to superimpose the Dreaming, a 'distinctly Aboriginal cultural construction' (p. 47), onto the 'real' reality of the physical landscape, causing the latter to recede from view, cloaked by the 'perceived' reality enshrined in the stories people tell, of ancestral beings and their activities. This, of course, flatly contradicts Pintupi ontology, which is premised on the fundamental *indissolubility* of the connection between persons and landscape, and on the assumption that phenomenal reality is open to direct perception whereas the order of the Dreaming is not, and can be apprehended only by way of its visible signs.[4]

The same contradiction is apparent in Nelson's account of the Koyukon. His experience of the discrepancy between the Koyukon attitude to the environment and that derived from his own 'Euro-American' background led him, he tells us, to endorse the perspective of cultural relativism, whose basic premise he sets out as follows:

> Reality is not the world as it is perceived directly by the senses; reality is the world as it is perceived by the *mind* through the medium of the senses. Thus reality in nature is not just what we see, but what we have *learned* to see.
>
> (1983: 239)

That we learn to see is not in doubt, but learning in this view entails the acquisition of cultural schemata for building representations of the world, in the mind, from data delivered by the senses. So the Koyukon, viewing the world in their mind's eye through the lens of received tradition, are supposed to see one reality; the Westerner, viewing it in terms of the concepts of scientific ecology, sees another. There is, Nelson concludes, no 'single reality in the natural world, . . . absolute and universal'. Yet not only is the existence of such a 'real' reality implied in the very notion that perceived realities are representations, in the mind, of a naturally given world 'out there', but this mentalist ontology also flies in the face of what the Koyukon themselves, by Nelson's own account, are trying to tell us.

This is all about watching and being watched (1983: 14–32). Knowledge of the world is gained by moving about in it, exploring it, attending to it, ever alert to the signs by which it is revealed. Learning to see, then, is a matter not of acquiring schemata for mentally *constructing* the environment but of acquiring the skills for direct perceptual *engagement* with its constituents, human and non-human, animate and inanimate. To recall a distinction I introduced in the last chapter, it is a process not of enculturation but of enskilment. If the Koyukon hunter notices significant features of the landscape of which the Western observer remains unaware, it is not because their source lies in 'the Koyukon mind' (Nelson 1983: 242) which imposes its own unique construction on a common body of sensory data, but because the perceptual system of the hunter is attuned to picking up information, critical to the practical conduct of his hunting, to which the unskilled observer simply fails to attend. That information is not in the mind but in the world, and its significance lies in the relational context of the hunter's engagement with the constituents of that world. Moreover, the more skilled the hunter, the more knowledgeable he becomes, for with a finely honed perceptual system, the world will appear to him in greater richness and profundity. New knowledge comes from creative acts of discovery rather than imagining, from attending more closely to the environment rather than reassembling one's picture of it along new conceptual lines.

It will at once be objected that I have taken no account of that vital component of knowledge that comes to people through their instruction in traditional lore, for example in the stories of the Dreaming among the Pintupi and of the Distant Time among the Koyukon. Do not these stories, along with the accompanying songs, designs, sacred objects and the like, amount to a kind of modelling of reality, a representation of the world that native people might consult as Westerners would consult a map? I think not. People, once familiar with a country, have no need of maps, and get their bearings from attending to the landscape itself rather than from some inner representation of the same. Importantly, Myers notes that among the Pintupi the meanings of songs remain obscure to those who do not already know the country, and that individuals who are new to an area are first instructed by being 'taken around, shown some of the significant places, and taught to avoid certain sites' (Myers 1986: 150). One might question what use songs, stories and designs could possibly have *as maps* if they are unintelligible to all but those who possess such familiarity with the landscape as to manage quite well without devices of this kind.

I do not believe, however, that their purpose is a representational one. Telling a story is not like weaving a tapestry to *cover up* the world or, as in an overworn anthropological metaphor, to 'clothe it with meaning'. For the landscape, unclothed, is not the 'opaque surface of literalness' (Ho 1991) that this analogy suggests. Rather, it has both transparency and depth: transparency, because one can see into it; depth, because the more one looks the further one sees. Far from dressing up a plain reality with layers of metaphor, or representing it, map-like, in the imagination, songs, stories and designs serve to conduct the attention of performers *into* the world, deeper and deeper, as one proceeds from outward appearances to an ever more intense poetic involvement. At its most intense, the boundaries between person and place, or between the self and the landscape, dissolve altogether. It is at this point that, as the people say, they become their ancestors, and discover the real meaning of things.

Conventional anthropological interpretation tends to range, on two sides of a dichotomy, peoples' practical-technical interaction with environmental resources in the context of subsistence activities, and their mytho-religious or cosmological construction of the environment in the context of ritual and ceremony. Hunters and gatherers are said to be distinctive, however, insofar as they do not seek physically to reconstruct the landscape to conform with their cosmological conceptions, but rather find these conceptions 'ready made' in the world as given. On these grounds they are supposed still to occupy a 'natural' rather than an 'artificial' or 'built' environment. Peter Wilson sets out this view very clearly:

> The hunter/gatherer pins ideas and emotions onto the world as it exists: the landscape is turned into a mythical topographical map, a grid of ancestor tracks and sacred sites, as is typical among Australian aborigines . . . A construction is put upon the landscape rather than the landscape undergoing a reconstruction, as is the case among sedentary peoples, who impose houses, villages, and gardens on the landscape, often in place of natural landmarks. Where nomads read or even find cosmological features in an already existing landscape, villagers tend to represent and model cosmic ideas in the structures they build.
>
> (1988: 50)

Once again, we find that the view of the landscape as culturalised space entails the naturalisation of hunting and gathering. Only as represented in thought is the environment drawn into the human world of persons; thus the practical business of life is reduced to material interactions in an alien world of nature, in which humans figure as 'mere organisms'.

Yet the people themselves insist that the real-world landscape in which they move about, set up camp and hunt and gather, is not alien at all but infused with human meaning – that this meaning has not been 'pinned on' but is there to be 'picked up' by those with eyes to see and ears to hear. They are, as their ethnographers have noted (with some surprise, else they would not have cared to remark on the fact), thoroughly 'at home' in the world. The Pintupi, Myers tells us, 'seem truly at home as they walk through the bush, full of confidence' (1986: 54). And the lands of the Koyukon, according to Nelson, 'are no more a wilderness than are farmlands to a farmer or streets to a city dweller' (1983: 246). As this statement implies, it is not because of his occupancy of a built environment that the urban dweller feels at home on the streets; it is because they are the streets of his neighbourhood along which he is accustomed to walk or drive in his everyday life, presenting to him familiar faces, sights and sounds. And it is no different, in principle, for the hunter-gatherer, as the inhabitant of an environment unscarred by human engineering. As I have remarked elsewhere, 'it is through *dwelling* in a landscape, through the incorporation of its features into a pattern of everyday activities, that it becomes home to hunters and gatherers' (Ingold 1996a: 116).

My argument is that the differences between the activities of hunting and gathering, on the one hand, and singing, storytelling and the narration of myth on the other, cannot be accommodated within the terms of a dichotomy between the material and the mental, between ecological interactions *in* nature and cultural constructions *of* nature. On the contrary, both sets of activities are, in the first place, ways of dwelling. The latter, as I have shown, amount not to a metaphorical representation of the world, but to a form of poetic involvement. But it is no different with the activities of hunting and gathering, which entail the same attentive engagement with the environment, and the same exploratory quest for knowledge. In hunting and gathering, as in singing and story-telling, the world 'opens out' to people. Hunter-gatherers, in their practices, do not seek to transform the world; they seek revelation. The intentions of non-human animals, for example, are revealed to Cree hunters in the outcomes of their endeavours. And Pintupi are forever alert to signs in the landscape that may offer new clues to ancestral activity in the Dreaming (Myers 1986: 67). In short, through the practical activities of hunting and gathering, the environment – including the landscape with its fauna and flora – enters directly into the constitution of persons, not only as a source of nourishment but also as a source of knowledge.

But reciprocally, persons enter actively into the constitution of their environments. They do so, however, from *within*. For the Pintupi, the world was created in the Dreaming, but the Dreaming is *trans*historical, not *pre*historical. The events of the Dreaming, though they occurred at particular places, are themselves timeless, each one stretched to encompass an eternity, or what Stanner (1965: 159) called 'everywhen'. And so the landscape, brought into being in these events, is movement out of time. People, as the temporal incarnation of ancestral beings, are not so much creators themselves as living on the *inside* of an eternal moment of creation. Their activities, which replicate on a much smaller scale the landforming activities of the ancestors, are therefore part and parcel of the becoming of the world, and are bound to follow the course set by the Dreaming: life, as the Pintupi say, is a 'one-possibility thing' (Myers 1986: 53). Likewise, Koyukon are bound to the course of the Distant Time, and must move with it, never against it (Nelson 1983: 240). This understanding of the landscape as a course to be followed could hardly be more different from the Western understanding of the natural environment as a resistance to be overcome, a physically given, material substrate that has first to be 'humanised', by imposing upon it forms whose origins lie in the imagination, before it can be inhabited.

WHAT DO HUNTERS AND GATHERERS ACTUALLY DO?

To this day, the anthropological status of hunters and gatherers has remained equivocal, to say the least. Though no-one would any longer deny them full membership of the human species, it is still commonly held that in deriving their subsistence from hunting and trapping 'wild' animals and gathering 'wild' plants, honey, shellfish and so on, they are somehow comparable in their mode of life to non-human animals in a way that farmers, herdsmen and urban dwellers are not. Nothing is more revealing of this attitude than the commonplace habit of denoting the activities of hunting and gathering by the single word 'foraging'. I am not concerned here with the narrow sense of foraging in which it has sometimes been contrasted with collecting (see, for example, Binford 1983: 339–46, Ingold 1986a: 82–7). I mean rather to draw attention to the way in which 'foraging' has been adopted in a very general sense as a shorthand for 'hunting and gathering', ostensibly on the grounds of simple convenience. 'Forager', it is argued, is less cumbersome than 'hunter-gatherer', and the term carries no unwarranted implications as regards the relative priority of animal and vegetable foods, or of male and female labour.

But the concept of foraging also has an established usage in the field of ecology, to denote the feeding behaviour of animals of all kinds, and it is by extension from this field that the anthropological use of the term is explicitly derived. Thus, introducing a volume of studies on 'hunter-gatherer foraging strategies', Winterhalder and Smith note that 'the subsistence patterns of human foragers are fairly analogous to those of other species and are thus more easily studied with ecological models' (1981: x). And it is precisely the definition of human foragers as those who do *not* produce their food that legitimates the comparison: 'Foraging refers inclusively to tactics used to obtain nonproduced foodstuffs or other resources, those not directly cultivated or husbanded by the human population' (Winterhalder 1981b: 16). In short, it appears that humans can be only either foragers or producers; if the former, their subsistence practices are analogous to those of non-human animals; if the latter, they are not. The producer is conceived to intervene in natural processes, from a position at least partially outside it; the forager, by contrast, is supposed never to have extricated him- or herself from nature in the first place.

I have argued in this chapter that the world as perceived by hunters and gatherers is constituted through their engagement with it, in the course of everyday, subsistence-related practices. These practices cannot be reduced to their narrowly behavioural aspect, as strategically programmed responses to external environmental stimuli, as implied in the notion of foraging. Nor, however, can they be regarded as planned interventions in nature, launched from the separate platform of society, as implied in the notion of production. *Neither foraging nor production is an adequate description of what hunters and gatherers do.* As an alternative, Bird-David suggests 'procurement':

> Distinguished from 'to produce' and 'production', as also from 'to forage' and 'foraging', 'to procure' (according to the Shorter Oxford Dictionary) is 'to bring about, to obtain

by care or effort, to prevail upon, to induce, to persuade a person to do something'. 'Procurement' is management, contrivance, acquisition, getting, gaining. Both terms are accurate enough for describing modern hunter-gatherers who apply care, sophistication and knowledge to their resource-getting activities.

(1992b: 40)

This is a suggestion I would endorse. The notion of procurement nicely brings out what I have been most concerned to stress: that the activities we conventionally call hunting and gathering are forms of skilled, attentive 'coping' in the world, intentionally carried out by persons in an environment replete with other agentive powers of one kind and another. The point may be most readily summarised by referring back to Figure 3.2. In the upper diagram, representing the Western ontology, foraging would be positioned as an interaction in the plane of nature, between the human organism and its environment, whereas production would appear as an intervention in nature from the separate plane of society. In the lower diagram, representing the hunter-gatherer ontology, there is but one plane, in which humans engage, as whole organism-persons, with components of the environment, in the activities of procurement.

My argument has been that the 'naturalisation' of the activities of hunting and gathering, as revealed in their apparently unproblematic redesignation as 'foraging', is a product of the 'culturalisation' of the perceived environment. In the case of hunter-gatherers of the tropical forest, we have seen how their perception of the forest environment, as being in some respects like a human parent, has been interpreted anthropologically as due to the application of a schema for metaphorically constructing it, and how, as a result, the forest itself and hunter-gatherers' interactions with it come to be excluded from the domain in which they relate to one another as persons. In the case of the northern hunters, we have likewise seen how the assumption that in their capacity as persons, humans can relate to animals only as the latter are represented within human intentional worlds, leads to the placement of real encounters of hunting beyond the bounds of these intentional worlds, in a separate domain designated as 'natural'. And finally, in examining Aboriginal perceptions of the landscape, we found that by treating the perceived world as culturalised space, the real-world landscape in which people live and move comes to be rendered as an indifferent and impersonal physical substrate, raw material for imaginative acts of world-making.

In short, a cultural constructionist approach to environmental perception, far from challenging the prevailing ecological models of hunting and gathering as foraging, actually reinforces them, creating by exclusion a separate logical space for organism–environment interactions wherein these models are appropriately applied. Those who oppose the designation of hunter-gatherers as foragers (for example, Bird-David 1992b: 38) often do so on the grounds that it makes them seem just like non-human animals, without however questioning the applicability of the foraging model to the animals themselves. I believe that by paying attention to what hunter-gatherers are telling us, this is just what we *should* be questioning, and in doing so laying down a challenge not only to cultural anthropology but to ecological science as well. We may admit that humans are, indeed, just like other animals; not, however, insofar as they exist as organisms rather than persons, as constituent entities in an objective world of nature presented as a spectacle to detached scientific observation, but by virtue of their mutual involvement, as undivided centres of action and awareness, within a continuous life process. In this process, the relations that human beings have with one another form just one part of the total field of relations embracing all living things (Ingold 1990: 220).

There can, then, be no radical break between social and ecological relations; rather, the former constitute a *subset* of the latter. What this suggests is the possibility of a new kind of ecological anthropology, one that would take as its starting point the active, perceptual engagement of human beings with the constituents of their world – for it is only from a position of such engagement that they can launch their imaginative speculations concerning what the world is like. The first step in the establishment of this ecological anthropology would be to recognise that the relations with which it deals, between human beings and their environments, are not confined to a domain of 'nature', separate from, and given independently of, the domain in which they lead their lives as persons. For hunter-gatherers as for the rest of us, life is given in engagement, not in disengagement, and in that very engagement the real world at once ceases to be 'nature' and is revealed to us as an environment for people. Environments are constituted in life, not just in thought, and it is only because we live in an environment that we can think at all.

Chapter Four

From trust to domination

An alternative history of human–animal relations

Just as humans have a history of their relations with animals, so also animals have a history of their relations with humans. Only humans, however, construct *narratives* of this history. Such narratives range from what we might regard as myths of totemic origin to supposedly 'scientific' accounts of the origins of domestication. And however we might choose to distinguish between myth and science, if indeed the distinction can be made at all, they have in common that they tell us as much about how the narrators view their own humanity as they do about their attitudes and relations to non-human animals. In this chapter I aim to show that the story we tell in the West about the human exploitation and eventual domestication of animals is part of a more encompassing story about how humans have risen above, and have sought to bring under control, a world of nature that includes their *own* animality.

In this story, a special role is created for that category of human beings who have yet to achieve such emancipation from the natural world: known in the past as wild men or savages, they are now more politely designated as hunters and gatherers. I shall be looking at how hunter-gatherers have come to be stereotypically portrayed, in Western anthropological accounts, as surviving exemplars of the 'natural' condition of mankind, and more particularly at how this is reflected in the depiction of hunters' relations towards their animal prey. I shall then go on to contrast this depiction with the understandings that people who actually live by hunting and gathering have of their relations with the environmental resources on which they depend: again, since our concern is specifically with relations towards animals, I shall concentrate on hunting rather than gathering whilst recognising, of course, that it is not a simple matter to determine where the former ends and the latter begins (Ingold 1986a: 79–100).

Taking the hunter-gatherer understandings as a baseline, I shall attempt to construct an alternative account of the transformation in human–animal relations that in Western discourse comes under the rubric of domestication. My concern, in particular, will be to contrast human–animal relations under a regime of hunting with those under a regime of pastoralism. And a leading premise of my account will be that the domain in which human persons are involved as social beings with one another cannot be rigidly set apart from the domain of their involvement with non-human components of the environment. Hence, any qualitative transformation in environmental relations is likely to be manifested similarly both in the relationships that humans extend towards animals and in those that obtain among themselves in society.

HUMANITY, NATURE AND HUNTER-GATHERERS

Let me begin, then, with the portrayal of the savage hunter-gatherer in Western literature.[1] There are countless instances, especially in the writings of nineteenth-century
anthropologists, of pronouncements to the effect that hunter-gatherers 'live like animals'
or 'live little better than animals'. Remarks of this kind carry force only in the context of
a belief that the proper destiny of human beings is to *overcome* the condition of animality
to which the life of all other creatures is confined. Darwin, for example, found nothing
shocking, and much to marvel at, in the lives of non-human animals, yet his reaction on
encountering the native human inhabitants of Tierra del Fuego, during his round-the-
world voyage in the *Beagle*, was one of utter disgust. 'Viewing such men', he confided to
his journal, 'one can hardly make oneself believe that they are fellow-creatures and inhabitants of the same world' (Darwin 1860: 216). It was not just that their technical inferiority
left them completely at the mercy of their miserable environment; they also had no control
over their own impulses and desires, being by nature fickle, excitable and violent. 'I could
not have believed', Darwin wrote, 'how wide was the difference between savage and civilised
man; it is greater than between a wild and domesticated animal, inasmuch as in man
there is a greater power of improvement' (1860: 208).

Now Darwin, like many of his contemporaries and followers, was in no doubt that
these human hunter-gatherers were innately inferior to modern Europeans. This is a view
that no longer commands acceptance today. If you wanted to compare, say, the innate
capacities of humans and chimpanzees, it should make no difference whatever whether
your human subjects were – say – Tasmanian Aboriginal hunter-gatherers or British airline
pilots.[2] Nevertheless the belief persists in many quarters that even though hunter-gatherers
are fully human so far as their species membership is concerned, they continue to live
alongside other animals within a pristine world of nature. Indeed this idea of hunters and
gatherers, as the human inhabitants of such a world, is virtually given by definition. To
see why this should be so, we need to return to that very dichotomy which Darwin used
as the measure of the distance from savagery to civilisation, namely that between the wild
and the domestic.

Hunting and gathering, of course, are terms that denote particular kinds of activities.
How, then, are these activities to be defined? The conventional answer is that hunters
and gatherers exploit 'wild' or *non-domesticated* resources, whereas farmers and herdsmen
exploit *domesticated* ones (see, for example, Ellen 1982: 128). The precise meaning of
domestication has remained a topic of scholarly debate for well over a century, and I shall
return in a moment to examine some of the suppositions that underlie this debate. Suffice
it to say at this point that every one of the competing definitions introduces some notion
of human control over the growth and reproduction of animals and plants. Wild animals,
therefore, are *animals out of control*. Hunter-gatherers, it seems, are no more able to achieve
mastery over their environmental resources than they are to master their own internal
dispositions. They are depicted as though engaged, like other animal predators, in the
continual pursuit of fugitive prey, locked in a struggle for existence which – on account
of the poverty of their technology – is not yet won. Indeed the ubiquity, in Western
archaeo-zoological literature, of the metaphors of pursuit and capture is extremely striking:
hunters forever pursue, but it is capture that represents the decisive moment in the onset
of domestication (Ducos 1989: 28). Feral animals, in turn, are likened to convicts on the
loose. Notice how the relation between predator and prey is presented as an essentially
antagonistic one, pitting the endurance and cunning of the hunter against the capacities

for escape and evasion of his quarry, each continually augmented by the other through the ratchet mechanism of natural selection. The encounter, when it comes, is forcible and violent.

Behind this opposition between the wild and the domestic there lies a much more fundamental metaphysical dualism – one that seems peculiar to the discourse which, as a convenient shorthand, we can call 'Western', to the extent of being its defining feature. This is the separation of two, mutually exclusive domains of being to which we attach the labels 'humanity' and 'nature'. All animals, according to the principle of this separation, belong wholly in the world of nature, such that the differences between species are differences within nature. Humans, however, are the sole exception: they are different because the essence of their humanity *transcends* nature; and by the same token, that part of them that remains *within* nature presents itself as an undifferentiated amalgam of animal characteristics (Ingold 1990: 210). Thus human beings, uniquely among animals, live a two-tier existence, half-in nature and half-out, both as organisms with bodies and as persons with minds. Now as Raymond Williams has pointed out:

> to speak of man 'intervening' in natural processes is to suppose that he might find it possible not to do so, or decide not to do so. Nature has to be thought of . . . as separate from man, before any question of intervention or command, and the method and ethics of either, can arise.
>
> (1972: 154)

It follows that when we speak of domestication as an intervention in nature, as we are inclined to do, humanity's transcendence over the natural world is already presupposed.

The same goes for the concept of production, classically defined by Friedrich Engels as 'the transforming reaction of man on nature' (1934: 34). In order to produce, humans have to achieve such command or mastery over nature as to be able to impress their own, calculated designs upon the face of the earth. Thus 'the further removed men are from animals, . . . the more their effect on nature assumes the character of premeditated, planned action directed towards definite preconceived ends' (Engels 1934: 178). In other words, to the extent that the human condition transcends nature, so nature herself comes to stand as raw material to human projects of construction. In their realisation, these projects establish a division, within the material world, between the natural and the artificial, the pristine and the man-made, nature-in-the-raw and nature transformed. Hunters and gatherers, as the human inhabitants of a still pristine environment, cannot produce, for in the very act of production the world is irreversibly altered from its natural state. The virgin forest, for example, becomes a neatly ordered patchwork of cultivated fields, naturally occurring raw materials are turned into tools and artefacts, and plants and animals are bred to forms that better serve human purposes. The field, the plough and the ox, though they all belong to the physical world, have been engineered to designs that in every case had their origins in the minds of men, in human acts of envisioning.

Since our present concern is with the history of human–animal relations, or rather with a particular narration of that history, I want to stress the way 'domestication' figures in this account as a feat of engineering, as though the ox were man-made, an artificial construction put together like the plough. Of course the possibility of actually engineering animals has opened up only very recently, and remains more in the realm of fiction than fact. Darwin, to his credit, was at pains to stress that the power of humans to intervene in natural processes is in reality rather limited: above all, humans cannot *create* novel variants, but can only select retroactively from those that arise spontaneously. 'It is an error', Darwin wrote, 'to speak of man "tampering with nature" and causing variability' (1875: 2). Nevertheless, and despite Darwin's careful distinction between intentional and unintentional selection, the belief has persisted that the husbandry of animals, to qualify at all as productive activity, must necessarily entail the deliberate, planned modification of the species involved. Now for pastoralists and farmers, who cannot exactly engineer the forms or behaviours of their animals and plants, the nearest they can come to it is 'controlled breeding' (Bökonyi 1969: 219; 1989: 22). And so it is in the modifications brought about by such breeding – or more technically by 'artificial selection' – that the essence of domestication has been supposed to lie. Thus it came to be assumed that to husband animals was, in essence, to breed them, both practices being lumped indiscriminately under the concept of domestication. Instances where one appeared without the other, such as the reindeer of northern Eurasian pastoralists which fall within the range of variation of the 'wild' form (Ingold 1980: Ch. 2), were dismissed as unstable, transitional states of 'semi-domestication'.

The separation of humanity and nature implicit in the definition of domestication as a process of artificial selection reappears in a competing definition which emphasises its social rather than its biological aspect. 'Domestication', Ducos writes, 'can be said to exist when living animals are integrated as objects into the socio-economic organisation of the human group' (1978: 54; 1989; see also Ingold 1986a: 113, 168, 233). They become a form of property which can be owned, inherited and exchanged. Property, however, is conceived here as a relation between persons (subjects) in respect of things (objects), or more generally, as a social appropriation of nature. Human beings, as social persons, can own; animals, as natural objects, are only ownable. Thus the concept of appropriation, just as the concept of intervention, sets humanity, the world of persons, on a pedestal above the natural world of things. As I have remarked elsewhere, in connection with the concept of land tenure, 'one cannot appropriate that within which one's being is wholly contained' (Ingold 1986a: 135). It follows that hunters and gatherers, characterised in Western discourse as exemplars of man in the state of nature, 'at or near the absolute zero of cultural development' (*ibid.*), can no more own their resources than they can intervene in their reproductive processes. The advent of domestication, in both senses, had to await the breakthrough that liberated humanity from the shackles of nature, a breakthrough that was marked equally by the emergence of institutions of law and government, serving to shackle *human* nature to a social order.

Implied here is the evolutionary premise that the level of being that sets mankind above the animal kingdom had to be *achieved*, in the course of an ascent from savagery to civilisation, just as it has to be achieved in the development of every individual from childhood to maturity.[3] That man's rise to civilisation was conceived to have had its counterpart in the domestication of nature is evident from the interchangeable use of the concept of culture to denote both processes. Edward Tylor's *Primitive Culture* of 1871, the first comprehensive study of human cultural variation, began with the words 'Culture or Civilisation', by which he meant the cultivation of intellectual potentialities common to humanity (1871, I: 1, see Ingold 1986b: 44). Darwin, for his part, introduced his equally compendious study, *The variation of animals and plants under domestication*, with the remark that 'from a remote period, in all parts of the world, man has subjected many animals and plants to domestication or culture' (1875: 2). The cultivation of nature thus appears as the logical corollary of man's cultivation of himself, of his own powers of reason and morality. As the former gave rise to modern domesticated breeds, so did the latter culminate in the emergence of that most perfect expression of the human condition, namely civil society.

Let me conclude this section by returning to Darwin's observation of the native inhabitants of Tierra del Fuego. When it came to his own kind, Darwin remained forever convinced of the necessity and inevitability of progress towards civilisation, yet he was unequivocal in his estimation that the Fuegians had not made it. In the spheres of religion, law, language and technology, they fell far short of a truly human level of existence. Thus:

> We have no reason to believe that they perform any sort of religious worship, . . . their different tribes have no government or chief, . . . the language of these people, according to our notions, scarcely deserves to be called articulate, . . . their [technical] skill in some respects may be compared to the instinct of animals, for it is not improved by experience.
>
> (1860: 208, 217–18)

Biologically, Darwin seems to be saying, these people are certainly human beings, they are of the same species as ourselves, yet in terms of their level of civilisation they are so far from *being human* that their existence may justifiably be set on a par with that of the animals. That being so, any influence that they may have had on the non-human animals in their environment, and on which they depend, cannot differ in kind from the influence that such animals have had on one another.

How hunters and gatherers relate to their environments

So much for the construction of hunter-gatherers, as *somewhat ambiguously* human, within the framework of concepts bequeathed by Western thought. Let me turn now to the hunter-gatherers themselves. How do those peoples who derive a livelihood, at least in part, from hunting and gathering, actually relate to the manifold constituents of their environments?

Much of our information about the traditional ways of life of hunters and gatherers – prior to their transformation or destruction in the wake of European invasion of their lands – comes from the writings of early anthropologists, missionaries, traders and explorers. They tended to depict hunter-gatherer life as a constant struggle for existence. Equipped with the most rudimentary technology in a harsh environment, hunters and gatherers were thought to have to devote every moment of their lives to the quest for food. In this respect, Darwin's description of the natives of Tierra del Fuego, apparently beset by hunger and famine and without the wit to improve their miserable condition, was entirely typical. More recent ethnographic studies, however, have shown this picture to be grossly exaggerated, if not entirely false. The new view of hunter-gatherer economy that emerged from these studies was put forward in its most outspoken form in a now celebrated article by Marshall Sahlins, originally presented to the 1966 Symposium on 'Man the Hunter', and provocatively entitled 'The original affluent society' (subsequently revised and published in Sahlins 1972: Ch. 1).

Unlike the individual in modern Western society who always wants more than he can get, however well-off he may be, the wants of the hunter-gatherer, Sahlins argued, are very limited. What one has, one shares, and there is no point in accumulating material property that would only be an impediment, given the demands of nomadic life. Moreover, for hunter-gatherers who know how to get it, food is always abundant. There is no concept of scarcity. Hunter-gatherers fulfil their limited needs easily and without having to expend very much effort. Two points go along with this. The first is an apparent lack of fore-sight, or of concern for the future. Hunter-gatherers, in Sahlins's depiction, take what they can get opportunistically, as and when they want it. And what they have they consume. The important thing, for them, is that food should 'go round' rather than that it should 'last out'. Whatever food is available is distributed so that everyone has a share, even though this means that there may be none left on the morrow. No attempt is made to ration food out from one day to the next, as explorers do when they go on expeditions. After all, for hunter-gatherers the 'expedition' is not time out from ordinary life but is rather life itself, and this life rests on the assumption that more food will eventually be found (Ingold 1986a: 211–12). The second point, which follows directly from this, is that hunter-gatherers are unconcerned about the storage of food. Stored surpluses impede mobility, and given that food is all around in the environment, hunter-gatherers treat the environment itself as their storehouse, rather than setting aside supplies of harvested food for the future.

One of the studies on which Sahlins drew for evidence in presenting this picture of hunter-gatherer affluence was that undertaken by James Woodburn, of the Hadza of Tanzania. But Woodburn himself, in a series of recent articles, has sought to qualify this view by distinguishing between different *kinds* of hunter-gatherer economy (Woodburn 1980, 1982, 1988). The major distinction is between what he calls *immediate-return* and *delayed-return* economies. In an immediate-return system, people go out on most days to obtain food, which they consume on the day they obtain it or very soon after. The equip-ment they use is simple and quickly made without involving much time or effort, nor do they invest any effort in looking after the resources they exploit. Moreover, there is little or no storage of harvested food. This picture, according to Woodburn, is consistent with the Hadza data, and also with Sahlins's general picture of hunter-gatherer affluence. In a delayed-return system, by contrast, there may be a substantial advance investment of labour in the construction of hunting or trapping facilities or (for fishermen) boats and nets. People might devote considerable effort to husbanding their resources, and there may also be extensive storage.

The significance of this distinction lies in what it suggests about peoples' commitments both to the non-human environment and to one another. Such commitments, Woodburn thinks, are likely to be far greater in a delayed-return system than in an immediate-return one. Obviously, people depend in an immediate-return system, just as much as they do in a delayed-return one, both on the resources of their environment and on the support of other people. But what is striking about the immediate-return system is the lack of investment in, or commitment towards, *particular* resources or persons. An individual, say in Hadza society, relies on other people in general, and on the resources of the environ-ment in general, rather than building up relationships with particular people and particular resources. As Woodburn puts it, 'people are not dependent on *specific* other people, for access to basic requirements' (1982: 434).

The more, however, that we learn about hunter-gatherer perceptions of the environ-ment, and of their relations with it, the more unlikely this picture of the immediate-return system seems. If what Woodburn says about the Hadza is correct, then they appear more as the exception than the rule. Over and over again we encounter the idea that the environ-ment, far from being seen as a passive container for resources that are there in abundance for the taking, is saturated with personal powers of one kind or another. It is alive.[4] And hunter-gatherers, if they are to survive and prosper, have to maintain relationships with these powers, just as they must maintain relationships with other human persons. In many societies, this is expressed by the idea that people have to *look after* or *care for* the country in which they live, by ensuring that proper relationships are maintained. This means treating the country, and the animals and plants that dwell in it, with due consideration and respect, doing all one can to minimise damage and disturbance.

Let me present one example, which will serve to direct our attention from the general context of hunters' and gatherers' relations with the environment towards the more specific context of the hunters' relations with their animal prey. The Cree of northeastern Canada, as we saw in Chapter One (pp. 13–14), suppose that animals intentionally present themselves to the hunter to be killed. The hunter consumes the meat, but the soul of the animal is released to be reclothed with flesh. Hunting here, as among many northern peoples, is conceived as a rite of regeneration: consumption follows killing as birth follows intercourse, and both acts are integral to the reproductive cycles, respectively, of animals and humans. However, animals will not return to hunters who have treated them badly in the past. One treats an animal badly by failing to observe the proper, respectful procedures in the processes of butchering, consumption and disposal of the bones, or by causing undue pain and suffering to the animal in killing it. Above all, animals are offended by *unnecessary* killing: that is, by killing as an end in itself rather than to satisfy genuine consumption needs. They are offended, too, if the meat is not properly shared around all those in the community who need it. Thus, meat and other usable products should on no account be wasted (see Feit 1973, Tanner 1979, Brightman 1993, cf. Ingold 1986a: 246–7).

This emphasis on the careful and prudent use of resources, and on the avoidance of waste, seems a far cry from the image, presented by Sahlins, of original affluence, of people opportunistically collecting whatever is on offer. Moreover the idea that success in present hunting depends on personal relationships built up and maintained with animal powers through a history of previous hunts, quite contradicts Woodburn's notion of immediate returns. For in the Cree conception, the meat that the hunter obtains now is a return on the investment of attention he put in on a previous occasion – when hunting the same animal or its conspecifics – by observing the proper procedures. Indeed it could be argued that in their concern to look after their environments, and to use them carefully, hunter-gatherers practise a conscious policy of conservation. They could, in other words, be said to manage their resources, as has actually been suggested in one recent collection of anthropological studies of North American and Australian hunter-gatherers, which was pointedly entitled *Resource Managers* (Williams and Hunn 1982).

Yet the environmental conservation practised by hunter-gatherers, if such it is, differs fundamentally from the so-called 'scientific' conservation advocated by Western wildlife protection agencies. Scientific conservation is firmly rooted in the doctrine, which I have already spelled out, that the world of nature is separate from, and subordinate to, the world of humanity. One corollary of this doctrine is the idea that merely by virtue of inhabiting an environment, humans – or at least civilised humans – are bound to transform it, to alter it from its 'natural' state. As a result, we tend to think that the only environments that still exist in a genuinely natural condition are those that remain beyond the bounds of human civilisation, as in the dictionary definition of a *wilderness*: 'A tract of land or a region . . . uncultivated or uninhabited by human beings'. Likewise the wild animal is one that lives an authentically natural life, untainted by human contact. It will, of course, have contacts with animals of many other, non-human species, but whereas these latter contacts are supposed to reveal its true nature, any contact with human beings is supposed to render the animal 'unnatural', and therefore unfit as an object of properly scientific inquiry. Juliet Clutton-Brock (1994) has drawn our attention to the way in which, by according to domestic animals a second-class status in this regard, the investigation of their behaviour has been impeded. Domestic animals, it seems, are to be exploited but not studied; wild animals to be studied but not exploited.

Scientific conservation operates, then, by sealing off portions of wilderness and their animal inhabitants, and by restricting or banning human intervention. This is like putting a 'do not touch' notice in front of a museum exhibit: we can observe, but only from a distance, one that excludes direct participation or active 'hands-on' involvement. It is consequently no accident that regions designated as wilderness, and that have been brought under externally imposed regulations of conservation, are very often regions inhabited by hunters and gatherers. Allegedly lacking the capability to control and transform nature, they alone are supposed to occupy a still unmodified, 'pristine' environment. The presence of indigenous hunter-gatherers in regions designated for conservation has often proved acutely embarrassing for the conservationists. For there is no way in which native people can be accommodated within schemes of scientific conservation except as *parts of the wildlife*, that is as constituents of the nature that is to be conserved. They cannot themselves be conservers, because the principles and practice of scientific conservation enjoin a degree of detachment which is incompatible with the kind of involvement with the environment that is essential to hunting and gathering as a way of life.

The sense in which hunters and gatherers see themselves as conservers or custodians of their environments should not, then, be confused with the Western scientific idea of conservation. This latter, as I have shown, is rooted in the assumption that humans – as controllers of the natural world – bear full responsibility for the survival or extinction of wildlife species. For hunter-gatherers this responsibility is inverted. In the last resort, it is those powers that animate the environment that are responsible for the survival or extinction of humans. Summarising the view of the Koyukon of Alaska, Richard Nelson writes:

> The proper role of humankind is to serve a dominant nature. The natural universe is nearly omnipotent, and only through acts of respect and propitiation is the well-being of humans ensured ... In the Koyukon world, human existence depends on a morally based relationship with the overarching powers of nature. Humanity acts at the behest of the environment. The Koyukon must move *with* the forces of their surroundings, not attempting to control, master or fundamentally alter them. They do not confront nature, they yield to it.
>
> (Nelson 1983: 240)

For the Koyukon, as for other hunting and gathering peoples, there are not two separate worlds, of humanity and nature. There is one world, and human beings form a rather small and insignificant part of it.

Given this view of the world, everything depends on maintaining a proper balance in one's relationships with its manifold powers. Thus, rather than saying that hunters and gatherers exploit their environments, it might be better to say that they aim to keep up a dialogue with it. I shall turn in the next section to what this means in terms of hunters' relations with animals. At this juncture, the point I wish to stress is that for hunters and gatherers, *there is no incompatibility between conservation and participation*. It is through a direct engagement with the constituents of the environment, not through a detached, hands-off approach, that hunters and gatherers look after it. Indeed, caring for an environment is like caring for people: it requires a deep, personal and affectionate involvement, an involvement not just of mind or body but of one's entire, undivided being. We do not feel forced in the social world – for example in the field of our relations with kin – to choose between either exploiting others for personal profit or avoiding all direct contact. Yet in the context of relations with animals, this is precisely the choice that is forced on us by the conventional dichotomy between wildness and domestication. It is time now to suggest some alternative terms.

FROM TRUST TO DOMINATION

Trust

It should by now be clear that the characterisation of hunting as the human pursuit of animals that are 'wild', though it speaks volumes about our Western view of hunters, is quite inappropriate when it comes to the hunters' view of animals. For the animals are not regarded as strange, alien beings from another world, but as participants in the same world to which the people also belong. They are not, moreover, conceived to be bent on escape, brought down only by the hunter's superior cunning, speed or force. To the contrary, a hunt that is successfully consummated with a kill is taken as proof of amicable relations between the hunter and the animal that has willingly allowed itself to be taken. Hunters are well-known for their abhorrence of violence in the context of human relations,[5] and the same goes for their relations with animals: the encounter, at the moment of the kill, is – to them – essentially *non*-violent. And so, too, hunting is not a failed enterprise, as it is so often depicted in the West: a failure marked by the technical inability to assert or maintain control; pursuit that is not ultimately crowned by capture. It is rather a highly successful attempt to draw the animals in the hunters' environment into the familiar ambit of social being, and to establish a working basis for mutuality and coexistence.

For hunters and gatherers, animals and plants in the environment play a nurturing role, as do human caregivers. This is the kind of understanding that Nurit Bird-David seeks to convey by means of her notion, introduced in the previous chapter (pp. 43–4), of 'the giving environment' (Bird-David 1990). Focusing on peoples of the tropical forest for whom gathering is rather more important than hunting, Bird-David suggests that hunters and gatherers model their relationships with life-giving agencies in their environments on the institution of sharing, which is the foundation for interpersonal relations within the human community. Thus in their nurturing capacity, these non-human agencies 'share' with you, just as you share what you receive from the environment with other people. Both movements, from non-human to human beings and among the latter themselves, are seen to constitute a single 'cosmic economy of sharing' (Bird-David 1992a). However, while people may indeed draw an analogy between the relations with animals and plants activated in hunting and gathering, and the relations among humans activated in sharing, it seems to me that these two sets of relations are, at a more fundamental level of principle, not just analogous but identical. This principle which, I maintain, inheres equally in the activities of sharing and in those of hunting and gathering, is that of *trust*.

The essence of trust is a peculiar combination of *autonomy* and *dependency*. To trust someone is to act with that person in mind, in the hope and expectation that she will do likewise – responding in ways favourable to you – so long as you do nothing to curb her autonomy to act otherwise. Although you depend on a favourable response, that response comes entirely on the initiative and volition of the other party. Any attempt to *impose* a response, to lay down conditions or obligations that the other is bound to follow, would represent a betrayal of trust and a negation of the relationship. For example, if I force my friend to assist me in my enterprise, this is tantamount to a declaration that I do not trust him to assist me of his own accord, and therefore that I no longer count him as a friend at all. Offended by my infidelity, his likely response will be to withdraw his favour towards me. Trust, therefore, always involves an element of risk – the risk that the other on whose actions I depend, but which I cannot in any way control, may act contrary to my expectations (see Gambetta 1988, for some excellent discussions of this point).

Now this combination of autonomy and dependency is, I believe, the essence of what is commonly reported in ethnographic studies of hunting and gathering societies under the rubric of sharing. People in hunter-gatherer communities *do* depend on one another for food and for a variety of everyday services, though these exchanges may be the surface expression of a deeper concern with *companionship*, characterised by Tom Gibson as 'shared activity in itself' (Gibson 1985: 393). Noteworthy in Gibson's account is the connection he draws between companionship and autonomy: 'a relationship based on companionship is voluntary, freely terminable and involves the preservation of the personal autonomy of both parties' (1985: 392). He contrasts this kind of relationship with the kind that is involuntary, non-terminable and places the parties under obligation (see Ingold 1986a: 116–17). Bird-David (1990) draws essentially the same contrast under the terms 'giving' and 'reciprocating', referring respectively to the relationships that hunter-gatherers and cultivators see themselves as having with the environment of the tropical forest. Clearly, both hunter-gatherers and cultivators depend on their environments. But whereas for cultivators this dependency is framed within a structure of reciprocal obligation, for hunter-gatherers it rests on the recognition of personal autonomy. In my terms, the contrast is between relationships based on *trust* and those based on *domination*. I shall turn to the latter in a moment, but first I should like to specify more precisely the meaning of trust in the context of relations between hunters and their animal prey.

I shall do so by drawing a further, analytic distinction between *trust* and *confidence* (following Luhmann 1988). Both terms are commonly and casually used in characterisations of hunter-gatherer attitudes towards the environment. Sahlins, for example, uses the terms freely and interchangeably in his account of the 'pristine affluence' of hunter-gatherer economic arrangements, marked, he claims, by

a *trust* in the abundance of nature's resources rather than despair at the inadequacy of human means. My point is that otherwise curious heathen devices became understandable by the people's *confidence*, a confidence which is the reasonable human attribute of a generally successful economy.

(1972: 29, my emphases)

Now Sahlins writes as though, for hunters and gatherers, the environment existed as a world of nature 'out there', quite separate from the world of human society and its interests. In this he uncritically projects onto the hunter-gatherer way of thinking a nature/society dichotomy which, as we have seen, is of Western provenance. According to this view, nature – which the people make no attempt to control or modify – is seen to go its own way, subject to ups and downs regardless of human actions or dispositions towards it. If it yields, or fails to yield, this is not because it has the hunter-gatherer in mind. And the hunter-gatherer has to assume that it *will* yield, since life itself is predicated on this expectation. The alternative, in Luhmann's words, 'is to withdraw expectations without having anything with which to replace them' (1988: 97).

Now all of us have to make these kinds of assumptions all the time: they are what enable us to get by in a world full of unforeseen and unconsidered dangers. The world may stop revolving or be knocked off course by a meteoric collision, but we have to assume that it will not, and for the most part the possibility never enters our heads. Likewise, according to Sahlins, hunter-gatherers assume the providence of nature and do not consider the possibility of starvation. It is this attitude that I denote by the concept of confidence. And the crucial aspect of confidence to which I wish to draw attention is that it presupposes no engagement, no active involvement on our part, with the potential sources of danger in the world, so that when trouble does strike it is attributed to forces *external* to the field of our own relationships, forces which just happen to set the 'outside world', under its own momentum, on a collision course with our expectations. But with the attitude that I denote by the concept of trust, it is quite otherwise. Trust presupposes an active, prior engagement with the agencies and entities of the environment on which we depend; it is an inherent quality of our relationships towards them. And my contention is that in this strict sense, trust rather than confidence characterises the attitude of hunters and gatherers towards their non-human environment, just as it characterises their attitude towards one another.

The animals in the environment of the hunter do not simply go their own way, but are supposed to act with the hunter in mind. They are not just 'there' for the hunter to find and take as he will; rather they *present themselves* to him. The encounter, then, is a moment in the unfolding of a continuing – even lifelong – relationship between the hunter and the animal kind (of which every particular individual encountered is a specific instance). The hunter hopes that by being good to animals, they in turn will be good to him.[6] But by the same token, the animals have the power to withhold if any attempt is made to coerce what they are not, of their own volition, prepared to provide. For coercion, the attempt to extract by force, represents a betrayal of the trust that underwrites the willingness to give. Animals thus maltreated will desert the hunter, or even cause him ill fortune. This is the reason why, as I mentioned above, the encounter between hunter and prey is conceived as basically non-violent. It is also the reason why hunters aim to take only what is revealed to them and do not press for more. To describe this orientation as 'opportunism' is misleading, for it is not a matter of taking what you can get but of accepting what is given. The same applies in the context of intra-community sharing: one may indeed ask for things that others have, but not for more. 'Practically, would-be-recipients request what they *see* in the possession of others and do not request them to produce what they do not appear to have' (Bird-David 1992a: 30).

By regarding the relation between hunters and their prey as one of trust, we can also resolve the problem inherent in Woodburn's distinction between immediate-return and delayed-return systems. Woodburn was concerned to discover the basis for the pronounced emphasis on personal autonomy in many hunter-gatherer societies, and he put it down to the lack of specific commitments and enduring relationships in an immediate-return economy. Yet we find that at least among hunters, people are enmeshed in highly particularistic and intimate ties with both human and non-human others. Contrary to expectations, however, their sense of autonomy is not compromised. Woodburn's error, as we can now see, was to assume that dependency on specific other people entails loss of autonomy. This is not necessarily so, for it is precisely in relations of trust that autonomy is retained *despite* dependency. But trust, as I have noted, inevitably entails risk, and this is as much the case in hunters' relations with animals as it is within the human community. Thus, of the 'other-than-human' persons that inhabit the world of the Ojibwa, Hallowell observes – taking up the perspective of an Ojibwa subject – that

> I cannot always predict exactly how they will act, although most of the time their behaviour meets my expectations ... They may be friendly and help me when I need them but, at the same time, I have to be prepared for hostile acts, too. I must be cautious in my relations with other 'persons' because appearances may be deceptive.
>
> (1960: 43)

That is why hunters attach such enormous importance to knowledge and its acquisition. This is not knowledge in the natural scientific sense, of things and how they work. It is rather as we would speak of it in relation to persons: to 'know' someone is to be in a position to approach him directly with a fair expectation of the likely response, to be familiar with that person's past history and sensible to his tastes, moods and idiosyncrasies. You get to know other human persons by sharing with them, that is by experiencing their companionship. And if you are a hunter, you get to know animals by hunting. As I shall show in Chapter Sixteen, the weapons of the hunter, far from being instruments of control or manipulation, serve this purpose of acquiring knowledge. Through them, the hunter does not transform the world, rather the world opens itself up to him. Like words, the hunter's tools are caught up in chains of personal (not mechanical) causation, serving to reveal the otherwise hidden intentions of non-human agents in a world where, recalling Feit's remark concerning the Cree, it is 'always appropriate to ask "who did it?" and "why?" rather than "how does that work?"' (1973: 116). In short, the hunter does not seek, and fail to achieve, control over animals; he seeks revelation. Robin Ridington has put the point concisely in his observation that hunter-gatherers, 'instead of attempting to control nature ... concentrate on controlling their relationship with it' (1982: 471).

Domination

It is quite otherwise with pastoralists.[7] Like hunters, they depend on animals, and their relationship with these animals may similarly be characterised by a quality of attentive, and at times even benevolent regard. Herdsmen do indeed care for their animals, but it is care of a quite different kind from that extended by hunters. For one thing, the animals are presumed to lack the capacity to reciprocate. In the world of the hunter, animals, too, are supposed to care, to the extent of laying down their lives for humans by allowing themselves to be taken. They retain, however, full control over their own destiny. Under pastoralism, that control has been relinquished to humans. It is the herdsman who takes life-or-death decisions concerning what are now 'his' animals, and who controls every other aspect of their welfare, acting as he does as both protector, guardian and executioner. He sacrifices them; they do not sacrifice themselves to him (Ingold 1986a: 272–3). They are cared for, but they are not themselves empowered to care. Like dependants in the household of a patriarch, their status is that of jural minors, subject to the authority of their human master (Ingold 1980: 96). In short, the relationship of pastoral care, quite unlike that of the hunter towards animals, is founded on a principle not of trust but of domination.[8]

These principles of relationship are mutually exclusive: to secure the compliance of the other by imposing one's will, whether by force or by more subtle forms of manipulation, is – as we have seen – an abrogation of trust, entailing as it does the denial rather than the recognition of the autonomy of the other on whom one depends. The very means by which the herdsman aims to secure access to animals would, for the hunter, involve a betrayal which would have the opposite effect of causing them to desert. The instruments of herding, quite unlike those of hunting, are of control rather than revelation: they include the whip, spur, harness and hobble, all of them designed either to restrict or to induce movement through the infliction of physical force, and sometimes acute pain (I return to these in Chapter Fifteen, pp. 306–8). Should we conclude, then, that while the concept of wildness is clearly inapplicable to describe the hunter's perception of animals with whom he enjoys a relation of trust and familiarity, the opposite concept of domestication – with its connotations of mastery and control – is perfectly apt to describe the pastoralist's relation with the animals in his herd?

The answer depends on precisely how we understand the nature of this mastery and control, and this, in turn, hinges on the significance we attach to the notion of physical force. Consider the slave-driver, whip in hand, compelling his slaves to toil through the brute infliction of severe pain. Clearly the autonomy of the slave in this situation to act according to his own volition is very seriously compromised. Does this mean that the slave responds in a purely mechanical way to the stroke of the whip? Far from it. For when we speak of the application of force in this kind of situation, we impute to the recipient powers of resistance – powers which the infliction of pain is specifically intended to overwhelm. That is to say, the use of force is predicated on the assumption that the slave is a being with the capacity to act and suffer, and in that sense a person. And when we say that the master causes the slave to work, the causation is personal, not mechanical: it lies in the *social* relation between master and slave, which is clearly one of domination. In fact, the original connotation of 'force' was precisely that of action intentionally directed against the resistance of another sentient being, and the metaphorical extension from the domain of interpersonal relations to that of the movements of inanimate and insentient things, like planets or billiard balls, is both relatively recent and highly specialised (see Walter 1969: 40 for a discussion of this point).

Now if by the notion of domestication is implied a kind of mastery and control similar to that entailed in slavery, then this notion might indeed be applicable to describe the pastoralist's relation with the animals in his herd. Richard Tapper argues, along precisely these lines, that where 'individual animals are taken out of their natural species community and subjugated to provide labour for the human production process, . . . their feeding under the control of their human masters', one may reasonably describe the 'human–animal relations of production' thereby established as 'slave-based' (Tapper 1988: 52–3). In those societies of the ancient world in which slavery was the dominant relation of production, the parallel between the domestic animal and the slave appears to have been self-evident. The Romans, for example, classified slaves and cattle, respectively, as *instrumentum genus vocale* and *instrumentum genus semi-vocale* (Tapper 1988: 59 fn. 3), while Vedic texts, according to Benveniste (1969: 48), have a term *pasu* for animate possessions that admits two varieties, quadrupedal (referring to domestic animals) and bipedal (referring to human slaves). Perhaps the most extraordinary piece of evidence comes from the work of the Japanese scholar, K. Maekawa, on the temple economy of Sumeria in the third millennium BC. From his analysis of Sumerian texts, Maekawa shows that the temple-state of Lagash maintained one population of captured female slaves to work as weavers, and another population of cattle for the supply of milk. In each population, female offspring were retained to secure its continuation, while male offspring were castrated and put to work: the men in hauling boats up-river, the oxen in pulling the plough (cited in Tani 1996: 404–5).

In a remarkable extension of the argument for the parallel between the domestic animal and the slave, Yutaka Tani has drawn attention to a technique for managing pastoral herds of sheep or goats that is widely distributed in the Mediterranean and Middle East. A selected male animal is castrated and trained to respond to the vocal commands of the shepherd. On rejoining the herd, this animal, known as a 'guide-wether', acts as an inter-mediary between the shepherd (the dominator) and his flock (the dominated). For while obedient to its master, the wether also sets an example, in its behaviour, which is followed by all the other animals in the flock. Now barring a small number of males kept for breeding purposes, most of these animals are female. The position of the wether, a castrated male charged with the guidance of a herd of females, is thus functionally anal-ogous to the position of the human eunuch, in the court of the emperor, charged with guarding the females of his harem. The reliability and trustworthiness of the eunuch, like that of the guide-wether, derives from his exclusion from the reproductive process. But despite his high rank, the eunuch remains a slave, wholly dependent on imperial favour for his position. Noting the similarity between the techniques of management employed, respectively, by the shepherd to control his flock and by the emperor to control his harem, Tani wonders whether the latter might be derived from the former (or, less probably, vice versa). The idea may seem far-fetched, and the historical evidence, as Tani admits, is inconclusive. Yet it seems more than coincidental that the technique of using the guide-wether is distributed 'in the same areas of the Mediterranean and Middle East as where the political institution of the eunuch first appeared and from where it diffused' (Tani 1996: 388–91, 403).

However obvious the parallel may have seemed, to people of the ancient world, between the domination and control of slaves and of pastoral herds, it is an idea that is deeply alien to modern Western thought. For viewing both kinds of relationship, with slaves and with livestock, through the lens of a dichotomy between humanity and nature, we are convinced that the master–slave relationship, occurring between human beings, exists on the level of society, whereas domestication amounts to a social appropriation of – or intervention in – the separate domain of nature, within which animal existence is fully contained. In a revealing comment, Marx argued that relations of domination, such as obtain between master and slave, cannot obtain between humans and domestic animals, because the latter lack the power of intentional agency: 'Beings without will, such as animals, may indeed render services, but their owner is not thereby lord and master' (1964: 102; see Ingold 1980: 88). Domination and domestication are here distinguished, on the premise that the one is a form of social control exercised over subject-persons, and the other a form of mechanical control exercised over object-things. But this is not, to my knowledge, a distinction that any pastoral people make themselves. They may rank animals hierarchically below humans, as in ancient society slaves were ranked hierarchi-cally below freemen, but they are not assigned to a separate domain of being. And although the relations pastoralists establish with animals are quite different from those established by hunters, they rest, at a more fundamental level, on the same premise, namely that animals are, like human beings, endowed with powers of sentience and autonomous action which have either to be respected, as in hunting, or overcome through superior force, as in pastoralism.

To sum up: my contention is that the transition in human–animal relations that in Western scholarly literature is described as the domestication of creatures that were once wild, should rather be described as a transition from trust to domination. I have suggested that the negative stereotype of the hunter's relation to his prey, marked by the absence of control, be replaced by a more positive characterisation as a certain mode of engagement. But I have also shown that the emergence of pastoralism does not depend, as orthodox definitions of domestication imply, upon humans' achieving a state of being that takes them above and beyond the world in which all other creatures live. Thus the transition from trust to domination is not to be understood as a movement from engagement to disengagement, from a situation where humans and animals are co-participants in the same world to one in which they hive off into their own separate worlds of society and nature. Quite to the contrary, the transition involves a *change in the terms of engagement.* Whether the regime be one of hunting or of pastoralism, humans and animals relate to one another not in mind or body alone but as undivided centres of intention and action, as whole beings. Only with the advent of industrial livestock management have animals been reduced, in practice and not just in theory, to the mere 'objects' that theorists of the Western tradition (who, barring the occasional pet, had little or no contact with animals in the course of their working lives) had always supposed them to be (Tapper 1988: 52–7). Indeed this objectification of animals, having reached its peak in the agro-pastoral industry, is as far removed from the relations of domination entailed in traditional pastoral care as it is from the relations of trust entailed in hunting.

Moreover, as alternative modes of relationship, neither trust nor domination is in any sense more or less advanced than the other. It is important, in particular, to guard against the tendency to think of relations based on trust as morally, or intrinsically 'good', and of those based on domination as intrinsically 'bad'. They are simply different. Trust, as I have shown, is a relation fraught with risk, tension and ambiguity. It is well to remember Hallowell's point, apropos Ojibwa ontology, that 'appearances my be deceptive' (1960: 43). The underside of trust, as Hallowell shows so clearly, is chronic anxiety and suspicion. Thus to argue that hunter-gatherer relations with the environment are based on a principle of trust is not to present yet another version of the arcadian vision of life in harmony with nature. Nor, by the same token, should the movement from trust to domination be regarded as one that replaced harmony by discord, or that set humanity on the path of its irrevocable alienation from nature. When hunters became pastoralists they began to relate to animals, and to one another, in different ways. But they were not taking the first steps on the road to modernity.

CONCLUSION

Writing of Koyukon hunters of Alaska, Nelson remarks that, for them, 'the conceptual distance between humanity and nature is narrow' (1983: 240). On the evidence of his own account, and many others, it would be more true to say that there is no conceptual distance at all, or rather that what *we* distinguish as humanity and nature merge, for them, into a single field of relationships. And indeed, we find nothing corresponding to the Western concept of nature in hunter-gatherer representations, for they see no essential difference between the ways one relates to humans and to non-human constituents of the environment. We have seen how both sharing (among humans) and hunting (of animals by humans) rest on the same principle of trust, and how the sense in which hunters claim to know and care for animals is identical to the sense in which they know and care for other human beings. One could make the same argument for pastoralism: I have shown elsewhere, in the case of northern Eurasian reindeer herdsmen, how the transition from hunting to pastoralism led to the emergence, in place of egalitarian relations of sharing, of relations of dominance and subordination between herding leaders and their assistants (Ingold 1980: 165–9). Evidently a transition in the quality of relationship, from trust to domination, affects relations not only between humans and non-human animals, but also, and equally, among human beings themselves. Hallowell's observation that in the world of the Ojibwa, 'vital social relations transcend those which are maintained with human beings' (1960: 43) could apply just as well to other hunting peoples, and indeed to pastoralists as well.

This observation, however, plays havoc with the established Western dichotomies between animals and society, or nature and humanity. The distinction between the human and the non-human no longer marks the outer limits of the social world, as against that of nature, but rather maps a domain within it whose boundary is both permeable and easily crossed. It comes as no surprise, then, that anthropology, as an intellectual product of the Western tradition, has sought to contain the damage by relativising the indigenous view and thereby neutralising the challenge it presents to our own suppositions. Thus we are told that the hunter-gatherer view is just another cultural construction of reality. When hunters use terms drawn from the domain of human interaction to describe their relations with animals, they are said to be indulging in metaphor (Bird-David 1992a). But to claim that what is literally true of relations among humans (for example, that they share), is only figuratively true of relations with animals, is to reproduce the very dichotomy between animals and society that the indigenous view purports to reject. We tell ourselves reassuringly that this view the hunters have, of sharing with animals as they would with people, however appealing it might be, does not correspond with what actually happens. For nature, we say, does not *really* share with man.[9] When hunters assert the contrary it is because the image of sharing is so deeply ingrained in their thought that they can no longer tell the metaphor from the reality. But *we* can, and we insist – on these grounds – that the hunters have got it wrong.

This strikes me as profoundly arrogant. It is to accord priority to the Western metaphysics of the alienation of humanity from nature, and to use *our* disengagement as the standard against which to judge *their* engagement. Faced with an ecological crisis whose roots lie in this disengagement, in the separation of human agency and social responsibility from the sphere of our direct involvement with the non-human environment, it surely behoves us to reverse this order of priority. I began with the point that while both humans and animals have histories of their mutual relations, only humans narrate such histories. But to construct a narrative, one must already dwell in the world and, in the dwelling, enter into relationships with its constituents, both human and non-human. I am suggesting that we rewrite the history of human–animal relations, taking this condition of active engagement, of being-in-the-world, as our starting point. We might speak of it as a history of human *concern* with animals, insofar as this notion conveys a caring, attentive regard, a 'being with'. And I am suggesting that those who are 'with' animals in their day-to-day lives, most notably hunters and herdsmen, can offer us some of the best possible indications of how we might proceed.

Chapter Five

Making things, growing plants, raising animals and bringing up children

> We have ... large and various orchards and gardens ... And we make (by art) in the same orchards and gardens trees and flowers to come earlier or later than their seasons, and to come up and bear more speedily than by their natural course they do. We make them also by art greater much than their nature, and their fruit greater and sweeter and of differing taste, smell, colour and figure, from their nature ... We have also parks and inclosures of all sorts of beasts and birds ... By art likewise we make them greater or taller than their kind is, and contrariwise dwarf them, and stay their growth; we make them more fruitful and bearing than their kind is, and contrariwise barren and not generative. Also we make them differ in colour, shape, activity, many ways.

So wrote Francis Bacon in 1624, outlining his Utopian vision of the *New Atlantis*, a society dedicated to the mastery of nature through rigorous application of the principles of rational science (Bacon 1965: 449–50). In this society every kind of living thing, both animal and vegetable, can be *made by art* so that it better serves human purposes. In what follows I aim to show how this notion of making has come to rest at the heart of what we mean by production, in relation not only to the manufacture of artefacts but also, and more especially, to the breeding – or 'artificial selection' – of plants and animals. The idea of production as making, I argue, is embedded in a grand narrative of the human transcendence of nature, in which the domestication of plants and animals figures as the counterpart of the self-domestication of humanity in the process of civilisation. I go on to consider how people who actually live by gardening, tilling the soil or keeping live-stock understand the nature of their activity, drawing on examples from South America, Melanesia and West Africa. Taking these understandings as a starting point, I shall then take a fresh look at what it means to cultivate plants and to husband animals. My conclu-sion is that the work of the farmer or herdsman does not *make* crops or livestock, but rather serves to set up certain conditions of development within which plants and animals take on their particular forms and behavioural dispositions. We are dealing, in a word, with processes of *growth*.

THE HUMAN TRANSFORMATION OF NATURE

According to the received categories of archaeological and anthropological thought, there are basically just two ways of procuring a livelihood from the natural environment, conventionally denoted by the terms *collection* and *production*. The distinction between them was first coined by Friedrich Engels. In a note penned in 1875, Engels pointed to production as the most fundamental criterion of what he saw as a kind of 'mastery' of the environment that was distinctively human: 'The most that the animal can achieve is to *collect*; man produces, he prepares the means of life . . . which without him nature would not have produced. This makes impossible any unqualified transference of the laws of life in animal society to human society' (1934: 308). The essence of production, for Engels, lay in the deliberate planning of activity by intentional and selfconscious agents. Animals, through their activities, might exert lasting and quite radical effects on their environments, but these effects are by and large unintended: the non-human animal, Engels thought, did not labour in its surroundings *in order* to change them; it had no conception of its task. The human, by contrast, always has an end in mind.

Curiously, however, whenever Engels turned to consider concrete examples of human mastery in production, he drew them exclusively from the activities of agriculture and pastoralism, through which plants, animals and the landscape itself had been demonstrably transformed through human design (1934: 34, 178–9). Opposing the foraging behaviour of non-human species to the human husbandry of plants and animals, Engels left a gap that could only be filled by calling into being a special category of humans known to him and his contemporaries as 'savages'. As a hunter of animals and a gatherer of plants, the savage had, as it were, come down from the trees but had not yet left the woods: suspended in limbo between evolution and history, he was a human being who had so far failed to realise the potential afforded by his unique constitution. Ever since, the humanity of hunter-gatherers has been somehow in question. They may be members of the species, *Homo sapiens*, but their form of life is such as to put them on a par with other animal kinds which also derive their subsistence by collecting whatever is 'to hand' in the environment. As the archaeologist Robert Braidwood wrote in 1957, 'a man who spends his whole life following animals just to kill them to eat, or moving from one berry patch to another, is really living just like an animal himself' (Braidwood 1957: 22).

This latent ambiguity also allowed the archaeologist, V. Gordon Childe, to take up the distinction between collection and production – in terms virtually identical to those proposed by Engels – to draw a line not between humans and animals, but between 'neolithic' people and their successors on the one hand, and 'palaeolithic' hunters and gatherers on the other. In crossing this line, the ancestors of present-day farmers, herdsmen and urban dwellers were alleged to have set in motion a revolution in the arts of subsistence without parallel in the history of life. Ushered in by the invention of the science of selective breeding, it was a revolution that turned people, according to Childe, into 'active partners with nature instead of parasites on nature' (1942: 55). Though contemporary authors might phrase the distinction somewhat differently, the notion of food-production as the singular achievement of human agriculturalists and pastoralists has become part of the stock-in-trade of modern prehistory. And understanding the origins of food-production has become as central a preoccupation for prehistorians as has understanding the origins of humankind for palaeoanthropologists: where the latter seek the evolutionary origins of human beings *within* nature, the former seek the decisive moment at which humanity *transcended* nature, and was set on the path of history.

Underlying the collection/production distinction, then, is a master narrative about how human beings, through their mental and bodily labour, have progressively raised themselves above the purely natural level of existence to which all other animals are confined, and in so doing have built themselves a history of civilisation. Through their transformations of nature, according to this narrative, humans have also transformed themselves. It is a fact about human beings, states Maurice Godelier, that alone among animals, they '*produce society in order to live*' – and in so doing, 'create history' (1986: 1, original emphases). By this he means that the designs and purposes of human action upon the natural environment – action that yields a return in the form of the wherewithal for subsistence – have their source in the domain of social relations, a domain of mental realities ('representations, judgements, principles of thought') that stands over and above the sheer materiality of nature (1986: 10–11).

Godelier goes on to distinguish five 'kinds of materiality', depending upon the manner and extent to which human beings are implicated in their formation. First is that part of nature which is wholly untouched by human activity; secondly there is the part that has been changed on account of the presence of humans, but indirectly and unintentionally; the third is the part that has been intentionally transformed by human beings and that depends upon their attention and energy for its reproduction; the fourth part comprises materials that have been fashioned into instruments such as tools and weapons, and the fifth may be identified with what we would conventionally call the 'built environment' – houses, shelters, monuments, and the like (Godelier 1986: 4–5). In this classification the critical division falls between the second and third kinds, for it is also taken to mark the distinction between the wild and the domestic. The third part of nature is taken to consist, primarily, of domesticated plants and animals, whereas the biotic components of the first and second parts are either wild or, at most, in a condition of pre-domestication. Moreover Godelier points to the domestication of plants and animals as a paradigmatic instance of the transforming action of humanity upon nature. This leaves us, however, with two unresolved problems.

The first concerns the status of hunters and gatherers who have sought not to transform their environments but rather to conserve them in a form that remains, so far as possible, unscarred by human activity. If, as Godelier claims, 'human beings have a history because they transform nature' (1986: 1), are we to conclude that humans who do not transform nature lack history? For his own part, Godelier resists this conclusion: 'I cannot see any theoretical reason to consider the forms of life and thought characteristic of hunters, gatherers and fishers as more natural than those of the agriculturalists and stockbreeders who succeeded them' (1986: 12). The activities of hunter-gatherers, he asserts, are like those of all human beings at all times, and unlike those of all non-human animals, in that they are prompted by mental representations that have their source in the intersubjective domain of society. Yet apart from the construction of tools and shelters (corresponding to the fourth and fifth kinds of materiality), these representations are not materialised in the physical substrate of nature. Hunter-gatherers have a history, but theirs is a history that is written neither in the pages of documents nor upon the surface of the land. It is inscribed exclusively upon the plane of mental rather than material reality. Overturning the classical conception of hunter-gatherers as arch-representatives of humanity in the state of nature, Godelier reaches the rather paradoxical conclusion that it is in their societies that the boundary between the mental and the material, between culture and nature, is most clearcut. The more that the material world is subordinated to the ends of art, the more the world of ideas is rendered in physical form, the less clearcut the nature/culture distinction appears to be (1986: 4).

The second problem is one to which Godelier alludes in a footnote, but fails to take further. It is that for most non-Western people, 'the idea of a transformation of nature by human beings has no meaning' (1986: 2, fn. 1). Thus the peoples of the past who were initially responsible for domesticating plants and animals must have had quite different ideas about what they were doing. In the next section I shall present a range of comparable ideas drawn from the ethnography of contemporary non-Western societies.

The point to stress at this juncture is that the idea of history as consisting in the human transformation of nature, like the ideas of nature itself and of society as an entity counterposed to nature, has a history of its own in the Western world. By tracing this history back to its roots we may find that it has grown out of a set of understandings very different from those familiar to us today, yet much closer to the apparently exotic cosmologies of non-Western 'others'.

It is beyond the scope of this chapter to document the history of Western thinking about humanity and nature (Glacken's [1967] massive treatise on the subject remains unsurpassed). Suffice it to note that the essence of the kind of thought we call 'Western' is that it is founded in a claim to the subordination of nature by human powers of reason. Entailed in this claim is a notion of making things as an imprinting of prior conceptual design upon a raw material substrate. Human reason is supposed to provide the form, nature the substance in which it is realised. We have already encountered this idea of making in the writings of Bacon, but more than two hundred years later it served as the fulcrum of Marx's theory of value, according to which it was the work of shaping up the material from its raw to its final state that bestowed value on what was already 'given' in nature. It made no difference, in principle, whether that work was represented by the labour of the artisan, in the manufacture of equipment, or by that of the farmer or stockbreeder, in the husbandry of plants and animals. Both were conceived as instances of productive making – the human transformation of nature.

Yet in arriving at his theory of value, Marx turned on its head an idea of even greater antiquity, though one whose systematic elaboration had to await the writings of the French Physiocrats, Quesnay and Turgot, in the eighteenth century. For these writers too, the role of the artisan was to imprint a rational design upon material supplied by nature. But in doing so, he created no new value. To the contrary, his work was understood to involve nothing more than a rearrangement of what nature had already brought into existence. The real source of wealth, according to Physiocracy, was the land, and lay in its inherent fertility. And for this reason, the activities of those who worked the land, in growing crops and raising animals, were understood to be fundamentally different in character from the activities of those whose tasks lay in the field of manufacture.

In an elegant analysis, Stephen Gudeman (1986: 80–4) has shown how the economic doctrines of Physiocracy were closely modelled on the theory of perception and cognition proposed some seventy years previously by John Locke. In Locke's economy of knowledge, the natural world is a source of raw sensations impinging upon the receptor organs of the passive human observer. The mind then operates on these received sensory data, separating and combining them to form complex ideas. In just the same way, according to the Physiocrats, the land furnishes its inhabitants with basic raw materials, to which human reason adds form and meaning. As Gudeman puts it, 'in this "intellectual" economics, agriculture is to artisanship as sensation was to mental operation' (1986: 83). The role of the farmer is to receive the substantive yield of the land, that of the artisan is to deliver the formal designs of humanity. Where the farmer's work is productive, in that it results in an influx of wealth to the human community, it is nevertheless passive since the creative agency in bringing forth this wealth was attributed to the land itself and, behind that, to divine intervention. Conversely the artisan's work is non-productive, since it adds nothing to human wealth, but is nevertheless active since it is impelled by reason (Gudeman 1986: 87).

In this view, although it would still be fair to describe the act of making things as a human transformation of nature, such making is not the equivalent but the very *opposite* of production, just as artisanship is the opposite of agriculture. Production is a process of growing, not making. The farmer, and for that matter the raiser of livestock, submits to a productive dynamic that is immanent in the natural world itself, rather than converting nature into an instrument to his own purpose. Far from 'impressing the stamp of their will upon the earth', to adopt Engels's imperialistic phrase (1934: 179), those who toil on the land – in clearing fields, turning the soil, sowing, weeding, reaping, pasturing their flocks and herds, or feeding animals in their stalls – are assisting in the reproduction of nature, and derivatively of their own kind.

In classical Greece, too, agriculture and artisanship were clearly opposed, belonging – as Vernant remarks (1983: 253) – 'to two different fields of experience which are to a large extent mutually exclusive'. The contrast between growing things and making things was delightfully phrased by the Sophist author Antiphon, writing in the fifth century BC, who invites us to imagine an old wooden bed, buried in the ground, taking root and sprouting green shoots. What comes up, however, is not a new bed, but fresh wood! Beds are made, but wood grows (Vernant 1983: 260). As a grower of crops rather than a maker of artefacts, the farmer was not seen to act upon nature, let alone to transform it to human ends. Work on the land was more a matter of falling into line with an overarching order, at once natural and divinely ordained, within which the finalities of human existence were themselves encompassed. Even were it technically possible to transform nature, the very idea would have been regarded as an impiety (Vernant 1983: 254).

If there is a certain parallel here with the doctrines of Physiocracy, despite the immense lapse of time, it is doubtless because both classical Greek and eighteenth century Physiocratic authors were able to draw on a fund of practical experience in working on the land. When it came to farming, they knew what they were talking about. But with regard to artisanship, their respective notions could not have been more different. For according to classical Greek writers, the forms which the artisan realised in his material issued not from the human mind, as constructs of a rational intelligence, but were themselves inscribed in the order of nature. Thus the idea of making as an imposition of rational design upon raw material would have been entirely alien to Greek thought. 'The artisan is not in command of nature; he submits to the requirements of the form. His function and his excellence is . . . to obey' (Vernant 1983: 294). This, of course, is the precise inverse of Godelier's assertion that in the husbandry of plants and animals, in making tools and constructing buildings – that is, in the production of the third, fourth and fifth kinds of materiality – it is nature that submits to the requirements of human form. The idea that production consists in action *upon* nature, issuing from a superior source in society, is an essentially modern one.

INDIGENOUS UNDERSTANDING: FOUR ETHNOGRAPHIC EXAMPLES

Our next step is to turn to consider some of the ways in which contemporary non-Western people understand their relations with cultivated plants and domestic animals. In what follows I shall present four ethnographic examples. The first is taken from Philippe Descola's (1994) study of the Achuar Indians of the Upper Amazon, the second draws on Marilyn Strathern's (1980) work on the people of the Mount Hagen region of the Papua New Guinea Highlands, and the third comes from a study by Walter van Beek and Pieteke Banga (1992) of the Dogon of Mali, in West Africa. For my fourth and final example I return to South America, and to the study by Stephen Gudeman and Alberto Rivera (1990) of the peasant farmers of Boyacá, in Colombia.

The Achuar of the Upper Amazon

The Achuar cultivate a great variety of plant species, of which the most ubiquitous is manioc, in gardens that have been cleared through a 'slash-and-burn' technique from primary forest. The focus of domestic life is the house, which stands at the centre of its garden, surrounded in turn by a vast expanse of forest. Though a man is expected to prepare a garden plot for each of his wives, the cultivation, maintenance and harvesting of plots is exclusively women's work. All members of the household regularly participate in gathering activities, which are concentrated in familiar areas of the forest within close reach of the garden. Beyond that is the zone of hunting, a risky space in which men dominate, and to which women venture only when accompanied by their husbands.

Gathering, for the Achuar, is a relaxed affair – an occasion for a pleasant day out. But hunting is a quite different matter. Men's relations with the animals they hunt are modelled on the human relation of affinity: like human in-laws, the creatures of the forest are inclined to be touchy, and their feelings have continually to be assuaged with liberal doses of seductive charm. Above all, it is necessary to keep on the right side of the 'game mothers', the guardian spirits of the animals, who exercise the same kind of control over their charges as do human mothers over their own children and domestic animals (Descola 1994: 257). Motherhood, however, also extends to a woman's relations with the plants she grows in her garden. She has, as it were, two sets of offspring, the plants in her garden and the children in her home, and since the two are in competition for the nurturance she can provide, relations between them are far from harmonious. Manioc, for example, is attributed with the power to suck the blood of human infants. Thus despite its peaceful appearance, the garden is as full of menace as is the surrounding forest (1994: 206).

Applying orthodox concepts of anthropological analysis, we might be inclined to oppose the forest and the garden along the lines of a distinction between the wild and the domesticated, as though the edge of the woods also marked the outer limits of the human socialisation of nature, and the point of transition at which production gives way to collection. But this, as Descola shows, would be profoundly at odds with Achuar understandings. For in the construction and maintenance of their gardens, the Achuar do not see themselves as engaged in a project of domesticating the pristine world of the forest; indeed the colonial image of the conquest of nature is entirely foreign to their way of thinking. For them, the forest is itself a huge garden, albeit an untidy one, and the relations between its constituents are governed by the same principles of domesticity that structure the human household, yet on a superhuman scale. The tension between garden plants and children mirrors, on a reduced scale, the tension between forest creatures and human hunters; likewise a woman's care for her crops and domestic animals is writ large in the care of the 'game mothers' for the species in their charge. In short, the Achuar garden figures as a microcosm of the forest: 'it is not so much the cultural transformation of a portion of wild space as the cultural homology in the human order of a cultural reality of the same standing in the superhuman order'. Human society is a scaled-down version of the society of nature, the garden plot 'temporarily realizes the virtualities of a homely wilderness' (Descola 1994: 220).

The people of Mount Hagen

The people of the Mount Hagen region of Papua New Guinea (henceforth 'Hageners') grow crops – especially taro, yams and sweet potato – in forest clearings; they also raise pigs. They have a word, *mbo*, for the activity of planting, which is also used for things that are planted such as cuttings pushed into the ground. By extension it can refer to any other point of growth within the general field of human relations: thus a breeding pig can be *mbo* in respect of the herd it will engender, and people can be *mbo* in respect of their placement in clan territory. The antithesis of *mbo* is *rømi*. This latter term is used for things or powers that lie beyond the reach of human nurture. The principal cultivated tubers have their wild counterparts, and these are *rømi*, as are wild pigs and other forest creatures. There are also *rømi* spirits who tend these wild plants and animals, just as people tend their gardens and pigs (Strathern 1980: 192). Indeed at first glance, the terms *mbo* and *rømi* seem to have their more or less exact equivalent in our conventional notions of 'wild' and 'domestic' respectively.

Completely absent from the Hagen conception, however, is the notion of a domestic environment 'carved out' from wild nature. *Mbo* does not refer to an enclosed space of settlement, as opposed to the surrounding bush or forest. Hageners do not seek to subjugate or colonise the wilderness; while the spirit masters of forest creatures have their spheres of influence as humans have theirs, the aim is 'not to subdue but to come to terms with them' (1980: 194). *Rømi* is simply that which lies outside the limits of human care and sociability. Significantly, while the opposed term *mbo* takes its primary meaning from the act of planting, it is not used for any other stage of the horticultural process, nor for garden land itself (1980: 200). In planting one does not transform nature, in the sense of imposing a rational order upon a given materiality. Rather, one places a cutting in the ground so that it may take root and grow.[1] As its roots extend into the soil, so the plant draws nourishment from its environment, gradually assuming its mature form.

Like the Achuar, Hageners draw a parallel between growing plants and growing children. The child, placed at birth within a field of nurture – as the plant is placed in the soil – steadily grows into maturity as a responsible, self-aware being, drawing sustenance from its relationships with others even as the latter, like the plant's roots, extend ever further outwards into the social environment (1980: 196). There is no sense, however, in which the child starts life as a thing of nature, to which a moral dimension of rules and values is added on through a process of socialisation. The child does not begin as *rømi*, and become *mbo*. It is *mbo* from the outset, by virtue of its planting within the field of human relationships. So too, in their cultivation of tubers and raising of pigs, Hageners do not impose a social order upon an environment consisting of 'nature in the raw'. They rather constitute, as inherently social, the very environment within which their plants and animals come into being, take root and grow to maturity.

The Dogon of Mali

Like many other African peoples (Morris 1995: 305–6), the Dogon draw a sharp contrast between the categories of *ana* (village) and *oru* (bush). In and around the village, people cultivate the staple crop of millet, and keep gardens of onions and tobacco. But they also depend on the bush in many ways. It is a source of firewood for cooking, brewing and firing pottery. Timber is needed, too, for building houses and granaries, and for fencing gardens. The bush also yields meat, relishes and treefruits, leaves for use as cattle fodder, and various medicinal herbs. However, the dependence of the village on the bush goes much deeper than this list of products would indicate. For in the Dogon view, the bush is nothing less than the source of life itself, and with it of all knowledge, wisdom, power and healing. But by the same token, it is greatly to be feared. It is a zone of movement and flux, in which all the fixedness and certainties of village life are dissolved. Everything shifts and changes – even trees and rocks can walk from place to place. The many spirits that roam the bush can exchange body parts with living people, human hunters venturing there become like the animals they hunt, and as they do so their existence in the present is swallowed up in a temporal horizon that merges past and future, life and death (van Beek and Banga 1992: 67–8).

Dogon cosmology envisages a kind of entropic system in which the maintenance of the village depends upon a continual inflow of vital force from the bush, which is worn down and used up in the process. If the village is a place of stability, where things stay put and proper distinctions are maintained, it is also a place of stagnation. In an almost exact inversion of the modern Western notion of food production as the manifestation of human knowledge and power over nature, here it is nature – in the form of the bush – that holds ultimate power over human life, while the cultivated fields and gardens are sites of consumption rather than production, where vital force is *used up*. 'Knowledge dissipates . . . and power evaporates unless reinvigorated from the bush' (van Beek and Banga 1992: 69).

Peasant farmers of Boyacá

The rural folk of Colombia say that it is the earth that gives them their food; the role of human beings is to assist it in bringing forth its crops. As one farmer is reported to have put it: 'Man helps the land; the earth produces the fruit' (Gudeman and Rivera 1990: 25). Likewise hens give eggs, sheep give lambs and cows calves. Here, too, the farmer is called upon to assist in the animals' labour much as a midwife assists at a birth. But the ultimate source of the 'strength' or 'force' (*la fuerza*) that enables people to work, animals to reproduce and crops to grow lies in the land itself. The earth is conceived as a repository of strength created and sustained by God (1990: 18). Thus crops draw strength from the land, humans in turn gain strength by consuming their crops (or the produce of animals whose strength was drawn from their consumption of fodder), and expend that strength in work on the land that enables it to yield up yet more of its strength to the cycle.

Gudeman and Rivera detect in this folk model distinct echoes of eighteenth-century Physiocracy. Indeed they go so far as to suggest that it offers a window on much earlier notions current among farming peoples of the Old World, which still resonate through the practices of Colombian rural folk as well as through the texts of European political economists. The Physiocratic view that only the land yields value, which the farmer harnesses on behalf of society, has its counterpart in the Colombian farmers' notion that human life is powered by the strength of the earth. Both views, moreover, invert the modern Western conception that sees in the land not an active agent but an inert source of raw materials to be shaped up to a human design. Marx wrote of the earth as foremost among the instruments of labour, and ever since we have tended to think of production as a process wherein land is placed in the service of humanity (Meillassoux 1972). But Colombian rural folk place themselves in the service of the land. And they regard their capacity to work not as some inner aspect of their being, as in the Marxian concept of 'labour-power', but as God's gift of strength, bestowed through the land and its produce, and expended in their activity (Gudeman and Rivera 1990: 103–4).

MAKING THINGS, FINDING THINGS AND GROWING THINGS

Let me now return to the opposition with which I began, between production and collection. There is no doubt that the primary meaning of production in the age of manufacture is, to recall Bacon's phrase, 'making by art'. The term refers, in other words, to the construction of artificial objects by rearranging, assembling and transforming raw materials supplied by nature. And if the opposite of 'to produce' is 'to collect', then collection must mean picking up one's supplies, as it were 'ready-made', from the environment. But how can you 'make' a pig, a yam, or a crop of millet? And how, for that matter, can such things be made in advance?

I believe this modern emphasis on production as making accounts for the special significance that tends to be attached to the so-called 'artificial selection' of plants and animals as the key criterion for distinguishing food-production from food-collection, and hence for determining the point of transition from hunting and gathering to agriculture and pastoralism. The ability that Bacon dreamed of, literally to 'make' an animal or plant in any way we want it, is only now coming to be realised due to developments in biotechnology and genetic engineering. For farmers and herdsmen of the past, it has never been a realistic possibility. What they could do, however, was isolate a breeding population within which they could select individuals for reproduction according to their conformity to an ideal type. Just as the distinction between the artefact and the naturally given object (such as a living organism) depends on the notion that the former is built upon a design that is extrinsic rather than intrinsic to the material (Monod 1972: 21), so likewise artificial selection can only be distinguished from natural selection on the grounds that it is guided by a 'preconceived end', an ideal suspended within the collective representations of the human community. This is probably why the notion of domestication has come to be so closely tied up with that of breeding: it is the closest thing to constructing the forms of plants and animals to blueprints of human design. And this, in turn, is why prehistorians investigating the origins of food-production are inclined to look for evidence of the morphological divergence of the plant or animal species in question from its original 'wild' form, as proof that production was going on.

This procedure, however, generates its own anomalies. For in many parts of the world, both in the past and still today, people are apparently engaged in the husbandry of plants and animals that do not differ appreciably from their wild counterparts. Kept as pets in the houses of the Achuar are a range of 'domestic wild animals' – various primates, birds and peccary (Descola 1994: 90). The forests of Highland New Guinea are full of wild domestic pigs, as well as a variety of plants that also appear in cultivated swiddens. And the fields of neolithic villagers in Southwest Asia were sown with 'domesticated wild barley' (Jarman 1972). Now the source of these anomalies lies in the very dichotomy between collection and production. In terms of this dichotomy, human beings must *either* find their food ready-made in nature *or* make it themselves. Yet ask any farmer and he or she will say, with good cause, that the produce of the farm is no more made than it is found ready-made. It is *grown*. So our question must be as follows. Granted that by making things we mean the transformation of pre-existing raw materials, *what do we mean by growing things*? On the answer to this question must hinge the distinctions between gathering and cultivation, and between hunting and animal husbandry.

Two common themes to emerge from the ethnographic cases presented in the previous section point towards a solution. First, the work that people do, in such activities as field clearance, fencing, planting, weeding and so on, or in tending their livestock, does not literally make plants and animals, but rather establishes the environmental conditions for their growth and development. They are 'mothered', nurtured, assisted – generally cosseted and helped along. Secondly, growing plants and raising animals are not so different, in principle, from bringing up children. Of course it is true that modern Western discourse, too, extends the notions of cultivation and breeding across human, animal and plant domains, referring in the human case to a refinement of taste and manners (Bouquet 1993: 189–90). Such refinement, however, is represented as a socially approved form of mastery over supposedly innate human impulses, and is the counterpart to the kind of mastery over the environment that is implied by the notion of domestication as the social appropriation of nature. When Achuar women compare their children to the plants in their gardens, or when Hageners use the language of planting for both children and pigs, they do not have this model of socialisation in mind. As Strathern puts it: 'the child grows into social maturity rather than being trained into it' (1980: 196). What each generation provides, whether in growing plants, raising animals or bringing up children, are precisely the developmental conditions under which 'growth to maturity' can occur.[2]

Where does this leave the distinctions between gathering and cultivation, and between hunting and animal husbandry? The difference surely lies in no more than this: the *relative scope of human involvement in establishing the conditions for growth*. This is not only a matter of degree rather than kind, it can also vary over time. Weeds can become cultigens, erstwhile domestic animals can turn feral. Moreover a crucial variable, I would suggest, lies in the temporal interlocking of the life-cycles of humans, animals and plants, and their relative durations. The lives of domestic animals tend to be somewhat shorter than those of human beings, but not so short as to be of a different order of magnitude. There is thus a sense in which people and their domestic animals grow older together, and in which their respective life-histories are intertwined as mutually constitutive strands of a single process. The lives of plants, by contrast, can range from the very short to the very long indeed, from a few months to many centuries.

Now as Laura Rival has pointed out, the planned intervention in and control over nature that we conventionally associate with the idea of domestication can only be envisaged in respect of plants 'whose growth is much faster relative to human growth and maturation processes' (Rival 1993: 648). It is as though humans could stand watch over the development of their crops without growing significantly older themselves. But the more slow-growing and long-lived the plant, the more artificial this assumption appears to be. In the case of the most enduring plants of all – such as certain large trees – the assumption becomes wholly untenable. Indeed for the most part, trees do not fit at all comfortably within the terms of the orthodox distinction between the wild and the domesticated, which may account for the curious fact that despite their manifest importance to people (as our Dogon example shows), they are all but absent from archaeological and anthropological discussions of the nature and origins of food production. Of an ancient tree that has presided over successive human generations it would seem more appropriate to say that it has played its part in the domestication *of* humans rather than having been domesticated *by* them.[3] In short, what is represented in the literature, under the rubric of domestication, as a transcendence and transformation of nature may be more a reflection of an increasing reliance on plants and animals that, by comparison with humans, are relatively fast-growing and short-lived.

I have suggested that regimes of plant and animal husbandry may best be distinguished in terms of the ways in which human beings involve themselves in establishing the conditions for growth. For example, in the cultivation of gardens, more is done to assist the growth of plants than when they are gathered from the bush. To grasp this idea, all that is required is a simple switch of perspective: instead of thinking about plants as part of the natural environment for human beings, we have to think of humans and their activities as part of the environment for plants. But behind this switch there lies a point of much more fundamental significance. If human beings on the one hand, and plants and animals on the other, can be regarded alternately as components of each others' environments, then we can no longer think of humans as inhabiting a social world of their own, over and above the world of nature in which the lives of all other living things are contained. Rather, both humans and the animals and plants on which they depend for a livelihood must be regarded as fellow participants in the *same* world, a world that is at once social and natural. And the forms that all these creatures take are neither given in advance nor imposed from above, but emerge within the context of their mutual involvement in a single, continuous field of relationships.[4]

With this conclusion in mind, let me return to Godelier's five kinds of materiality, which were also distinguished according to the manner and extent of human involvement in their existence. In what way does Godelier's formulation differ from our own? The answer is that for Godelier, the formative role of humans lies in their capacity as beings who, to various degrees, act *upon*, intervene *in*, or do things *to*, a domain of nature that is external to their socially constituted selves. According to the argument I have presented, by contrast, human beings do not so much transform the material world as play their part, along with other creatures, in the world's transformation of itself (I return to this formulation in Chapter Eleven, pp. 200–1). In this view, nature is not a surface of materiality upon which human history is inscribed; rather history is the process wherein both people and their environments are continually bringing each other into being. This is one way of interpreting Marx's celebrated yet enigmatic remark that 'history itself is a *real* part of *natural history* – of nature developing into man' (Marx 1964: 143, original emphases). By the same token, it is also man developing into nature. Or in other words, human actions in the environment are better seen as incorporative than inscriptive, in the sense that they are built or enfolded into the forms of the landscape and its living inhabitants by way of their own processes of growth.

I have been concerned, in this chapter, to dissolve the conventional dichotomy between production and collection. In so doing, however, I seem to have ended up with another, equally intractable dichotomy, namely between making and growing. I have observed that in the tradition of Western thought, the idea of making – understood as the inscription of conceptual form upon material substance – has been extended from the manufacture of artefacts to the breeding of plants and animals, as exemplified in the passage from Bacon's *New Atlantis* with which I began. It has even been extended to the raising of children – insofar as this is regarded as a process of socialisation whereby approved norms and values are superimposed upon the raw material of new-born human infants. In every case it is supposed that a design or representation that has its source in the domain of society is imprinted upon the substrate of external nature. In arguing against this view, I have suggested that bringing up children or raising livestock, just as much as the cultivation of crops, is a process in which plants, animals or people are not so much made as grown, and in which surrounding human beings play a greater or lesser part in establishing the conditions of nurture.

I have but one further point to make in conclusion. The orthodox Western account, as we have seen, extends the idea of making from the domain of inanimate things to that of animate beings. I want to suggest, quite to the contrary, that the idea of growing might be extended in the reverse direction, from the animate to the inanimate. What we call 'things', too, are grown. In practice, there is more to the manufacture of artefacts than the mechanical transcription of a design or plan, devised through an intellectual process of reason, onto an inert substance. For as I shall show in Chapter Eighteen, the forms of artefacts are not given in advance but are rather generated in and through the practical movement of one or more skilled agents in their active, sensuous engagement with the material. That is to say, they emerge – like the forms of living beings – within the relational contexts of the mutual involvement of people and their environments. Thus there is, in the final analysis, no absolute distinction between making and growing, since what we call 'making things' is, in reality, not a process of transcription at all but a process of growth.

Chapter Six

A circumpolar night's dream

Sometime a horse I'll be, sometime a hound,
A hog, a headless bear, sometime a fire;
And neigh, and bark, and grunt, and roar, and burn,
Like horse, hound, hog, bear, fire, at every turn.
> William Shakespeare, *A Midsummer
> Night's Dream* (3, i, 97–100)

INTRODUCTION: OF THINGS AND BEINGS

We are accustomed to calling animals and plants 'living things'. But we call ourselves 'human beings'. Let us agree that plants and animals, human and non-human, are all organisms. The question then arises: is an organism a thing or a being? This is by no means an issue of mere semantics, for on the answer hangs our understanding of life itself. If life is a property of things, then it must be reducible to some internal principle, the possession of which distinguishes the class of objects we call organisms from classes of other kinds, and which – from its position within the organism – drives the latter's development and its interactions with the environment. But if life is tantamount to being, then we have to regard the organism not so much as a living thing than as the material embodiment of a certain way of being alive. In other words, we should think of the organism not as containing life, or expressing it, but as emergent within the life process itself.

Now natural science, including the science of evolutionary biology, has developed in the West as an inquiry into the objective properties of things. Thus the applicability of evolutionary biology to humans depends upon our accepting that they, in a sense, are things as well. Yet *they are us*, and were we but things, how would we be able to recognise ourselves for what we are? Paradoxically, if organisms are things, then to see ourselves as organisms we must be *more* than organisms. Indeed it is precisely by this 'excess' that we are inclined to define the scope of our common humanity. Whereas an animal such as a bear or a chimpanzee is all organism, the human being is said to be an organism 'plus . . .' (Collins 1985). Its organic nature is supposedly topped up with some additional factor – call it mind or self-awareness – that can be found not by external observation but only by the knowledge we have of ourselves as possessing specific identities, feelings, memories and intentions.

Herein lies the curious, split-level image of human existence which is such a characteristic feature of modern thought and science. Surely, as science insists, humans are part of nature. They are biological organisms, composed of the same stuff, and having evolved according to the same principles, as organisms of every other kind. Like other creatures, they are born, grow old and die, they must eat to live, protect themselves to survive and mate to reproduce. But if that were all there is to it, how could there be science? It would seem that the very possibility of a scientific account of humankind as a species of nature is only open for a creature for whom being is knowing, one that can so detach its consciousness from the traffic of its bodily interactions in the environment as to treat the latter as the object of its concern. To be human in this sense – to exist as a knowing subject – is, we commonly say, to be a *person*. So is the scientist a person rather than an organism? How can we exist both inside the world of nature and outside of it, as organisms and persons, at one and the same time?

There seems to me to be only one way out of the paradoxes and contradictions entailed in modern science's attitude to humanity. This is to build on the premise that all organisms, including human ones, are not things but beings. As beings, persons *are* organisms, and being organisms, they – or rather we – are not impartial observers of nature but participate from within in the continuum of organic life. In order to demonstrate the possibility of an account of the living world founded on this premise, and to spell out some of its implications, I shall draw in this chapter on one particular anthropological study of how people in a non-Western society perceive themselves and the world around them. This is the account by A. Irving Hallowell of what it means to be a person among the northern Ojibwa, indigenous hunters and trappers of the forests to the east of Lake Winnipeg and north of Lake Superior in Canada.[1]

Hallowell's article, 'Ojibwa ontology, behavior and world view' (OO), first published in 1960, is in my estimation one of the great classics of northern circumpolar ethnography.[2] I have turned to it over and over again for inspiration, and every reading has yielded some new insight. I must emphasise, however, that what follows is not intended as a contribution to Ojibwa ethnography. I have not carried out fieldwork in the region, nor do I have the deep familiarity with the literature on these people that would qualify me for such a task. Rather, I offer some reflections which, though stimulated by a reading of Hallowell's work, are primarily motivated by the goal set out above – that is, of restoring human beings to the organic lifeworld in a way that does not, at the same time, reduce them to mere objects of nature. These reflections are not, however, entirely without ethnographic substance, for they resonate both with themes that crop up with remarkable regularity in the literature on northern circumpolar societies,[3] and with my own outlook which has undoubtedly been shaped by the experience of working in this region.

ANIMALS AS PERSONS

It is customary, in the West, to assume that to speak of persons is to tell of the thoughts, intentions and actions of human beings. 'Person' and 'human' are all but synonyms – to the extent that to ask whether non-human animals can be persons seems almost perverse. Nevertheless, people in Western societies do very often treat animals, or speak of them, *as if* they were persons. Let me briefly present two examples of this tendency. The first lies in attitudes towards household pets. Many people who are convinced that, as a general rule, animals cannot be persons, are quick to make an exception of their pets. But if you ask them why pets are persons, or at least rather like persons, whereas other animals are not, they will probably say that on account of having been raised in human households, virtually as members of the family, these particular animals have become almost human themselves. They are credited with human feelings and responses, spoken to and expected to understand, given names, put through life-cycle rituals, and sometimes even dressed in clothing. Thus, far from softening or obscuring the boundary between humanity and animality, the special treatment of pets constitutes the exception that proves the rule: namely that, in the West, to be a person is to be human. Animals can only be persons to the extent that some of our humanity has, so to speak, 'rubbed off' on them through close contact with human members of the household. And just as the animal can never become *fully* human, its personhood, too, can never be more than partially developed. That is why pets are often treated as somehow retarded, locked in perpetual childhood. However old they are, they are never allowed to grow up, but are rather treated as cases of arrested development.

The second example of the Western tendency to liken animals to persons concerns fables, especially those composed for children. Our story-books are full of tales in which human characters are turned or turn themselves into wolves, bears, mice, frogs, birds, fish, and a host of other creatures. Some of these stories are of great antiquity. But whatever they may have meant for people in the distant past, for contemporary audiences and readers there is never any suggestion that they are anything *but* stories. The animal characters, often depicted in strikingly human form, stand in metaphorically for human ones, and serve to illustrate distinctively human dispositions and foibles – the cunning fox, the innocent deer, the conceited toad, the noble lion, and so on. In short, the animal characters are used to deliver a commentary on the nature of *human* society. Moreover no child, raised in contemporary Western society, would make the mistake of confusing such animal stories with natural history books, of supposing that 'The Princess and the Frog' is an observer's account of the behaviour of amphibians, or that 'Little Red Riding Hood' is an account of the habits of the wolf. Children are taught, at a very early age, to distinguish between telling stories and recounting the 'facts'.

Both these examples, of pet-keeping and fables, illustrate a propensity, technically known as anthropomorphism, to ascribe human qualities to non-human beings. In the one case, the ascription is metonymic (the animal is an extension of the human), in the other case it is metaphoric (the animal substitutes for the human). Either way, so long as we continue to assume that only humans can truly be persons, the attribution of personhood to animals is bound to be anthropomorphic.[4] The Ojibwa, however, do not make this assumption. Persons, in the Ojibwa world, can take a great variety of forms, of which the human is just one. They can also appear in a variety of animal guises, as meteorological phenomena such as thunder or the winds, as heavenly bodies such as the sun, and even as tangible objects such as stones that we would have no hesitation in regarding as inanimate. None of these manifold forms in which persons appear is any more basic, or 'literal', than the others. Moreover, as we shall see, persons can be encountered not only in waking life but also, and equally palpably, in dreams and in the telling of myths. And most importantly, they can change their form. Indeed for the Ojibwa this capacity for metamorphosis is one of the key aspects of being a person, and is a critical index of power: the more powerful the person, the more readily a change of form may be effected.

Though persons may appear in animal form, not all animals are persons. One can usually tell if an animal is a person, because its behaviour will be out of the ordinary. But some animals are always extraordinary. One such is the bear. The hunter, on encountering a bear, will act towards it as a person who can understand what is being said and will respond according to its own volition (OO, p. 36). There is nothing in the least anthropomorphic about this. The hunter is not regarding the bear as if it were human. To the contrary, it is perceived to be unequivocally ursine. Unlike the pet in a Western society, the personhood of the bear does not depend upon its previous contacts with humans – indeed it need not have had any such contacts at all. For the same reason, the bear is just as much a 'full person' as is the human hunter. Ojibwa relate to persons in animal form as grown-ups, not as children. And whereas anthropomorphised animal-persons in the West are treated as beings that need to be looked after and controlled by their human guardians, the animal-persons in the environment of the Ojibwa are considered to be on the same level as, if not more powerful than, human beings themselves.

Likewise, the animals that figure as persons in the traditional narratives of the Ojibwa are not anthropomorphic characters. Their tales, like our own, are replete with incidents in which humans turn into animals, or marry animals, or give birth to animals, and vice versa. But these are not fables, nor are they intended to deliver an allegorical commentary on the human condition. They are tales about events that really took place, in the histories of real persons, and in the same world that people ordinarily experience in the course of their quotidian lives. What they recount is based on detailed, accurate observation of the landscape, of weather conditions and of the behaviour of animals. The mythological figure of the Thunder Bird, for example, can make itself manifest in the form of a peal of thunder or a kind of hawk. There is a striking correspondence between the normal seasonal occurrence of thunderstorms and the period during which migratory birds wintering in the south appear in Ojibwa country. In one myth, a man who marries a Thunder Bird woman and goes off to live with his in-laws (the mythic 'masters' of various species of hawk) finds himself having to eat what they call 'beaver', but what to him are frogs and snakes – which are, indeed, the principal foods of the sparrow hawk.[5] And the nests of the Thunder Birds can be physically identified in the landscape as collections of stones in high, inaccessible locations (OO, pp. 32–3).

In short, what distinguishes the Thunder Bird from any ordinary hawk is nothing like what, for us, distinguishes the Wolf of Little Red Riding Hood from the wolf of the forest. The distinction is not between animals of fantasy and of fact, but rather between animals that are persons and animals that are not. Animal persons are no more fantastic than human ones. Ojibwa do, nevertheless, differentiate between narratives of past experience of these two sorts of person. Hallowell calls them 'myths' and 'stories' respectively (OO, pp. 26–7). Stories recount events in the lives of human beings, from the anecdotal to the legendary. Myths, by contrast, tell of the lives of non-human persons – or, to be more precise, the myths *are* these persons, who, in the telling, are not merely commemorated but actually made present for the assembled audience, as though they had been brought to life and invited in. For this reason, the narration of myth is a ritualised event, and there are restrictions on who can tell it and when it can be told. But despite these formalities, myths are no less true, or more phantasmagoric, than stories. The difference is simply that in myths, the protagonists are persons of the 'other-than-human' class, otherwise known and addressed by the inclusive kinship term, 'grandfathers'.

OTHER-THAN-HUMAN GRANDFATHERS

All persons, whether human or not, share the same fundamental structure. This structure consists, in Hallowell's words, of 'an inner vital part that is enduring and an outward form which can change' (OO, p. 42). The inner essence, or soul, holds the attributes of sentience, volition, memory and speech. Any being that possesses these attributes is a person, irrespective of the intrinsically unstable form in which it appears. Now while human persons and other-than-human grandfathers are alike in this regard, such that no absolute division in kind can be drawn between them, they do differ in degree – that is, in the amount of power a person possesses and hence in their capacity for metamorphosis. Grandfathers are more powerful than living humans. Most powerful are the Sun, the Four Winds, the Thunder Birds, and the spirit 'masters' of all the different species of animals. These beings are immortal, but can change their form with relative ease, appearing now as a human, now as an animal, now perhaps as some meteorological phenomenon – as we have seen with the Thunder Bird. In myth the Bird can figure as a man or woman, in dreams it shows up as a hawk, in waking life it announces its presence as a thunder-clap. By contrast, only the most powerful human persons, such as sorcerers and shamans, can change into a non-human form and make it back again – and then only with some danger and difficulty. Sorcerers, for example, can transform themselves into bears in order better to pursue their nefarious activities.

However for most humans, metamorphosis means death: indeed the only change of form that *all* humans undergo is brought about upon their demise. As with any meta-morphosis, death involves an alteration of manifest appearance, while the vital essence of the person continues its existence in some other form. Spirits of the dead are that much more powerful, and can manifest themselves in the guise of either ghosts (which may be seen or heard) or animals, often birds.[6] But whereas the power of human persons always increases when they die, there is only one way in which they can grow in power during their lifetimes, and that is through the guardianship or tutelage of one or more grandfa-thers. For men in particular, grandfatherly assistance is considered crucial for coping with the vicissitudes of life. In the past, every boy, on reaching puberty, would embark upon a prolonged period of fasting. Alone in the forest, he would hope to dream of his future guardian, from whom he would receive blessings that would see him through all kinds of difficulties in later life – so long as he met certain necessary obligations towards the grand-father concerned. In one account, for example, a boy encountered a human-like figure in his dream, who then turned into a golden eagle. This person was the 'master' of the eagles. The boy, too, was transformed into an eagle in his dream – thus winged and feathered, he flew to the south with his new protector, before returning to the point whence he originally departed (Hallowell, *Culture and Experience* (CE), 1955, p. 178).

Now the idea that a human being can be turned into a bear prowling in the forest, or an eagle soaring in the sky, is simply inconceivable within the normal canons of Western thought. Any creature born of human parents, it is supposed, is bound within the limi-tations of the human bodily frame, whatever environmental circumstances may be encountered during its lifetime. It is these bodily specifications that are fixed and enduring, whereas ways of thinking, feeling, speaking and behaving – adding up to what is conven-tionally known as 'culture' – are variable, even within the life-history of a single individual. This seems to be the precise inverse of the Ojibwa model of the person, according to which it is the variable body that clothes a constant spiritual essence comprising the powers of self-awareness, intentionality, sentience, and speech. In their encounter with Euro-Americans, Ojibwa were evidently troubled by the incompatibility between these different ontologies of personal being. John Tanner, a white man who grew up among Ojibwa people during the early nineteenth century and subsequently wrote of his experiences, claimed that the ursine sorcerer, prowling around at night, was actually a man *dressed up* in a bear skin (CE, p. 177). This, and other similar statements by both native and non-native informants, may be understood, according to Hallowell, as 'rationalizations advanced by individuals who are attempting to reconcile Ojibwa beliefs and observation with the disbelief encountered in their relations with whites' (OO, p. 37).

Rendering metamorphosis as a kind of dressing up is certainly one way of explaining it – or rather, explaining it away – in terms that Westerners would understand. The person's bodily form does not *actually* change, it is merely concealed beneath an outer clothing, a disguise. Yet as Viveiros de Castro has noted (1998), the description of metamorphosis as an enclothing of the soul, far from being a peculiar response to ontological disjuncture, is very widely reported in the ethnography of native Amerindian peoples. Contrary to Hallowell's interpretation, it seems that the idea of dressing up is not, in itself, foreign to indigenous understanding. What is foreign is rather the idea that the function of clothing is to disguise or conceal. In Amerindian cosmology, clothing does not cover up the body, it *is* a body (Viveiros de Castro 1998: 482). It serves, in other words, not to conceal but to enable, furnishing the distinctive equipment – including skills and dispositions as well as anatomical devices – by which a person can carry on a particular kind of life in the world. Viveiros de Castro (*ibid.*) likens the adoption of a specific bodily form to the diver's donning of a wet-suit, the purpose of which is not to disguise the wearer as a fish, but to enable him to swim like one. Thus metamorphosis is not a covering up, but an *opening up*, of the person to the world. A person who can take on many forms can turn up in all kinds of situations, now in one form, now in another, each one affording a different perspective. The greater the person's powers of metamorphosis, the wider the range of their practical possibilities of being, and hence the more extensive the breadth of their experience and the scope of their phenomenal presence.

The idea that by clothing himself with the bodily forms of one animal after another, the wearer is enabled to proceed through a series of trials calling for diverse strengths and capabilities, is beautifully illustrated by an Ojibwa story collected by Homer Huntington Kidder in the 1890s. The storyteller was Jacque LePique, a character of mixed parentage and fluent in English and Canadian French as well as Ojibwa and Cree. The tale concerns a man named Iron Maker who, along with eleven companions, sank to the bottom of a lake after their boat had capsized. Following an encounter at the lake bottom with an old man, an old woman and a snake, Iron Maker found himself gasping for breath at the surface of the water.

> He thought of the beaver, whereupon the beaver came to him and gave him his body. He swam towards the shore, but before he could reach it, he felt himself losing the power to keep the shape of the beaver. So he thought of the otter. Then the otter gave him his body, and in that form he reached land.
>
> There Iron Maker found himself naked in his own body. It was freezing weather . . . He would have died of cold but for the help of four other animals which, one after another, lent him their bodies to get home: First the bear, in whose shape he went a good way, then the lynx, then the raccoon, and after that the ox (buffalo).
>
> When Iron Maker no longer had the power to keep the shape of the ox, he was pretty near his lodge. He ran home naked and fell at the door half dead with cold.
>
> (in Bourgeois 1994: 69)

Like Puck in Shakespeare's *Midsummer Night's Dream* – whose lines head this chapter, and who threatened to appear in the forms, successively, of a horse, a hound, a hog, a headless bear and a fire – Iron Maker made it home from the bottom of the lake, first as a beaver, then as an otter, then as a bear, a lynx, a raccoon and an ox.

Now all of this leaves us with a problem of the following kind. We may accept that a person can change their form at will, knowing all the while that the character in question exists, like Shakespeare's Puck, only as a *dramatis persona* in a masque or play, who is actually being impersonated by an ordinary human actor. But if I were to report, in all sincerity, having encountered such a character as Puck or Iron Maker in real life, I doubt whether much credence would be given to my claims. People would say that if I was not actually lying, then I must be suffering from delusions, leaving me incapable of telling fact from fantasy, or reality from dreams. Yet these are precisely the sorts of claims that Ojibwa make. Are they, then, lying or deluded?

Accusations of both kinds have been levelled often enough, against Ojibwa people and others who think like them, reinforcing the stereotype of the primitive Indian who can neither think logically nor be trusted. Anthropologists, by temperament and training, are inclined to be rather more sympathetic to native accounts. By and large, however, they adopt an expository strategy not unlike that of the theatre-goer attending a performance of Shakespeare's *Dream*, amounting to a willing suspension of disbelief. This strategy makes it possible to get on with the job of understanding what people are telling us, without our having to worry about whether there is any foundation in reality for what they have to say (see Chapter One, p. 14). Hallowell himself does just this, when he argues that what, for the Ojibwa, are attributes of personhood form part of a comprehensive 'worldview' that is projected onto reality-as-we-know-it. His concern is to understand the world view, not the fundamental nature of reality. Yet he goes on to stress that Ojibwa do not, themselves, 'personify' natural objects (OO, p. 29). For example, the sun is perceived as a person of the 'other-than-human' class; it is not perceived initially as a natural object onto which 'person' attributes are subsequently projected. It is not, in other words, *made* into a person; it is a person, period.

Now there is more than a hint of duplicity here. It would be a mistake, says Hallowell, to suppose that Ojibwa personify objects, yet from his standpoint as an anthropological observer, this appears to be precisely what they are doing. Evidently what Hallowell takes to be a particular cultural construction of an external reality is, in Ojibwa eyes, the only reality they know. For the Ojibwa, the sun is a person because it is experienced as such; for Hallowell the sun is not *really* a person but is constructed as such in the minds of the Ojibwa. And if it is not really a person, then it cannot really undergo metamorphosis. By this move, Ojibwa metaphysics appear to pose no challenge to our own ontological certainties. Turning our backs on what Ojibwa people say, we continue to insist that 'real' reality is given independently of human experience, and that understanding its nature is a problem for science. Must we then conclude that the anthropological study of indigenous understandings, whatever its intrinsic interest, can tell us nothing about what the world is really like, and that it therefore has no bearing on natural scientific inquiry?

LIVING THINGS AND BEING ALIVE

This question returns us to the paradox I raised in the introduction. The notion that persons, as beings in the world, can appear in both human and other-than-human forms may sound strange, but it is not half as strange as the notion that to become a person – to be in a position to know and reflect upon the nature of existence – means taking oneself *out* of the world. The challenge for us now is to bring the person, as it were, back 'down to earth', to restore it to the primary context of its engagement within an environment. Taking this condition of engagement as our point of departure, can we find some way of making sense of Ojibwa understandings concerning such matters as metamorphosis? Can we, in other words, ground these understandings in the real experience of persons in a lifeworld rather than attributing them to some overarching cosmological schema for its imaginative reconstruction? To begin to address this challenge, we need to go back to a question which is even more fundamental than that of what makes a person. What makes something alive, or animate?

Hallowell recounts a fascinating anecdote concerning the nature of stones:

> I once asked an old man: Are *all* the stones we see about us here alive? He reflected a long while and then replied, 'No! But *some* are.' This qualified answer made a lasting impression on me.

(OO, p. 24)

Now Hallowell had been led to ask this question on account of a peculiarity in the grammatical structure of the Ojibwa language. Like other languages in the Algonkian family to which it belongs, a formal distinction is allegedly made in this language between 'animate' and 'inanimate' nouns. Stones are grammatically animate, and Hallowell was keen to know why. The answer he received, however, was puzzling in two respects. First, there is the general question of how something as apparently inert as a stone can possibly be alive. But secondly, why should some stones be animate and others not? As Hallowell recognises (OO, p. 23), the categorical distinction between animate and inanimate is not one that Ojibwa articulate themselves, but was rather imposed by Western linguists who brought with them their own conventional understanding of what these terms mean. Before attempting to resolve the puzzle of the stones, we have, therefore, to pause to consider the meaning of the animate as a category of Western thought.

Ever since Plato and Aristotle, it has been customary in the West to envisage the world of nature as made up of a multitude of discrete objects, things, each with its own integrity and essential properties. These things may be grouped into classes of varying degrees of inclusiveness on the basis of selected properties that they are perceived to possess in common. One major class, known as 'animate', comprises all those things that are said to possess the property of life. All remaining things, that do not possess this property, are 'inanimate'. There has been much debate about what it takes for something to be alive: vitalists argued for the existence of some mysterious life-force that they thought was infused into all organisms; mechanists dismissed the idea as unscientific hocus-pocus, but in their enthusiasm to reduce organisms to clockwork they virtually dissolved the animate into the category of the inanimate. The problem was only resolved, after a fashion, by the discovery of the DNA molecule, popularly hailed as the 'secret of life', which seemed to offer a basis for distinguishing living things that satisfied the objective canons of natural science. Throughout all this debate, however, one fundamental idea has remained unquestioned, namely that life is a qualifying attribute of objects. We look for it in a world that already consists of things-in-themselves, whose essential nature is given without regard to their positioning and involvement within wider fields of relations.

Now these are the kinds of things – stones, trees, birds, and so on – that are denoted by words of the class grammarians call 'nouns'. Thus to place the Ojibwa word for stone in the grammatical category 'animate noun' is to assume that so far as the language is concerned, all stones are things with the essential attribute of life. The same would go for trees, the sun and moon, thunder, and artefacts like kettles and pipes, the words for which are likewise placed in the 'animate' class (OO, p. 23). Judging from his qualified response, this is something that even the old man whom Hallowell questioned on the matter would have found hard to accept. Reflecting on his answer, Hallowell concludes that 'the Ojibwa do not perceive stones, in general, as animate, any more than we do. The crucial test is experience. Is there any personal testimony available?' (OO, p. 25). And indeed, such testimony can be adduced: Hallowell heard tell of an instance in which, during a ceremony, a stone was observed to roll over and over, following the master of the ceremony around the tent, another in which a boulder with contours like a mouth would actually open its 'mouth' when tapped by its owner with a knife, and yet another where a man asked a particular stone whether it belonged to him and received a negative response!

The critical feature of all these examples is that the liveliness of stones emerges in the context of their close involvement with certain persons, and relatively powerful ones at that. Animacy, in other words, is a property not of stones *as such*, but of their positioning within a relational field which includes persons as foci of power.[7] Or to put in another way, the power concentrated in persons enlivens that which falls within its sphere of influence. Thus the animate stone is not so much a living thing as a 'being alive'. This immediately makes sense of the old man's remark, for whether a stone is alive or not will depend upon the context in which it is placed and experienced. It also explains why animacy is attributed to artefacts (like kettles and pipes) that are closely bound up with the lives of persons. But by the same token, it makes a nonsense of the categorical distinction between living and non-living things. It is simply not the case, as Scott Atran confidently asserts, that people universally divide 'natural objects' into two classes, such that every object either is, or is not, of a 'living kind' (Atran 1990: 56). The point is not that Ojibwa draw classificatory distinctions along different lines, but rather that in their ontology, life is not a property of objects at all, but a condition of being.

Indeed strictly speaking, there are no 'natural objects' in the Ojibwa world to classify. As Mary Black has shown through a reanalysis of Hallowell's ethnography, it is not by their natures that Ojibwa identify the objects in their everyday environment, as though each were independently endowed with a fixed combination of distinctive features. Rather these objects are apprehended 'in terms of characteristics that *define them* as unstable, changing and inconsistent'. The nature of the things one encounters, their essence, is not given in advance but is revealed only 'after-the-fact', and sometimes only after the lapse of some considerable period of time, in the light of subsequent experience – which of course may differ from one person to another. This Ojibwa way of dealing with perception is, as Black puts it, fundamentally *antitaxonomic*, reducing to a shambles any attempt to bring it within the bounds of a neatly ordered system of classificatory divisions (Black 1977a: 101–4). Black's own field research, conducted among the Ojibwa in the 1960s, lends support to these conclusions. The one thing on which her informants were agreed was in their dismissal of the tidy classifications of formal linguistic analysis. They did not regard classes such as animate and inanimate as mutually exclusive, and objects could freely shift from one class to the other, depending on the context (Black 1977b: 143).

Most significantly for our current concerns, Black also notes that the Ojibwa term *bema.diziwa.d*, which comes closest to 'living things', literally translates as 'those who continue in the state of being alive'. Yet the term might be more accurately glossed, she suggests, as 'those who have power'. Now Hallowell tells us that the Ojibwa word for life 'in the fullest sense', including health, longevity and good fortune, is *pimädäziwim*. As such, it is something that every person strives to achieve (OO, p. 45). But life in this sense is not given, ready-made, as an attribute of being that may then be expressed in one way or another. It is rather a project that has continually to be worked at. Life is a task.[8] As an ongoing process of renewal, it is not merely expressive of the way things are, but is the very *generation* of being. And power, in effect, is the potential of the life process to generate beings of manifold forms. Thus conceived, it is a property not of individuals in isolation but of the total field of relations in which they are situated. Only within such a field can a person strive for *pimädäziwim* (OO, p. 48).

Let me return, for a moment, to the case of the rolling stone that followed its master around the ceremonial tent. On what grounds was it judged to be alive? Clearly, the critical criterion was that it had been observed to move. It did not move of its own volition, since it was controlled by the power of the master; nevertheless the stone acted, it was not acted upon – for example by being pushed or pulled. But once again, in coming to terms with this phenomenon, we must be wary of the characteristically Western assumption that the world is full of things which may or may not move of their own accord, depending on whether they are of the animate or inanimate class. As we have seen, it would make no more sense to the Ojibwa than it does to us to suppose that the stone exists as a living thing, as though the property of life were an aspect of its substantive nature, of its 'thinginess', *as distinct* from its movement in the world.[9] The movement is not an outward expression of life, but is the very process of the stone's being alive. The same could be said of trees, which are included in Hallowell's list of things formally classified in Ojibwa grammar as 'animate' (OO, p. 23). The Western biologist would doubtless be more inclined to regard the tree than the stone as a 'living thing', by appeal to some aspect of its substantive nature such as DNA or carbon chemistry. For the hunter in the woods, however, what makes a tree alive are its distinctive movements as they are registered in experience: the swaying of its boughs in the wind, the audible fluttering of leaves, the orientation of branches to the sun. Recall that the winds and the sun are persons for the Ojibwa, and can move trees much as powerful humans can move stones.

Different beings, whether or not they qualify as persons, have characteristic patterns of movement – ways of being alive – which reveal them for what they are. The sun, for example, has its own regular pattern of rising and setting, a regularity that, in Hallowell's words, 'is of the same order as the habitual activities of human beings' (OO, p. 29). If we were to consider the sun in abstraction from its observed movement across the sky, then it would indeed appear to be a mere physical body, and its movement a mechanical displacement. But this is not how it is presented to us in immediate experience. Rather, the movement is as much a part of the way the sun is as my own habitual movements are of the way I am. And these movements, of the sun in the heavens, of trees in the wind, of animals and human beings as they go about their everyday tasks, do not take place against the backdrop of a nature that is fixed, with its locations and distances all laid out in advance. For they are part and parcel of that total life process, of continuous generation, through which the world itself is forever coming into being. In short, living beings do not move upon the world, but move along with it.[10] I return to this theme in Chapter Eleven (pp. 198–201).

THE MEANING OF EXPERIENCE

At this point I would like to return to Hallowell's observation, apropos the vitality of stones, that 'the crucial test is experience' (OO, p. 25). What are we to understand by this key word, 'experience'? And what, precisely, is being tested? One approach to answering these questions might be to argue as follows. There exists on the one hand a real world 'out there', customarily called nature, whose forms and composition are given quite independently of the human presence, and on the other hand a world of ideas or mental representations, which bears a relation of only partial correspondence to this external reality. Some things in the world are not represented in the mind, but some images in the mind have no counterpart in the real world. It is experience that mediates between the two worlds, providing both the raw material – in the form of sensory data – from which ideas are constructed, and the opportunities to test them by empirical observation. Thus at first glance we might form the impression that a certain stone actually moved; this could then be checked by further examination which would either confirm or refute the initial hypothesis.

For the Ojibwa, however, knowledge does not lie in the accumulation of mental content. It is not by representing it in the mind that they get to know the world, but rather by moving around in their environment, whether in dreams or waking life, by watching, listening and feeling, actively seeking out the signs by which it is revealed. Experience, here, amounts to a kind of sensory participation, a coupling of the movement of one's own awareness to the movement of aspects of the world. And the kind of knowledge it yields is not propositional, in the form of hypothetical statements or 'beliefs' about the nature of reality, but personal – consisting of an intimate sensitivity to other ways of being, to the particular movements, habits and temperaments that reveal each for what it is. Indeed such knowledge, closely analogous to that which the skilled craftsman has of his raw material, is not easily articulated in propositional form, and would seem to be devalued by any attempt to do so – to disembed it from its grounding in the context of the knower's personal involvement with the known. This is probably the reason why a young man who, through a dream encounter, has secured the blessing of an other-than-human 'grandfather', is forbidden under normal circumstances to speak of his experience in any detail (OO, p. 46). You keep such things to yourself – although others can tell, from your subsequent attitudes and behaviour, that you have a new guardian in your life.

'The concept of the "natural"', Hallowell tells us, 'is not present in Ojibwa thought' (OO, p. 28).[11] Experience, therefore, cannot mediate between mind and nature, since these are not separated in the first place. It is rather intrinsic to the ongoing process of *being alive to the world*, of the person's total sensory involvement in an environment. What then does experience put to the test? Let me try to answer this question by way of another example. Visual sightings of the Thunder Bird in its hawk-like manifestation are exceedingly rare, yet one boy's report of such a sighting – initially greeted with some scepticism – was finally accepted when his description was found to match precisely that offered by another man who had encountered the same bird in a dream (OO, p. 32, see also Callicott 1982: 305). People can lie about their encounters with other-than-human persons, sometimes with dire consequences, but in this case the boy must have been telling the truth. How, otherwise, could he have described the bird so accurately? However the conditions of truth, in this case, lie not in the correspondence between an external reality and its ideal representation, but in the authenticity of the experience itself. Rather than confirming the factual existence of the Thunder Bird as an experience-independent datum of nature, the boy's vision was proof of his exceptional powers of perception. It is these powers that are being constantly tested by experience.

Moreover experiences of this kind are formative. They contribute to the shaping of a person's own sense of self, and of their attitudes and orientations towards the world. Or in short, experience is intrinsic to the generative process wherein persons – both human and other-than-human – come into being and pursue the goal of life, each within the field of their relations with others. And as Hallowell pointed out in his classic article on 'The self and its behavioral environment' (CE, Ch. 4), the process is a mutual one. The formation of the self is, at one and the same time, the formation of an environment for that self, and both emerge out of a common process of maturation and personal experience. Through this process, 'an intelligible behavioral environment has been constituted for the individual that bears an intimate relation to the kind of being he knows himself to be and it is in this behavioral environment that he is motivated to act' (CE, pp. 85–6). The self, in this view, is not the captive subject of the standard Western model, enclosed within the confines of a body, and entertaining its own conjectures about what the outside world might be like on the basis of the limited information available to it. On the contrary, for Hallowell – as indeed for the Ojibwa who have exercised such an obvious and profound influence on his thought – the self exists in its ongoing engagement with the environment: it is *open* to the world, not closed in.

At first glance, however, this view of the self seems inconsistent with the structure of personhood that Hallowell attributes to the Ojibwa. Recall that this structure consists of an inner part that endures and an outward appearance that is susceptible to transformation. Does this not imply that the self is enclosed within its bodily garb? We have already seen how the Ojibwa, in common with many other Amerindian peoples, liken the body to a suit of clothing donned by the soul. Not infrequently, indeed, it is compared to a box-like container. But just as clothing does not necessarily imply disguise or cover-up, so containment is not equivalent to enclosure, confinement, or immobilisation. Rather, the body as container is conceived as a kind of vehicle that serves to extend the spatiotemporal range of a person's movement, influence and experience. Thus what Hallowell, in his characterisation of the Ojibwa person, calls its inner essence is not trapped inside the outward form but rather lies behind it – behind the superficial world of appearances. To penetrate beneath the surface of the person is not, then, to go inside into the mind rather than outside into the world. It is rather to dissolve the very boundary that separates mind from world, and ultimately to reach a level where they are one and the same. Nothing better illustrates this point than the difference between Western and Ojibwa interpretations of dreaming.

DREAMING AND METAMORPHOSIS

People in the West are encouraged to think of dreams as hallucinations, comprising a stream of free-floating images that exist only in the interiority of the unconscious mind, a mind that is freed during sleep from its bodily bearings in the real world. Thus we consider the dreamworld to be the very opposite of the solid, physical world 'out there', just as illusion is opposed to reality, fantasy to fact. For the Ojibwa, by contrast, the world of dreams, like that of myth, is continuous with that of one's waking life. Just as myths are understood as the past experiences of other-than-human persons, so dreams are among the past experiences of human selves (CE, p. 181). In their dreams, humans meet the grandfatherly protagonists of myth, and carry on activities with them in a familiar landscape, albeit viewed from an unfamiliar perspective, revealing secrets of the environment that one may not have noticed before but whose presence is invariably confirmed by subsequent inspection. This is not to say that Ojibwa confuse dream experiences with those they have while wide awake. The difference is that in dreams, the vital essence of the person – the self – is afforded a degree of mobility, not only in space but also in time, normally denied in waking life. While the body of the sleeper is readily visible at some fixed location, the self may be roaming far afield (OO, p. 41). A sorcerer, for example, may be observed lying asleep in his tent, but in his dream he meets you while you were out hunting in the forest. And sure enough, when you were hunting recently, you had an unnerving encounter with a bear. The bear was the sorcerer, who was 'bearwalking' (OO, p. 36).[12]

Both Western and Ojibwa people might agree that in a certain sense, dreaming liberates the mind from its bodily housing. But whereas in the Western conception, this amounts to a taking leave of reality, for the Ojibwa it allows complete freedom of movement *within* the earthly and cosmic space of ordinary life (Callicott 1982: 304). The dreaming mind, far from cutting its already tenuous and provisional connection with the real world, is able to penetrate that world to the point where mind and world become indistinguishable. This difference of interpretation has its roots in fundamental ontological assumptions. Mainstream Western philosophy starts from the premise that the mind is distinct from the world; it is a facility that the person, presumed human, brings to the world in order to make sense of it. When it is not busy making sense of the world, during 'time off', it dreams. For the Ojibwa, on the other hand, the mind subsists in the very involvement of the person in the world. Rather than approaching the world from a position outside of it, the person in Ojibwa eyes can only exist as a being *in* the world, caught up in an ongoing set of relationships with components of the lived-in environment. And the meanings that are found in the world, instead of being superimposed upon it by the mind, are drawn from the contexts of this personal involvement. Thus the dreaming self in its nocturnal journeys, far from taking a break from the demands of coping with reality, sets out in search of meanings that will help to make sense of the experiences of waking life.

With these observations in mind, let me return to the problem of metamorphosis. How are we to respond to the objections of the sceptic to the effect that whatever people may say, humans cannot *really* turn into eagles or bears, or thunder into a kind of hawk, or vice versa? From an Ojibwa perspective, this objection is not so much false as beside the point. Metamorphosis may not occur in ordinary waking life, but it certainly occurs in dreams. And as Hallowell is at pains to stress, 'there is nothing psychologically abstruse about the incorporation of dreams into the category of self-related experiences' (CE, p. 96). The awareness of the self is as phenomenally real when one is dreaming as when one is awake, and these dream experiences are built into the constitution of the self by memory processes that are no different from those working on the experiences of waking life. Consider the case of the boy who, in the midst of a storm, witnessed the Thunder Bird in its hawk-like guise. What if he was only dreaming? Even when awake, we too can sometimes let our imaginations wander, and see things that are not 'really' there. But from the point of view of the experience of the self, it makes no difference whether the boy was awake, day-dreaming or actually asleep. He still saw the bird, was moved to wonder by its presence, and remembered the encounter for the rest of his life. Experiences undergone when asleep are just as much a part of autobiographical memory as are experiences when awake (OO, p. 42).

If, then, we accept that whether awake or asleep, the person's encounters are those of a being-in-the-world, it follows, as Hallowell puts it, 'that metamorphosis can be *personally* experienced' (CE, p. 180). Far from covering over a solid substrate of literal reality with layer upon layer of illusion, what dreams do is to penetrate beneath the surface of the world, to render it transparent, so that one can see into it with a clarity and vision that is not possible in ordinary life. In dreams, for the Ojibwa, the world is opened up to the dreamer, it is *revealed*. This is why they attach such a tremendous importance to dreaming as a source of knowledge, for the knowledge revealed through dreams is also a source of power. Of course this knowledge is of a different kind from what people in the West call science. As I pointed out in the introduction to this chapter, the very project of natural science is premised on the detachment of the human subject from the world that is the object of his or her inquiry. The Ojibwa, starting off from the opposite premise – that the subject can exist only as a being *in* the world – have arrived at something quite different: not a natural science but a poetics of dwelling (on this contrast, see Chapter One, pp. 25–6). And it is within the context of such a poetics that Ojibwa ideas about metamorphosis, the personhood of the sun, the winds and thunder, the liveliness of stones, and so on, should be understood.

THE SOUNDS OF SPEECH

I shall return, in the conclusion to this chapter, to the relation between poetics and science. Before doing so, I should like to elaborate further on the contrast between Western and Ojibwa models of the person with particular reference to the criterion which, more than anything else, is adduced to justify claims to the unique status of humanity: namely the capacity for speech. For the Ojibwa, according to Hallowell, the essential powers of person-hood include, besides speech, sentience, volition and memory. Those of us brought up in the Western tradition of thought would have no particular problem with this idea. We *do* have a problem, however, when it comes to the attribution of these powers to non-human animals, and even more of a problem in attributing them to things that we would regard as inanimate. To give a lead into this problem, let me recount one more anecdote from Hallowell's Ojibwa study. An old man and his wife are sitting in their tent, and a storm is raging outside. There is thunder and lightning. The thunder comes in a series of claps. The old man listens intently. Then he turns to his wife and asks, quite casually and in a matter-of-fact tone of voice, 'Did you hear what was said?' 'No', she replies, 'I didn't catch it' (OO, p. 34). What are we to make of this?

Certainly, so long as we remain with a Western view of the nature of sentience, voli-tion, memory and speech, the story seems incredible. The language of agency that we are accustomed to use posits a being, the agent, who is endowed with will and purpose, and whose existence and identity are given independently of any action that he or she chooses to initiate. Thus I may or may not choose to speak, or I may decide to say one thing rather than another, but as a being with intentions and purposes – that is, as a person – I am not the same as my speech. Likewise I may choose to clap my hands, but as a phys-ical event in the world, the clap exists apart from myself – the person who claps. Notice the similarity between this notion of agency, as an inherent attribute of persons as distinct from their overt behaviour, and the notion of animacy built into the Western notion of 'living things', which, as we have already seen, construes life as a substantive property of objects as distinct from their movement in the world.

Does the thunder, then, clap like I do? Though we might say 'the thunder claps', we know perfectly well that we are speaking figuratively, as though there were some being in the heavens with intentions and purposes rather like our own, and who claps like a human person, except on a more awesome scale. In reality, we are sure there is no such cosmic being. And to get around the problem of how something can occur without an agent to produce it, we may use an alternative form of words, such as 'there was a clap of thunder'. The point is that thunder does not exist separately from its clap, in the way that I am supposed to exist separately from mine. Rather, the clap *is* thunder; it is the acoustic form of thunder's phenomenal presence in the world. Through the clap, the thunder audibly exists for those who hear it. Let me put this contrast in another way, while keeping for the moment to the terms of the Western model of personal agency. When I speak, or for that matter when I clap, it is because I have an idea. My concern is to communicate that idea, and I do so by means of coded signs or signals which travel in the medium of sound. By converting ideas in the mind into physical impulses in the world, information is transmitted. But the thunder is *not* transmitting a message. Of course it affects us; we are moved by the sound, perhaps a little scared. But we do not look for a message in the sound or ask, as did the old man in Hallowell's story, 'Did you hear what was said?'

As this example shows, Western thought systematically distinguishes the sounds of speech, along with other sound-producing gestures whose purpose is to give outward expression to inner ideas or mental states, from the sounds of nature that are just there but have not been produced by anybody. My clap and the thunderclap fall on either side of this division. And the dichotomy between interior mental states and their outward physical or behavioural expression that underwrites this conception of the distinctiveness of speech also applies to the way we tend to think about other aspects of personhood – sentience, volition, memory. Thus volition implies the intentionality of action, but Western thought sees intentionality as residing not in the action itself but in a thought or plan that the mind places before the action and which the latter is supposed to execute. Likewise we are inclined to think of memory as a store of images in the mind, rather than of remembering as an activity situated in the world. And we talk about sentience in terms of inner states or 'feelings', instead of focusing on the perceptual activity of feeling the world around us. In short the self, as the locus of ideas, plans, memories and feelings, seems to exist as a substantive entity quite independently of where it is and what it does.

Behind all this is a model of the person which, as we have already seen, identifies the self with an interior intelligence, the conscious mind, enclosed by its physical container, the body. According to this model, the body picks up sensory signals from the world around it and passes them to the mind, which processes them to form images or representations. Through a logical manipulation of these representations, the mind formulates plans of action, which are then passed as instructions for the body to execute in the world. The mind itself may be envisaged as many-layered, with outer layers of consciousness covering over deeper, more subterranean levels of the unconscious. Locked up in there, directly known only to ourselves, are our thoughts, feelings and memories, which can only be released, and made known to others, by way of their bodily enactment in speech and gesture. The Ojibwa model of the person, however, is quite different. As shown schematically in Figure 6.1, this model does not posit the self in advance of the person's entry into the world; rather, the self is constituted as a centre of agency and awareness in the process of its active engagement within an environment. Feeling, remembering, intending and speaking are all aspects of that engagement, and through it the self continually comes into being.

In short, the Ojibwa self is *relational* (Bird-David 1999: S77–8). If we were to ask where it is, the answer would not be 'inside the head rather than out there in the world'. For the self exists, or rather becomes, in the unfolding of those very relations that are set up by virtue of a being's positioning *in* the world, reaching out into the environment – and connecting with other selves – along these relational pathways. Taking this view of the person, as Hallowell does, it is clear that no physical barrier can come between mind and world. 'Any inner–outer dichotomy', he asserts, 'with the human skin as boundary, is psychologically irrelevant' (CE, p. 88). But this is precisely the dichotomy, as we have seen, by which speech and similar expressive gestures are conventionally distinguished from

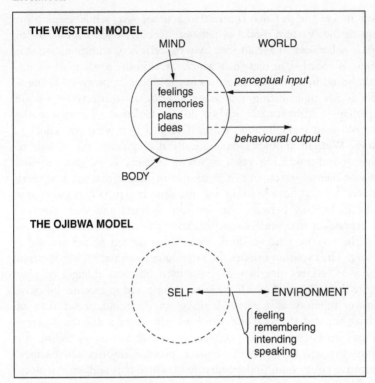

THE WESTERN MODEL

MIND   WORLD

perceptual input

feelings
memories
plans
ideas

behavioural output

BODY

THE OJIBWA MODEL

SELF ◄─────► ENVIRONMENT

feeling
remembering
intending
speaking

Figure 6.1 Western and Ojibwa models of the person.

the sounds of nature. To take Hallowell at his word means having to adopt a quite different view of speech, not as the outward expression of inner thoughts, but as one of the ways in which the self manifests its presence in the world. Thus when I speak or clap, I myself am not separate from the sound I produce – of my voice or the mutually percussive impact of my hands. These sounds are part of the way I am, they belong to my being as it issues forth into the environment. In other words, speech is not a mode of transmitting information or mental content; it is a way of *being alive*.

Now if we take this view of speech, there is no longer anything so odd about supposing, as the Ojibwa do, that thunder can speak, and that other people can hear. The rumbling of thunder is the manifestation of its presence in the world, just as the sounds of human speaking, singing, clapping or drumming are manifestations of ours. Likewise in 'conjuring performances' (Hallowell 1942, 1976: 459), when the voices of grandfatherly other-than-human persons are heard to issue from the interior of a barrel-shaped tent which is constantly shaken about by their activity, each character makes his presence felt, and is recognised by the audience, on account of the peculiarity of his speech, including features of voice, vocabulary and intonation. Thus the world in which the Ojibwa dwell is polyglot, full of beings with their own diverse styles of speaking or singing.[13] As people move through the forest in hunting, or hear myths being recited, or sit around the outside of the conjuring lodge, they constantly listen out for the sounds that are the signatures of these manifold life-forms, and respond with speech-sounds of their own. Non-human sounds like thunder or animal calls, the voices of other-than-human persons, and the speech of human beings are alike in that they not only have the power to move those who hear them, but also take their meaning from the contexts in which they are heard. In these respects, no fundamental line of demarcation can be drawn between the sounds of nature and of human speech.

Is there any significance, then, in the fact that the thunder was heard instead of seen? There is a long tradition in the history of Western thought, which I review at length in Chapter Fourteen, of distinguishing between vision and hearing along the lines that the former is remote and objective, cutting the viewer off from things seen, whereas the latter is intimate and subjective, establishing a kind of interpenetration or resonance between the listener and the world. There are some hints, in Hallowell's account, that the Ojibwa might make a similar kind of distinction. Thus he tells us that under no circumstances can the inner essence of the person, the soul, be a direct object of visual perception. 'What can be perceived visually is only that aspect of being that has some form or structure . . . The only sensory mode under which it is possible to directly perceive the presence of souls . . . is the auditory one' (CE, pp. 179–80). This is why the other-than-human persons of the shaking tent ceremony are heard but never seen. So far as the audience is concerned these persons *are* their voices, just as thunder *is* its clap. In both cases sound is of the essence of being rather than its outward expression. However there are counter-indications, too, that Ojibwa might not, or at least not always, make such a radical distinction between seeing and hearing.

One such indication is that ghosts, the outward form of spirits of the dead, can be heard as well as seen. They are known to whistle (CE, p. 174). But more significantly, the notion that vision presents us with a world of objective forms rests upon an assumption that is incompatible with the relational model of the person presented above. This assumption, which is implicit in most studies of visual perception by Western psychologists, is that seeing things involves the formation of images in the mind on the basis of sensory data drawn from the play of light upon the retinal surfaces of the eyes. Now in an earlier section on the meaning of experience for the Ojibwa, I showed that for a being who is alive to its surroundings, experience does not mediate between things in the world and representations in the mind, but is intrinsic to the sensory coupling, in perception and action, of the awareness of the self to the movement of those features of the environment selected as foci of attention. This view of experience calls for a quite different understanding of vision. It would be premised on the notion of the perceiver as an active participant in an environment rather than a passive recipient of stimuli, one whose vision penetrates the world rather than holding up a mirror to it. David Smith, writing of the Chipewyan of the northwest Canadian subarctic, has drawn attention to the importance of precisely this kind of vision to their 'bush sensibility'. The hunter and trapper, making his way through bush or forest, has at all times to *watch what is going on*. Yet as Smith also shows, regarded as a form of dynamic, sensory resonance, seeing does not differ in principle from hearing, and when it comes to people's pragmatic, first-hand experience of moving around in the environment, they are so closely intertwined as to be inseparable (Smith 1998: 413–14, see also Chapter Fourteen, pp. 276–81). I suspect that this is as true for the Ojibwa as it is for the Chipewyan, and therefore that vision and hearing are not, in fact, sharply differentiated in their practice.[14]

Before leaving the topic of hearing and speech, one more issue remains to be dealt with. It arises from Hallowell's remark, apropos the old man's questioning of his wife about the thunder, that 'he was reacting to this sound in the same way as he would respond to a human being, whose words he did not understand' (OO, p. 34). We have seen that the Ojibwa lifeworld is polyglot, inhabited by manifold beings each with their own particular pattern of speech. It is tempting to compare these different patterns to the diverse languages of human communities, as though understanding the sounds of thunder, the winds, the various forms of animal life, and so on were a problem of translation, of rendering meanings expressed in a multitude of foreign tongues in terms of one's own. Was the old man, then, asking his wife to translate for him? Were the words of the thunder spoken so quickly that, with his imperfect grasp of the language, he failed to grasp what had been said? Now the metaphor of translation implies a certain view of language or speech, as a vehicle for the outward expression of inner ideas. To translate is, then, to 'carry across' an idea encoded in one expressive medium into the terms of another. I have argued, however, that in attributing the power of speech to thunder, Ojibwa do not suppose that it is trying to transmit ideas to humans, but rather that its presence in the world, like that of other beings whether human or other-than-human, can take an acoustic form. Responding to that presence with sensitivity and understanding is not therefore a matter of translation. It is more a matter of empathy.

Consider, for example, the response of a mother to the cry of her baby. Because of the special relationship between them, she *hears* that cry – it is immediately intelligible to her in a way that the cries of other infants are not. To be understood, the cry does not first have to be rendered intelligible through translation into a language that she and others can comprehend. I would suggest that the old man in Hallowell's story may have heard the thunder in the same way. He, too, must have had a special relationship with the Thunder Bird. Indeed in one of his last papers on the Ojibwa, first published in 1966, Hallowell adds a crucial qualification to his earlier interpretation of the story of the old man, the old woman and the thunder. 'By and large', he observes, 'the Ojibwa do not attune themselves to receiving messages every time a thunderstorm occurs'. Thus to understand the old man's response we have to realise that he had had previous contacts with the Thunder Bird in the dreams of his puberty fast (Hallowell 1976: 459). He was therefore sensitised to the sound of thunder in a way that ordinary Ojibwa (including his wife) were not. He could empathise with it. Of course, total empathy is as impossible to achieve as perfect translation. But they proceed in quite different ways. Rather than shifting into another register of expression, the achievement of empathy means taking on another way of being. Full understanding, in short, is attained *not through translation but through metamorphosis*. And this happens, above all, in dreams.

NATURALISM AND ANIMISM

Are the Ojibwa animists? In recent anthropology the concept of animism has had a rather bad press, on account of its liberal use in the past to brand, as primitive superstition, systems of belief which allegedly attribute spirits or souls to things, living or non-living, which to any rational, thinking person are 'obviously' mere objects of nature (for a review of these usages, see Bird-David 1999: S67–8). Philippe Descola, however, suggests a way of considering animism that is rather more respectful of indigenous understandings. Animism, he writes, is 'a kind of objectification of nature [which] endows natural beings not only with human dispositions, granting them the status of persons with human emotions and often the ability to talk, but also with social attributes – a hierarchy of positions, behaviours based on kinship, respect for certain norms of conduct' (Descola 1992: 114). Though Descola draws his ethnographic illustrations from Amazonian societies, this characterisation of what he calls 'animic systems' would seem readily applicable to the

Ojibwa case as depicted in Hallowell's account. Critically, in such a system, relations between persons – that is, *social* relations – can override the boundaries of humanity as a species. Thus, as Hallowell reports, 'the world of personal relations in which the Ojibwa live is a world in which vital social relations transcend those which are maintained with human beings' (OO, p. 43). To this one might add that a person's social relations are carried on in the same space as, and are continuous with, relations with other constituents of their environment, that is with non-persons. There is, then, no radical break between the domains of social and ecological relations.

Following Descola's lead, we might set out to draw a systematic comparison between the animism of peoples like the Ojibwa and the naturalism of Western thought and science. Whereas animism takes the relational character of the world as an ontological *a priori*, against which the 'naturalness' of beings – the material forms in which they appear – stands out as unstable and problematic, naturalism takes it for granted that nature really exists, as an ontological domain of order and necessity where things are what they are, in themselves. Against this world of nature, it is the status and the forms of human culture that appear problematic (Descola 1996a: 88, see also Viveiros de Castro 1998: 478). Yet for Descola, animism and naturalism (along with totemism, consideration of which I reserve for the next chapter) may be regarded as alternative 'schemata of praxis', in other words as 'mental models which organise the social objectivation of non-humans' (1996a: 87). This appeal to the language of mental models, to the idea of accommodating beings that are really non-human into schemes of representation that construct them as social and therefore human, belongs squarely within a naturalist ontology, and it is from this that the terms of the comparison are derived. For what these terms do is to preserve a space for 'really natural' nature which is unaffected by the diverse constructions that the human mind might place upon it. Thus the comparison between naturalism and animism, since it is done on naturalism's terms, is hardly a fair or balanced one (see Chapter Three, pp. 41–2).

My purpose in this chapter has been to redress the balance. Instead of trying to comprehend Ojibwa understandings within a comparative framework which already presupposes the separation of mind and nature, I have been concerned to place the mode of understanding of Western science within the context of the primary existential condition, revealed in Ojibwa thought and practice, of being alive to the world. Let me summarily take stock of these two approaches. The first posits a world 'out there' full of objects, animate and inanimate. The life process of animate objects, being the expression of their essential nature (nowadays understood as their genetic constitution) under given environmental conditions, is understood to be purely consequential, an 'effect' (see Chapter One, p. 19). Hence an additional principle, of mind or consciousness, has to be invoked to account for the powers of intentionality and awareness that we normally attribute to persons. In animic systems such as those of the Ojibwa, these powers are said to be projected onto non-human kinds. So long as we follow Descola in assuming that in reality, they are reserved for human beings, such projection is bound to be anthropomorphic. If, in other words, only humans *really* have intentions, to represent non-humans such as bears *as though* they were persons with intentions is necessarily to represent them as human (see Kennedy 1992: 9). That is why Descola builds a component of anthropomorphism into his very definition of animism, as a system that endows natural beings with human capacities. Only beings thus endowed, it seems, can have social relations.

Working from an Ojibwa notion of animacy, not as an empirical property of things but as an existential condition of being, my argument has followed an alternative path.

This has been to envisage the world from the point of view of a being within it, as a total field of relations whose unfolding is tantamount to the process of life itself. Every being emerges, with its particular form, dispositions and capacities, as a locus of growth – or in Ojibwa terms, as a focus of power – within this field. Mind, then, is not added on to life but is immanent in the intentional engagement, in perception and action, of living beings with the constituents of their environments. Thus the world is not an external domain of objects that I look *at*, or do things *to*, but is rather going on, or undergoing continuous generation, with me and around me. As such primary engagement is a condition of being, it must also be a condition of knowledge, whether or not the knowledge in question is deemed to be 'scientific'. All properly scientific knowledge rests upon observation, but there can be no observation without participation – without the observer's coupling the movement of his or her attention to surrounding currents of activity. Thus the approach I have followed here is not an *alternative* to science, as animism is to naturalism; it rather seeks to restore the practices of science to the contexts of human life in the world. For it is from such contexts that all knowledge grows.

This approach has two further implications that I would like briefly to explore. The first takes us back to the question of anthropomorphism, the second concerns what I shall call the 'genealogical model'. Natural science, as von Bertalanffy has put it (1955: 258–9), approaches the world through a 'progressive de-anthropomorphization', that is, through the attempt to expunge from its notion of reality all that can be put down to human experience. Thus purified, nature is revealed to a detached human reason as a domain of things in themselves. Now Ojibwa ontology, too, could be said to entail a process of de-anthropomorphisation, but this operates in a quite different direction. Instead of severing the link between reality and human experience, Ojibwa ontology recognises the reality of the experience of other-than-human beings.[15] All experience depends on taking up a position in the world, tied to a particular form of life, but for the Ojibwa the human is but one form out of many. This, of course, undermines the core assumption that Descola brings to his characterisation of animic systems as inherently anthropomorphic, namely that experience depends upon powers of awareness and intentionality that mark their possessors as uniquely human.

The genealogical model is a way of thinking about the relations between animate beings which rests on the idea that every such being is specified, in its essential nature, prior to commencing its life in the world. According to the model, the elements of the specification are received as a kind of endowment, passed on independently of the being's interaction with its environment. And it is in the passing on or 'inheritance' of this endowment, from generation to generation, that relations are constituted. I shall consider this model and its implications at length in Chapter Eight. Suffice it to say at this point that the model is central not only to the way modern biology conceives of species and their phylogenetic connections, but also to the conventional anthropological understanding of kinship. Thus a simple line on a kinship diagram indicates that some component of the essence of a person is received, by transmission, at the point of conception, ahead of that person's growth in an environment. Now from the genealogical model, it is easy to derive the following propositions: first, membership of the human – or any other – species is fixed by birth; secondly, the animals most closely related to humans are those (namely the great apes) with which they have the closest genealogical connections; and thirdly, human kinship relations cannot crosscut the species barrier.

From the Ojibwa perspective, none of these propositions is valid. We have seen that beings can change from one species-form to another, that the animals closest to humans are those such as bears and eagles which are fellow participants in the same life-world, and that one specific category of kin – namely 'grandfathers' – admits persons of both human and other-than-human kinds. Ojibwa ontology, however, is incompatible with the genealogical model at a more fundamental level. For if the forms of beings are not expressed but generated within the life process, then these forms cannot be passed on as part of any context-independent specification. One cannot, in other words, lay down the form that a being will take independently of the circumstances of its life in the world. Kinship, in particular, is not about handing down components of a person-specification, but about the ways in which other persons in my environment, through their presence, their activities and the nurturance they provide, contribute to the process of my own growth and wellbeing. And since these others may be non-human as well as human, there is nothing in the least strange about the extension of kinship relations across the species boundary, nor do we have to set up a distinction between 'real' and 'fictive' kinship in order to accommodate cases of this kind. To receive blessings from my other-than-human grand-fathers, it is not necessary to suppose that I am descended from them in the genealogical sense.

Conclusion

Ever since Darwin, Western science has cleaved strongly to the view that humans differ from other animals in degree rather than kind. Yet it is a view that has raised more problems than it has solved. For if we ask on what scale these differences of degree are to be measured, it turns out to be one that places human beings unequivocally at the top. It is the scale of the rise of reason, and its gradual triumph over the shackles of instinct. Where Darwin differed from many (though by no means all) of his predecessors was in both attributing powers of reasoning to sub-human animals and recognising the powerful sway of instinct even on the behaviour of humans beings. As he argued in *The Descent of Man* (1871, Chs 3 and 4), the beginnings of reason can be found far down in the scale of nature, but only with the emergence of humanity did it begin to gain the upper hand. In short, for Darwin and his many followers, the evolution of species in nature was also an evolution that progressively liberated the mind from the promptings of innate disposition. Moreover in bringing the rise of science and civilisation within the compass of the same evolutionary process that had made humans out of apes, and apes out of creatures lower in the scale, Darwin was forced to attribute the ascendancy of reason in the West to innate endowment, a conclusion that is utterly unacceptable today. Modern science has responded, by and large, by dissociating the historical process of civilisation from the evolution of the species, thereby compromising the thesis of continuity. Humans are made to appear different in degree, not kind, from their evolutionary antecedents by attributing the movement of history to a process that differs in kind, not degree, from the process of evolution!

I have been searching, in this chapter, for a way of understanding the continuity of the relations between human beings and all the other inhabitants of the earth which does not fall foul of the difficulties of the argument by degree – an argument that is unashamedly anthropocentric in taking human powers of intellect as the measure of all things, that can only comprehend the evolution of species in nature by supposing an evolution of reason that takes them out of it, and that, if applied consistently, is incompatible with any ethical commitment to shared human potential. I have tried to show that the ontology of a non-Western people, the Ojibwa, points the way towards a solution. I do not mean to suggest for one moment that the Ojibwa orientation to life in the world is without paradoxes of its own. Nor would I wish to argue that it offers a viable substitute for science. Earlier, I suggested that what the Ojibwa have arrived at is not an alternative science of nature but a poetics of dwelling. In the past, there has been a tendency to write off such poetics as the outpourings of a primitive mentality that has been superseded by the rise of the modern scientific worldview. My conclusion, to the contrary, is that scientific activity is always, and necessarily, grounded in a poetics of dwelling. Rather than sweeping it under the carpet, as an embarrassment, I believe this is something worth celebrating, and that doing so will also help us do better science.

Chapter Seven

Totemism, animism and the depiction of animals

INTRODUCTION

Art, it is often supposed, is one of the hallmarks of humanity. It reveals a capacity, common to all human beings, to disengage consciousness from the current of lived experience, so as to treat that experience as an object of reflection. Such reflection is the work of the imagination, and its products are symbolic representations. In visual art, these representations are expressed in painting, drawing and sculpture. Throughout history, in cultures around the world, non-human animals have always figured as key topics of artistic representation. Indeed from earliest times, human beings seem to have been fascinated by their diverse forms and movements, and to have desired to express this aesthetic appreciation in visual media.

What I have just set out is a fairly conventional view, not only in the academic disciplines of archaeology, anthropology and art history but also, I think, more widely among those of us who have been raised within the conventions of the Western 'art world'. I believe, however, that it is almost entirely false, and in this chapter I want to show why. My argument, in a nutshell, is that it results from the retrojection, onto the entire field of pre-modern or non-Western societies, of notions of humanity and animality, of culture and nature, and of art as representation, that have their source in Western modernity. The field of non-Western 'art' is vast, and obviously I cannot deal with it all. Instead, I shall confine my attention to the paintings, drawings and carvings of certain peoples conventionally known in anthropological literature as 'hunters and gatherers'. This is not the place to debate the validity of the category; the important point for our present purposes is that people who hunt and gather for a subsistence generally have an extremely close and intimate knowledge of the landscape and its plant and animal inhabitants, on whose continuity or regeneration their life depends. They stand, if you will, at the opposite extreme from the affluent Westerner who may find the wild animal a beautiful thing to look at, whether directly or more often through the lens of a camera, so long as it remains at a safe distance which precludes any closer involvement.

In order to avoid the unwanted connotations of the concept of 'art', I shall refer to the animal-like figures that hunter-gatherers draw, paint or carve as 'depictions'. Though far from ideal for the purpose, it is the most neutral term I can find. Obviously, to say of a figure that it depicts an animal is to suggest that it bears some iconic resemblance to the creature in question. It does not necessarily follow, however, that the one *represents* the other (Gibson 1979: 279–80). But if depictions are not representations, what are they? How else are we to interpret the correspondence between the figure and the animal it evokes? The answers to these questions, I argue, depend upon ways of understanding the relationships between human beings, animals and the land. To show how this is so, I intend to contrast two such understandings, which I denote by the terms 'totemism' and 'animism'. These should be taken as labels of convenience only, and I should move at once to correct the misleading impression to which adding the '-ism' is apt to give rise, namely that the terms refer to coherent and explicitly articulated doctrinal systems. They are, of course, nothing of the sort, but rather orientations that are deeply embedded in everyday practice. Or to put it another way, they are not so much systems *to* which people relate as immanent in their ways of relating.

Furthermore, I have no wish to become embroiled in arguments about the extent to which the diverse beliefs and practices that have been brought under the respective rubrics of totemism and animism share features in common. Suffice it to say that my view of totemism rests largely on my reading of ethnographic material from Australian Aboriginal societies, and my view of animism has its basis in the ethnography of the circumpolar North. Ironically, the word 'totem' actually comes from the language of the Ojibwa, a native people of northern North America whose basic ontology, as we saw in the last chapter, is unquestionably animic. It entered the anthropological literature by way of an account written by the Englishman J. K. Long, who was trading with the Ojibwa towards the end of the eighteenth century, as a label for systems of ritual and belief that associate particular social groups, such as clans, with particular natural species, usually of animals. For various reasons, internal to the history of social anthropology, the *locus classicus* for such systems subsequently shifted from North America to Australia. More recent ethnographic studies of Australian Aboriginal societies showed, however, that the association of clans with species is a corollary of a more fundamental set of linkages between people, land and ancestral beings. Both for ethnographers of the region and for Aboriginal people themselves, it is to these linkages that the concept of totemism has come to refer, and this is the sense in which I will use the term here.[1]

In what follows I begin by spelling out the contrast between totemism and animism, and go on from there to show how first the totemic ontology, and then the animic one, are reflected in the depiction of animals. This, in turn, provides a basis for their systematic comparison. Finally, I return to the orthodox view spelled out in the introductory paragraph in order to show why it is so wrong, and to replace it with a more satisfactory alternative. The activities of hunters and gatherers that lead to the production of what we in the West call 'art' should, I argue, be understood as ways not of representing the world of immediate experience on a higher, more 'symbolic' plane, but of probing more deeply into it and of discovering the significance that lies therein.

TOTEMISM AND ANIMISM

At the most fundamental level, the contrast is about the relative priority of form and process. With a totemic ontology, the forms life takes are already given, congealed in perpetuity in the features, textures and contours of the land. And it is the land that harbours the vital forces which animate the plants, animals and people it engenders. With an animic ontology, to the contrary, life is itself generative of form. Vital force, far from being petrified in a solid medium, is free-flowing like the wind, and it is on its uninterrupted circulation that the continuity of the living world depends. In the following paragraphs I elaborate on this contrast in more detail.

Throughout Aboriginal Australia, people's sense of being is grounded in the understanding that the fundamentals of existence were laid down in an era known conventionally as the Dreaming. During this era, which both underwrites the living present and encompasses it as but a moment of eternity, the initially shapeless earth was inhabited by beings of immense scale and power who roamed across its surface, shaping it with the impress of their movements and depositing something of their creative essence at place after place as they passed along. These beings are said to be ancestral to all currently living creatures, whether human or non-human. But the relationship between the ancestors and their living progeny is not a genealogical one. That is to say, there is no line of descent, passing through a series of intermediate steps, that would connect the one to the other, nor is any living generation further removed from the ancestors than its predecessors. For every living being, according to the Aboriginal conception, draws its essential form and substance directly from the land, and the land, in turn, embodies the creative powers of the ancestors. Human beings and other creatures come and go: they emerge from the land, live out their time, and are reincorporated into it when they die. But the land is always there, and will continue to bring forth new life so long as those who dwell upon it – by fulfilling their custodial responsibilities towards it, or 'looking after' it in the proper way – do not allow its powers to be dissipated. It is this understanding of the relationship between the ancestors, the land which is the enduring form of their presence, and the living beings it engenders, that I call 'totemic'.

Among the native peoples of the circumpolar North the land does not have quite the same significance that it has in Aboriginal Australia. For the powers that bring forth life, instead of being concentrated in the land itself, are rather distributed among the manifold beings that inhabit it. There is no power source, analogous to the totemic ancestors of Aboriginal cosmology, that subtends the life process itself. Consequently, animate beings are engendered not by the land but reciprocally, by one another. Far from revealing the shape of a world that already exists, as it were, out of time, life is the temporal process of its ongoing creation. The world of this 'animic' understanding is home to innumerable beings whose presence is manifested in this form or that, each engaged in the project of forging a life in the way peculiar to its kind. But in order to live, every such being must constantly draw upon the vitality of others. A complex network of reciprocal interdependence, based on the give and take of substance, care and vital force – the latter often envisaged as one or several kinds of spirit or soul – extends throughout the cosmos, linking human, animal and all other forms of life. Within this network, the generation of animate form in any one region necessarily entails its dissolution in another. Vitality must be surrendered here so that it may be reconstituted there. For this reason, no form is ever permanent; indeed the transience or ephemerality of form is necessary if the current of life is to keep on flowing. All of existence is suspended in this flow. Borne along in the current, beings meet, merge and split apart again, each taking with them something of the other. Thus life, in the animic ontology, is not an emanation but a generation of being, in a world that is not pre-ordained but incipient, forever on the verge of the actual.

Having set out the basic contrast between totemism and animism, I now want to consider how it bears upon the relation between human beings and non-human animals. How, for example, is it reflected in the attitudes of hunters towards their prey? In a totemic system, to hunt (or to refrain from hunting) animals of a particular species is part of the proper way of living one's life on the land according to a pre-established order of things. Thus the relation between human and animal is subsumed by the relation of both to the ancestral powers of which they are the living incarnations. People of course have to hunt (as well as gather) to secure a livelihood, but the actual pursuit of animals lacks cosmological significance. It is, as Philippe Descola writes, 'a quite mundane activity of food procurement' (1996: 95). While it helps to keep people fed it does not, in itself, establish their presence in the world. It is in dwelling upon the land – in the senses both of inhabiting it and of sustained focal attention towards its ancestral essence in acts of ceremony – that people forge their sense of being. In an animic system, on the other hand, hunting effects the circulation of vital force between humans and animals and thus contributes directly to the regeneration of the lifeworld of which both are part. The animals offer something of their potentiality and substance to human beings so that the latter may live, while humans, in return, through the proper treatment of the animals in death, ensure the release of their life force and hence their subsequent reincarnation. Human life, which in the totemic ontology is predicated upon the immortality of the land, is here predicated upon the mortality of animals. In the animic ontology, the killing and eating of game is far more than mere provisioning; it is world-renewing.

Let me put the contrast in another way. The totemic world is essential, the animic world dialogical. When an Australian Aboriginal man proclaims himself to be a kangaroo, he means that he – along with other persons who share this affiliation – actually partakes of the same substance as the kangaroo. The connection, in other words, lies in the essential consubstantiality of members of the human group, and of the animal species, all of whom derive the lineaments of their being from the same place in the landscape in which is deposited the creativity of the kangaroo ancestor. But what of the shaman, in a northern circumpolar society, who walks abroad as a bear? Recall that the animic cosmos is populated by beings of both human and non-human kinds engaged in ongoing mutual interaction. Animals, like humans, are supposed to form their own communities, and members of each can visit the communities of the other. From a perspective located within the human community, non-human beings will appear in their animal guise. However upon 'crossing over' to the animal side, a man will see his hosts as creatures like himself, while to the people back home he will now appear in animal form. In short, in the dialogue between human and animal, each in turn takes up the point of view of the other, becoming temporarily other to his or her own people. The shaman, in animic society, is a person of exceptional power, who can move with relative ease across the human–animal interface. But particular animals may also be credited with similar powers: indeed right across the circumpolar North, the bear is regarded as such a one. If the bear can appear human, so too, the human shaman can show up as a bear (see Figure 7.1). Whether you see one or the other depends on where you are looking from; in other words it has to do not with the substance of being but with the relative positioning of self and other in contexts of dialogue.

Figure 7.1 An Inuit man and a polar bear cordially greet one another. Drawing by Davidialuk Alasuaq, from the personal collection of Professor Bernard Saladin d'Anglure.

From B. Saladin d'Anglure, Nanook, super-male, *Signifying animals: human meaning in the natural world*, ed. R. Willis, 1990, p. 179.

Now one of the principal reasons why the shamans of animic society make their often arduous journeys to the communities of non-human animals is to recover vitality that may have been lost, due to some untoward circumstance, to the 'other side'. Such loss is generally experienced in the form of serious illness, and by bringing vitality back to the sufferer the shaman aims to effect a cure. Another reason may be to negotiate with the spirit masters, who control the disposition of animals, for their release to human hunters. To make the crossing to the animal domain, the shaman has to avail himself of the assistance of bodies other than his own. Animals of various kinds, known as his 'helpers', carry his inner being aloft on its journey, yet all the while his corporeal body remains where it stands. The shaman's liberation from the constraints of his bodily bearing in the human world is generally achieved through going into trance. In this state, the normal boundaries between human and animal are dissolved. However, such 'out-of-body' experience has no place within a totemic system, for the simple reason that the unity of human and animal, in a totemic ontology, lies in their very consubstantiality. A man does not have to leave his body to take on that of his totem, for his own body and that of his totem share the same essence whose ultimate source, as we have seen, lies in the land. Whereas the animist must go beyond the body to transcend the human-animal distinction, the totemist finds the distinction dissolved at the very core of his being – within the body, not beyond it. Human and animal, separated in life, are reunited on death and burial, that is through the ultimate return of the body to the land from which it grew (see Figure 7.2).

THE DEPICTION OF ANIMALS

Now that we have established the basic contrast between totemic and animic ontologies, our next, and principal problem is to consider how each, in turn, bears upon the depiction of animals. As a lead into the problem, consider the two depictions reproduced in Figures 7.3 and 7.4. The first was executed on bark by the Australian Aboriginal painter Namerredje Guymala, one of a group of Kunwinjku-speaking painters residing in the town of Oenpelli in Western Arnhem Land. It dates from about 1975. The second was drawn on paper around the same time by Davidialuk Alasuaq, an

Figure 7.2 This bark painting by Djawada Nadjongorle, a Kunwinjku Aboriginal artist from Western Arnhem Land, Australia, juxtaposes the figures of a dead human spirit and the sand monitor, *Varanus gouldii*. The juxtaposition vividly brings out the unification, in death, of human and animal, joined by their shared ancestral essence.

Figure 7.3 Painting of an antilopine kangaroo with *mimih* spirit, by Namerredje Guymala, c.1975.

Inuit from Povungnituk in northern Quebec. On the face of it, both appear to depict hunting scenes. The animal in Figure 7.3 is an antilopine kangaroo, and in the top right corner is a figure of undoubtedly human form, spear-thrower in hand, on the point of launching a spear towards the head of his victim. The animal in Figure 7.4 is a caribou, which stares directly at the Inuit hunter crouching half-concealed in the undergrowth. The hunter is about to loose an arrow from his bow to dispatch the caribou. Now in both pictures, there is actually more going on than immediately meets the eye. The first, as I shall show, is not really a hunting scene at all. The second, though it does indeed describe an encounter between hunter and prey, also catches a moment of reflection in a dialogue between two sentient beings, each of whom is offering something to the other while wondering about the other's intentions. I begin with the former.

Painting the ancestors: Aboriginal Australia

It is obvious, looking at Figure 7.3, that the depictions of the anthropomorphic hunter and of the kangaroo that he appears to be spearing follow quite different conventions.[2] The hunter is portrayed as a diminutive, stick-like figure, caught in an unstable posture that conveys a powerful sense of movement. He is clearly doing something, using tools, engaging in an activity. The kangaroo, by contrast, does not appear to be doing anything at all. It is depicted in limp, static profile, resembling nothing so much as a perfectly preserved fossil in a slab of stone. Not only is it shown on a much larger scale than is the hunter, but the artist has also chosen to concentrate on the animal's bodily architecture – on its design, morphology and the internal layout of its organs – rather than on the dynamics of movement, posture and behaviour. A particularly remarkable characteristic of the depiction is its use of so-called 'X-ray' style to display the principal features of anatomy, including the heart and lungs, liver, and intestinal tract, as well as the backbone (Taylor 1996: 135–7). Indeed the static, anatomical portrayal of the animal contrasts so strikingly with the dynamic, postural portrayal of the hunter that it seems almost calculated to draw attention to the former's existential status as an *inanimate* being, as opposed to the animacy of the latter. The kangaroo, whatever else it may be supposed to be, is not a living creature.

Figure 7.4 Inuit hunter and caribou. Drawing by Davidialuk Alasuaq, from the personal collection of Professor Bernard Saladin d'Anglure.

From B. Saladin d'Anglure, *Inuit and caribou*, published by Université Laval, Canada, 1979, p. 61.

The figure of the hunter in this painting, though human-like in appearance, in fact depicts a spirit being, one of a class of such beings known as *mimih*. Wispish and delicate but nevertheless agile, *mimih* are believed to inhabit crannies in the rocky escarpment that dominates the landscape of Western Arnhem Land. From their abodes within the rock face they carry on a form of life precisely parallel to that of ordinary living humans, engaging in such activities as hunting, fighting and ceremonials. It was through observing the practices of these spirits that people in the past learned, among other things, how to hunt, to cook, to divide up game in the proper way, and to dance. But above all, *mimih* taught them how to paint. Small red monochrome paintings of *mimih* figures abound on the walls of caves in the escarpment. Many of these, as a matter of fact, are extremely old and are thought by archaeologists to have been produced between nine and eighteen thousand years ago, though the exact dating remains a subject of some controversy. Kunwinjku people, however, assert that the figures were painted by *mimih* themselves, and that they accurately portray both their bodily appearance and their customary activities (Taylor 1996: 89, 183–4).

So much for the figure of the hunter, but what about the figure of the kangaroo? This could be read on two levels. On the one hand the kangaroo is a perfectly ordinary animal, which is hunted and killed for food. Long ago, *mimih* used to hunt kangaroo to eat, as humans do today, and many stories are told of their exceptional skill and prowess in this regard (Carroll 1977: 123–5, Taylor 1996: 134). Yet paradoxically, these stories have virtually nothing to say about the activity of hunting itself, and focus almost exclusively on the procedure for cutting up and cooking the animal once it has been killed. Likewise in depictions of *mimih* hunters apparently spearing kangaroos, such as that in Figure 7.3, neither the behaviour of the animal on encountering the hunter, nor its attitude in death, is portrayed. It is rather shown as if already dead, and collapsed upon the ground. The area enclosed by the body profile is schematically divided into sections by double parallel lines, which also indicate the way in which the carcass should be cut up for presentation to various categories of kin. The picture can thus be interpreted as a kind of instruction manual, carrying the imprimatur of the *mimih* spirits, for butchery and distribution. In some pictures, the animal is shown already dismembered into several pieces (Carroll 1977: 123). As the distribution of cuts follows the paths of kinship, so the image of the divided animal body provides a kind of scheme or template for the enactment of significant human relationships (Taylor 1996: 199, 225–7). But neither in the pictures nor in the accompanying stories is there a sense of the animal as anything other than mere meat, or of the hunt as an encounter entailing any kind of relationship between one animate being and another.

Read on another level, however, the figure of the kangaroo is a portrayal of no ordinary animal. It depicts, rather, an ancestral being, one of many whose world-shaping activities are recounted in the stories of the Dreaming. The ancestral standing of such beings is usually indicated by means of a 'geometric' internal division of the body area into triangular or rhombic panels which are filled in with fine cross-hatching (Taylor 1996: 139–43). This cross-hatching produces a shimmering effect that is understood as an emanation of the ancestral power immanent in the depiction: the closest equivalent in Western experience, perhaps, is the brilliance of a stained glass window lit up by sunlight.[3] In the painting shown in Figure 7.3 these features are not pronounced, and so it is probably not intended to be interpreted on this level. But many other paintings on the same theme, complete with a *mimih* hunter in the corner, do depict the kangaroo in a vividly 'ancestral' light (Taylor 1996: 23, 180). Once again the animal is portrayed, by contrast to the hunter, as fundamentally inanimate. This does not mean, however, that it is dead rather than alive, as in the first-level reading. Ancestral beings are inanimate in the same way as is the land they energise: their presence *underlies* the cycle of life and death in which the existence of all mortal creatures, both human and animal, is suspended.

Now painting, whether on cave walls or bark shelters, is one of the ways through which the order of the Dreaming is presented to humans. Another way is through their observation of the landscape itself, created as it was through ancestral activity. One can, rather literally, 'follow' the story of creation either by walking about over the landscape and attending to its features, or by similarly roaming with one's eyes across the surface of the picture. It might be suggested, on these grounds, that the painting should be understood as a kind of map of the landscape. Thus the body of the ancestral being, depicted in the form of an animal (the kangaroo), would stand for the landscape in its totality, and its internal divisions to places and the relations between them, and between their respective inhabitants. Yet while there is certainly a correspondence between the form of the painting and the morphology of the landscape, it would not be right to suppose that the one *represents* the other. Rather, both landscape and painting exist on the same ontological level, as alternative ways in which an underlying, ancestral order is *revealed* to human experience (Taylor 1996: 229–32, see Morphy 1991: 221–2, 237). The immobility of the animal in the painting, then, is strictly equivalent to the permanence of the landscape: the movement is entirely on the side of the painter through whose work the form of the ancestral being is gradually unveiled, just as it is on the side of the hunter who makes his way through the terrain.

But likewise in the painting, the movement appears to be wholly on the side of the *mimih* spirit as it clambers over the motionless body of the ancestral creator being. Like ordinary humans, *mimih* have no creative power of their own but are bound to an already established order of things. And in these spirits living humans see the reflections of themselves. Thus the relation between the *mimih*-figure and the ancestral kangaroo in the painting is precisely analogous both to that between the painter and the world as it is revealed through his work, and to that between the hunter and the landscape over which he roams in pursuit of game. The human painter, depicting the *mimih*, paints his own reflection as it looks back at him from the rock face. It is almost a self-portrait, but not quite, for the human's activity of painting is reflected back as the spirit's activity of hunting. In this the equivalence between hunting and painting, as alternative ways of opening up an ancestral order to visual perception, is perfectly epitomised – though I should stress again that hunting, in Aboriginal understanding, is primarily a kind of movement on the land rather than something you do to, or with, animals. This interpretation, incidentally, immediately makes sense of Kunwinjku assertions to the effect that the original *mimih* paintings were produced by the spirits themselves. But ancestral beings do not paint themselves; they simply *are*, and are revealed in the enduring forms of their creation.

Three further stylistic features of totemic depiction follow from what I have said so far. First, animal-like figures are not generally arranged together to form a narrative scene. For to show such a figure engaged in any kind of activity, on its own or with others, would be fundamentally incompatible with both readings of what it depicts, whether the dead body of a creature that has been hunted and killed or the body of an ancestral being metamorphosed into the landscape. It is true that in some compositions, animal figures appear in symmetrically disposed pairs (Taylor 1996: 164), but this appears to be in the interests of formal balance rather than due to any narrative requirements. Once again, this is in striking contrast to paintings of anthropomorphic *mimih* figures, both ancient and recent, which often show many figures together engaged in a variety of activities (Carroll 1977: 122–5, Taylor 1996: 188). Secondly, the animal is specified, in pictorial form, by a fixed profile or silhouette which itself frames the painting. For what is depicted is not a particular being situated within a world, but rather the world as it is enfolded within a particular being. The bodily limits of the being are therefore the limits of the world. There is nothing beyond. Admittedly, in Figure 7.3 the portrait of the *mimih* spirit lies outside the profile of the animal. But as we have seen this portrait, rather like a signature in the corner of a modern Western work of art, is a projection of the identity of the painter rather than a disclosure of the underlying order of the world, and in this sense is not really part of the picture at all. Thirdly, since there is nothing beyond the body profile, we must look to what is *inside* it – to the relations between its divisions and between these and the whole – to understand the significance of the painting. Where, for example, an ancestral being is credited with the creation of sacred objects to be used in ceremonies, these objects are indicated in paintings as organs internal to the ancestral body in its animal form, rather than as implements in its hands (Taylor 1989: 379–80). Here, too, there is an obvious contrast with depictions of *mimih*, which are often shown brandishing tools and weapons that serve to indicate the activities in which they are engaged (Taylor 1996: 187–9).

In order to reinforce my general argument about the static nature of totemic depictions and their association with the morphology of the landscape, I should like to refer briefly to two other painting traditions from Aboriginal Australia, both very different from that of Western Arnhem Land which has been the focus of my discussion up to now. Among peoples of the desert regions of Central Australia, such as the Walbiri, Pintupi and Luritja, animal forms do not appear at all. What are depicted, in the past by being drawn or sculpted in the sand, and nowadays painted in acrylic on board, are not ances-tral beings themselves but the permanent traces of their activity.[4] A horseshoe-shaped motif, for example, indicates the impression that was left in the ground where the kangaroo ancestor sat down to rest; a pair of parallel wavy lines is the path left in the sand by the ancestral python, and a cluster of small circles are the eggs laid by the ancestral lizard. To each of these motifs there correspond specific features of the landscape: the kangaroo's resting place is a water-hole, the snake's track a creek-bed, the python's eggs a patch of rounded boulders (Layton 1985: 437–8). In sand-drawings and paintings, graphic elements of this kind are linked by connecting lines into a kind of network, and the various routes that can be traced through the network correspond to the paths taken by ancestral beings as they travelled from place to place, creating the landscape as they went.

Now in these depictions from the Australian Central Desert, just as in those from Western Arnhem Land, nothing is going on, or being done. They portray a world that is already made, not one in the making. Yet the two traditions of painting seem to be the exact inverse of one another. In the first we see an unbounded ground, but no animal figures – only 'black holes' corresponding to their enduring imprints in the surface of the earth. In the second we see bounded animal figures, but no ground – there is nothing beyond them. Further reflection, however, shows these to be mutually exclusive alterna-tives. For to combine figure and ground – that is, to show the animal figures and their imprints in the landscape *together* in the same composition – would at once be to convert it into a narrative scene of the world-in-creation. Suppose, for example, that we were to take a figure depicting the ancestral kangaroo and place it upon a line of horseshoe-motifs to show its track. The effect would be to turn the figure inside out: no longer enfolding the world in its being, the kangaroo ancestor would be portrayed instead as a being in the world, engaged in the activity of journeying from place to place with its character-istic alternation of movement and rest. If, on the other hand, we were to take a depiction of the line of ancestral travel and the impressions left along the way, and add to it an image of the kangaroo-being itself, then the latter would – by its very presence – indi-cate that the depiction is of a world-shaping journey that is still ongoing rather than over and done with. To portray a world whose formation is complete, the agents of creation have either to be removed from the scene, thus demonstrating that their work is finished, or shown metamorphosed into the forms of their own creation, in which case the world itself becomes one with the immobilised bodies of its creators, each of which incorporates the whole in a particular aspect. The first solution has been adopted by the painters of the Central Desert, the second by those of western Arnhem Land.

Among the peoples of the Western Kimberleys of northwestern Australia, we find yet another solution.[5] In this case the figures in paintings, which are found on the walls of certain caves, are immobile like the landscape because they are actually fused with it. That is to say, they are as tied to the sites in which they occur as are the rock faces that bear them. The principal figures depicted in these paintings are anthropomorphic creator beings known as *Wandjina*. These beings are of bulbous, rotund build, somewhat resembling the human neonate, which gives the impression that they would be incapable of supporting themselves, let alone of autonomous movement. The head is usually surrounded by a broad, halo-like band often divided by lines that radiate outwards. Having neither mouths with which to breathe or sing, nor ears to hear, they are clearly inanimate, while their large round eyes stare vacantly out from the rock face. The *Wandjina* figures are often accompanied by similarly lifeless figures of animal form, depicting the species that they are supposed to have originally brought into being. According to Aboriginal legend, having shaped the landscape through their activities in the Dreaming, the *Wandjina* eventually came to rest at particular sites where they can still be seen. At these sites, they literally painted themselves into the cave walls. Living humans paint too, of course: thus every clan is responsible for the regular retouching of the *Wandjina* in its own country, in order to keep them in good condition. For if a painting were to fade and disappear, so would the being it depicts, and with it would go the life-giving energy which it imparts to the land. Painting as retouching, in short, is not just a matter of disclosing an already created world, but of conserving or looking after it.

Both in appearance and in status, the *Wandjina* of the Kimberleys are at the opposite end of the scale from the *mimih* of Arnhem Land. *Mimih*, as we have seen, are mobile, and in ancient times they used the walls of caves as convenient surfaces on which to depict their everyday activities in a straightforwardly narrative style, subsequently copied by human beings. But the *Wandjina* did not paint pictures of themselves *on* the rock, they painted themselves *into* it. In the painting, they metamorphosed into their own depictions. *Wandjina* figures, in short, are not depictions *of* anything. Rather, they *are* what they depict, the creator beings themselves, forever immobilised in the rock face. Comparing the *mimih* figures with the animal forms of ancestral beings in the paintings of Western Arnhem Land, we have seen that in the first case depiction is a mode of narration, and in the second a mode of revelation. In the *Wandjina* of the Kimberleys, by contrast, depiction is a mode of being.

Carving the spirits: the circumpolar North

Now let me return to Figure 7.4, and from the totemic ontology of Aboriginal Australia to the very different, animic system of northern circumpolar societies – exemplified in this instance by the Inuit. There is no doubt that the drawing depicts a narrative scene. Critically, it is one in which the animal is just as much a participant as the human hunter. Both are clearly situated in an environment, with a ground surface and scrub vegetation. There is, indeed, a world of difference between the observation of a living animal in its normal environment and the examination of its anatomical form, as though it were laid out before you like a corpse. On a surface reading, this is what distinguishes the figure of the caribou in Davidialuk Alasuaq's picture from Namerredje Guymala's rendering of the kangaroo. The picture is a finely observed portrayal of the characteristic posture and behaviour of the caribou when it encounters the hunter face to face. It is a fact well known both to hunters and to biologists who have set out to study caribou behaviour by scientific methods, that at the point when the animal becomes aware of the close presence of a potential predator, whether human or non-human, it stands still, turning to stare directly at its pursuer (see Chapter One, p. 13). The attitude of the animal at this point, and the tension and suspense of the moment, are beautifully caught in the picture.

From my discussion in Chapter One, it will be recalled that native people have a particular explanation for why the caribou stands its ground. This is the moment, they say, at which the animal intentionally offers itself up to the hunter. This leads us to a deeper reading of the drawing of the caribou in Figure 7.4, which once again contrasts with the 'inside' reading of the figure of the kangaroo in Kunwinjku painting. Recall that the latter reveals a motionless essence, embodied in the land, upon which is founded the life-cycles of ordinary, mortal creatures. The depiction of the caribou, to the contrary, reveals powers of agency, intentionality, and sentience embodied in a living, moving being. On this reading, the human hunter relates to the animal as one such being to another, and the encounter is a moment in the ongoing dialogue between them. Among hunters who take this view of animals, there is a general feeling that one should not kill an animal that does not consent to be taken. To kill without the animal's active connivance would be an act of violence, carrying the threat of equally violent retribution in the future. How, then, can a hunter know for sure whether an animal means to give itself up or not? This dilemma, a very real one in the experience of Inuit and other northern hunting peoples, is fundamentally what the drawing is about. Let us take a closer look at what is going on.

Like humans, animals reveal their identities and intentions through their behaviour. But the animal in the picture is behaving suspiciously. Specifically, it has a sprig of willow clenched between its jaws. With this, it seems to be trying to say something. But what? Could it be a warning of some kind? The hunter does not know for sure. Uncertain about the caribou's intentions towards him he turns his eyes away from its gaze, and does not shoot. Another picture by Davidialuk Alasuaq, reproduced in Figure 7.5, shows what could have happened had he done so. Here the arrow has already penetrated the body of the caribou, whose forelegs are giving way in a posture that vividly portrays its imminent death. But look at the faces of the hunter and his prey! The man stares at us with an expression of wide-eyed terror. As for the animal, the skin and fur covering of its head has been pulled back to reveal a wolf-like visage, with round eyes, a long, thin snout and bared fangs. The gentle caribou has turned into a frightening predator, and we are left wondering who, in fact, is hunting whom.[6]

Now animals that appear thus, with the head covering removed or retracted, are known as 'hoodless' (*nasaittuq*).[7] Generally, they are individuals that have been maltreated in one way or another by humans in the past, and therefore harbour some malice towards them. I have already shown how, in an animic system, the regeneration of the lifeworld depends

Figure 7.5 On killing a hoodless caribou. Drawing by Davidialuk Alasuaq, from the personal collection of Professor Bernard Saladin d'Anglure.

From B. Saladin d'Anglure, *Inuit and caribou*, published by Université Laval, Canada, 1979, p. 63.

upon the maintenance of balance in the reciprocal give-and-take of vital force. Animals give life to humans, but humans should receive only what is offered rather than seek to extract vitality by forcible or violent means. For otherwise the animals, seeking equally violent recompense, would be turned from life-givers to life-takers. This is precisely what has happened in the case of the hoodless caribou depicted in Figure 7.5. Significantly *nasaittuq*, if killed, are deemed to be inedible: as potential eaters of human beings they cannot be eaten *by* humans – not, at least, without courting considerable danger.

However the image of the retractable hood tells us something more, about the way in which living beings are generally thought to be constituted in animic systems. Despite considerable variation in the detail, a fundamental division is always recognised into two parts: an interior, vital part that is the source of all awareness, memory, intention and feeling, and an exterior, bodily covering that provides the equipment and confers the powers that are necessary to conduct a particular form of life.[8] The first is continuous through time, the second is inherently unstable. Creatures of the sea, for example, can exchange fins and flippers for the armature of a terrestrial quadruped, or vice versa: whales, say the Yup'ik of Alaska, can turn into wolves (Fienup-Riordan 1994: 74–5), but behind the altered bodily form and lifestyle lies a continuity of being. Now for animals in their own communities, as for humans in theirs, the body is transparent. Beings perceive and interact with one another directly, wearing their feelings and intentions, so to speak, 'on the surface', and above all – as we shall see – on the face. However it is not ordinarily possible for a human being to perceive a living animal in this way: its true face remains concealed behind the bodily covering. To witness it 'face-to-face', with its hood removed, one must already have crossed over from the human to the animal domain. Indeed a common theme of stories all around the circumpolar North is of how a traveller, having lost his or her bearings in the human world, strays or is lured into the abode of a certain animal, whereupon the latter stands revealed in its inner being. For the traveller, this is a dangerous, indeed potentially fatal predicament. One may never make it back to the company of humankind. Small wonder, then, that the hunter depicted in Figure 7.5 looks scared. For not only does the hoodless caribou, its predatory intentions revealed, pose a direct threat to life and limb, but also the very sight of it casts a pall of uncertainty over his existential status as a human being.

In short, the faces of animals are visible only to humans who have taken up the subject positions of the animals themselves, and who have therefore – in the eyes of other humans – actually *turned into* animals. Only shamans have the power to do this intentionally and with relative impunity. Human beings can, however, invoke the presence of animals in their midst by means of masks. Here, in effect, it is the animal, whose inner being or spirit is revealed on the surface of the mask, which takes up the subject position of a human, namely that occupied by the mask-bearer. The carving of wooden masks depicting the faces of animals and other non-humans, for display in dances and ceremonies, is widespread among the indigenous peoples of the circumpolar North. In some regions, such as among Inuit and Yup'ik people of Alaska, and on the American northwest coast, the construction of masks reached quite extraordinary degrees of elaboration. This is not the place for a detailed analysis of their symbolic content.[9] I want merely to make three general observations about the depiction of animals in masks. First, the central component of every mask, around which all else revolves, is a face. Secondly, the mask is not a disguise intended to hide the identity of the bearer. Thirdly, in appearance, the masks often show little obvious resemblance to the animals whose spirits they are supposed to depict.

As a surface, the face has some very peculiar properties. I can feel my own face, and others can see it. But it remains invisible to me. Where others see my face, I see the world. Thus the face is the visible appearance, in others' eyes, of my own subjective presence as an agent of perception. It is, if you will, the *look* of human being. By the same token, the face-depicting mask is the look of non-human being. Both face and mask are the phenomenal forms of 'the Other as Subject', that is, as the 'second person' whom one would address as 'you' and who would respond in kind (Viveiros de Castro 1998: 483). Now when the hunter in Figure 7.5 witnessed the caribou with its hood drawn back, what he saw was the animal's real face. However, far from its having been unmasked, as a conventional understanding of masking as disguise or cover-up would lead us to expect, *the mask was what was revealed*. In other words, the mask is not the skin and fur of the hood but the face itself. As visible manifestations of inner being, face and mask are ontologically equivalent. Thus a being can no more look through a mask than it can look through its own face. There is no face peering out from behind the mask. In effect the identity of the human mask-bearer is not so much disguised as displaced by the mask he carries. For this reason, in masked dances the eyes of the bearers should be downcast – rendered passive in order to make way for the active perceptual powers of the mask (Fienup-Riordan 1987).[10]

Moreover, precisely because the mask's purpose is to reveal the true, or spirit face of the animal rather than to conceal that of its human bearer behind an animal disguise, its appearance is nothing like the animal's facial covering. The standard features of the mask-face include eyes, mouth and nostrils. On perceiving these features we are inclined to regard the face as human, or at least human-like, in appearance, and there is some evidence that native people did the same, thus supposing that animal spirits are human in form (Oosten 1992: 115–16). Yet the faces on many masks are so grotesquely distorted that they bear no more resemblance to the human visage than to that of any other creature, and mask-makers were certainly not constrained by any conventions of realism. Their aim, it seems, was not to depict any attributes of morphology or behaviour that might be drawn from empirical observation of the animal in question, but rather to capture the underlying character and personal idiosyncrasies attributed to the spirit that has assumed its form. This was done by inflecting the curve of the mouth, the splay of the nostrils or the slant of the eyes in recognisable ways. Some masks have hinged flaps of outwardly naturalistic appearance, but these are designed to open up so as to disclose the face, effecting a transformation precisely equivalent to the caribou's removal of its hood. Other masks achieve the same effect through visual punning or figure–ground reversal: thus a whale's-tail mask looks realistic enough when viewed from one angle, but from another the contours of the tail turn out to reveal a mouth, nose and browridges (Ray 1967: 212 and Plate 52, Oosten 1992: 128–9, see also Carpenter 1966: 224).

It is in the matter of clothing, not masks, that considerations of animals' diverse bodily forms, and of the behavioural capacities that go along with them, come to the fore. Circumpolar hunters attach great importance to clothing, dressing up in the skins and furs of the animals they have killed. Of course they have to keep warm, but there is more to it than that. We have seen that animals' bodily covering is understood as so much equipment which enables them to lead the kinds of lives they do. Human beings differ from other animals in that they are born naked, without any covering. To survive, they must clothe themselves with animal bodies, and in so doing, they can also draw on the effectivities these bodies confer (see Chapter Six, p. 94). Very often, parts of the animal skin would be tailored to cover corresponding parts of the human body: thus the skin of the head would be made into a hood, that of the legs into trousers and boots, and so on (Chaussonnet 1988: 213). In short, whereas animals take body-skin *off* to reveal themselves in their inner being, humans put it *on* in order to function in the world.[11] This is the difference between the bear and the man in Figure 7.1. The man wears a coat, leaving his face and hands uncovered. The bear, however, has uncovered his face and hands by peeling back the skin. The one, in a sense, dresses up, the other dresses down. Dressing in skin clothing, however, is very different from wearing a mask. For the mask is distinguished from clothing precisely as the inner being of the animal is distinguished from its exterior body. Dressed in its skin, the human acquires the effectivities of the animal; donning the mask, the human makes way for the spirit of the animal.

Before leaving the subject of masks, I should like to comment on a curious feature of masks from the Kuskokwim-Yukon area of Alaska. One such is illustrated in Figure 7.6A. This is an example of the type of mask referred to above, with hinged doors that open to reveal a face. Painted on the inside surface of each door are quite realistic, silhouette depictions of seals (on the left) and caribou (on the right). Now the mask-face belongs to a *tunghak*, one of the spirit 'masters' or keepers of game animals. Evidently, the *tunghak* has its charges in mind, since even with the shutters closed the seal and caribou figures dance before its eyes. Now it is often said in these parts that a hunter, if he is to succeed, should likewise keep the animals he will pursue at the forefront of his thoughts. Thinking of animals is one of the ways of keeping up a proper relationship with them; conversely the animals, if well regarded, will think positively of humans. Yup'ik hunters, according

Figure 7.6 Two masks from the Kuskokwim-Yukon area of Alaska, from Nelson (1983 [1896–7]: Plates 50 and 51). The first (A) depicts a spirit master of the animals (*tunghak*). According to Nelson (1983: 406) the animal figures on the inside left shutter are seals; Ray, however, claims they are whales (1967: 65). A colour photograph of the same mask appears in Fitzhugh (1988: 306 fig. 435), but in this the figures on the left appear too worn to be identified with certainty. The second mask (B) depicts a salmon, with its back cut away to reveal the face of the salmon's *inua*, or spirit.

From E. W. Nelson, *The Eskimo about Bering Strait*, published by Smithsonian Institution Press, 1983, p. 408.

to Fienup-Riordan, 'admonished young men to "keep the thought of seals" foremost in their minds as they shoveled snow, carried out trash, and hauled water' (1994: 53). So whatever he is doing, whether actually out hunting or engaged in routine domestic chores, the animals should always be there before a man's mind's eye. Hunters, as we might say, typically have animals 'on the brain'. In the extraordinary, bird-like hunting helmets traditionally worn by the Aleut, adorned with exquisitely lifelike animal figurines carved from ivory, and sometimes painted with narrative depictions of hunting scenes as well, this became almost literally true (Rousselot, Fitzhugh and Crowell 1988: 152, 164–5). But the carving of realistic animal figurines is a practice of truly circumpolar distribution, and – besides the significance attached to masks and clothing – is probably one of the most distinctive features of animic depiction. I would like to conclude this section with a few words about it.

In my analysis of the animal depictions of Western Arnhem Land, I showed how the activity of painting can be compared, in a certain sense, to that of hunting. In the circumpolar North there is a similar parallel between carving and hunting. Yet the similarity hides a contrast, for in the experience of the carver, hunting is not so much a movement through the terrain as a mode of relating to animals. The important thing in hunting is never to impose one's will upon animals, to force them against their inclinations. When it is ready, but not before, the animal reveals itself to the hunter, who can then gracefully receive its gift of bodily substance. In just the same way, carving is not the wilful imposition of preconceived form on brute matter, but a process in which the carver is continually responsive to the intrinsic qualities of the material, to how it wants to be. The following passage, in which Edmund Carpenter describes an Inuit carver at work, could almost have been written of the hunter on the ice:

> As the carver holds the unworked ivory lightly in his hand, turning it this way and that, he whispers, 'Who are you? Who hides there?' And then: 'Ah, Seal!' . . . Then he brings it out: seal, hidden, emerges. It was always there: He did not create it. He released it: he helped it step forth.
>
> (1966: 206)

If painting, for the people of Western Arnhem Land, is a way of focusing attention on the land and its immanent ancestral powers, then carving for the Inuit and other peoples of the North is a way of keeping animals in mind. Moreover it is the process – of dwelling on the animals in one's thought – that is important, rather more than the products – the carvings themselves – which are readily lost or discarded (Carpenter 1966: 212).

This interpretation helps us to make sense of two outstanding features of carved animal figurines: their minute size and their realism (Figure 7.7). Among carvings from the so-called Dorset Culture, dating to as early as 800 BC, Carpenter notes that one – of a ptarmigan – 'is scarcely larger than the head of a match', another – of a running bear, complete with claws – 'is less than three-eighths of an inch high', and a third – of a glaucous gull – 'weighs less than one-sixtieth of an ounce'. Yet each was so accurate that there could be no doubt about the species depicted (1966: 218). These tiny objects are the material embodiments of thoughts, or more strictly they *are* thoughts. For the carver would not separate thinking in the head from thinking with the hands, nor, consequently, would he distinguish the products of these respective activities. But as embodied thoughts, carvings are of such a microcosmic scale that they can be turned around in the hand as can images in the mind. They are not designed to be set upon a pedestal and looked at, indeed most will not stand up unless artificially mounted. Rather, like memories, they are held close to the person – generally fastened to the clothing – and are carried around with that person wherever he or she goes. Indeed the relation between the hunter and the miniature figurines he carries is precisely analogous to that between the *tunghak* depicted in the mask shown in Figure 7.6A and the tiny animal figures painted on its inside doors. Both the mask-spirit who has seals and caribou to bestow, and the hunter who has hopes of receiving them, have animals in mind.

These little animals are like tokens in the ongoing relationship of give and take between human hunters and the spirit beings on whose continued generosity the supply of game depends. They are, in that sense, equivalent to the animals actually killed in the hunt, and this accounts for the realism of their depiction. Equally lifelike figures are frequently carved on hunting and other equipment: knife-handles, harpoon heads, toggles, lamps, bowls and containers, and sundry other items could all be ornamented in this way. As Fitzhugh explains, throughout northern North America (and for that matter, in the Eurasian North as well), 'hunting art, the ornamentation of weapons, and the use of ritual hunting clothing were the hunter's way of asking for the gift of an animal rather than overpowering it physically or spiritually' (1988: 310–11). It should come as no surprise, then, that among Australian Aboriginal hunter-gatherers, who have no such reciprocal ties with animal-donors, the ornamentation of equipment is conspicuously absent. Indeed in the relation between the ancestral beings of Western Arnhem Land and the tiny *mimih* spirits we find the precise inverse of the relation, among northern circumpolar hunters, between human or spirit beings and the little animal tokens that they carry. Where the human-like *mimih* adheres to the much larger body of the zoomorphic ancestral being, the carved animal figurine adheres to the clothing of the hunter, and the painted animal silhouette to the mask of the spirit.

SOME MORE COMPARISONS

I have shown that perhaps the most fundamental contrast between the totemic and animic depiction of animals is between a

Figure 7.7 Miniature waterfowl carved in walrus ivory by Inuit of the Ungava District, northern Quebec; from Turner (1979 [1889–90]: 96 fig. 63). The species depicted include loons, eider ducks, geese, sea pigeons, and guillemots. Turner writes: 'It is readily discerned, in most instances, what position and action of the bird was intended to be represented. The last shows in the plainest possible manner that the loon is just starting to swim from an object which has given it alarm'.

From L. M. Turner, *Ethnology of the Ungava District*, published by Presses Coméditex, Quebec, 1979.

focus on morphology and anatomy in the former, and on posture, movement and behaviour in the latter. It would be a mistake to infer from this, however, that in totemic society, people know and experience the land, and the ancestral beings that shaped it, only by their final immobile forms. And it would be equally mistaken to infer that in animic society, animals and other non-human beings are known and experienced only by way of their mobility. After all, the animal spirit whose face is carved on a mask is no more shown to be 'doing something' than is the ancestral being whose profile is painted on rock or bark. Neither the painting nor the mask *depicts* movement. The difference between them, however, is that in totemic depiction the significant movement lies in the process of painting itself, whereas in animic depiction it is imparted to the finished object, the mask.

In their ceremonies Australian Aboriginal people re-enact, through song, dance and storytelling, the events of ancestral world-creation. Dance steps, in particular, mime the original movements of the ancestral beings, and are closely modelled on the characteristic postures and gestures of the animals whose forms they take. In storytelling, the narrator may move a finger across the sand in imitation of the movement of the ancestral hero of the story, leaving a trace that has its counterpart in the landscape which the hero shaped in its journey. Now like dancing and storytelling, painting, too, is a performance. The movement of painting is congealed in the depiction just as that of the storyteller is congealed in the traces of his gestures in the sand, or that of the dancers in the imprint of their feet upon the earth. But the analogy is between painting, dancing and storytelling, not between paintings, dances and stories. The painter does not, in his picture, seek to portray the actions of ancestral beings, as do dancers in their steps and storytellers in their words. But like them, he seeks to re-enact ancestral activity – to 'go over' it again and again, quite literally in the case of retouching – in the very movement of his work. Thus while painting *is* an activity, paintings do not *depict* activity.

Carving, of course, is an activity too. But among Inuit and Yup'ik of Alaska, where the making of masks was most highly elaborated, the carving itself was rather quickly and furtively done so, it was said, as not to offend the spirits depicted (Ray 1967: 52). A shaman who had experienced a vision of the spirit in question would often commission an expert carver to do the work for him, according to his instructions. Once completed, the mask would be hidden away, only to be revealed in the ceremony for which it was intended. Here, borne aloft by a dancer and animated by his movements, the mask would come to life, to be witnessed by the audience as a being in their midst. Thus while the Yup'ik or Inuit mask of an animal spirit, in itself, no more depicts activity than does the Australian Aboriginal painting of a totemic ancestor, the former is perceived as a dynamic, mobile presence whereas the latter is perceived as a static locus of congealed power. This difference maps directly onto the basic distinction between totemic and animic ontologies with which I began. It therefore furnishes an explanation for the remarkable ethnographic fact that masks, which are such a striking feature of the animic societies of the circumpolar North, are conspicuously absent from the totemic societies of Aboriginal Australia.

In preparation for dances and ceremonies, however, Australian Aboriginal people do apply painted designs to their own bodies, and it is perhaps to these, rather than to paintings on external surfaces, that the masks of northern circumpolar societies should be compared. Among the Kunwinjku of Western Arnhem Land, the painted body bears the same pattern, consisting of a division into panels filled in with cross-hatching, that is also applied to painted depictions of ancestral beings in their animal forms, thereby establishing the essential consubstantiality of the two (Taylor 1996: 118–19). Thus decorated, a ritual participant becomes the living embodiment of the being whose distinctive pattern he or she bears. So too, the Inuit masked dancer takes on the *persona* of the spirit-being whose face is depicted on the mask he carries. But the similarity hides a crucial contrast. In the masked dance one being, the spirit, takes the place of another, the dancer. In Aboriginal ceremony, to the contrary, the identities of participants merge with those of the beings whose deeds they enact. The mask, in short, effects a displacement, whereas the body painting effects a reincorporation. The one asserts a metaphorical relation of formal substitution, the other a metonymical link of substantial identity.

Almost exactly the same contrast was suggested by Andrew and Marilyn Strathern, in a comparison of modes of self-decoration in the Mount Hagen area with those of the Sepik River and elsewhere in Papua New Guinea. Sepik peoples carve elaborate figures and masks, the people of Hagen do not:

> The process of decoration in Hagen is not representational but metonymical: that is, when Hageners wish to associate themselves with magically powerful things, such as birds, they do not construct masks, carvings or paintings of these. Instead they actually take the *parts* of the birds, their feathers, and attach these to themselves as decorations.
>
> (Strathern and Strathern 1971: 176–7)

Likewise, Australian Aboriginal body decoration enhances the power and vitality of humans through direct contact with ancestral substance, whereas the carved masks of northern circumpolar peoples invoke the presence of non-human sources of power, namely animal spirits, with which humans must perforce transact in order to keep vitality in circulation. In this connection it is significant that disposable parts of animals such as feathers, down and hair, which are used for decoration in both traditions, are attached directly to the body in Aboriginal Australia, but are invariably attached to masks in the circumpolar North.

While body painting can be contrasted along one dimension with masks, along another it can be contrasted with clothing. For northern circumpolar hunters, as we have seen, the body is conceived as a covering that provides the wherewithal to conduct a certain form of life. By 'dressing up' in the bodies of animals, humans can draw on the practical effectivities they confer. Painting the body, however, is quite different from clothing it, for rather than surrounding it with an envelope of capacities, painting serves to bring out, or render visible, its inner constitution. This contrast, in turn, enables us to explain the difference between two quite distinct styles of so-called 'X-ray' depiction. Kunwinjku painters, as we have seen, concentrate on the *insides* of the animal body: its internal parts and organs and their positioning in relation to one another (see Figure 7.3). In the northern style, on the other hand, the X-ray view always reveals what is *inside* the body – its spiritual inhabitant – invariably manifested as a face. An example is shown in Figure 7.6B, another mask from the Kuskokwim-Yukon region of Alaska. The mask portrays the body of the salmon in a somewhat flattened form, but the back has been cut away to reveal the facial features of the salmon's spirit. Quite unlike the totemic style of X-ray depiction, exemplified by Kunwinjku painting, in which the emphasis is on the body's enduring essence, its *bones*; in the animic style of the Yup'ik the body figures as a *skin* that enclothes its spiritual inhabitant. The former style is no more interested in the face than is the latter with the details of internal skeletal architecture.

Finally, there is a contrast to be drawn between painting and carving as techniques of depiction. Australian Aboriginal people were traditionally skilled carvers, yet with the exception of some crude specimens intended for the tourist market (Layton 1992a: 151–2), they did not carve animal figures. Northern circumpolar people, conversely, knew very well how to paint, and they applied paint to – among other things – their carved masks. But painted depictions of animals or other beings are remarkably rare. I would like to suggest that the difference between painting and carving might be related to that between the totemic focus on the land and the animic focus on its living inhabitants. This suggestion is admittedly speculative, and doubtless calls for a good deal of qualification and refinement. Nevertheless, the parallel between painting, as a movement that 'goes over' and transforms a surface, and the movement of ancestral beings going over and transforming the surface of the earth, seems more than coincidental. Likewise, there is a remarkable affinity between carving, as a way of bringing out the form immanent in a lump of material, be it ivory, wood or stone, and the animic understanding of being as immanent within the manifold appearances of the lifeworld. I have shown, moreover, that while painting is akin to hunting in the totemic context, where to hunt is to make one's way over the land, carving is akin to hunting in the animic context, where to hunt is to engage in a dialogue with its non-human inhabitants.

CONCLUSION

Up to now I have been concerned with the differences between totemic and animic depiction. To conclude, it is time to turn to what they have in common. This is most easily expressed in terms of what they are *not*. In a word, they are not representational. Neither in their painting nor in their carving do people seek to reconstruct the material world they know, through their mundane subsistence pursuits of hunting and gathering, on a higher plane of cultural or symbolic meaning. Whether their primary concern be with the land or its non-human inhabitants, their purpose is not to represent but to reveal, to penetrate beneath the surface of things so as to reach deeper levels of knowledge and understanding. It is at these levels that meaning is to be found. There is no division, here, between 'ecology' and 'art', as though hunting were merely a matter of organic provisioning and carving or painting gave vent to the free play of the symbolic imagination. This division, along with the dualism of nature and culture on which it rests, is of modern provenance, and it lies behind the conventional notion of the work of art as proof of a uniquely human capacity for creative thought and expression.

It is commonly believed that art, like language, is a species universal whose evolutionary emergence marked the advent of humanity itself. This belief, however, belongs to a Western myth of origin which, like all such myths, does more to legitimate the present than shed light on the past. Projecting onto our hunter-gatherer forbears the capacities for everything we most value in contemporary civilisation, the entire course of history – including the history of art – is revealed as the glorious but pre-ordained movement of their progressive fulfilment.[12] The famous paintings of Lascaux or Chauvet surprise us because they seem better than they ought to be at such an early epoch, but we never doubt that they are art. Of course we know nothing about how the people who painted these pictures, some 30,000 years ago, felt about animals, ancestors and the land. It is, however, extremely unlikely that they subscribed to the hierarchical ranking of humanity over nature that leads contemporary Western observers to celebrate their achievement as the high point of artistic development in prehistory. Such ranking would certainly have been utterly inconceivable within the totemic and animic ontologies that I have discussed here.

To be sure, hunters and gatherers have been painting and carving figures of one kind or another for thousands of years. But only in recent times, now that their paintings and carvings have entered the Western 'art world' – where they attract curiosity, admiration and sometimes high prices – have these people begun to engage in the production of art in the conventional art-world sense of objects for sale or for display in museums and galleries. Hunters and gatherers of the past were painting and carving, but they were not 'producing art'. To understand the original significance of what they were doing, I contend, we must cease thinking of painting and carving as modalities of the production of art, and view art instead as one rather peculiar, and historically very specific objectification of the activities of painting and carving. We are right to admire the skills of Australian Aboriginal painters, and of Inuit and Yup'ik carvers. Like all skills, they are acquired through practice and training within an environment. They are not, however, culturally specific dialects of a naturally evolved, and developmentally preconstituted 'capacity for art'. The existence of such a capacity is a figment of the Western imagination.

Chapter Eight

Ancestry, generation, substance, memory, land

INTRODUCTION

'Indigenous or aboriginal peoples', according to a recent United Nations document, 'are so-called because they were living on their lands before settlers came from elsewhere' (United Nations 1997: 3). At the time of colonisation, they were the original inhabitants. This is no guarantee, of course, that their forbears had not, during some earlier wave of population movement, displaced a yet earlier people, nor is it to deny that people of settler origin might develop deep and lasting attachments to the land. But these possibilities raise some awkward questions. Does not the conflation of the two terms, indigenous and aboriginal, merely perpetuate a thoroughly Eurocentric image of the precolonial world as a mosaic of cultures and territories that was already fixed in perpetuity before history began? And is it reasonable to withhold indigenous status from persons who were born and raised in a country, among people who likewise have a lifelong familiarity with it, on no other grounds than that many generations previously, their ancestors had arrived from somewhere else?[1] Behind both questions is a more fundamental issue about what it actually means to be an 'original inhabitant'. Suppose – as is widely the case – that the people who were already living on the land when the settlers arrived are no longer alive today. On what grounds can contemporary generations partake of the 'originality' of their predecessors?

In the official organs of the United Nations and the International Labour Organisation (ILO), this question is answered in terms of *descent*. Thus the document cited above goes on to explain, in the same passage, that indigenous peoples 'are the descendants – according to one definition – of those who inhabited a country or a geographical region at the time when people of different cultures or ethnic origins arrived'.[2] This answer, however, intro-duces paradoxes of its own. For the descendants of these prior inhabitants of the country need no longer live there. Indeed in many cases a substantial majority do not. The very idea that originality can be passed on by descent, along chains of genealogical connec-tion, seems to imply that it is a property of persons that can be transmitted, rather like a legacy or endowment, independently of their habitation of the land. On the other hand, this very habitation is claimed as the root source of aboriginal identity. How, then, can an identity that lies in people's belonging to the land reappear as a property that belongs to them? There is a profound contradiction here, which it is my purpose in this article to explore. It turns, as I shall argue, on the interpretation of five terms that have been central to the debate on indigenous peoples, as conducted by academics, policy-makers and representative organisations of the peoples themselves. They are: ancestry, generation, substance, memory and land.

I aim to show that the meanings of these terms are linked, within this debate, by way of their common grounding in what I shall call the 'genealogical model'. I begin by spelling out this model, and the assumptions it entails: that original ancestry lies at the point where history rises from an ahistorical substrate of 'nature'; that the generation of persons involves the transmission of biogenetic substance prior to their life in the world; that ancestral experience can be passed on as the stuff of cultural memory, enshrined in language and tradition; and that the land is merely a surface to be occupied, serving to support its inhabitants rather than to bring them into being. I go on to argue that the genealogical model fundamentally misrepresents the ways in which the peoples whom *we* class as indigenous – that is, who are regarded as such from a sympathetic, anthropologically informed perspective – actually constitute their identity, knowledgeability, and the environments in which they live. I suggest an alternative, *relational* approach to interpreting the five key terms which is more consonant with these people's lived experience of inhabiting the land. In this approach, both cultural knowledge and bodily substance are seen to undergo continuous generation in the context of an ongoing engagement with the land and with the beings – human and non-human – that dwell therein. I conclude that it is in confronting the need to articulate their experience in an idiom compatible with the dominant discourses of the state that people are led to lay claim to indigenous status, in terms that nevertheless systematically invert their own understandings.

Before proceeding further I should enter two qualifications. First, it may reasonably be objected that formal attempts to define the indigenous can only be understood in the political context of peoples' struggles, against the odds, to restore their security, dignity, well-being and self-esteem after years of marginalisation and oppression. The intent and meaning of any definition, in other words, must lie in the effort to reconfigure the relations between a historically disadvantaged and numerically under-represented minority and the encompassing nation state (Saugestad 1998: 31). To focus exclusively on criteria of eligibility – let alone on one particular criterion, that of descent – in isolation from the contexts of their application, surely misses the point. My response to this objection is simply to stress that what follows is not intended as a contribution to the analysis of the relations between indigenous minorities and nation states. Rather, I take one particular definition of indigenous status, formulated by the ILO, as an example of a way of thinking about what it means to be indigenous which, I believe, is symptomatic of more fundamental patterns of thought. It is these underlying patterns that I aim to explore. To observe that people face a genuine dilemma in articulating their aspirations within the hegemonic discourse of their erstwhile oppressors is not to question the worth or the integrity of their political project. They may indeed have no alternative.

The second qualification concerns the connection between the genealogical model and the troublesome notion of modern or Western thought. The examples on which I draw come predominantly from studies of hunting and gathering societies. In such societies, people are rarely concerned with tracing paths of genealogical ancestry and descent. Yet we know from ethnography that in a great many agricultural and pastoral societies, the narration of such paths is a major preoccupation. Do agriculturalists and pastoralists, then, operate with a genealogical model? Is this, to revert to an older anthropological terminology, what distinguishes 'tribal' from 'band-level' societies? By and large, I think not. As a first hypothesis, I would suggest that genealogical thinking in agricultural and pastoral societies is carried on within the context of a relational approach to the generation of knowledge and substance. That is to say, it is embedded in life-historical narratives of the deeds of predecessors, of their movements and emplacements, and of their interventions

– oftentimes from beyond the grave – in the lives of successors. The genealogical model turns this logic on its head. Here, genealogical connection becomes the context both for thinking about relationships and for their enactment, rather than vice versa. Such a model is indeed characteristic of Western modernity. But I would hesitate to attribute it exclusively to the modernist episteme. Modern thought cannot have sprung, fully fashioned, from nowhere, but must owe something to more deep-seated and enduring forms of consciousness. As a second hypothesis, I would suggest that the genealogical model is an aspect of just such a form and that it belongs, in this respect, with the generative conditions for modernity rather than with modernity *per se*. To test either of the aforementioned hypotheses, however, would call for a major investigation that lies well beyond the scope of the present chapter.

THE GENEALOGICAL MODEL

Ancestry

One of the most potent images in the intellectual history of the Western world has been that of the tree (Deleuze and Guattari 1988: 18). We use tree diagrams to represent hierarchies of control, schemes of taxonomic division, and above all, chains of genealogical connection. It is the tree as genealogy that specifically concerns me here. Early drawings of such trees in the Western tradition draw copiously on Biblical imagery, depicting the family of man as so many branches radiating from a trunk whose roots are planted firmly in the land. Here, at the base of the trunk, lies the autochthonous Adam, the first man – who, as St Paul declared in his Epistle to the Corinthians, is unequivocally 'earthy'. Despite the revolution wrought by evolutionary theory in our conceptions of time and of humankind's place in nature, this basic picture has remained little changed (Bouquet 1995: 42–3). Thus Alfred Kroeber, in his *Anthropology* of 1948, used the Biblical figure of the 'tree of the knowledge of good and evil', rooted in the Garden of Eden, to illustrate his view of the history of human culture as a tree whose branches – unlike those of its neighbour, the 'tree of life' – could grow together as well as split apart (see Figure 8.1). Contemporary palaeo-anthropologists continue to delve in the earth for human origins, and while the earliest ancestors of man are no longer thought to have been specially created but rather to have arisen by way of an evolutionary phylogeny that is itself depicted as a vast genealogical tree, they remain uniquely placed at the roots of history: in possession of the full suite of human capacities, yet still committed – like all other creatures – to a life wholly confined within the natural world.

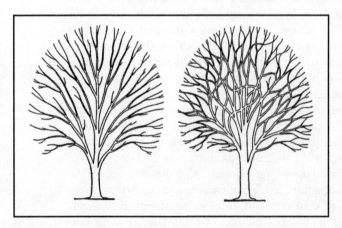

Figure 8.1 'The tree of life and the tree of the knowledge of good and evil – that is, of human culture'.

Reproduced from *Anthropology* by A. L. Kroeber, Harcourt Brace Jovanovich, 1948, p. 260.

Almost invariably, these ancestors are portrayed as hunter-gatherers. Like the earthy Adam, they are supposed to remain *of* the land, as opposed to cultivators who, having broken through the bounds of nature and 'branched out' over the territories of the globe, proceed to settle *upon* it. This opposition, between people *of* and *on* the land, continues to inform public awareness, in the West, of the difference between indigenous people and colonists. The former are seen to embody, in their present way of life, the ancestral condition of those who were 'there first', at the point where history began. Concern for the heritage of indigenous peoples is thus tempered by a perception that they, in turn, represent an essential part of the heritage of global humanity. Their place is understood to lie at the foot of the tree of human culture. As culture rises from the land, branching out into its many lines, so history rises up from the ground of nature. That history, however, is conceived as one of colonisation. In the popular conception, colonists – by the very fact of their occupation of the land – inevitably establish their domination over indigenes, just as culture is bound to dominate nature. Land is there to be occupied, but does not itself contribute to the constitution of its occupants. It therefore lies outside of history.

How, then, is the connection established between ancestral humans and contemporary indigenes? The answer, as we have already seen, is generally couched in the idiom of descent. Present-day indigenous people, it is supposed, are in some sense 'the same' as the people who were there at the very beginning, because the former are descended from the latter. There is, however, a striking contrast between the image of the tree, 'rising up', and that of descent as 'going down', and it is probably no accident that images of the first kind tend to dominate in progressivist accounts of the advance of human civilisation, whereas images of the latter kind appear in more relativistic accounts of the continuity and diversification of local tradition. Certainly, ever since W. H. R. Rivers introduced what he called the 'genealogical method' into anthropological inquiry, it has been conventional to upend the tree, placing its roots at the top (Bouquet 1995: 42–3; 1996). The effect of this inversion, however, is to erase the image of the tree as a living, growing entity, branching out along its many boughs and shoots, and to replace it with an abstract, dendritic geometry of points and lines, in which every point represents a person, and every line a genealogical connection. Thus a vertical line connecting two points, A and B, stands for the proposition, 'person B is descended from person A'.[3] My question, which goes to the heart of anthropological studies of kinship, is: what, exactly, is implied by this line? Or to rephrase the question in negative terms, what does it leave out?

Generation

To begin with the positive part of the answer: the implication is that the essential or substantive components of personhood are 'handed on', fully-formed, as an endowment from predecessors. Their origins, in other words, lie in the completed past, rather than in the present lives of recipients. From this it follows that the practical activities of people in the course of their lives – in relating to others, making artefacts and inhabiting the land – are not themselves generative of personhood but are rather ways of bringing already established personal identities into play. And this, in turn, answers our question in its negative formulation. For if the essential elements of personhood are given by virtue of genealogical connection, independently of the situational contexts of human activity, then a person's location on a genealogical chart – in which every line is a link in a chain of descent – says nothing about his or her actual placement *in the world*.[4] As every person in the chain is but an intermediary, passing on to successors the rudiments of being received from predecessors, what each does in his or her life – though it may influence the possibility of transmission – has no bearing on its content. The circumstances of your existence could affect whether you have many, few or no descendants, but not what you pass on to them. A genealogy therefore presents a history of persons in the very peculiar form of a history of *relatedness*, which unfolds without regard to people's *relationships* – that is to their experience of involvement, in perception and action, with their human and non-human environments. I shall return to the distinction between relatedness and relationship, since it is critical for my argument.

What we have just discovered, cleverly concealed behind the apparently innocent graph of the line of descent, is an assumption that persons are brought into being – that is, generated – independently and in advance of their entry into the lifeworld, through the bestowal of a set of ready-made attributes from their antecedents. This assumption lies at the very core of the genealogical model, and all its remaining features can be derived from it. In particular, it implies that the generation of persons is not a life process. On the contrary, life and growth are conceived as the enactment of identities, or the realisation of potentials, that are already in place. It is descent, the passing down of the components of being underwriting one life-cycle to the site of inauguration of another, that generates persons. Thus the genealogical model, in separating out the generation of persons from their life in the world, also splits the descent-line from the life-line. In so doing it establishes the conventional notion of the *generation*, defined by the Oxford English Dictionary as 'offspring of the same parent regarded as a step in a line of descent from an ancestor'. Whereas life goes on within each generation, descent crosses from one generation to the next in a cumulative, step-by-step sequence (Figure 8.2).

With each new generation, those preceding it regress ever further into the past. Life, however, is lived in the present. Thus the present is set over against the past along the lines of generational succession and replacement. The confinement of life to the present leaves the past lifeless or extinct. Philippe Descola catches the essence of this view, so characteristic of modernity, in his observation that 'the present exists for us only thanks to the inexorable abolition of the past from which it proceeds' (1996b: 226). The idea of the past as an age that is spent, and that has no further part to play in what is to come, is one of the hallmarks of genealogical thinking. But in separating the descent-line from the life-line, the genealogical model also divorces time from being. The events that follow one another along a line of descent, like beads on a string, do not take place in the lives of persons, they *are* persons. The existence of each is collapsed into the moment of the event it represents. And these events, in turn, are suspended in a time that is abstract and chronological (Ingold 1986b: 128–9). The same logic that maps being upon the plane of the present also stretches time to eternity, yielding the classic dichotomy between synchrony and diachrony.

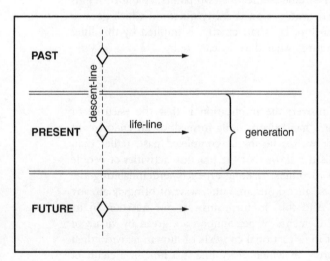

Figure 8.2 The relation between descent-line, life-line and generation, according to the genealogical model.

Arrayed diachronically in linear sequence, reaching back to 'time immemorial', persons of the past are removed from their present descendants by a distance measured out in generations.

Substance

Now it is commonly supposed that the total endowment a person-to-be receives, by way of descent, can be divided into two components, respectively material and ideational. The first comprises the ingredients of bodily substance; the second the contents of cultural memory. It was once customary to speak of the former in terms of kinds – or colours – of 'blood', a usage preserved in the technical concept of consanguineal kinship (connection based on 'shared blood') as well as in a multitude of expressions of everyday currency in the Western world (Schneider 1968: 23–5, Bouquet 1993: 17–21). Nowadays, one is as likely to hear it said of some feature of a person that it is 'in the genes' as to be told that it is 'in the blood'. But the sense of such pronouncements has hardly been altered by the substitution of genetic for sanguinary metaphors. If anything, the science of genetics has not so much challenged as taken on board – and in turn lent authority to – the founding principles of the genealogical model, namely that persons embody certain attributes of appearance, temperament and mentality by virtue of their ancestry, and that these are passed on in a form that is unaffected by the circumstances or achievements of their life in the world. These principles underly the belief, for example, in a species-wide human nature which has come down to us more or less unchanged from its evolutionary origins in the Pleistocene era, while remaining immune to the upheavals of history (see Chapter Twenty-one).

Where, however, the very same principles are adduced to justify a narrower claim to ethnic distinctiveness, based on the assertion of common descent from an 'original' ancestral population, the claim is bound to take on implicitly – if not explicitly – racial overtones. This should come as no surprise, since the concepts of race and of generation, in the specific sense of procreation implied by the genealogical model, are etymologically linked, both derived from the Latin *generare*, 'to beget' (Wolf 1994: 1). All attempts to ascribe indigenous identity on the criterion of descent have been plagued by the problem of miscegenation, and by concern over the degrees of racial impurity to which this is perceived to give rise. What proportion of colonists can one number among one's ancestors while yet qualifying as an indigenous person? If indigenous people are marked out by their common possession of an ancestral essence, how can some persons claim to be more indigenous than others? In practice, efforts to accommodate the real complexities of genealogical connection within essentialist categorisations based on the sharing of substance through descent have invariably led to the endless ramification of ever finer lines of discrimination and exclusion whose imposition – which may have real consequences for those affected in terms of access to resources and arenas of decision-making – appears increasingly arbitrary.

Memory

Turning from the transmitted component of bodily substance to the ideational component of cultural memory, we find the assumptions of the genealogical model replicated, once again, in an approach to culture as a corpus of traditional wisdom, handed down as a legacy from the past, and which is applied or expressed, rather than actually generated, in the contexts of present activity. This approach has venerable anthropological antecedents, and continues to inform much contemporary discussion. Culture, it is commonly said, consists of 'what one needs to know in order to behave as a functioning member of one's society'.[5] Notice how, in this view, the acquisition of cultural knowledge is clearly distinguished from the practicalities of its use that come under the rubric of 'functioning'. What divides acquisition from functioning is none other than the division, inherent in the genealogical model, between the generation of persons and their life in the world. As the descent-line is split off from the life-line, so the intergenerational transmission of knowledge is distinguished from environmentally situated experience. And in psychology as in biology, mainstream science has incorporated the principles of the model into its own conceptual frame. Thus a distinction is posited between 'social learning', by which information is copied into the head of the novice, and 'individual learning', born of the experience of putting it into practice (I return to this distinction in Chapter Twenty-one, pp. 386–7). The former takes place *across* generations; the latter is confined *within* each generation. A glance at Figure 8.2 reveals the congruence between these concepts and the terms of the genealogical model.

What does all this imply about memory? If culture is taken to consist of a body of acquired information that is available for transmission independently of the contexts of its application in the world, then memory must be something like an inner cabinet of the mind, in which this information is stored and preserved from the vagaries of everyday life. Whatever people do, or wherever they go, they carry the contents of memory with them. It is an encyclopaedic resource on which they can continually draw for guidance on how to proceed in a manner appropriate to the circumstances in which they find themselves. Remembering, then is a matter of retrieving from storage – or 'calling up' – items of information relevant to the situation at hand. Critically, this implies that objects of memory pre-exist, and are imported into, the contexts of remembering. They are already present, in some representational form, within the native mind. Thus, far from bringing memories *into* being, remembering serves to bring *out*, or to disclose, knowledge that has been there from the start. In short, from the perspective of the genealogical model, remembering is no more generative of the contents of memory than is life activity generative of the person. And this, in turn, means that if people share memories, it is not because of their mutual involvement in joint activity within a certain environment, but because their knowledge has come down to them from the same ancestral source, along the lines of common descent. They are bound by an identity not only of bodily substance but also of cultural tradition – by both inheritance and heritage.

Land

If the sharing of substance and memory by dint of common descent is what makes people the same, then what makes them different? Here I want to argue that one of the key entailments of the genealogical model is that *difference is rendered as diversity*. That is to say, the model leads us to compare individuals in terms of such qualities as they may possess, by virtue of their essential natures, irrespective of their positioning *vis-à-vis* one another in the world. Diversity is the measure of difference as construed within a comparative project of this kind, one that presumes a world already divided into discrete, unit entities – 'things-in-themselves' – which may then be grouped into classes of progressively higher order on the basis of perceived likeness. This classificatory exercise gives rise to the familiar tree-diagrams of taxonomy, with their roots in the highest, most inclusive levels and branches reaching out into lower levels of ever finer discrimination. Where it is further supposed that every individual derives the specifications of its essential nature by *descent*, then the taxonomic tree readily translates into a genealogical one.

To be sure, the translation is not perfect – a fact that has ignited fierce and still unresolved controversies among scholars engaged in the reconstruction of both evolutionary phylogenies and cultural (especially philological) histories. These controversies need not detain us here:[6] they have to do with the method of reconstruction but do not touch the more fundamental assumption that difference arises from the accumulation of minor variations along lines of descent in the content of transmitted information, whether biogenetic or cultural, due to errors in the process of intergenerational transcription. In genetics these errors are known as mutations; analogous forms of miscopying have often been suggested for the histories of language and culture. Assuming, then, that difference increases with genealogical distance, we might reasonably conclude that one indigenous person is more like another from the same ethnic group than a colonist whose ancestors came from elsewhere, but more like the latter – who is, after all, a fellow human being – than, say, a chimpanzee. But these similarities and differences have absolutely nothing to do with the life-histories of the individuals whom we are comparing: where they have lived, what they have done, or whether they share any experiences in common. Their source, in other words, lies not in current fields of relationship but in past histories of relatedness.

Now as we have already seen, a person's position within such a history – that is, their *genealogical* position – is fixed quite independently of their position and involvement in the lifeworld. It follows that the difference between the indigenous person and the colonist, insofar as it is attributable to descent, does not reflect their respective modalities of habitation of the land. Indeed the land, conceived in its broadest sense as a field of dwelling for beings of all kinds, human and non-human, simply has no place at all within a genealogically inspired conception of biocultural diversity. If each and every individual is constituted by the sum total of bodily substance and cultural knowledge received down the line from ancestors, then the land itself can be no more than a kind of stage upon which is enacted a historical pageant consisting of the succession of generations. At no point does it enter directly into the constitution of persons – with one exception, namely at the mythical point of autochthonous origin. And this takes us back to the question of ancestry.

The genealogical model, it seems, presents us with a stark choice. Either we grant indigenous peoples their historicity, in which case their existence is disconnected from the land, or we allow that their lives are embedded in the land, in which case their historicity is collapsed into an imaginary point of origin. In the first option, an original connection to the land is converted into an object of memory that is handed down as a heritable attribute of individuals without further regard to its source. In the second, it is as though indigenous people lived in suspended animation in a prehistoric world of unadulterated nature which the rest of humanity has long since left behind. Land and history, in short, figure as mutually exclusive alternatives. For indigenous people themselves, by contrast, it is in their relationships with the land, in the very business of dwelling, that their history unfolds. Both the land and the living beings who inhabit it are caught up in the same, ongoing historical process. To comprehend this process, we need a different, relational model, and it is to this that I now turn.

THE RELATIONAL MODEL

Ancestry

'We're tired of trees', sigh Gilles Deleuze and Félix Guattari in a moment of exasperation. 'They've made us suffer too much' (1988: 15). In place of the arborescent, dendritic imagery of the genealogical model they offer an alternative figure, that of the *rhizome*. This is to be envisaged as a dense and tangled cluster of interlaced threads or filaments, any point in which can be connected to any other. Whether the image is botanically accurate need not concern us here.[7] It has the virtue of giving us a way of beginning to think about persons, relationships and land that gets away from the static, decontextualising linearity of the genealogical model, and allows us to conceive of a world in movement, wherein every part or region enfolds, in its growth, its relations with all the others. 'The rhizome', as Deleuze and Guattari repeatedly insist, 'is an antigenealogy' (1988: 11, 21). To put it more positively, it is a progeneration, a continually ravelling and unravelling relational manifold. I believe that a relational model, with the rhizome rather than the tree as its core image, better conveys the sense that so-called indigenous people have of themselves and of their place in the world. In what follows, I review the five terms of my earlier discussion – ancestry, generation, substance, memory, land – in the light of this alternative model. To begin with the first, our question is: what is the meaning of ancestry in a rhizomatic world where the rudiments of being are not transmitted along arboreal lines of genealogical connection?

Part of the difficulty we have in addressing this question lies in the sheer multiplicity of possible answers. Here I suggest just four. Ancestors can be ordinary humans who lived in the past, or spirit inhabitants of the landscape, or mythic other-than-human characters, or original creator beings. As an illustration of the first possibility, consider the following passage in which Signe Howell describes the myriad signs that the Chewong of Malaysia discern as they move around in their jungle environment. 'These may be paths made by animals, a fruit tree planted by an ancestor, stones which are inhabited by potentially harmful beings, fallen tree-trunks, the place where an event in a particular myth took place, etc.' (1996: 132). The ancestor mentioned in this passage was an ordinary human predecessor whose activity, in this case of planting a tree, left an enduring token in the landscape. But his contribution to successors was not to hand anything down by way of substance or memory (thereby converting 'successors' into 'descendants'); it was rather to play a small part, along with the innumerable other beings – human, animal, spiritual – that have inhabited the forest at one time or another, in creating the environment in which people now live, and from which they draw their sense of being. Passing by the fruit tree, contemporary Chewong may be reminded of the ancestor's erstwhile presence and deeds, but it is in such acts of remembrance, not in any transmitted endowment carried in their bodies and minds, that he lives on.

The second possibility may be illustrated by means of an example from Nurit Bird-David's account of the Nayaka of Tamil Nadu, South India. 'Nayaka refer', she reports, 'to the spirits that inhabit hills, rivers, and rocks in the forest and to the spirits of their immediate forefathers alike as *dod appa* ("big father") and *dod awa* ("big mother")' (1990: 190, see also Chapter Three, pp. 43–4). For anthropological analysts primed with the genealogical model of kinship, such usages have caused no end of trouble. Surely, it is argued, people cannot really be descended from beings embodied in features of the landscape, as they are from their own forefathers. Classically, anomalies of this kind have been dealt with by constructing a special category of 'fictive kinship' which is modelled on, but nevertheless fundamentally distinct from, the 'real' kinship founded in genealogical connection. But the people themselves, for whom there is no anomaly, are telling us something quite different. It is that the role of parents is not, as the genealogical model implies, to pass on to their offspring the essential specifications of personhood in advance of their entry into the lifeworld, but rather – by their presence, their activities and the nurturance they provide – to establish the necessary conditions in the environment for their children's growth and development. This is what kinship is all about. And since the spirit inhabitants of the land contribute to human well-being equally, and on the same footing, as do human forbears, providing both food, guidance and security, they too can be 'big' fathers and mothers. As such, they are ancestors of a sort, albeit ones that are alive and active in the present.[8]

For an illustration of the third possibility, we can return to A. Irving Hallowell's ethnography of the Ojibwa of Berens River, Manitoba, which I have already considered at length in Chapter Six. The characters of Ojibwa myths are known collectively by a term, *ätíso'kanak*, that translates as 'our grandfathers'. They include the Sun, the Four Winds, and the 'masters' of various animal species. Despite their mythic status, these 'other-than-human' characters are entirely real in Ojibwa experience. They are regarded, according to Hallowell, 'as living entities who have existed from time immemorial. While there is genesis through birth and temporary or permanent form-shifting through transformation, there is no outright creation' (1960: 27). In other words, the other-than-human grandfathers have been there all along, living a parallel existence to ordinary humans with whom they may enter into close and, for the latter, lifelong relationships. Just like human grandfathers, they are a source of protection, and especially of wisdom. But this wisdom, gained above all through dream experience, takes the form not of knowledge that is 'passed down' but of a heightened perceptual awareness that reveals the world of one's waking life in a new or enriched light. Crucially, Ojibwa make no more claim to be descended from their grandfathers than do Nayaka to be descended from the spirits of the landscape. Grandfathers are ancestors because they were there before you, and because they guide you through the world. In that sense you follow them. But you are not descended from them.

The fourth and final possibility is most fully elaborated in the ethnography of Aboriginal Australia. The ancestors celebrated in Aboriginal myth and ceremony were creator beings who, in their world-forming activities, roamed across the face of the earth, emerging onto the surface here, going 'back in' there, and travelling from place to place – though in no particular direction – in between. The landscape itself is a reticulate maze of criss-crossing lines of ancestral travel, with the most significant localities at its nodal points. Localities identified by particular landscape features – hills, rocks, gullies, waterholes and so on – embody the ancestors' powers of creativity and movement in a congealed form. It is these powers, in turn, that engender living persons. Through conception, birth or long-term residence a person incorporates the essence of a locality into his or her own being, even to the extent of substantial identity. A nice illustration of the point comes from Nancy Munn's (1970) study of the Pitjantjatjara of the Australian Western Desert. On the subject of birthmarks – which are called *djuguridja*, 'of or pertaining to the ancestors' – Munn recalls one woman explaining that a mark on her body was also to be found on a particular ancestral rock at her birthplace. 'The rock was the transformed body of the ancestor lying down and the marking was originally his hair' (Munn 1970: 146). In this case there is indeed a bond of substance between the ancestor and the living person, but it is not

one of descent. Following Munn, it might better be described as a kind of reverse metamorphosis, in which the subject-turned-object (the ancestor transformed into the rock in
the Dreaming) becomes an object-turned-subject (the rock imprinting upon the body of
the living person at birth).

Now if there is one thing that our four examples have in common, it is that in no
case can the connections between ancestors and living people be described in terms of a
dendritic geometry of points and lines. Indeed there are no points as such. Every being
is instantiated in the world as the line of its own movement and activity: not a movement from point to point, as though the life-course were already laid out as the route
between them, but a continual 'moving around', or coming and going. Significant moments
– births, deaths, encounters with animals or spirits, coming out of the ground or going
back in – are constituted *within* this movement, where the life-lines of different beings
cross, interpenetrate, appear or disappear (only, perhaps, to reappear at some other
moment). Try to depict the relations between beings, ancestral and living, in the form of
a tree, and its boughs would intertwine, grow together as well as split apart, in a profu-
sion of cross-cutting connections. Indeed our tree, comprehensively entangled in such
transverse ties, would cease to look like a tree at all, and take on all the appearance of a
rhizome! As Deleuze and Guattari observe, 'transversal communications between different
lines scramble the genealogical trees' (1988: 11).[9] Our next task is to examine the implications of this rhizomatic view for the concept of generation.

Generation

We have seen that the genealogical model collapses the life of each person into a single
point, which is connected to other such points by lines of descent. A relational model
presents us with precisely the opposite picture. There are no lines of descent linking successive 'generations' of persons. Rather, persons are continually coming into being – that is,
undergoing generation – in the course of life itself. To put it in a nutshell: whereas in
the genealogical model life is encompassed within generations, in the relational model
generation is encompassed within the process of life. But this also entails a radically
different conception of the person. According to the genealogical model, every person is
a substantive entity, whose particular make-up is a function of biogenetic and cultural
specifications received from predecessors, prior to its involvement with other entities of
like or unlike kinds. By contrast, the relational model situates the person in the lifeworld
from the very start, as a locus of self-organising activity: not a generated entity but a site
where generation is going on.[10] Perhaps no-one has expressed the point better than a Cree
man from the James Bay region, who, as will be recalled from Chapter Three (p. 51),
explained to the ethnographer, Colin Scott, that to be a person is to live, and that life
(*pimaatisiiwin*) is a process of 'continuous birth' (Scott 1996: 73).

This, too, is what I had in mind in positively redescribing the antigenealogical,
rhizomatic character of the lifeworld as *progenerative*. Entailed here is a distinction between
pro-generation and procreation. The latter term captures the sense of begetting implied
when we say that one being is descended from another. It suggests a one-off event: the
making of something absolutely new out of elements derived from immediate antecedents.
By progeneration, in contrast, I refer to the continual unfolding of an entire field of relationships within which different beings emerge with their particular forms, capacities and
dispositions. Consider, for example, the relations between human hunters and their animal
prey. Thinking genealogically, one would suppose that as humans beget humans, so moose

(say) beget moose – so long as hunters leave sufficient animals alive to ensure their procreative replacement. Not so, however, for the Rock Cree of northern Manitoba, whose understanding of human–animal relations has been richly documented by Robert Brightman (1993). Cree say that moose present themselves willingly to be killed by hunters, and in that way contribute actively to the production of human existence. But conversely, hunters, in their treatment of kills in consumption and disposal of the remains, bring it about that the vitality of animals is restored, and so contribute to the production of animal existence. As Brightman explains, 'hunter and prey successively renew each other's lives, and, indeed, each seems to realize its innate nature in the transaction, the hunter as supplicant and the animal as benefactor' (1993: 188).

Here, hunting – including acts of killing, consumption and disposal – is the very epitome of progeneration. In the unfolding of the relation between hunters and prey both humans and animals undergo a kind of perpetual rebirth, each enfolding into its inner constitution the principle of its relationship to the other. Actual events of birth and death, therefore, are merely moments in the progenerative process, points of transition in the circulation of life. Once again, this conclusion stands in stark contrast to the images of life and death evoked by the genealogical model. For according to this model, as we have seen, life does not cross generations, but is expended in the present, in the procreative project of forwarding the elements needed to get it restarted in the future.[11] In each successive generation, the life-cycle begins at the point of conception and ends at death. When a person dies his or her life is over, finished. With a relational model, by contrast, life does not start or stop. To borrow a phrase from Deleuze and Guattari, it is a matter of 'coming and going rather than starting and finishing' (1988: 25). Particular persons may come and go, but the life process continues. All of existence is suspended in this process. Animals come when, following the successful hunt, they enter the human community, they go again with the eventual disposal of the remains. But the animal that has gone has not ceased to be: it still exists, albeit in another form. And for this reason, there is always the possibility of its return. As one Cree hunter told Brightman, 'they say it just comes up again and again' (1988: 240).

What goes for animals also goes for human beings. It should come as no surprise, therefore, that the relational model tends to be associated with ideas of reincarnation and cyclical rebirth. When an old person dies, it does not mark the end of a generation, which will henceforth recede ever further into the past as it is buried under layer after layer of new people. The fact that deceased persons are no longer present does not mean that they belong to a past that has been irrevocably left behind, but rather that they have departed from the living, along a path that takes them to what is often conceived as another land. Co-presence may be temporally bounded, but existence is not. Or to put it in another way, the past may be absent from the present but is not extinguished by it. Death punctuates, but does not terminate, life. Writing of the Yup'ik Eskimos of Alaska, Ann Fienup-Riordan notes that 'death as a final exit had no place in [their] system of cosmological reproduction ... Birth into the land of the dead was ultimately the source of continuing life' (1994: 250). Thus, far from calling for the replacement of one generation by another, death affirms the continuity of the progenerative process. Life is not compacted, as the genealogical model implies, into a linear sequence of procreative moments suspended in time, but is itself intrinsically temporal. As the philosopher Henri Bergson wrote, 'wherever anything lives, there is, open somewhere, a register in which time is being inscribed' (1911: 17). And the life of every being, as it unfolds, contributes at once to the progeneration of the future and to the regeneration of the past.

Substance

I have suggested that from a relational perspective, persons should be understood not as procreated entities, connected to one another along lines of genealogical connection or *relatedness*, but rather as centres of progenerative activity variously positioned within an all-encompassing field of *relationships*. Every such centre, as Rom Harré puts it, is 'a site from which a person perceives the world and a place from which to act' (1998: 3). It is from their emplacement in the world that people draw not just their perceptual orientations but the very substance of their being. Conversely, through their actions, they contribute to the substantive make-up of others. Such contributions are given and received throughout life, in the context of a person's ongoing relationships with human and non-human components of the environment. Thus, far from having their constitution specified in advance, as the genealogical model implies, persons undergo histories of continuous change and development. In a word, they *grow*. Indeed more than that, they are *grown*. By this I mean that growth is to be understood not merely as the autonomous realisation of pre-specified developmental potentials, but as the generation of being within what could be called a sphere of nurture.[12] It is the role of ancestors, as our earlier examples demonstrated, to establish this sphere by way of their presence and their activity, rather than to pass on the rudiments of being *per se*. That is to say, ancestors grow their successors, although the latter are not literally descended from them. But this nurturing role is not limited to ancestors: ordinary living persons, too, contribute reciprocally to the conditions of each other's growth as embodied beings. It is in these contributions, as we have seen, that their kinship consists.

Now while each person is at the centre of their own field of perception and action, the position of this centre is not fixed but moves relative to others. As it does so, it lays a trail. Every trail, however erratic and circuitous, is a kind of life-line, a trajectory of growth. This image of life as a trail or path is ubiquitous among peoples whose existential orientations are founded in the practices of hunting and gathering, and in the modes of environmental perception these entail. Persons are identified and characterised not by the substantive attributes they carry into the life process, but by the kinds of paths they leave. Beings of extraordinary power, such as the world-shaping ancestors of Australian Aboriginal cosmology or the other-than-human persons of the Ojibwa, can be recognised from their unusual paths which can, for example, leave indelible impressions on the landscape or even disappear underground. In the world of the Yup'ik Eskimos, one class of extraordinary persons, the *tenguirayulit*, are so fleet of foot that they can literally take off, leaving a trail of wind-blown snow in the trees (Fienup-Riordan 1994: 80). While the paths of ordinary human beings and other terrestrial animals remain on ground level, even plants deposit trails in the form of roots and runners in the wake of their advancing tips. Batek women from Pahang, Malaysia, say that the roots of wild tubers 'walk', as humans and other animals do (Lye 1997: 159). This may seem an odd idea to us, but only because we think of walking as the spatiotemporal displacement of already completed beings from one point to another, rather than as the movement of their substantive formation within an environment. Both plants and people, we could say, 'issue forth' along lines of growth, and both exist as the sum of their trails (see Wagner 1986: 21).

Putting together all the trails of all the different beings that have inhabited a country – human, animal and plant, ordinary and extraordinary – the result would be a dense mass of intersecting pathways, resembling nothing so much as a rhizome. This is not to rule out the possibility that particular growth configurations may be dendritic in form.

After all, among hunters and gatherers who inhabit a forest environment, some of the most important persons can be trees! This is beautifully demonstrated in Tuck Po Lye's recent study of the Batek, to which I referred a moment ago. For the Batek, trees are people. They possess agency and sociality. They can be both nurturing and protective, and dangerous (Lye 1997: 156–63). But of course there is a world of difference between the real, living tree in the forest and the abstract tree of the genealogical model. For the former is caught up in a dense network of entanglements with the vegetation that clings to it, the animals that forage and nest in it, and the humans that live under it. In short, the tree is but one part of that vast rhizome that is the forest as a whole. Only when it is abstracted from these rhizomatic entanglements does it appear in its 'pure', dendritic form.

I have already shown that a person's genealogical position is fixed independently of their location in the lifeworld. By contrast, every position in the total network of trails or life-lines is itself an emplacement. Lye draws explicitly on the 'rhizomatic epistemology' of Deleuze and Guattari to explain how, for the Batek, places are constituted as nodes in the endless comings and goings of people, each characterised by its particular assemblage of relations, and connected to all the others both socially and physically. 'Important place-names, trails and familiar campsites, like the roots of a rhizome, integrate diverse elements of the forest and serve as passageways for the ongoing experiences of people' (1997: 166). Among hunters and gatherers generally, the most significant places are where the paths of different beings intersect, or perhaps merge for a while before diverging again. It is here that exchanges of substance occur, for example in episodes of hunting, where the trails of human and animal cross and from which each leaves bearing something of the substance of the other, or of gathering, where people pick and consume the fruit of a tree once planted by an ancestor. Among themselves human persons exchange substance through feeding and being fed, in the nurturance and sharing that characterises the everyday life of a camp – which may be envisaged, in turn, as a place upon which the trails of many people temporarily converge.

Once again, this relational understanding inverts the genealogical model. Instead of thinking of substance as passing along a line of transmission connecting lives that – confined within their respective generations – proceed in parallel but never join, persons are conceived as passing along lines of movement and exchanging substance at the places where their respective paths cross or commingle. 'Throughout their lives', as Bird-David puts it, persons 'perpetually coalesce with, and depart from, each other' (1994: 597).[13] I have attempted to depict the contrast schematically in Figure 8.3; however in limiting the picture to a mutually constitutive encounter between two persons, A and B, it has been drastically oversimplified. In reality, as Fienup-Riordan says for the Yup'ik, 'the variety of persons and creatures that one might encounter in one's path is immense' (1994: 87). All of these beings may further one's growth and development, not only through contributions of substance, but also by way of the experiences they afford.

Thus the contrast shown in Figure 8.3 applies just as well to the growth of knowledge as to that of bodily substance. Knowledge, from a relational point of view, is not merely applied but generated in the course of lived experience, through a series of encounters in which the contribution of other persons is to orient one's attention – whether by means of revelation, demonstration or ostention – along the same lines as their own, so that one can begin to apprehend the world for oneself in the ways, and from the positions, that they do. In every such encounter, each party enters into the experience of the other and makes that experience his or her own as well. One shares in the process of knowing, rather

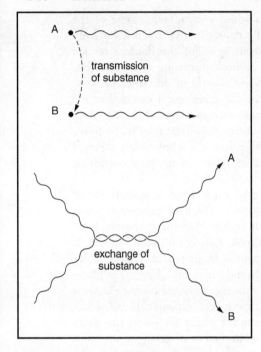

Figure 8.3 Schematic contrast between the transmission of substance according to the genealogical model, and the exchange of substance according to the relational model. For simplicity, the diagram depicts only two persons, A and B.

than taking on board a pre-established body of knowledge. Indeed in this education of attention, nothing, strictly speaking, is 'handed down' at all. The growth and development of the person, in short, is to be understood relationally as a *movement along a way of life*, conceived not as the enactment of a corpus of rules and principles (or a 'culture') received from predecessors, but as the negotiation of a path through the world (see Chapter Thirteen).

Memory

With this, we are led to pose a question about memory not unlike the one posed earlier, about ancestry. There we asked: what is the meaning of ancestry in a lifeworld where the elements of a person's substantive make-up are not passed on along lines of descent? The question that concerns us now is: what is the meaning of memory in a world of experience where the rudiments of knowledge are not handed down along analogous lines of cultural transmission? A large part of the answer hinges on our understanding of language. For according to the genealogical model, it is above all thanks to language that the concepts and values of a culture are transmitted from one generation to the next. Not only does this presuppose that cultural knowledge exists in the form of a corpus of transmissible, context-free representations; it also implies that the words of language take their meanings from their attachments to these representations, quite apart from the situations of their utterance in speech. The purpose of speaking, then, is to render explicit, or publicly accessible, meanings that would otherwise remain confined within the interiority of the mind – nevertheless only to those who share the language and are therefore in a position to decode the messages conveyed therein.[14] It follows that the loss of a language inevitably leads to the loss of the knowledge expressed in it, which will die out with the last generation of speakers. Much concern over the disappearance of indigenous languages is fuelled by a fear that with them will go traditions that have been handed down from time immemorial, severing once and for all the increasingly tenuous threads that connect present humanity to its ancestral past.

If, however, as the relational model implies, the source of cultural knowledge lies not in the heads of predecessors but in the world that they point out to you – if, that is, one learns by discovery while following in the *path* of an ancestor – then words, too, must gather their meanings from the contexts in which they are uttered. Moving together along a trail or encamped at a particular place, companions draw each other's attention, through speech and gesture, to salient features of their shared environment. Every word, spoken in context, condenses a history of past usage into a focus that illuminates some aspect of the world. Words, in this sense, are instruments of perception much as tools are instruments of action. Both conduct a skilled and sensuous engagement with the environment that is sharpened and enriched through previous experience. The clumsiness of the novice in handling unfamiliar tools is matched, as every anthropological fieldworker knows, only by his incomprehension of spoken words. What the novice lacks, however, and the knowledgeable hand possesses, is not a scheme of conceptual representations for organising the data of experience but rather the perceptual sensitivity that enables him to discern, and continually to respond to, those subtle variations in the environment whose detection is essential to the accomplishment of ongoing activity. From this point of view, and contrary to the tenets of the genealogical model, speech is not so much the articulation of representations as the embodiment of *feeling*. It is a way, as Maurice Merleau-Ponty once put it, 'for the human body to sing the world's praises and in the last resort to live it' (1962: 187). I return to this point in Chapter Twenty-three (pp. 408–10).

But to live the world is also to inhabit it. Thus a way of speaking is, in itself, a way of living in the land. Far from serving as a common currency for the exchange of otherwise private mental representations, language celebrates an embodied knowledge of the world that is already shared thanks to people's mutual involvement in the tasks of habitation. It is not, then, language *per se* that ensures the continuity of tradition. Rather, it is the tradition of living in the land that ensures the continuity of language. Conversely, to remove a community of speakers from the land is to cut the language adrift from its generative source of meaning, leaving it as the vestige of a form of life that has long since been overtaken by its representation as an *object* of memory. In this regard, the assumptions of the genealogical model have had fateful consequences for the peoples it construes as indigenous. For so long as it is supposed that the language, and the traditions encoded therein, can be passed along like a relay baton from generation to generation, it appears to make no difference *where* the people are. On these grounds, administrations have often seen no principled objection to moving their 'indigenous' peoples off the land, or greatly restricting their access, whether in the interests of industrial development or wildlife conservation. It did not occur to them that such displacement might rupture the continuity of tradition or cut the people off from their pasts.

I have already shown that traditional knowledge, in the genealogical conception, comprises an inventory of transmitted items that are stored in memory, from which they may be accessed as required, and expressed in speech or practice. From a relational perspective, by contrast, knowledge subsists in practical activities themselves, including activities of speaking. And just as to follow a path is to remember the way, so to engage in any practice is, at the same time, to remember how it is done. Thus hunters and gatherers, following in the paths of their ancestors as they make their way through the terrain, remember as they go along. The important thing, so far as they are concerned, is that the process should keep on going, not that it should yield precise replicas of past performance. Indeed 'keeping it going' may involve a good measure of creative improvisation. A skill well remembered is one that is flexibly responsive to ever-variable environmental conditions. Thus there is no opposition, in the terms of the relational model, between continuity and change. Change is simply what we observe if we sample a continuous process at a number of fixed points, separated in time. The growth of an organism, for example, is continuous, but if we compare its appearance at different times it will appear to have changed. So too, the growth of knowledge, conceived relationally, is an aspect of the growth of persons, in the contexts of their involvement with one another and with the environment. Just because people are doing things differently now, compared with the way they did them at some time in the past, does not mean that there has been a rupture of tradition or a failure of memory. What would really break the continuity, however, would be if people were forcibly constrained to replicate a pattern fixed by genealogical descent, or to 'traditionalize the traditional', as Bjørn Bjerkli has nicely put it (1996: 18). The effect would be similar to that of a needle becoming stuck in the groove of a record. One could not keep the music going.

We are now in a better position to answer the question I posed at the start of this section. For if knowledge is not received from predecessors in advance of its application in the world, then objects of memory cannot pre-exist acts of remembering. Nor can such acts be understood as purely cognitive operations, of calling up representations already installed within the mind. On the contrary, it is through the activity of remembering that memories are *forged*. This activity, moreover, is tantamount to the movement of the person through the world. Memories, then, are generated along the paths of movement that each person lays down in the course of his or her life. Earlier, I pointed out that in the terms of the relational model, the progeneration of the future is also a regeneration of the past. Another way of putting this would be to say that the growth of knowledge is, at one and the same time, the production of memory. Journeying forward along a path or trail, one is also taken back to places imbued with the presence of ancestors. 'Trails', as Lye observes in her study of the Batek, 'are routes to remembrance just as they are routes to knowledge'. She recalls one Batek man pointing out a particular trail to her. 'That', he is reported to have said, 'is a trail of the old people. So when people feel *ha?ip* [longing] for the old people, they come back here and use the trail so that they can remember the old people' (Lye 1997: 149).

One more example, from the other side of the world, may be drawn from Richard Nelson's study of the Koyukon of Alaska (Nelson 1983: 243). He describes how he was taken by an old woman to see a place in the forest where, long ago, the late Chief Henry and his wife Bessie had their fishing camp. Looking closely, one could make out dark bands on the birch trees, where the bark had been removed from which Bessie used to make baskets, and axe marks on the rotting stumps of trees that Chief Henry had felled. Examining these signs, which an untrained eye would have passed over completely, Nelson's companion began to talk a little sadly about the deceased couple and their activities. She spoke of the skill and sensitivity that enabled Chief Henry to select wood with the best grain for making sleds or snowshoes, or Bessie to weave excellent baskets from birchbark. Yet this same sensitivity, grounded in an intimate familiarity with the country and its inhabitants, also enabled the old woman, in her turn, to recognise the signs of the couple's erstwhile presence in an otherwise featureless and overgrown patch of forest. Memories may be forged with words, and artefacts with tools; both, however, are the fruits of a certain way of living in the land. For the old woman this way of life was not just an *object* of memory, represented and passed down in oral tradition, but also a *practice of remembering*, embedded in the perception of the environment.

Land

What, then, given this relational view of growth and remembrance, makes people more or less the same or different? Not their genealogical proximity as determined by a past history of relatedness, but the extent to which their own life-histories are intertwined through the shared experience of inhabiting particular places and following particular paths in an environment. Common involvement in spheres of nurture, rather than any principle of shared descent, creates likeness. Persons, as we have seen, are to be understood from this perspective not as preconstituted – or procreated – entities, but rather as *loci* of growth, of the progenerative unfolding of the entire field of relationships within which each comes into being. The source of their differentiation is to be found in this unfolding. There is no room, within such a view, for the kind of classificatory project that groups individuals on the basis of whatever intrinsic characteristics they might happen to possess, by virtue of their biogenetic inheritance or cultural heritage, irrespective of their life in the world. Thus ethnic and racial classifications are as foreign to relational thinking as are the genealogically conceived taxonomies devised by biologists for the classification of living things. It is not by their inner attributes that persons or organisms are identified, but by their positions *vis-à-vis* one another in the relational field (Ingold 1993a: 229). The relational model, in short, *renders difference not as diversity but as positionality*.[15]

The idea of a field of relationships may seem highly abstract, far removed from the reality of entities and events 'on the ground'. Yet it is the very dominance of the genealogical model in our thinking, I would argue, that leads us to suppose that things exist, in the real world, independently of their relations. The relational model overturns this understanding. To exist, it asserts, is already to be positioned in a certain environment and committed to the relationships this entails. Reality, then, is relational through and through. The relational field is no abstraction but the very ground from which things grow, and take on the forms they do. Another word for this ground is *land*. Up to now I have spoken of beings of various kinds as 'inhabiting' the land. This should not be taken to imply mere occupancy, as though inhabitants, already endowed by descent with the attributes of substance and memory that make them what they are, were slotted into place like pegs on a peg-board. Positions in the land are no more laid out in advance for persons to occupy, than are persons specified prior to taking them up. Rather, to inhabit the land is to draw it to a particular focus, and in so doing to *constitute* a place. As a locus of personal growth and development, however, every such place forms the centre of a sphere of nurture. Thus the generation of persons within spheres of nurture, and of places in the land, are not separate processes but one and the same. In the relational model, as Leach has put it, 'kinship is geography' (Leach 1997: 36).

All this has implications for our ideas about permanence and replacement. Recall that according to the genealogical model, life is encompassed within generations. Every organism comes with its allotted lifespan, and has eventually to make way for copies of itself if its kind is to continue. Life, in short, is conceived as but a means to the end of procreative replacement. The land, by contrast, since it is supposed to contain or support living things, cannot itself be alive. For if every form of life exists *upon* the land, then the land must be inanimate. It does not, therefore, have to be replaced; it is simply, and permanently *there*, an enduring surface over which generation after generation of individuals pass like cohorts on the march. The relational model, on the other hand, does not counterpose the land to its inhabitants along the axis of a dichotomy between the animate and the inanimate. A founding premise of the model is that life, rather than being an internal property of persons and things, is immanent in the relations between them. It follows that the land, comprised by these relations, is itself imbued with the vitality that animates its inhabitants. The important thing is to ensure that this vitality never 'dries up'. As hunters and gatherers have explained to their ethnographers, with remarkable consistency, it is essential to 'look after' or care for the land, to maintain in good order the relationships it embodies; only then can the land, reciprocally, continue to grow and nurture those who dwell therein.

This perspective gives us a view of the land quite unlike the inert and timeless, two-dimensional substrate of the genealogical model. It figures rather as an immense tangle of interlaced trails – an all-encompassing rhizome – which is continually ravelling here, and unravelling there, as the beings of which it is composed grow, or 'issue forth', along the lines of their relationships. I have referred to this ravelling and unravelling as a process of progeneration. Every being, in the course of its life history, works in the first place to keep the progenerative process going rather than to secure its own procreative replacement. Thus there is no opposition, here, between history and land. Both carry the same intrinsic temporality. Woven like a tapestry from the lives of its inhabitants, the land is not so much a stage for the enactment of history, or a surface on which it is inscribed, as *history congealed*. And just as kinship is geography, so the lives of persons and the histories of their relationships can be traced in the textures of the land.

CONCLUSION

> Indigenous peoples regard all products of the human mind and heart as interrelated, and as flowing from the same source: the relationships between the people and their land, their kinship with the other living creatures that share the land, and with the spirit world. Since the ultimate source of knowledge and creativity is the land itself, all of the art and science of a specific people are manifestations of the same underlying relationships, and can be considered as manifestations of the people as a whole.

So writes Erica-Irene Daes on behalf of the Working Group on Indigenous Populations, which was established in 1982, under the auspices of the United Nations, to hear the views of the representatives of such populations on the issue of the protection of their collective 'heritage' (Daes 1997: 3). In this passage she offers a cogent and succinct restatement of the relational perspective. Yet it also contradicts, point by point, the 'official' definition of what it means to be indigenous, with which I began. To recapitulate: this definition classifies as indigenous the descendants of people who were already inhabiting some country or region at the time when colonists arrived from elsewhere. The axiom, formulated so clearly by Daes, that indigenous peoples draw their being from their relationships with the land, is here brushed aside in favour of a claim based purely and simply on proof of prior presence, judged in terms of a linear concept of time and history.

The fact that a certain region was home to a population of human beings prior to its colonial settlement tells us nothing about how these 'original inhabitants' understood their relationships to the land. They may of course have felt themselves to have been connected to other components of the lifeworld in the way the relational model suggests. But for contemporary people to claim indigenous status on the criterion of *descent* from this ancestral population is tantamount to an admission that for them, 'living in the land' is no more than a distant memory. For the principle of descent implies, as we have seen, that people do *not* draw their substance and knowledge from the land, or from their relationships with it, but rather from their immediate genealogical antecedents. At the same time it rules out the possibility of any real kinship with other creatures that share the land, and reduces the activity of dwelling to mere occupancy. In short, the appeal to descent as a basis on which to ascribe indigenous identity contravenes those very understandings that for the indigenous groups themselves, are most fundamental to their way of life. Indeed it seems that a sense of being founded on people's relationships to the land is bound to be compromised by its articulation in terms of a model that treats these relationships as no more than epiphenomena of genealogically transmitted, biogenetic and cultural attributes.

To describe indigenous people as those who were 'there first' is to situate them within a history conceived as a narrative of colonial conquest and state formation. It is a designation, as André Béteille comments, that 'acquires substance when there are other populations in the same region that can reasonably be described as settlers or aliens' (1998: 188). In the eyes of the settlers who went on to take possession of their lands, these earlier inhabitants may well have seemed like archetypal 'natives'. In a sense, then, the official definition of indigenous status faithfully reflects the self-perception of the non-indigenous populations of nation states, as descendants of settlers who founded the nations they represent on alien soil. In these terms, contemporary indigenes are descendants of the colonially dispossessed. Indeed the categorical opposition of indigenous and non-indigenous populations, conceived respectively as the descendants of natives and settlers, is itself a construction of colonialism. For the genealogical model is fundamentally a colonial model, with its notion of the land as a surface to be occupied, of the lifeworld as a country to which people can move in order to take up residence, bringing their endowments of heritable substance and knowledge with them, and of generation as serial replacement, such that the present takes over from, and extinguishes, the past.

To conclude: we are left with the question of why people should feel the need to articulate claims to indigenous status in terms that, by their own accounts, are incompatible with their experience and understanding of the world. The answer, I believe, is that these people are compelled to operate in a modern-day political context in which they are also citizens of nation states. The genealogical model is deeply implicated in the discourse of the state: indeed it is the principal source of legitimation for the state's sovereign entitlement to defend and administer its territory in the name of the nation. For the state, the land belongs to the national heritage, and is held in trust by each generation of citizens on behalf of their descendants. If it is by appeal to common heritage that the citizens of the state are made to appear the same – that is, to share a national identity – then only by stressing their separate heritage can encapsulated groups express their difference. The construction of indigenous status upon the principle of descent is thus, as I have argued elsewhere, 'a product of the representation of difference in the discourse of homogeneity' (Ingold 1993a: 218). In this construction, the very relationships within which persons are positioned and from which they derive their identity and belonging are recast as the outward expressions of inner, inherited properties or attributes that *belong to them*. It is in the attempt to recover a lost or threatened sense of relational identity in attributional terms that people come to define themselves, and to be defined by others, as 'indigenous'.

Part II

Dwelling

INTRODUCTION

The chapters in this part explore various aspects of what I have called the *dwelling perspective*. By this I mean a perspective that treats the immersion of the organism-person in an environment or lifeworld as an inescapable condition of existence. From this perspective, the world continually comes into being around the inhabitant, and its manifold constituents take on significance through their incorporation into a regular pattern of life activity. It has been rather more usual, in social and cultural anthropology, to suppose that people inhabit a world – of culture or society – to which form and meaning have already been attached. It is assumed, in other words, that they must perforce 'construct' the world, in consciousness, before they can act in it. I refer to this view as the *building perspective*. Each chapter explores some aspect of the contrast between the building and dwelling perspectives, in relation to such topics as the significance of architecture, the perception of the landscape, the idea of environmental change, the practice of wayfinding, and the properties of vision and hearing. In order to lay a foundation for these explorations, however, I begin in Chapter Nine with a general introduction to anthropological theories of perception and cognition. The fundamental question that all such theories seek to address is the following: why should people from different cultural backgrounds perceive the world in different ways?

In the first part of the chapter I outline the history of anthropological attempts to answer this question, starting with the classical work of Emile Durkheim, through influential statements by Edmund Leach, Clifford Geertz and Mary Douglas, to the more recent development of the field known as cognitive anthropology. Throughout this history, the assumption has persisted that people construct the world, or what for them is 'reality', by organising the data of sensory perception in terms of received and culturally specific conceptual schemata. But in recent anthropology, this assumption has been challenged by advocates of 'practice theory', who argue that cultural knowledge, rather than being imported into the settings of practical activity, is constituted within these settings through the development of specific dispositions and sensibilities that lead people to orient themselves in relation to their environment and to attend to its features in the particular ways that they do. In the second part of Chapter Nine, I assess the relevance for anthropological understanding of alternative approaches drawn from cognitive science, ecological psychology and phenomenology. Though my conclusion is that anthropology has more to gain from an alliance with ecological psychology than with cognitive science, and that such an alliance accords well with a phenomenology of dwelling, there are still problems to be faced in overcoming the dichotomy between culture and biology, in reconciling a phenomenology of the body with an ecology of mind, and in translating the overall theoretical perspective into a practicable programme of research.

Chapter Ten explores how a dwelling perspective might affect our understanding of the similarities and differences between the ways in which human beings and other animals create environments for themselves. I am concerned, in particular, with the meaning of architecture, or that part of the environment conventionally described as 'built'. I start by documenting the transition in my own thinking from a 'building perspective', according to which worlds are made before they are lived in, to a 'dwelling perspective', according to which the forms people build, whether in the imagination or on the ground, only arise within the current of their life activities. Drawing on Jakob von Uexküll's notion of *Umwelt*, I show how we might distinguish between human and non-human constructions in the terms of the building perspective, on the basis of the presence or absence of an intentional project of design. This argument, however, implies the existence of some kind of threshold in human evolution, beyond which our ancestors were able to author their own projects. This idea has motivated the search for a point of origin for humanity in general, and for human architecture in particular. Through the adoption of a dwelling perspective, influenced by the philosophy of Martin Heidegger, I show that the point of origin is illusory. There can, then, be no absolute distinction between 'natural' and 'artificial' structures. Buildings, like other environmental structures, are never complete but continually under construction, and have life-histories of involvement with both their human and non-human inhabitants. Whether, at a certain point in its life history, a structure looks to us like a building or not will depend on the extent and nature of human involvement in its formation.

In Chapter Eleven I turn to what I consider to be the unifying themes of archaeology and sociocultural anthropology: namely, landscape and temporality. This chapter is an attempt to show how the temporality of the landscape might be understood by way of a dwelling perspective. I first set out to clarify the meaning of 'landscape' by contrast to the concepts of land, nature, space and environment. I then introduce the notion of 'taskscape' to denote a pattern of dwelling activities. The intrinsic temporality of the taskscape, I argue, lies in its rhythmic interrelations or patterns of resonance. At first glance the opposition between landscape and taskscape seems to mirror that, in the field of art, between painting and music. However by considering how taskscape relates to landscape, the distinction between them is ultimately dissolved, and the landscape itself is shown to be fundamentally temporal. I illustrate the thesis of the temporality of the landscape through an analysis of the scene depicted by Pieter Bruegel the Elder in his painting *The harvesters*. In conclusion, I criticise the view that a properly cultural ecology would be one that would go beyond strictly pragmatic concerns with the conditions of adaptation to focus on the multiple layers of symbolic meaning with which people cover over their environments. For meaning, I contend, does not cover the world but is immanent in the contexts of people's pragmatic engagements with its constituents. But the discovery of meaning in the landscape has to begin from a recognition of its temporality, and in this lies the essence of archaeological investigation.

The significance of the contrast between building and dwelling perspectives for cosmological conceptions of 'the earth' is my theme in Chapter Twelve. I argue that the image of the earth as a globe, implied in such phrases as 'global environmental change', is one that actually expels humanity from the lifeworld, such that rather than the environment surrounding *us*, it is we who have surrounded *it*. Far from reintegrating human society into the world of nature, the idea of the earth as a solid globe of opaque materiality marks their final separation. Thus the biodiversity of locally distributed life-forms presents itself to a universal, globally distributed humanity. The conservation ethic entailed in such a global vision, which places nature on the inside and humanity on the outside, is at once eco*centric* and anthropo*circumferential*. Against this, I examine the contrasting image of the sphere, conjuring up a transparent lifeworld which is perceived by its inhabitants from within. This image, which is characteristic of the cosmologies of pre-modern societies, is genuinely anthropocentric, but in a way that counterposes neither humanity and nature, nor the local and the global. I show how the shift from a spherical to a global perspective marks the triumph of technology over cosmology. But it also leads to the systematic disempowerment of local communities, taking from them – in the name of preserving biodiversity – the responsibility to care for their own environments.

From my discussion of the landscape and of the topological image of the globe in Chapters Eleven and Twelve, it is clear that in the building perspective (as in the genealogical model of Chapter Eight) the earth is presented to humanity as a surface to be occupied rather than a world to be inhabited. It is further supposed that the disposition of things and places on this surface is known by representing it, either in the mind or on paper, in the form of a map. Thus to know where one is entails identifying one's current position with a corresponding location on the map, and to find one's way from one position to another is to navigate by means of it. In Chapter Thirteen I take a critical look at the notion of the map, and its application in anthropological studies of wayfinding and navigation. I argue that while dwelling in the world entails movement, this movement is not between locations in space but between places in a network of coming and going that I call a region. To know one's whereabouts is thus to be able to connect one's latest movements to narratives of journeys previously made, by oneself and others. In wayfinding, people do not traverse the surface of a world whose layout is fixed in advance – as represented on the cartographic map. Rather, they 'feel their way' *through* a world that is itself in motion, continually coming into being through the combined action of human and non-human agencies. I develop a notion of mapping as the narrative re-enactment of journeys made, and of maps as the inscriptions to which such re-enactments may possibly give rise. However, the building perspective enshrined in modern science splits mapping into the phases of mapmaking and map-using, and likewise splits wayfinding into the twin projects of cartography and navigation.

In Chapter Fourteen I turn to a problem in the anthropology of the senses. Does a building perspective imply the hegemony of vision? Is hearing the predominant sense of dwelling? To regain an appreciation of human dwelling in the world is it necessary to rebalance the sensorium, giving greater weight to the ear, and less to the eye, in the ratio of the senses? Many philosophers and historians have noted the 'ocularcentrism' of the Western tradition, its privileging of sight over the other senses as a source of human knowledge. Anthropologists, for their part, have stressed the importance of hearing in the sensorium of many non-Western peoples. Yet the comparison remains couched in terms of a dichotomy between vision and hearing whose roots lie firmly in the intellectual history of the West. In the terms of this dichotomy, vision is distancing, objectifying, analytic, and atomising; hearing is unifying, subjective, synthetic and holistic. Vision represents an external world of being, hearing participates in the inwardness of the world's becoming: the former is inherently static, the latter suspended in movement. Whereas one hears sound, one does not see light, but only the things off whose surfaces light is reflected. This is why hearing is supposed to penetrate the inner, subjective domain of thought and feeling in a way that vision cannot. It is also why Western thought, for all its dependence on the written word, and in apparent contradiction to its elevation of sight as the 'noblest' of the senses, has tended to treat writing (which is seen) as inferior to speech (which is heard).

But ethnography suggests that people in non-Western societies do not regard vision and hearing as radically opposed, but rather as virtually interchangeable. Nor does their apparent emphasis on understanding through sensory participation rather than external observation entail a bias towards hearing over vision. For many, vision remains paramount. But it is a vision that is non-representational, a matter of watching rather than seeing. Like hearing, it is caught in the flow of time and bodily movement. One can, in short, dwell just as fully in the world of visual as in that of aural experience: indeed for the most part these worlds are one and the same. That this point has been missed in the anthropology of the senses is due to its tendency to treat sensory experience as but a vehicle for the expression of extra-sensory, cultural values. The key question, I conclude, is: what is the relationship between the cultural evaluation of the senses and the ways in which they are practically deployed in acts of perception?

Chapter Nine

Culture, perception and cognition

There is one question that, perhaps more than any other, motivates anthropological inquiry. Take people from different backgrounds and place them in the same situation; they are likely to differ in what they make of it. Indeed such difference is something that every anthropologist experiences in the initial phases of fieldwork. But why should this be so? How do we account for it? In their attempts to answer this question, anthropologists have come up against some of the most contested issues in the psychology of perception and cognition. My purpose in this chapter is to show how they have dealt with these issues. The chapter is divided into two parts. In the first part I trace something of the history of the problem over the past century of anthropological thought. In the second, I go on to assess the relevance for anthropological understanding of alternative approaches drawn from cognitive science, ecological psychology and phenomenology. This is a considerable agenda, and in the space of a single chapter I can do no more than touch on the many questions raised.

I

SOCIAL ANTHROPOLOGY

In British social anthropology (as distinct from American cultural anthropology) thinking about perception and cognition goes back to the classical work of Emile Durkheim, himself one of the founding fathers of what was then the new science of sociology. In his manifesto for the new discipline, *The rules of sociological method* (first published in 1895), Durkheim adamantly opposed all attempts to explain social phenomena in terms of the psychological properties of individuals. As he famously declared, 'every time a social phenomenon is directly explained by a psychological phenomenon, we may rest assured that the explanation is false' (1982[1895]: 129). If sociology is a kind of psychology, Durkheim thought, its object of study must be the mind of society, not of the individual. This mind, the consciousness of the collectivity, was supposed to have emergent properties of its own, in no way reducible to the given properties of individuals as inscribed in human nature. But it was not until the concluding chapter of his greatest work, *The elementary forms of the religious life*, that Durkheim explicitly spelled out the relation between the consciousness of the individual and that of the collectivity – 'the highest form of the psychic life' (1976[1915]: 444). He did so in terms of a thoroughgoing distinction between sensation and representation.

The distinction was made on two grounds. The first lies in the contrast between the ephemerality of sensations and the durability of representations. Every sensation, Durkheim argued, is tied to a particular moment that will never recur, for even if – at a subsequent point in time – the thing perceived has not changed, the perceiver will no longer be the same. We are nevertheless able to represent our experience, and so to know what we have perceived, by catching perceptual images that would otherwise float by on the stream of consciousness within the mesh of a system of concepts that remains somehow aloof from this sensory agitation (in a 'different portion of the mind', Durkheim suggested, that is more calm and serene). Like language, which is the medium in which concepts are expressed ('for every word translates a concept'), the conceptual system has a kind of stability: it endures, whilst the stream of consciousness flows on (Durkheim 1976[1915]: 433).

Secondly, whereas sensations are private and individual, representations are public and social. Since sensations consist in the reactions of the organism to particular external stimuli, there is no way in which a sensation can be made to pass directly from one individual consciousness to another. If people are to share their experiences they must talk about them, and to do that these experiences must be represented by means of concepts, which in turn may be expressed in words whose meanings are established within a community of speakers by verbal convention. Thus collective representations serve as a kind of bridge between individual consciousnesses that are otherwise closed to each other, furnishing them with a means of mutual understanding. 'The concept is an essentially impersonal representation; it is through it that human intelligences communicate' (Durkheim 1976[1915]: 433–4).

Following Durkheim's lead, British social anthropologists carried on with the comparative study of collective representations – otherwise known as 'social structures' – without paying much attention to the psychological premises on which such study rested. Fifty years later, two of the most influential social anthropologists of the day, Edmund Leach and Mary Douglas, could still pose the problem of perception and cognition in very much the same terms. Given that the world of our immediate, sensory experience is a formless and continuous flux in which nothing is the same from one moment to the next, how can we know what we perceive? To recognise specific objects and events in the external world, Leach claimed, the flux has to be cut up into bounded chunks: thus thought fragments the continuum of life as it is lived, and the diversity of culture lies precisely in the manifold ways in which the continuum can be cut. Leach's first explicit statement of this theory of perception and cognition was presented in an article on 'Anthropological aspects of language', published in 1964. Here he argued that the categories of language provide the 'discriminating grid' which, laid over the continuous substrate of raw experience, enables the speaker to tell one thing from another, and so to see the world 'as being composed of a large number of separate things, each labelled with a name' (1964: 34). As the child learns its mother-tongue, thereby taking on board a conventional system of named categories, so its environment literally takes shape before its very eyes.

Two years later, Mary Douglas published her seminal study, *Purity and danger*. Here, too, we find the same basic idea: that in perception the world is constructed to a certain order, through the imposition of culturally transmitted form upon the flux of experience.

> As perceivers we select from all the stimuli falling on our senses only those that interest us, and our interests are governed by a pattern-making tendency ... In a chaos of shifting impressions, each of us constructs a world in which objects have recognisable shapes, are located in depth, and have permanence.
>
> (1966: 36)

As with Leach, the roots of Douglas's thinking lie in Durkheim's theory of knowledge. This theory, as we have seen, effectively divides the human subject into two mutually exclusive parts. One part, fully immersed in the sensate, physical world, is continually bombarded by stimuli which are registered in consciousness as a 'chaos of shifting impressions'. The other part, however, stands aside from this engagement, and is untouched by it. Here are located the conceptual categories that sort the sensory input, discarding or suppressing some elements of it while fitting the remainder into a pre-existing, socially approved schema. Crucially, then, perception is a two-stage phenomenon: the first involves the receipt, by the individual human organism, of ephemeral and meaningless sense data; the second consists in the organisation of these data into collectively held and enduring representations.

CULTURAL ANTHROPOLOGY

The rigid distinction between social and psychological phenomena that British social anthropology took from Durkheim was not matched by the parallel, North American tradition of cultural anthropology. The founder of this latter tradition, Franz Boas, consistently adopted the position that the patterned integration of culture, as a system of habits, beliefs and dispositions, is achieved on the level of the individual rather than having its source in some overarching collectivity, and is therefore essentially psychological in nature. Accordingly, American cultural anthropologists of the mid-twentieth century paid a great deal of attention to the way in which the individual personality is fashioned out of the cultural materials available to it. In two respects, however, subsequent developments led to the establishment of a view of perception and cognition more closely in line with that espoused by British writers. The first lay in the separation of culture, as a body of transmissible knowledge, from patterns of observable behaviour. Already in the writings of Clyde Kluckhohn, and in the review of concepts of culture that Kluckhohn compiled in collaboration with Alfred Kroeber, we find a stress on culture as an internalised system of rules and meanings *as distinct* from manifest behaviour patterns and their artefactual products (Kluckhohn 1949: 32, Kroeber and Kluckhohn 1952: 114). And in 1957, Ward Goodenough confirmed this separation in his much cited definition of culture as 'whatever it is one has to know or believe in order to operate in a manner acceptable to [a society's] members' (cited in D'Andrade 1984: 89).

The distinction between culture and behaviour was once again reiterated, this time by Clifford Geertz, in an influential article first published in 1966, on 'The impact of the concept of culture on the concept of man'. Culture, Geertz argued, 'is best seen not as complexes of concrete behavior patterns – customs, usages, traditions, habit clusters – ... but as a set of control mechanisms – plans, recipes, rules, instructions (what computer engineers call "programs") – for the governing of behavior' (Geertz 1973: 44). He nevertheless took strong exception to the view, attributed to Goodenough, that the place to find these control mechanisms is inside the heads of individuals.[1] Herein, then, lay the second development: having split culture from behaviour, the former was removed from the minds of individuals and reinscribed on the level of the collectivity. In a move redolent of Durkheim's earlier formulation, Geertz insisted that the domain of cultural symbols is social rather than psychological, public rather than private. Their natural place of abode is in the intersubjective space of social interaction – 'the house yard, the marketplace, and the town square' – whence they are 'used to impose meaning upon experience' (1973: 44–5). For any one individual, the range of symbolic meanings which can be drawn upon is more or less given by what is current in the community into which he or she is born. But without the guidance provided by significant symbols, human beings would be hopelessly lost, unable to establish their bearings in the world. For unlike other creatures whose activities are more closely controlled by innate response mechanisms, humans depend on a substantial input of additional information, learned rather than innate, in order to function adequately in their normal environments. 'Undirected by culture patterns – organized systems of significant symbols – man's behavior would be virtually ungovernable, a mere chaos of pointless acts and exploding emotions, his experience virtually shapeless' (Geertz 1973: 46).

Despite his different intellectual roots, in American cultural anthropology rather than British social anthropology, Geertz came to conclusions remarkably similar to those that were being drawn at the same time by Douglas, and that I have already touched upon. Both Geertz and Douglas took culture to comprise a framework of symbolic meanings, common to a community and relatively impervious to the passage of time and generations, which gives shape to the raw material of experience and direction to human feeling and action. Thus to return to our original question: if two individuals from different backgrounds, placed in the same environment, construe it in different ways, the reason would be that each has brought a different symbolic system to bear in organising the same material of sensory experience. Granted, then, that every community has its own particular system for the organisation of experience, anthropological attention naturally came to focus on cultural variation in the organisational principles involved. Geertz, as we have seen, claimed that such principles were to be found in the publicly accessible space of social discourse, and not in the interiority of the mind. But others, taking their cue more directly from Goodenough, insisted that cultural cognition can only take place by way of shared conceptual schemata lodged in the minds of individuals. Their aim was to uncover these schemata, and it gave rise, in the late 1960s, to a field of inquiry known rather generally as 'cognitive anthropology', though in a narrower and more restricted form as 'ethnoscience' (Tyler 1969).

COGNITIVE ANTHROPOLOGY

The problem for the cognitive anthropologist, Tyler explains, 'is to discover how other people create order out of what appears to him to be utter chaos' (1969: 6). They do so, it is supposed, by grouping the infinitely variable phenomena of the experienced world into a finite set of named, hierarchically ordered classes. This is done by attending only to those perceptual cues that differentiate things as belonging to one class rather than another, while ignoring those that would indicate the uniqueness of every member of a class. But the ordering principles that govern this process of selective attention are given in the mind, not in the world. 'There is nothing', Tyler asserts, 'in the external world which demands that certain things go together and others do not' (1969: 7). In other words, the principles of classification are arbitrary and subjective with regard to the world whose phenomena are to be classified. They are to be discovered through the formal analysis of responses provided by native informants to a series of questions of the form 'is this thing here a kind of X?', 'what other kinds of X are there?', 'is X a kind of Y?', and so on, all of which are designed by the investigator to elicit precisely the distinctions he or she is looking for.

Despite early promise, the project of cognitive anthropology soon ran into difficulties. An enormous amount of effort was put into mapping out rather limited semantic domains

– for example of kinship terms, plant and animal taxonomies or colour classifications –
without bringing any comparable advance in understanding how people actually negotiate
their relationships with one another, and with their non-human environments, in the usual
course of everyday life. It became apparent that the key to such negotiation lay in a certain
flexibility in the use of concepts and a sensitivity to context that was disregarded by formal
semantic analysis. The neatly ordered paradigms and taxonomies yielded by this method
of analysis seemed to be artefacts of anthropologists' techniques of controlled elicitation
rather than having any counterpart in the cognitive organisation of the people studied.
The specialised tasks of naming and discrimination that the latter were expected to perform
were not, after all, ones that they would have ordinarily encountered. Indeed the ability
to name things correctly is but a small and relatively insignificant part of what a person
needs to know in order to get by in the world, so that the greater part of cultural knowledge had still to be uncovered. Above all, cognitive anthropology was unable to grasp the
source of human motives: one learned no more from an analysis, say, of kinship terminology about people's feelings for one another than one might learn from the grammar
of a language about why its speakers say the things they do.

In recent years, and partly in response to these objections, cognitive anthropology has
resurfaced in a new guise, as the investigation of what are now called 'cultural models'.
Introducing a seminal volume of essays on *Cultural models in language and thought*, Naomi
Quinn and Dorothy Holland define such models as 'presupposed, taken-for-granted models
of the world that are widely shared . . . by the members of a society and that play an
enormous role in their understanding of that world and their behaviour in it' (1987: 4).
They differ from the classificatory schemas identified by earlier cognitive anthropologists
in three major ways. First, rather than dividing up the continuum of experience into
named categories, cultural models offer a description of the world framed in terms of
networks of interconnected images or propositions, in which objects, events and situations
take on regular, prototypical forms. Actual experience in the real world is then organised
by matching it to the prototypical scenarios built into the simplified worlds of the cultural
models, and these, in turn, furnish conventional guidelines for action. Secondly, although
linguistic data provide important clues to underlying cultural knowledge, it cannot be
assumed that word meanings stand to components of the cultural model in a simple relation of one-to-one correspondence. The relation is rather complex and indirect, and can
only be grasped through an analysis of the richly textured material of ordinary discourse.
Thirdly, cultural models – to the extent that they are fully internalised – do not merely
describe or represent the world, they also shape people's feelings and desires. That is to
say, they can have 'motivational force' (D'Andrade 1992: 28). As Claudia Strauss argues,
in her introduction to a recent volume dedicated to the demonstration of this point, the
realm of cognition is inseparable from the realm of affect; thus cultural models should be
understood as 'learned, internalised patterns of thought-feeling' (Strauss 1992: 3).

Despite these fairly radical revisions, the programme of cognitive anthropology remains
basically unchanged. Starting from the premise that culture consists in a corpus of inter-
generationally transmissible knowledge, as distinct from the ways in which it is put to use
in practical contexts of perception and action, the objective is to discover how this knowledge is organised. Moreover the assumptions on which the programme rests are much as
they were in Durkheim's day. They are that cognition consists of a process of matching
sensory experience to stable conceptual schemata, that much if not all of the order that
people claim to perceive in the world – and especially the social world – is imposed by
the mind rather than given in experience, that people are able to understand one another

to the extent that their cultural orderings are founded on consensus (such that the limits of consensus define the boundaries of society), and that the acquisition of such orderings involves a process of internalisation. These assumptions have not, however, gone unchallenged – indeed there is a powerful movement within contemporary anthropology that would reject them altogether. One of the most influential figures in this movement has been Pierre Bourdieu, who in a series of works has attempted to show how cultural knowledge, rather than being imported by the mind into contexts of experience, is itself generated within these contexts in the course of people's involvement with others in the practical business of life. Through such involvement, people acquire the specific dispositions and sensibilities that lead them to orient themselves in relation to their environment and to attend to its features in the particular ways that they do. These dispositions and sensibilities add up to what Bourdieu calls the *habitus* (1990: 52–65).[2]

THE THEORY OF PRACTICE

Like the 'cultural model' of cognitive anthropology, the *habitus* of Bourdieu's theory of practice could be described as a pattern of thought-feeling. The similarity ends there, however. For thinking and feeling, in Bourdieu's account, do not go on in an interior subjective (or intersubjective) space of images and representations but in the space of people's actual engagement in the settings of practical activity. Whereas cultural models are supposed to exist independently of, and prior to, their application in particular situations of use – such as in doing things or making things, or in the interpretation of experience – the *habitus* exists only as it is instantiated in the activity itself. In other words, the *habitus* is not expressed in practice, it rather *subsists* in it.[3] What Bourdieu has in mind is the kind of practical mastery that we associate with skill – a mastery that we carry in our bodies and that is refractory to formulation in terms of any system of mental rules and representations. Such skill is acquired not through formal instruction, but by routinely carrying out specific tasks involving characteristic postures and gestures, or what Bourdieu calls a particular body *hexis*. 'A way of walking, a tilt of the head, facial expressions, ways of sitting and of using implements' – all of these, and more, comprise what it takes to be an accomplished practitioner, and together they furnish a person with his or her bearings in the world (Bourdieu 1977: 87). And if people from different backgrounds orient themselves in different ways, this is not because they are interpreting the same sensory experience in terms of alternative cultural models or cognitive schemata, but because, due to their previous bodily training, their senses are differentially attuned to the environment.

In the anthropological study of cognition this kind of approach is perhaps best represented in the work of Jean Lave. Her book *Cognition in Practice* (1988) is a manifesto for an 'outdoor psychology' – that is, a psychology that would take as its unit of analysis 'the whole person in action, acting within the settings of that activity' (1988: 17). Cognition, in Lave's view, is not a process that goes on 'inside the head', whose products are representations that bear some complex relation to the world outside, but rather a social activity that is situated in the nexus of ongoing relations between persons and the world, and that plays its part in their mutual constitution. It is a process wherein both persons, as knowledgeable social agents, and the settings in which they act, continually come into being, each in relation to the other. Thus thinking is inseparable from doing, thought is 'embodied and enacted', and cognition is 'seamlessly distributed across persons, activity and setting' (1988: 171). To study cognition is to focus on the *modus operandi* not of the mind, in organising the bodily data of sense, but of the whole body-person in the business of dwelling in the world. And if knowledge is shared it is because people work together, through their joint immersion in the settings of activity, in the process of its formation.

What, then, becomes of the models and schemata of the cognitive anthropologists? Are they merely artefacts of analytic abstraction, products of attempts by anthropological observers to represent manifest behaviour as the output of formal programmes? Or do they, to the contrary, offer clues to basic truths about the way the human mind works? The answers to these questions hinge on more fundamental differences of approach which divide psychologists as much as anthropologists. Roughly speaking, the division is between advocates of cognitive science on the one hand, and their critics on the other, who find inspiration in an ecological or phenomenological perspective on perception and cognition. These differences of approach, and some of their implications for anthropology, are reviewed in the next part of this chapter.

II

COGNITIVE SCIENCE

In the field of psychology, cognitive science emerged as an alternative to behaviourism in the 1950s, alongside the development of the digital computer. Its founding axioms are that people come to know what is 'out there' in the world by representing it in the mind, in the form of 'mental models', and that such representations are the result of a computational process working upon information received by the senses. The functioning of the mind, then, can be compared to the operation of a computer program, and the relation between mind and brain to that between the program and the 'hardware' in which it is installed (Johnson-Laird 1988). But the computing analogy also found its way into cognitive anthropology – I have already referred to Geertz's (1973: 44) likening of cultural control mechanisms to computer software – where it was similarly supposed that the mind is equipped with programmes that construct internal representations of the environment from the data of sensation, and deliver appropriate plans for action (D'Andrade 1984: 88–9). Whereas cognitive scientists, however, have by and large been concerned to discover universals of human cognition, which are attributed to innate structures established in the course of evolution under natural selection, cognitive anthropologists have sought to account for human perception and action in terms of acquired schemata or programmes that differ from one culture to another.

How, then, should we view the relation between these two projects? Are they contradictory or mutually compatible? D'Andrade (1981: 181–2) tackles this issue by considering the fit between *programmes* and *processors*. By programmes he means the informational content of transmitted culture – what is 'passed along' from generation to generation. By processors he means the apparatus of acquisition that makes such transmission possible, an apparatus that is assumed to be common to all human minds. According to this division, cognitive anthropology is concerned with the diversity of cultural content, and with the way in which its organisation is constrained by invariant properties of the processing devices that govern its acquisition, while cognitive psychology is concerned with the structure and functioning of the devices themselves, and the way in which they work on all kinds of information (including cultural information). This formulation, however, begs a critical question. Granted that mental representations are the products of a processing of information by acquired cultural programmes, what is the source of the processing apparatus of which these programmes are themselves products? This apparatus, it seems, must already be in place prior to the acquisition of culture; hence its design and operation must be innately specified. In short, the theory that all human cognition is grounded in culturally specific schemata can hold only on condition that human beings come universally pre-equipped with the structures necessary to enable these schemata to be acquired in the first place.

This is precisely the conclusion reached by Dan Sperber (1985), in the context of his critique of cultural relativism – the doctrine, long ascendant in anthropology, that people in different cultures inhabit different cognitive (or rather, cognisable) worlds, each with its own criteria of rationality and judgement. Relativists argue that just as every non-human animal species, depending on its evolved cognitive organisation, can only know the world in its own particular way, so also every human culture is locked into the cognitive framework of a unique worldview. But whereas species differences supposedly have a genetic basis, cultural differences are assumed to be entirely independent of genetic constraint. Thus cultural relativists tend to imagine that theirs is a position opposed to an innatist view of the human mind, and that evidence for the diversity of incommensurate worldviews only goes to prove that the underlying structures of human cognition are genetically underdetermined and malleable to the effects of experience.

Yet in this, Sperber shows, they are mistaken. Relativists, he contends, have failed to attend to the psychological implications of their assumption that human behaviour is rooted in tradition rather than heredity. Had they done so, they would have realised that a creature capable of taking on not just one form of life but *any one* of a very large number of possible alternative forms would require more rather than less by way of innate programming. On the basis of a formal logical argument, Sperber concludes that 'the greater the diversity of the cultures that humans are capable of acquiring, the greater the complexity of the innate learning abilities involved' (1985: 43). Thus the relativists' appeal to human cultural diversity is not at all contrary to the universalist claims of cognitive science; rather it depends upon them.

Though the logic of Sperber's argument may be impeccable, it rests on a foundation that is far from secure – namely, that cultural knowledge takes the propositional (or semi-propositional) form of *beliefs*, 'representations acquired through social communication and accepted on the ground of social affiliation' (1985: 59). Underlying the commonsense understanding of the culturally competent actor is supposed to lie a huge database of such representations, which provide all the information necessary to generate appropriate responses under any given environmental circumstances. Yet as many critics of cognitive science have pointed out, and as the failure of attempts to replicate human skills in the design of expert systems has amply demonstrated (Dreyfus and Dreyfus 1987), even the simplest and most routine of everyday tasks are refractory to codification in propositional form. By and large, these tasks are not represented (save in the notebooks of observers), nor are such representations communicated in learning situations. Most cultural learning takes place through trial-and-error and practice, albeit in socially structured situations, and although beginners may need to follow rules, these rules structure the situation of learning and do not themselves form any part of the content of what is learned. For the skilled practitioner consults the world, rather than representations (rules, propositions, beliefs) inside his or her head, for guidance on what to do next.[4] As Andy Clark puts it, why should we go to the trouble of modelling the world when 'we can use the world as its own best model' (Clark 1997: 29–30, see also Chapman 1991: 20)?

Faced with the evident artificiality of depicting cultural knowledge in algorithmised form as a set of programmes, acquired by means of a processing device that is somehow constituted in advance of ontogenetic development, cognitive science has come up with an alternative model of the way the mind works. Instead of positing one giant processor with a massive capacity for information storage and retrieval, it is suggested that the mind consists of a very large number of small, simple processors, massively interconnected, all operating in parallel, and receiving inputs and delivering outputs to each other along the countless pathways linking them. Crucially, a system so constituted can learn from experience, not by taking on new informational content, but by adjustments to the differential strengths of the connections among processing units. In other words, knowledge is acquired through the establishment of particular patterns of connection: any processor may therefore be involved in the representation of diverse experiences; conversely the representation of any experience may be distributed across many processors (Johnson-Laird 1988: 174). This so-called 'connectionist' model of the mind has a certain anthropological appeal – thus cognitive anthropologists such as D'Andrade (1990: 98–9) have noted that the properties of cultural models are precisely what would be expected from the operation of parallel processing networks, while Bloch (1991) has suggested that the acquisition of practical skills may best be understood in terms of the development of tightly connected networks dedicated to particular domains of cognition (for a more extended review, see D'Andrade 1995: 143–9).

Despite its greater realism, connectionism remains open to much the same criticisms that have been levelled against earlier versions of artificial intelligence (Dreyfus 1992). For ultimately, it is still grounded in the Cartesian ontology that is basic to the entire project of cognitive science – an ontology that divorces the activity of the mind from that of the body in the world. Thus the body continues to be regarded as nothing more than an input device whose role is to receive information to be 'processed' by the mind, rather than playing any part in cognition itself. And beyond that, the world is supposed to exist as a domain of problems to be solved, or as a field for the enactment of solutions reached, rather than as a resource for problem solving (Clark 1997: 83–4). Connectionists, Clark admits, 'inherit a distressing tendency to study disembodied problem solving and to opt for abstract, symbolically defined input-output mappings' (1997: 80). What they fail to recognise is that the processing loops that yield intelligent action are not confined to some interior space of mind, confined within the skull, but freely penetrate both the body and its environment. This failure is deeply rooted in the history of twentieth-century psychology. It lies, as Edward Reed (1987: 144–5) has shown, in the founding assumptions of the behaviourist theory that cognitive science claims to have overthrown: namely that perception is based on discrete bodily sensations touched off by external stimuli, and that action is based on the corresponding bodily responses.

The objection to behaviourism was that, as a theory, it was incomplete: the simple linkage of stimulus and response was considered insufficient to account for the knowledgeability of actors or the productivity of their actions. To complete the picture, cognitive scientists posited a mental processing device that would convert the stimulus input into knowledge, and generate plans for the delivery of meaningful responses. There is however another way out of behaviourism, and this is to treat the perceiving organism not as a passive recipient of stimuli but as an active agent who purposively seeks out information that would specify the meaningful properties of his or her environment. This was the path taken by James Gibson in his pioneering studies of visual perception, and in doing so he laid the foundations for an approach, known as 'ecological psychology', which is radically opposed, in almost every respect, to the project of cognitive science.

ECOLOGICAL PSYCHOLOGY

The point of departure for ecological psychology is the proposition that perceptual activity consists not in the operation of the mind upon the bodily data of sense, but in the intentional movement of the whole being (indissolubly body and mind) in its environment. The emphasis on movement is critical. Cognitive science assumes a static perceiver who has nothing to go on but transient patterns of sensory excitation that are, in themselves, quite insufficient to specify the objects and events that gave rise to them. Thus the problem of perception, for the cognitive scientist, is to show how these ephemeral and fragmentary sense data are reconstructed, in terms of pre-existing schemata or representations, into a coherent picture of the world. But for Gibson, sensations do not, as such, constitute the data for perception (Gibson 1979: 55). Rather, what the perceiver looks for are constancies underlying the continuous modulations of the sensory array as one moves from place to place. In visual perception, for example, we do not see patterns of light but objects in our environment. We do so because, as we move about, the pattern of light reaching the eyes from reflecting surfaces in the environment (that is, the 'optic array') undergoes a gradual transformation. It is the invariants that underly this transformation, and not the momentary patterns of stimulation themselves, that specify what we see. Indeed it is Gibson's contention that the invariant relations that structure the modulations of an optic array for a moving observer contain all the information necessary to specify the environment. Perception, then, is a matter of extracting these invariants. The perceiver has no need to reconstruct the world in the mind if it can be accessed directly in this way.

Certain implications follow. First, if perception entails movement, then it must be a mode of action rather than a prerequisite for action. For Gibson, perception is an active and exploratory process of information pickup; far from working on sensations already received, it involves the continual movement, adjustment and reorientation of the receptor organs themselves. What is important, he argues, 'is the looking, listening, touching and sniffing that goes on when the perceptual systems are at work' (1982[1976]: 397–8). Secondly, if perception is a mode of action, then what we perceive must be a direct function of how we act. Depending on the kind of activity in which we are engaged, we will be attuned to picking up particular kinds of information. The knowledge obtained through direct perception is thus *practical*, it is knowledge about what an environment offers for the pursuance of the action in which the perceiver is currently engaged. In other words, to perceive an object or event is to perceive what it *affords*. Perhaps the most fundamental contribution of Gibson's approach to perception lay in his insight that the information picked up by an agent in the context of practical activity specifies what are called the 'affordances' of objects and events in the environment (Gibson 1979: 127–43).

Thirdly, the information that is potentially available to an agent is inexhaustible: there is no limit to what can be perceived. Throughout life one can keep on seeing new things in an otherwise permanent world, not by constructing the same sense data according to novel conceptual schemata, but by a sensitisation or 'fine-tuning' of the perceptual system to new kinds of information. Novel perceptions arise from creative acts of discovery rather than imagining, and the information on which they are based is available to anyone attuned to pick it up. Finally, and following from the above, one learns to perceive in the manner appropriate to a culture, not by acquiring programmes or conceptual schemata for organising sensory data into higher-order representations, but by 'hands-on' training in everyday tasks whose successful fulfilment requires a practised ability to notice and to respond fluently to salient aspects of the environment. In short, learning is not a transmission of information but – in Gibson's (1979: 254) words – an 'education of attention'. As such, it is inseparable from a person's life in the world, and indeed continues for as long as he or she lives.

There are clear parallels between the ecological critique, in the field of psychology, of cognitive science and the critique by practice theorists of cognitive anthropology, which I reviewed in the first part of this chapter. Both Gibson's ecological psychology and Bourdieu's theory of practice set out to re-embed perception and cognition within the practical contexts of people's ongoing engagement with their environments in the ordinary course of life. And both seek to escape from the sterile Cartesian dualisms of mind and nature, subject and object, intellection and sensation, and so on. Yet while the impact of Bourdieu's work in social and cultural anthropology has been immense, the relevance of Gibsonian ecological psychology to anthropological theory has been little explored. An obvious reason for the discrepancy lies in the fact that Gibson himself devoted scant attention to the specifically social and cultural dimensions of human life, preferring – if anything – to downplay the significance of the distinction between human beings and other animals. In developing his theory of affordances, Gibson did devote a brief section to 'other persons and animals' in the environment of the perceiver, noting that they have the peculiar capacity to 'act back' or, literally, to *interact* with the perceiver. Thus 'behavior affords behavior, and the whole subject matter of psychology and of the social sciences can be thought of as an elaboration of this basic fact' (Gibson 1979: 135). But beyond suggesting that the perception of mutual affordances in social life involves the same principles of information pickup as are involved in the perception of inanimate objects, Gibson did not pursue further the implications of this rather sweeping statement.

A recent attempt to develop this neglected aspect of the Gibsonian programme has been made by Edward Reed (1988a). The crux of his argument is that social agents can not only directly perceive their mutual affordances for one another, but also *share* their direct perception of other constituents of the environment. Attuned through prior training and experience to attending to similar invariants, and moving in the same environment in the pursuit of joint activities, they will pick up the same information (Reed 1988a: 119–20, see Gibson 1982[1967]: 412). Thus, contrary to the axioms of cognitive anthropology, the communion of experience that lies at the heart of sociality does not depend upon the organisation of sensory data, initially private to each perceiver, in terms of an objective system of collective representations. Rather, sociality is given from the start, *prior* to the objectification of experience in cultural categories, in the direct, perceptual involvement of fellow participants in a shared environment (Ingold 1993a: 222–3). This, indeed, is what makes anthropological fieldwork possible, for it allows the fieldworker and local people to inhabit a common ground of experience, even though each may bring to bear a radically different conceptual frame to the task of its interpretation. As Michael Jackson notes, 'by using one's body in the same way as others in the same environment one finds oneself informed by an understanding which may then be interpreted according to one's own custom or bent, yet which remains grounded in a field of practical activity and thereby remains consonant with the experience of those among whom one has lived' (1989: 135).

The environment of joint practical activity should not, however, be confused with the physical world of 'nature' (Gibson 1979: 8). For the world can appear in this latter guise only to a creature that can disengage itself – or imagine itself to be disengaged – from the processes of its own material life. But the world we inhabit does not confront us, it surrounds us. This does not mean that it is any less real; the environment, however, is reality constituted in *relation* to the beings whose environment it is. As I have argued elsewhere (Ingold 1992a), Gibsonian psychology offers a way of thinking about human-environmental relations that dispenses with the conventional dichotomy between naturally given and culturally constructed worlds. According to convention, it is necessary to distinguish between the 'real' environment, as it is presented to detached, scientific observation, and the 'perceived' environment as it is built up through a selective response to stimuli (Brookfield 1969: 53). In anthropology, the distinction is commonly expressed by means of a contrast between the 'etic' level of objective description and the 'emic' level on which the environment is made meaningful by cultural subjects.[5] Yet from a Gibsonian perspective, it is apparent that the world becomes a meaningful place for people through being *lived in*, rather than through having been constructed along the lines of some formal design. Meanings are not attached by the mind to objects in the world, rather these objects take on their significance – or in Gibson's terms, they afford what they do – by virtue of their incorporation into a characteristic pattern of day-to-day activities. In short, far from being inscribed upon the bedrock of physical reality, meaning is immanent in the relational contexts of people's practical engagement with their lived-in environments.

Phenomenology

It is at this point that ecological psychology makes contact with an older, Continental European tradition of philosophical inquiry, broadly characterised as phenomenological, and represented above all in the works of Martin Heidegger and Maurice Merleau-Ponty. Just as the point of departure, for Gibson, had been the perceiver-in-his/her-environment, so likewise these philosophers set out from the premise that every person is, before all else, a being-in-the-world. And their intellectual agenda, like that of Gibson, was fundamentally antagonistic to the kind of rationalism whose contemporary manifestation, in the field of psychology, is cognitive science. Yet in some ways they went even further. For all his emphasis on perception as a process that is continually going on, Gibson assumed that the world which the perceiver moves around in and explores is relatively fixed and permanent, somehow pre-prepared with all its affordances ready and waiting to be taken up by whatever creatures arrive to inhabit it.[6] From a phenomenological standpoint, by contrast, the world emerges with its properties alongside the emergence of the perceiver in person, against the background of involved activity. Since the person is a being-in-the-world, the coming-into-being of the person is part and parcel of the process of coming-into-being of the world.

Consider, for example, Heidegger's critique of Cartesianism (reviewed in Dreyfus 1991: 109–27). Heidegger begins by distinguishing two ways in which the world may 'show up' to a being who is active within it: availableness and occurrentness. The former is evident in our everyday use of the most familiar things around us, which, absorbed into the current of our activity (as indeed, we are ourselves), become in a sense transparent, wholly subordinate to the 'in-order-to' of the task at hand. The latter refers to the way in which things are revealed in their essential nature to an observer who self-consciously stands back from the action, assuming a stance of contemplative detachment or disinterested reflection. Now Cartesian ontology, which takes as its starting point the self-contained subject confronting a domain of isolable objects, assumes that things are initially encountered in their pure occurrentness, or brute facticity. The perceiver has first to make sense of these occurrent entities – to render them intelligible – by categorising them, and assigning to them meanings or functions, before they can be made available for use. Heidegger, however, reverses this order of priority. For a being whose primary condition of existence is that of dwelling in the world, things are initially encountered in their availableness, as already integrated into a set of practices for 'coping' or getting by. To reveal their occurrent properties, things have to be rendered *un*intelligible by stripping away the significance they derive from contexts of ordinary use. This, of course, is the explicit project of natural science, which seeks to describe and explain a world which the rest of us are preoccupied with living in. Yet the scientist, like everyone else, is a being-in-the-world, and scientific practice, as any other skilled activity, draws unselfconsciously upon the available. Thus even science, however detached and theoretical it may be, takes place against a background of involved activity. The total disengagement of the subject from the world, from which Cartesianism charts a process of building up from the occurrent to the available, is therefore a pure fiction which can only be reached by extrapolating to the point of absurdity a progressive reduction from the available to the occurrent.

If, as Heidegger seems to suggest, self and world merge in the activity of dwelling, so that one cannot say where one ends and the other begins, it surely follows that the intentional presence of the perceiving agent, as a being-in-the-world, must also be an *embodied* presence. This was the principal contention of Merleau-Ponty in his massive treatise, dating from 1945 [trans. 1962], on the *Phenomenology of perception*. 'The body', Merleau-Ponty wrote, 'is the vehicle of being in the world, and having a body is, for a living creature, to be involved in a definite environment, to identify oneself with certain projects and be continually committed to them' (1962: 82). Like Heidegger, Merleau-Ponty was concerned to reverse the ontological priorities of Cartesian rationalism. Just as for Heidegger, the available is the ground upon which we may seek to reveal the properties of the occurrent, so for Merleau-Ponty our knowledge of the body as a physical thing – as a mere conduit or target of the mind's attention – is grounded in a more fundamental awareness, pre-objective and pre-conscious, which is given by the existential condition of our total bodily immersion, from the start, in an environment. Only because we are thus immersed in the world can we imagine ourselves as existing separately from it. The problem of perception lies in understanding the nature of this immediate pre-objective experience, itself a precondition for objective thought. Accordingly, Merleau-Ponty sought to uncover 'underneath the objective and detached knowledge of the body that other knowledge which we have of it by virtue of its always being with us and of the fact that *we are our body*' (1962: 206, my emphasis). In this latter sense, the body is neither object nor instrument, it is rather the *subject* of perception.

In recent years, albeit somewhat belatedly, many anthropologists have begun to read Merleau-Ponty with renewed interest. Though there is nothing particularly novel about anthropological concerns with the body and its symbolism, much work in this field is marked by a tendency to treat body praxis as a mere vehicle for the outward expression of meanings emanating from a higher source in culture or society. This is true, for example, of the writings of Mary Douglas. In line with her general thesis, reviewed in the first part of this chapter, of the cultural construction of experience, Douglas holds that the body is a medium whose forms – whether adopted in movement or repose – 'express social pressures in manifold ways' (1970: 93). As Jackson has eloquently shown, this 'subjugation of the bodily to the semantic' diminishes the body and its experience in two ways. First, body movements – postures and gestures – are reduced to the status of signs which direct the analyst in search of what they stand for, namely *extra*-somatic cultural meanings. Secondly, the body is rendered passive and inert, while the active role of mobilising it, putting it to use and charging it with significance is delegated to a knowing subject which is both detached from the body and reified as 'society' (Jackson 1989: 122–3). The first reduction fails to recognise that gestures, whatever they might be held to symbolise, delineate their own meanings through their embeddedness in social and material contexts of action. The second reduction ignores a consideration pivotal to Merleau-Ponty's phenomenology: that the body is given in movement, and that bodily movement carries its own immanent intentionality. Indeed it is because of this intentionality that the subject's action is, at one and the same time, a movement of perception (1962: 110–11).[7]

Drawing inspiration from Merleau-Ponty, Jackson (1989) calls for studies that would take as their focus the 'body subject' in its dealings with the world. In similar vein, and linking Merleau-Ponty's concerns with perception to Bourdieu's with practice, Thomas Csordas (1990) puts the case for the establishment of a 'paradigm of embodiment' in anthropological inquiry. Far from treating the body as an *object* of study, this paradigm would be launched from the postulate that 'the body is to be considered as the *subject* of culture, or in other words as the existential [as opposed to the cognitive] ground of culture' (1990: 5). In its promise to collapse the Cartesian dualities between mind and body, subject and object, the paradigm holds a certain appeal for many anthropologists whose familiarity with indigenous, non-Western understandings – which are not generally concordant with such dualities – predisposes them to adopt a critical attitude towards the foundational assumptions of Western thought and science. Not everyone has been won over, however, as is evident from the continuing strength of cognitive anthropology, and from the pronouncements of anthropologists such as Bloch (1991), D'Andrade (1995) and Sperber (1996) who see a role for anthropology in an interdisciplinary alliance with cognitive science. Moreover, as I shall show by way of conclusion, there remain three major obstacles to the further development of the phenomenological approach.

CONCLUSION

The first obstacle has to do with the problematic status of biology. Even anthropologists who would readily accept the idea of embodiment as a paradigm for the study of culture, and who denounce the mind/body distinction, tend to balk at attempts to soften the conventional dichotomy between culture and biology (for example, Csordas 1990: 36). In effect, the dichotomy remains as strong as it always was; only the body has been repositioned. Formerly placed with the organism on the side of biology, the body has now reappeared as a 'subject' on the side of culture. Far from collapsing the Cartesian dualism of subject and object, this move actually serves to reproduce it. Moreover it leaves the organism bodiless, reduced to an inchoate mass of biological potential. The embodiment of culture, in short, leads to nothing less than the disembodiment of the organism! Indeed to posit some kind of biological residuum that exists prior to, and independently of, the culturally constituted body is to resort to the very objectivism that a phenomenological approach claims to repudiate (Morton 1995). It seems to me that to consolidate the theoretical gains brought by the paradigm of embodiment, one final step has yet to be taken: that is, to recognise that the body *is* the human organism, and that the process of embodiment is one and the same as the development of that organism in its environment.

This leads to the second obstacle, which is that the cause of dissolving the division between body and mind is ill-served by emphasising one term to the exclusion of the other. One could, in principle, speak just as well of enmindment as of embodiment, to emphasise the way in which the body and its surroundings are incorporated into those processing loops that underwrite human powers of agency and intentionality. Body and mind, after all, are not two separate things but two ways of describing the same thing – or better, the same process – namely the environmentally situated activity of the human organism-person (see Chapter Nineteen, pp. 352–3). Mind, as Gregory Bateson always insisted, is not 'in the head' rather than 'out there in the world', but immanent in the active, perceptual engagement of organism and environment (Bateson 1973). Indeed the distance between a Merleau-Pontyan phenomenology of the body and what Bateson christened the 'ecology of mind' is not as great as might first appear.

Finally, even if it is agreed that a phenomenological approach offers a richer and more 'experience-near' (Geertz 1984: 124) account of human life in the world than do the more formal, 'experience-distant' concepts of cognitive science, the problem remains of translating this approach into a programme of research that would give us a more accurate idea than we presently have of how people routinely succeed, in their everyday, skilful 'coping', in performing with ease actions that are far beyond the capabilities of any machine yet devised. It is easy to pour scorn on the efforts of researchers in artificial intelligence to replicate the processes at work in the human brain, but as Dreyfus admits (1992: xliv), no one knows how the brain does it, nor are philosophers in any way equipped to provide the answers.

What we can say, however, is that the effect of taking the agent-in-an-environment rather than the isolated, self-contained individual as our point of departure is to collapse not only the venerable Durkheimian distinction between the individual and society, but also the division – which has traditionally rested on this distinction – between the two disciplines of anthropology and psychology. I can see no further intellectual justification for continuing to separate these disciplines. For we now recognise that such processes as thinking, perceiving, remembering and learning have to be studied within the ecological contexts of people's interrelations with their environments. We recognise, too, that the mind and its properties are not given in advance of the individual's entry into the social world, but are rather fashioned through a lifelong history of involvement in relationships with others. And we know that it is through the activities of the embodied mind (or enminded body) that social relationships are formed and reformed. Psychological and social processes are thus one and the same. And the discipline that will be called into being to study these processes, whatever we choose to call it, will be the study of how people perceive, act, think, know, learn and remember within the settings of their mutual, practical involvement in the lived-in world.

Chapter Ten

Building, dwelling, living:

How animals and people make themselves at home in the world

This chapter is partly autobiographical, and describes my own attempts over the last few years to find a satisfactory way of understanding the relationships between people and their environments. It is incomplete, in the sense that I cannot claim to have yet found, or that I will ever find, final answers to the questions that are bothering me. Indeed, if one of the main conclusions of what I have to say is that so-called 'ends' or 'goals' are but landmarks on a journey, then this must apply as much to my own thinking and writing as to everything else that people do in the world. The most fundamental thing about life is that it does not begin here or end there, but is always *going on*. And for the same reason, as we saw in Chapter One (p. 20), environments are never complete but are continually under construction. My purpose here is to consider the implications of this point with regard to our ideas about the similarities and contrasts between human beings and other animals in the ways in which they go about creating environments for themselves. I am concerned, in particular, with the meaning of architecture, or of that part of the environment which is conventionally described as 'built'.

In recent years, my own ideas have undergone something of a sea change, which is where the autobiographical element comes in. I began with a view that was – and indeed still is – fairly conventional in anthropology, one that sets out from the premise that human beings inhabit discursive worlds of culturally constructed significance, laid out upon the substrate of a continuous and undifferentiated physical terrain. If I differed from my colleagues, at least in social anthropology, it was in my concern to spell out the implications of this premise for the distinction between human beings and non-human animals. I felt sure that the models developed by ecologists and evolutionary biologists to account for the relations between organisms and their environments must apply as well to the human as to any other species, yet it was also clear to me that these models left no space for what seemed to be the most outstanding characteristic of human activity – that it is intentionally motivated. Human intentions, I argued, are constituted in the intersubjective domain, of relationships among *persons*, as distinct from the domain in which human beings, as biological *organisms*, relate to other components of the natural environment. Human life, I therefore proposed, is conducted simultaneously in two domains – a social domain of interpersonal relations and an ecological domain of inter-organismic relations – so that the problem is to understand the interplay between them (Ingold 1986a: 9).

Starting out from two quite reasonable propositions – that human beings are organisms, and that human action is intentionally motivated – I thus ended up with what appeared to be a thoroughly *unreasonable* result: that unlike all other animals, humans live a split-level existence, half in nature, half out; half organism, half person; half body, half mind. I had come out as an unreconstructed Cartesian dualist, which is perhaps not so surprising when you remember that the intellectual division of labour between the natural sciences and the humanities – and within anthropology between its biological and sociocultural divisions – rests on a Cartesian foundation. Something, I felt, must be wrong somewhere, if the only way to understand our own creative involvement in the world is by taking ourselves out of it. Eventually, it dawned on me that although the problem was an anthropological one, it would require more than an anthropological solution: what is needed is a completely new way of thinking about organisms and about their relations with their environments; in short, a new ecology. And it is towards this new ecology that I have been groping.

In this task, I have gained inspiration from three principal sources. The first comes from biology, and consists in the work of the handful of courageous scholars – principally developmental biologists – who have been prepared to challenge the hegemony of neo-Darwinian thinking in the discipline (e.g. Ho and Saunders 1984, see also Oyama 1985). The second lies in what is known as 'ecological psychology', an approach to understanding perception and action that is radically opposed to the cognitivist orientation of the psychological mainstream (Gibson 1979, Michaels and Carello 1981). And the third comes from philosophical writing of a broadly phenomenological bent, above all the works of Martin Heidegger (1971) and Maurice Merleau-Ponty (1962).[1] Although developed independently, in the different disciplinary contexts of biology, psychology and philosophy, these three approaches have much in common. Though I cannot now explore the commonalities in detail, I want to highlight just two of them that are rather central to what I shall have to say. First, all three approaches reverse the normal order of priority – normal, that is, in the history of Western thought – of form over process. Life, in this perspective, is not the revelation of pre-existent form but the very process wherein form is generated and held in place. Secondly, the three approaches adopt as their common point of departure the agent-in-its-environment, or what phenomenology calls 'being in the world', as opposed to the self-contained individual confronting a world 'out there'. In short, they maintain that it is through being inhabited, rather than through its assimilation to a formal design specification, that the world becomes a meaningful environment for people.

In what follows, I refer to this position as the 'dwelling perspective', by contrast to the more conventional position from which I began, and which I shall call the 'building perspective'. Thus the movement in my own thinking has been from the building perspective to the dwelling perspective. To document this movement, I shall start by spelling out the first of these perspectives, and its implications for the way we understand the construction of the built environment, in greater depth. I shall then explain what is entailed in adopting a dwelling perspective in its place. Finally, I shall consider how this shift from a building perspective to a dwelling perspective bears upon the concept and meaning of architecture.

CONSTRUCTING ENVIRONMENTS AND MAKING WORLDS

Our initial problem may be framed by juxtaposing two statements, the first of which will be familiar to anthropological readers, the second much less so. 'Man', Clifford Geertz has declared, 'is an animal suspended in webs of significance he himself has spun' (1973: 5). One is led to suppose that non-human animals are not so suspended. Spiders spin webs, and do indeed suspend themselves in them, but their webs are tangible objects – they catch flies, not thoughts. But now consider this passage from the delightful but little

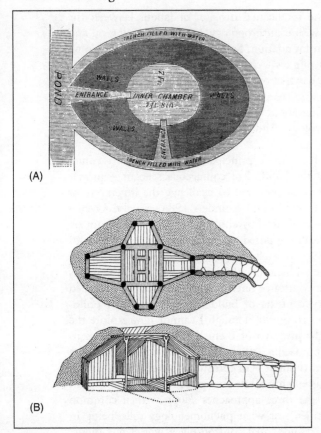

(A)

(B)

Figure 10.1 Human and animal architecture. (A) Ground plan of beaver lodge (from Morgan 1868: 142); (B) Floor plan and cross-section of Eskimo house, Mackenzie region (from Mauss and Beuchat 1979: 4).

known text of Jakob von Uexküll, *A Stroll through the Worlds of Animals and Men*: 'As the spider spins its threads, every subject spins his relations to certain characters of the things around him, and weaves them into a firm web which carries his existence' (1957: 14). Now the subjects of which von Uexküll speaks are not merely human, nor even close to human. Indeed he begins his stroll with a particular species of parasitic tick! If, as it would seem, what Geertz says of humankind applies equally to ticks, then what – if anything – *does* distinguish human from non-human environments?

Though it might be said, with Nelson Goodman (1978), that human beings are makers of worlds, this only begs the question of how human acts of world-making differ from the processes whereby non-human animals fashion their environments. It was this question that initially led me to focus on the meaning of the built environment: not, that is, on what a built environment means, but on what it means to say that an environment is built. How can we distinguish an environment that is built from one that is not? It is all very well to define the built environment, as do Denise Lawrence and Setha Low in a recent review, to include 'any physical alteration of the natural environment, from hearths to cities, through construction by humans' (1990: 454). But why should the products of human building activity be any different, in principle, from the constructions of other animals? Or to phrase the same question in another way, by what right do we conventionally identify the artificial with the 'man-made'? And where, in an environment that bears the imprint of human activity, can we draw the line between what is, and is not, a house, or a building, or an instance of architecture (Pearson and Richards 1994: 2)?

My first efforts to deal with these questions all hinged on a crucial distinction, which I thought quite unproblematic at the time, between design and execution. The argument ran roughly as follows: imagine a mollusc shell, a beaver's lodge and a human house. All have been regarded, at one time or another, as instances of architecture. Some authors would restrict architecture to the house, others would include the lodge – as an example of 'animal architecture' (von Frisch 1975) – but exclude the shell, others would include all three forms. The usual argument for excluding the shell is that it is attached to the body of the mollusc, whereas for something to count as an artefact it must be detached from the body. The shell, it is said, 'just grows' – there is nothing the mollusc can or need do about it. The beaver, by contrast, works hard to put its lodge together: the lodge is a product of the beaver's 'beavering', of its activity. Likewise the house is a product of the activities of its human builders. In their respective forms, and levels of complexity, they need not be that different (Figure 10.1). Should we, then, conclude that the lodge is beaver-made just as much as the house is man-made?

To this question I answered in the negative (Ingold 1986b: 345–6; 1988b: 90). Wherever they are, beavers construct the same kinds of lodges and, so far as we know, have always done so. Human beings, by contrast, build houses of very diverse kinds, and although certain house forms have persisted for long periods, there is unequivocal evidence that these forms have also undergone significant historical change. The difference between the lodge and the house lies, I argued, not in the construction of the thing itself, but in the origination of the *design* that governs the construction process. The design of the lodge is incorporated into the same programme that underwrites the development of the beaver's own body: thus the beaver is no more the designer of the lodge than is the mollusc the designer of its shell. It is merely the *executor* of a design that has evolved, along with the morphology and behaviour of the beaver, through a process of variation under natural selection. In other words, both the beaver – in its outward, phenotypic form – and the lodge are 'expressions' of the same underlying genotype. Richard Dawkins (1982) has coined the term 'extended phenotype' to refer to genetic effects that are situated beyond the body of the organism, and in this sense, the lodge is part of the extended phenotype for the beaver.

Human beings, on the other hand, are the authors of their own designs, constructed through a self-conscious decision process – an intentional selection of ideas. As Joseph Rykwert has put it: 'unlike even the most elaborate animal construction, human building involves decision and choice, always and inevitably; it therefore involves a project' (1991: 56). It is to this project, I maintained, that we refer when we say that the house is *made*, rather than merely constructed. I even went so far as to extend the argument to the domain of toolmaking, criticising students of animal behaviour for their assumption that wherever objects are manifestly being modified or constructed for future use, tools are being made. They are only being made, I claimed, when they are constructed in the imagination prior to their realisation in the material (Ingold 1986a: 40–78). But if the essence of making lies in the self-conscious authorship of design, that is in the construction of a project, it follows that things can be made without undergoing any actual physical alteration at all. Suppose that you need to knock in a nail but lack a hammer. Looking around the objects in your environment, you deliberately select something best suited to your purpose: it must be hard, have a flat striking surface, fit in the hand, and so on. So you pick up an appropriate stone. In this very selection, the stone has 'become' a hammer in that, in your mind's eye, a 'hammer-quality' has been attached to it. Without altering the stone in any way, you have made a hammer out of it.[2] In just the same manner, a cave may come to serve as a dwelling, a stretch of bare flat land as an airstrip, or a sheltered bay as a harbour.

To deal with situations of this kind, I chose the term *co-option*. Thus the stone was co-opted, rather than constructed, to become a hammer. It follows that there are two kinds of making: co-optive and constructive. In co-optive making an already existing object is fitted to a conceptual image of an intended future use, in the mind of a user. In constructive making this procedure is reversed, in that the object is physically remodelled to conform more closely to the pre-existing image. Indeed it seemed that the history of things – of artefacts, architecture and landscapes – could be understood in terms of successive, alternating steps of co-option and construction. We press into service what we find around us to suit our current purposes, we proceed to modify those things to our own design so that they better serve these purposes, but at the same time our objectives – or adaptive requirements – also change so that the modified objects are subsequently co-opted to quite other projects for which they are perceived to come in handy, and so on and on. Exactly the same model has been applied to account for the evolution of organisms – Darwin himself used it in his book on orchids (1862: 348).[3] To adopt terms suggested by Stephen J. Gould and Elisabeth Vrba (1982), structures *ad*apted for one purpose may be *ex*apted for another, subsequently undergoing further adaptation, only to be exapted for yet another purpose ... The difference is just that in the case of organic evolution, the selection involved is natural rather than intentional (Ingold 1986b: 200–2).

It was in searching around for ways to express these ideas that I came across the writings of Jakob von Uexküll, Estonian-born aristocrat and a founding figure in the fields of both ethology and semiotics, to whose *Stroll through the Worlds of Animals and Men*, first published in 1934, I have already referred. Reacting against the mechanistic biology of the day, von Uexküll argued that to treat the animal as a mere assemblage of sensory and motor organs is to leave out the subject who uses these organs as tools, respectively, of perception and action:

> We who still hold that our sense organs serve our perceptions, and our motor organs our actions, see in animals ... not only the mechanical structure, but also the operator, who is built into their organs, as we are into our bodies. We can no longer regard animals as mere machines, but as subjects whose essential activity consists in perceiving and acting ... All that a subject perceives becomes his *perceptual world* and all that he does, his *effector world*. Perceptual and effector worlds together form a closed unit, the *Umwelt*.
>
> (1957: 6)

For von Uexküll, the *Umwelt* – that is, the world as constituted within the specific life activity of an animal – was to be clearly distinguished from the environment, by which he meant the surroundings of the animal as these appear to the indifferent human observer. We human beings cannot enter directly into the *Umwelten* of other creatures, but through close study we may be able to imagine what they are like. But the reverse does not hold: the non-human animal, because it cannot detach its consciousness from its own life-activity, because it is always submerged within its own *Umwelt*, cannot see objects as such, for what they are in themselves. Thus for the animal, the environment – conceived as a domain of 'neutral objects' – cannot exist (Ingold 1992a: 43).

Towards the end of his stroll, von Uexküll invites his readers to imagine the manifold inhabitants of an oak tree. There is the fox, who has built its lair between the roots; the owl, who perches in the crotch of its mighty limbs; the squirrel, for whom it provides a veritable maze of ladders and springboards; the ant, who forages in the furrows and crags of its bark; the wood-boring beetle who feeds and lays its eggs in passages beneath the bark, and hundreds of others (Figures 10.2 and 10.3). Each creature, through the sheer fact of its presence, confers on the tree – or on some portion of it – a particular quality or 'functional tone': shelter and protection for the fox, support for the owl, a thoroughfare for the squirrel, hunting grounds for the ant, egg-laying facilities for the beetle. The same tree, thus, figures quite differently within the respective *Umwelten* of its diverse inhabitants. But for none of them does it exist *as a tree* (von Uexküll 1957: 76–9). Now consider the forester, who is measuring up the tree to estimate the volume of timber it will yield. For him, the tree figures as a potential source of valuable raw material, whereas for the little child – again to follow von Uexküll's example (pp. 73–5) – it seems to be alive and to reveal a frightening aspect. But these different perceptions are not tied, as they are for non-human animals, to the *modus operandi* of the organism. Human beings do not construct the world in a certain way by virtue of what they are, but by virtue of their own conceptions of the possibilities of being. And these possibilities are limited only by the power of the imagination.

Herein, it seemed to me, lay the essential distinction I was seeking between the respective ways in which the subjective existence of human and non-human animals is suspended in 'webs of significance'. For the non-human, every thread in the web is a relation between it and some object or feature of the environment, a relation that is set up through its own practical immersion in the world and the bodily orientations that this entails. For the human, by contrast, the web – and the relations of which it consists – are inscribed in a separate plane of mental representations, forming a tapestry of meaning that *covers*

Figure 10.2 Fox, owl and oak tree

From Jakob von Uexküll 'A Stroll through the Worlds of Animals and Men,' in *Instinctive Behavior*, 1957, pp. 76–7, illustrations by G. Kriszat.

over the world of environmental objects. Whereas the non-human animal perceives these objects as immediately available for use, to human beings they appear initially as occurrent phenomena to which potential uses must be *affixed*, prior to any attempt at engagement. The fox discovers shelter in the roots of a tree, but the forester sees timber only in his mind's eye, and has first to fit that image in thought to his perception of the occurrent object – the tree – before taking action. Or to take another example, suggested recently by Maurice Bloch, the 'swidden plot' exists as an image in the mind of the horticulturalist, who has to match that image to an observed stand of uncut forest prior to transforming it into a field (Bloch 1991: 187). As mental representations, the timber and the swidden plot belong to the 'intentional worlds' (cf. Shweder 1990: 2) of the forester and the farmer; as occurrent phenomena, the oak tree and the stand of forest belong to the physical environment of 'neutral objects'. It has been conventional, in anthropological and other writings of Western academic provenance, to refer to these worlds, of human values and purposes on the one hand, and of physical objects on the other, by means of the shorthand terms, culture and nature, respectively. And in a paper written

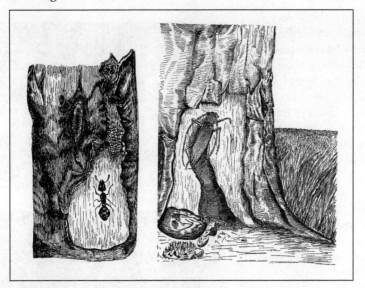

Figure 10.3   Ant, bark-boring beetle and oak tree

From Jakob von Uexküll 'A Stroll through the Worlds of Animals and Men,' in *Instinctive Behavior*, 1957, pp. 78–9, illustrations by G. Kriszat.

in 1987, I concluded that 'making is equivalent to the cultural ordering of nature – the inscription of ideal design upon the material world of things' (Ingold 1989: 506). This statement, I confess, is now a source of considerable embarrassment.

THE BUILDING PERSPECTIVE

In my defence, I can only say that I was singing a tune that has been sung by most anthropologists, in one form or another, for decades, in the context of an encounter with students of animal behaviour whose theories had no place for agency or intentionality at all, except as an epiphenomenal effect of innate predisposition.[4] This tune is what I earlier called the 'building perspective', and I should now like to elaborate on this perspective with reference to anthropological work other than my own. For a founding statement, we could turn once again to Geertz, and to his assertion that culture – or at least that kind of culture taken to be the hallmark of humanity – consists in 'the imposition of an arbitrary framework of symbolic meaning upon reality' (1964: 39). Reality, that which is imposed upon, is envisioned here as an external world of nature, a source of raw materials and sensations for diverse projects of cultural construction. Following from this, a distinction is commonly made between the *real* environment that is given independently of the senses, and the *perceived* environment as it is reconstructed in the mind through the ordering of sense data in terms of acquired, cognitive schemata. Other conventional oppositions that encode the same distinction, and that we have already encountered (see Chapter Three, p. 41, and Chapter Nine, p. 168), are between 'etic' and 'emic', and between 'operational' and 'cognised'. The starting point in all such accounts is an imagined *separation* between the perceiver and the world, such that the perceiver has to reconstruct the world, in the mind, prior to any meaningful engagement with it.

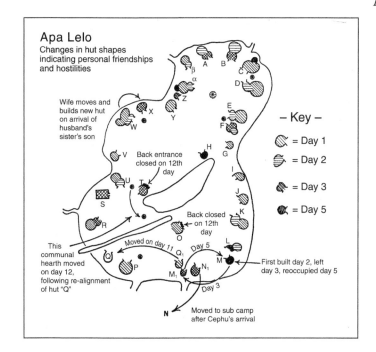

Figure 10.4 The Mbuti Pygmy camp of Apa Lelo

From C. M. Turnbull, *Wayward servants*, published by Eyre & Spottiswoode, 1965, p. 357.

Here, then, is the essence of the building perspective: that worlds are made before they are lived in; or in other words, that acts of dwelling are preceded by acts of worldmaking. A good example of this approach comes from the introduction to Maurice Godelier's book, *The mental and the material* (1986). Here, Godelier is concerned with the proper translation of the Marxian concepts *Grundlage* and *Überbau*, usually rendered in English as 'infrastructure' and 'superstructure'. He likens the *Überbau* to a building: 'The *Überbau* is a construction, an edifice which rises on foundations, *Grundlage*; and it [the *Überbau*] is the house we live in, not the foundations' (pp. 6–7). Human beings, then, inhabit the various houses of culture, pre-erected upon the universal ground of nature – including the universals of *human* nature. For another example, I would like to turn to Peter Wilson's *The domestication of the human species* (1988). In this book, Wilson argues that the most significant turning point in human social evolution came at the moment when people began to live in houses. Roughly speaking, this marks a division between hunters and gatherers, on the one hand, and agriculturalists and urban dwellers, on the other. 'Hunter-gatherers', Wilson writes, 'create for themselves only the flimsiest architectural context, and only the faintest line divides their living space from nature'. All other societies, by contrast, 'live in an architecturally modified environment', inhabiting houses and villages of a relatively enduring kind, structures that – even when abandoned – leave an almost indelible impression in the landscape. In essence, Wilson is distinguishing between societies with architecture and societies without it.

This is a bold generalisation, and like all such, it is an easy target for empirical refutation. That is not my concern, however. I am rather concerned to expose the assumptions entailed in making the distinction between an 'architecturally modified environment' and what is

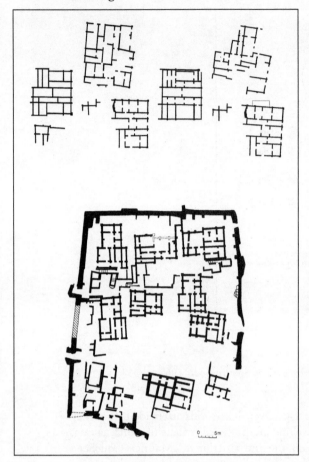

Figure 10.5 Building plans of three periods from the ancient Mesopotamian site of Tell es-Sawwan.

From J. Mellaart, *The Neolithic of the Near East*, published by Thames and Hudson, London 1975.

simply called 'nature'. For it is on this distinction that Wilson's entire argument rests. One objection to it immediately comes to mind. To be sure, the physical arrangement and formal properties of a hunter-gatherer encampment may be very different from those of a permanent village settlement. By way of example, compare the plan, shown in Figure 10.4, of the Mbuti Pygmy camp of Apa Lelo, in the Ituri forest of Zaire, with the plans shown in Figure 10.5 of the ancient Mesopotamian village site of Tell es-Sawwan. In the first case the spatial structure of settlement is loose, informal, and sensitive to the changing state of interpersonal relations between cliques, hosts and visitors. In the second it is tightly packed, geometrically regular, and appears to impose fairly tight constraints on the disposition of people and activities. Moreover, compared with the substantial buildings of the village settlement, the constructions of the hunter-gatherers are scarcely more that shades and windbreaks. Most of life, for hunter-gatherers, goes on around dwellings rather than in them. Nevertheless, the fact remains that hunter-gatherers do build shelters of various kinds. So who are we to say that they have no architecture? And if they do not, how are we to comprehend their building activity?

The answer that emerges from Wilson's account is that among hunter-gatherers, erecting shelters is one of a suite of activities, along with food-collecting, cooking, toolmaking and repair, childminding, and so on, that constitute the daily round for these people. Thus building activity is part and parcel of life in an environment that is already *given* in nature, and that has not itself been artificially engineered. With village architecture, by contrast, nature has to a degree been covered over or transformed, so that what immediately confronts people is not a natural environment but – in Wilson's words – 'an environment of their own making, the cultural' (1988: 8). If hunter-gatherers build as part of their adaptation to the given conditions of the natural environment, villagers adapt to the conditions of an environment that is already built. Either way, the environment is given in advance, as a kind of container for life to occupy. Where, as among hunter-gatherers, building is a part of everyday life, it is not supposed to have any lasting impact on the environment; where, as among villagers, the environment has been manifestly built, the buildings are apparently made before life begins in them. This, of course, is the architect's perspective: first plan and build the houses, then import the people to occupy them.

What, then, of the dwellings of nomadic pastoralists? A recent study comparing pastoral tent dwellings and village houses in Turkey and Iran by the archaeologist, Roger Cribb (1991), found that despite differences in the building materials used and the flexibility they afford, the tent and the house were virtually identical in their underlying organisational templates. What really distinguished the house from the tent was the degree to which the imposed, cultural design – shared by villagers and nomads alike – is actually translated into enduring, material structures. For such structures do not get built overnight; they grow cumulatively in the course of a settlement's continuous occupation, such that 'each new alteration or addition builds on a series of existing structures'. But in the case of a pastoral nomadic camp, 'each occupation is a fresh event', so that the camp 'has no such history but remains permanently retarded in the initial stages of the normal developmental cycle [of the settlement]' (1991: 156). Thus, although pastoralists carry a basic organisational template with them, there is little opportunity for its enduring physical realisation before the camp picks up and moves off somewhere else, where the occupation process starts all over again. In such cases, building never proceeds beyond the first phase of temporary habitation (Ingold 1992c: 795–6).

In a statement that epitomises the building perspective, Amos Rapoport writes that 'the organisation of space cognitively precedes its material expression; settings and built environments are thought before they are built' (1994: 488). In the case of villagers, the environment is ready-built. In the case of nomadic pastoralists, it would seem, the environment, though thought, is never more than partially built. As for the hunter-gatherers, it appears that the building hardly gets started at all: indeed Rapoport refers to the camp sites of Aboriginal people of the Australian Central Desert as exemplars of the situation where the environment is thought but *never* built. On these grounds, as we saw in Chapter Three (pp. 56–7), they are supposed to inhabit a 'natural' rather than an 'artificial' environment.

THE SEARCH FOR ORIGINS

Having spelled out the essence of the building perspective, let me now return to my earlier observation, comparing the forms of the beaver's lodge and the human house, that the first is tied, as it were, to the nature of the beaver itself, whereas the second is both historically and regionally variable. Among non-human animals, it is widely supposed, there can be no significant change in built form that is not bound to evolutionary changes in the essential form of the species. With human beings, by contrast, built form is free to vary independently of biological constraint, and to follow developmental pathways of its own, effectively decoupled from the process of evolution. In his famous paper of 1917, on 'The Superorganic', Alfred Kroeber declared: 'Who would be so rash as to affirm that ten thousand generations of example would convert the beaver from what he is into a carpenter or a bricklayer – or, allowing for his physical deficiency in the lack of hands, into a planning engineer!' (1952: 31). Yet human beings, through practice, example and a good measure of ingenuity, coupled with their ability to transmit their acquired know-how across the generations and to preserve it in long-term memory, have learned all these trades, and many more besides.

However, this argument implies some kind of threshold in the evolution of our own kind, at which point our ancestors were sufficiently endowed with the qualities of intelligence and manual dexterity to become the authors of their own projects of building. Taking off from this point, the history of architecture must be supposed to have proceeded from the earliest dwellings to the modern construction industry, the species-specific nature of the human organism remaining all the while unchanged. But what *was* the earliest dwelling? According to Kenneth Bock, an event in the history of architecture – such as the construction of a Gothic vault – differs from an event in the evolution of species 'in that the former involves formation of intent or purpose on the part of an actor while the latter does not' (1980: 182). The same idea is implied by Joseph Rykwert when he suggests that the essence of architecture lies in 'taking thought about building' (1991: 54). But how did it come about that, at some decisive moment, our ancestors began to think about what they built?

As Rykwert shows, in his study of the notion of the 'primitive hut' in the history of architecture, this is a question that has long exercised the minds of Western thinkers. And the title of his book, *On Adam's House in Paradise* (1972), nicely conveys the mythic quality of the many speculative answers that have been proposed. Reproduced in Figure 10.6 is one of the more delightful images of 'the first hut', taken from the work of the great French architectural theorist, Eugène Viollet-le-Duc, *Histoire de l'habitation humaine*, published in 1875 (Viollet-le-Duc 1990: 26). Architecture began, for Viollet-le-Duc, when the problem of the need for shelter was met through the procedures of rational planning. In his tale of the building of the first hut the secret is revealed to a hapless primitive tribe, the Nairitti, by a progressive time-traveller by the name of Epergos, bestowed upon them as a gift of his superior intelligence. For Viollet-le-Duc, as for many others, Rykwert notes, it was 'the difference of conception, the attachment of meaning to his task, that distinguishes man's first attempts [at building] from those of the instinctually driven beasts' (1972: 22). These attempts may have been decidedly inferior to the constructions of animals, nevertheless they marked the turning point at which humanity was set upon the road to culture and civilisation.

The search for the first building continues to this day, though it is informed by a much better knowledge both of the archaeological traces left by early human or hominid populations, and of the behaviour of those species of animals – namely the great apes – most closely related to humankind. One of the most peculiar and distinctive aspects of the behaviour of chimpanzees, gorillas and orang-utans is their habit of building so-called 'nests'. In functional terms, they are not really nests at all: every individual animal builds its own nest afresh, each evening, and uses it for the sole purpose of sleeping. Nor does the nest site mark any kind of fixed point in the animal's movements; it may be built anywhere, and is abandoned the next morning (Groves and Sabater Pi 1985: 23). Nevertheless, assuming that the common ancestor of apes and humans would have had a similar habit, attempts have been made to trace an evolutionary continuum from this nesting behaviour to the residential arrangements of prototypical human groups (of which the camps of contemporary hunter-gatherers have frequently been taken as the closest exemplars, on the grounds of the presumed similarity of ecological context).

Comparing the nesting patterns of apes with the camping patterns of human hunter-gatherers, Colin Groves and J. Sabater Pi note some striking differences. The human 'nest', if we may call it that, is a fixed point for the movements of its several occupants, and a place to which they regularly return. In other words, it has the attributes of what the ethologist, Heini Hediger, would call 'home': it is a 'goal of flight' and a 'place of maximal security' (Hediger 1977: 181). There is a difference, too, in the respective ways in which apes and humans go about building their accommodation. For one thing, apes use material that comes immediately to hand, normally by a skilful interweaving of growing vegetation to form an oval-shaped, concave bed; whereas humans collect suitable materials from

Figure 10.6 The first hut, as depicted by Viollet-le-Duc.

From *The architectural theory of Viollet-le-Duc: readings and commentary*, edited by M. F. Hearn, published by MIT Press, 1990, p. 26.

a distance, prior to their assembly into a convex, self-supporting structure. For another thing, the ape makes its nest by bending the vegetation around its own body; whereas the human builds a hut, and then enters it (Groves and Sabater Pi 1985: 45). There is a sense, as Hediger remarks, in which apes build from the 'bottom up', seeking support for rest and sleeping, whereas humans build from the 'top down' seeking shelter from sun, rain or wind (1977: 184). Yet there are also remarkable similarities between ape and human living arrangements, in the overall number and layout of nests or huts and in the underlying social organisation, and on the grounds of these similarities, Groves and Sabater Pi feel justified in arguing that human campsites are but elaborations of a generalised ape pattern. All the critical differences – the functioning of the site as a home-base, the collection of material prior to construction, the technique of building from the outside – can be put down, they think, to one factor, namely the human ability 'to visualise objects in new configurations, and to bring these configurations into being on the basis of that mental picture' (1985: 45).

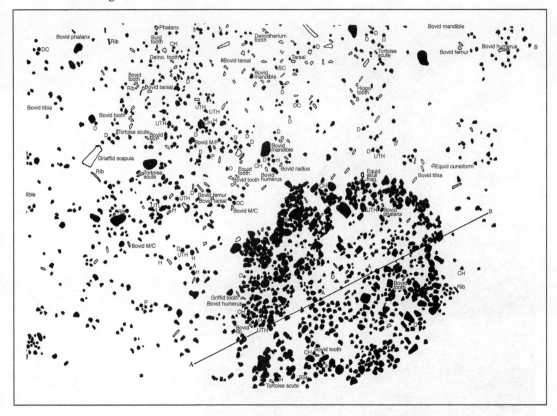

Figure 10.7 The 'stone circle' from Bed I of Olduvai Gorge.

From M. D. Leakey, *Olduvai Gorge* (volume three), published by Cambridge University Press, 1971.

   Though in substance based on fact rather than fantasy, the form in which this argument is cast is virtually identical to that of Viollet-le-Duc's tale of the building of the first hut. Equipped, albeit by natural selection rather than providential intervention, with foresight and intelligence, the first builders set to work to execute a plan that was already formed as a picture in their imagination. They had solved the problem of shelter in their minds, prior to putting the solution into practical effect. It is in this light that we can understand the extraordinary significance that has been attached to the so-called 'stone circle' discovered at the famous site of Olduvai Gorge in Tanzania, and dated to some 1.75 million years ago (Figure 10.7). In her interpretation of the circle, Mary Leakey writes that in its general appearance, it 'resembles temporary structures often made by present-day nomadic peoples who build a low stone wall round their dwellings to serve either as a windbreak or as a base to support upright branches which are bent over and covered with either skins or grass' (1971: 24). A photograph of such a dwelling, from the Okombambi people of Southwest Africa, is provided to substantiate the comparison. As always in these matters, the specific interpretation has been challenged. What has not been challenged, however, is the frame of mind that leads us to suppose that if the interpretation were correct, we would have at last discovered the *real* 'first hut', and with it not just the origins of architecture, but the point of transition to true humanity.

For it is the structure of our thought, not the patterning of the archaeological record, that sets up a point of origin at the intersection of two axes, one of evolutionary change – leading from ancestral pongids and hominids to human beings, the other of historical change – leading from Palaeolithic hunting and gathering to modern industry. (Why this should be so is a matter to which I return in Chapter Twenty-one, pp. 388–90.) To explode the myth of the first hut thus requires nothing less than the dissolution of the dichotomy, which in modern scholarship separates the biological sciences from the humanities, between evolution and history, or between the temporal processes of nature and culture. Before indicating how this might be done, I need to introduce what I have called the 'dwelling perspective'.

THE DWELLING PERSPECTIVE

For this purpose I turn to Martin Heidegger's evocative essay, 'Building Dwelling Thinking', on which I have drawn for my title (Heidegger 1971: 145–61). In this essay, Heidegger asks what it means to build and to dwell, and what the relation is between these two – between building and dwelling. He begins with what might be taken as the hegemonic view, as enshrined in the discourse of Western modernity. This is that building and dwelling are separable but complementary activities, related as means to ends. We build houses so that we may dwell in them (or, as is usual in industrial society, some people build houses for other people to live in). To dwell, in this sense, means merely 'to occupy a house, a dwelling place'. The building is a *container* for life activities, or more strictly for certain life activities, since there are other kinds of activity that go on outside houses, or in the open air. Yet, Heidegger asks, 'do the houses in themselves hold any guarantee that *dwelling* occurs in them?' (1971: 146). To clarify matters, let us call the physical structure, the building in itself, the *house*; and the setting within which people dwell the *home* (Lawrence 1987). Heidegger's question can then be rephrased as follows: what does it take for a house to be a home (Pearson and Richards 1994: 6)? Merely to pose the question in this form suggests that there must be more to dwelling than the mere fact of occupation. What, then, does it mean, 'to dwell'?

Heidegger tackles the issue through an exercise in etymology. The current German word for the verb 'to build', *bauen*, comes from the Old English and High German *buan*, meaning 'to dwell'. Though this original meaning has been lost, it is preserved in such compounds as the English 'neighbour', meaning one who dwells nearby. Moreover, this sense of dwelling was not limited to one sphere of activity among many – to domestic life, say, as opposed to work or travel. Rather it encompassed the whole manner in which one lives one's life on the earth; thus 'I dwell, you dwell' is identical to 'I am, you are'. Yet *bauen* has another sense: to preserve, to care for, or more specifically to cultivate or to till the soil. And then there is the third sense: to construct, to make something, to raise up an edifice. Both these modern senses of building – as cultivation and as construction – are thus shown to be encompassed within the more fundamental sense of dwelling. In the course of time, however, this underlying sense has fallen into disuse, such that *bauen* has come to be reserved exclusively for cultivation and construction. Having forgotten how the latter activities are grounded in dwelling, modern thought then *rediscovers* dwelling as the occupation of a world already built.

In short, where before, building was circumscribed within dwelling, the position now appears reversed, with dwelling circumscribed within building. Heidegger's concern is to regain that original perspective, so that we can once again understand how the activities of building – of cultivation and construction – belong to our dwelling in the world, to the way we are. 'We do not dwell because we have built, but we build and have built because we dwell, that is because we are dwellers . . . To build is in itself already to dwell . . . *Only if we are capable of dwelling, only then can we build*' (Heidegger 1971: 148, 146, 160, original emphases). I take this to be the founding statement of the dwelling perspective.[5] What it means is that the forms people build, whether in the imagination or on the ground, arise within the current of their involved activity, in the specific relational contexts of their practical engagement with their surroundings. Building, then, cannot be understood as a simple process of transcription, of a pre-existing design of the final product onto a raw material substrate. It is true that human beings – perhaps uniquely among animals – have the capacity to envision forms in advance of their implementation, but this envisioning is itself an activity carried on by real people in a real-world environment, rather than by a disembodied intellect moving in a subjective space in which are represented the problems it seeks to solve (see Chapter Twenty-three, pp. 418–19). In short, people do not import their ideas, plans or mental representations into the world, since that very world, to borrow a phrase from Merleau-Ponty (1962: 24), is the homeland of their thoughts. Only because they already dwell therein can they think the thoughts they do.

To argue that the forms of buildings arise as a kind of crystallisation of human activity within an environment clearly puts paid to my initial dichotomy between design and execution. No longer can we assume, with Christopher Alexander, that form is 'the ultimate object of design' (1964: 15), as though the one issued quite automatically and unproblematically from the other. To the contrary, a dwelling perspective ascribes the generation of form to those very processes whose creativity is denied by that perspective which sees in every form the concrete realisation of an intellectual solution to a design problem. Where, then, does this leave the constructions of non-human animals? The argument is equally damaging to the conventional biological account, which holds that the outward, phenotypic form – not just of the animal itself, but of the constructions making up its 'extended phenotype' – is the expression of a solution to some specific problem of adaptation, already reached by natural selection, and transferred to the animal at the point of conception, encrypted in the materials of heredity – the genes. That design is thus imported into the organism, as a kind of 'evolved architecture' (Tooby and Cosmides 1992), prior to the organism's development within an environmental context, is indeed one of the great delusions of modern biology. For as I shall show in Chapter Twenty-one, the forms of organisms are in no way prefigured in their genes but are the emergent outcomes of environmentally situated development processes.

For any animal, the environmental conditions of development are liable to be shaped by the activities of predecessors. The beaver, for example, inhabits an environment that has been decisively modified by the labours of its forbears, in building dams and lodges, and will in turn contribute to the fashioning of an environment for its progeny. It is in such a modified environment that the beaver's own bodily orientations and patterns of activity undergo development. The same goes for human beings. Human children, like the young of many other species, grow up in environments furnished by the work of previous generations, and as they do so they come literally to carry the forms of their dwelling in their bodies – in specific skills, sensibilities and dispositions. But they do not carry them in their genes, nor is it necessary to invoke some other kind of vehicle for the inter-generational transmission of information – cultural rather than genetic – to account for the diversity of human living arrangements.

We can now see how, by adopting a dwelling perspective – that is, by taking the animal-in-its-environment rather than the self-contained individual as our point of departure – it is possible to dissolve the orthodox dichotomies between evolution and history, and between biology and culture. For if, by evolution, we mean differentiation over time in the forms and capacities of organisms, then we would have to admit that changes in the bodily orientations and skills of human beings, insofar as they are historically conditioned by the work of predecessors (along with the enduring products of that work, such as buildings), must themselves be evolutionary. And if, by cultural variation, we mean those differences of embodied knowledge that stem from the diversity of local ˙developmental contexts, then far from being superimposed upon a substrate of evolved human universals, such variation must be part and parcel of the variation of all living things, which has its source in their enmeshment within an all-encompassing field of relations. It is not necessary, then, to invoke one kind of theory, of biological evolution, to account for the transition from nest to hut, and another kind, of cultural history, to account for the transition from hut to skyscraper. For once history is itself recognised as an evolutionary process, the point of origin constituted by the intersection of evolutionary and historical continua disappears, and the search for the first hut – for the beginnings of architecture, history and true humanity – becomes a quest after an illusion.[6]

THE HOUSE AS ORGANISM

Let me conclude by returning to von Uexküll's oak tree. Suppose that it stands, not in the forest, but in the precincts of a house. Now at first glance we might have no hesitation in regarding the house, but not the tree, as a building, or an instance of architecture. For surely the house, as Godelier puts it, belongs to 'that part of nature which is transformed by human action and thought [and] owes its existence to conscious human action on nature' (1986: 5, see also Chapter Five p. 79). The tree, on the other hand, has no such debt to humanity, for it has grown there, rooted to the spot, entirely of its own accord. On closer inspection, however, this distinction between those parts of the environment that are, respectively, built and unbuilt seems far less clear. For the form of the tree is no more given, as an immutable fact of nature, than is the form of the house an imposition of the human mind. Recall the many inhabitants of the tree: the fox, the owl, the squirrel, the ant, the beetle, among countless others. All, through their various activities of dwelling, have played their part in creating the conditions under which the tree, over the centuries, has grown to assume its particular form and proportions. And so, too, have human beings, in tending the tree's surroundings.

But the house also has many and diverse animal inhabitants – more, perhaps, than we are inclined to recognise. Sometimes special provision is made for them, such as the kennel, stable or dovecote. Others find shelter and sustenance in its nooks and crannies, or even build there. And all, in their various ways, contribute to its evolving form, as do the house's human inhabitants in keeping it under repair, decorating it, or making structural alterations in response to their changing domestic circumstances. Thus the distinction between the house and the tree is not an absolute but a relative one – relative, that is, to the scope of human involvement in the form-generating process.[7] Houses, as Suzanne Blier notes (1987: 2), are living organisms. Like trees, they have life-histories, which consist in the unfolding of their relations with both human and non-human components of their environments. To the extent that the influence of the human component prevails, any feature of the environment will seem more like a building; to the extent that the non-human component prevails, it will seem less so.

Building, then, is a process that is continually going on, for as long as people dwell in an environment. It does not begin here, with a pre-formed plan, and end there, with a finished artefact. The 'final form' is but a fleeting moment in the life of any feature, when it is matched to a human purpose, likewise cut out from the flow of intentional activity. As the philosopher Alfred North Whitehead once remarked, 'from the moment of birth we are immersed in action, and can only fitfully guide it by taking thought' (1938: 217). And this applies, with equal force, to 'taking thought about building', the definitive characteristic of the architectural attitude. We may indeed describe the forms in our environment as instances of architecture, but for the most part we are not architects. For it is in the very process of dwelling that we build.

Chapter Eleven

The temporality of the landscape

PROLOGUE

I adhere to the view that social or cultural anthropology, biological anthropology and archaeology form a necessary unity – that they are all part of the same intellectual enterprise. I am not concerned here with the link with biological or 'physical' anthropology, but what I have to say does bear centrally on the unifying themes of archaeology and sociocultural anthropology. I want to stress two such themes, and they are closely related. First, human life is a process that involves the passage of time. Secondly, this life-process is also the process of formation of the landscapes in which people have lived. *Time* and *landscape*, then, are to my mind the essential points of topical contact between archaeology and anthropology. My purpose, in this chapter, is to bring the perspectives of archaeology and anthropology into unison through a focus on the temporality of the landscape. In particular, I believe that such a focus might enable us to move beyond the sterile opposition between the naturalistic view of the landscape as a neutral, external backdrop to human activities, and the culturalistic view that every landscape is a particular cognitive or symbolic ordering of space. I argue that we should adopt, in place of both these views, what I have called a 'dwelling perspective', according to which the landscape is constituted as an enduring record of – and testimony to – the lives and works of past generations who have dwelt within it, and in so doing, have left there something of themselves.

For anthropologists, to adopt a perspective of this kind means bringing to bear the knowledge born of immediate experience, by privileging the understandings that people derive from their lived, everyday involvement in the world. Yet it will surely be objected that this avenue is not open to archaeologists concerned with human activities in the distant past. 'The people', it is said, 'they're dead' (Sahlins 1972: 81); only the material record remains for their successors of our own time to interpret as best they can. But this objection misses the point, which is that *the practice of archaeology is itself a form of dwelling*. The knowledge born of this practice is thus on a par with that which comes from the practical activity of the native dweller and which the anthropologist, through participation, seeks to learn and understand. For both the archaeologist and the native dweller, the landscape tells – or rather *is* – a story, 'a chronicle of life and dwelling' (Adam 1998: 54). It enfolds the lives and times of predecessors who, over the generations, have moved around in it and played their part in its formation. To perceive the landscape is therefore to carry out an act of remembrance, and remembering is not so much a matter of calling up an internal image, stored in the mind, as of engaging perceptually with an environment that is itself pregnant with the past. To be sure, the rules and methods of engagement employed respectively by the native dweller and the archaeologist differ, as do the stories they tell. Nevertheless, insofar as both seek the past in the landscape, they are engaged in projects of fundamentally the same kind.[1]

It is of course part of an archaeological training to learn to attend to those clues which the rest of us might pass over (literally, when they are below the surface), and which make it possible to tell a fuller or a richer story. Likewise native dwellers, along with their anthropological companions, learn through an education of attention. The novice hunter, for example, travels through the country with his mentors, and as he goes, specific features are pointed out to him. Other things he discovers for himself, in the course of further forays, by watching, listening and feeling. Thus the experienced hunter is the *knowledge-able* hunter (see Chapter Three, pp. 55–6). He can tell things from subtle indications that you or I, unskilled in the hunter's art, might not even notice. Called upon to explicate his knowledge, he may do so in a form that reappears in the work of the non-native ethnographer as a corpus of myths or stories, whereas the archaeologist's knowledge – drawn from the practices of excavation rather than hunting – may appear in the seemingly authoritative form of the site report. But we should resist the temptation to assume that since stories are stories they are, in some sense, unreal or untrue, for this is to suppose that the only real reality, or true truth, is one in which we, as living, experiencing beings, can have no part at all. Telling a story, as I observed in Chapter Three (p. 56), is not like unfurling a tapestry to *cover up* the world, it is rather a way of guiding the attention of listeners or readers *into* it. A person who can 'tell' is one who is perceptually attuned to picking up information in the environment that others, less skilled in the tasks of perception, might miss, and the teller, in rendering his knowledge explicit, conducts the attention of his audience along the same paths as his own.

Following that preamble, I shall now go on to lay out the burden of my argument. This is presented in four principal sections. In the first two, I attempt to specify more precisely what I mean by my key terms – landscape and temporality. I argue that temporality inheres in the pattern of dwelling activities that I call the taskscape. In the third section I consider how taskscape relates to landscape and, ultimately by dissolving the distinction between them, I proceed to recover the temporality of the landscape itself. Finally, I draw some concrete illustrations of my arguments from a well-known painting by Bruegel, *The harvesters*.

LANDSCAPE

Let me be begin by explaining what the landscape is *not*. It is not 'land', it is not 'nature', and it is not 'space'. Consider, first of all, the distinction between land and landscape. Land is not something you can see, any more than you can see the weight of physical objects. All objects of the most diverse kinds have weight, and it is possible to express *how much* anything weighs relative to any other thing. Likewise, land is a kind of lowest common denominator of the phenomenal world, inherent in every portion of the earth's surface yet directly visible in none, and in terms of which any portion may be rendered quantitatively equivalent to any other (Ingold 1986a: 153–4).[2] You can ask of land, as of weight, how much there is, but not what it is like. But where land is thus quantitative and homogeneous, the landscape is qualitative and heterogeneous. Supposing that you are standing outdoors, it is what you see all around: a contoured and textured surface replete with diverse objects – living and non-living, natural and artificial (these distinctions are both problematic, as we shall see, but they will serve for the time being). Thus at any particular moment, you can ask of a landscape what it is like, but not how much of it there is. For the landscape is a plenum, there are no holes in it that remain to be filled in, so that every infill is in reality a reworking. As Meinig observes, one should not overlook 'the powerful fact that life must be lived amidst that which was made before' (1979a: 44).

The landscape is not 'nature'. Of course, nature can mean many things, and this is not the place for a discourse on the history of the concept. Suffice it to say that I have in mind the rather specific sense whose ontological foundation is an imagined separation between the human perceiver and the world, such that the perceiver has to reconstruct the world, in consciousness, prior to any meaningful engagement with it. The world of nature, it is often said, is what lies 'out there'. All kinds of entities are supposed to exist out there, but not you and I. We live 'in here', in the intersubjective space marked out by our mental representations. Application of this logic forces an insistent dualism, between object and subject, the material and the ideal, operational and cognised, 'etic' and 'emic'. Some writers distinguish between nature and the landscape in just these terms – the former is said to stand to the latter as physical reality to its cultural or symbolic construction. For example, Daniels and Cosgrove introduce a collection of essays on *The iconography of landscape* with the following definition: 'A landscape is a cultural image, a pictorial way of representing or symbolising surroundings' (1988: 1).

I do not share this view. To the contrary, I reject the division between inner and outer worlds – respectively of mind and matter, meaning and substance – upon which such distinction rests. The landscape, I hold, is not a picture in the imagination, surveyed by the mind's eye; nor however is it an alien and formless substrate awaiting the imposition of human order. 'The idea of landscape', as Meinig writes, 'runs counter to recognition of any simple binary relationship between man and nature' (Meinig 1979b: 2). Thus, neither is the landscape identical to nature, nor is it on the side of humanity against nature. As the familiar domain of our dwelling, it is *with* us, not *against* us, but it is no less real for that. And through living in it, the landscape becomes a part of us, just as we are a part of it. Moreover, what goes for its human component goes for other components as well. In a world construed as nature, every object is a self-contained entity, interacting with others through some kind of external contact. But in a landscape, each component enfolds within its essence the totality of its relations with each and every other. In short, whereas the order of nature is explicate, the order of the landscape is implicate (Bohm 1980: 172).

The landscape is not 'space'. To appreciate the contrast, we could compare the everyday project of dwelling in the world with the rather peculiar and specialised project of the surveyor or cartographer whose objective is to *represent* it. No doubt the surveyor, as he goes about his practical tasks, experiences the landscape much as does everyone else whose business of life lies there. Like other people, he is mobile, yet unable to be in more than one place at a time. In the landscape, the distance between two places, A and B, is experienced as a journey made, a bodily movement from one place to the other, and the gradually changing vistas along the route. The surveyor's job, however, is to take instrumental measurements from a considerable number of locations, and to combine these data to produce a single picture which is *independent* of any point of observation. This picture is of the world as it could be directly apprehended only by a consciousness capable of being everywhere at once and nowhere in particular (the nearest we can get to this in practice is by taking an aerial or bird's-eye view). To such a consciousness, at once immobile and omnipresent, the distance between A and B would be the length of a line plotted between two points that are simultaneously in view, that line marking one of any number of journeys that could potentially be made (cf. Bourdieu 1977: 2). It is as though, from an imaginary position above the world, I could direct the movements of my body within it, like a counter on a board, so that to say 'I am here' is not to point from somewhere to my surroundings, but to point from nowhere to the position on the board where my body happens to be. And whereas actual journeys are made through a landscape, the board on which all potential journeys may be plotted is equivalent to space.[3]

There is a tradition of geographical research (see, for example, Gould and White 1974) which sets out from the premise that we are all cartographers in our daily lives, and that we use our bodies as the surveyor uses his instruments, to register a sensory input from multiple points of observation, which is then processed by our intelligence into an image that we carry around with us, like a map in our heads, wherever we go. The mind, rather than reaching into its surroundings from its dwelling place within the world, might be likened in this view to a film spread out upon its exterior surface. The sense of space implicated in this cartographic view of environmental perception may be illuminated by means of an analogy drawn from the linguistics of Ferdinand de Saussure. To grasp the essence of language, Saussure invites us to picture thought and sound as two continuous and undifferentiated planes, of mental and phonic substance respectively, like two sides of a sheet of paper. By cutting the sheet into pieces (words) we create, on one side, a system of discrete concepts, and on the other, a system of discrete sounds; and since one side cannot be cut without at the same time cutting the other, the two systems of division are necessarily homologous so that to each concept there corresponds a sound (Saussure 1959: 112–13).

Now when geographers and anthropologists write about space, what is generally implied is something closely akin to Saussure's sheet of paper, only in this case the counter-side to thought is the continuum not of phonic substance but of the surface of the earth. And so it appears that the division of the world into a mosaic of externally bounded segments is entailed in the very production of spatial meanings. Just as the word, for Saussure, is the union of a concept with a delimited 'chunk' of sound, so the place is the union of a symbolic meaning with a delimited block of the earth's surface. Spatial differentiation implies spatial segmentation. This is not so of the landscape, however. For a place in the landscape is not 'cut out' from the whole, either on the plane of ideas or on that of material substance. Rather, each place embodies the whole at a particular nexus within it, and in this respect is different from every other.

A place owes its character to the experiences it affords to those who spend time there – to the sights, sounds and indeed smells that constitute its specific ambience. And these, in turn, depend on the kinds of activities in which its inhabitants engage. It is from this relational context of people's engagement with the world, in the business of dwelling, that each place draws its unique significance. Thus whereas with space, meanings are *attached* to the world, with the landscape they are *gathered from* it. Moreover, while places have centres – indeed it would be more appropriate to say that they *are* centres – they have no boundaries. In journeying from place A to place B it makes no sense to ask, along the way, whether one is 'still' in A or has 'crossed over' to B (Ingold 1986a: 155). Of course, boundaries of various kinds may be drawn in the landscape, and identified either with natural features such as the course of a river or an escarpment, or with built structures such as walls and fences. But such boundaries are not a condition for the constitution of the places on either side of them; nor do they segment the landscape, for the features with which they are identified are themselves an integral part of it. Finally, it is important to note that no feature of the landscape is, of itself, a boundary. It can only become a boundary, or the indicator of a boundary, in relation to the activities of the people (or animals) for whom it is recognised or experienced as such.

In the course of explaining what the landscape is not, I have already moved some way towards a positive characterisation. In short, the landscape is the world as it is known to those who dwell therein, who inhabit its places and journey along the paths connecting them. Is it not, then, identical to what we might otherwise call the environment? Certainly the distinction between landscape and environment is not easy to draw, and for many purposes they may be treated as practically synonymous. It will already be apparent that I cannot accept the distinction offered by Yi-Fu Tuan, who argues that an environment is 'a given, a piece of reality that is simply there', as opposed to the landscape, which is a product of human cognition, 'an achievement of the mature mind' (Tuan 1979: 90, 100). For that is merely to reproduce the dichotomy between nature and humanity. The environment is no more 'nature' than is the landscape a symbolic construct. Elsewhere, I have contrasted nature and environment by way of a distinction between reality *of* – 'the physical world of neutral objects apparent only to the detached, indifferent observer', and reality *for* – 'the world constituted in *relation* to the organism or person whose environment it is' (Ingold 1992a: 44). But to think of environment in this sense is to regard it primarily in terms of *function*, of what it affords to creatures – whether human or non-human – with certain capabilities and projects of action. Reciprocally, to regard these creatures as organisms is to view them in terms of their principles of dynamic functioning, that is as organised systems (Pittendrigh 1958: 394). As Lewontin succinctly puts it (1982: 160), the environment is 'nature organised by an organism'.

The concept of landscape, by contrast, puts the emphasis on *form*, in just the same way that the concept of the body emphasises the form rather than the function of a living creature. If the body is the form in which a creature is present as a being-in-the-world, then the world of its being-in presents itself in the form of the landscape. Like organism and environment, body and landscape are complementary terms: each implies the other, alternately as figure and ground. The forms of the landscape are not, however, prepared in advance for creatures to occupy, any more than are the bodily forms of those creatures independently specified in their genetic make-up. Both sets of forms are generated and sustained in and through the processual unfolding of a total field of relations that cuts across the emergent interface between organism and environment (Goodwin 1988). Having regard to its formative properties, we may refer to this process as one of embodiment.

Though the notion of embodiment has recently come much into fashion, there has been a tendency – following an ancient inclination in Western thought to prioritise form over process (Oyama 1985: 13) – to conceive of it as a movement of *inscription*, whereby some pre-existing pattern, template or programme, whether genetic or cultural, is 'realised' in a substantive medium. This is not what I have in mind, however. To the contrary, and adopting a helpful distinction from Paul Connerton (1989: 72–3), I regard embodiment as a movement of *incorporation* rather than inscription, not a transcribing of form onto material but a movement wherein forms themselves are generated (Ingold 1990: 215). Taking the organism as our focus of reference, this movement is what is commonly known as the life-cycle. Thus organisms may be said to incorporate, in their bodily forms, the life-cycle processes that give rise to them. Could not the same, then, be said of the environment? Is it possible to identify a corresponding cycle, or rather a series of interlocking cycles, which builds itself into the forms of the landscape, and of which the landscape may accordingly be regarded as an embodiment? Before answering this question, we need to turn to the second of my key terms, namely 'temporality'.

TEMPORALITY

Let me begin, once again, by stating what temporality is *not*. It is not chronology (as opposed to history), and it is not history (as opposed to chronology). By chronology, I mean any regular system of dated time intervals, in which events are said to have taken place. By history, I mean any series of events which may be dated in time according to their occurrence in one or another chronological interval. Thus the Battle of Hastings was an historical event, 1066 was a date (marking the interval of a year), and records tell us that the former occurred in the latter. In the mere succession of dates there are no events, because everything repeats; in the mere succession of events there is no time, as nothing does. The relation between chronology and history, in this conception, has been well expressed by Kubler: 'Without change there is no history; without regularity there is no time. Time and history are related as rule and variation: time is the regular setting for the vagaries of history' (1962: 72).

Now in introducing the concept of temporality, I do not intend that it should stand as a third term, alongside the concepts of chronology and history. For in the sense in which I shall use the term here, temporality entails a perspective that contrasts radically with the one, outlined above, that sets up history and chronology in a relation of complementary opposition. The contrast is essentially equivalent to that drawn by Alfred Gell (1992: 149–55) between what he calls (following McTaggart) the A-series, in which time is immanent in the passage of events, and the B-series, in which events are strung out in time like beads on a thread. Whereas in the B-series, events are treated as isolated happenings, succeeding one another frame by frame, each event in the A-series is seen to encompass a pattern of retensions from the past and protentions for the future. Thus from the A-series point of view, temporality and historicity are not opposed but rather merge in the experience of those who, in their activities, carry forward the process social life. Taken together, these activities make up what I shall call the 'taskscape', and it is with the intrinsic temporality of the taskscape that I shall be principally concerned in this section.

We can make a start by returning for a moment to the distinction between land and landscape. As a common denominator in terms of which constituents of the environment of diverse kinds may be rendered quantitatively comparable, I compared land with weight. But I could equally have drawn the comparison with *value* or with *labour*. Value is the denominator of commodities that enables us to say how much any one thing is worth by comparison with another, even though these two things may be quite unlike in terms of their physical qualities and potential uses. In this sense, the concept of value (in general) is classically distinguished from that of *use*-value, which refers to the specific properties or 'affordances' of any particular object, that commend it to the project of a user (Ingold 1992a: 48–9, cf. Gibson 1979:127, Marx 1930: 169). Clearly, this distinction, between value and use-value, is precisely homologous to that between land and landscape. But if we turn to consider the work that goes into the making of useful things, then again we can recognise that whilst the operations of making are indeed as unlike as the objects produced – involving different raw materials, different tools, different procedures and different skills – they can nevertheless be compared in that they call for variable amounts of what may simply be called 'labour': the common denominator of productive activities. Like land and value, labour is quantitative and homogeneous, human work shorn of its particularities. It is of course the founding premise of the labour theory of value that the amount of value in a thing is determined by the amount of labour that went into producing it (I return to this theme in Chapter Seventeen, pp. 326–8).

How, then, should we describe the practices of work in their concrete particulars? For this purpose I shall adopt the term 'task', defined as any practical operation, carried out by a skilled agent in an environment, as part of his or her normal business of life. In other words, tasks are the constitutive acts of dwelling. No more than features of the landscape, however, are tasks suspended in a vacuum. Every task takes its meaning from its position within an ensemble of tasks, performed in series or in parallel, and usually by many people working together. One of the great mistakes of recent anthropology – what Reynolds (1993: 410) calls 'the great tool-use fallacy' – has been to insist upon a separation between the domains of technical and social activity, a separation that has blinded us to the fact that one of the outstanding features of human technical practices lies in their embeddedness in the current of sociality. It is to the entire ensemble of tasks, in their mutual interlocking, that I refer by the concept of *taskscape*. Just as the landscape is an array of related features, so – by analogy – the taskscape is an array of related activities. And as with the landscape, it is qualitative and heterogeneous: we can ask of a taskscape, as of a landscape, what it is like, but not how much of it there is. In short, the taskscape is to labour what the landscape is to land, and indeed what an ensemble of use-values is to value in general.

Now if value is measured out in units of money, and land in units of space, what is the currency of labour? The answer, of course, is *time* – but it is time of a very peculiar sort, one that must be wholly indifferent to the modulations of human experience. To most of us it appears in the familiar guise of clock-time: thus an hour is an hour, regardless of what one is doing in it, or of how one feels. But this kind of chronological time does not depend upon the existence of artificial clocks. It may be based on any perfectly repetitive, mechanical system, including that (putatively) constituted by the earth in its axial rotations and in its revolutions around the sun. Sorokin and Merton (1937), in a classic paper, call it 'astronomical' time: it is, they write, 'uniform, homogeneous; . . . purely quantitative, shorn of qualitative variations'. And they distinguish it from 'social time', which they see as fundamentally qualitative, something to which we can affix moral judgements such as good or bad, grounded in the 'rhythms, pulsations and beats of the societies in which they are found', and for that reason tied to the particular circumstances of place and people (1937: 621–3; see also Chapter Seventeen, pp. 325–6). Adopting Sorokin and Merton's distinction, we could perhaps conclude that whereas labour is measured out in units of astronomical time, or in clock-time calibrated to an astronomical standard, the temporality of the taskscape is essentially social. Before we can accept this conclusion, however, the idea of social time must be examined a little more closely.

In my earlier discussion of the significance of space, I showed that in the cartographic imagination, the mind is supposed to be laid out upon the surface of the earth. Likewise in the chronological perspective, time appears as the interface between mind and 'duration' – by which is meant an undifferentiated stream of bodily activity and experience. Taking time in this sense, Durkheim famously likened it to 'an endless chart, where all duration is spread out before the mind, and upon which all possible events can be located in relation to fixed and determinate guidelines' (1976 [1915]: 10). Rather like Saussure's sheet of paper, it could be compared to a strip of infinite length, with thought on one side and duration on the other. By cutting the strip into segments we establish a division, on the one hand, into calendrical intervals or dates, and on the other hand, into discrete 'chunks' of lived experience, such that to every chunk there corresponds a date in a uniform sequence of before and after. And as every chunk succeeds the next, like frames on a reel of film, we imagine ourselves to be looking on 'as time goes by', as though we could take up a point of view detached from the temporal process of our life in the world and watch ourselves engaged now in this task, now in that, in an unending series of present instants. Whence, then, come the divisions which give chronological form to the substance of experience? Durkheim's answer, as is well known, was that these divisions – 'indispensable guidelines' for the temporal ordering of events – come from *society*, corresponding to the 'periodical recurrence of rites, feasts, and public ceremonies' (p. 10). Thus for Durkheim, time is at once chronological *and* social, for society itself is a kind of clock, whose moving parts are individual human beings (Ingold 1986b: 341).

This is not, however, the way we perceive the temporality of the taskscape. For we do so not as spectators but as participants, in the very performance of our tasks. As Merleau-Ponty put it, in reckoning with an environment, I am 'at my task rather than confronting it' (1962: 416). The notion that we can stand aside and observe the passage of time is founded upon an illusion of disembodiment. This passage is, indeed, none other than our *own* journey through the taskscape in the business of dwelling. Once again we can take our cue from Merleau-Ponty: 'the passage of one present to the next is not a thing which I conceive, nor do I see it as an onlooker, I effect it' (1962: 421). Reaching out into the taskscape I perceive, at this moment, a particular vista of past and a future; but it is a vista that is available from this moment and no other (see Gell 1992: 269). As such, it *constitutes* my present, conferring upon it a unique character. Thus the present is not *marked off* from a past that it has replaced or a future that will, in turn, replace it; it rather gathers the past and future into itself, like refractions in a crystal ball. And just as in the landscape, we can move from place to place without crossing any boundary, since the vista that constitutes the identity of a place changes even as we move, so likewise can we move from one present to another without having to break through any chronological barrier that might be supposed to separate each present from the next in line. Indeed the features that Durkheim identified as serving this segmenting function – rites, feasts and ceremonies – are themselves as integral to the taskscape as are boundary markers such as walls or fences to the landscape.

The temporality of the taskscape is social, then, not because society provides an external frame against which particular tasks find independent measure, but because people, in the performance of their tasks, *also attend to one another*. Looking back, we can see that Durkheim's error was to divorce the sphere of people's mutual involvement from that of their everyday practical activity in the world, leaving the latter to be carried on by individuals in hermetic isolation. In real life, this is not how we go about our business. By watching, listening, perhaps even touching, we continually feel each other's presence in the social environment, at every moment adjusting our movements in response to this ongoing perceptual monitoring. For the orchestral musician, playing an instrument, watching the conductor and listening to one's fellow players are all inseparable aspects of the same process of action: for this reason, the gestures of the performers may be said to *resonate* with each other. In orchestral music, the achievement of resonance – or what Schutz (1951: 78) called a 'mutual tuning-in relationship' – is an absolute precondition for successful performance. But the same is true, more generally, of social life (Wikan 1992, Richards 1996). Indeed it could be argued that in the resonance of movement and feeling stemming from people's mutually attentive engagement, in shared contexts of practical activity, lies the very foundation of sociality.

Let me pursue the analogy between orchestral performance and social life a little further since, more than any other artistic genre, music mirrors the temporal form of the taskscape.

I want, by means of this analogy, to make three points. First, while there are cycles and repetitions in music as in social life, these are essentially rhythmic rather than metronomic (on this distinction, see Young 1988: 19). It is for precisely this reason that social time, *pace* Durkheim, is *not* chronological. A metronome, like a clock, inscribes an artificial division into equal segments upon an otherwise undifferentiated movement; rhythm, by contrast, is intrinsic to the movement itself. Langer has argued that the essence of rhythm lies in the successive building up and resolution of tension, on the principle that every resolution is itself a preparation for the next building-up (1953: 126–7). There may of course be rests or sustained notes within a piece, but far from breaking it up into segments, such moments are generally ones of high tension, whose resolution becomes ever more urgent the longer they are held. Only our last exhalation of breath is not a preparation for the next inhalation – with that, we die; similarly with the last beat the music comes to an end. Social life, however, is never finished, and there are no breaks in it that are not integral to its tensile structure, to the 'ebb and flow of activity' by which society itself seems to breathe (Young 1988: 53).

My second point is that in music as in social life, there is not just one rhythmic cycle, but a complex interweaving of very many concurrent cycles.[4] While it reflects the temporal form of social life, music in fact represents a very considerable simplification, since it involves only one sensory register (the auditory), and its rhythms are fewer and more tightly controlled. In both cases, however, since any rhythm may be taken as the tempo for any of the others, there is no single, one-dimensional strand of time. As Langer puts it: 'life is always a dense fabric of concurrent tensions, and as each of them is a measure of time, the measurements themselves do not coincide' (1953: 113). Thus the temporality of the taskscape, while it is intrinsic rather than externally imposed (metronomic), lies not in any particular rhythm, but in the network of interrelationships between the multiple rhythms of which the taskscape is itself constituted. To cite a celebrated anthropological example: among the Nuer of southern Sudan, according to Evans-Pritchard, the passage of time is 'primarily the succession of [pastoral] tasks *and their relations to one another*' (1940: 101–2, my emphasis). Each of these relations is, of course, a specific resonance. And so, just as social life consists in the unfolding of a field of relationships among persons who attend to one another in what they do, its temporality consists in the unfolding of the resultant pattern of resonances.

Thirdly, the forms of the taskscape, like those of music, come into being through movement. Music exists only when it is being performed; it does not pre-exist, as is sometimes thought, in the score, any more than a cake pre-exists in the recipe for making it. Similarly, the taskscape exists only so long as people are actually engaged in the activities of dwelling, despite the attempts of anthropologists to translate it into something rather equivalent to a score – a kind of ideal design for dwelling – that generally goes by the name of 'culture', and that people are supposed to bring with them into their encounter with the world. This parallel, however, brings me to a critical question. Up to now, my discussion of temporality has concentrated exclusively on the taskscape, allowing the landscape to slip from view. It is now high time to bring it back into focus. I argued in the previous section that the landscape is not nature; here I claim that the taskscape is not culture. Landscape and taskscape, then, are not to be opposed as nature to culture. So how are we to understand the relation between them? Where does one end and the other begin? Can they even be distinguished at all?

If music best reflects the forms of the taskscape, it might be thought that painting is the most natural medium for representing the forms of the landscape. And this suggests that an examination of the difference, in the field of art, between music and painting might offer some clues as to how a distinction might possibly be drawn between taskscape and landscape as facets of the real world. I begin by following up this suggestion.

TEMPORALISING THE LANDSCAPE

At first glance the difference seems obvious: paintings do not have to be performed, they are presented to us as works that are complete in themselves. But on closer inspection, this contrast appears more as an artefact of a systematic bias in Western thought, to which I have already alluded, that leads us to privilege form over process. Thus the actual work of painting is subordinated to the final product; the former is hidden from view so that the latter alone becomes an object of contemplation. In many non-Western societies, by contrast, the order of priority is reversed: what is essential is the act of painting itself, of which the products may be relatively short-lived – barely perceived before being erased or covered up. This is so, for example, among the Yolngu, an Aboriginal people of northern Australia, whose experience of finished paintings, according to their ethnographer, is limited to 'images fleetingly glimpsed out of the corner of the eye' (Morphy 1992: 187). The emphasis, here, is on painting as *performance*.[5] Far from being the preparation of objects for future contemplation, it is an act of contemplation in itself. So, too, is performing or listening to music. Thus all at once, the contrast between painting and music seems less secure. It becomes a matter of degree, in the extent to which forms endure beyond the immediate contexts of their production. Musical sound, of course, is subject to the property of rapid fading: speeding outwards from its point of emission, and dissipating as it goes, it is present only momentarily to our senses. But where, as in painting, gestures leave their traces in solid substance, the resulting forms may last much longer, albeit never indefinitely.

Returning now from the contrast between music and painting to that between taskscape and landscape, the first point to note is that no more than a painting is the landscape given ready-made. One cannot, as Inglis points out, 'treat landscape as an object if it is to be understood. It is a living process; it makes men; it is made by them' (1977: 489). Just as with music, the forms of the landscape are generated in movement: these forms, however, are congealed in a solid medium – indeed, to borrow Inglis's words again, 'a landscape is the most solid appearance in which a history can declare itself' (*ibid.*). Thanks to their solidity, features of the landscape remain available for inspection long after the movement that gave rise to them has ceased. If, as Mead argued (1977 [1938]: 97), every object is to be regarded as a 'collapsed act', then *the landscape as a whole must likewise be understood as the taskscape in its embodied form*: a pattern of activities 'collapsed' into an array of features.

But to reiterate a point made earlier, the landscape takes on its forms through a process of incorporation, not of inscription. That is to say, landscape formation is not a matter – as James Weiner would have it (1991: 32) – of transforming 'a sheer physical terrain into a pattern of historically experienced and constituted space and time', as though the physical world pre-existed as a blank slate, a mere substrate of formless materiality, awaiting the impress of cultural significance. Human beings do not, in their movements, inscribe their life histories upon the surface of nature as do writers upon the page; rather, these histories are woven, along with the life-cycles of plants and animals, into the texture of the surface itself (see Chapter Eighteen, pp. 347–8). Thus the forms of the landscape arise alongside those of the taskscape, within the same current of activity. If we recognise a man's gait in the pattern of his footprints, it is not because the gait preceded the foot-prints and was 'inscribed' in them, but because both the gait and the prints arose within the movement of the man's walking.

Since, moreover, the activities that comprise the taskscape are unending, the landscape is never complete: neither 'built' nor 'unbuilt', it is perpetually under construction. This is why the conventional dichotomy between natural and artificial (or 'man-made') compo-nents of the landscape is so problematic. Virtually by definition, an artefact is an object shaped to a pre-conceived image that motivated its construction, and it is finished at the point when it is brought into conformity with this image. What happens to it beyond that point is supposed to belong to the phase of use rather than manufacture, to dwelling rather than building. But the forms of the landscape are not pre-prepared for people to live in – not by nature nor by human hands – for it is in the very process of dwelling that these forms are constituted. We may recall here Heidegger's remark, already cited in the last chapter, that 'to build is in itself already to dwell' (1971: 146). Thus the landscape is always in the nature of work in progress.

My conclusion that the landscape is the congealed form of the taskscape does enable us to explain why, intuitively, the landscape seems to be what we *see* around us, whereas the taskscape is what we *hear*. To be seen, a thing need do nothing itself, for the optic array that specifies its form to a viewer consists of light reflected off its outer surfaces. To be heard, on the other hand, a thing must actively emit sounds or, through its move-ment, cause sound to be emitted by other objects with which it comes into contact. Thus, outside my window I see a landscape of houses, trees, gardens, a street and pavement. I do not hear any of these things, but I can hear people talking on the pavement, a car passing by, birds singing in the trees, a dog barking somewhere in the distance, and the sound of hammering as a neighbour repairs his garden shed. In short, what I hear is *activity*, even when its source cannot be seen. And since the forms of the taskscape, suspended as they are in movement, are present *only* as activity, the limits of the taskscape are also the limits of the auditory world. (While I deal here only with visual and aural perception, we should not underestimate the significance of touch, which is important to all of us but above all to blind people, for whom it opens up the possibility of access to the landscape – if only through proximate bodily contact.)

This argument carries an important corollary. Whereas both the landscape and the taskscape presuppose the presence of an agent who watches and listens, the taskscape must be populated with beings who are themselves agents, and who reciprocally 'act back' in the process of their own dwelling. In other words, the taskscape exists not just as activity but as *inter*activity. Indeed this conclusion was already foreshadowed when I introduced the concept of resonance as the rhythmic harmonisation of mutual attention. Having said that, however, there is no reason why the domain of interactivity should be confined to the movements of human beings. We hear animals as well as people, such as the birds and the dog in my example above. Hunters, to take another example, are alert to every sight, sound or smell that reveals the presence of animals, and we can be sure that the animals are likewise alert to the presence of humans, as they are also to that of one another. On a larger scale, the hunters' journeys through the landscape, or their oscillations between the procurement of different animal species, resonate with the migratory movements of terrestrial mammals, birds and fish. Perhaps then, as Reed argues, there is a fundamental difference between our perception of animate beings and inanimate objects, since the former – by virtue of their capacity for autonomous movement – 'are *aware* of their surroundings (including us) and because they *act* on those surroundings (including us)'

(Reed 1988a: 116). In other words, they afford the possibility not only of action but also of interaction (cf. Gibson 1979: 135). Should we, then, draw the boundaries of the taskscape around the limits of the animate?

Though the argument is a compelling one I find it unsatisfactory, for two reasons in particular. First, as Langer observes, 'rhythm is the basis of life, but not limited to life' (1953: 128). The rhythms of human activities resonate not only with those of other living things but also with a whole host of other rhythmic phenomena – the cycles of day and night and of the seasons, the winds, the tides, and so on. Citing a petition of 1800 from the seaside town of Sunderland, in which it is explained that 'people are obliged to be up at all hours of the night to attend the tides and their affairs upon the river', Thompson (1967: 59–60) notes that 'the operative phrase is "attend the tides": the patterning of social time in the seaport follows *upon* the rhythms of the sea'. In many cases these natural rhythmic phenomena find their ultimate cause in the mechanics of planetary motion, but it is not of course to these that we resonate. Thus we resonate to the cycles of light and darkness, not to the rotation of the earth, even though the diurnal cycle is caused by the earth's axial rotation. And we resonate to the cycles of vegetative growth and decay, not to the earth's revolutions around the sun, even though the latter cause the cycle of the seasons. Moreover these resonances are *embodied*, in the sense that they are not only historically incorporated into the enduring features of the landscape but also developmentally incorporated into our very constitution as biological organisms. Thus Young describes the body as 'an array of interlocking (or interflowing) cycles, with their own spheres of partial independence within the solar cycle' (1988: 41). We do not consult these cycles, as we might consult a wrist-watch, in order to time our own activities, for the cycles are inherent in the rhythmic structure of the activities themselves. It would seem, then, that the pattern of resonances that comprises the temporality of the taskscape must be expanded to embrace the totality of rhythmic phenomena, whether animate or inanimate.

The second reason why I would be reluctant to restrict the taskscape to the realm of living things has to do with the very notion of animacy. I do not think we can regard this as a property that can be ascribed to objects in isolation, such that some (animate) have it and others (inanimate) do not. For life is not a principle that is separately installed inside individual organisms, and which sets them in motion upon the stage of the inanimate. To the contrary, as I have argued elsewhere, life is 'a name for *what is going on* in the generative field within which organic forms are located and "held in place"' (Ingold 1990: 215). That generative field is constituted by the totality of organism–environment relations, and the activities of organisms are moments of its unfolding. Indeed once we think of the world in this way, as a total movement of becoming which builds itself into the forms we see, and in which each form takes shape in continuous relation to those around it, then the distinction between the animate and the inanimate seems to dissolve. The world itself takes on the character of an organism, and the movements of animals – including those of us human beings – are parts or aspects of its life-process (Lovelock 1979). This means that in dwelling in the world, we do not act *upon* it, or do things *to* it; rather we move along *with* it. Our actions do not transform the world, they are part and parcel of the world's transforming itself. And that is just another way of saying that they belong to time.

For in the final analysis, everything is suspended in movement. David Reason expresses the point in an eloquent passage that could stand as a summary of all I have argued so far:

Landscapes change; and change is itself an intrinsic aspect of our experience of land-scape. The landscape is a polyrhythmic composition of processes whose pulse varies from the erratic flutter of leaves to the measured drift and clash of tectonic plates. Relative to the human span, the view before us seems composed of fleeting, ephemeral effects which create a patina of transience on apparently stable forms.

(1987: 40)

As this passage reveals, what appear to us as the fixed forms of the landscape, passive and unchanging unless acted upon from outside, are themselves in motion, albeit on a scale immeasurably slower and more majestic than that on which our own activities are conducted. Imagine a film of the landscape, shot over years, centuries, even millennia. Slightly speeded up, plants appear to engage in very animal-like movements, trees flex their limbs without any prompting from the winds. Speeded up rather more, glaciers flow like rivers and even the earth begins to move. At yet greater speeds solid rock bends, buckles and flows like molten metal. The world itself begins to breathe. Thus the rhythmic pattern of human activities nests within the wider pattern of activity for all animal life, which in turn nests within the pattern of activity for all so-called living things, which nests within the life-process of the world.

At each of these levels, as Mae-Wan Ho shows, coherence is founded upon resonance (Ho 1989: 18–20). Reminding us of Whitehead's maxim, that there is 'no holding nature still and looking at it', Ho argues that the world is not anything we can look at but a process that we are part of. Ultimately, then, by re-placing the tasks of human dwelling in their proper context within the process of becoming of the world as a whole, we can do away with the dichotomy between taskscape and landscape – only, however, by recognising the fundamental temporality of the landscape itself.[6]

THE HARVESTERS

In order to provide some illustration of the ideas developed in the preceding sections, I reproduce here a painting which, more than any other I know, vividly captures a sense of the temporality of the landscape. This is *The harvesters*, painted by Pieter Bruegel the Elder in 1565 (Figure 11.1). I am not an art historian or critic, and my purpose is not to analyse the painting in terms of style, composition or aesthetic effect. Nor am I concerned with the historical context of its production. Suffice it to say that the picture is believed to be one of a series of twelve, each depicting a month of the year, out of which only five have survived (Gibson 1977: 147). Each panel portrays a landscape, in the colours and apparel appropriate to the month, and shows people engaged in the tasks of the agricultural cycle that are usual at that time of year. *The harvesters* depicts the month of August, and shows field hands at work, reaping and sheafing a luxuriant crop of wheat, whilst others pause for a midday meal and some well-earned rest. The sense of rustic harmony conveyed in this scene may, perhaps, represent something of an idealisation on Bruegel's part. As Walter Gibson points out, Bruegel was inclined to 'depict peasants very much as a wealthy landowner would have viewed them, as the anonymous tenders of his fields and flocks' (1977: 157–8). Any landowner would have had cause for satisfaction in such a fine crop, whereas the hands who sweated to bring it in may have had a rather different experience. Nevertheless, Bruegel painted during a period of great material prosperity in the Netherlands, in which all shared to some degree. These were fortunate times.

Figure 11.1 *The harvesters* (1565) by Pieter Bruegel the Elder.
The Metropolitan Museum of Art, Rogers Fund, 1919 (19.164).

We are accustomed, by the conventions of modern society, to describe our experience of landscape as though we were viewing a picture. What I am about to suggest, however, is precisely the reverse. Rather than treating the world as its own painting I should like you, the reader, to regard this painting by Bruegel as though it were its own world, into which you have been magically transported. Imagine yourself, then, set down in the very landscape depicted, on a sultry August day in 1565. Standing a little way off to the right of the group beneath the tree, you are a witness to the scene unfolding about you. And of course you hear it too, for the scene does not unfold in silence. So used are we to thinking of the landscape as a picture that we can look *at*, like a plate in a book or an image on a screen, that it is perhaps necessary to remind you that exchanging the painting for 'real life' is not simply a matter of increasing the scale. What is involved is a fundamental difference of orientation. In the landscape of our dwelling, we *look around* (Gibson 1979: 203).[7] In what follows I shall focus on six components of what you see around you, and comment on each insofar as they illustrate aspects of what I have had to say about landscape and temporality. They are: the hills and valley, the paths and tracks, the tree, the corn, the church, and the people.

The hills and valley

The terrain is a gently undulating one of low hills and valleys, grading off to a shoreline that can just be made out through the summer haze. You are standing near the summit of a hill, from where you can look out across the intervening valley to the next. How, then, do you differentiate between the hills and the valley as components of this landscape? Are they alternating blocks or strips into which it may be divided up? Any attempt at such division plunges us immediately into absurdity. For where can we draw the boundaries of a hill except along the valley bottoms that separate it from the hills on either side? And where can we draw the boundaries of a valley except along the summits of the hills that mark its watershed? One way, we would have a landscape consisting only of hills, the other way it would consist only of valleys. Of course, 'hill' and 'valley' are opposed terms, but the opposition is not spatial or altitudinal but kinaesthetic. It is the movements of falling away from, and rising up towards, that specify the form of the hill; and the movements of falling away towards, and rising up from, that specify the form of the valley. Through the exercises of descending and climbing, and their different muscular entailments, the contours of the landscape are not so much measured as *felt* – they are directly incorporated into our bodily experience. But even if you remain rooted to one spot, the same principle applies. As you look across the valley to the hill on the horizon, your eyes do not remain fixed: swivelling in their sockets, or as you tilt your head, their motions accord with the movement of your attention as it follows its course through the landscape. You cast your eyes first downwards into the valley, and then upwards towards the distant hill. Indeed in this vernacular phrase, to 'cast one's eyes', common sense has once again grasped intuitively what the psychology of vision, with its metaphors of retinal imagery, has found so hard to accept: that movement is the very essence of perception. It is *because*, in scanning the terrain from nearby into the distance, your downward glance is followed by an upward one, that you perceive the valley.

Moreover someone standing where you are now would perceive the same topographic panorama, regardless of the time of year, the weather conditions and the activities in which people may be engaged. We may reasonably suppose that over the centuries, perhaps even millennia, this basic topography has changed but little. Set against the duration of human memory and experience, it may therefore be taken to establish a baseline of permanence. Yet permanence, as Gibson has stressed, is always relative; thus 'it is better to speak of persistence under change' (Gibson 1979: 13). Although the topography is invariant relative to the human life-cycle, it is not itself immune to change. Sea-levels rise and fall with global climatic cycles, and the present contours of the country are the cumulative outcome of a slow and long drawn out process of erosion and deposition. This process, moreover, was not confined to earlier geological epochs during which the landscape assumed its present topographic form. For it is still going on, and will continue so long as the stream, just visible in the valley bottom, flows on towards the sea. The stream does not flow between pre-cut banks, but cuts its banks even as it flows. Likewise, as we have seen, people shape the landscape even as they dwell. And human activities, as well as the action of rivers and the sea, contribute significantly to the process of erosion. As you watch, the stream flows, folk are at work, a landscape is being formed, and time passes.

The paths and tracks

I remarked above that we experience the contours of the landscape by moving through it, so that it enters – as Bachelard would say – into our 'muscular consciousness'. Reliving the experience in our imagination, we are inclined to recall the road we took as 'climbing' the hill, or as 'descending' into the valley, as though 'the road itself had muscles, or rather, counter-muscles' (Bachelard 1964: 11). And this, too, is probably how you recall the paths and tracks that are visible to you now: after all, you must have travelled along at least some of them to reach the spot where you are currently standing. Nearest at hand, a path has been cut through the wheat-field, allowing sheaves to be carried down, and water and provisions to be carried up. Further off, a cart-track runs along the valley bottom, and another winds up the hill behind. In the distance, paths criss-cross the village green. Taken together, these paths and tracks 'impose a habitual pattern on the movement of people' (Jackson 1989: 146). And yet they also arise out of that movement, for every path or track shows up as the accumulated imprint of countless journeys that people have made – with or without their vehicles or domestic animals – as they have gone about their everyday business. Thus the same movement is embodied, on the side of the people, in their 'muscular consciousness', and on the side of the landscape, in its network of paths and tracks. In this network is sedimented the activity of an entire community, over many generations. It is the taskscape made visible.

In their journeys along paths and tracks, however, people also move from place to place. To reach a place, you need cross no boundary, but you must follow some kind of path. Thus there can be no places without paths, along which people arrive and depart; and no paths without places, that constitute their destinations and points of departure. And for the harvesters, the place to which they arrive, and whence they will leave at the end of the day, is marked by the next feature of the landscape to occupy your attention . . .

The tree

Rising from the spot where people are gathered for their repast is an old and gnarled pear-tree, which provides them with both shade from the sun, a back-rest and a prop for utensils. Being the month of August, the tree is in full leaf, and fruit is ripening on the branches. But this is not just *any* tree. For one thing, it draws the entire landscape around it into a unique focus: in other words, by its presence it constitutes a particular place. The place was not there before the tree, but came into being with it. And for those who are gathered there, the prospect it affords, which is to be had nowhere else, is what gives it its particular character and identity. For another thing, no other tree has quite the same configuration of branches, diverging, bending and twisting in exactly the same way. In its present form, the tree embodies the entire history of its development from the moment it first took root. And that history consists in the unfolding of its relations with mani-fold components of its environment, including the people who have nurtured it, tilled the soil around it, pruned its branches, picked its fruit, and – as at present – use it as something to lean against. The people, in other words, are as much bound up in the life of the tree as is the tree in the lives of the people.[8] Moreover, unlike the hills and the valley, the tree has manifestly grown within living memory. Thus its temporality is more consonant with that of human dwelling. Yet in its branching structure, the tree combines an entire hierarchy of temporal rhythms, ranging from the long cycle of its own germi-nation, growth and eventual decay to the short, annual cycle of flowering, fruiting and foliation. At one extreme, represented by the solid trunk, it presides immobile over the passage of human generations; at the other, represented by the frondescent shoots, it resonates with the life-cycles of insects, the seasonal migrations of birds, and the regular round of human agricultural activities (Davies 1988). In a sense, then, the tree bridges the gap between the apparently fixed and invariant forms of the landscape and the mobile and transient forms of animal life, visible proof that all of these forms, from the most permanent to the most ephemeral, are dynamically linked under transformation within the movement of becoming of the world as a whole.

The corn

Turning from the pear-tree to the wheat-field, it is no longer a place in the landscape but the surrounding surface that occupies your attention. And perhaps what is most striking about this surface is its uniformity of colour, a golden sheen that cloaks the more elevated parts of the country for as far as the eye can see. As you know, wheat takes on this colour at the particular time of year when it is ripe for harvesting. More than any other feature of the landscape, the golden corn gathers the lives of its inhabitants, wherever they may be, into temporal unison, founded upon a communion of visual experience. Thus whereas the tree binds past, present and future in a single place, the corn binds every place in the landscape within a single horizon of the present. The tree, we could say, establishes a vivid sense of duration, the corn an equally vivid sense of what Fabian (1983: 31) calls *coevalness*. It is this distinction that Bachelard has in mind when he contrasts the 'before-me, before-us' of the forest with the 'with-me, with-us' of fields and meadows, wherein 'my dreams and recollections accompany all the different phases of tilling and harvesting' (Bachelard 1964: 188). You may suppose that the sleeper beneath the tree is dreaming of corn, but if so, you may be sure that the people and the activities that figure in his dream are coeval with those of the present and do not take him back into an encounter with the past.[9]

Where the corn has been freshly cut, it presents a sheer vertical front, not far short of a man's height. But this is not a boundary feature, like a hedge or fence. It is an inter-face, whose outline is progressively transformed as the harvesters proceed with their work. Here is a fine example of the way in which form emerges through movement. Another example can be seen further off, where a man is engaged in the task of binding the wheat into a sheaf. Each completed sheaf has a regular form, which arises out of the coordinated movement of binding. But the completion of a sheaf is only one moment in the labour process. The sheaves will later be carried down the path through the field, to the haycart in the valley. Indeed at this very moment, one woman is stooped almost double in the act of picking up a sheaf, and two others can be seen on their way down, sheaves on their shoulders. Many more operations will follow before the wheat is eventually transformed into bread. In the scene before you, one of the harvesters under the tree, seated on a sheaf, is cutting a loaf. Here the cycle of production and consumption ends where it began, with the producers. For production is tantamount to dwelling: it does not begin here (with a pre-conceived image) and end there (with a finished artefact), but is *continuously going on*.

The church

Not far off, nestled in a grove of trees near the top of the hill, is a stone church. It is instructive to ask: how does the church differ from the tree? They have more in common, perhaps, than meets the eye. Both possess the attributes of what Bakhtin (1981: 84) calls a 'chronotope' – that is, a place charged with temporality, one in which temporality takes on palpable form. Like the tree, the church by its very presence constitutes a place, which owes its character to the unique way in which it draws in the surrounding landscape. Again like the tree, the church spans human generations, yet its temporality is not inconsonant with that of human dwelling. As the tree buries its roots in the ground, so also people's ancestors are buried in the graveyard beside the church, and both sets of roots may reach to approximately the same temporal depth. Moreover the church, too, resonates to the cycles of human life and subsistence. Among the inhabitants of the neighbourhood, it is not only seen but also heard, as its bells ring out the seasons, the months, births, marriages and deaths. In short, as features of the landscape, both the church and the tree appear as veritable monuments to the passage of time.

Yet despite these similarities, the difference may seem obvious. The church, after all, is a *building*. The tree, by contrast, is not built, it grows. We may agree to reserve the term 'building' for any durable structure in the landscape whose form arises and is sustained within the current of human activity. It would be wrong to conclude, however, that the distinction between buildings and non-buildings is an absolute one. Where an absolute distinction is made, it is generally founded on the assumption that built form, rather than having its source within nature, is superimposed by the mind upon it. That assumption, however, presupposes the separation of mind and nature. But from the perspective of dwelling there is no such separation. It is evident, from this latter perspective, that the forms of buildings, as much as of any other features of the landscape, are neither given in the world nor placed upon it, but emerge within the self-transforming processes of the world itself. With respect to any feature, the scope of human involvement in these processes will vary from negligible to considerable, though it is never total (even the most engineered of environments is home to other species). Thus to recall our conclusion from the last chapter, what is or is not a building is a relative matter; moreover as human involvement may vary in the life history of a feature, it may be *more or less* of a building in different periods.

Returning to the tree and the church, it is clearly too simple to suppose that the form of the tree is naturally given in its genetic make-up, whereas the form of the church preexists, in the minds of the builders, as a plan which is then realised in stone. In the case of the tree, we have already observed that its growth consists in the unfolding of a total system of relations constituted by the fact of its presence in an environment, from the point of germination onwards, and that people, as components of the tree's environment, play a not insignificant role in this process. Likewise the 'biography' of the church consists in the unfolding of relations with its human builders, as well as with other components of its environment, from the moment when the first stone was laid. The final form of the church may indeed have been prefigured in the human imagination, but it no more issued from the image than did the form of the tree issue from its genes. In both cases, the form is the embodiment of a developmental or historical process, and is rooted in the context of human dwelling in the world.

In the case of the church, moreover, that process did not stop when its form came to match the conceptual model. For as long as the building remains standing in the landscape, it will continue – as it does now – to figure within the environment not just of human beings but of a myriad of other living kinds, plant and animal, which will incorporate it into their own life-activities and modify it in the process. And it is subject, too, to the same forces of weathering and decomposition, both organic and meteorological, that affect everything else in the landscape. The preservation of the church in its existing, 'finished' form in the face of these forces, however substantial it may be in its materials and construction, requires a regular input of effort in maintenance and repair. Once this human input lapses, leaving it at the mercy of other forms of life and of the weather, it will soon cease to be a building and become a ruin.

The people

So far I have described the scene only as you behold it with your eyes. Yet you do not only look, you listen as well, for the air is full of sounds of one kind and another. Though the folk beneath the tree are too busy eating to talk, you hear the clatter of wooden spoons on bowls, the slurp of the drinker, and the loud snores of the member of the party who is outstretched in sleep. Further off, you hear the swish of scythes against the cornstalks and the calls of the birds as they swoop low over the field in search of prey. Far off in the distance, wafted on the light wind, can be heard the sounds of people conversing and playing on a green, behind which, on the other side of the stream, lies a cluster of cottages. What you hear is a taskscape.

In the performance of their particular tasks, people are responsive not only to the cycle of maturation of the crop, which draws them together in the overall project of harvesting, but also to each other's activities as these are apportioned by the division of labour. Even within the same task, individuals do not carry on in mutual isolation. Technically, it takes only one man to wield a scythe, but the reapers nevertheless work in unison, achieving a dance-like harmony in their rhythmic movements. Similarly the two women carrying sheaves down into the valley adjust their pace, each in relation to the other, so that the distance between them remains more or less invariant. Perhaps there is less co-ordination between the respective movements of the eaters, however they eye each other intently as they set about their repast, and the meal is a joint activity on which all have embarked together, and which they will finish together. Only the sleeper, oblivious to the world, is out of joint – his snores jar the senses precisely because they are *not* in any kind of rhythmic relation to what is going on around. Without wakeful attention, there can be no resonance.

But in attending to one another, do the people inhabit a world of their own, an exclusively *human* world of meanings and intentions, of beliefs and values, detached from the one in which their bodies are put to work in their several activities? Do they, from within such a domain of intersubjectivity, look at the world outside through the window of their senses? Surely not. For the hills and valley, the tree, the corn and the birds are as palpably present to them (as indeed to you too) as are the people to each other (and to you). The reapers, as they wield their scythes, are *with* the corn, just as the eaters are *with* their fellows. The landscape, in short, is not a totality that you or anyone else can look at, it is rather the world in which we stand in taking up a point of view on our surroundings. And it is within the context of this attentive involvement in the landscape that the human imagination gets to work in fashioning ideas about it. For the landscape, to recall the words of Merleau-Ponty (1962: 24), is not so much the object as 'the *homeland* of our thoughts'.

EPILOGUE

Concluding an essay on the ways in which the Western Apache of Arizona discover meaning, value and moral guidance in the landscape around them, Keith Basso abhors the tendency in ecological anthropology to relegate such matters to an 'epiphenomenal' level, which is seen to have little or no bearing on the dynamics of adaptation of human populations to the conditions of their environments. An ecology that is fully *cultural*, Basso argues, is one that would attend as much to the semiotic as to the material dimensions of people's relations with their surroundings, by bringing into focus 'the layers of significance with which human beings blanket the environment' (Basso 1984: 49). In rather similar vein, Denis Cosgrove regrets the tendency in human geography to regard the landscape in narrowly utilitarian and functional terms, as 'an impersonal expression of demographic and economic forces', and thus to ignore the multiple layers of symbolic meaning or cultural representation that are deposited upon it. The task of decoding the 'many-layered meanings of symbolic landscapes', Cosgrove argues, will require a geography that is not just human but properly *humanistic* (Cosgrove 1989: 120–7).

Though I have some sympathy with the views expressed by these writers, I believe that the metaphors of cultural construction they adopt have an effect quite opposite to that intended. For the very idea that meaning *covers over* the world, layer upon layer, carries the implication that the way to uncover the most basic level of human beings' practical involvement with their environments is by stripping these layers away. In other words, such blanketing metaphors actually serve to create and perpetuate an intellectual space in which human ecology or human geography can flourish, untroubled by any concerns about what the world means to the people who live in it. We can surely learn from the Western Apache, who insist that the stories they tell, far from putting meanings upon the landscape, are intended to allow listeners to place themselves in *relation* to specific features of the landscape, in such a way that their meanings may be revealed or disclosed. Stories help to open up the world, not to cloak it.

And such opening up, too, must be the objective of archaeology. Like the Western Apache – and for that matter any other group of people who are truly 'at home' in the world – archaeologists study the meaning of the landscape not by interpreting the many layers of its representation (adding further layers in the process) but by probing ever more deeply into it. Meaning is there to be *discovered* in the landscape, if only we know how to attend to it. Every feature, then, is a potential clue, a key to meaning rather than a vehicle for carrying it.[10] This discovery procedure, wherein objects in the landscape become clues to meaning, is what distinguishes the perspective of dwelling. And since, as I have shown, the process of dwelling is fundamentally temporal, the apprehension of the landscape in the dwelling perspective must begin from a recognition of its temporality. Only through such recognition, by temporalising the landscape, can we move beyond the division that has afflicted most inquiries up to now, between the scientific study of an atemporalised nature, and the humanistic study of a dematerialised history. And no discipline is better placed to take this step than archaeology. I have not been concerned here with either the methods or the results of archaeological inquiry. However to the question, 'what is archaeology the study *of* ?', I believe there is no better answer than 'the temporality of the landscape'. I hope, in this chapter, to have gone some way towards elucidating what this means.

Chapter Twelve

Globes and spheres
The topology of environmentalism

My purpose in this chapter is no more than to try out a rather embryonic idea. It concerns the significance of the image of the globe in the language of contemporary debate about the environment. Though the image has long been deployed in geopolitical contexts, and even longer in connection with navigation and astronomy, my impression is that its use as a characterisation of the *environment* is rather recent. I have in mind such phrases, which slip so readily off the tongues of contemporary policy-makers, as 'global environmental change'. One is immediately struck by the paradoxical nature of this phrase. An environment, surely, is that which surrounds, and can exist, therefore, only in relation to what is surrounded (Ingold 1992a: 40). I do not think that those who speak of the global environment mean by this the environment surrounding the globe. It is *our* environment they are talking about, the world as it presents itself to a universal humanity. Yet how can humans, or for that matter beings of any other kind, possibly be surrounded by a globe? Would it not be fairer to say that it is we who have surrounded *it*?

My idea is that what may be called the global outlook may tell us something important about the modern conception of the environment as a world which, far from being the ambience of our dwelling, is turned in upon itself, so that we who once stood at its centre become first circumferential and are finally expelled from it altogether (Figure 12.1). In other words, I am suggesting that the notion of the global environment, far from marking humanity's reintegration into the world, signals the culmination of a process of separation.

The image of the globe is familiar to all of us who have gone through a Western schooling and are used to studying models upon which are drawn, in outline, the continents and oceans, and the gridlines of latitude and longitude. We are taught that this is what the earth looks like, although none of us, with a handful of significant exceptions, has ever seen it. By and large, life is lived at such close proximity to the earth's surface that a global perspective is unobtainable. The significant exceptions comprise, of course, that privileged band of astronauts who have viewed the earth from outer space. In a sense,

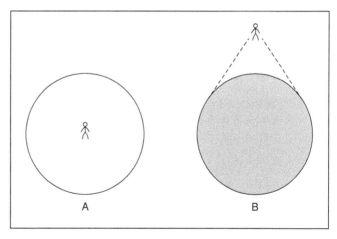

Figure 12.1 Two views of the environment: (A) as a lifeworld; (B) as a globe.

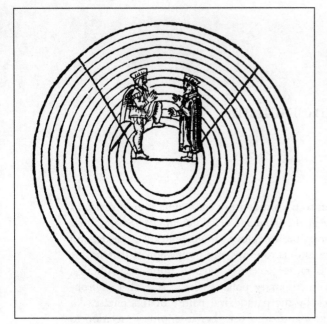

Figure 12.2 The fourteen spheres of the world, as drawn by Giovanni Camillo Maffei of Solofra in his *Scala Naturale* (Venice, 1564). Giovanni's patron, the Count of Altavilla, is shown beginning his ascent through the spheres.

the astronaut's relation to the real globe seen through the window of the spacecraft mirrors the schoolchild's relation to the model globe in the classroom: in both cases the world appears as an object of contemplation, detached from the domain of lived experience. For the child the world is separately encapsulated in the model; for the astronaut life is separately encapsulated, albeit temporarily, in the space module. My point with this comparison is a simple one: with the world imaged as a globe, far from coming into being in and through a life process, it figures as an entity that is, as it were, presented to or confronted by life. The global environment is not a lifeworld, it is a world apart from life.

Before pursuing the implications of this view, I should like to introduce an alternative image of the world which, at least in European thought, is of far more ancient provenance. This is the image of the sphere. Something of the difference in connotation between 'globe' and 'sphere' is suggested in their very acoustic resonance: 'globe' is hard and consonantal; 'sphere' soft and vocalic. A globe is solid and opaque, a sphere hollow and transparent. For the early astronomers, of course, the cosmos itself was seen to be comprised of a series of such spheres, at the common centre of which stood man himself. The idea was that as man's attention was drawn ever outward, so it would penetrate each sphere so as to reach the next. This is illustrated in Figure 12.2, taken from the *Scala Naturale* of Giovanni Camillo Maffei, published in Venice in 1564, and dedicated to the Count of Altavilla. Here there are fourteen concentric spheres which – Maffei tells us – may be envisaged to form a giant stairway, the ascent of which affords, step-by-step, a comprehensive knowledge of the universe. In the picture, the Count is shown taking the first step, under Maffei's direction (see Adams 1938: 58–9).

Unlike the solid globe, which can only be perceived as such from without, spheres – as is clear from this figure – were to be perceived from within. The global view, we might say, is centripetal, the spherical view centrifugal. Nor is it any accident that the perception of the spheres was imaged in terms of listening rather than looking. Visual perception, insofar as it depends on the reflection of light from the outer surface of things, implies both the opacity and inertia of what is seen and the externality of the perceiver. The spheres, being transparent, could not be seen, but undergoing their own autonomous rotations about the common centre, they could be heard: thus the motion of the spheres was supposed to make a harmonious sound that could be registered by the sufficiently sensitive ear. Dating back to Pythagoras and subsequently taken up by Plato and Aristotle, the notion of the 'music of the spheres' was passed on to the Middle Ages through the writings of Boethius, and became integral to the ideas of the Renaissance, starting with Marsilio

Ficino in the fifteenth century (Hallyn 1993: 232). Still today, it is commonly argued that the space of auditory perception is spherical in form, a sphere that surrounds (without enclosing) the listener at its centre. Thus whereas we appear to be on the edge of visual space looking *in* with the eye, we are always at the centre of auditory space listening *out* with the ear (Schafer 1985: 88, 94; cf. Ihde 1976, Carpenter and McLuhan 1960). The globe is to the sphere, according to this argument, as vision is to hearing.[1]

The idea of the spherical cosmos is by no means exclusive to the history of European thought. Let me present one further example, taken from Fienup-Riordan's (1990) account of the lifeworld of the Yup'ik Eskimos. Her cross-sectional depiction of the cosmos as perceived by the Yup'ik, reproduced in Figure 12.3, bears an uncanny resemblance to Maffei's diagram. At the centre is the dwelling, from which roads lead in various directions through the several surrounding spheres.

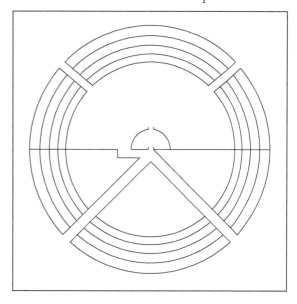

Figure 12.3 Yup'ik cosmology in cross section.

Reproduced from *Eskimo essays: Yup'ik lives and how we see them*, by A. Fienup-Riordan, published by Rutgers University Press, 1990, p. 111.

A person journeying far enough in any direction would eventually arrive at a point where the earth folded back up into the skyland, the home of the spirits of the game . . . Not only was the earth encompassed by a canopy from above, but below its thin surface resided the spirits of the dead, both animal and human, each in separate villages. Four or five 'steps' separated these two distinct but related domains.

(Fienup-Riordan 1990: 110)

Notice how in this image the surface of the earth, far from bounding the world externally, is but a thin and permeable membrane dividing the world internally, between upper and lower hemispheres.

What I hope to have established, at least in outline, is that the lifeworld, imaged from an experiential centre, is spherical in form, whereas a world divorced from life, that is yet complete in itself, is imaged in the form of a globe. Thus the movement from spherical to global imagery is also one in which 'the world', as we are taught it exists, is drawn ever further from the matrix of our lived experience. It appears that the world as it really exists can only be witnessed by leaving it, and indeed much scientific energy and resources have been devoted to turning such an imaginative flight into an achieved actuality. One consequence is the alleged discrepancy between what, in modern jargon, are called 'local' and 'global' perspectives. Insofar as the latter, afforded to a being outside the world, is seen to be both real and total, the former, afforded to beings-in-the-world (that is, ordinary people) is regarded as illusory and incomplete. Retrieving from my shelves a geology textbook published in 1964 – two years before the earth was first photographed from space – I read on the very first page that 'races of men [whose] horizons are limited to a tribal territory, the confines of a mountain valley, a short stretch of the coast line, or the congested blocks of a large city' can have no conception of the true nature and extent of the world about them (Putnam 1964: 3). If true knowledge is to be had by looking *at* the world, this statement is self-evidently valid. My point, however, is that this speculist assumption is precisely what has given us the imagery of the world as a globe. And it is this assumption, too, that privileges the knowledge we get from school by looking at model globes over the knowledge we get from life by actively participating in our surroundings.

Do not misunderstand me. I am not some latter-day flat-earther or pre-Copernican. I do not mean to deny that the earth takes the form of a globe – something that has been known, if not universally accepted, at least from the time of Pythagoras – or that it is one of a number of planets revolving around a rather insignificant star. My question is how it came to pass that this globe, the planet we call Earth, was taken to be an environment, or what my geology textbook called 'the world about us'.

We can take a cue from the writings of Immanuel Kant who, in his *Critique of pure reason*, drew a sophisticated analogy between the topological form of the earth and that of the universe as a whole – that is, the 'world' conceived as the domain of all possible objects of knowledge. Kant first places himself in the shoes of one ignorant of the fact that the earth is global in form:

> If I represent the earth as it appears to my senses, as a flat surface, with a circular horizon, I cannot know how far it extends. But experience teaches me that wherever I may go, I always see a space around me in which I could proceed further.
>
> (1933: 606)

One is thus in the hapless position of realising that one's knowledge is limited, but of having no way of knowing just how limited it is. Once it is recognised, however, that the earth is a globe, and given a knowledge of its diameter, it is immediately possible to calculate, from first principles, its surface area. And so, even though – as we traverse the surface – new horizons are always opening up, not only can we work out, by subtraction, how much there remains to be discovered, but also every fresh observation can be slotted into position, in relation to each and every other, within a complete, unifying spatial framework. Thus, to obtain a comprehensive knowledge of the environment, we must already have in mind an image of the globe, or come pre-equipped with what Kant called 'an extended concept of the whole surface of the earth', onto which may be mapped the data of experience (see Richards 1974: 11). Moreover the same applies to knowledge in general, which the mind sees as arrayed upon the surface of a sphere, at once continuous and limited in extent: 'Our reason is not like a plane indefinitely far extended, the limits of which we know in a general way only; but must rather be compared to a sphere, the radius of which can be determined from the curvature of the arc of its surface . . .' (Kant 1933: 607). In this analogy, the topology of the earth's surface comes to stand for the fundamental idea, which the mind is said to bring to experience, of the unity, completeness and continuity of nature. Here, surely, is to be found the very essence of the global outlook.

Let us, then, compare an imaginary Kantian traveller, journeying across the globe in search of new experiences to fit into his overall conception, with the Yup'ik Eskimos, in whose cycles of everyday and seasonal movement the cosmos, as they see it (Figure 12.3), is continually being re-created (Fienup-Riordan 1990: 110–11). For both, the earth provides the ground on which they move, but whereas for the Yup'ik, this movement is conducted within the world, the Kantian traveller, for whom the world is a globe, journeys upon its outer surface. It is at this surface, the interface between world and mind, sensation and cognition, that all knowledge is constituted. Not only is the surface a continuous one, it also lacks any centre. Anywhere upon it can serve, in principle, equally well as a point of origin or as a destination. Thus if the 'world about us' is the globe, planet earth, it is not a world *within* which we dwell, as is the Yup'ik world depicted with the house at its centre, but one *on* which we dwell. The globe, of course, does have a centre, yet a journey to the centre of the earth, as immortalised in Jules Verne's celebrated novel, is a voyage into the unknown, a domain of strange and terrifying primordial forces.

In short, from a global perspective, it is on the surface of the world, not at its centre, that life is lived.[2] As a foundational level of 'physical reality', this surface is supposed already to have been in existence long before there was any life at all. Then somehow, through a series of events of near-miraculous improbability, there appeared on it first life and then, very much later, consciousness. These appearances are commonly pictured in terms of the addition of extra layers of being to that basic layer represented by the earth's surface: hence the tripartite division into lithosphere, biosphere and noosphere, corresponding respectively to the inorganic substance of rocks and minerals, the organic substance of living things and the superorganic substance of human culture and society.

Although spherical imagery is employed here, the spheres are defined as layered surfaces that successively *cover over* one another and the world, not as successive horizons disclosed from a centre. And the outer wrapping is none other than the human mind and its products. This picture (see Figure 12.4) is the complete obverse of the medieval conception illustrated in Figure 12.2. The difference may be considered in relation to the genesis of meaning. The world which the Count of Altavilla is setting out to explore in Maffei's diagram is itself a world of meaning which, through a kind of sensory attunement, an education of attention, will be gradually revealed to him as he proceeds from one level of understanding to the next. This world – like the world of the Dreaming in Aboriginal Australia (see Chapter Three, p. 56) – has properties of both transparency and depth: not only can one see into it, but also the more one looks the further one sees. By contrast, the world depicted in Figure 12.4, insofar as it corresponds to 'planet Earth', consists of pure substance, physical matter, presenting an opaque and impenetrable surface of literal reality *upon which* form and meaning are overlain by the human mind. That is to say, meaning does not lie in the relational context of the perceiver's involvement in the world, but is rather inscribed upon the outer surface of the world by the mind of the perceiver. To know the world, then, is a matter not of sensory attunement but of cognitive reconstruction. And such knowledge is acquired not by engaging directly, in a practical way, with the objects in one's surroundings, but rather by learning to represent them, in the mind, in the form of a *map*.

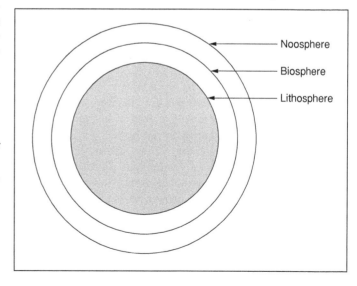

Figure 12.4 Lithosphere, biosphere and noosphere.

I reserve discussion of the notions of mapping and mapmaking for the next chapter. It is sufficient to note, here, the immediate connection between the apprehension of the world as a solid globe and the idea, commonly encountered even in anthropological literature, of the environment as a substrate for the external imposition of arbitrary cultural form. The world becomes a *tabula rasa* for the inscription of human history.

The familiar globes of geography classrooms provide a vivid example of such inscription or covering over. Though the sea is painted blue, the continental land-masses are frequently painted in a mosaic of contrastive colours, representing the territories of nation states. Thus, we are led to think, has the order of human society wrapped itself around the face of the world. Yet that order, we know, has its roots in the history of colonialism, and the attendant voyages of (principally maritime) discovery and exploration. The image of the world as a globe is, I contend, a colonial one. It presents us with the idea of a preformed surface *waiting to be occupied*, to be colonised first by living things and later by human (usually meaning Western) civilisation. Through travel and exploration, it is said, mankind has conquered the globe. Having now filled it up, and still multiplying in numbers at an alarming pace, we are urgently searching around, not just in fantasy but also in fact, for new worlds to colonise. Not only, then, does it appear that the world existed prior to life; it also appears that life can hop from world to world and even – like a parasitic vector flying between successive hosts – exist temporarily in worldless suspension.

The idea that the world exists prior to the forms of life that come to occupy it, and hence that each of these life-forms is itself separately encoded in a context-free vehicle, a kind of free-floating capsule that can carry form from one site of occupation to another, is deeply entrenched in both biological and anthropological thought. In biology it appears as the doctrine of genetic preformation, according to which every organism may be specified, independently of the environmental context of its development, as a unique configuration of self-replicating elements (genes). Through a process of variation under natural selection, organisms are supposed to evolve in ways that make them better adapted to the conditions of their environments, yet the very notion of adaptation implies that these conditions are specifiable in advance, in terms of a set of exogenous parameters quite distinct from the endogenous, genetically fixed parameters of the adapting organisms. There is thus one set of specifications for life, and another set for the world (see Lewontin 1983). In anthropology, cultural information is made to play much the same role as is played by the genes in biology. Again, there is one set of specifications for the forms of life that are carried around – as it used to be said – 'inside people's heads'. And there is another set for the environment, often identified with 'nature' or 'the physical world', upon which these forms are inscribed. And if we ask 'What kind of world is this, that is an environment for every form of life yet external to all of them?', the answer, as we have seen, is planet Earth, the globe.

Moreover, once the world is conceived as a globe, it can become an object of appropriation for a collective humanity. In this discourse, we do not belong to the world, neither partaking of its essence nor resonating to its cycles and rhythms. Rather, since our very humanity is seen to consist, in essence, in the transcendence of physical nature, it is the world that belongs to us. Images of property abound. We have inherited the earth, it is said, and so are responsible for handing it on to our successors in reasonably good condition. But like the prodigal heir, we are inclined to squander this precious inheritance for the sake of immediate gratification. Much of the current concern with the global environment has to do with how we are to 'manage' this planet of ours. That it is ours to manage, however, remains more or less unquestioned. Such management is commonly described in the language of intervention. But to intervene in the world, as we have already had occasion to note (Chapter Four, p. 63), implies the possibility of our choosing not to do so (Williams 1972: 154). It implies that human beings can launch their interventions from a platform above the world, as though they could live *on* or *off* the environment, but are not destined to live *within* it. Indeed, this rendering of action towards the environment as planned intervention in nature is fundamental to the Western notion of production (see Chapter Three, pp. 58–9). History itself comes to be seen as a process wherein human producers, through their transforming reaction on nature, have literally constructed an environment of their own making.

The idea is epitomised in the title of an influential volume, published in 1956, called *Man's role in changing the face of the earth* (Thomas *et al.* 1956). There are two points about this title to which I wish to draw attention. The first is that with the world envisaged as planet Earth, it is its *face* that is presented to humanity as the substrate for the latter's transforming interventions. This recalls my earlier observation that in the global outlook, life appears to be lived upon the outer surface of the world rather than from an experiential centre within it. The world does not surround us, it lies beneath our feet.[3] The second point concerns the notion of change. It is not of course the case, as was believed by some of the early advocates of uniformitarianism, that the earth has persisted since the beginning of time in homeostatic equilibrium, at least until humans came along to upset the balance. On the contrary, it has been – and continues to be – racked by geological forces acting on such a scale as to make the most impressive feats of human engineering seem puny by comparison. These earth-shaping processes, however, are considered to be immanent in the workings of nature. They are what the world undergoes. But in speaking of the role of humanity, the world appears as an *object* of transformation. Change figures as what is done to the planet by its present owner-occupiers, human beings. It is thus exogenous rather than endogenous, not nature transforming itself, but nature transformed through the imposition of non-natural, human design.

This is what is meant when, in 'changing the face of the earth', the universal agent – 'man' – is said to have replaced the natural environment with one which is, to an ever-greater extent, *artificial*. Thus the construction of the human order appears to entail the destruction of the natural one, as production entails consumption. We are, today, increasingly concerned to limit what are perceived to be the destructive consequences of human activity. My point, however, is that the very notions of destruction and damage limitation, like those of construction and control, are grounded in the discourse of intervention. That is to say, they presume a world already constituted, through the action of natural forces, which then becomes the object of human interest and concern. But it is not a world of which humans themselves are conceived to be a part. To them, it is rather presented as a spectacle. They may observe it, reconstruct it, protect it, tamper with it or destroy it, but they do not dwell in it. Indeed, what is perhaps most striking about the contemporary discourse of global environmental change is the immensity of the gulf that divides the world as it is lived and experienced by the practitioners of this discourse, and the world of which they speak under the rubric of 'the globe'. No-one, of course, denies the seriousness of the problems they address; there is good reason to believe, however, that many of these problems have their source in that very alienation of humanity from the world of which the notion of the global environment is a conspicuous expression.

This point brings me back to the distinction, mentioned earlier, between 'local' and 'global' perspectives. The difference between them, I contend, is not one of hierarchical degree, in scale or comprehensiveness, but one of kind. In other words, the local is not a more limited or narrowly focused apprehension than the global, it is one that rests on an altogether different mode of apprehension – one based on practical, perceptual engagement with components of a world that is inhabited or dwelt-in, rather than on the detached, disinterested observation of a world that is merely occupied. In the local perspective the world is a sphere, or perhaps a nesting series of spheres as portrayed in Figures 12.2 and 12.3, centred on a particular place. From this experiential centre, the attention of those who live there is drawn ever deeper *into* the world, in the quest for knowledge and understanding. It is through such attentive engagement, entailed in the very process of dwelling, that the world is progressively revealed to the knowledge-seeker. Now different centres will, of course, afford different views, so that while there is only one global perspective, indifferent to place and context, the number of possible local perspectives is potentially infinite. This does not mean, however, that they are in any sense incomplete, or that they represent no more than fragments of a total picture. It is only when we come to represent local differences in terms of a globalising discourse that the centre from which each perspective is taken is converted into a boundary within which every local view is seen to be contained. The idea that the 'little community' remains confined within its limited horizons from which 'we' – globally conscious Westerners – have escaped results from a privileging of the global ontology of detachment over the local ontology of engagement.

To the extent that it has been used to legitimate the disempowerment of local people in the management of their environments, this idea has had serious practical consequences for those amongst whom anthropologists have conducted their studies. To adopt a distinction from Niklas Luhmann (1979), it might be argued that the dominance of the global perspective marks the triumph of technology over cosmology. Traditional cosmology places the person at the centre of an ordered universe of meaningful relations, such as that depicted by Maffei (Figure 12.2), and enjoins an understanding of these relations as a foundation for proper conduct towards the environment. Modern technology, by contrast, places human society and its interests outside what is residually construed as the 'physical world', and furnishes the means for the former's control over the latter. Cosmology provides the guiding principles for human action *within* the world, technology provides the principles for human action *upon* it. Thus, as cosmology gives way to technology, the relation between people and the world is turned inside out (Figure 12.1), so that what was a cosmos or lifeworld becomes a world – a solid globe – externally presented to life. In short, the movement from spherical to global imagery corresponds to the undermining of cosmological certainties and the growing belief in, and indeed dependence upon, the technological fix. It is a movement from revelation to control, and from partial knowledge to the calculated risk.

Let me add one further comment in conclusion. I have written throughout as though the characterisations of the environment, respectively, as globe and sphere were irrevocably opposed, and thus mutually exclusive. But this is not really so, since each view contains the seeds of the other. To regard the world as a sphere is at once to render conceivable the possibility of its logical inverse, the globe; and of course vice versa. We could say that both perspectives are caught up in the dialectical interplay between engagement and detachment, between human beings' involvement in the world and their separation from it, which has been a feature of the entire history of Western thought and no doubt of other traditions as well. Concretely, this is perhaps most clearly manifest in the architectural form of the dome (Smith 1950). A sphere on the inside, a globe on the outside, this form has a cosmic resonance of near-universal appeal. But for any society, at any period of its history, we may expect one perspective to be ascendant, and the other to be associated with its more or less muted undercurrent. And my sense of the contemporary discourse on the environment in the West is that it continues to be dominated by global imagery associated with the triumph of modern science and technology, but that it is under increasing threat from those – including many anthropologists – who would turn to local or indigenous cosmologies of engagement for sources of insight into our current predicament.

Postscript

Since this chapter was written, two further strands have emerged along which I think the argument can be extended. One is to relate the image of the globe, discussed here, with that of the tree, which is currently pervasive in the representation of biodiversity. The second is to show how the distinction between globe and sphere, as alternative topologies of environmental awareness, crosscuts the conventional dichotomy, as it appears in contemporary environmentalist debates, between ecocentrism and anthropocentrism.

The image of living things as arrayed upon the branches of a tree will already be familiar from my discussion of the genealogical model in Chapter Eight (pp. 134–5). The definitive feature of the model, I argued, is that every creature is specified in its essential nature through the bestowal of attributes passed down along lines of descent, independently and in advance of its placement in the world. The idea that the world is presented to life as a surface to be occupied, at once continuous and finite in extent – in short, as the surface of a globe – is simply the obverse of this notion. The intrinsic connection between the geological image of the world as a globe and the biological image of life as a tree is beautifully illustrated in an engraving by Johannes Christian Bendorp, dating from the turn of the nineteenth century (reproduced in Bouquet 1995: Figure 2.6). Said to depict the Tree of Jesse, it shows a bay tree – on whose trunk and branches are arrayed all the descendants of Adam and Eve – springing from a point on the surface of a solid globe. The precise location of this point is immaterial; what is significant, however, is the inscription below, which reads: 'God created the whole family of man from one blood, to inhabit the entire Earth' (Bouquet 1995: 51). Thus the Earth, as a globe, is there to be colonised by those who 'branch out' over it, along their several lines of descent.

Now one of the consequences of the genealogical model, as I showed in Chapter Eight (pp. 138–9), is that difference is rendered as diversity. Thus living things are classified and compared, and their kinds enumerated, in terms of intrinsic properties that they are deemed to possess by virtue of genealogical connection, irrespective of their positioning in relation to one another in an environment. This is the basis for the modern concept of biodiversity. It follows, however, that this very concept is founded in a global perspective. In other words, the mode of apprehension that would reveal the totality of living things as a catalogue of biodiversity is also one that reveals the world as a globe in the purview of a universal humanity. That is why the human species is itself so conspicuously absent from mainstream conceptions of global biodiversity. Species can only be enumerated in the natural world by a humanity that has set itself above and beyond it, and that – being simultaneously everywhere and nowhere – can set the whole of nature in its sights. So far as human differences are concerned, these are typically understood in terms of a concept of cultural diversity that is seen as *analogous* to biodiversity rather than as an extension of it. And the analogy, of course, serves only to reinforce the belief that whatever differences may exist between peoples, on account of their divergent histories of descent, are superimposed upon a humanity that is common to all.

To pick up the second strand: contemporary discussions concerning human rights and responsibilities towards the environment, above all in global geopolitical arenas, have tended to revolve around a pivotal opposition between the positions of so-called *anthropocentrism* and *ecocentrism*. By anthropocentrism is usually meant an attitude which values all things non-human – all inanimate and animate components of the environment barring other people – solely as instrumental means to the realisation of exclusively human ends. Against this, ecocentrism is defined as that attitude which credits the world of nature – and above all, of living things in their interrelationships – with an intrinsic value quite independently of the purposes and activities, and even of the presence, of human beings. Yet despite (or perhaps because of) their conventional opposition, these two positions share more in common than meets the eye. Both presuppose a global perspective. For both, 'there is just one big environment', identified with the order of nature (Cooper 1992: 167). But by its very vastness, this all-embracing environment is profoundly alien to human experience. It is, as David Cooper puts it, 'much too big' to be lived in. One cannot relate to its components. The environment we relate to, by contrast, is the one that surrounds us, that constitutes our milieu and our ambience. And this is spherical rather than global in its topology.[4]

Since we are human, the world around us must necessarily be anthropocentric: this, in itself, implies no lack of participation, nor does it entail an instrumental attitude. Indeed it is decidedly odd that the term 'anthropocentrism' should have been adopted to denote an attitude that, more than any other, *withdraws* human life from active participation in the environment. It is an attitude that might be more accurately described as 'anthropocircumferentialism'. The term may be an impossibly cumbersome one; nevertheless I believe we need it, if only to distinguish the discursive construction of the environment characteristic of modern Western thought and science from the many pre-modern and non-Western cosmologies that are anthropocentric in the strict sense of placing the human being at the hub of a dwelt-in world, a centre of embodied awareness that reaches out, through the activity of the senses, into its surroundings. Thus the shift from anthropocentrism to anthropocircumferentialism is tantamount to the withdrawal of the human presence from the centre to the periphery of the lifeworld (Figure 12.1). And ecocentrism, finally, is just the other side of the coin from anthropocircumferentialism. For once humanity is placed on the outside, *surrounding* the global environment, then the environment – now surrounded rather than surrounding – no longer holds any place for human beings.

Chapter Thirteen

To journey along a way of life

Maps, wayfinding and navigation

INTRODUCTION

Everyone has probably had the experience, at some time or other, of feeling lost, or of not knowing in which way to turn in order to reach a desired destination. Yet for most of the time we know where we are, and how to get to where we want to go. Ordinary life would be well-nigh impossible if we did not. It remains a challenge, however, to account for everyday skills of orientation and wayfinding. This challenge is compounded by the considerable potential for misunderstanding surrounding the question of what it actually *means* to know where one is, or the way to go. For the map-using stranger, making his way in unfamiliar country, 'being here' or 'going there' generally entails the ability to identify one's current or intended future position with a certain spatial or geographic location, defined by the intersection of particular coordinates on the map. But a person who has grown up in a country and is conversant with its ways knows quite well where he is, or in what direction to go, without having to consult an artefactual map. What, then, does he have that the stranger lacks? According to a view that has found wide support in the literatures of geography and psychology, there is no difference in principle between them. Both are map-users. For both, knowing where one is means identifying one's position in the world with a location on the map. The difference is just that the native inhabitant's map is held not in the hand but in the head, preserved not on paper but in memory, in the form of a comprehensive spatial representation of his usual surroundings. At any moment, it is supposed, he can access this mental or 'cognitive' map, and determine his location in terms of it.

In this chapter I shall argue, to the contrary, that there is no such map, and that the belief in its existence is a consequence of the mistaken attribution to native people of a sense of what it means to know one's whereabouts that effectively treats them as strangers in their own country. Indeed the native inhabitant may be unable to specify his location in space, in terms of any independent system of coordinates, and yet will still insist with good cause that he knows where he is. This, as I shall show, is because places do not have locations but histories. Bound together by the itineraries of their inhabitants, places exist not in space but as nodes in a matrix of movement. I shall call this matrix a 'region'. It is the knowledge of the region, and with it the ability to situate one's current position within the historical context of journeys previously made – journeys to, from and around places – that distinguishes the countryman from the stranger. Ordinary wayfinding, then, more closely resembles storytelling than map-using. To use a map is to navigate by means of it: that is, to plot a course from one *location* to another in *space*. Wayfinding, by contrast, is a matter of moving from one *place* to another in a *region*. But while it would be wrong, or at least misleading, to liken the countryman's knowledge to a map, there is a certain parallel to be drawn between the processes of knowing and mapping. Both are environmentally situated activities, both are carried out along paths of travel, and both unfold over time. Just as wayfinding has to be distinguished from navigation, however, so also mapping must be distinguished from mapmaking. For the designs to which mapping gives rise – including what have been variously categorised as 'native maps' and 'sketch maps' – are not so much representations of space as condensed histories. Thus, to put my thesis in a nutshell, knowing is like mapping, not because knowledge is like a map, but because the products of mapping (graphic inscriptions), as those of knowing (stories), are fundamentally *un*-maplike. What follows is an elaboration of this argument.

COGNITIVE MAPS

At the most general level, the question of how people find their way around may be posed in terms of two alternative metaphors. Following David Rubin (1988: 375), I call the first a complex-structure metaphor, and the second a complex-process metaphor. The former, which has long been dominant in cognitive psychology, holds that even before the individual steps forth into the environment, he has already had copied into his mind – through some mechanism of replication – a comprehensive description of its objects, features and locations, and the relations between them. This, of course, is the cognitive map. Having determined his current whereabouts and desired destination within the map, and having plotted the route between them, his actual movement from place to place is a perfectly straightforward, indeed almost mechanical matter of executing the prescribed course. Getting from A to B, in short, is explained through the harnessing of a simple process, of bodily locomotion, to a complex structure, the mental map. With a complex-process metaphor, on the other hand, little or no pre-structured content is imputed to the mind. Instead, wayfinding is understood as a skilled performance in which the traveller, whose powers of perception and action have been fine-tuned through previous experience, 'feels his way' towards his goal, continually adjusting his movements in response to an ongoing perceptual monitoring of his surroundings. What the first approach explains through positing an isomorphism between structures in the world and structures in the mind, the second explains as the unfolding of a field of relations established through the immersion of the actor-perceiver within a given environmental context. This is the approach favoured by ecological psychology, and it is the one I follow here.

Before pursuing an ecological approach to wayfinding, however, it is worth reflecting on the circumstances in which the notion of the cognitive map came to be introduced in the first place. At that time, some half a century ago, psychology was still in the grip of the behaviourist paradigm. Animals, including human beings, were supposed to respond more or less automatically, in ways conditioned by previous experience, to particular environmental stimuli. Seeking to verify this simple model, psychologists devised numerous experiments in which their star laboratory animal – the humble rat – was induced to run through a variety of mazes. Starved at the outset, having successfully negotiated the maze the rat would be rewarded with food from a box. The idea was that through repeated trials, the animal would learn to take one particular path rather than another at each successive 'choice-point' along the route. The whole route would then be remembered as a chain of conditioned responses, such as right or left turns, triggered by the successive appearance of particular stimuli in the form of gateways in the maze. But rats are enterprising creatures, and they often found ways of subverting the experimenters' intentions.

They would, for example, manage to climb out of the maze near the start by pushing back the cover and then run directly over the top to the food box, where they would climb back down and eat. This caused some consternation in the behaviourist camp, since according to the stimulus–response model they should have had no idea of the direction in which to head off in search of food, knowing no other way than the familiar route through the maze, with all its twists and turns.

To further test the rats' abilities, psychologist Edward C. Tolman and his collaborators devised what they called a 'spatial orientation' experiment (Tolman, Ritchie and Kalish 1946). A maze was first set up as shown in Figure 13.1. Starting at A, the animals had to run across an open circular table, then through the alley CD, and finally along the roundabout route through E and F to reach the food box at G. Once they were accustomed to this, the original maze was replaced with the apparatus shown in Figure 13.2. Starting again at A, the animals ran across the circular table and down the alley, only to find it blocked at one end. After returning to the table and exploring a little way down the other radiating paths, each rat would eventually choose to run all the way out along one of them. The overwhelming majority opted for path number 6 – the path that would take them to precisely the same spot where, in the original set-up, the food box had been located. This experiment seemed to provide convincing evidence that in their training for the first maze, the rats had not merely learned a fixed sequence of steps that would lead them reliably towards their goal. Rather, as Tolman hypothesised, they must have built up 'something like a field map of the environment', upon which could be traced all possible routes and paths and their relationships. Having located their own position and that of the food box in terms of this map, the rats were able to select the path, in the second maze, that led directly from the one to the other. In light of this ability it was clearly inadequate, Tolman reasoned, to liken the animal's central nervous system – as the behaviourists had done – to a telephone switchboard such that every incoming stimulus simply 'dials up' the appropriate response. The brain was to be compared, instead, to a 'map control room' where stimulus-based information would be collected and collated, and where the routes would be plotted that would finally determine the animal's overt behavioural responses (Tolman 1948: 192).

Despite its provocative title, Tolman's 1948 paper – 'Cognitive maps in rats and men' – had much to say about rats but virtually nothing about human beings. Ironically, what little Tolman *did* have to say about humans had nothing to do with their abilities of orientation and wayfinding, but with certain psychopathologies which, he thought, could be attributed to regimes of child training that blocked the development of properly comprehensive cognitive maps. Ending on a high moral tone, Tolman preached that only by inculcating the paramount virtues of reason and tolerance could our

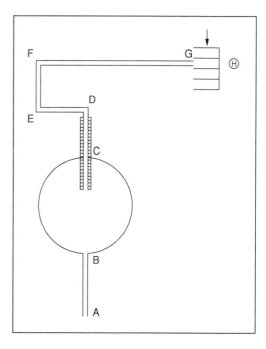

Figure 13.1 The spatial orientation experiment: the original maze.

After Tolman, Ritchie and Kalish, Studies in spacial learning I, *Journal of Experimental Psychology*, 36, 1946.

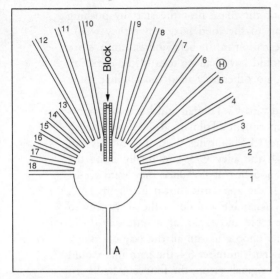

Figure 13.2 The spatial orientation experiment: the replacement maze.

After Tolman, Ritchie and Kalish, Studies in spacial learning I, *Journal of Experimental Psychology*, 36, 1946.

children be furnished with maps sufficiently broad and comprehensive to cope with 'that great God-given maze which is our human world' (1948: 208). It is hard to know what the rats would have made of this! Be that as it may, more recent work by James and Carol Gould on the wayfinding abilities of honey bees helps to put the rats' capacities in perspective. For it turns out that what rats can do, bees can do too: namely, make their way directly to a food source, along a course never taken before. And they can do this without involving anything that we might dignify by terms like 'thought', 'reason' or 'imagination'. The Goulds sound an appropriate note of scepticism when they remark that the calculation a bee would have to undertake in order to plan an optimal route would not be beyond a simple computer. There is no obvious reason why the bee, or for that matter the rat, should have any more of an understanding of the task before it than the computer, or why its solution should call for any intelligence whatsoever (Gould and Gould 1988: 224–5).

Here is what the Goulds did with their bees. First, a group of foragers were trained to fly to a feeding station in some woods out of sight of the hive. Later, individuals about to set off from the hive to the feeder were captured and transported, in an opaque container, to another location well off from their regular route and from which the feeder, likewise, was hidden from view. Here they were released. It was found that the bees flew straight from this location to the feeder, along what can only have been an entirely novel route for them. There is no way in which they could have done this, had they been constrained to follow a fixed sequence of steps between accustomed landmarks – as stipulated by the stimulus-response model. Instead, the Goulds suggest, the bee does what we would do under similar circumstances: 'she would use nearby landmarks to figure out where she is, determine in which direction her goal lies, and then depart directly towards it' (Gould and Gould 1988: 109). She navigates, in other words, in terms of a cognitive map. That humans do likewise was suggested by experiments conducted by Worchel (cited by Oatley 1977: 539–40), who led his subjects blindfold along two sides of a right-angled triangle and then told them to make their way back along the hypoteneuse – a task they completed with considerable accuracy. The ability to update one's position on the cognitive map, and thereby to keep on target despite twists and turns, is – according to Keith Oatley – the basis for any kind of navigation, whether on land or at sea. But whatever the conditions under which it is carried out, navigation 'is a complex cognitive skill' (Oatley 1977: 537).

Comparing what the Goulds say about bees with what Oatley says about humans, we find more than a hint of double standards. Confronted with essentially the same task, its successful accomplishment by humans is attributed to complex skills whereas bees apparently do it on autopilot. I do not mean to deny that human wayfinding is a highly complex, skilled process. But there seems good reason to suppose that it is skilled precisely to the extent that it goes *beyond* the simple computational operations described by cognitive map theorists. For the environment within which people find their way about is not, as Tolman would have it, a 'great God-given maze', with all its landmarks, routes, openings and obstructions already laid out in advance. It is rather an immensely variegated terrain of comings and goings, which is continually taking shape around the traveller even as the latter's movements contribute to its formation. To hold a course in such an environment is to be attentive at all times to what is going on around you, and to respond in ways that answer to your purpose. This is probably as true of rats, in their ordinary environment, as it is of human beings in theirs. Rats are sensitive and intelligent creatures, and if their performance in experimental mazes manifests a basic computational capacity but no real skill, this is only because the artificial set-up in which they find themselves is a highly impoverished one that deprives them of any opportunity for the exercise of normal powers of discrimination and judgement.

WHAT IS A MAP ANYWAY?

The core assumption of the cognitive approach to orientation and wayfinding is, as we have seen, that perceptually salient aspects of the structure of the world are copied into an analogous structure in the mind (Rubin 1988: 375). This copy is said to be a map, or at least to be maplike in form. But why should this particular metaphor have been adopted, rather than some other? Why maps rather than, say, pictures or images? What is the difference between a map of the world and a picture or image of the world? Any general definition of a map, say Arthur Robinson and Barbara Petchenik, 'must be based on its being simply a representation of things in space' (1976: 15). Yet a perspective drawing would satisfy this criterion, and we would surely not describe such a drawing as a map. One possible approach to defining a map, in contradistinction to the perspectival image, is suggested by Alfred Gell (1985). The approach rests on the idea that maps encode beliefs or propositions about the locations of places and objects that are true (or taken to be true) independently of where one is currently positioned in the world. An example of such a proposition might be that 'Edinburgh is north of London'. One could issue statements to this effect whether one was in London, Edinburgh, or anywhere else for that matter, and they would all be equally valid. In Gell's terms, these statements – each of which is a *token* of the proposition in question – are *non-indexical*, in that their truth conditions are not bound to the place where they are made.

Accordingly, Gell proceeds to define the map as 'any system of spatial knowledge and/or beliefs which takes the form of non-token-indexical statements about the spatial locations of places and objects' (1985: 278–9). Now a person equipped with knowledge in this form ought, in principle, to be able to figure out just how the world should look from any selected point of observation. If I were hiking in the mountains, for example, I should be able to state how the various peaks would appear arrayed before me, were I standing on a particular summit. Such statements, however, since they hold good only for the view from that summit, and none other, are *indexical* of the place. Any set of beliefs and propositions whose tokens are indexical in this sense, having regard for what is where for a subject positioned at a certain location, comprises what Gell calls an *image* (1985: 280). Thus the difference between the image and the map comes to hinge on the criterion of the indexicality or non-indexicality of its tokens. If our knowledge consisted only of images – that is, of token-indexical spatial propositions – then, to follow Gell's argument, we would never be able to hold any coherent idea about our own location in space, or about the locations of other places relative to ourselves. We know where we are, not because what we see around us matches to a certain mental image, but because this image has itself been uniquely derived from an underlying map, at a point defined by a given set of spatial coordinates that are indifferent to our own movement. As we travel from one place to another, we pass through a sequence of images, each of which is specific to – and in turn permits us to identify – a particular location along the way. But the map, from which all these images are generated, remains the same wherever we are.

I shall return in due course to what Gell has to say about the nature of navigation and wayfinding. For the moment I want to focus on the implications of this way of distinguishing between the map and the image. It is certainly true, as Gell intimates, that the mere possession of a map, whether mental or artefactual, will not help you to find your way around unless you can use it to generate location-specific images for comparison with immediate perceptual experience. It is also true that no map will do the work that cognitive theorists expect of it unless the information it encodes is invariant with respect to the location of the percipient. Consider Oatley's assertion, for example, that the essence of navigation lies in the 'ability to update one's position within the cognitive map while travelling' (1977: 539). How could this possibly be done if the map keeps changing as one goes along? Oatley himself confuses the issue, when he speaks of the navigator's cognitive map as 'a process, not just a picture' (p. 546). For if the navigator is to look to the map for directions, it can be neither process nor picture, neither embodying his own movement nor representing any particular scenes along the route. 'We only update maps', as Gell observes, 'when the geography of the world changes, not whenever we move about ourselves' (1985: 274). Ultimately, the justification for extending the map metaphor into the domain of cognition must lie in the assumption, more often than not unstated, that what the map affords is a representation of things in space that is independent of any particular point of view.

This assumption, however, raises problems of its own. One of the difficulties that cartographers often face in their attempts to explain the nature of maps is that the very fields, of cognition and communication, from which they might find appropriate analogues have already seized upon the map as an analogue from cartography. 'When non-cartographic writers use the term "map"', as Robinson and Petchenik say, 'they seem to mean that it is possible to take isolated incidents, experiences, and so on, and arrange them intellectually so that there is some coherence, some total relation, instead of individual isolation' (1976: 4). Thus scientists refer to their theories as maps, into which can be fitted the data of observation, while anthropologists are inclined to attribute a similar maplike quality to culture and society (for example, Leach 1976: 51), on the grounds that it furnishes an overarching framework of concepts and categories for the organisation of otherwise fragmentary sensory experience. These, and many other similar metaphorical usages make it appear natural and self-evident that *actual* maps should function in the same way, as schematic representations of the real world, which do not index any position but upon which it should be possible to plot the position of everything in relation to everything else. Now most people in Western societies, educated since their schooldays in the conventions of modern cartography, probably do tend to think of maps as representations of this kind. But whether the artefacts and inscriptions that have at one time or another been designated as maps actually satisfy the requirement of non-indexicality, is moot. The question, in short, is: are maps maplike?

David Turnbull, arguing from the perspective of a sociologist of science, makes a compelling case to the effect that they are not. The idea that maps are independent of any point of view, that the propositions they encode are equally valid wherever one stands in the world, is, Turnbull contends, a myth – though it is one that has been avidly cultivated in the name of science and objectivity (Turnbull 1989: 15). The reality is that no map, however 'modern' or sophisticated the techniques of its production, can be wholly divorced from the practices, interests and understandings of its makers and users. Or to put it another way, every map is necessarily embedded in a 'form of life'. And to the extent that it is so embedded, it must fail on the criterion of non-indexicality. As Turnbull explains, 'all maps are in some measure indexical, because no map, representation or theory can be independent of a form of life' (1989: 20). At first glance, this argument seems to run directly counter to Gell's insistence that a representation can only be a map insofar as the propositions encoded therein are *non*-indexical. Closer examination, however, reveals a certain slippage in the meaning of indexicality. Is indexing a place the same as indexing a form of life? If the map discloses a perspective or 'point of view', is this a view *in* the world, as it appears from a particular place, or a view *of* the world, filtered through the concepts, categories and schemata of a received cultural tradition? Could a map be non-indexical in the first sense and indexical in the second?

Consider an example to which both Gell and Turnbull refer. Micronesian mariners,[1] who are used to voyaging across hundreds of miles of open sea between often tiny islands, know the bearing of any island from any other by its so-called 'star course' – that is, by a list of stars whose successive rising or setting points, during the night, indicate the direction in question. The expert mariner has committed to memory an entire compendium of star courses, each unique to a particular pair of islands, and it is in this compendium, according to Gell, that his 'map' consists. Now it is clearly the case that any statement of the course between one island A, and another island B, will not depend for its validity on one's current position at sea. Thus star courses 'have the essential map property of non-token-indexicality; they do not change truth value according to where they are uttered' (Gell 1985: 284). Yet it is also fair to say, with Turnbull, that the principles upon which the Micronesian mariner's map is constructed are securely embedded within the percepts and practices of traditional seafaring, and therefore that it requires a knowledge of this cultural context to be able to 'read' and understand the map. It would appear, in short, that while the map indexes a tradition, it is non-indexical with regard to location. The same, moreover, could be said of 'modern' maps, constructed on scientific principles with the aid of sophisticated technological gadgetry. Modern science and technology, as Turnbull remarks (1991: 36), are as dependent on tradition for their successful transmission as is Micronesian seafaring lore. And no more than Micronesian maps can modern maps be understood without taking into account 'the world view, cognitive schema or the culture of the mapmaker' (Turnbull 1989: 20).

There is, however, something deeply paradoxical about this argument. For to separate tradition from locality, or culture from place, is also to divorce traditional knowledge from the contexts of its production in the environmentally situated experience of practitioners. Thus the form of life is reduced to a 'world view' or 'cognitive schema' – a set of rules and representations for the organisation of sensory experience that individuals carry in their heads and that are available for transmission independently of their bodily activity in the world. It is as though culture were *received* along lines of traditional transmission from ancestors, and *imported* into the sites of its practical application. But this is to fall right back into the classical view of culture as a map, the analogy – as Bourdieu (1977: 2) points out – 'which occurs to an outsider who has to find his way around in a foreign landscape and who compensates for his lack of practical mastery, the prerogative of the native, by the use of a model of all possible routes'. So here is the paradox: actual maps are made to appear indexical with regard to cultural tradition only by a rendering of culture as non-indexical with regard to locality. The placing of maps within their cultural context is paralleled by the *dis*placing of culture from its context in the lifeworld. How, then, are we to resolve this dilemma? How can we hold on to the commonsense notion that maps retain a certain invariance as we move about, that they do not continually recompose themselves to reflect the particularities of wherever we happen to be, while yet recognising their embeddedness in locally situated practices? My answer, in brief, will be that what maps index is *movement*, that the vision they embody is not local but *regional*, but that the ambition of modern cartography has been to convert this regional vision into a *global* one, as though it issued from a point of view above and beyond the world.

HOW TO SEE THE WORLD FROM EVERYWHERE AT ONCE

When you stand at a particular spot, everything appears from a certain angle, while much of the environment will likely be hidden from view behind prominent foreground features. Stand at another spot, and things will appear differently. In order to have any conception of the overall configuration of one's environment, it would seem necessary to be in possession of some kind of totalising scheme into which every one of these location-specific perceptual images could be integrated. This, as we have seen, is an argument commonly adduced to justify positing the existence of cognitive maps. It is an argument, however, that assumes a snapshot theory of vision, as if one could only ever see, in perspective, from a fixed point of observation. 'Is not to see', as Merleau-Ponty asks rhetorically, 'always to see from somewhere?' He proceeds to answer, however, in the negative (Merleau-Ponty 1962: 67). To take up his own example, the house next door may be viewed from this side or that, from inside or outside, or even from up above if one were to fly overhead. But what I see is none of these appearances; it is the house *itself*, in all its concrete actuality. The form of the house is progressively disclosed to me as I move around and about, and in and out, not as the sum of a very large number of images, arrayed in memory like frames on a reel of film, but as the envelope of a continually changing perspectival structure. Observation, Merleau-Ponty claims, consists not in having a fixed point of view on the object, but 'in varying the point of view while keeping the object fixed' (1962: 91). Thus the house is not seen from somewhere but from nowhere – or rather from everywhere (pp. 67–9).

In keeping with his ecological approach to visual perception, James Gibson presents an argument along very similar lines. Animals and people, Gibson writes, see as they move, not just in the intervals between movements. Such ambulatory vision takes place along what he calls a 'path of observation'. A path is to be understood not as an infinite series of discrete points, occupied at successive instants, but as a continuous itinerary of movement. Thus the environment one sees is neither 'seen-at-this-moment' nor 'seen-from-this-point'. On the contrary, 'what one perceives is an environment that surrounds one, that is everywhere equally clear, that is in-the-round or solid, and that is all-of-a-piece' (Gibson 1979: 195–7). But if the features of this environment are revealed as one travels along paths of view, rather than projected from a sequence of points of view, where do these paths begin, and where do they end? And if we see not at this moment in time, but over a certain period, how long is this period? Such questions cannot be precisely answered. Of a minor feature we might say, after only cursory exploration, that we have seen it all. But of a complex, varied and extensive terrain, although we may have criss-crossed it along innumerable paths, we may still feel there is more to be discovered. As for our perception of the environment as a whole, what else can this be than the outcome of a lifetime's observation, along all the paths we have ever taken? This is what Gibson means when he asserts that perceiving the world over a sufficient length of time, and along a sufficiently extended set of paths, is tantamount to perceiving it 'as if one could be everywhere at once' (p. 197).

It is critically important to distinguish this sense of omnipresence from that implied by the conventional notion of the 'bird's-eye view' (Gibson 1979: 198–9). The latter, of course, has nothing to do with the way birds in flight actually see, but rather describes how we imagine the world would look from a point of observation so far above the earth's surface that the entire territory with which we are familiar from journeys made at ground level could be taken in at a glance. The higher one goes, it is supposed, the more one's vision transcends the locational constraints and narrow horizons of the view from the ground. And by the same token, the more apparently maplike it becomes. Robinson and Petchenik are right to point out that the analogy between the map and the bird's eye view is potentially misleading, not only because of their different geometries of projection, but also because the map is 'a construction, an abstraction, an arrangement of markings that relates to spatial "reality" only by agreement, not by sensory testability' (1976: 53). Nevertheless, anyone who has flown over familiar country by plane will have been astonished, on the one hand, by how strange it looks, and on the other, by how closely the view from the window resembles a topographic map of the same territory. There is nothing strange, however, about the environment perceived from everywhere, in the sense adduced by Merleau-Ponty and Gibson, nor do you have to leave the ground to perceive it in this way. It is not a view from 'up there' rather than 'down here', but one taken *along* the multiple paths that make up a country, and along which people come and go in the practical conduct of life. Our perception of the environment as a whole, in short, is forged not in the ascent from a myopic, local perspective to a panoptic, global one, but in the passage from place to place, and in histories of movement and changing horizons along the way.

The same point could be made, following Edward Casey (1996: 30), through a contrast between *vertical* and *lateral* modes of integration. In the vertical mode, embraced by modern cartography as well as by cognitive map theorists, local particulars obtained by observation on the ground are fitted within an abstract conception of space so as to form a representation of the world as though one were looking down upon it from 'up above'. While the eyes of the body remain close to the ground, the mind's eye – which is witness to this maplike representation – is up with the birds. The lateral mode of integration, by contrast, presupposes no such division between mind and body. For the work of integration is performed by the organism as a whole as it moves around, purposefully and attentively, from place to place. Such movements do not merely connect places that are already located in terms of an independent framework of spatial coordinates. Rather, they bring these places into being as nodes within a wider network of coming and going. Casey refers to this network of interplace movement as a *region* – that is, 'an area concatenated by peregrinations between the places it connects' (1996: 24). Evidently, when Gibson speaks of perceiving the environment from everywhere at once, that 'everywhere' is neither space, nor a portion of space, but a region in this sense. Likewise, every 'somewhere' is not a location in space but a position on a path of movement, one of the matrix of paths comprising the region as a whole. In short, whereas everywhere-as-space is the world as it is imagined from a point of view above and beyond, everywhere-as-region is the world as it is experienced by an inhabitant journeying from place to place along a way of life.

This idea of the region may be illustrated by means of three ethnographic examples. Among the Walbiri, an Aboriginal people of western central Australia, the entire country is perceived 'in terms of networks of places linked by paths' (Munn 1973a: 215). Originally laid down through the movements of ancestral beings in that formative era known as the Dreaming, these paths are continually retraced in the journeys of the living people who take after them. As they relate the stories of these journeys, Walbiri men and women may draw web-like figures in the sand whose basic components are lines and circles. Every line conveys a journey to or from camp, while every circle conveys the act of making camp by walking all around it. Rather similarly for the Ongees, a group of hunter-gatherers inhabiting the island of Little Andaman in the Bay of Bengal, places are brought into being at the confluences of the paths of movement of humans, animals and spirits. Asked by the ethnographer, Vishvajit Pandya, to draw the places where humans and spirits live, Ongee informants responded by sketching lines of movement (straight for humans, wavy for spirits), leading to the demarcation of the various places at their intersections.[2] The world of the Ongees, Pandya concludes, 'is not a preconstituted stage on which things happen, but rather an area or region created and constructed by the ongoing practice of movement' (Pandya 1990: 777). My third example is taken from A. Irving Hallowell's study of the Saulteaux (Ojibwa), hunters and trappers of the Berens River district near Lake Winnipeg in Canada. In Saulteaux experience, to move in a certain direction is always to travel from place to place. This is so not only for human persons, but also for the sun, the moon and the winds, all of which are held to be persons of a kind. Thus 'what we refer to abstractly as cardinal directions are to them the *homes* of the winds, the places they come from. Similarly, east is thought of as the place where the sun rises; west, the place where it sets; south is the place to which the souls of the dead travel, and the place from which the summer birds come' (Hallowell 1955: 191). For the Saulteaux, then, as indeed for the Ongee and the Walbiri, 'everywhere' is not a space but a region concatenated by the place-to-place movements of humans, animals, spirits, winds, celestial bodies, and so on.

KNOWING AS YOU GO

We can now return to the paradox I introduced earlier. If our knowledge of the environment is embedded in locally situated practices, how come that it retains a certain constancy as we move about? If all knowledge is context-dependent, how can people take their knowledge with them from one context to another? For clues towards a resolution I turn once again to the work of David Turnbull. One of Turnbull's aims is to break down the conventional distinction between so-called indigenous knowledge and Western science. He does so by emphasising that *all* knowledge, of whatever kind and historical provenance, is generated within a 'field of practices' (1989: 61). And since practices must be carried out by particular people in particular places, all knowledge – including that which we call science – must be inherently local. Let me set aside for the time being the contrary thesis, which Turnbull confusingly appears to entertain at the same time, that the context for both indigenous and scientific knowledge is something like a worldview or cognitive schema, by nature detached from the local sites of its practical expression. I have already drawn attention to the dangers of falling back on a concept of culture that divorces knowledge and its transmission from environmentally situated experience. My present concern is with another difficulty in Turnbull's argument. For while on the one hand, he insists that a common characteristic of all knowledge systems is their 'localness', he also argues, on the other, that what is critical to the growth and reproduction of any knowledge system is the work that goes into moving its diverse components – including practitioners, their know-how and skills, technical devices and standards of evaluation – from one local site of knowledge production to another (Turnbull 1993a: 30).

Consider the case of Western science. According to what might be called the 'official' view of science, data recorded by means of standardised procedures in diverse locations are fitted into a framework of theory consisting of propositions that are strictly non-indexical with regard to place. What happens in practice, however, is a good deal more messy. Not only is it unclear where data collection ends and theory building begins, but also there is no unified body of theory under which all of experience can be subsumed. Rather, there are as many theoretical growth-points as there are sites of practical investigation, and the character of each is conditioned by circumstances peculiar to each place. Much of the labour of science, Turnbull argues, lies in attempts to establish the connectivity and equivalence that would render procedures developed and results obtained in one local context applicable in another (1993a: 37). But if science calls for the constant movement of personnel, knowledge and techniques from place to place, and the assemblage, in each, of inputs of heterogeneous provenance, how can it also share the characteristic of localness? As a system of knowledge, science cannot be rooted in any particular place or places, but must rather emerge from the total network of interplace relations constituting its field of practice. Furthermore, if that is so for science, then it should be equally so for any other knowledge system. As Turnbull himself puts it, 'all knowing is like travelling, like a journey between the parts of a matrix' (1991: 35). So what is this matrix? It is, of course, a *region* in the sense defined above – that is, as the sum of journeys made.

My point is that knowing, like the perception of the environment in general, proceeds along paths of observation. One can no more know *in* places than travel in them. Rather, knowledge is regional: it is to be cultivated by moving along paths that lead around, towards or away from places, from or to places elsewhere. Conceived as the ensemble of such place-to-place movements, the notion of region, far from denoting a level of generalisation intermediate between local particulars and global universals, offers a way out of this kind of dichotomous and hierarchical thinking. As every place, through the movements that give rise to it, enfolds its relations to all others, to be somewhere *is* to be everywhere at once. Rephrased in our terms, what Turnbull proposes is a compelling argument to the effect that all knowledge systems, including science, are integrated laterally rather than vertically. The philosopher Joseph Rouse makes much the same point in arguing that 'we go from one local knowledge to another rather than from universal theories to their particular instantiations' (Rouse 1987: 72). In light of the foregoing considerations, I would prefer to say that we *know as we go*, from place to place. This does not, however, alter the basic point, which is that science is distinguished from other systems of knowledge by the lengths to which it goes to present itself *as if* it were vertically integrated, as if the scientist's task were to fit data to theory rather than to put the knowledge that has brought him to one place to work in setting off towards another. To create this illusion, science has to suppress, or to hide from view, the social labour involved in establishing equivalences and connections across places (Turnbull 1996: 62). In this, moreover, it is aided and abetted by modern cartography, which has been similarly concerned to establish its scientific credentials through its claim to produce accurate and objective representations of a world 'out there'.

Cartographers, like scientists, and indeed like practitioners of any other knowledge system, draw their material from all manner of sources, through both direct observation and inquiry into local tradition. The collection and collation of this material may take them – or agents operating on their behalf – on innumerable and often lengthy journeys. None of this, however, appears in the final form of the modern, 'scientific' map. To the contrary, one of the most striking characteristics of the modern map is its elimination, or erasure, of the practices and itineraries that contributed to its production (Turnbull 1996: 62). In the words of Michel de Certeau, 'the map, a totalising stage on which elements of diverse origin are brought together to form a tableau of a "state" of geographical knowledge, pushes away into its prehistory or into its posterity, as if into the wings, the operations of which it is the result or the necessary condition' (1984: 121). Just as science, in the official view, is charged with the task of integrating site-specific data into an overarching, unified framework of theory, so the mission of cartography is ostensibly one of representing the 'geographic facts' on the ground within a single, universal system of spatial coordinates (Edney 1993: 55). The ideal is a perfect congruence between the world and its representation, and progress is measured by the degree of approximation towards it. Thus in the work of the modern cartographer, knowledge generated through movement from place to place within a region is presented *as if* it issued from a totalising vision above and beyond the world. In short, cartography transforms everywhere-as-region, the world as experienced by a mobile inhabitant, into everywhere-as-space, the imaginary 'bird's-eye view' of a transcendent consciousness.

The same transformation, of course, is worked on the ordinary perception of the environment by the theory of cognitive maps. As in the modern artefactual map, so too in its 'mental' analogue, all those movements of coming and going through which people develop a knowledge of their environment are pushed into the wings, to recall de Certeau's phrase, leaving the map as a *fait accompli*, final and complete, the product of a process of making that begins with the layout of the world and ends with that layout copied into the mind. Any journeys undertaken beyond that point are supposed to belong to the phase of mapusing rather than mapmaking, and therefore to play no further part in the formation of the map itself. The traditional Micronesian seafarer, in this view, is just as much a mapuser as is the modern marine navigator with his charts and compass, even though his skill 'is entirely mental and perceptual, using no instruments of any kind' (Oatley 1977: 537). But whereas modern artefactual maps have their authors, designers or manufacturers, the origins of traditional mental maps appear lost in the mists of time. Indeed to say of such maps that they are 'traditional' is virtually tantamount to an admission that they have no maker or makers, but rather that they 'make themselves' – or that like myths, following Lévi-Strauss's celebrated aphorism, they 'think themselves out' through the medium of men's minds and without their knowledge (Lévi-Strauss 1966a: 56). In any case the assumption is that the map is made before it is used, that it already exists as a structure in the mind, handed down as part of a received tradition, prior to the traveller's venturing forth into the world.

My contention, to the contrary, is that people's knowledge of the environment undergoes continuous formation in the very course of their moving about in it. To return to a distinction which I introduced at the outset, this is to account for such knowledge in terms of the generative potentials of a complex process rather than the replication of a complex structure. That process consists in the engagement of the mobile actor-perceiver with his or her environment. As I have already suggested, we know *as* we go, not *before* we go. Such ambulatory knowing – or knowledgeable ambulating – cannot be accommodated within the terms of the conventional dichotomy between mapmaking and map-using. The traveller or storyteller who knows as he goes is neither making a map nor using one. He is, quite simply, *mapping*. And the forms or patterns that arise from this mapping process, whether in the imagination or materialised as artefacts, are but stepping stones along the way, punctuating the process rather than initiating it or bringing it to a close. My perspective, in short, accords with what Robert Rundstrom has called 'process cartography', in which mapping is seen as 'open-ended, ongoing, always leading to the next instance of mapping, the next map' (Rundstrom 1993: 21). In what follows, I first show in more detail how mapping differs from mapmaking. I then turn to the distinction between mapping and map-using. All wayfinding, I argue, is mapping; all navigation map-using. Thus mapping is to map-using as wayfinding to navigation. The overall structure of the argument is summarised in Figure 13.3.

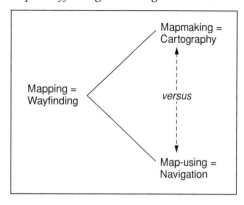

Figure 13.3 The relations between mapping, mapmaking and map-using: a summary.

MAPPING IS NOT MAPMAKING

'Mapping' and 'mapmaking', according to Denis Wood, 'do not mean the same thing' (1992: 32). The difference, in his view, is akin to that between speaking and writing. Wood thinks of mapping as a *capacity* universal to humans, established along with other capacities of the human mind-brain through a process of evolution under natural selection. But the fact that all human beings are capable of mapping does not mean that they all make maps. Likewise, just because all humans can speak does not mean they all write. Whereas mapping, like speaking, might be regarded as a 'universal expression of individual existence', mapmaking, like writing, has to be seen as 'an unusual function of specifiable social circumstances arising only within certain social structures' (Wood 1993a: 50). In other words, the emergence of mapmaking belongs not to the evolution of humanity but to its history. Yet the difference between mapping and mapmaking, just as that between speaking and writing, is for Wood a very fine one. It is not the difference between outwardly expressing an idea and 'capturing' that expression in an alternative medium. For one thing, mapping is no more the externalisation of a map that already exists in the mapper's head than is speaking the externalisation of a thought. Rather, both mapping and speaking are genres of performance that draw their meanings from the communicative contexts of their enactment. It follows, for another thing, that neither mapmaking nor writing can serve to transcribe pre-existent thoughts or mental representations onto paper. The map, like the written word, is not, in the first place, the transcription of anything, but rather an *inscription*. Thus mapping gives way to mapmaking at the point, not where mental imagery yields an external representation, but where the performative gesture becomes an inscriptive practice (Wood 1993a: 53).

Wood illustrates his argument with a nice example. Two boys have been playing rollerblade hockey. At home over dinner, one explains the layout of the court by gesturing with his hands and fingers over a place mat. The other does the same at school, to impress a friend, but in this case (it is during an art class) he gestures with pencil in hand, over a sheet of paper. Whereas nothing remains of the first boy's gestures on the mat, those of the second leave a trace in the form of an inscription, a sketch-map, that can be preserved and reproduced indefinitely beyond the context of its production. We may suppose that the two boys were of equal ability, and moreover that the first would have had ready access to pencil and paper had he needed it. So why did the second make a map and the first not? The answer, for Wood, lies in the nature of the communicative situation. In general, just as much as in this exemplary instance, it is the situation – at once social and political – that calls for the map. And while the difference between gesturing with an inscribing tool and gesturing without might seem slight, the socio-political consequences are immense. It is the 'fine line of . . . inscription', Wood concludes, 'that differentiates . . . mapping . . . from mapmaking, and mapping *societies* from mapmaking *societies*, in the latter of which it is the inscriptive property of the artefactual map that permits it to serve the interests of the power elites who control the mapmaking process (as well as those who would contest them)' (1993a: 53).

Now while I agree with Wood that there is an important distinction to be made between mapping and mapmaking, I would draw it along different lines. Before doing so, however, we need to be more precise about the meaning of mapping. Wood himself seems unable to make up his mind whether the term refers to a cognitive capacity, to actual movement in the environment, or to the narrative reenactment of journeys made. At one point he tells us that mapping 'is the way we humans make and deploy mental maps' (1992: 32), while at another he dismisses the concept of the mental map only to declare that mapping 'is really just . . . getting around' (1993a: 53). Yet in his example of the two boys, mapping appears to consist neither in having a pre-existent 'map in the head', nor in bodily move-ment on the ground, but in a kind of retrospective storytelling. It seems to me that the notion of an evolved capacity for mental mapping is deeply flawed. One could hardly expect any such capacity to spring, fully formed, from an individual's genetic make-up, in advance of his or her entry into the lifeworld. It would rather have to undergo devel-opment in the very unfolding of the individual's life within an environment. Thus the life-historical process of 'getting around' – or in a word, wayfinding – would appear to be a condition for the emergence of a 'mapping capacity', rather than a consequence of its application. This leaves us with the third sense of mapping – the retelling of journeys made (or possibly the rehearsal for journeys to be made) – as perhaps the most appro-priate. I admit, however, that the distinction between wayfinding and mapping is not hard and fast. For one way of retelling the story of a journey is to retrace one's steps, or the steps of ancestors who made the journey in the past. In effect, since travelling from one place to another means remembering the way, all wayfinding is mapping, though not all mapping is wayfinding. I return to this point below.

For the time being, let us continue to regard mapping as the re-enactment, in narrative gesture, of the experience of moving from place to place within a region. In this sense, both boys in Wood's example were engaged in mapping. The fact that one left no trace whereas the other produced a lasting inscription has no appreciable bearing on the nature of the activity as such. The sketch-map that emerged, as the trace of the second boy's gestures, was a more or less incidental by-product of the mapping process, not its ultimate goal. Rundstrom makes much the same point in his account of mapping among Inuit of the central and eastern Canadian Arctic. An Inuit traveller, returning from a trip, could recount every detail of the environment encountered along the way, miming with his hands the forms of specific land and sea features. Such gestural performance, after a long journey, could last many hours. It could also, given appropriate tools and materials, generate an inscription. Many of these inscriptions were produced at the instigation of Western explor-ers who made contact with the Inuit. They were often astonished at the accuracy of what they regarded as 'native maps'. But for Inuit mappers it was the performance that mattered

– 'the recapitulation of environmental features' – rather than any material artefacts or inscriptions to which it gave rise (Rundstrom 1990: 165). Undoubtedly the vast majority of maps that have ever been produced in human societies, like those of the Inuit, have been improvised on the spot within a particular dialogic or storytelling context, and without any intention for their preservation or use beyond that context. This applies, for example, to the web-like sand drawings of the Walbiri, to which I have already referred (Munn 1973b: 196). 'Most maps for most of the time', as Wood observes, 'have probably been ephemeral, scratched in sand or snow, or, if committed to a more permanent medium, immediately crunched up and thrown away' (1993b: 83, see Lewis 1993: 99).

In the course of producing such a map, the mapper takes his interlocutors on a tour of the country, and as he does so his moving hand, which may or may not hold an inscribing implement, traces out the paths taken and the sights or landmarks encountered along the way. Of the maps produced in aboriginal times by the Saulteaux, Hallowell notes that 'their purpose was not to delineate a section of the country as such, but to indicate a route to be followed, and the emphasis was upon a succession of landmarks roughly indicated in their relations to one another' (Hallowell 1955: 195). Malcolm Lewis's studies of native North American and Inuit maps have shown that they invariably rest on deictic principles: that is, they *point* to things, revealing aspects of how they look as one proceeds along a path of observation from 'here' to 'there' (Lewis 1993: 102). Even in contemporary Western societies, whose inhabitants are bombarded on a daily basis with images founded upon cartographic geometries of plane projection – where they live, as Wood puts it, 'map-immersed in the world' (1992: 34) – people continue to describe their environment, to themselves and others, by retracing the paths of movement they customarily take through it rather than by assigning each of its features to a fixed location in space. 'When we are asked for directions', as Barbara Belyea notes, 'few of us can resist pointing and waving our arms, or tracing the traveller's route over the surface of his map. *The gesture becomes a part of the map*, a feature of its reception' (Belyea 1996: 11, my emphasis). It may be misleading, Belyea suggests, to liken the inscriptive process to writing, as though the purpose of the exercise were to represent the features of the landscape in the same way that writing is supposed to represent the spoken word. For the graphs on the map are not representations of anything. Every line is rather the trace of a gesture, which itself retraces an actual movement in the world. To read the map is therefore to follow the trace as one would the path of the hand that made it.[3]

The analogy between mapping and writing, however, may be closer than Belyea thinks. For much of its history, at least in the Western world, writing was understood not as the representation of speech but as a means by which what has been said or told could be committed to memory (Carruthers 1990). Throughout the Middle Ages, as David Olson notes, 'written records were thought of and treated as reminders rather than representations' (Olson 1994: 180). And the same was true of medieval maps, which served as memoranda of itineraries, providing directions and advice to the traveller who would undertake the same journey (de Certeau 1984: 120). In the history of writing as in that of mapping, remembering gradually gave way to representation over the same period – from the fifteenth to the seventeenth century – that also saw the rise of modern scientific discourse. De Certeau has shown how, in the course of this transition, the map 'slowly disengaged itself from the itineraries that were the conditions of its possibility'. For some time, maps would continue to be illustrated with pictures of ships, landforms, people and beasts of various descriptions, winds and currents, and the like. Subsequently dismissed as quaint decorations, these figures were really fragments of stories, telling of the journeys, and the incidents that took place along them, from which the map resulted. But eventually, the map won out over these pictorial figurations, eliminating all remaining traces of the practices that produced it (de Certeau 1984: 120–1). Thus the making of maps came to be divorced from the experience of bodily movement in the world.[4] The cartographer has no need to travel, indeed he may have no experience whatever of the territory he so painstakingly seeks to represent. His task is rather to assemble, off-site, the information provided to him – already shorn of the particular circumstances of its collection – into a comprehensive spatial representation. It is of course no accident that precisely the same task is assigned, by cognitive map theorists, to the mind in operating upon the data of sense.

It is at the point where maps cease to be generated as by-products of story-telling, and are created instead as end-products of projects of spatial representation, that I draw the line between mapping and mapmaking. In effect, mapmaking suppresses, or 'brackets out', both the movements of people as they come and go between places (wayfinding), and the re-enactment of those movements in inscriptive gesture (mapping). It thereby creates the appearance that the structure of the map springs directly from the structure of the world, as though the mapmaker served merely to mediate a transcription from one to the other. I call this the cartographic illusion (see Figure 13.4). One aspect of this illusion lies in the assumption that the structure of the world, and so also that of the map which purports to represent it, is fixed without regard to the movement of its inhabitants. Like a theatrical stage from which all the actors have mysteriously disappeared, the world – as it is represented in the map – appears deserted, devoid of life. No-one is there; nothing is going on. Suppose, for example, that I describe a journey I have made by tracing a path with my finger over the surface of a topographic map. Once the map has

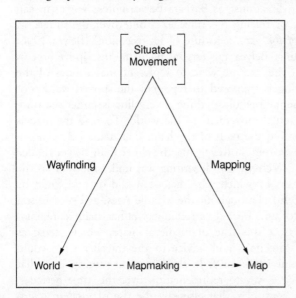

been folded and put away, nothing of this would remain. So far as the map's representation of the world is concerned, I may as well have never made the trip. Had I, alternatively, traced my path with a pencil, the resulting lines would be deemed to have added nothing to the map, but rather to have defaced it. To restore the map, they would have to be rubbed out! Either way, *my gesture does not become part of the map* but is excluded from it, as is my original movement from the world it represents.[5] This is in marked contrast to the maps of native North American Indians and Inuit, as described by such scholars as Lewis, Rundstrom and Belyea, which actually *grow*, line by line, with every additional gesture. So do the charts used by Micronesian seafarers, which 'literally get larger, coconut-palm rib by cowrie shell, and stick by stone'

Figure 13.4 The cartographic illusion. The environmentally situated movement entailed in both wayfinding and its narrative re-enactment (mapping) is bracketed out to create the illusion that the form of the map arises, in mapmaking, as a direct transcription of the layout of the world.

(Wood 1992: 31). And so, too, do our own sketch-maps. In these instances the development of the map, as a 'pattern of interconnected lines' (Belyea 1996: 6), parallels that of the region, as a network of coming and going. But the modern topographic map does not grow or develop, it is *made*. And just as the process of its production is eliminated from the final form of the product, so the world it describes is not a world in the making, but one ready-made for life to occupy.

It is this, finally, that lies behind the distinction between the map and the picture, as alternative descriptions of the same country. For those of us schooled in the conventions of modern cartography, the distinction may seem obvious enough. Maps are supposed to furnish an objective record of the disposition of things in space, that is strictly independent of any point of view, whereas pictures show how these things might be experienced by a subject positioned somewhere in that space, or moving through it (Turnbull 1989: 15). It is widely believed, as Svetlana Alpers observes, that 'maps give us the measure of a place and the relationship between places, quantifiable data, while landscape pictures are evocative, and aim rather to give us some quality of a place or the viewer's sense of it. One is closer to science, the other is art'. Anything on the map that evokes the experience of place or movement is dismissed by the scientific cartographer as 'mere decoration'; anything in the picture that conveys factual information about spatial location is dismissed by the artist as 'mere topography' (Alpers 1983: 124–6). But for the Dutch painters and draughtsmen of the seventeenth century, who are the subjects of Alpers's study, these boundaries between maps and pictures, and between science and art, would have made little sense. Mapping and picturing were, for them, one and the same, having as their common aim 'to capture on a surface a great range of knowledge and information about the world' (1983: 122). As mapmaking triumphed over mapping, however, and as cartographers sought to dissociate themselves professionally from artists, so maps were stripped of their pictorial attributes. Thus historians of cartography, viewing the development of mapmaking in retrospect, are able to present it as having progressed from being an 'art' to being a 'science', replacing subjective fancy with hardwon and independently verifiable factual information (Edney 1993: 56). Art, in the words of Brian Harley, was gradually 'edged off the map' (Harley 1989: 4). But to edge art off the map is also to edge human actor-perceivers off the world, to push their direct, sensory experience into the wings, and to consign their narratives of movement and travel to the realms of fable, fantasy and hallucination.

WAYFINDING IS NOT NAVIGATION

'Navigation', writes Edwin Hutchins, 'is a collection of techniques for answering a small number of questions, perhaps the most central of which is "Where am I?"' (Hutchins 1995: 12). So – to return to a question I raised at the outset – what does it mean to know where one is? What would one need to know in order to feel that the question has been satisfactorily answered? First of all, according to Hutchins, one must possess some representation of space – a map – whether internal or external, inscribed in the mind or on a sheet of paper, within which every object or feature in one's environment is assigned a determinate location. One has then to be able to establish a coherent set of correspondences between what is depicted on the map and what is visible in one's surroundings. From these it should be possible to identify one's current position in the world with a specific location on the map. Only then has the question of where one is been answered (Hutchins 1995: 12–13). Alfred Gell, in an article to which I have already referred, argues along much the same lines. To know where one is, in Gell's view, it is not enough to have formed a perceptual image of the environment as seen from some place. This image has to be matched to that generated from the map (mental or artefactual) at a particular spatial location. 'Navigation', according to Gell, 'consists of a cyclic process whereby images generated from maps are matched up against perceptual information, and perceptual images are identified with equivalent coordinates on a map' (1985: 280). This process of matching is essentially the same as what Hutchins means by 'establishing correspondences', such as, for example, when we say 'this here' (pointing to contours on the map) corresponds to 'that there' (pointing to the outline of a hill on the horizon).

Now while Gell takes as his principal ethnographic example the classic case of Micronesian seafaring, Hutchins chose to study the practices of nautical navigation on board a large modern naval vessel. Both writers insist, however, that reduced to its bare essentials, navigation is a cognitive task that all of us face all the time as we find our way about, whether at sea or on land. Navigational techniques may of course be distinguished, as Gell admits, both in terms of their complexity and the volume of information handled, and in terms of the extent to which this information is published or transmitted by rote memorisation. But none of this, he claims, alters the fact that 'the essential logical processes involved in all way-finding, from the most elementary and subliminal, to the most complex and laborious, are identical' (Gell 1985: 286). For Hutchins, likewise, we are all navigators in our everyday lives, as the following passage reveals:

> When the navigator is satisfied that he has arrived at a coherent set of correspondences, he might look to the chart and say 'Ah, yes; I am here, off this point of land.' *And it is in this sense that most of us feel we know where we are.* We feel that we have achieved reconciliation between the features we see in our world and a representation of that world.
>
> (1995: 13, my emphasis)

Yet as soon as Hutchins takes us on board ship, and introduces us to the work of the navigators on the bridge, things look rather different. For it turns out that establishing correspondences between features on the chart and features in the environment is extremely difficult, and calls for specialised skills that can only be acquired through lengthy training and hands-on experience. To reconcile the chart with the territory, as Hutchins explains, one has to imagine how the world would look from a point of view – that of the 'bird's eye' – from which it is never actually seen, save from an aircraft or satellite. The ordinary passenger, untutored in the techniques of navigation, is quite unable to do this, and may confess to being baffled by maps and charts. He cannot, in other words, translate from his on-board experience of motion as 'moving through a surrounding space' to the depiction of motion on the chart as 'that of an object moving across a space'. Navigators, on the other hand, become so used to thinking of the movement of the ship from this peculiar perspective – as if they were manoeuvring it about like a counter on a game-board – that they find it difficult to imagine this movement, any more, from the ordinary passenger's perspective (Hutchins 1995: 62).

I intend to argue, in accord with Hutchins's ethnography but contrary to his general claim, that we are no more navigators in our everyday lives – in finding our way around in a familiar environment – than we are cartographers when we retrace these movements in narrative. Navigation (or map-*using*) is, I contend, as strange to the ordinary practices of wayfinding as is cartography (or map*making*) to ordinary practices of mapping. It would be hard to imagine why we should find the navigator's charts so baffling, or why his skills should be so specialised, if they were but analogues of cognitive structures and capacities that we use all the time. Thus Gell, along with others who have had resort to the notion of cognitive maps, is surely wrong to regard wayfinding and navigation as processes of a similar or even identical kind. For when we move about, we do not normally think of ourselves as piloting our bodies across the surface of the earth, as the navigator pilots his ship across the ocean. Nor do we have to think in this way in order to know, at any moment, where we are. This is because the question 'Where am I?' is not ordinarily answered in terms of a location in space, determined by the intersection of an independent set of coordinates. Hutchins to the contrary, it is *not* in this sense that most of us feel we know where we are. Indeed I may know precisely where I am and yet have no idea of my geographic location. For it is not by assigning the position where I currently stand to certain spatial coordinates that an answer to the 'where' question is arrived at, but rather by situating that position within the matrix of movement constitutive of a region.

To amplify this point, let me compare two, admittedly fictional, scenarios. In the first you are walking with a friend through unfamiliar terrain, equipped with a topographic map. Arriving at a place that affords a good panoramic view, your friend stops to ask, 'Where are we?' You look around, pointing to various landmarks which you proceed to correlate with markings on the map. Finally, indicating with a finger a particular spot on the map's paper surface, you declare 'We are here'. In the second scenario, you are walking in familiar country around your home, with a companion who is a stranger to the area. Once again, on arrival at a certain place, your companion puts the same question, 'Where are we?' You may respond in the first instance with a place-name. But then, realising that the name alone leaves him none the wiser, you might go on to tell a story about the place – about your own association with it, about other people who have lived and visited there, and about the things that happened to them. Now in the second case you have no need to consult an artefactual map, nor would it be of any avail to you, not because you have resort instead to a map inside your head, but because knowing your present whereabouts has nothing to do with fixing your location in space. As someone who has lived in a country, and is used to its ways, knowing where you are lies not in the establishment of a point-to-point correspondence between the world and its representation, but in the remembering of journeys previously made, and that brought you to the place along the same or different paths. In the first scenario, of course, you have no knowledge of this kind. Having never visited the country before you do not know where you are, in the sense you do when on home ground, even though you may be able to locate your own position, and that of everything else, with pin-point accuracy on your map.

For those who know a country, in short, the answers to such basic questions as 'Where am I?' and 'Which way should I go?' are found in narratives of past movement. It is in this respect, as noted earlier, that wayfinding and mapping become one and the same: to follow a path is also to retrace one's steps, or the steps of one's predecessors. And in this respect, too, wayfinding differs fundamentally from navigation, just as mapping differs from map-using. For when navigating in a strange country by means of a topographic map, the relation between one's position on the ground and one's location in space, as defined by particular map coordinates, is strictly synchronic, and divorced from any narrative context. It is possible to specify where one is – one's current location – without regard to where one has been, or where one is going. In ordinary wayfinding, by contrast, every place holds within it memories of previous arrivals and departures, as well as expectations of how one may reach it, or reach other places from it. Thus do places enfold the passage of time: they are neither of the past, present or future but all three rolled into one. Endlessly generated through the comings and goings of their inhabitants, they figure not as locations in space but as specific vortices in a current of movement, of innumerable journeys actually made. Taking this view of place as my starting point, I now want to show how wayfinding might be understood not as following a course from one spatial location to another, but as a movement in *time*, more akin to playing music or story-telling than to reading a map.

PATHS, FLOWS AND THE PASSAGE OF TIME

The inspiration for this move comes from Gibson, and follows from his insight – which I explored in an earlier section – that the environment is perceived not from multiple points of view but along a path of observation. Rejecting both of the dominant psycho-logical approaches to wayfinding, as chains of conditioned responses to environmental stimuli and as navigation by means of cognitive maps, Gibson proposes an alternative, 'the theory of reversible occlusion' (1979: 198). In brief, the theory states that one knows the way in terms of the specific order in which the surfaces of the environment come into or pass out of sight as one proceeds along a path. Suppose, for example, that you are walking along a street in town, or through a valley in the countryside. The surfaces you can see – the facades of buildings in the one case, or the ground rising on either side in the other – comprise a *vista*. As Gibson explains, a vista is 'a semienclosure, a set of unhidden surfaces, . . . what is seen from here, with the proviso that "here" is not a point but an extended region'. But now, as you turn the corner into another street, or reach the brow of the ridge at the head of the valley, a new set of surfaces, previously hidden, looms into view, while those of the original vista disappear from sight. The passage from one vista to another, during which the former is gradually occluded while the latter opens up, constitutes a *transition*. Thus to travel from place to place involves the opening up and closing off of vistas, in a particular order, through a continuous series of reversible transitions. It is through this ordering of vistas, Gibson maintains, that the structure of the environment is progressively disclosed to the moving observer, such that he or she can eventually perceive it from everywhere at once (Gibson 1979: 198–9).

Gibson's notion of wayfinding through reversible occlusion has been further developed in recent work by psychologist Harry Heft (1996). We have already seen how the forms of environmental features are revealed as the envelopes of a continually modulating pers-pective structure along a path of observation. Now this flow of perspective structure, as Heft points out, also specifies the observer's own movements relative to the layout of the environment. As every path of travel gives rise to its own distinctive flow pattern, so every such pattern uniquely specifies a certain path. To find one's way, Heft argues, means to travel along a particular route so as to generate or recreate the flow of perspective structure peculiar to the path leading to one's destination (1996: 122). One remembers the route as a succession of vistas connected by transitions, rather as one might remember a piece of music as a series of thematic sections linked by bridge passages. Just as with musical performance, wayfinding has an essentially *temporal* character (1996: 112): the path, like the musical melody, unfolds over time rather than across space. In this connection, it is important to remind ourselves of Gibson's contention that every path should be conceived as a unitary movement, and not as a potentially infinite set of adjacent points (Gibson 1979: 197). In music, a melodic phrase is not just a sequence of discrete tones; what counts is the rising or falling of pitch that gives shape to the phrase as a whole. Likewise in wayfinding, the path is specified not as a sequence of point-indexical images, but as the coming-into-sight and passing-out-of-sight of variously contoured and textured surfaces.

In this respect, too, the theory of wayfinding advanced here differs profoundly from that which Gell has caricatured under the rubric of 'mapless practical mastery', and which he attributes, *inter alia*, to Bourdieu (Gell 1985; see Bourdieu 1977: 2). 'We can suppose', writes Gell, 'that practical mastery of the environment consists of possessing complete knowledge of what the environment looks like from all practically-available points of view'. The master traveller, equipped with such knowledge, remembers the journey from A to B as a 'chain of linked landscape images', each particular to a certain point along the route, selected from the total stock of images filed in memory. As he proceeds on his way he will pause, every so often, to check that what he sees from the spot where he stands corresponds to the image he has on file (Gell 1985: 274–5). Our argument, to the contrary, is that mastery consists in knowing what the environment looks like from all practically available *paths* of view, that what the traveller remembers are vistas and transitions rather than location-specific images, and that keeping track is a matter of regenerating the flow of perspective structure over time. Now for Gell the theory of mapless practical mastery, taken on its own, could not possibly work, since it would leave the traveller bereft of any means to formulate navigational decisions. It is all very well to know that you are currently where you ought to be – that what you see around you matches your expectations for a certain stage in your journey. But this alone will not tell you in which direction to go to reach the next checkpoint. Nor, if what you see does *not* match any of the images in the chain for the particular journey you are making, do you have any way of working out how to get back on track. In short, to go from A to B, or from any point to any other along the way, you need to be able to ascertain their relative locations in space. And this, Gell reasons, requires a map.

If it were true that all wayfinding consisted of navigation between fixed points, Gell's argument would be unassailable. But it is not. Ordinary movement in a familiar environment lacks the stop-go character of navigation, in which every physical or bodily manoeuvre (displacement in space) is preceded by a mental or calculative one (fixing the course). 'Finding one's way' is not a computational operation carried out prior to departure from a place, but is tantamount to one's own movement through the world. To recapitulate my earlier point, we know *as* we go, not *before* we go. Thus the operation is not complete until one has reached one's final destination: only then can the traveller truly claim to have found his way. The notion of 'finding' has here to be understood in its original sense of exploratory movement, at once improvisatory and assured, guided by past experience and by a continual monitoring of fluctuations not only in the pattern of reflected light but also in the sounds and 'feel' of the environment. There is no better illustration of this than the example that Gell himself uses in an attempt to prove, to the contrary, that wayfinding is based on the execution of pre-formulated 'navigational decisions' (1985: 282). This is the case of Micronesian seafaring. In a classic paper on the subject, Thomas Gladwin describes how, at every moment during a voyage, the mariner is attentive to 'a combination of motion, sound, feel of the wind, wave patterns, star relationships, etc.', all of which – through comparison with remembered observations from past experience – translates into 'a slight increase or decrease in pressure on the steering paddle, or a grunted instruction to slack off the sail a trifle' (Gladwin 1964: 171–2). Quite unlike the European navigator, with his charts and compass, the Micronesian seafarer feels his way towards his destination by continually adjusting his movements in relation to the *flow* of waves, wind, current and stars.[6] In this respect his activity does not differ in principle from that of the terrestrial traveller who responds to the flow of perspective structure as he journeys through a landscape. Both are essentially engaged in projects of wayfinding rather than navigation: thus Hallowell's observation that for the Saulteaux, direction always has the meaning of 'toward such-and-such a place', is paralleled by Gladwin's that the Micronesian mariner proceeds as if he were constantly within sight of land (Hallowell 1955: 190–1, Gladwin 1964: 173). And once it is recognised that the wayfinder's multi-sensory monitoring is of flows, not images, and that flows specify paths and not spatial locations, Gell's objections to the idea of mapless practical mastery fall away.

Micronesian seafaring resembles terrestrial wayfinding in one other critical respect: every journey is apprehended and remembered as a movement through time rather than across space. Islands, for the mariner, are not pinned down to specific spatial or geographic locations, nor does he imagine his craft to be covering the distance over a planar surface from one such location to another. Throughout the voyage he remains, apparently stationary, at the centre of a world that stretches around as far as the horizon, with the great dome of the heavens above. But as the journey proceeds the island of embarkation slips ever farther astern while the destination island draws ever closer. At the same time an island off to one side, selected as a point of reference for the voyage, is supposed to swing past the boat, falling as it does so under the rising or setting positions of a series of stars. The fact that the reference island (*etak*) is normally invisible below the horizon, and may not even exist at all, has been a source of puzzlement to many interpreters who – assuming that the mariner's task is to navigate from one spatial location to another – have proposed that the *etak* is used to obtain a locational fix. Nothing in what the mariners themselves have to say, however, suggests that it serves any such purpose. The alleged bearing of the *etak* does not enter into any numerical computation. Rather, pointing to the *etak* is the mariner's way of indicating where he is in terms of the temporal unfolding of the voyage as a whole (Hutchins 1995: 87–8). We have already seen how, in terrestrial wayfinding, a route from one place to another is remembered as a temporally ordered sequence of vistas. In much the same way, the Micronesian mariner remembers an inter-island voyage as a sequence of *etak* segments, each of which begins as the reference island falls under one particular star and ends as it falls under the next in line. At any movement, the mariner will know what segment he is in. As it swings beneath the horizon, from segment to segment, the *etak* island marks in its movement the passage of time, just as do the sun, moon and stars overhead, in theirs. Completion of the penultimate segment should bring the mariner, at length, to the final '*etak* of sighting', as the island for which he is bound hoves into view.

THE WORLD HAS NO SURFACE

One further contrast remains to be drawn between wayfinding and navigation, and it takes us back to the cartographic notion of the map as a representation of some portion of the earth's surface. The following 'official' definition of the map, issued by the International Cartographic Association, is exemplary:

> A map is a representation normally to scale and on a flat medium, of a selection of material or abstract features on, or in relation to, the surface of the Earth or of a celestial body.
>
> (cited in Robinson and Petchenik 1976: 17)

Now the idea that the world is presented to the traveller as a surface to be traversed presupposes the specialised, 'bird's-eye view' of the cartographer or navigator. Indeed the world can only be perceived to have an exterior surface by a mind that is situated above and beyond it. In ordinary wayfinding however, whether on land or at sea, the world is apprehended from within. One makes one's way *through* it, not over or across it. Of course the traveller encounters surfaces of diverse kinds – of solid ground, water, vegetation, buildings, and so on – and it is largely thanks to the responses of these surfaces to light, sound and the pressure of touch that he perceives the environment in the way he does. For the mariner the ocean, with its subtle differences of tint and colour, sculpted by the wind into waves and ripples, and breaking up around the boat into foam and spray, presents an infinitely variegated and ever changing surface. Likewise for the pedestrian, making his way along a forest track, the surface of the ground is a patchwork of mud, furrowed by the imprint of previous journeys, puddles, fallen leaves, broken boughs, and outcropping rocks and stones. These are surfaces, however, *in* the world, not *of* the world. That is to say, they are formed on the interface, not between matter and mind, but between solid or liquid substance and the gaseous medium (air) in which humans live and breathe, and which affords movement and sensory perception.[7] In short for its manifold inhabitants, journeying along their respective ways of life, the world itself *has no surface*.

I noted earlier the parallel between the tracing of paths on the ground in wayfinding and the tracing of lines on paper (or in sand, snow, etc.) in mapping: indeed to the extent that all wayfinding is mapping, these are one and the same. Our conclusion, however, that for the mapper or wayfinder the world has no surface, calls for some qualification of the view, for which I argued above, that mapping is an inscriptive process. This need not be so. If a map consists of a network of interconnected lines, each corresponding to a path of movement through the world, there is no necessary reason why these lines should be inscribed on a surface. One could think of the gesturing hand, in mapping, as a weaving hand rather than a drawing hand, and of the result as something more akin to a cat's cradle than a graph. The lines of the map could be threads, wires or sticks. Micronesian mariners used coconut leaf ribs to map the intersecting courses of ocean swells (Turnbull 1991: 24). Or to take a familiar example from a contemporary urban context, one could construct a route map for the London Underground out of stiff wire, soldered at the intersections, and it would serve just as well as the conventional printed versions. The fact that the map is generally reproduced on paper is a matter of obvious practical convenience, but not of logical necessity. The meaning of the map lies entirely in its routes and intersections, whereas the paper surface has no significance whatsoever. To read the map is to trace a continuous path from one station to another, without regard to their respective locations on the surface. With the modern topographic map it is quite otherwise, for in this case the paper surface of the map stands for nothing less than the *surface of the earth*. One of the most revealing indicators of this change in the significance of the map-surface, corresponding to the transition from mapping to mapmaking, lies in the appearance of frame boundaries. Native maps, as Belyea points out (1996: 6), are never framed. A line or border drawn around and enclosing such a map would have no meaning. The frame of the topographic map, by contrast, defines the portion of the earth's surface that the map purports to represent. Thus the appearance of borders around the map corresponds to the disappearance of the itineraries and practices that give rise to it.

CONCLUSION

There is a paradox at the heart of modern cartography. The more it aims to furnish a precise and comprehensive representation of reality, the less true to life this representation appears. 'To present a useful and truthful picture', as Mark Monmonier writes, 'an accurate map must tell white lies' (Monmonier 1991: 1). But the reason for the discrepancy between truth and accuracy is not quite what Monmonier claims it to be. It is not that the map must leave things out if critical information is not to be drowned in a welter of ever finer particulars. It is rather that the world of our experience is a world suspended in movement, that is continually coming into being as we – through our own movement – contribute to its formation. In the cartographic world, by contrast, all is still and silent. There is neither sunlight nor moonlight; there are no variations of light or shade, no clouds, no shadows or reflections. The wind does not blow, neither disturbing the trees nor whipping water into waves. No birds fly in the sky, or sing in the woods; forests and pastures are devoid of animal life; houses and streets are empty of people and traffic. To dismiss all this – to suggest that what is excluded in the cartographic reduction amounts, in Monmonier's words, to a 'fog of detail' – is perverse, to say the least (Wood 1992: 76). For it is no less than the stuff of life itself. Were one magically transported into the looking-glass world behind the map, one would indeed feel lost and disoriented, as in a fog. But the fogginess is a function not of the amount or density of detail but of the arrestation of movement. Detached from the flow of which each is but a moment, details settle like an opaque precipitate upon the surface of the earth. Little wonder, then, that the cartographer feels the need to sweep them up, or that the navigator prefers to brush them aside in plotting a course!

The ordinary wayfinder, on the other hand, is not generally troubled by detail. Quite to the contrary, the richer and more varied the texture of the environment, the easier it is to find one's way about. But above all, wayfinding depends upon the attunement of the traveller's movements in response to the movements, in his or her surroundings, of other people, animals, the wind, celestial bodies, and so on. Where nothing moves there is nothing to which one can respond: at such times – as before a storm, or during an eclipse – the experienced traveller can lose his bearings even in familiar terrain. These observations should finally lay to rest the cartographic illusion, namely that the world is pre-prepared as a stage upon which living things propel themselves about, from one location to another. Life, in this view, is an internal property of objects, transported upon the exterior surface of a lifeless earth. In the view I have set forth here, by contrast, the world is *not* ready-made for life to occupy. Contrary to the assumptions of cartographers and cognitive map theorists, life is not contained within things, nor is it transported about. It is rather laid down along paths of movement, of action and perception. Every living being, accordingly, grows and reaches out into the environment along the sum of its paths. To find one's way is to advance along a line of growth, in a world which is never quite the same from one moment to the next, and whose future configuration can never be fully known. Ways of life are not therefore determined in advance, as routes to be followed, but have continually to be worked out anew. And these ways, far from being inscribed upon the surface of an inanimate world, are the very threads from which the living world is woven.

Chapter Fourteen

Stop, look and listen!

Vision, hearing and human movement

ON HEARING SOUNDS, AND SEEING THINGS

Near the house where I grew up was a path I often took, which crossed a railway line. Beside the track was a notice which advised the pedestrian to 'stop, look and listen' before attempting to cross the line. I may not always have followed this advice as closely as I should, but at least I knew what it meant. To me, as doubtless to others who walked that path, it made perfectly good sense. In the absence of automatic signalling arrangements, how else is one to know whether a train is coming save by looking and listening? Only later did I discover that what is obvious to pedestrians is, to philosophers, utterly baffling. To be sure, the philosopher might admit, our knowledge of the world can only come through some form of perception. Yet it seems that the one thing we cannot perceive is perception itself. You may claim to see a train, but only by way of the light that reaches your eyes. And you hear it only by way of the sound that reaches your ears. So how can you know that the train exists at a certain distance, as a detached material object, behind the perceptual images, shaped in light and sound, that you have of it? And if it exists only in your perception – in your eyes and ears, or even in your thoughts – then how can it run you down? Nor is that all. Looking and listening, we receive one set of sensations through the eyes, and another, quite different set through the ears. Supposing that our knowledge is ultimately founded on sensory experience, how do we know that the sights and sounds that come to our notice are all manifestations of the same thing, the train, that is bearing down on us? If we hear sounds rather than things (like trains), then how do I know that *this* sound I hear belongs to *that* train I see?

These are among the most ancient of philosophical conundrums, and it is not my intention to resolve them here. I do mean to suggest, however, that the way in which they are posed bears the imprint of a certain way of imagining the human subject – namely, as a seat of awareness, bounded by the skin, and set over against the world – that is deeply sedimented in the Western tradition of thought. The problem of perception, thus, is one of how anything can be translated or 'cross over' from the outside to the inside, from the macrocosm of the world to the microcosm of the mind. This is why visual and aural perception are usually described, in the writings of philosophers and psychologists, as processes of *seeing* and *hearing*. Sight begins at the point where light enters the eyes of the stationary perceiver, hearing at the point where sound strikes his ears – at the interface, in short, between outside and inside. Yet the notice beside the railway tracks did not advise the pedestrian to 'stand, see and hear'. It advised him to 'stop, look and listen': that is, to interrupt one bodily activity, of walking, and to initiate another, of looking-and-listening (as I show later, these are better regarded as aspects of one activity than as two distinct activities). In what, then, does this activity consist? Not in opening the eyes, since these are open anyway; nor in opening the ears, since they cannot be closed save by stopping them with the fingers. It consists, rather, in a kind of scanning movement, accomplished by the whole body – albeit from a fixed location – and which both seeks out, and responds to, modulations or inflections in the environment to which it is attuned. As such, perception is not an 'inside-the head' operation, performed upon the raw material of sensation, but takes place in circuits that cross-cut the boundaries between brain, body and world.

But I am running ahead of myself. There is much ground to be cleared before the idea of perception outlined above can be substantiated. To begin this clearance we need to inquire more closely into the assumptions we tend to make about our experiences of seeing and hearing. You can attempt to find out what these are by performing a simple thought experiment. Suppose you are standing beside the tracks as a train is passing. You see the locomotive and the coaches hurtling by, you hear the roar of the engine followed by the clickety-clack of bogies as they roll over joints in the rail. These sights and sounds are ordinarily so entangled in your experience that it is not easy to tell them apart, to imagine what the train would look like without the noise it makes, or what it would sound like without the appearance it presents. But you could try, nevertheless. Picture yourself blindfolded, or on a pitch dark night, such that the visual component of experience is eliminated. The sound of the approaching train, as it swells, seems to assault and ultimately to overwhelm every fibre of your being. You cannot resist being swept along with it until eventually, as the train recedes into the distance, you are left stranded by the trackside, breathless and dizzy, in exactly the same spot where, in truth, you had been standing all along! But now, as a second experiment, picture yourself with your ears stopped, so as to cut out the auditory component of experience. This time the train appears to pass before your eyes as though it were a spectre whose very existence lies in dimensions other than those of the world to which you belong. You see it, you register its presence and its passing, but you are not *moved* by it. The vision is just another sighting to add to your collection.

If the results of these admittedly fictitious experiments have any validity, they suggest that far from being equivalent and mutually substitutable, vision and hearing are radically opposed, as different as is standing on the river bank, watching the water flow by, from being tossed in with the current. As a participant observer in the event constituted by the train's passing the spot where you stand, at the intersection of the path and the tracks, it would seem that whereas you participate aurally, you observe visually. Indeed the notion that sound can get inside you and shake you up, in a way that light cannot, has a long and distinguished pedigree in the history of ideas. Time and again, the ears are imagined topologically as openings in the head that actually allow the sound to seep in and touch the innermost surfaces of being. The eyes, by contrast, are supposed to be backed by screens that let no light through, leaving the mind in the dark – like the inhabitants, in Plato's celebrated allegory, of a cave who can see nothing but shadows on the walls cast by the light of their own fire. Sound, it is said, reaches directly into the soul, whereas in vision all one can do is reconstruct a picture of what the outside world might be like, on the basis of light-induced sensations. But by the same token, we are more readily convinced that we hear sound than that we see light. The objects of vision, we suppose, are not sources or manifestations of light but the *things* that light illuminates for us. The objects of hearing, on the other hand, are not things but sounds or sources of sound.[1]

True, there have been dissenting voices. One of them was Martin Heidegger. In his essay on 'The origin of the work of art', Heidegger argued that only when we divert our attention away from things, or listen abstractly (as we might, say, to classical music, with our eyes closed), do we hear 'bare sound'. In ordinary life, he insisted, we do not hear sounds but things themselves – the door shutting in the house, the storm in the chimney, the Mercedes as distinct from the Volkswagen (Heidegger 1971: 26). So too, Heidegger would have said, we hear the train before the noise it makes. But this view is not easily reconciled with everyday experience. For what we claim to hear, at least when we speak of these matters, is the slamming of the door, the whistling of the wind, the humming or chugging of the car engine, and the roar of the locomotive. Slamming, whistling, humming, and so on are words that describe not things but actions or movements which, because of the vibrations they set up, we actually sense as noises of various kinds. Or to take another example, consider the word 'cuckoo'. This is, in the first place, an onomatopoeic rendering of a sound that I have often heard in the countryside, and which always seems to emanate from a far-off, undisclosed location in the woods. We say the cuckoo is a bird, but in my experience the bird exists, purely and simply, as its sound. I have never seen one (except in illustrated books on ornithology). But only through being seen does the cuckoo come to be apprehended as a thing that makes a sound, instead of the sound itself.[2]

In due course I shall proceed to qualify the idea that we see things before light, and hear sound before things. I shall do so by showing that sound, strictly speaking, is no more an object of hearing than is light an object of vision. Rather, just as to say there is light is another way of saying that one can see, so also, to say there is sound is another way of saying that one can hear. Light and sound are, in essence, the undersides of the experiences of seeing and hearing respectively. Now as blind people are able to tell us, it is in fact possible to hear things as well as to see them. And for sighted people, the eyes are as much a part of the perceptual system for listening as are the ears part of the system for looking. To that extent, vision and hearing are not so much disparate as interchangeable. But behind the discovery, whether visual or auditory, of a world already made there lies a deeper, pre-objective level of perception, a level at which sensory awareness rides on the cusp of the very movement of the world's coming-into-being. At this level, as I shall show, the experiences of vision and hearing are not mutually substitutable in the way that – for example – the signed language of the deaf is substitutable for oral speech. Instead, they are virtually indistinguishable: vision *is* a kind of hearing, and vice versa. This argument eventually leads me to reject the thesis that attributes the dominance of objective thinking in the West to an obsession with the eye. For the moment, however, let me continue with the contrast between seeing and hearing, as this is commonly understood, in order to examine its implications for our understanding, first, of persons and things; secondly, of language, speech and writing; and thirdly, of the sensory practices of people in non-Western societies.

VISION OBJECTIFIES, SOUND PERSONIFIES

Of all the implications of the contrast between vision and hearing, the most consequential has been the notion that vision, since it is untainted by the subjective experience of light, yields a knowledge of the outside world that is rational, detached, analytical and atomistic. Hearing, on the other hand, since it rests on the immediate experience of sound, is said to draw the world into the perceiver, yielding a kind of knowledge that is intuitive, engaged, synthetic and holistic. For those who would celebrate positive scientific inquiry as the crowning achievement of the human spirit, vision is undoubtedly the superior sense. Yet for all that, it is not to be trusted. The visual path to objective truth, it seems, is paved with illusions. Precisely because vision yields a knowledge that is indirect, based on conjecture from the limited data available in the light, it can never be more than provisional, open to further testing and the possibility of empirical refutation.[3] But while we can never be certain of what we see, there is no doubt about what we hear. Since sound speaks to us directly, hearing does not lie. We do not suffer from aural as we do from optical illusions (Rée 1999: 46). In short, when it comes to affairs of the soul, of emotion and feeling, or of the 'inwardness' of life, hearing surpasses seeing as understanding goes beyond knowledge, and as faith transcends reason.

Nothing better illustrates these attitudes to vision and hearing, so deeply embedded in Western sensibilities, than these lines from the 'Foreword' to Victor Zuckerkandl's classic study of musical perception, *Sound and Symbol*. Here he is comparing the demeanour of the blind and the deaf:

> The quietness, the equanimity, the trust, one might almost say the piety, so often found in the blind are in strange contrast to the irritability and suspicion encountered among so many of the deaf . . . It seems as if, by the very fact that the blind man trusts himself to the guidance of the ear instead of the eye, other modes of connection with the world are revealed to him, modes that are otherwise overshadowed by the dominance of the eye – as if, in the realms with which he thus comes into contact, man were less alone, better provided for, more at home, than in the world of visible things to which the deaf man is directed and to which an element of foreignness always clings.
>
> (1956: 3)

As a stereotypic depiction of the behaviour of blind and deaf people this passage is, of course, outrageous. It says much, however, about how we are inclined to view hearing as warm, connecting and sympathetic; and sight as cold, distancing and unfeeling. No wonder, then, that numerous commentators have sought to lay the ills of modern Western civilisation at the door of its alleged obsession with vision (Jay 1993a, Levin 1988, 1993). More than any other modality of perception, they say, vision leads us to objectify our environment, to regard it as a repository of things, alien to our subjective selves, that are there to be seized by the eyes, analysed by science, exploited by technology, and dominated by power. If only we could redress the balance by restoring hearing to its proper place in the sensorium, it is claimed, we might hope to regain a more harmonious, benevolent and empathetic awareness of our surroundings. Then, perhaps, we may rediscover what it means to *belong*.[4]

These laments are not new; to the contrary, the denigration of vision is as ancient as is its elevation to the top of the hierarchy of the senses. As Don Ihde points out, in his study of the phenomenology of sound, 'there is an old and deeply held tradition that vision "objectifies", and, contrarily but not so widely noted, there is a tradition which holds that sound "personifies"' (Ihde 1976: 21). To this latter tradition belong the claims of many classical scholars that the very word, 'person', is derived from the Latin verb *personare*, meaning literally 'to sound through'. Whether the derivation is etymologically well founded need not concern us;[5] what count are rather the reasons that make it so compelling. These, I contend, lie in its concordance with a widely held notion that behind the visible aspect of the person, above all the face, lies an inner being that reveals itself through the voice. In speaking, the voice 'sounds through' from the inside to the outside; in hearing it conversely penetrates from the outside to the inside. Where vision places us *vis-à-vis* one another, 'face-to-face', leaving each of us to construct an inner representation of the other's mental state on the basis of our observations of outward appearance, voice and hearing establish the possibility of genuine intersubjectivity, of a participatory communion of self and other through shared immersion in the stream of sound. Vision, in this conception, defines the self individually in *opposition* to others; hearing defines the self socially in *relation* to others.

THE WRITTEN WORD AND THE SOUNDS OF SPEECH

Nowhere is the ambivalence surrounding attitudes to vision and hearing more evident than in Western ideas about language, and above all about the distinction between speech and writing. The distrust of writing is a recurrent theme throughout the history of Western thought. Ever since Plato and Aristotle, philosophers have tended to regard writing as an exterior, visible facade for the inner sonic reality of spoken words. Plato, in the *Phaedrus* (274–7), has Socrates declare that writing provides no more than 'the appearance and not the reality of wisdom' (Plato 1973). For Aristotle, only the spoken word truly represents mental experience, while the written word stands for the spoken one (Aristotle 1938: 115). Rousseau, for whom writing was 'nothing but the representation of speech', complained bitterly (in writing of course) about the prestige and attention accorded by his contemporaries to writing when it was no more than a contrived and inauthentic cover for the real thing (Derrida 1974: 36). And two of the giants of twentieth-century linguistics held to much the same opinion. For Bloomfield (1933: 21) writing was 'merely a way of recording language by visible marks', while according to Saussure (1959: 23), 'language and writing are two distinct systems of signs; the second exists for the sole purpose of representing the first'. In a famous image (Figure 14.1), Saussure located language at the interface between thought and sound, as though human consciousness – the realm of ideas – hovered over an ocean of sound like air over water (1959: 112).

There is, in all these pronouncements, an implicit prioritisation of hearing over vision, as though the former gave access to intimacies of human experience to which the latter could only offer a pale reflection. 'The only true bond', as Saussure wrote, is 'the bond of sound' (1959: 25).[6] Ironically, however, at the very same time that writing is rendered as having no other purpose than the modelling of speech in a visible medium, the apprehension of speech is itself modelled on the inspection of the written word. Thus a visual bias

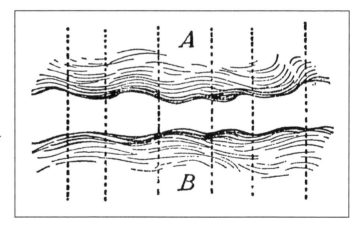

Figure 14.1 Saussure's depiction of language at the interface between a plane of thought (A) and a plane of sound (B). The role of language is to cut the interface into subdivisions, as indicated by the vertical dashed lines, thereby establishing a series of relations between particular ideas and particular sounds. 'Visualize the air in contact with a sheet of water', says Saussure; 'if the atmospheric pressure changes, the surface of the water will be broken up into a series of divisions, waves; the waves resemble the union of thought with phonic substance'.

From F. de Saussure, *Course in general linguistics*, New York: The Philosophical Library, 1959, p. 112.

enters, as it were by the back door, into our very notion of what language *is*. Recall that the underlying assumption, shared by both champions of visual perception and their critics, is that we do not see light but the objects it illuminates. You may not be able to read, for example, without a source of illumination, but what you see is not the light but the words on the page. Likewise, you cannot hear speech unless it is voiced in sound. However your familiarity with the written word leads you to believe that what you hear is not the sound itself but the words shaped in it. 'Language-as-word', as Ihde notes, 'even while sounding, does not draw attention to itself *as* sound' (1976: 161). Rather, the sound 'yields up' or delivers the words we claim to hear. Thus it is supposed that words can be extracted from the medium of sound, and can be preserved, whether as impressions in the mind or as inscriptions on the page, independently of their sounding.

Language, it seems, is the exception that proves the rule that we see things (not light), and hear sounds (not things). When we listen to music, we attend to the sound *as such*, for it is surely in the sound, no more and no less, that the music consists. But when it comes to speech, we are inclined to treat hearing as a species of vision – a kind of seeing with the ear, or 'earsight' – that reacts to sound in the same way that eyesight reacts to light. Thus we are convinced that we apprehend words, not sound. It is almost as though the sounds of speech were seen rather than heard. This, of course, is exactly what Saussure had in mind when he described the verbal signifier – the pattern of sound as registered in the psyche – as a *sound-image* (1959: 66). So far as he was concerned, we recognise a word of speech in the same way that we do a word of writing, by matching the perceived pattern to a pre-existing mental schema. But what if we had never seen a word, if we had no notion of a word as an object of vision? Granted that our familiarity with writing leads us to model the hearing of the spoken word upon the sight of the written one, how might the power of speech have been experienced by people with no knowledge of writing, or for whom the written word was meant to be disseminated, at most, through being read aloud rather than through its reproduction in print?

In his influential study, *The Gutenberg Galaxy*, Marshall McLuhan (1962) argued that the invention of the printing press ushered in an entirely new era in the history of human culture, marked by the absolute dominance of the eye, and with it a bias towards a way of thinking that is objective and analytic, and that follows a linear path of explicit logical connections. Even before the introduction of print technology, during the preceding 'chiro-graphic' stage of culture, the substitution of written for spoken words had begun to tip the balance between sight and hearing in favour of the former. But among peoples at an 'oral-aural' level of culture, to whom writing was unknown, the ear exercised an over-whelming tyranny over the eye (McLuhan 1962: 28). And so too, McLuhan maintained, their thought lacked the logical elaboration, analytic discrimination and objectivity that, in the literate West, are normally considered to be the hallmarks of rationality. Building on these ideas, one of McLuhan's associates, Walter Ong, sought to derive all the essential characteristics of 'orally based thought and expression' from the features that distinguish hearing from vision. Oral culture, he claimed, is aggregating, harmonic and holistic rather than dissecting, analytic and atomistic; concrete and situationally specific rather than abstract and context-independent; and focused on persons rather than things. Hearing binds people together in community; vision isolates the individual *vis-à-vis* the world. Finally, 'the interiorizing force of the oral word relates in a special way to the sacral, to the ultimate concerns of existence'. With the ascendancy of vision, however, religion gives way to secular science (Ong 1982: 73–4).

In their placing of oral cultures and literate civilisations on either side of a 'great divide', both McLuhan and Ong effectively reproduced a dichotomy between oral participation and visual observation that, as I have already shown, is deeply embedded within the Western tradition. Thus sound, according to Ong, registers the interiority of things in a way that is impossible with light, which merely reflects off their outer surfaces. The following passage is exemplary:

> Sight isolates, sound incorporates. Whereas sight situates the observer outside what he views, at a distance, sound pours into the hearer . . . Vision comes to a human being from one direction at a time . . . When I hear, however, I gather sound from every direction at once: I am at the center of my auditory world, which envelops me, establishing me at a kind of core of sensation and existence . . . You can immerse yourself in hearing, in sound. There is no way to immerse yourself similarly in sight.
>
> (Ong 1982: 72)

It is in his contention that the listener in a 'primarily oral' culture hears words *as sound*, rather than as images shaped in sound, that Ong takes issue with Saussure (1982: 17). People in such a culture, 'totally untouched by any knowledge of writing or print', do not hear words as if they were looking at them. In their speech, every word is a fugitive movement carried on the crest of a sound that 'exists only when it is going out of existence'. It was writing, Ong contends, that tied words down and made them appear thing-like, as 'quiescent objects . . . for assimilation by vision' (1982: 91). Thus writing transforms the word rather than, as Saussure thought, merely representing it in an alternative medium.

VISION AND HEARING IN ANTHROPOLOGY

Another of McLuhan's collaborators was the anthropologist Edmund Carpenter. Writing on the basis of fieldwork conducted among the Aivilik Eskimo (Inuit) of Southampton Island in the Canadian arctic, Carpenter claimed that the world of the Inuit is defined, above all, by sound rather than by sight (Carpenter 1973: 33). To inhabit such a world is not to look out upon a space of ready-made objects, but to participate from the inside in the perpetual movement of their generation. There are, strictly speaking, no things in the Inuit world, only beings, which establish their presence, first and foremost, by way of their ongoing actions. Hearing is the resonant coupling of these actions with the movement of the listener's attention. Thus Inuit hear sound rather than things, and are moved by the sound itself, as they are by song. Indeed the distinction between speech and song, so central to the literate conception of language, would make no sense to them (Carpenter 1966: 212; I return to this distinction in Chapter Twenty-three, pp. 407–10). Speaking and singing are actions which, like hunting or carving, 'bring out' or release aspects of being into the fullness of the acoustic space surrounding the person. Unlike the framed, pictorial space surveyed by the eye, acoustic space is 'dynamic, always in flux, creating its own dimensions moment by moment' (1973: 35, see also Carpenter and McLuhan 1960). Its form – as we recall from Chapter Twelve (pp. 210–11) – is that of a sphere, extending outwards from the person equally in all directions. But this sphere has no outer surface or boundary: it does not pre-exist and enclose the speaker and listener but rather takes shape around them in the very process of their auditory engagement with one another and with the environment.

Between them, McLuhan, Carpenter and Ong effectively laid the foundations for a currently vibrant field of inquiry that has come to be known as the anthropology of the senses (Stoller 1989, Howes 1991a, Classen 1993, 1997). It is true that certain aspects of their programme have come in for justified criticism from anthropological quarters: the attribution of pre-logical mentalities to 'tribal' societies at the oral-aural level, the relative neglect of other sensory modalities besides sight and hearing, and the consequent elision of differences among cultures on either side of the 'great divide' between orality and literacy (Howes 1991b: 172–3, Classen 1997: 403–4). However the basic idea, that cultures can be compared in terms of the relative weighting of the senses through which people perceive the world around them, has been retained. Thus it is not so much in *what* they perceive as in *how* they perceive that cultures differ. It will no longer do to identify cultural variations with alternative worldviews, as though everyone perceived their surroundings in the same way (visually, by viewing it) but saw different things on account of their drawing on different models for organising the data of perception into representations. For the very idea that the world is known by representing it in the mind is bound up with assumptions about the pre-eminence of vision that are not applicable cross-culturally. Below I briefly review three studies in the anthropology of the senses, all of which accord particular prominence to hearing. The first, by Paul Stoller, is of the Songhay of Niger, in West Africa; the second, by Anthony Seeger, is of the Suyá of Mato Grosso, Brazil; and the third, by Alfred Gell, is of the Umeda of Papua New Guinea.

For the Songhay, Stoller asserts, sound 'is a foundation of experience'. Unlike vision, which sets up a distance between the spectator and the object seen, sound 'penetrates the individual and creates a sense of communication and participation' (1989: 103, 120). To show how this is so, Stoller examines the significance that Songhay attach to the sounds of two kinds of musical instruments – the *godji* (monochord violin) and *gasi* (gourd drum) – both played during possession ceremonies, of the praise-poetry that accompanies these ceremonies, and of words spoken in sorcery. The *godji* produces a high-pitched cry, whereas the *gasi*, depending on how it is beaten, produces a 'clack' or a 'roll'. Both people and spirits are excited by these sounds, finding them irresistible. Indeed for the Songhay, the cries of the violin, and the clacks and rolls of the drum, *are* the voices of spirits that, in rituals of possession, penetrate and shake up the bodies of those possessed. And while the instruments are sounding, the praise-singer (*sorko*) recites the names of the spirits, shouting them directly into the ears of the intended medium. The sonic force of the shout affects the medium's body much as wind affects fire, igniting it into paroxysms that indicate the onset of possession (Stoller 1989: 108–12). In sorcery, too, it is the actual sound of the magical incantation that powerfully works its effects, whether for good or ill, on the body of the victim or patient. The magical word *is* sound, which exists (and goes out of existence) in the act of its enunciation. As such, it is a phenomenon of the same order as the cry, clack or roll of the musical instrument, or the shout of the praise-singer. In every case it is the sound itself that people hear, and to which they respond. This sound is supposed to have an existence of its own, 'separate from the domains of human, animal and plant life' (1989: 112).

Among the Suyá, according to Seeger, the faculty of hearing is valued very highly, as are the complementary faculties of speech and song. Speech is distinguished from song in Suyá classification, not however in terms of the detachment of words from sound, but as poles on a continuum of alternative combinations of 'phonetics, text, time, tone and timbre' (Seeger 1987: 46, 51). The significance accorded to hearing, as well as to speech and song, is highlighted through the massive expansion of the earlobes and (for men) the lower lips, into which are inserted large discs of wood or rolled palm leaf. The word *ku-mba*, in the Suyá language, translates not only as 'to hear' but also as 'to understand' and 'to know'. It is the ability to 'hear-understand-know' well that defines the person as a fully social being. And where we might describe the memory even of spoken words in visual terms, as images in the mind, Suyá describe even a visual phenomenon such as a weaving pattern, that has been learned and remembered, as lodged in the ear (Seeger 1975: 213–14). The sense of sight, to the contrary, is associated in Suyá thinking with morally delinquent, anti-social tendencies. A person possessed of extraordinary powers of hearing is a paragon of virtue, but someone with extraordinary vision is a witch. The witch sees everything – his is a transparent world that offers no barriers to sight. 'He can look up and see the village of the dead in the sky; he can look down and see the fires of the people who live under the earth; and he can look around and see enemy Indians in their own villages far away' (1975: 216). In their elaboration of hearing as the morally superior sense, and their distrust and fear of people with vision, Suyá seem to establish 'some kind of opposition between vision and social virtue' which, Seeger suggests, may have reson-ances elsewhere – even in the traditions of the West (1975: 222).

The Umeda, like many other peoples of Papua New Guinea, inhabit an environment of dense, and virtually unbroken forest, in which things are visible only at close range, normally within a few tens of metres. Such an environment, Gell argues, 'imposes a reorganisation of sensibility', giving pride of place to hearing, along with smell (Gell 1995: 235). Thus out hunting, Umeda walk with their eyes to the ground, listening for game instead of looking for it, since it is by their sounds that animals announce their existence and presence in the world of the hunter. This is not a world of preconstituted, visual-spatial objects but is rather apprehended dynamically. Not only animals and plants, but also landscape features such as ridges, knolls and pools, are grasped in the first place as movements rather than static forms. Alert to these movements, the body resonates rather like a sounding cavity, and responds in kind through its own activity of speech (1995: 240). Thus the sound of the spoken word echoes to the movement of the being or feature in the environment to which it corresponds, giving rise to the 'phonological iconism' which, as Gell shows, is such a pronounced feature of the Umeda language. Through their speech, Umeda do not point to and label things in the world 'out there', but continually bring the world into being around themselves, even as they are continually brought into being through their own immersion in an ambience of sound. But Gell goes further, to propose that the predominance of hearing over seeing leads to a 'bias towards the expres-sion of sympathy towards community members' (1995: 235). The 'auditory' culture of the Umeda, Gell claims, is a 'culture of sympathy'.

THE ANTHROPOLOGY OF THE SENSES: A FIRST CRITIQUE

What is so striking about the studies reviewed above is that in all three, a radical contrast is established between hearing and vision along lines which, as we have seen, are already sharply drawn within the Western tradition. Among the criteria of distinction, to reca-pitulate, are that sound penetrates whereas sight isolates, that what we hear are sounds that fill the space around us whereas what we see are things abstracted or 'cut out' from the space before us, that the body responds to sound like a resonant cavity and to light like a reflecting screen, that the auditory world is dynamic and the visual world static, that to hear is to participate whereas to see is to observe from a distance, that hearing is social whereas vision is asocial or individual, that hearing is morally virtuous whereas vision is intrinsically untrustworthy, and finally that hearing is sympathetic whereas vision is indifferent or even treacherous. Yet there are puzzles and inconsistencies which suggest that these distinctions may reflect more upon the preconceptions of anthropological analysts than upon the actual sensory experience of the peoples among whom they have worked. Indeed it is hard to avoid the suspicion, voiced by Nadia Seremetakis (1994: 124), that in the imputation to non-Western 'Others' of heightened auditory (along with tactile and olfactory) sensibilities, they are being made to carry the burden of sensory modalities exiled from the sensory structure of Western modernity on account of the latter's attribution to the hegemony of vision.

Stoller, for example, devotes a whole chapter to arguing the need for anthropologists to transform themselves from ethnographic 'spectators into seers',[7] by opening up to the world of the other and allowing themselves to be penetrated by it. So convinced is he, however, that 'a person's spatialized "gaze" creates distance' that he can follow his own advice only by learning to *hear*, rather than to see, as the Songhay do (1989: 120). In this, his approach is entirely in accord with the convention that to attain real knowledge one must abandon the illusions of vision and yield to the guidance of the ear. The true 'seer' of the Western tradition is the blind prophet: in Seeger's words, 'one who physically cannot see' (1975: 222). Yet by Seeger's own account, this is not so for the Suyá, among whom the witch is certainly a seer rather than a spectator, albeit of a morally undesirable complexion. For the witch's all-around sight does not view the world from the outside, but opens it up from the inside. A similar inconsistency between analytic preconception and native experience appears in Gell's study of the Umeda. For having reasserted the now familiar proposition that 'hearing is (relatively) *intimate*, concrete, and tactile, whereas vision promotes abstraction', he goes on to tell us that Umeda themselves 'treat sight . . . as a climactic sense with connotations of *intimacy* and danger' (1995: 235, 239, my emphases). The intimacy of sight, for Umeda, lies in close-range, eye-to-eye contact, and its danger is linked to the ever present possibility of sorcery attack. An angry glance can terrify the one to whom it is directed. Umeda, it seems, would be the last to agree that vision promotes abstraction!

Commenting on the Suyá case, David Howes suggests that 'there may be a connection between aurality and sociability, on the one hand, and visuality and individuality (or an "asocial disposition"), on the other'. This connection, he argues, might even be rephrased as a general law: 'the more a society emphasizes the eye, the less communal it will be; the more it emphasizes the ear, the less individualistic it will be' (Howes 1991b: 177–8). Once again, however, this 'law' merely reproduces a homology between two dualities, individual versus social and seeing versus hearing, that has long been axiomatic in the Western tradition. And it glosses over fundamental differences between Western and (for example) Suyá understandings, both of the 'asocial individual' and of vision. The Suyá 'witch' is not at all, as Howes (1991b: 177) thinks, the counterpart of the Western 'individual'. For one thing, the witch's vision penetrates the world rather than catching reflections off its outer surfaces; for another he does not stand, as does the Western individual, *vis-à-vis* others in society, but embodies in his being the active negation of sociality as a principle of relationship. In this sense the witch is more *anti*-social than *a*social.

Like the Suyá witch, the shaman among the Inuit possesses extraordinary powers of vision, though these could be used for beneficial as well as harmful ends. He, too, is a seer rather than a spectator, whose sight could open up pathways into the parallel worlds of animals and spirits. In the cosmology of the Yup'ik Eskimos, according to Anne Fienup-Riordan, 'vision was an act constituting knowledge, and witnessing was a potentially creative act' (1994: 316). The Eskimo cosmos, it transpires, teems with ever-watchful eyes. Among Inuit generally, there is a close association between seeing and hunting: it is through his clear and penetrating sight that the hunter initiates an encounter with the game animal, which in turn is consummated with the animal's willingly offering itself to the hunter (Oosten 1992: 130). These observations bring us back to Carpenter's seminal study of Inuit sensory experience. Why, in the face of overwhelming evidence for the centrality of eyesight to the Inuit perception of their environment, did Carpenter nevertheless insist to the contrary that, for them, the eye is subservient to the ear (Carpenter 1973: 33)? Could it be because he took with him into his study a preconceived notion of vision, as analytic and reflective rather than active and generative (Schafer 1985: 96), that was fundamentally incompatible with his fine appreciation of the dynamic potential and spherical topology of the Inuit lifeworld? And if, as Inuit ethnography suggests, it is perfectly possible to combine the perception of a lifeworld of this kind with a thorough-going ocularcentrism, albeit of a kind radically different from that with which we are familiar in the West, then how can we any longer attribute such perception to the predominance of hearing over sight in the balance of the senses?

Recall that it is on precisely these grounds that Gell accounts for the Umeda perception of animals, plants and the landscape. Judging from the descriptions of Gell and Carpenter, the parallels between the ways in which Umeda and Inuit constitute their worlds of experience are remarkably close. Their respective environments, however, could hardly be more different: dense, tropical forest as against treeless, arctic tundra. It is scarcely surprising that in these conditions, the Umeda hunter should be obliged to rely on his ears, and the Inuit hunter on his superior eyesight. Indeed Carpenter admits that when his Inuit companions used their eyes, 'it was often with an acuity that amazed me' (1973: 36). Yet to the extent that he depends on powers of vision rather than hearing, the Inuit hunter does not, in consequence, find his relation with the world turned inside out. He remains, like his Umeda counterpart, at the centre of a dynamic cosmos, caught up in the process of its perpetual generation. Beings do not, all at once, appear to him inert and thinglike, nor does the hunter feel himself any more an observer, or any less a participant.

Thus in comparing the sensory profile of Inuit or Umeda – or for that matter, Songhay or Suyá – with that of the West, it is clear that what is at stake is not the priority of vision over hearing, but the understanding of vision itself. Evidently, the primacy of vision cannot be held to account for the objectification of the world. Rather the reverse; it is through its co-option in the service of a peculiarly modern project of objectification that vision has been reduced to a faculty of pure, disinterested reflection, whose role is merely to deliver up 'things' to a transcendent consciousness. But while the eye, as Theodor Adorno argued, has had to get used to perceiving a reality of objects (or more specifically, of commodities), the ear has lagged behind in this development. There is something almost 'archaic', says Adorno, about hearing (Adorno 1981: 99). One of the ironies of the contemporary critique of visualism is that in calling for the restoration of hearing to its rightful place in the ratio of the senses, it actually reproduces this opposition between hearing and vision, and with it the very narrow and impoverished concept of vision to which its enlistment in the project of modernity has brought us. Having installed vision as the chief instrument of objective knowledge, leaving hearing to float in the primordial realms of emotion and feeling, we know what it means to hear sound but have effectively lost touch with the experience of *light*. To show how this has come about, I turn in the next section to a figure whose thinking is widely acknowledged to occupy a pivotal place in this transition – René Descartes.

THE OPTICS OF DESCARTES

Descartes began his *Optics* of 1637 by proclaiming his enthusiasm for the telescope. 'Since sight', he wrote, 'is the noblest and most comprehensive of the senses, inventions which serve to increase its power are undoubtedly among the most useful there can be' (1988: 57). And what more wonderful invention could one imagine than the telescope, which has so enhanced the power of sight as to open up whole new vistas for the human understanding of nature and the universe? In according pride of place among the senses to vision, Descartes was following in the footsteps of a long line of philosophers, reaching back to Plato and Aristotle.[8] Despite continuing doubts concerning the reliability of sight, as opposed to hearing, the superiority of both vision and hearing over the so-called 'contact' senses of touch, taste and smell was never in question. So far, I have had nothing to say about the latter. Taste and smell raise a whole gamut of problems of their own which lie beyond my present concerns, and while I admit that they would have to be included in any discussion of human sensory experience that claimed to be truly comprehensive, I do not intend to deal with them further here. But I can no longer put off some consideration of touch. For in treatments of perception in the Western philosophical tradition, it is above all to touch rather than hearing that sight has been compared. And in this, Descartes was no exception. Indeed it was through an analogy with touch that he chose to introduce the workings of vision.

Descartes invites us to consider a man who, blind from birth, is well practised in the art of perceiving objects around and about him through the medium of a stick. What happens is this. When the tip of the stick impacts upon an object (whether due to the movement of the stick, the object or both), a mechanical impulse is passed to the hand, whence it is further registered in the region of the brain from which the nerves of the hand originate. These excitations in the brain then provide the data upon which is done a mental act of calculation. Suppose, for example, that the blind man wishes to judge the distance of an object, which he touches at the same point with two sticks, one held in each hand. Knowing the distance between his hands, and the angle formed by each stick with the line connecting them, it is a simple matter to work out how far the object lies from the body. As Descartes himself remarks, the mental computational task involved in the estimation of distance calls for 'a kind of reasoning quite similar to that used by surveyors when they measure inaccessible places by means of two different vantage points' (1988: 67).

The import of the analogy is that for Descartes, this is precisely equivalent to what happens in vision. All you have to do is to substitute rays of reflected light for sticks, and the two eyes for the two hands.[9] Fluctuations in the patterns of reflected light reaching the eyes, due to the movement either of environmental objects or of the eyes themselves, are registered at the back of the retina, and thence in the part of the brain where the optic nerve-fibres have their source. The mind – or what Descartes calls the soul (in French, *âme*) – then gets to work on these patterns of excitation, resulting in that awareness of objects that allows us to claim to 'see' them. In defence of Descartes, it is important to recognise two aspects of this account which are often overlooked. First, it was plain to him that perception – whether visual or tactile – depended on movement. Were there no movement of the body and its sensory organs relative to the environment, nothing would be perceived. Ironically, this point has been lost in much of the subsequent psychology of vision, only to be rediscovered by advocates of an ecological approach to visual perception who adopt an explicitly anti-Cartesian stance. I return to this below. Secondly,

Descartes did not, as is commonly supposed, argue that the function of the eyes is to establish internal representations of external objects, which are then available for inspection by the mind. Indeed he was well aware of the absurdity of having to posit another set of eyes, inside the brain, to view the internal image. Whatever reaches the brain, and leads us to have sensory awareness of objects, no more *resembles* those objects than do the movements of the blind man's stick resemble the objects with which it comes into contact (1988: 64).[10]

It remains the case, however, that for Descartes, the act of perception naturally divides into two stages: the first leading from the physical encounter with an object to a pattern of nervous excitation in the brain; the second leading from these nervous impulses to a mental awareness of the object in the perceiver's line of sight. In which of these two stages, then, does the essence of vision reside? The comparison with touch suggests the former. Thus vision uses eyes and light-rays, touch uses hands and sticks. At a critical juncture in his exposition, however, Descartes shifts his ground. For it transpires that it is no longer in the work of the eyes that the essence of vision lies, but rather in the operations of the mind upon the deliverances of the senses. 'It is the soul which sees', he declares, 'and not the eye; and it does not see directly, but only by means of the brain' (1988: 68). Initially introduced as an active mode of bodily exploration of the environment, vision – as it were – 'goes indoors', and perforce has to build a picture of the outside world on the basis of intelligence received via the nervous system. Nor need this intelligence be received exclusively by way of the eyes. As a purely cognitive faculty, vision can also work upon the data of touch. Equipped with a stick, or even with bare hands, the blind can see! So can sighted people, walking without a light on a pitch dark night (1988: 58).

Thus we reach the extraordinary conclusion that vision, now conceived as an exclusively intellectual achievement, is no longer conditioned in any way by the embodied experience of inhabiting an illuminated world.[11] The role of light, being precisely equivalent to that of the blind man's stick, is to effect a purely mechanical transduction. One does not see light, any more than the blind man sees his stick. Rather one sees things *by means of* the light and the stick. For what is registered in the brain, in the form of patterns of nervous excitation, is information not about light, or about the stick, but about the bodies in the environment with which it comes into contact, or off which it is deflected. Once this information is inside the brain, at the point where vision proper begins, the light – like the stick – has done its job, and plays no further part in the proceedings by virtue of which the perceiver comes to 'see' the world spread out before him. At this point the eyes, that look but cannot see, hand over to the 'I', the Cartesian *cogito*, who sees but cannot look. Through the medium of light, my eyes can touch the world, and be touched by it; but *I* cannot. Yet I can see. Evidently, then, the superiority of vision over touch is not that of one sense over another, but that of cognition over sensation. This is why Descartes chose to explain sight by making an example of the blind man. It was his way of showing that light, in itself, is incidental to vision.

ON THE MEANING OF LIGHT

All this, however, still leaves us with a puzzle. If the power of sight lies in the cognitive operations of the mind rather than the physical work of the eyes, then why should Descartes have been so excited by the telescope, which surely augments the power of the eyes but does nothing to assist the mind? It is the soul which sees, says Descartes. But the telescope, which is not a computing device, does not help the soul to see! Were we to maintain, to the contrary, that the power of sight lies first and foremost in the work of the eyes and not the operations of the mind, then the telescope might indeed be of some assistance, yet by Descartes' own argument there would no longer be any reason to elevate the sense of sight over the contact sense of touch. If one could, with all equanimity, substitute sticks for light rays, then what is so special about eyesight? The ambivalence, in Descartes' account, between eye and mind as the primary locus of seeing, or in other words between vision as bodily *observation* and as mental *speculation* (Jay 1993a: 29), was never resolved, and remains with us to this day. Moreover it has become entangled in our thinking with another, equally puzzling dilemma, concerning the very significance of the word 'light'. Does it refer to rectilinear rays which, reflected off the surfaces of things, strike the eyes and thereby give rise to certain sensations? Or does its meaning lie in the subjective experience that we have in consequence of these sensations, of a luminosity within which things are given to consciousness as 'visible objects'? Does light, in short, shine in the world or in the mind?

For the philosophers of antiquity, this question did not arise, or not at least in this form. Their physics was one that placed the figure of sentient man at the centre of the cosmos, and each chapter of physics corresponded to a particular area of bodily sensation. One such chapter was optics. It was about how knowledge of the surrounding world could be obtained through the eye. Light, denoted by the term *lux*, was both the source of illumination and the medium in which this knowledge was supposed to be represented. As such it originated from the centre, with man, rather than from the cosmic periphery. But the Copernican revolution overthrew this anthropocentric cosmology. By the first half of the seventeenth century, when Descartes was writing, humankind had been relegated to the periphery of a universe that was supposed to run on principles entirely indifferent to human sensibilities. The task of physics was now to discover these principles. Among them are those whereby some physical impulse is propagated that, along with other effects, stimulates a reaction in the eyes. This impulse came to be known as *lumen*. Now when Descartes tells us that it is the soul that sees in the light of reason, rather than the eye in the light of the physical world, the light he is referring to is clearly the *lux* of the ancients – the light that shines in the mind.[12] But when to the contrary, as throughout the *Optics*, he speaks of light as reflected rays that excite the eye, he evidently intends to refer to the *lumen* of the physicists. The paradox of the *Optics* is that while vision 'goes indoors', from the world to the mind, light 'goes outdoors' from the mind to the world. And as Descartes showed, this external light – *lumen* – is the one thing we cannot see. The result is a curious disjunction between light and sight: the former on the outside, the latter on the inside, of an interface between mind and world. In short, sight begins where light ends.

Although more than three centuries have passed since Descartes was writing, we are still no clearer about the meaning of light. From contemporary physics we learn that light is a form of radiation that consists of waves or photons. This is to understand light in the sense of *lumen*. Yet most people, naturally enough, continue to equate light – as the thinkers of antiquity did – with the *lux* that illuminates the world of their perception. They are convinced, however, that this *lux* is the same as the physicists' *lumen*, and therefore that it has an external existence quite independent of their own eyes. Thus it is said that light travels from external objects to the eyes, and that we see because of it. And it is supposed that even if we close our eyes, the environment is still illuminated, as it was before. Yet we know that in fact, whatever reaches the eyes from outside (waves, photons) gets no further than the back of the retina. And the experience on which we report, of an illuminated world, is apparently possible thanks to what goes on beyond that point, in the optic nerves and the brain. So is there light only in consequence of the stimulation of the retinal surface? Does it exist only on the hither side of eyesight? And if so, how can we claim, at one and the same time, that light *reaches* the eyes from afar? Physics has colluded in this confusion, though in the reverse direction. For notwithstanding its redefinition from a physiology of the senses to an objective science of nature, it continues to describe as 'optics' that branch of study dealing with light and its propagation, even though in practice it has nothing whatever to do with the eye.

Vasco Ronchi, in the introduction to his *Optics* of 1957, illustrates these problems in the conception of light by drawing an intriguing parallel with sound. The equivalent of the distinction between *lumen* and *lux* is, in this case, that between mechanical vibration in the external medium and the sound we claim to hear when our ears are placed within its field of action. By rights, there should be no such thing as a physics of sound. For as there is no sound without an ear and a brain, the study of sound – that is, acoustics – could be undertaken only by combining the physics of vibratory motion with the physiology of the ear and the psychology of aural perception. Yet physicists, anxious to reserve acoustics for themselves, and not to get mixed up with subjective phenomena of mind and perception, persist in equating the vibrations that induce in the listener an experience of sound with the sound itself, thus perpetuating the error that 'sound is actually a physical, not a mental phenomenon' (Ronchi 1957: 17). And so everyone else is happy to go along with the illusion that sound actually travels through the air and is received as such by the listener, when in fact all that reach the ears are vibrations and there is no sound until these have been transformed into nerve impulses and carried to the mind-brain.

But if there is really no sound in the physical world beyond the brain, are we to conclude that this world is *silent*? And likewise, if there is really no *lux* in the external world, are we to conclude that the world 'out there' is *dark*? This is, indeed, the conclusion to which Ronchi moves. Our minds are filled with sound and light, even though neither vibrations nor rays reach there, while the vibrant and radiant world is actually silent and dark. Yet what can silence mean in a world without ears, or darkness in a world without eyes? Questions about the meaning of light, as of sound, are surely wrongly posed if they force us to choose between regarding light and sound as either physical or mental phenomena. They are wrongly posed because they continue to regard the organs of sense as gateways between an external, physical world and an internal world of mind.

Thus Ronchi, like Descartes before him, thinks of vision as a process that starts with a movement in the world which, via a propagation of waves or particles that happen to enter the eyes, causes impulses to travel along the optic nerves to the brain, and ends with these impulses being 'turned over to the mind' which – on the basis of a comparison with information already in its possession – 'creates a luminous and colored figure' (Ronchi 1957: 288). According to this view, a physiology of vision can tell us about what happens on the far side of the 'turn-over' point, and a psychology of vision can tell us what happens on the near side. Neither kind of account, however, can embrace the 'turning over' itself. How it is that nervous impulses are passed to the mind – or how they 'tickle' the soul, as Descartes rather quaintly put it (1988: 65) – remains a mystery.

It is my contention that there is no such interface between eye and mind. Far from starting with incident radiation and finishing up with a mental image, the process of vision consists in a never-ending, two-way process of engagement between the perceiver and his or her environment. This is what we mean when we speak of vision, colloquially, as 'looking' or 'watching'. And what Ronchi presents as a turn-over point is not that at all, but a critical nexus in this process. It is at this nexus, rather than on either the near or the far side of it, that the phenomenon we know as 'light' is generated. This phenomenon is not the objective, external *lumen*, nor is it the subjective, interior *lux*. It is rather a phenomenon of experience, of that very involvement in the world that is a necessary precondition for the isolation of the perceiver as a subject with a 'mind', and of the environment as a domain of objects to be perceived. Establishing this understanding of the process of vision and of the nature of light will be our next task.

THREE TWENTIETH-CENTURY THINKERS

In order to set out the groundwork for an alternative metaphysics of vision, I shall embark in what follows on a kind of theoretical triangulation. I do this by reviewing the ideas of three mid-twentieth-century thinkers, all of whom had important things to say about vision which were critical, in one way or another, of Descartes. The first, Hans Jonas, went out of his way to stress the differences between vision, hearing and touch as sensory modalities. For him, vision was indeed the superior sense, due not to its identification with reason, but to its peculiar phenomenal properties. The second, James Gibson, rejected the two-stage model of visual perception, and with it the classic Cartesian dualism of body and mind. Gibson argued that perception is an activity not of the mind, upon the deliverances of sense, but of the whole organism in its environmental setting. Vision is not, then, indirect, as Descartes maintained, but direct. The third, Maurice Merleau-Ponty, has perhaps gone further than any other recent thinker in recognising that vision is not just a matter of seeing things but is crucially an experience of light. Refusing to set up any absolute boundary, or line of demarcation, between the perceiver and the perceived, Merleau-Ponty held that light is tantamount to what we experience, in vision, as an opening up of the body onto the world.

Hans Jonas

The distinctiveness of sight, for Jonas, lies in three properties that are unique to this sensory modality: namely, simultaneity, neutralisation and distance (Jonas 1966: 136). The first refers to the ability to take in the world at a glance, so that a manifold that is present all at once can likewise be apprehended all at once. Neither hearing nor touch can achieve this. Reiterating a well-established view that we have already encountered, Jonas argues that whereas one can see things, one hears only sounds rather than the entities whose activity gives rise to them. Thus one hears the bark but not the dog, whose presence can only be inferred on the basis of non-acoustic information. And there is no sound that is not suspended in the current of time. The duration of the sound one hears is the same as that of one's hearing it; what is disclosed over time is also apprehended over time. True, distinct sounds may coexist or be juxtaposed, but each belongs to one of several 'strands' proceeding concurrently, and cannot be apprehended apart from the temporal flow. Arrest the flow and what you have is not a coherent snapshot, but a collection of atomic fragments. Touch shares with hearing this quality of temporality, at least so far as the perceiver is concerned. Yet unlike hearing, the data of touch can be synthesised to reveal the stable presence of objects. In this respect, touch comes closer to vision: thus, up to a point, the blind can achieve with their hands what the sighted achieve with their eyes. Nevertheless, the difference between touch and vision remains fundamental. The discovery of objects through touch necessitates an active exploration of the environment: this calls for movement and takes time. With vision you have only to open your eyes, and the world is there, already spread out as a ground for any further exploration of it. Only with vision, therefore, is it possible to distinguish being from becoming, and hence to entertain a concept of change. For hearing and touch, since they can know the world only through the movement of perceptual activity, there is neither change nor stasis, only becoming (Jonas 1966: 136–45).

The second property of sight, what Jonas calls neutralisation, lies in the disengagement between the perceiver and the seen. Touching something entails an action on your part, to which the object responds according to its nature. Hearing presupposes an action on the part of the object which generates the sound, to which you respond according to your sensibility. Thus while the balance of agency shifts from the subject (in touch) to the object (in hearing), there is in both an engagement between them, of a kind that is entirely absent from vision. The object need do nothing to be seen, since the source of the light by which it is revealed lies elsewhere. And to see the object one does not have to take up an attitude towards it. 'In seeing', Jonas writes, 'the percipient remains entirely free from causal involvement in the things to be perceived' (1966: 148). Thus vision is neutralising since it reveals the object simply for what it is. What is lost in terms of an intuitive understanding of the connectedness of things is gained in terms of objectivity. Rather than *affecting* the perceiver, as touch and hearing do, vision offers to the perceiver an *image* which, handed over to thought, can be manipulated at will, without further consequence for the object itself. But precisely because of their neutralisation, the objects of vision are in a sense 'mute', since in revealing their presence they do not speak to us or address human concerns (Jonas 1966: 145–9).

The third property of sight, spatial distance, is relatively self-evident. In an environment free from obstruction we can see a long way. Touch does not extend beyond the reach of the body, augmented perhaps by sticks or other such prostheses. Sound carries further, but has its limits, and is especially susceptible to distortion at the margins. Moreover when I hear a far-off sound, though I may be able to estimate the direction and distance of its source from where I now stand, I still have no idea – from the acoustic information alone – of what lies in between. It is peculiar to vision, by contrast, that it reveals not only distant objects, but also an encompassing landscape that stretches out from my present location to the horizon. I could, then, set out along a path that would take me to any one of these objects, with some foreknowledge of what to expect along the way (Jonas 1966: 149–52). Yet in an appendix, Jonas adds a crucial qualification to this argument. As he now admits, vision would never reveal the world in the way it does, arranged in depth and stretching away from us, were we not already used to moving through it, and in so doing, incorporating its features into structures of tactile awareness. Touch, in a word, confirms the materiality of the visible. Hence the motility of the body is a factor in the very constitution of vision and of the seen world. At first glance, this proposition seems at odds with the thesis of the simultaneity of visual perception: that the world can be taken in at a glance, from a fixed standpoint. Jonas's solution to the paradox is to argue that we are able to view the world as a spectacle, from a position of rest, precisely *because* we do so in the light of the 'accumulated experience of performed motion' (1966: 154) resulting from a history of previous activities. In short, the dynamics of bodily movement establish the essential foundation for the static experience of vision, but are not themselves part of that experience (Jonas 1966: 152–6).

James Gibson

With this last point, Gibson would have found himself in fundamental disagreement. Movement, in his view, is as integral to vision as it is to touch; moreover there is no need for the one sense to be *validated* by the other (Gibson 1966: 55). I shall not here attempt a full review of Gibson's ecological approach to visual perception, as others have done so elsewhere (Michaels and Carello 1981, Reed 1988b; see also Chapter Nine, pp. 166–8). However there are three aspects of this approach that I am particularly concerned to bring out here. First, I shall explain more precisely what Gibson meant by saying that visual as well as other modalities of perception are direct rather than indirect. Secondly, I show how Gibson's conception of the senses as perceptual systems, rather than as stimulus-specific registers of experience, renders the distinctions between vision, hearing and touch far less clearcut than we are inclined to think. Thirdly, I want to explore the specific argument by which Gibson denies that we ever see light as such. In this, I suggest, his ideas are still firmly rooted in the Cartesian tradition.

For Descartes, it will be recalled, the mind is unable to mingle with the world. Locked within the confines of a body, all it can do is to perform various calculative manoeuvres, on the basis of stimuli registered in the brain, in order to build up a more or less accurate representation of the world outside. This is what Descartes meant by describing perception – whether visual or tactile – as indirect. Gibson maintains, to the contrary, that perception is direct. By this he does not mean that it can somehow bypass the brain; any such suggestion would obviously be absurd. His point is rather that we should cease thinking of perception as the computational activity of a mind within a body, and regard it instead as the exploratory activity of the organism within its environment. As such, it does not yield images or representations. It rather guides the organism along in the furtherance of its project. The perceptually acute organism is one whose movements are closely tuned and ever responsive to environmental perturbations. For this reason, visual perception can never be disinterested or purely contemplative, as Jonas claimed. *What* we see is inseparable from *how* we see, and how we see is always a function of the practical activity in which we are currently engaged.

On the face of it Gibson would seem to agree with Descartes, that sight and touch are strictly comparable as modes of sensory contact with the environment. 'In many respects', he writes, 'the [haptic] system parallels vision' (1966: 134). Moreover we have seen that Gibson's view that perception of any kind depends on movement of the perceiver relative to the perceived also finds resonances in Descartes. Beneath the apparent convergence, however, their respective positions are diametrically opposed. For on the axis of contrast that Jonas draws between neutralisation and engagement, and which for him distinguishes sight from touch, the Cartesian perspective would join touch with sight on the side of neutralisation, whereas the Gibsonian perspective joins sight with touch on the side of engagement. Or to sum up:

	Touch	Sight
Descartes:	Neutralisation	Neutralisation
Jonas:	Engagement	Neutralisation
Gibson:	Engagement	Engagement

It would be wrong, Gibson argues, to think of the eyes, the ears or the sensitive surfaces of the skin simply as loci for banks of receptor cells that are, in turn, hooked up to centres of projection in the brain. Rather, they are to be understood as integral parts of a body that is continually on the move, actively exploring the environment in the practical pursuit of its life in the world. Sight, for instance, is not an effect of the stimulation of photo-receptors in the retina, coupled to processors in the visual cortex. It is rather an achievement of a system that also encompasses the neuromuscular linkages controlling the movement and orientation of the *organs* in which the receptors are located. These organs may be specified on a number of levels of increasing inclusivity: thus 'the eye is part of a dual organ, one of a pair of mobile eyes, and they are set in a head that can turn, attached to a body that can move from place to place'. Together these organs comprise what Gibson calls the *perceptual system* for vision (Gibson 1979: 53, cf. 1966). Much of this is shared with the system for hearing, and with that for touch. The head, for example, is common to vision and hearing: the action of turning the head so as to balance the auditory input from a sound source to the two ears, located on each side, also turns the eyes, at the front, so that they are oriented directly towards the source. As this example demonstrates, the perceptual systems not only overlap in their functions, but are also subsumed under a total system of bodily orientation (Gibson 1966: 4, 49–51; 1979: 245). Looking, listening and touching, therefore, are not separate activities, they are just different facets of the same activity: that of the whole organism in its environment.

Hence the idea, proposed by Jonas, that having made a thorough exploration of the world through movement, relying on the sense of touch, one could then stop still and take it in at a glance through the eyes, would have made no sense to Gibson. This is for two reasons: first, that we explore the world with our eyes open (and even when we stop we look about); and secondly, that vision does not yield a snapshot, or even a series of snapshots. It rather yields an appreciation of objects 'in the round'. We do not see an object, any more than we feel it, from a single point of view. Rather, by 'running our eyes over it' – as we might run our fingers over it in tactile perception – we discover its form as the envelope of a movement, that is of the continuous modulation of the array of reflected light reaching the eyes. Indeed it is because vision, like touch, takes place over time along what Gibson calls a 'path of observation' (1979: 197), that we can see aspects of objects which, at any particular moment, may be hidden by occluding edges. And since the information yielded by the operation of perceptual systems is specific to the things encountered, rather than to the particular sensory keyboard that is activated, a switch in the balance of stimulation – say from the tactile to the visual – may make little appre-ciable difference to what is actually perceived. Of course the *sensations* of vision are not the same as those of touch and hearing. But the 'patterns in the flux of sound, touch, and light from the environment', which specify the objects of one's attention, may be strictly equivalent (Gibson 1966: 54–5; 1979: 243).

This argument carries an important corollary. For if what we see is delineated by the patterning or modulation of reflected light as it is picked up by the moving organs of sight, then the one thing we never actually see must be light itself. To the question, 'Of all the possible things that can be seen, is light one of them?', Gibson answers categori-cally in the negative (1979: 54). Rather, he says, we see *things* by means of light. In view of Gibson's resolutely anti-Cartesian stance, this conclusion – which is fully in accord with Descartes' views on the matter – comes as something of a surprise. Indeed he admits to being vexed by the question of how certain phenomena seem to announce their pres-ence directly, as radiant light, rather than by way of the illumination of their surfaces (1966: 220). Is this not how we come to perceive a flaming fire, a candle lamp, the sun and moon, a shaft of sunlight through the clouds, a rainbow, the glare of the sun reflected from a glossy surface, or the scintillations of light off water? Intuitively, it seems that in every one of these cases light is just what we *do* see. Yet for each, Gibson has his answer: the fire and the lamp are 'specific objects and are so specified', as are the celestial bodies. We do not really see shafts of sunlight, but only illuminated particles in the air. Dazzled by the sun, what we actually perceive is a 'fact about the body', namely its excessive optical stimulation, experienced as a kind of pain. As for rainbows, scintillations and the like, these 'are all manifestations of light, not light as such' (1979: 55).

But as the examples mount up, Gibson's defence becomes less and less plausible. In what sense can we possibly regard a flame as an object? Ignoring the knowledge of science and schoolbooks, how are the sun and moon specified?[13] When it comes to beams of sunlight, common sense tells us that we see the light by way of airborne particles, and not vice versa. If excessive optical stimulation causes pain, does this make it any less an experience of light? What if the glare were less intense, and caused no appreciable discomfort: would we, then, cease to be aware of it? Finally, it is difficult to see how 'manifestations of light' can possibly be distinguished from 'light as such' without resorting to a highly reductive notion of what light actually is. Indeed this is precisely what Gibson does. 'All we ever see', he insists, 'is the environment or facts about the environment, never *photons or radiant energy*' (1979: 55, my emphasis). Gibson's 'light', in short, is the *lumen* of modern physics.[14] At no point does he ever think of it as anything other than a kind of energetic impulse, a source of stimulation that, if it exceeds a certain threshold, causes photoreceptor cells to 'fire'. The resulting sensations, he insists, do not in themselves constitute the basis for visual perception. No amount of light will cause us to see, unless that light is structured on account of its reflection from illuminated surfaces in the environment. Thus light carries the information for perception, but is never perceived *as such*.

Maurice Merleau-Ponty

It is here, above all, that Gibson's ecological psychology parts company with the phenomenology of Merleau-Ponty. Though they speak very different intellectual languages, there is much in common between what Gibson and Merleau-Ponty have to say. For both, the senses exist not as distinct registers whose separate impressions are combined only at higher levels of cognitive processing, but as aspects of functioning of the whole body in movement, brought together in the very action of its involvement in an environment. Any one sense, in 'homing in' on a particular topic of attention, brings with it the concordant operations of all the others. In his *Phenomenology of Perception*, Merleau-Ponty compares this integration of the senses in action to the collaboration of the eyes in binocular vision (1962: 230–3). Just as the unity of the object of vision is not the result of some 'third person process' which produces a single image out of two monocular images, but is rather given in the way the two eyes 'are used as a single organ by one single gaze', so the unity of a thing as an 'inter-sensory entity' lies not in the mental fusion of images founded on different registers of sensation, but in the bodily synergy of the senses in their convergent striving towards a common goal. Thus 'my gaze, my touch and all my other senses are together the powers of one and the same body integrated into one and the same action' (1962: 317–18). In short, for Merleau-Ponty as for Gibson, it is in their collaborative bearing on features of the world, rather than their common accountability to processing centres in the mind, that the senses are conjoined.

Like Gibson, too, Merleau-Ponty regards touch and vision as comparable modes of sensory engagement with the environment. This is not to say they are equivalent, since each brings with it 'a structure of being that can never be exactly transposed' (1962: 225). That is why formerly blind persons, whose sight has been restored, initially find their predicament so bewildering: tactile experience turns out to be a poor guide to the visual world, not because it is relatively impoverished but because the tactile world is differently *structured* (1962: 222–4). Nevertheless, Merleau-Ponty surmises that the visual gaze functions as a 'natural instrument' of perception in much the same way as does the blind man's stick (1962: 153). The analogy, of course, is drawn from Descartes. Yet in his celebrated essay on 'Eye and mind', Merleau-Ponty takes it as the starting point for an all-out attack on the whole Cartesian programme (Merleau-Ponty 1964a: 169–78). His objection, however, is not to the comparison of the visual gaze to the tactile probe, but to the idea that both are harnessed to the project of constructing internal representations of an external reality. The truth, he maintains, is quite otherwise. For like the stick, the gaze is caught up in a dialogic, exploratory encounter between the perceiver and the world, in which every movement on the part of the perceiver is a questioning, and every reaction on the part of the perceived is a response. Thus 'the gaze gets more or less from things according to the way it questions them, ranges over or dwells on them' (1962: 153).

Both Gibson and Merleau-Ponty are adamant in their rejection of the Cartesian idea of vision, in Merleau-Ponty's words, 'as an operation of thought that would set up before the mind a picture or a representation of the world' (1964a: 162). Indeed the perceiver, they would say, has no need for such a picture in order to act in a way that is attuned to the features of his or her surroundings. Since my body inhabits the world, and since – to all intents and purposes – I and my body are one and the same (Merleau-Ponty 1962: 206), it follows that I, too, am an inhabitant of the world rather than of a space inside my head. And for the same reason, I can always consult the world to orient my movements, rather than an internal cognitive representation. Like Gibson, Merleau-Ponty stressed that while there cannot be vision without movement, this movement must also be visually guided: it must 'have its antennae, its clairvoyance' (1964a: 162). But whereas Gibson asked how it is possible for the perceiver to see objects in the environment, Merleau-Ponty went one step further back. For how could there be an environment full of objects, he asked, except for a being that is already immersed in the lifeworld, in 'the soil of the sensible' (1964a: 160), and therefore caught up in a visual field that is pre-objectively given? Such involvement must be ontologically prior to the objectification of the environment that Gibson takes as his point of departure. In short, before 'I see *things*' must come 'I can *see*'. So what does it mean, to see?

Merleau-Ponty's essay 'Eye and mind', his last published work, is an attempt to answer this question. The arguments of the essay are not easy to follow, but one can get the gist of them by performing a simple experiment. Close your eyes for a while, and then open them again. Do you have the impression that you are staring out upon the world through a hole (or perhaps two holes) in the front of your head? Is it as though you were looking through the windows of your unlit house, having opened the shutters?[15] Far from it. Rather, it seems that you are out there yourself, shamelessly mingling with all you see, and flitting around like an agile spirit from one place to another as the focus of your attention shifts. It is as if the walls and ceiling of your house had simply vanished, leaving you out in the open. In short, you experience seeing not as seeing *out*, but as *being* out – until, that is, you close your eyes again, at which point the spirit is instantly captured and put back inside, imprisoned in the dark and eery confines of a shuttered enclosure, your head. For Descartes the light of the mind (*lux*) was in this darkness, which is why he thought the blind could see. But experience teaches us differently. It is, as Merleau-

Ponty writes, that through vision 'we come into contact with the sun and the stars, that we are everywhere all at once'. Or again, vision 'is the means given me for being absent from myself' (1964a: 186–7). We now have a clue to what Merleau-Ponty meant by his repeated insistence on the indistinguishability of the seeing and the seen, or the 'sensor and the sensible' (cf. 1962: 214). This is primordially evident in the case of my body, which both sees and is seen, but equally true of the whole 'fabric of the world' in which it is caught up. And we can understand what he means by the assertion that vision is not *of* things but happens *among* them. For it is constitutive of the whole perceptual field, drawn around myself at its centre, which both they and I inhabit.

All this is a far cry from the picture that Jonas paints of the immobile and detached spectator, contemplating a world with which he has no causal involvement whatever. Returning to an opposition that I have already introduced in the context of my initial discussion of the anthropology of the senses, Merleau-Ponty replaces the image of the spectator with that of the *seer*. 'Immersed in the visible by his body', he writes, 'the seer does not appropriate what he sees; he merely approaches it by looking, he opens himself to the world' (1964a: 162). Raise your eyelids, and you find yourself, almost literally, 'in the open'. Indeed, this little phrase perfectly captures what Merleau-Ponty portrays as the magic – or delirium (1964a: 166) – of vision. We live in visual space from the inside, we inhabit it, yet that space is already outside, open to the horizon. Thus the boundary between inside and outside, or between self and world, is dissolved. The space of vision both surrounds us and passes through us (1964a: 178). Elsewhere, Merleau-Ponty imagines himself gazing up at the blue sky:

> As I contemplate the blue of the sky I am not *set over against* it as an acosmic subject; I do not possess it in thought, or spread out towards it some idea of blue such as might reveal the secret of it ... I am the sky itself as it is drawn together and unified, and as it begins to exist for itself; my consciousness is saturated with this limitless blue.
>
> (1962: 214, original emphases)

Compare this with Gibson, who answers his own question of how one might visually perceive 'a luminous *field*, such as the sky?', with the response: 'To me it seems that I see the sky, not luminosity as such' (1979: 54).

The sky presents a problem for Gibson precisely because he is unable to countenance the environment in any other way than as a world of objects 'set over against' the perceiver, and revealed through the patterns of ambient light reflected from its opaque, outer surfaces. Yet the sky has no surface. It is not a thing, like a building or a tree, off which light rebounds. On the contrary, the sky is openness or transparency itself, sheer luminosity, against which things stand out by virtue of their opacity or closure. To suppose, as Gibson does, that one sees the sky as distinct from its luminosity is like pretending that one hears thunder rather than its sound, or feels the wind rather than a current of air. What is thunder if not sound, or the wind if not airflow? On hearing thunder, or feeling the wind, it is as though one's very being mingles with the surrounding medium and resonates with its vibrations. Likewise, sunlight and moonlight present themselves to vision, in Merleau-Ponty's words, as 'kinds of symbiosis, certain ways the outside has of invading us and certain ways we have of meeting this invasion' (1962: 317). This is not to reduce light to radiant energy or photons, as in a physicalist description; nor is it to conclude, on the other extreme, that light shines only in the mind while the world might as well be pitch dark. It is to recognise that for persons who can see, light is the *experience* of inhabiting the world of the visible, and that its qualities – of brilliance and shade, tint and colour, and saturation – are variations upon this experience.[16]

Perhaps Gibson was right, after all, to say that we do not see light 'as such', since light is not an object. It rather constitutes, for the sighted, the pre-objective foundation of existence, that commingling of the subject with the world without which there could not be visible things, or 'facts about the environment', at all. Light, in short, is the ground of being out of which things coalesce – or from which they stand forth – as objects of attention. Thus as Merleau-Ponty writes (1964a: 178), we do not so much see light as see *in* it. And for all who can see in it, the experience of light is perfectly real. Indeed we have no more reason to doubt the reality of light than we have to question the experience of blindness for those who *cannot* see in it. Yet we are all too ready to take it for granted: it is the very familiarity of our experience, of that openness to the world sensed as light, that causes it to hide from us. So busily preoccupied are we with all the things that vision reveals to us that we forget the foundational experience upon which it rests. The process of seeing in light is swallowed up by its products, objects of sight. And by the same token, the joy and astonishment of the discovery that 'I can *see*' gives way to the mundane indifference of 'I see *things*'. The message of Merleau-Ponty is that we need to reverse this perspective, to recover the sense of vision that is original to our experience of the world, and that is a precondition for its objectification.[17]

This, finally, is what motivates the work of the painter. A painting, for Merleau-Ponty, is not just another object of vision. You do not look at it, nor do you see it, as you would any ordinary thing. Rather, you 'see according to it, or with it' (1964a: 164). Like all sighted people, painters see in light, and it is the inspiration for their work. They cannot afford to dismiss their experience as an illusion, and nor can we, unless we wish to write off the history of painting as an aberration caused by the overstimulation of excessively susceptible minds (1964a: 186–7). However the painter's vision, Merleau-Ponty insists, 'is not a view from the *outside*, a merely "physical-optical" relation with the world'. It is rather a 'continued birth', as though at every moment the painter opened his eyes to the world, like a new-born infant, for the first time. The birth of his vision is, at one and the same time, the 'concentration or coming-to-itself of the visible'. And so the painting to which it gives rise is an embodiment of this creative movement: it does not *represent* things, or a world, but shows 'how things become things, how the world becomes a world' (1964a: 167–8, 181).[18] Thus to see with, or according to, a painting is to question the ordinariness of our everyday perception of objects, to rekindle in us the astonishment of vision, and to remind us that there are things in the world to be seen only because we first can see.

In the course of this review of the ideas of our three thinkers – Jonas, Gibson and Merleau-Ponty – we have progressed from a notion of vision as a mode of *speculation*, to one of vision as a mode of *participation*, and finally to one of vision as a mode of *being*. For Jonas the visual world is presented to the disinterested observer as a scene or spectacle; for Gibson it becomes an environment that surrounds the engaged participant but whose preformed surfaces nevertheless remain closed and impenetrable to the eye. For Merleau-Ponty the visual world is given to subjective experience as a cosmos that is open and transparent, that one can see into rather than merely look at, and that continually comes into existence around the perceiver. As we have already seen, recent debates in both anthropology and philosophy concerning the role of the senses in human societies have tended to assume that vision is inherently speculative, and have paid little heed to the possibility of alternative modalities. When it comes to touch and especially sound, however, a quite different view prevails, and this has led to the positing of a great sensory divide between visual perception on the one hand, and auditory and tactile perception on the other, and with it, between Western societies in which the former allegedly dominates, and non-Western societies which are said to be given over to the latter. My aim, now, is to replace the orthodox, speculative notion of vision with a participatory or existential one. Once this is done, the 'great divide' simply vanishes.

THE HEARING EYE AND THE SEEING EAR

After that long excursion into theories of vision, our immediate priority must be to return to sound and hearing. Earlier on, I cited a passage from the work of the musicologist Zuckerkandl, *Sound and Symbol* (1956), in which he contrasts the properties of sight and hearing by way of a rather gross characterisation of the attitudes of deaf and blind people. I shall consider what such people have to say about their own sensory experience in the following section. For the moment, however, I intend to look rather more closely at Zuckerkandl's study, for two reasons. First, I want to bring out the close parallels between the way Zuckerkandl speaks of the musical experience of sound, and the way Merleau-Ponty speaks of the painterly experience of light. These experiences, it turns out, are virtually identical. Secondly, although Zuckerkandl maintains that vision and hearing are generally opposed, he admits that this is not universally so, and towards the end of his study he speculates that this opposition may not have been given from the start, either in the development of the individual or in the evolution of human culture. If he is right in supposing that vision split off from hearing in the course of an evolution towards modern Western civilisation, then it is clearly inadmissible to retroject the resulting distinction between these sensory modalities onto humanity at large.

For the most part, Zuckerkandl is quite categorical about the difference between the way in which the world is perceived through the eye and through the ear. The eye reinforces a barrier separating two domains: the inner domain of the mind or consciousness, and the outer domain of the world. It keeps things at a distance. They stay 'out there', fixed in their proper places in an overall spatial array that can be mapped out in terms of intervals and boundaries. The space of vision is one from which you, the viewer, are excluded, a space where things are but you are not. Thus the visual experience of space is essentially disjunctive. The domains of 'inner' and 'outer', as Zuckerkandl writes, 'face each other like two mutually exclusive precincts on either side of an impassable dividing line'. But in hearing, the distinction between 'precincts' is transformed into one between 'directions'. In the inward direction, the world penetrates consciousness; in the reverse, outward direction, consciousness penetrates the world (1956: 368–9). In place of the barrier that the eye throws up around the perceiving subject, the ear builds a bridge which allows a two-way flow of sensory traffic. When you see things that are far away, they are perceived to be *at* a distance, but when you hear far-off sounds they seem to be *coming from* a distance (p. 291). The space of hearing, then, is not set over against you, the listener, but streams towards you and into you. It is a space not of places but of flows, where nothing can be divided and nothing measured. Your auditory experience is essentially participatory, one of immersion in a 'boundless indivisible oneness' (p. 336). And so the quality 'out there', that we experience in vision, is replaced by the quality 'from-out-there-toward-me-and-through-me'. Or in other words, the step from visual to auditory perception is 'like a transition from a static to a fluid medium' (p. 277).

What I find so remarkable about Zuckerkandl's account of hearing is that it matches point by point, almost down to the details of the rhetoric, what Merleau-Ponty has to say about vision. We have only to recall Merleau-Ponty's conception of visual space as both 'surrounding' and 'passing through' the perceiver, of consciousness as 'saturated' with luminosity, of the seer as 'immersed' in the visible, of the outside 'invading' us and of our 'meeting this invasion' (1962: 214, 317; 1964a: 162, 178). Echoing Zuckerkandl's notion of inward and outward currents, Merleau-Ponty speaks of an 'inspiration and expiration of Being, action and passion so slightly discernible that it becomes impossible to distinguish between what sees and what is seen' (1964a: 167). Revealing, too, is the fact that in order to convey the sense of what he means by vision, Merleau-Ponty has occasional recourse to auditory metaphor – the precise reverse of the use of visual metaphor to describe auditory experience that we have already encountered in the Saussurian notion of the sound-image. 'Quality, light, colour, depth', he writes, 'are there only because they awaken an echo in our body and because the body welcomes them' (1964a: 164). If for Saussure it sometimes seems as though the sounds of speech were seen and not heard, for Merleau-Ponty it can seem as though we listen with the eyes. In other words, though our experience may be one of seeing in light, it is nevertheless an experience that has all the qualities of hearing.

This thought had also occurred to Zuckerkandl. It arises in the context of a discussion of the pros and cons of either playing or listening to music with the eyes closed. According to one view, the eye is so closely implicated in a particular apprehension of space, occupied by 'corporeal things in their places', that it actively inhibits our involvement in the fluid space of forces that music opens up to us. It holds us back, and makes us unwilling to entrust ourselves with the whole of our being to sound. But Zuckerkandl is not fully convinced. Is it really necessary, he asks, to blind ourselves temporarily in order properly to hear? Is vision capable only of seeing things in their places? 'Can the eye perhaps hear too?' (1956: 341). Zuckerkandl believes that it can, albeit exceptionally, and that there are indeed 'activities of the eye that go beyond the function of seeing a thing in a place – and go beyond it in a particular direction, *which it seems natural to compare with the mode of perception of the ear*' (p. 344, my emphases). To exemplify the point Zuckerkandl imagines himself, just as had Merleau-Ponty before him, gazing into the blue sky. What he sees is not a 'thing out there' but 'boundless space, in which I lose myself'. But whereas Merleau-Ponty uses this example to illustrate the coalescence of the perceiver and the world which he takes to be fundamental to apprehending the space of vision, Zuckerkandl uses it to clarify his conception of auditory space! For him, the experience one has, looking up at the sky, is precisely what it means to hear.

It seems, then, that the kind of opening up to the world that Merleau-Ponty calls seeing is more or less identical to that which Zuckerkandl calls hearing. In Zuckerkandl's book, everything that Merleau-Ponty has to say about painterly vision would fall under the rubric of 'hearing with the eyes'. Indeed it is above all in the realm of painting, he thinks, that we find a perception of forces and dynamic relations strictly akin to the hearing of tones in music. The space of the picture, along with the things represented therein, 'is not simply set off from the observer; rather it opens itself to him, takes him into itself, passes into him' (Zuckerkandl 1956: 345). But reversing the perspective, all of what Zuckerkandl says about hearing could be regarded, from Merleau-Ponty's angle, as 'seeing with the ears'. This expectation is confirmed in the *Phenomenology of Perception*, where Merleau-Ponty devotes special attention to 'the sight of sounds'. Thus 'when I say that I see a sound, I mean that I echo the vibration of the sound with my whole sensory being' (1962: 234). This equivalence of seeing and hearing, however, raises an intriguing question. When we hear with the eyes, or conversely when we see with the ears, is the experience one of light or sound?

Before we can answer this question, we have first to recognise that sound is no more a physical impulse that arrives from outside than it is a purely mental, 'inside the head' phenomenon. Indeed everything we have said about light applies to sound also. Like light, sound exists neither on the inner nor on the outer side of an interface between mind and world. It is rather generated as the experiential quality of an ongoing engagement between the perceiver and his or her environment. Sound is the underside of hearing just as light is the underside of vision; we hear in one as we see in the other. Now it would be foolish to suggest that gazing up at the sky yields anything other than an experience of light. Yet as seeing is tantamount, in this case, to hearing, it would be equally foolish to deny that it could also, and at the same time, be experienced as sound. Poets, as Zuckerkandl points out, have never had any difficulty with the idea (1956: 341). A particularly eloquent example of the sight of sound, or hearing with the eye, is offered by the poet David Wright, who speaks of how he 'hears' things, or rather movements, which most of us take to be silent:

> I take it that the flight of most birds, at least at a distance, must be silent ... Yet it *appears* audible, each species creating a different 'eye-music', from the nonchalant melancholy of seagulls to the staccato flitting of birds.
>
> (Wright 1990: 12)

The particular poignancy of this example derives from the fact that Wright is himself deaf. He cannot therefore hear with the ears, as other people do. But for precisely that reason, his visual experience has an auditory dimension that is missing for most people with normal hearing, placed in similar situations.

Much has been made of the phenomenon of synaesthesia, the apparent capacity of certain perceivers to register an experience in one sensory modality on the basis of sensations delivered in another. The synaesthetic may, for example, claim to see certain forms or colours on hearing a musical melody, or to hear particular sounds on watching a silent movement. Wright's report of hearing the flight of distant birds might well be taken as an instance of the latter. Yet built into the very definition of synaesthesia is a two-fold distinction between sensation and perception on the one hand, and between discrete sensory modalities on the other. Following both Gibson and Merleau-Ponty, I have suggested that the eyes and ears should not be understood as separate keyboards for the registration of sensation but as organs of the body as a whole, in whose movement, within an environment, the activity of perception consists. 'My body', as Merleau-Ponty puts it, 'is not a collection of adjacent organs but a synergic system, all the functions of which are exercised and linked together in the general action of being in the world' (1962: 234). Sight and hearing, to the extent that they can be distinguished at all, are but facets of this action, and the quality of the experience, whether cast in light or sound, is intrinsic to the bodily movement entailed, rather than possessed 'after the fact' by the mind. So if I hear the flight of birds it is because, following their course across the sky, the movement of my own body – of my eyes, of my hand, indeed of my entire posture – resonates with theirs. From this point of view, the 'problem' of synaesthesia simply vanishes.

For Zuckerkandl, too, when Dante speaks of Hell as 'a place dumb of all light', or when Goethe declares that light 'trumpets', they are referring not to synaesthesia but to 'a real perception through the eyes, but which nevertheless has the characteristics of hearing' (1956: 341). Under all normal circumstances, Zuckerkandl maintains, this kind of perception is overshadowed by the ordinary sight of things, and re-emerges only during rare moments of ecstasy when the boundary between the perceiver and the world appears to dissolve. But for the new-born baby, opening its eyes upon the world for the first time, or the previously blind person to whom sight has been restored through a medical procedure, the experience must be overwhelming. As William James wrote, with acknowledgement to Condillac, 'The first time we see *light* . . . we *are* it rather than see it' (James 1892: 14). Light – or 'I can see', which is another way of saying the same thing – is in this situation quintessentially an experience of being. Ihde notes that the first impressions of a blind person, on gaining sight, are often reported to be akin to those of listening: the patient 'is impressed by what we might call the *flux* and *flow*' (Ihde 1976: 63).[19] For the baby, of course, there are not yet *things* to be seen, for the separation of the self from the world, and the consequent process of objectification, have hardly begun. But long before it first opens its eyes, the baby can already hear quite well. For every new-born, as Schafer says (1985: 96), hearing precedes vision. Thus while Berger (1972: 7) may be right to say that in the life of the child, 'seeing comes before words', it is still the case that the infant hears the sounds of speech, and above all its mother's voice, long before it can see. It is therefore entirely understandable that the earliest visual perception should be experienced as a hearing with the eyes.

The conclusion to be drawn from this, as Zuckerkandl recognises, is that the 'normal' function of the eye – 'the perception of things in places' – is not given from the start but is the result of a development in the field of vision, 'whose earlier stages are not so sharply differentiated from hearing as later ones' (1956: 342). From this conclusion, Zuckerkandl launches into an argument which, by his own admission, is entirely speculative, but which is nevertheless of profound significance for the anthropology of the senses. If vision gradually diverges from hearing in the life-history of the individual, could this not also occur, along the same lines and through similar stages, in the evolution of culture? Could the congruence of sight and hearing, so quickly overtaken in individual development, have once characterised an entire epoch? And could it persist, perhaps, in the 'magical abilities of . . . primitives, . . . based upon a direct seeing of space as force, a dynamic communication between within and without'? If so, then 'we should have in music the miraculous echo of a world that once lay open to sight' – a world that otherwise survives only in the visual arts, especially painting (1956: 343–5). While the ontogenetic and evolutionary assumptions built into this argument, and especially the identification of 'primitive' perception with that of children, may no longer be acceptable today, Zuckerkandl's remarks nevertheless suggest something very important, namely, that the distinction between vision and hearing, as generally understood in the Western tradition, is not natural or universal to humanity but the outcome of a specific historical development. In comparisons between Western and non-Western societies, therefore, the distinction cannot form part of the explanation for differences in sensory experience, but is part of what has to be explained.

THE SENSORY EXPERIENCE OF BLIND AND DEAF PEOPLE

It is now time to return to the two thought experiments with which I began. To recall, in the first you listen blindfold to the sound of an oncoming train; in the second you watch it pass with your ears plugged. In the one case, you suppose, the sound gets inside you and shakes you up; in the other it is as though the train glided by in a world apart from the one you inhabit. Now these experiments do indeed tell us much about the ways we imagine vision and hearing to work. But they turn out to be a poor guide to what is actually going on, at least in the case of people whose eyes and ears are functioning normally. Seeing with the ears stopped is qualitatively different from seeing without, for the simple reason that a good deal of the information controlling the movements of the *organs* of sight, including the eyes, head and whole body, is picked up by hearing. Without that information, vision is disoriented, which is precisely why, in the second experiment, your visual attention seemed so detached from the train's movement. Conversely, hearing blindfold is qualitatively different from hearing with one's eyes open, for although the ears (unlike the eyes) are immobile relative to the head, hearing is affected by head and body movements which are partially guided by information picked up by the operations of sight. Again, it is the lack of such information, and the ensuing loss of auditory control, that accounts for the violence with which the sound of the unseen train seems to assault your senses.

If our experiments mislead us when it comes to normal vision and hearing, could they nevertheless tell us something about the experience of people who are deaf or blind? Is the deaf person, of necessity, an impassive observer of things in a world from which he or she feels somewhat alienated? And are the blind, conversely, participants in a world in which all is movement and becoming, yet inevitably at the mercy of its currents? Such views are commonly encountered; I have already cited, as an example, a passage to this effect from Zuckerkandl. They are not, however, supported by the testimony of blind and deaf people themselves. These people do not feel that their experience of the world is any less complete, or has any less integrity, than that of anyone else. In this respect it is quite unlike the experience of normally sighted and hearing persons, on finding themselves suddenly but temporarily blinded or deafened. Is it the case, then, that those for whom blindness or deafness is a permanent condition compensate for the lack of one sense by augmenting the powers of those remaining? Once again, the answer appears to be 'no'. Indeed David Wright, speaking as one who is profoundly deaf, argues that the theory of compensation is a mistake, and an irritating one at that (Wright 1990: 12, 111). It is in error for two reasons: first, aural perception actually deteriorates when it is not oriented by vision, and vice versa; and secondly, the theory mistakes a heightened sensitivity to specific movements – aural or gestural – which are critical for the interpretation of what is going on for a general enhancement of the sense as a whole. Blind and deaf people, like everyone else, sense the world with their whole body, and like everyone else, too, they have to cope with the resources available to them. But their resources are more limited, and for this there is absolutely no compensation. The life of the blind person, as John Hull puts it, 'is experienced as being intact, although the scope of activity has in many ways become smaller'. It is not like a round cake from which a substantial slice has been cut out. It is more like a smaller cake (Hull 1997: xii).

Granted that the experience of the blind or deaf person is not any particular segment, or 'cut', of the total experience of the visually and aurally unimpaired, but is a totality of a very different kind, I believe (with Ihde 1976: 44) that we can still learn a great deal about how visual and auditory perception work – even for people with normal sight and hearing – from a comparison of these different experiences. The comparison is of course complicated by the fact that there are individual variations in degrees of blindness and deafness. In what follows I shall assume the total non-functioning of eyes and ears respectively. I begin with blindness, drawing on the superb and extremely moving account by John Hull of his own experience of going blind, and of adjusting to this condition, as an adult. The account is revealing in two ways. First, it highlights features of visual perception that we normally rely on but tend to take for granted, by bringing out the problems that ensue from their absence. Secondly, it reveals unexpected properties of aural perception that are critical for the blind, but which may be equally at work among sighted people although not recognised for what they are. Apropos the first, I shall focus on eye-to-eye contact; apropos the second, I shall consider the phenomenon of echolocation. As a prelude to both, however, a few general remarks are in order about how blind and sighted people, respectively, perceive the space around them.

Being blind

There is much in Hull's account that corroborates the ideas of Hans Jonas, reviewed in an earlier section. The perception of the blind person, dependent as it is on touch and hearing, is fundamentally suspended in the current of time. Visual space is presented to the sighted all at once, but tactile space has to be assembled by the blind, bit by bit, through a repetitive and time-consuming exploration with the fingers. Thus the blind person may take days 'to discover what the sighted person will grasp in a split second' (Hull 1997: 183). Acoustic space is similarly temporal. Unlike the objects of touch, however, which can always be touched again, the manifold inhabitants of acoustic space have an ephemeral nature, passing in and out of existence along with the sounds they make. This is not a world of being – 'the silent, still world where things simply are' – but a world of becoming where there is only action, and where every sound marks a locus of action (pp. 72–3). In this world, 'sounds come and go in a way that sights do not' (pp. 145–6). So do the agents, especially people, who make the sounds. As a sighted person, I can see when someone else is in the room before he or she begins to speak or approaches to shake my hand. But for the blind person, the voice or handshake comes from nowhere. One has the feeling of being grasped or accosted, unable either to resist or to choose one's assailant (p. 87). Other people, with their voices and tactile gestures, appear suddenly and disappear equally abruptly. 'The intermittent nature of the acoustic world', Hull writes, 'is one of its most striking features' (p. 73). The seen world can never escape one's eyes, it is always there, and one can return to it again and again. But the world of sound escapes as fast as it comes into being. And the sound that has passed can never be recovered (p. 145).

Can the blind person, then, ever enjoy an experience comparable to that of the sighted, of being placed in something like a landscape that can be taken in as a totality, with its infinitely variegated surfaces, contours and textures, inhabited by animals and plants, and littered with objects both natural and artificial? There is one circumstance in which this is possible, in Hull's experience, namely when it is *raining*. For the sounds of raindrops, which are perceived to come not from any particular point but from all quarters at once, reveal in every detail the surfaces on which they fall. 'Rain', Hull writes, 'has a way of bringing out the contours of everything; it throws a coloured blanket over previously invisible things; instead of an intermittent and thus fragmented world, the steadily falling rain creates continuity of acoustic experience . . . This is an experience of great beauty' (1997: 26–7). There is indeed a certain parallel between the ecstasy of hearing that Hull describes and what, for the sighted, I have described as the astonishment of vision, when the world is revealed to the seer as though the fog in which it had been enveloped were lifted, and he or she were gazing upon on it for the first time. Rain does for the blind what sunshine does for the sighted, bathing the world in sound as the sun bathes it in light. Immersed in the audible, to borrow and adapt Merleau-Ponty's words, the listener opens himself to the world: 'My body and the rain intermingle, and become one audio-tactile, three-dimensional universe, within which and throughout the whole of which lies my awareness' (Hull 1997: 120).

Now in my earlier discussion of the maxim 'vision objectifies, sound personifies', I noted that it is closely bound in the Western tradition with a certain construction of the person, according to which an inner essence, identified with the voice, is supposed to hide behind – but nevertheless to sound through – an outer mask identified with the face. The voice can be heard, the face seen – unless, that is, one is in the company of another who happens to be blind. Yet the view is commonly expressed that for the blind their inability to see the faces of others can be a positive advantage. For they are not, like the rest of us, susceptible to outward impressions. Thus did David Hume, in the eighteenth century, address a blind acquaintance, the Edinburgh poet Thomas Blacklock: 'Your passion ... will always be better founded than ours, who have sight: we are so foolish as to allow ourselves to be captivated by exterior beauty: nothing but beauty of the mind can affect you' (cited in Rée 1999: 40). In our present times the blind French writer Jacques Lusseyran takes the same view: the blind inhabit a world 'free of the deception of physical appearances, where what and how something is said reveals its true purpose' (cited in Hill 1985: 109). But in Hull's experience matters are not that simple. For him the face is not a mask but is as intimately bound up with the life and identity of the self as is the voice. And of all the components of the face, the most revealing, and the topic of our greatest attention and fascination, are the eyes.

If there is a critical difference between face and voice, it is not so much that one is seen and the other heard, than that you can hear your own voice whereas you cannot see your own face. 'I live in the facial expressions of the other', writes Merleau-Ponty, 'as I feel him living in mine' (1964b: 146). From this stems what John Berger calls 'the reciprocal nature of vision' – a reciprocity that is even more fundamental, in Berger's view, than that of spoken dialogue. For in eye-to-eye contact, he writes, 'the eye of the other combines with our own eye to make it credible that we are part of the visible world' (Berger 1972: 9).[20] Thus your visibility, your identity, indeed your very existence as a person, is confirmed in the sight of others. In normal circumstances, to see another person is to know you can be seen by them; to see a place is to know that you could, in principle, be seen by someone standing there. But when the other person is blind the reciprocity of vision breaks down. Suppose that I am sighted and you are blind: while I can see your face, I am also aware that you are not looking at me. It seems that I am not there for you. But not being able to see the faces of others leads you to imagine that others, conversely, cannot see you. Hull vividly describes the nagging fear of having no face, the loss of consciousness associated with perceived invisibility. 'Because I cannot see, I cannot be seen ... It would make no difference if my whole face disappeared. Being invisible to others, I become invisible to myself'. It requires a real effort of will, if you are blind, to remind yourself that you can still be seen (Hull 1997: 51–2).

Far from leading to deep intersubjectivity, to a greater sense of belonging, connectedness and participation, as the received stereotype implies, blindness results – at least in Hull's experience – in an overwhelming feeling of distance and withdrawal. 'People', as he puts it, 'become mere sounds', and 'sounds are abstract' (1997: 21, 48). For him, quite contrary to conventional wisdom, vision personifies, whereas sound objectifies. Hull writes as one who has been fully blind for only a few years: he knows very well what it is like to be able to see the faces of others, and what he says must surely resonate with the experience of every sighted person. Why then, against all the evidence of our senses, do we cling to the illusion that sight is inimical to sociality, that it individualises, isolates and abstracts? Is it because we take, as a prototypical scenario of vision, the situation of looking *at* an inert, opaque object, rather than that of looking *into* the eyes of an active, lively subject – whose eyes are also looking into one's own? If so, does this not provide further proof of what has already become apparent from my first critique of the anthropology of the senses: namely, that it is not vision that objectifies the world, but rather the harnessing of vision to a project of objectification that has reduced it to an instrument of disinterested observation? Our very familiarity with the reciprocal, intersubjective nature of vision, it seems, has conspired to hide it from us. It becomes the tacit ground against which is projected an explicit image of vision as the sight of things.

Blind people, of course, cannot see things any more than they can see faces. But they can listen to them. Blind participants in a study conducted by Miriam Hill reported listening to mailboxes, signs, openings, doors, posts, poles and trees, as well as 'the sounds that bounce off buildings' (Hill 1985: 102). The ability to perceive objects in this way, beyond the reach of touch, seems to be based on a principle of echolocation. Just as for the sighted, recalling Gibson's argument, the presence and forms of environmental objects are revealed through modulations in the array of reflected light reaching the eyes of a moving observer, so for the blind they are revealed through modulations in the array of reflected sound. Yet it is not only the ears that are at work in this process. 'What the blind person experiences in the presence of an object', as Lusseyran explains, 'is pressure' (cited in Hill 1985: 107). Hull reports on precisely the same experience, describing the pressure as sometimes so intense that one instinctively wants to put up a hand to the face to protect oneself.

> One shrinks from whatever it is. It seems to be characterised by a certain stillness in the atmosphere. Where one should perceive the movement of air and a certain openness, somehow one becomes aware of a stillness, an intensity instead of an emptiness, a sense of vague solidity.
>
> (Hull 1997: 23)

For the blind actor-musician Tom Sullivan, it seemed that he could feel, on his face, waves of air that had been pushed away by the body during movement and returned at an angle from some obstacle (Sullivan and Gill 1975: 68). He called this 'facial vision'. Not surprisingly, it does not work well in windy weather (Hill 1985: 103).

There is some doubt, then, as to whether facial vision is a form of hearing or of touch: indeed the phenomenon raises in a peculiarly acute form the problem of the distinction between these sensory modalities. Hull claims that 'the sense of pressure is upon the skin of the face, rather than upon or within the ears' (1997: 24). Elsewhere he describes the sensation of being in an empty building as one that goes beyond mere hearing; 'there must be a certain sensitivity of the entire body to vibrations and to air pressure as well as to inaudible echoes' (p. 85). Evidently the same vibrations which, as they excite the membrane of the ear, are discerned as sound can also excite receptors distributed over the skin, but are then discerned as 'pressure'. Paul Rodaway (1994: 50) regards facial vision as a form of 'global touch', by which he means the body's general contact with the environment, across all its surfaces. But as he points out, it could just as well be described as a subtle form of auditory perception. The implication, that we hear not just with the ears but with the whole body, is, as we shall see in a moment, of great significance for understanding the sensory experience of the deaf. For the present, I should like to conclude my discussion of the experience of blindness with three points.

First, the clear distinction that sighted people are inclined to make between touch and hearing may in fact be a *consequence* of vision, and of the precise delineation of tangible surfaces, at the interface between solid objects and the surrounding medium, that it affords. This may be why the multimodal feeling-hearing of the blind, which is neither touch, echo, nor motion but a blending of all of these, may be so hard for the sighted to grasp (Hill 1985: 104). Secondly, the commonplace supposition that vision is inherently spatial and hearing inherently temporal needs to be qualified. Through the principle of echolocation, hearing *can* disclose a world of stable forms – of things in their places – just as vision can. And while it is true that such disclosure depends upon the perceiver's motion relative to the perceived, the same is equally true of vision (Rodaway 1994: 124–5). In essence, both looking and listening are aspects of a movement that, being generative of both space and time, is ontologically prior to any opposition we might draw between them. Thirdly, it seems probable that even sighted people, albeit unawares, are significantly guided by echo-location or 'facial vision' (Ihde 1976: 67–70). They simply do not pay any attention to it. As Rée writes, for all of us 'becoming acquainted with buildings or landscapes is partly a matter of getting to know their acoustic profiles – listening to the sounds they produce and the echoes they give back' (1999: 53). To be at home in a place, especially in the dark, means knowing how it sounds and resounds.[21] Thus listening is just as much a means of active inquiry and of orienting oneself in the world as is looking.

Being deaf

Turning now to the experience of the deaf, there are two aspects of what Wright aptly calls 'deafmanship' (1990: 113) on which I want to focus. For the first, I return to the point that we hear with the whole body, in order to bring out the range of auditory experience even for people who, like Wright himself, have no use of the ears whatever. Secondly, I refer to the sign language of the deaf, in order to show that the contrast between hearing and vision as sensory modalities of verbal communication is far less fundamental than is commonly supposed. On the first point, and judging from Wright's autobiographical account, it seems that deafness is never absolute in the way that blindness can be (Wright 1990: 9, see Ihde 1976: 45, Rée 1999: 36–7). This is because what we experience as sound is caused by vibrations in surrounding media and surfaces, to which the ears are not alone in responding. Standing on a resonant surface such as wooden floorboards, one can 'hear' approaching footsteps through the feet. But one cannot do this if the surface is, say, of stone or concrete. In speech, one hears the sound of one's own voice, in part, through an internal conduction of vibrations set up in the bones of the head. Insofar as these vibrations bypass the mechanism of the ear, they may still be sensed by a speaker who is deaf. In addition, deaf people can judge the quality of their voice by placing a finger to their neck, at the location of the larynx, and they can likewise 'hear' the sound of a musical instrument, radio or record player by touching the sound box or amplifier (Rée 1999: 36).

But in these instances of 'touch-hearing', what is heard is nothing like the complete sound as it would be experienced by a listener whose ears are functioning normally. Much depends on the particular resonant properties of the surfaces with which one comes into contact, principally through the hands and feet. As a rule, however, the sound 'comes across as a blurred bumble of noise' (Wright 1990: 9). Timbre and pitch are indeterminate, but there is an overwhelming concentration on frequencies at the lower end of the spectrum. The sounds that can be 'heard' at these frequencies tend to be abrupt and percussive, like explosions or the noise of heavy machinery. Since they cannot be placed within the finely differentiated acoustic field of background and foreground sounds such as is revealed by the ears, it is hard to pin them down to specific sources or locations. They tend, rather, to appear and disappear, suddenly and without warning. Moreover low-frequency external noise, picked up through bodily vibration, is easily confused with that generated internally in the course of normal metabolic and respiratory processes – of the kind that the doctor can 'hear' by means of a stethoscope (Rodaway 1994: 100–1, Rée 1999: 53–4).

Besides this touch-hearing, however, Wright reports on another kind of experience of sound, registered not through feeling but through *sight*. Only where nothing moves, as on a perfectly calm day, does the world appear to be shrouded in total silence. Upon the slightest movement, this silence is shattered. I have already referred to such experience as an instance of the 'sight of sound', exemplified in Wright's observation that 'birds, flying, sing with wings instead' (1990: 3, 11–12). Yet he admits that this 'visionary noise', unlike the palpable sensations of touch-hearing, is actually a thing of the imagination. It does not really exist. I have to say that I am not convinced by the implied distinction between real and imaginary sound. For even the sounds that people with normal hearing routinely describe as real are no less phenomena of lived experience, and it is perfectly clear from Wright's description of vision-hearing that the sounds he sees are, for him, every bit as vivid as are the sounds that other people hear, for them. Wright himself wonders whether his eye for sound may owe something to unconscious childhood memories, for deafness did not strike him until the age of seven. He recalls that at the time, he did not notice he was deaf, and only gradually became aware of his condition on account of his inability to pick up the sounds of unobservable movements like the ticking of a clock (1990: 22, see Rée 1999: 37). In the case of visible movements, the fact that his ears had ceased to function made no perceptible difference, at least at first, to what he heard. This surely furnishes compelling evidence for the view that even for the aurally unimpaired, hearing is critically guided by the 'antennae' of sight. And it fits with Hull's observation that when people go blind, their hearing does not improve but rather deteriorates (Hull 1997: 117).

Now when people are speaking to one another, the movements of their speech may be visible in the face, and especially the lips. This is the basis for the skill of lip-reading. It is normal, too, for speech to be accompanied, and amplified in its expressive force, by visible gestures of the hands. In communities of the deaf, gestural systems have been elaborated to the point of constituting languages in their own right, fully commensurate with spoken ones. These are conventionally known as signed languages (Armstrong, Stokoe and Wilcox 1995). Neither speech nor sign has quite the intimacy of eye-to-eye contact, since in both cases there is a functional differentiation, within the overall bodily system of perception and action, between the organs of sense and motion. In speech the division is between the ears and the voice; in sign it is between the eyes and hands. But as speech and sign are formally equivalent in this regard, the possibilities of establishing a direct, mutual involvement of self and other through sign must be just as great as they are through speech. This is the point at which to remind ourselves of what McLuhan, Ong and their followers have to say about the properties of thought and expression in the oral-aural modality. For setting aside the likelihood of deaf signers' familiarity with the written word, there seems no good reason to doubt that these properties should be attributable to the manual-visual modality as well.

Recall that for Ong, people in a primarily oral culture hear words not as things, as though they were looking at them, but as sound. Similarly for deaf signers, gestures are movements to be watched, not objects to be looked at (Armstrong, Stokoe and Wilcox 1995: 83–4). There is no holding them still for inspection. Like speech sounds, signed gestures exist only in their passing. The fact that they are seen and not heard makes them no less fleeting, no more thing-like, than spoken sounds. Moreover the movements of the hands in gesture respond to visually perceptible movements in the signer's surroundings much as, in the oral context, speech sounds resonate to the properties of the acoustic environment, yielding the 'gestural iconism' that is such a pronounced feature of the signed language of the deaf – the precise counterpart of the phonological iconism in the speech of supposedly 'auditory' cultures such as the Umeda (Gell 1995: 247–8). Taking all these parallels into account, we can only come to the same conclusion as Jonathan Rée, in his study of the history of deaf education. 'The idea that there is a metaphysical gulf dividing communication by visible gestures from communication by audible words', he writes, 'is a fantasy without foundation, a hallucination rather than a theory' (Rée 1999: 323–4).

McLuhan and Ong, of course, were above all concerned to contrast the properties of speech and *writing*. Their mistake, as should now have become clear, was to imagine that these contrasting properties could be deduced from the differences between hearing and vision. The critical feature of writing, by which it is distinguished from both sign and speech, is that it is inscribed upon a durable surface. Is it, then, their inscription, and not just their visibility, that renders words as things? Not exactly, for the perception of inscriptions as objects depends upon a still more limited set of conditions. The trace of a gesture, such as the calligrapher's brush stroke, may be apprehended as a movement in just the same way as the gesture itself. In this, the reader's eye follows the trace as it would follow the trajectory of the hand that made it. The written word is perceived as a thing only when it is read not as the *trace* of a visible gesture but as the *representation* of a vocal one. Thus, lurking behind the argument that writing leads us to see words as 'quiescent objects' (Ong 1982: 91) lies an assumption, still widespread even among linguists, that the only proper languages are spoken languages, and therefore that writing exists for the sole purpose of representing the sounds of speech. This phonocentric assumption betrays a deep-seated and obstinately persistent prejudice to the effect that manual signing is an imperfect form of communication that scarcely qualifies as 'language' at all.[22] And it is precisely this disqualification of gesture from language proper that has given rise to the idea that language can be made visible in no other way than through the representation of speech in writing.

THE INTERCHANGEABILITY OF VISUAL AND AUDITORY PERCEPTION

In conversation with Georges Charbonnier, the painter André Marchand describes his perception of the visible world as one in which he is already submerged, and which opens up to him, as it were, on the inside:

> For example, in a forest, I have felt many times that it was not I who was looking at the forest. On some days I have felt that it was the trees that were looking at me, that were speaking to me. For myself, I was there . . . listening.[23]
>
> (Charbonnier 1959: 143)

This experience is surely familiar to anyone who has wandered in the woods. There are two aspects of it to which I want to draw attention. First, it lends compelling support to the idea of the reciprocity of vision, to which I have already alluded in connection with the ordeals of blindness. Unable to see, the blind person becomes convinced of his own invisibility, as though his very existence were thrown into question. Conversely, to 'be there', to have a presence in the world, and so to be able to see, is to exist in the sight of others. Thus we feel that the trees around us have eyes and are looking at us, for if they were not, where would *we* be? Secondly, notice how readily Marchand slips from the language of sight to that of sound. The trees look, but they may as well be speaking; we watch, but we might as well be listening. It is to this interchangeability of visual and auditory perception that I now wish to turn.

I begin with a musicological example, which takes us back to Zuckerkandl's question of whether it is preferable to listen to music with the eyes open or closed. In his autobiography, the composer Igor Stravinsky argues passionately for the former view. 'I have always had a horror', he writes, 'of listening to music with my eyes shut, with nothing for them to do. The sight of the gestures and movements of the various parts of the body producing the music is fundamentally necessary if it is to be grasped in all its fullness' (Stravinsky 1936: 72). Watching the movements of the drummer, the violinist or the trombonist gives shape and direction to our hearing, which would otherwise be empty and aimless. We hear less well with the eyes closed, according to Stravinsky (and as Hull also found with the onset of his blindness), since we lose this visual steering of auditory perception. Cut loose from the bodily movement of its production, musical sound appears abstract and incorporeal. It has often been remarked of hearing that it is a passive sense, that all it can do is succumb to imperatives issuing from the outside world. Jonas, for example, maintains that 'in hearing, the percipient is at the mercy of environmental action' (1966: 139), while for Adorno, hearing appears 'dozy and inert' (1981: 100). It is just this kind of passive hearing, as 'mere supine susceptibility' (Rée 1999: 53), that Stravinsky attributes to those who like to listen to music with their eyes shut. Such people, as he caustically remarks, far from listening to the music itself, prefer to 'abandon themselves to the reveries induced by the lullaby of its sounds' (1936: 73). They allow the sound to wash over them – or to 'float through experience', as Ihde (1976: 78) puts it – oblivious to the fact that it is being produced by players with instruments. Once we open our eyes, however, we cease to be mere consumers of sound, and join silently in the process of its production. Hearing is roused from its slumber, and becomes active and engaged.

This leads us to a conclusion of paramount importance. If hearing is a mode of participatory engagement with the environment, it is not because it is opposed in this regard to vision, but because we 'hear' with the eyes as well as the ears. In other words, *it is the very incorporation of vision into the process of auditory perception that transforms passive hearing into active listening.* But the converse also applies: it is the incorporation of audition into the process of visual perception that converts passive spectating into active looking or watching. That is why Marchand found that in looking at the trees – which were also looking at him – he was also silently listening to them. He was 'looking' with the ears as well as the eyes. Marchand's experience would be entirely familiar to the Koyukon people, who follow a life of hunting, trapping and fishing in the forests of Alaska. They 'live in a world that watches', according to their ethnographer Richard Nelson, 'in a forest of eyes' (1983: 14). But it is a forest of ears as well. The principal trees of the forest, namely spruce and birch, as well as many of its diverse animal inhabitants, are invested with spirits which, like people, can hear as well as see. That is why, for the Koyukon, it is always important to be careful in what you say, so as not to cause any offence. They see because you see; they hear because you hear. But whether on the side of people or spirits, it is the element of auditory attention that converts vision into watchfulness.

Among the Yup'ik Eskimos, too, there was a similar awareness that people are constantly under the watchful scrutiny of spirits. The cosmos itself (*ella*) – sentient, knowing and responsive – was conceived as an immense eye, but it was one that could hear as well as see. It could also smell. Thus for their own and everyone else's safety, mourners and menstruating women were subject to restrictions such that they 'remained odorless, inaudible, immobile, and invisible to the eye of *ella*' (Fienup-Riordan 1994: 248). The knowledge that the eye of *ella* was watching, and that human activities were visible to the spirit world, controlled every aspect of everyday Yup'ik life. To witness a spirit directly was to see it as a *face* which, like the cosmos itself, was circular in form and centred on the eyes. However the face was not a mask covering over the *persona* of the spirit, and through which its voice could be heard. To the contrary, the face would be revealed through a process of unmasking akin to the retraction of a hood – a dissembling of outward appearance as given to ordinary, quotidian vision so as to uncover the being within. To encounter another person 'face-to-face' was not, therefore, to be set over against them, as in the image of the *vis-à-vis*, but to be enveloped in the intense, intersubjective intimacy of eye-to-eye contact. Unmasked, the eyes of the spirit would literally catch the glance of the beholder in their sight. But this implies that as an aspect of being, the face is as much on the 'inside' as is the voice. If the voice is the sound of being, then the face is its look.[24] And hence, too, to listen to another person, whether human or spirit, is equivalent to looking at them. As one Yup'ik man explained: 'A speaker will not scold you for looking at him too much. But looking all the time while someone is teaching, that is how one must keep listening' (Joe Beaver, in Fienup-Riordan 1994: 316). To this, Fienup-Riordan adds that 'watching a person's face . . . was particularly revealing'.

Some sort of distinction is nevertheless entailed, here, between two kinds – or levels – of vision: on the one hand, the ordinary sight of pre-existing things that comes from moving around in the environment and detecting patterns in the ambient light reflected off its outer surfaces; on the other hand, the revelatory sight experienced at those moments when the world opens up to the perceiver, as though he or she were caught up in the movement of its birth. This distinction is effectively equivalent to the one I introduced earlier, in comparing the theories of visual perception of Gibson and Merleau-Ponty, between vision as a mode of *participation* and as a mode of *being*. In neither case can vision be radically separated from hearing. In the former, as I have shown, it is the co-option of hearing by vision that turns merely contemplative seeing into active looking or watching. In the latter, our inquiry into the convergences between what Merleau-Ponty and Zuckerkandl have to say, respectively, about the painterly apprehension of light and the musical apprehension of sound, showed that they were, in principle, all but indistinguishable. To illustrate the contrast between these two levels of vision, and the different relations with hearing involved in each, I turn briefly to another example.

Earlier, I told of how I know the cuckoo by its sound, and that only through being seen does it come to be perceived as a thing that makes a sound. Among the Ojibwa, indigenous hunters and trappers of the Canadian North, there is said to be a bird whose sound, as it swoops across the sky, is a peal of thunder. Few have seen it, and those who have are credited with exceptional powers of revelatory vision (Hallowell 1960: 32; see Chapter Six, pp. 92–3, 99, for a more detailed account based on Hallowell's ethnography). What is the difference, then, between seeing a cuckoo and seeing a thunderbird? Birdwatchers would surely be among the first to recognise the importance of hearing to active, exploratory vision. Listening out for birdsong and other sounds – the beating of wings, or the rustling of leaves – the watcher's sight homes in on the source from which these sounds issue. Thus the organs of hearing constitute an auditory guidance system that serves to orient vision towards its target. The enigma of the call, *cuc-koo*, emanating from somewhere in the trees, is resolved as soon as we spot the bird that is producing it. Naming the bird by the sound of its call, we regard it as just another individual of a species, a living thing, whose presence and activity, moreover, are unaffected by the watcher's neutralising gaze.

The thunderbird, by contrast, is not a thing of any kind. Like the sound of thunder, it is a phenomenon of experience. Though it is by thunder that the bird makes its presence heard, this sound is not *produced* by the thunderbird as the cuckoo produces its call. For the thunder *is* the bird, in its sonic incarnation. Therefore to see it is not to resolve the cosmic mystery of the sound, as though one could take a step back from one's involvement in the world and say 'Oh, so that's where it's coming from!' One is rather drawn further in. The bird presents itself to vision as an experience of light in just the same way that it presents itself to hearing as an experience of sound. If sound, here, is intrinsic to sight, this is not because it guides vision towards its object but because *hearing is seeing*. As a specific form of the experience of light, the thunderbird is not set over against the perceiver as an object of vision, but invades the perceiver's consciousness, whence it is generative of his or her own capacity to see. Much the same could be said of the experience of sunlight or moonlight, and indeed the sun and moon are apprehended by the Ojibwa, along with the thunderbird, as beings of similar kind. They are, in short, not so much visible things as manifestations of light.

Whereas in Western society such revelatory vision is the province of the painter, in many non-Western societies it is closely associated with the activities of the shaman. The metamorphosis of sound into light and vice versa – that is, hearing with the eyes and seeing with the ears – is peculiarly characteristic of shamanic practice. A fascinating example of this phenomenon has been documented among the Shipibo-Conibo Indians of eastern Peru by Angelika Gebhart-Sayer (1985). In a ritual of healing the shaman, suitably entranced, becomes conscious of an aura of radiant light that seems to float towards him, covering the surfaces on which it falls with elaborately reticulate, geometric designs. Where they touch his lips, these luminescent designs are at once converted into melodious song. The shaman sings along with his attendant spirits, and other villagers (who hear only the shaman's voice) join in, following his example. As the combined voices are wafted through the air, they turn once more (though only in the shaman's sight) into designs that penetrate the patient's body and settle there, becoming ever clearer as the cure proceeds (Gebhart-Sayer 1985: 162–4). The shaman's songs, as Gebhart-Sayer puts it, 'can be heard in a visual way, . . . and the geometric designs may be seen acoustically' (p. 170).

The designs themselves are of extraordinary intricacy, and were once recorded on cotton fabric sheets bound into 'books' – leading to speculation that the Indians in this region might have possessed a form of hieroglyphic writing. None of these books survive today, but the villagers among whom Gebhart-Sayer carried out her fieldwork recalled that an old man from a nearby village, the son-in-law of a shaman, had kept a school exercise book whose pages were filled with minute red and black patterns. One woman remembered how, as a child, she had managed secretly to get hold of the book and to copy four of the designs before being caught and scolded by her grandmother. She claimed never to have forgotten them, and was able to redraw them from memory (Gebhart-Sayer 1985: 155). One of her drawings is reproduced in Figure 14.2. It is not hard to see why European observers should have been moved to compare such graphs to writing. It seems, on the face of it, that the Shipibo-Conibo shaman apprehends the sounds of song in much the

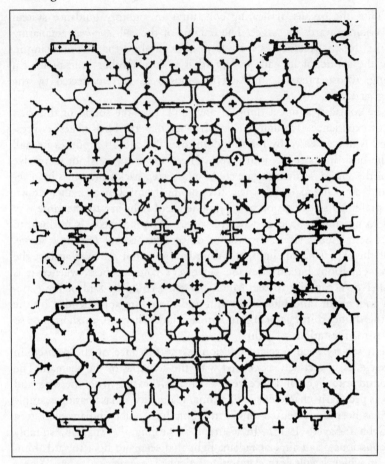

Figure 14.2 One of the designs from the sacred book of a Shipibo-Conibo shaman, drawn from memory by a woman from the village of Caimito in 1981.

Reproduced from A. Gebhart-Sayer, The Geometric Designs of the Shipibo-Conibo in Ritual Context, *Journal of Latin American Lore*, 11: 2, 1985, p. 158.

same way that people in the literate West are supposed to apprehend the sounds of speech – that is, as if they were looking at them. The geometric design lodged in the shaman's vision bears an uncanny resemblance to the Saussurian 'sound-image'. And if the written word is a transcription of the image from the mind onto paper, could not the same be said of the graphic designs in the shaman's 'books'?

It is true that in a sense, the Indian shaman 'sees' songs, and that in another sense, people raised in the Western tradition of print literacy 'see' spoken words. But the senses of seeing adduced in these two instances could not be more different. This difference corresponds, rather precisely, to the way in which Western thinkers have conventionally distinguished vision from hearing. To recall Zuckerkandl's formulation, it is the difference between the experience of a world 'out there', and that of a world coming 'from-out-there-toward-me-and-through-me' (Zuckerkandl 1956: 368). For the Westerner to see words is to apprehend them as things, exterior objects to be grasped by way of the images or representations that are formed of them in the mind. The shaman's vision, by contrast, is not a seeing of things but an experience of light, which is felt to be streaming towards him and into him. As it does so it turns to sound. It is at the interface where inflowing light is converted into outflowing sound that the designs are generated in his perception. In the healing ritual, this conversion takes place upon the shaman's lips. Thus where the design is inscribed upon a surface, such as cotton fabric or paper, that surface is transformed into an interface of the same kind as the lips. This immediately makes sense of native claims to the effect that the surface, with its designs, speaks directly to the person who 'reads' it (Gebhart-Sayer 1985: 154).

If this is indeed reading, then it is more akin to lip-reading than to the reading of the written word. In the graphic traces on the page of the shaman's book the voice is rendered visible, just as it is, for the deaf lip-reader, in the movements of the speaker's lips and face. As the eye of the beholder follows the traces, his lips move to pronounce the corresponding sounds. This interpretation is corroborated by Peter Gow, in a study of reading and writing among another native people of the Peruvian Amazon, the Piro. The study focuses on the story of one man, Sangama, reputed to be the 'first Piro who could read'. According to the story, told in the 1940s by his younger cousin Zumaeta, Sangama used to pick up printed books and newspapers and read them, 'his eyes following the letters and his mouth moving' (Gow 1990: 91). What he saw, however, were not words on paper. He saw the paper itself as the red painted lips of a woman, speaking to him. And he was convinced that this was what his European bosses saw when they read their newspapers: 'When the white, our patron, sees a paper, he holds it up all day long, and she [the paper] talks to him ... The white does that every day' (in Gow 1990: 92–3). If Europeans were predisposed to treat Indian designs as an instance of writing, what could be more natural than for the Indian, Sangama, to treat the printed texts of European books and newspapers as instances of design? Sangama's claim to be able to read, as Gow shows, was based on his understanding of shamanic practice. In accord with this understanding, he approached the graphs on the page not as 'representations' or 'symbols' of vocal sounds, but as the voice itself, shining forth as a pattern of light. It is probably along these lines, too, that we should interpret Seeger's observation that among the Suyá, another Amazonian people, visual designs such as weaving patterns are seen acoustically. On learning such a design, they say 'It is in my ear' (Seeger 1975: 214).

THE ANTHROPOLOGY OF THE SENSES: A SECOND CRITIQUE

We can now pick up the threads of my critique of the anthropology of the senses, from where I left off earlier in this chapter. The common flaw, running through all the work in this field that I have reviewed so far, lies in its naturalisation of the properties of seeing, hearing and other sensory modalities, leading to the mistaken belief that differences between cultures in the ways people perceive the world around them may be attributed to the relative balance, in each, of a certain sense or senses over others. Thus it is supposed that where vision predominates, people will apprehend the world in one way, and where hearing predominates they will apprehend it in another. This approach is exemplified in the work of David Howes, who formulates the key question in the anthropology of the senses as follows: 'What is the world like to a culture that takes actuality in less visual, more auditory or olfactory, gustatory or tactile terms than those to which we are accustomed?' (Howes 1991a: 6). By 'we' he means people of modern Western societies, steeped in a hyper-visual aesthetic that turns the world into a spectacle laid out before the 'detached and observing eye' (Romanyshyn 1989: 31). As an antidote to this kind of spectacular vision, epitomised by the representational techniques of linear perspective, Howes invites us to consider the graphic designs of the Shipibo-Conibo Indians, such as the one reproduced in Figure 14.2. Unlike the perspective drawing where everything is geometrically fixed in its proper place, these designs, he says, fairly *pulsate* (Howes 1991a: 5).

What is the explanation for this contrast? Why should the impact of Shipibo-Conibo shamanic designs be so very different from that of the drawings of Renaissance draftsmen? For Howes the answer lies in the 'pluri-sensorial' quality of the Shipibo-Conibo aesthetic, as against the 'almost exclusively visual' aesthetic of the West. He seems to think that vision is an inherently objectifying sense, that it naturally sets things off at a distance from the observer, but that these distancing effects can be counteracted by adding liberal doses of non-visual experience to the sensory mix. Thus in shamanic healing, the luminescent designs mingle with songs and fragrances to bring about a cure, whereas in the viewing of Renaissance art sounds and smells are screened out, leading to a stultification of the non-visual senses and a corresponding stepping up of 'the natural power of the eye to survey things from afar' (Howes 1991a: 5–6). This is hardly a convincing argument, however. For one thing, it is no more in the nature of the eye that it should function as an instrument of detached speculation than that it should open the seer to experiences of the most intimate revelation. Besides, it is simply not the case that people in Western societies exercise their powers of sight in an environment sheltered from acoustic and olfactory stimuli. Certainly, the sight of designs moves the Shipibo-Conibo shaman to song, and the odours of selected plants form an important part of the ambience of the healing ritual (Gebhart-Sayer 1985: 171–2). Yet who would deny the power of fragrance and song, alongside visual images of sacred significance, in the Catholic Mass? The aesthetic experience of the Western church-goer is surely just as 'pluri-sensorial' as that of the participant in a Shipibo-Conibo ceremony. Adding more sounds and smells will not make any difference to the way he or she sees.

If the centrality that the Western tradition accords to the eye were due to nothing more than an inattention to hearing, along with touch, taste and smell, then it could be easily corrected. So far as hearing is concerned, we would have only to speak up in praise of sound – which, in itself, would be no bad thing (Ihde 1976: 9). But as Ihde points out, the situation is complicated by the fact that the reduction *to* vision, in the West, has been accompanied by a second reduction, namely the reduction *of* vision. One cannot escape this reduction, inherent in the rhetoric of visualism, simply by erecting an antivisualism in its place (Ihde 1976: 21, see Feld 1996: 96). For its source lies not in any bias towards the eye over other organs of sense, but in what Johannes Fabian (1983: 123) calls a particular 'cognitive style' – one that is likely to prejudice our understanding of all kinds of perceptual experience, whether predominantly visual or not. It is in this style, rather than in anything to do with the ratio of the senses, that we find the answer to our question of how Renaissance drawing differs in its impact from Shipibo-Conibo design. Incorporated into Western techniques of depiction, it leads us to equate vision with visualisation – that is with the formation, in the mind, of images or representations of the world. Incorporated into techniques of anthropological analysis, however, this very same cognitive style is what leads us to regard the process whereby people 'make sense' of their world as a cultural construction of reality.

At the heart of this approach is a representationalist theory of knowledge, according to which people draw on the raw material of bodily sensation to build up an internal picture of what the world 'out there' is like, on the basis of models or schemata received through their education in a particular tradition. The theory rests on a fundamental distinction between physical and cultural dimensions of perception, the former having to do with the registration of sensations by the body and brain, the latter with the construction of representations in the mind. And despite vigorous protestations to the contrary (Howes 1991b: 169–70), the anthropology of the senses remains fully committed to this version of Cartesian mind/body dualism. It turns out that it is not, after all, concerned with the varieties of sensory experience, generated in the course of people's practical, bodily engagement with the world around them, but with how this experience is ordered and made meaningful within the concepts and categories of their culture. Moreover the same logic that divides bodily sensation from mental representation, as a physical rather than a cultural fact, also reifies the senses as aspects of a universal human nature. In its movements and responses, such as in looking, listening and touching, the body may furnish symbolic resources for projects of cultural cognition, but it is not from these bodily processes themselves that culture springs. In short, to adopt a useful distinction from Csordas (1990: 40 fn. 2), the body with its various senses is taken to comprise the cognitive rather than the existential ground of culture (see also Chapter Nine, pp. 169–70).

This position is exemplified by Constance Classen, in her book *Worlds of Sense* (1993). Her concern here is quite explicitly with the expressive rather than the practical significance of sensory experience – that is, with the ways in which such experience may be selected, metaphorically, to 'stand for' the central concepts and values of a culture. These values and concepts add up to what she calls the *sensory model*. Thus Western culture, for example, has fastened on the experience of vision to signify the value of objective knowledge. In another culture, with a different sensory model, core values might be expressed through metaphors of hearing, or touch. This is what Classen means by the cultural 'shaping', or 'conditioning', of perception. 'Sensory models', as she insists, 'are cultural models, and sensory values are cultural values'. But just because here vision, or there touch or hearing, have been singled out as vehicles for symbolic elaboration, this does not mean that people will see, hear or touch any differently in consequence. Whether the mode of engagement with the environment of greatest practical importance to people is looking, listening, or touching, or some amalgam of these, is immaterial. What is important, so far as the 'cross-cultural exploration of sensory orders' is concerned, is that the meanings and understandings of the world gained through perceptual activity are *expressed symbolically* by way of metaphors drawn from one or another domain of sensory experience (1993: 135–7, see also Classen 1997).

The same objectification of the bodily experiences of looking, listening and touching, and their conversion into metaphorical resources for the expression of extra-somatic, cultural values, is also evident in the work of Howes. To his credit, Howes does recognise that human beings are not simply endowed by nature with ready-made powers of perception, but that these powers are rather cultivated, like any skill, through practice and training in an environment. For this reason they can vary from one individual to another, even within a single society. The musician, for example, may develop a fine sense of hearing, and the chef an equally subtle sense of taste, even though both may belong – as they do in the West – to a society that is inclined to describe the knowledge and judgement of each through metaphors of sight. We could even expect that these variations of sensory skill would be manifested neurophysiologically in the differential development of the cerebral cortex, such that were we to map the surface of the human body on a scale that varies in proportion to the space that each region takes up in the cortex, the resulting figure – known as the 'sensory homunculus' (see Figure 14.3) – would differ, say, from the musician to the chef, reflecting their contrasting 'sensory profiles'.[25] For Howes,

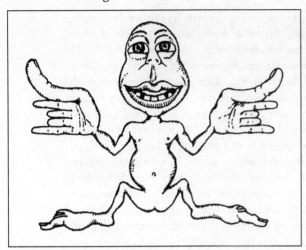

Figure 14.3 The sensory homunculus, an illustration of how the surface of the body is represented in the somatosensory cortex. Larger areas of the cortex are devoted to the more sensitive parts of the body, such as the fingers and lips.

however, these individual variations in practical, perceptual ability are simply irrelevant. He wants to show how the 'map of the senses' differs, not between individuals, but between whole cultures or societies (Howes 1991b: 168–9).

The effect of this move is to uphold a notion of cultures as consisting in systems of collective representations, over and above the conditions and contexts of practical life within which people develop and embody their own skills of action and perception. Howes sets out his position on the matter as follows:

Differences among individuals (by age, sex, occupation, or temperament) only take on meaning against the background of the culture to which they belong. It is the sense in which *whole* societies can be classified as more tasteful than others, ... or more aurally than visually minded, ... that is of primary interest to the 'anthropology of the senses'.

(1991b: 168, original emphasis)

In an 'aurally minded' society, for example, people would express their ideas of knowledge or understanding by drawing on metaphors from the realm of acoustic experience. Where we, in our 'visually minded' society, say 'I see what you mean', they might say 'I hear what you mean'. But this implies nothing about the relative development of their powers of hearing or seeing. Thus Howes is fatally confused in supposing that what he envisages as a 'cultural map of the senses' is merely a scaled-up version of the sensory homunculus (1991b: 168–9). For as the level of analysis shifts from the individual to society as a whole, so the domain that is 'mapped' is no longer of bodily but of conceptual space. Instead of tracing a set metonymical connections between the sense organs and regions of the brain, the 'cultural map' establishes a system of metaphorical correspondences between the material realm of sensory experience and the ideal realm of mental representations. To grasp the logic of this, one has only to substitute a 'plane of sense' for the 'plane of sound' in Saussure's depiction of language (see Figure 14.1).

Like the earlier anthropology of the body (see Jackson 1989: 123; Chapter Nine, pp. 169–70), the anthropology of the senses – as presented in the work of scholars such as Howes and Classen – seems determined to leave lived, sensory experience behind in the search for what it stands for, namely the incorporeal 'ideas' and 'beliefs' of a culture. Far from helping us to understand how the whole body perceives, and how meaning is generated within the contexts of its activities of looking, listening and so on, this approach reduces the body to a locus of objectified and enumerable senses whose one and only role is to carry the semantic load projected onto them by a collective, supersensory subject – namely society – and whose balance or ratio may be calculated according to the proportion of the load borne by each.[26] Now in criticising this approach, I do not intend to downplay the importance of examining the ways in which sensory metaphors are mobilised in discourse. The fact that we say 'I see what you mean' is surely significant. But in resorting to this figure of speech, I am not expressing one thing, a concept of understanding, in terms of another, a specific objectification of the bodily sensation of sight. I am rather inviting you to compare the experience of unison arising from our mutual engagement in verbal dialogue to the experience, with which both you and I are familiar, of unison between perceiver and perceived in the activity of watching or looking. But what if you were *not* familiar with the latter experience? What if you were blind?

For Howes and Classen, whether or not you can actually see, or just how one's sensory capacities are practically deployed in activities of perception, is beside the point so far as the sensory characterisation of a whole society is concerned. These are merely questions of individual idiosyncrasy. Fieldwork among the 'aurally minded', in a society which has elected to articulate its core values by means of metaphors of hearing, will not tell us anything about the experience of the blind. But as Hull shows, in a meditation upon the blind person's response to the expresssion 'I see what you mean', matters are not that simple. Should he refrain from using the expression? That, Hull remarks, would be absurd. To opt out of the verbal conventions of one's society would be to compound one disability with another. Yet he cannot avoid the fact that the expression, which invites comparison between his understanding and a form of perceptual experience which he does not share with his interlocutors, does not have quite the same resonance for him as it has for them. There is, he says, 'a subtle shift in the whole character of communication between sighted and blind people' (Hull 1997: 26).

The lesson to be learned from this is that the verbal conventions of a society do not come ready-made, nor are they simply superimposed upon the experience of its members so as to 'make sense' of it. Rather, they are continually being forged and reforged in the course of people's efforts to make themselves understood – that is to 'make sense' of *themselves* to others. They do this by drawing comparisons between their own sensory practices and experiences and those attributable to their fellows. I suppose you are familiar, as I am, with the sound of thunder and the sight of lightning. I want you to understand what it felt like when I stood by the railway tracks as the train passed by. 'It thundered past me', I say, 'in a flash'. But in having recourse to this metaphor, it is my *experience* that I want to convey to you, not some conceptual prototype of a 'passing train' for which the auditory and visual sensations of thunder and lightning happen to provide apt vehicles of symbolic expression. Instead of abandoning the lived experience of individuals for the collective sensory consciousness of society, it is surely to this creative interweaving of experience in discourse, and to the ways in which the resulting discursive constructions in turn affect people's perceptions of the world around them, that an anthropology of the senses should primarily direct its attention. 'Making sense', in short, lies not in the subjection of human nature to social conditioning (Classen 1993: 5), but in the involvement of whole persons with one another, and with their environment, in the ongoing process of social life.

EPILOGUE

Martin Jay closes his monumental study of attitudes to vision in the recent history of Western thought, above all in the Francophone tradition of scholarship, with the following words:

> The trip began by acknowledging . . . how ineluctible . . . is the modality of the visible, not merely as perceptual experience, but also as cultural trope. It thus seemed fruitful

to follow the unfolding of a loose discourse about visuality, rather than to try to document actual transformations in sensual practices.

(Jay 1993a: 587)

If there is one, principal conclusion to be drawn from my critique of the anthropology of the senses, it is that any attempt to separate out the discourse surrounding vision from the actual practices of looking, watching and seeing is unsustainable. The same, indeed, goes for any other sensory modality. For what is discourse, if not a narrative interweaving of experience born of practical, perceptual activity? The meanings to which it gives rise, as I have shown, are not added 'on top' of lived, bodily experience, but lie in the ways in which the strands of this experience are woven together. Historians of philosophy are surely deceiving themselves in imagining that what has been thought and written *in terms* of the senses can be neatly partitioned off from what has been lived and felt *through* them. As Rée says, 'the historical development of philosophy will never make much sense if it is treated as a bloodless struggle between great books, with all the local flavours, fragrances, noises, temperatures, and colours of ordinary experience left out' (1999: 383).

Indeed the conceit of the philosopher who would write a history of vision without regard to how people actually see mirrors that of the physicist who would construct an optics that makes no reference to the eye. Both, in effect, reproduce a dichotomy between mind and nature, within which all knowledge takes the form of representations of reality. It is through its assimilation to this framework that vision has come to be characterised, by admirers and detractors alike, as having a natural propensity to turn whatever it encounters into objective 'things', to be grasped dispassionately from a distance (Levin 1988: 98). And having been cast in this role, as either the hero or the villain of the drama of modernity, any tendency towards imagining the world as a domain of exterior objects, to be seized by the senses and analysed by the mind, is automatically construed as 'visualism' (Fabian 1983: 106–7). It is as though vision had been compelled to take on the mantle of a particular cognitive style, and all the virtues and vices that go with it. Naturally, critics of visualism have concentrated on the vices (Jenks 1995). David Levin, for example, insists that vision is 'the most reifying of all our perceptual modalities' (1988: 65),[27] whose hegemony in modern society can be linked to a will to power, technoscientific exploitation and political surveillance. And while he admits that vision might have its more open, caring or gentle side, this is to be found only on the margins, in the 'play of shadows and reflections' which reveal to us that 'we are, after all, phenomena of light' (pp. 429, 431).

However, to make the charge against vision stick, as Stephen Houlgate shows, one would have to show that seeing in *actual practice*, rather than as imagined by philosophers, harboured within itself a tendency towards reification (Houlgate 1993: 98–9). One would, in other words, have to breach those artificial barriers that separate life from discourse, allowing the realities of experience to intrude upon the hallowed turf of intellectual debate. Anthropologists do this all the time, indeed the creative tension between theoretical speculation and lived experience is the very driving force of anthropological inquiry. Historians of philosophy, on the other hand, are loath to mix the two, fearing that any move in that direction would threaten the integrity of their own, essentially literary project. That is why philosophical critics of visualism would never dream of asking the kind of question with which a hard-nosed psychologist like Gibson, for example, begins his study of visual perception: 'How do we see the environment around us?' (Gibson 1979: 1). For them, the answer is already presupposed: to see is to reduce the environment to objects that are to be grasped and appropriated as representations in the mind. The irony is that this answer, which critics of visualism are inclined to take for granted, has its source in the very Cartesian epistemology that they seek to dethrone. What they offer, then, is not an account of visual practice, but a critique of modernity dressed up as a critique of the hegemony of vision.

From the arguments and evidence presented in this chapter I hope to have shown that the case against vision is comprehensively disproven. Indeed it should never have been brought in the first place. It is as unreasonable to blame vision for the ills of modernity as it is to blame the actor for crimes committed, on stage, by the character whose part he has the misfortune to be playing. With Houlgate (1993: 106, 111), I believe that the responsibility for reducing the world to a realm of manipulable objects lies not with the hegemony of vision but with a 'certain narrow conception of thought'. And it is this conception, too, that has led to the reduction of vision – that is, to its construal as a sensory modality specialised in the appropriation and manipulation of an objectified world. Through this reduction, as I have shown, vision came to be opposed to hearing. But there is nothing natural or pre-ordained about this opposition: as often as it is reasserted in academic books, it is belied by our own experience. It is my contention that by exploring the common ground between vision and hearing, rather than by abandoning the one for the other through a 'turn to listening' (Levin 1993: 3–4), we may be guided not only towards a better appreciation of the richness and depth of visual experience, but also towards a more generous, open-ended and participatory understanding of thought.

Part III

Skill

INTRODUCTION

In Western society we tend to think of art and technology as separate fields of endeavour, and the study of each has been built on different foundations. The chapters in this part suggest ways in which this separation might be overcome, by taking as a point of departure the skilled practices of socially situated agents. The first three chapters represent successive stages in my attempts to rethink the technical. It was in drafting the essay which now appears as Chapter Fifteen that it dawned on me that the opposition between intellectual design and mechanical execution, in terms of which discussions of human and animal toolmaking and tool-using have traditionally been couched, is in fact a phenomenon of Western modernity. Instead of assuming that technical operations are, by their very nature, mechanical, I argue in this chapter that the machine is an outcome of the historical development of the forces of production accompanying the growth of industrial capitalism. In this development the relations between workers, tools and raw material have been transformed, such as to replace subject-centred skills with objective principles of mechanical functioning. It is to these principles that the modern concept of technology refers. I show how the emergence of this concept was bound up with the rise of a mechanistic cosmology that separated design from construction, and reduced skilled making to 'merely technical' execution. Thus whereas in the artisan's handling of his tools, the movements of their working points are guided by his own perception, the motions of the machine, and any tools attached to it, are predetermined.

I conclude that the transition, in the history of human technicity, from the hand-tool to the machine, is not from the simple to the complex, but is rather tantamount to the withdrawal of the producer, in person, from the centre to the periphery of the productive process. It is a history, in other words, not of complexification but of externalisation. In Chapter Sixteen I consider how this conclusion might affect our understanding of the technical capabilities of hunters and gatherers. Classically portrayed as people with the simplest of technologies, it would be closer to the mark to say that hunter-gatherers have no technology at all. That is to say, their lives are not bound, as is so often suggested, to the operational requirements of a predetermined 'techno-environmental system'. Rather, the success of their way of life depends upon their possession of acutely sensitive skills of perception and action. Yet as properties of persons, developed in the contexts of their engagement with other persons or person-like agencies in the environment, technical skills are themselves constituted within the matrix of social relations. Hence, insofar as they involve the use of tools, these must be understood as links in chains of personal rather than mechanical causation, serving to draw components of the environment into the sphere of social relations rather than to emancipate human society from the constraints of nature. Their purpose, in short, is not to control but to reveal.

Herein lay the second step in my rethinking of the technical. Having first recognised that hunting, for example, entails the practice of a skill rather than the operation of a technology, the stage was set for my realisation that technical relations, in pre-industrial societies, are embedded in social relations. It follows that the process of externalisation is also a process of disembedding of the technical from the social, ultimately giving rise to the modern, institutionalised separation of technology and society. Returning, however, to the context of modern industrial society, I began to think that this picture of a progressive evolution from skill to technology, in which the craftsman or artisan gradually gives way to the machine operative, is too simple. In Chapter Seventeen I present an alternative to this evolutionary model, while at the same time linking the discussion of tools and technicity to the issues of time and temporality adumbrated in Chapter Eleven. Following a classic article by historian E. P. Thompson, the transition from pre-industrial to industrial society has often been depicted as one in which a task-oriented time, grounded in the rhythms of social life, has been replaced by the mechanical regimen of the clock. Drawing on ethnographic studies of locomotive drivers I show, to the contrary, that task-orientation remains central to the experience of work in industrial society, even though the reality of that experience is systematically denied by the Western discourse of freedom and necessity. Indeed, clock time is as alien to people of industrial as it is to those of pre-industrial societies: the only difference is that the former have to deal with it. Likewise the machine operative of industrial society remains a skilled practitioner: his skill, however, lies in coping with machines rather than in their operation, and what it produces is not commodities for the owner of capital but his own personal and social identity.

In Chapter Eighteen I return to a theme already introduced in Chapter Five, concerning the difference between making things and growing things. There I was concerned to show what it means to say that the herdsman's animals, or the farmer's crops, are grown rather than made. I now take up the suggestion that artefacts, too, may be grown, and that in this sense they are not so very different from living organisms. To illustrate the argument I consider the weaving of a coiled basket. Conventionally, we regard weaving as a kind of making. Could we not, however, reverse the argument, and regard making as a kind of weaving? The effect of this reversal – which is precisely equivalent to our strategy, in Part II, of regarding building as a kind of dwelling – would be to place the emphasis on the skilled character of the form-generating process rather than upon the final form of the object produced. Evidently, a basket is not made through the forcible imposition upon material substance of some pre-existent design, included among the collective representations of a cultural tradition, as the standard notion of artefacts as items of 'material culture' would lead us to believe. For in weaving, a surface is built up rather than transformed, and the spiral form of the basket emerges through the rhythmic repetition of movement in the weaving process rather than originating in the maker's mind. Indeed, despite their different geometrical properties, there is a close parallel between the generation of spirals in artefacts (such as the basket) and in living organisms (such as in the shell of a gastropod). Just as the form of the organism is not prefigured genetically but arises through a process of growth within a morphogenetic field, so the form of the artefact is not prefigured culturally but arises through the unfolding of a field of forces that cuts across its developing interface with the environment.

Chapter Nineteen takes us back to the modern dichotomy between art and technology which, I argue, stands in the way of an appreciation of the true nature of technical skill.

To specify more precisely what I mean by skill, I highlight five critical dimensions of any kind of skilled practice. First, intentionality and functionality are immanent in the practice itself, rather than being prior properties, respectively, of an agent and an instrument. Secondly, skill is not an attribute of the individual body in isolation but of the whole system of relations constituted by the presence of the artisan in his or her environment. Thirdly, rather than representing the mere application of mechanical force, skill involves qualities of care, judgement and dexterity. Fourthly, it is not through the transmission of formulae that skills are passed from generation to generation, but through practical, 'hands-on' experience. Finally, skilled workmanship serves not to execute a pre-existing design, but actually to generate the forms of artefacts. Through a comparison of the looping skills involved in making string bags among Telefolmin people of Central New Guinea and the nest-building skills of the male weaverbird, I show that these dimensions of skill are equally evident in both cases. The conventional notion that the birds' activity is due to instinct whereas humans are guided by the dictates of culture is therefore inadequate. In both cases, the pattern of regular movement generates the form. And in both, the fluency and dexterity of this movement is a function of skills that are developmentally incorporated into the *modus operandi* of the body, through practice and experience in an environment. But this leaves us with a still unanswered question. How *do* the skills of human beings differ from those of non-human animals?

In a famous footnote to *Capital*, Karl Marx compared the history of human technology to the history of organic adaptation as described by Darwin in *The Origin of Species*. The comparison suggests three further questions. First, how – if at all – can we distinguish the evolution of technology from its history? Secondly, is there anything inherently progressive about technical change? And thirdly, are there grounds for supposing that such change is governed by a mechanism analogous to that of variation under natural selection? In Chapter Twenty I address each of these three questions in turn. The first takes us back to the problem of origins, already raised in Chapter Ten. Was there some take-off point in human evolution beyond which technology acquired a dynamic of its own, and could go on developing without any further change in human capacities? On the second question, I show that estimations of technological complexity are meaningless unless account is taken not just of material toolkits but also of the knowledge and skills required to operate them. Finally, while the analogies between technical change and organic evolution are suggestive, the way in which they are commonly drawn suggests that what changes is a *design* for the technical artefact, comparable to the organic genotype, rather than the form of the object itself. Our conclusion from Chapter Eighteen, however, is that the forms of artefacts, like those of organisms, arise through processes of growth within fields of relationships. To account for change in artefactual forms, therefore, we have to understand how these fields, and their generative potentials, are constituted and transformed over time.

Now if the same logic is to be applied to organisms, then we have to think about organic evolution in general, and human evolution in particular, in a completely new way. I attempt such a rethinking in Chapter Twenty-one. It is conventional, in palaeoanthropology, to distinguish between the process of evolution, leading from ancestral pongid and hominid forms to 'anatomically modern humans', and the process of history, leading from the Palaeolithic hunter-gatherer past to modern science and civilisation. I argue that this distinction is untenable. Comparing walking and cycling, as modes of locomotion, and speech and writing, as modes of communication, I show that these capacities cannot be opposed as, respectively, biologically innate and culturally acquired. They are, in every case, embodied skills, incorporated into the human organism through a process of development. Thus the differences we call cultural are themselves biological. The reasons for the separation of biology and culture in orthodox theory lie in the identification of the former with a formal genetic 'endowment'. But form, I argue, is not received by the organism-to-be at the point of conception, but generated within the dynamic functioning of developmental systems. And through contributing to the environmental conditions of development for successor generations, organisms – including human beings – actively participate in their own evolution.

There can, then, be no specification of the essential form of humanity independent of the relational contexts in which human beings *become*. The notion of the 'anatomically modern human' is an analytic fiction, derived through the retrojection, onto the Palaeolithic past, of a concept of recent historical provenance in the West. I suggest an alternative approach to human evolution, starting from the inescapable condition of human beings' involvement in their diverse environments. This approach is taken one step further in Chapter Twenty-two, which focuses on the controversial issue of language origins. It has been customary, in discussions of this issue, to distinguish speech, as a universal human capacity, from the manifold languages of particular communities. It is supposed that the former is a product of evolution under natural selection, and is transmitted genetically, thereby establishing the cognitive foundations, in successive generations, for the acquisition of the latter through a parallel process of cultural transmission. But this distinction between genetic and cultural transmission, I maintain, is a consequence of the attempt to treat both speech in general, and languages in particular, as formal, rule-governed systems. This, in turn, betrays the scriptist bias of modern linguistic theory: the tendency to assimilate the spoken utterance, in its pure or ideal form, to the sentence of writing.

I propose a different view. Instead of regarding speech and language, respectively, as innate capacity and acquired competence, I maintain that speaking should be treated as a variety of skilled practice, with all the generic properties of skill outlined in Chapter Nineteen. Through a focus on skill as embodied knowledge we are able to dispense with the troublesome dichotomy between innate and acquired characters. But this also has the effect of dissolving the distinction between evolution and history, and with it, the point of origin constituted by their intersection. The notion of 'language origins' is thus shown to have itself originated within the current of modern thought, alongside the rationalisation of language associated with print literacy. However this same current has also yielded the three key terms – namely 'technology', 'language' and 'intelligence' – which generally frame contemporary accounts of the evolution of human cognition. Of course, in all societies people use tools and talk to one another, and these and other activities represent creative ways of coping in the world. But to say that everyday tool-using is a behavioural instantiation of technology, or that spoken dialogue is an instantiation of language, or even that creative activity is an instantiation of intelligence, is already to make certain rather problematic assumptions.

I conclude, in Chapter Twenty-three, by spelling out what these assumptions are and by suggesting how we might construct an alternative account that would dispense with them. This we could do by examining the relation, in human evolution, not between technology, language and intelligence, but between craftsmanship, song and imagination. I argue that song, far from being put together from separate linguistic and musical components, is rather a performative unity that is decomposed into these components through the imposition of a concept of language of modern origin. In just the same way, the modern concept of technology decomposes craftsmanship into the separate components of rational-technical operations and expressive art. To focus on song and craftsmanship rather than language and technology is to foreground the poetic and performative aspects of speech and tool-use that have been marginalised by rationalism. Neither speech nor tool-use can be understood as the mechanical output of a mental constructional or problem-solving device, such as a technological or linguistic 'intelligence'. Both, however, involve imagination, understood as the activity of a being whose verbal creativity and puzzle-solving is carried on within the context of involvement in a real world of persons, objects and relations. I am, indeed, such a being, and one of the results of my activity is this book.

Chapter Fifteen

Tools, minds and machines

An excursion in the philosophy of technology

THE TECHNICAL AND THE MECHANICAL

Do machines make history? In an article that takes this question as its title, Heilbroner (1967) identifies it as 'the problem of technological determinism'. That technology has to do with the construction and application of machinery may seem obvious to people in industrial societies. But what are we to make of history prior to the machine age? Were there machines about, shaping the course of history, in the days when virtually all tools were operated by hand, and when virtually all the power to operate them came from human muscles? What is the difference between tool use and machine performance, and how does it affect the involvement of the human subject in the act of making? Reflecting on these questions, one is bound to inquire into the nature of the machine, and into the broader applicability of the relatively modern concept of technology, particularly in analyses of pre-industrial or non-Western societies. Such an inquiry touches on important issues in the philosophy of technology, and has considerable historical and anthropological implications. In our own age the concept of technology has become such an established part of thinking on humanity and the 'human condition' that we are inclined to use it as a window through which to view tool-assisted practices of all kinds, past and present, Western and non-Western, human and animal. Thus we imagine that where tools are being used *there must exist a technology*. But what, exactly, is entailed in this assumption? How does it affect our understanding of what it means to make things? And how might this understanding be changed if we were to regard the use of tools not as the operation of a technology but as an instance of skilled practice?

Let me begin with a brief etymological prelude. The word 'technology' is a compound formed from two words of classical Greek provenance, namely *tekhnē*, which meant the kind of art or skill that we associate with craftsmanship; and *logos*, which meant roughly a framework of principles derived from the application of reason. Just occasionally, *tekhnē* and *logos* were combined in classical literature to denote the art of reason, or the skill involved in rhetorical debate. But in contemporary usage the meaning of technology is just the reverse: namely, the rational principles that govern the construction of artefacts – or more simply, the reason of art rather than the art of reason. In this sense, the term did not come into regular use until well into the seventeenth century (Mitcham 1979). And it is no accident that its coinage coincided with the radical transformation in Western cosmology ushered in by such figures as Galileo, Newton and Descartes. For the specific achievement of these pioneers of modern natural science was to establish the idea that the universe itself is a vast machine, and that through a rational scientific understanding of its principles of functioning, this machine could be harnessed to serve human interest and purposes. Thus technology came to be seen as the application of the mechanics of nature, derived through scientific inquiry, to the ends of art.

The shift from the classical concept of *tekhnē* to the modern concept of technology has brought about a profound change in the way we think about the relation between human beings and their activity. In its original, Aristotelian conception, *tekhnē* meant 'a general ability to make things intelligently' (Bruzina 1982: 167), an ability that depends upon the craftsman's or artisan's capacity to envision particular forms, and to bring his manual skills and perceptual acuity into the service of their implementation. But with the adoption of a mechanistic view of nature, the activity of making began to take on a quite different aspect. The image of the artisan, immersed with the whole of his being in a sensuous engagement with the material, was gradually supplanted by that of the operative whose job it is to set in motion an exterior system of productive forces, according to principles of mechanical functioning that are entirely indifferent to particular human aptitudes and sensibilities.

The artisan, of course, knows what he is making, and works to clear standards of perfection. He may be less than clear, however, about the methods by which his results are achieved, and is often quite unable to specify these methods with any precision. The operative, on the other hand, is guided in his activity by formal and explicit rules of procedure whose validity is independent of the specific ends to which they are applied. These rules, grounded in the general principles of mechanics, furnish the *logos* of *tekhnē*, the rationalisation of the process of production that was lacking from the craftsman's art (Mitcham 1979: 182). The effect of this rationalisation, however, is to remove the creative part of making from the context of physical engagement between workman and material, and to place it antecedent to this engagement in the form of an intellectual process of design. A thoroughgoing distinction is thus introduced between the design of things and their construction. The thing, we say, is virtually 'conceived' in advance of its realisation in practice. According to one view, these phases of design and construction correspond to the separate provinces of engineering and technology respectively (Mitcham 1978: 230). The engineer, in Mitcham's words, 'is not so much one who actually makes or constructs an artifact, as one who directs, plans or designs', whereas the technician or technologist has the knowledge and proficiency to execute designs rather than to conceive them.

This dichotomy between conception and execution is institutionalised, however, in many other domains of modern society. It is apparent, for example, in the opposition between architecture and the building industry: the architect, classically a 'master-builder', is now a creator of structures that are left to the industry to put up. The architect designs the house, the builder implements the architect's design. One creates but does not implement; the other implements but does not create (Coleman 1988: 15–16). An identical logic, incidentally, underwrites the distinction in natural science between theoretical conjecture and experimental observation. And significantly, the process by which the architect or theoretical scientist arrives at novel ideas, as distinct from their subsequent implementation or testing, is often described as more akin to art – a term once synonymous with practical skill but now opposed to technology as the spontaneous work of the human imagination to the mechanical execution of predetermined operational sequences. Where excellence in the one field is attributed to genius, in the other it is attributed to expertise. Thus, constituted by its opposition to design, technique is reduced to the 'merely technical', and ultimately to the mechanical.

Now in the classical conception, *tekhnē* and *mēkhanē* were opposed as skills to the various mechanical devices which assist their application. In the modern view, by contrast,

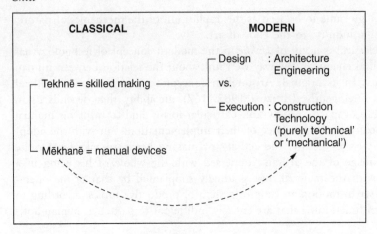

Figure 15.1 A comparison of classical and modern conceptions of the technical.

the technical has joined the mechanical, meaning 'an instrumentality of a particular sort, namely, that which can be separated from the specific context of human experience and sensibility as operative in making' (Bruzina 1982: 167). To borrow, with some modification, a diagram from Bruzina, classical and modern understandings of the technical may be compared as shown in Figure 15.1. With this reduction of skilled making, *tekhnē*, to 'purely technical' execution, the performance is no longer seen to issue from the hand and eye of the concrete, experiencing human subject, and acquires a kind of objectivity and independence from human agency. For whereas the work of making originates with the craftsman or artisan, the operative is merely accessory to processes whose specification has been laid down in advance. It is this *separability* of constructive work from the context of sensory experience that gives it the quality of being mechanical. With the machine, as Bruzina puts it, 'the entire work-action becomes something that can be dealt with independently of human being in its properties and principles of function' (1982: 170). Whether or not the work is actually powered by human muscles is beside the point. Whatever the motive force, where the movements of an instrumental apparatus in the execution of a given design are independently prescribed in its initial conditions, and follow a set course, we are dealing with a machine performance. And the prescriptions embodied in the machine, derived through the application of scientific law, are of course technological.

THE DEFINITION OF TECHNOLOGY

A cursory review of the literature in the history and philosophy of technology reveals a plethora of approaches to the definition of its subject matter, not unlike that in anthropology surrounding the definition of culture. Both disciplines have faced an uphill task in their search for a concept, whether of technology or culture, whose meaning transcends the very historical and ethnological variation they aim to document, and of which their own inquiries are a part. Thus definitions of technology differ widely, depending on whether the intent is to embrace the totality of human works, in all societies and during all epochs, or to mark the specific historical transformations that gave rise to the concept in the first place. Bruzina exemplifies the latter approach, in advancing his thesis that 'only when making by way of the instrumental device becomes principally a machine perform-ance, and the minding of it principally science, does *tekhnē/ars* become *technology* in the proper sense of the word' (1982: 171). He is subsequently still more explicit about the term's historical specificity: 'technology is the action of making when the knowledge that guides it is explicit science as that has developed since the time of Galileo' (1982: 178). Cardwell is likewise careful to distinguish 'technology', as a neologism of the seven-teenth century, from the previous, and more elementary 'technics'. He associates the emergence of technology with a mechanistic ontology that led to the practice of technics 'becoming self-conscious and at the same time increasingly science-based' (Cardwell 1973: 360).

This approach to the definition of technology leads inevitably to the problem of its relation with science. I do not intend to dwell at any length on this controversial issue. It suffices to draw a broad distinction between those who would not credit technology with any autonomous knowledge base of its own but rather regard it as the practical appli-cation of knowledge that belongs essentially to science, and those for whom technology exists as a knowledge system in its own right, alongside science but no more dependent on it than is science on technology. An instance of the former position is the definition with which Singer, Hall and Holmyard preface their massive *History of Technology*. It is a history, they claim, of 'how things are commonly done or made' and 'what things are done or made' (1954–8, I: vii). The knowledge that underlies both the 'how' and the 'what' is conspicuously absent from their definition. It is assumed that such knowledge pertains to science, not to technology. And yet the definition is intended to be applicable to the entire sweep of human history, beginning with the origins of language and the first man-made tools. If technology is all toolmaking and tool-using, guided only during the modern era by scientific knowledge, we are left wondering – with Layton (1974) – what kind of knowledge could have informed the making activities of pre-modern societies. Layton's own position accords with the second of the two approaches outlined above: he defines technology as 'systematic knowledge of the industrial arts' (1974: 3), both distinct from and complementary to science. More recently, Adams (1996) has taken a similar view, arguing that at no point in its history has technology ever been the mere imple-mentation of scientific knowledge. Rather, Adams claims, scientists and technologists have distinctive ways of knowing and thinking, and have coexisted in a relationship that, though tense and awkward, has always been two-way.

For other writers, technology is effectively equivalent to the field of operation of human labour, together with the products to which it gives rise. Drucker, for example, defines technology 'as human action on physical objects or as a set of physical objects charac-terised by serving human purposes. Either way the realm and subject matter of the study of technology would be human work' (1970: 39). But to equate technology with work is to render it redundant as a conceptual category. It might make more sense to say that human work is the *context* for the study of technology. Mitcham's suggestion that 'the term [technology] be stipulated to refer to the human making and using of material artefacts in all forms and aspects' (1978: 232) suffers from the same problem of over-generality, and the same unnecessary conflation of technology with the labour-process. There seems to be no way to prevent the concept of technology from spilling over from a narrow focus on tools and techniques to embrace the entire field of human endeavour. Is there anything, the sceptic might ask, about human life and activity that is not tech-nological? If not, what need have we for the concept of technology at all? Beyond stating the obvious, how does it help us to know that *everything* is technological?

Another family of definitions focus explicitly on the idea of technology as a corpus of knowledge, as distinct both from the productive activities in which it is put to use, and from the artificial products of such activity. Burns recognises that there is a major discrepancy between historical and sociological usages that link technology to the rise of science and mechanised industry in the modern Western world, and the much broader usage of anthropologists and archaeologists who would apply the concept to peoples of all times and places. In the former usage, technology is 'the body of knowledge about (a) scientific principles and discoveries and (b) existing and previous industrial processes'; in the latter it is 'the body of knowledge available for the fashioning of implements of all kinds, for the practice of crafts and manual skills . . ., and for the extraction and collection of materials of all kinds' (Burns 1964: 716). In a classic anthropological statement, Firth defines the technological system as the 'material equipment, and body of knowledge at command of the participants in the economy' (1939: 78). And according to Merrill, technologies are 'bodies of skills, knowledge, and procedures for making, using and doing useful things', or more broadly, 'technology . . . connotes the practical arts' (1968: 576).

Now skills, knowledge and procedures could all be regarded as parts of human culture, leading Margolis to observe that 'culture is both the context of technology and the genus of which the technological cannot be more than a determinate species' (1978: 27). Non-human animals, of course, may be credited with both perceptual knowledge and practical intelligence; however it is widely believed that they lack the symbolic intelligence which is a prerequisite for the intentional design of novel forms (invention) and for their transmission by teaching rather than imitative learning. At the root of this capacity for symbolically mediated thought and instruction, according to Margolis, is language: thus for him, technology is 'the practical capacity of a creature that has mastered language and that can consider alternative ways of acting and making' (1978: 28). In this sense, far from being limited to certain societies and periods, technology might be considered a human universal, 'roughly characterized as the intersection of practical knowledge and ideology' (Margolis 1978: 34). I have myself argued, along rather similar lines, that while technology consists of knowledge encoded in symbols, it is knowledge only in a certain aspect, as models *for* rather than *of* (Geertz 1973: 93–4), and that knowledge becomes technology by virtue of a 'practical orientation to the material world' that simultaneously converts neutral objects into useful equipment (Ingold 1986a: 43).

Perhaps the most comprehensive characterisation of technology in recent literature comes from McGinn: 'it is', he writes, 'a form of activity that is fabricative, material product-

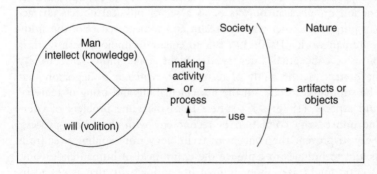

Figure 15.2 Modes of technology

After C. Mitcham, Types of technology, *Research in Philosophy and Technology* 1, 1978, p. 234.

making or object-transforming, purposive (with the general purpose of expanding the realm of the humanly possible), knowledge-based, resource-employing, methodical, embedded in a sociocultural-environmental influence field, and informed by its practitioners' mental sets' (1978: 190). As a definition this is hopelessly cumbersome; it does however have the advantage of providing a convenient checklist of factors that need to be considered in any complete account of the human labour-process as it is involved in the production of things. In order to resolve the definitional turmoil revealed in the foregoing discussion, a necessary first-step is surely to separate out the components of purpose, knowledge, activity and artefacts that are implicated in productive work. Mitcham distinguishes between technology-as-objects, technology-as-process, technology-as-knowledge and technology-as-volition, linking them together in the form of a diagram reproduced here as Figure 15.2 (Mitcham 1978: 233–4). I find this a helpful place from which to start.

OBJECT, PROCESS, KNOWLEDGE AND VOLITION

'Technology-as-objects' encompasses the entire range of fabricated items intended for some use or other, including – in Mumford's classification (1946: 11) – tools, utensils, utilities, apparatus and machines. Mumford brings all of these under his notion of 'technics', a term which we could well retain to denote the area of overlap between *instruments* and *artefacts*. An instrument, or 'tool' in the broadest possible sense, is any object that can be turned to account by an animal (not necessarily human) in the realisation of its project (Ingold 1986a: 47). Many instruments, even human ones, are in no sense constructed for a purpose: I have one such beside me as I write, a stone recovered from a pebble beach which I use as a paperweight. The stone is a tool but not a technic. Likewise the earth is not a technic, even though Marx referred to it (not without a hint of absurdity) as 'the most general instrument of labour . . . since it provides the worker with a platform for all his operations' (1930: 173). On the other hand there are artefacts which, though fabricated in accordance with an already existing design, are not designed to be used in any further project of fabrication. A piece of sculpture is an artefact, so is a cake, but neither of them is a technic.

The second mode of technology in Mitcham's scheme, 'technology-as-process', includes most importantly the activities we commonly denote as making and using. Of course in making one thing we commonly use another, though the reverse does not hold (Mitcham 1978: 253, Ingold 1986a: 58). The key element here is that of skill, defined by Feibleman as 'proficiency in the use of artefacts' (1966: 318). It is this element that makes tailoring and weaving, to use Marx's example, 'qualitatively different productive activities', although both involve the expenditure of physical and mental effort, and 'in this sense are both of them human labour' (Marx 1930: 13). Note however that skilled activity does not necessarily result in the production of objects, nor need it involve their manipulation: the violinist performs on her instrument, but the dancer performs with her own body. Clearly, therefore, technique must be conceptually disengaged from technics. But we face a more difficult problem when we come to the distinction – if one can be made – between skill and intelligence, or between technique and technology in the third of Mitcham's modes, as knowledge.

One possible formulation of this distinction is suggested by David Pye (1964: 55). He regards skill simply as a 'particular application of dexterity', in contrast to what he calls 'know-how', which refers to the capacity of the craftsman to envision forms in advance of their implementation. I have suggested elsewhere that the priority of know-how over skill could mark a critical threshold in the evolution of human constructive abilities, making possible the design of new forms and thus greatly speeding up the tempo of cultural change (Ingold 1986a: 31). Edwin Layton makes a rather similar distinction between skill and knowledge, while insisting that you cannot have one without the other: 'Technique means detailed procedures and skill and their application. But complex procedures can only come into being through knowledge. Skill is the "ability to use one's knowledge effectively". A common synonym for technology is "know-how". But how can there be "know-how" without knowledge?' (1974: 33–4). Layton identifies the 'central purpose of technology' as design, 'an adaptation of means to some preconceived end'. Originating as a conception in the designer's mind, it is converted by degrees into detailed blueprints, which in turn are translated into tools and artefacts. Technology, Layton suggests, may be viewed as the entire spectrum from ideas, through blueprints and techniques, to things (1974: 37–8).

The fourth of Mitcham's 'modes of technology', as volition, is the least developed and most problematic. It expresses the crucial fact that human labour is, by and large, *purposive* activity (Marx 1930: 170). Yet as we shall see, the will that instigates production is not necessarily the will of the producer. The craftsman of capitalist manufacture certainly knows what he is making, and handles his tools accordingly. In that sense he is personally involved in his work in a way that the machine operative is not (Feibleman 1966: 321). But that capacity to envision and implement, depending as it does on acquired skills of perception and action, is not his to command, for along with his bodily energy it forms part of the labour power contracted to the employer. Thus the alienation of labour power under capitalist relations of production did not, at least prior to the introduction of industrial machinofacture, entail any split between the capacities of mind and body. Rather, the line of division lies between the capacities of the whole person, inseparably mind and body, and the agency that puts these capacities to work. In short, to say that a man works from his own *knowledge* is not the same as saying that he works of his own *volition*. This is a point to which I shall return, in the context of a comparison between the 'subjective' labour organisation of manufacture and the 'objective' organisation of machinofacture. But first we have to look more closely at the distinction between machines and ordinary tools.

ON THE DIFFERENCES BETWEEN MACHINES AND TOOLS

To define the machine is no simple matter, since the term has undergone important changes in its meaning from antiquity to the present day. Originally connoting an 'instrument for lifting heavy weights', using the principles of wheel and axle, lever and inclined plane, but empowered by the human body through the hand, in its modern sense the machine is often distinguished from the tool on the grounds that it draws on a source of power outside the body, and is not manually operated (Mitcham 1978: 235–6, 271–2 fn. 16). Thus the notion of the tool has come to be reserved for that aspect of a device that is activated by human agency, whereas 'machine', in Mitcham's words, commonly 'denotes an instrument in its human independence, or at least that aspect of the device which is not dependent on man' (1978: 236). This view is not far removed from Mumford's earlier contention that 'the essential distinction between a machine and a tool lies in the degree of independence in the operation from the skill and motive power of the operator: the tool lends itself to manipulation, the machine to automatic action' (Mumford 1946: 10).

Taking the 'degree of independence' as a variable, we could envisage a continuum whose poles are on the one hand the human body, performing operations unassisted by any extra-somatic aids whatever, and on the other hand the automaton, in which not only the motive power but also the operational constraints are packaged within the same artificial system. Just such a continuum was envisaged by André Leroi-Gourhan in his monumental work on *Gesture and Speech*. He divided the continuum into five stages, arranged in an evolutionary sequence, beginning with that of manipulative action, in which the practitioner works with bare hands. This is followed by the hand's exerting a direct motor function, by moving the tool in its grasp. In the third stage the hand exercises an indirect motor function, by applying force to a device, such as a spring, crank, lever or pulley cable, that in turn moves the tool. In the fourth the hand works to harness the energy of a non-human power source, which in turn directly or indirectly moves the tool, as with animal traction, water-driven mills, and so on. Finally, in fully automatic action, there is nothing for the hand to do but to set off a programmed process by pushing a button or throwing a switch (Leroi-Gourhan 1993: 242–9). The whole process may be seen as a gradual displacement of technical operations from the human organism onto the artificial machine, a displacement that Leroi-Gourhan calls 'exteriorisation'. For Leroi-Gourhan, however, the exteriorisation of technical operations did not fundamentally alter their nature. In the routine manipulation of hand tools, he believed, the body functions to all intents and purposes like a machine; or to put it the other way around, the workings of the machine effectively mimic those of the living body, of which it is but an 'improved artificial copy' (1993: 269).

Writing a century before Leroi-Gourhan, Karl Marx had also embarked upon a comparison between the human handling of tools and machine performance. But he had come to precisely the opposite conclusion. Crucial to handling, in Marx's terms, is that the worker does not just apply motor force but actually guides the movement of the tool, watching as he works, and making continual adjustments in response both to environmental perturbations and to his perceptual monitoring of the developing form. In the machine, by contrast, responsibility for the movements of the tool – or what has now become the device's 'working point' – is transferred from dextrous hands to a mechanism that is indifferent to its surroundings and answerable only to instructions that have been fed into it in advance. Once the guidance of the working point is relinquished to the machine, Marx argued, it is more or less incidental whether the motive power comes from human muscles, from non-human animals such as horses (whose substitution for humans in this capacity gave rise to the notion of 'horse-power'), or from wind, water, steam, electricity or whatever (Marx 1930: 396–7). Thus a machine may still be hand-operated, but when the hand delivers only muscle-power and not skilled constraint – that is, when the technically effective gesture ceases to be coupled to immediate sensory perception – the tool or working point is no longer 'handled' in Marx's sense. The essential distinction, as he put it, lies 'between a man as a simple motor force and as a worker who actually handles tools' (1930: 395).

Bearing this distinction in mind, we may observe that the transition from hand tool to automatic machine can take two alternative courses, as shown schematically in Figure 15.3. The diagram is constructed from three binary oppositions, between (1) human (–) and non-human (+) power; (2) skilled (–) and mechanical (+) constraint; and (3) somatic (–) and extra-somatic (+) working points. With the hand tool (a), the working point is a detached instrument, but the hand that holds it not only delivers a bodily power but also guides the motion of the tool. With the automaton (d), these human functions have

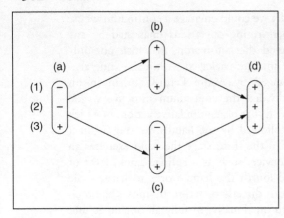

Figure 15.3 Routes of transition from hand tool to automaton.

been entirely supplanted by the apparatus. Of the two intermediate cases, (b) and (c), the first comprises what are often called 'machine tools', which, though driven from an external power-source, still call for skilled manipulation by an operator. An example is the power-drill. But in the second case, of 'man-powered machines', the opposite situation obtains, for the constraint is mechanical, while human beings merely supply the motive power, for example by working a treadle, turning a crank, or operating a pump-handle. The line of distinction between manpower and skilled constraint thus places (c) on the side of the machine, but leaves (b) on the side of the tool.

There are, it is true, certain devices that appear at first glance to resist classification in these terms. Consider for example the pedal-powered potter's wheel. Not only does the potter provide the motive force, but he also shapes the pot using his fingers, unaided by any other instruments whatever. The wheel is surely a detached device, yet the power, the skill and the working point are all supplied by the human operator. The paradox presented by this instance is resolved by recognising that in operating his wheel, the potter is really working two systems simultaneously. One, driven by the body via the feet, generates the rotary motion of the pot, and requires no skill (barring perhaps a speed control). The other is a skilled system comprised by the intimate co-ordination of manual, visual and tactile functions. Technically, therefore, the wheel is a machine, operated in conjunction with a somatic tool, the hand. The situation with regard to the woodworker's lathe is similar, except that since wood is not pliable as is clay, the hand operates through the medium of a chiseling tool. It is important to recognise such compound systems for what they are, since even the total automation of one component need not in any way reduce the element of human 'handling' of the other component. This is a point to which I shall return.

MOTORS, TRANSMITTERS AND WORKING PARTS

A complete machine, according to Marx, 'consists of three essentially distinct parts, the motor machine, the transmitting mechanism, and the mechanical tool or working machine' (1930: 393). This was no new idea: when Marx was writing it was already part of the orthodoxy of French mechanical instruction, supported by the authority of the geometer-engineer, Jean-Victor Poncelet (1788–1867). 'The science of machines', as Poncelet had written, 'consists of the science of tools, the science of motors, and the science of communicators or modifiers of movement' (Poncelet 1844, III 11, my translation). Besides noting the interchangeability of manpower and machine-power, Marx devoted some attention to the functional equivalence of manually-operated and machine-operated tools or working parts. The spindles of the spinning machine, the knives of the chopping machine and the saws of the sawing machine are all immediately recognisable as the counterparts of tools once manipulated by hand, albeit much modified to fit in with the requirements of the apparatus. But emancipated from the bodily restrictions of manual operation, such tools could increase in number or scale by several orders of magnitude. The spinner can operate only one wheel at a time, whereas the spinning jenny has up to eighteen spindles going simultaneously; the steam-hammer has a head just like the hammer of the blacksmith, but as Marx observed, 'such a heavy one that Thor himself could not wield it' (Marx 1930: 408). Nevertheless, despite their gargantuan proportions, mechanised tools carry out 'the same operations which the manual worker of former days carried out with tools of a like kind' (1930: 394).

Thus with regard to both motive power and working parts, the difference between tools and machines is one of degree rather than kind. For Marx the essential, qualitative difference, as we have seen, lies in the substitution of a mechanically determining system for a skilled system of constraint (on this distinction, see Pye 1964: 53–4). Curiously, however, the latter criterion does not enter into Marx's initial specification of the components of the complete machine, whereas the 'transmitting mechanism', which does appear as the third term of his specification – alongside motive power and working parts – receives no further mention at all. This mechanism, corresponding to the 'communicators' and 'modifiers' of Poncelet, consists of pulleys, cog-wheels, belts, gears, etc., all of which impart motion to the tool. In the case of manually operated tools, the transmission function is of course performed by the links and joints of the human skeleton. Empowered by the muscles, its characteristic movements are of a reciprocating, back-and-forth nature, and these are transmitted directly – via the handle of the tool – to its working point. But machines, unlike tools, 'typically achieve their effect by means of rotary rather than reciprocating motions' (Mitcham 1978: 239, cf. Mumford 1946: 80). Now rotary movement does not come naturally to the body: it is acquired only with difficulty and is always discontinuous. As Lynn White observed: 'continuous rotary motion is typical of inorganic matter, whereas reciprocating motion is the sole form of movement found in living things' (1962: 115). Hence a necessary step in the transition from hand tools to man-powered machines – from (a) to (c) in Figure 15.3 – was the incorporation of an artificial mechanism that would convert reciprocating to rotary motion. Such a mechanism is the crank, and its discovery represents one of the most important moments in the early development of machinery (White 1962: 103–17).

Is there, then, any connection between the substitution – by means of a transmitting mechanism – of rotary for reciprocating motion, and the substitution of mechanical determination for skilled constraint? Or to put the question another way: can a tool or working point be handled if its motion is fundamentally distinct from the motion of the hand as an empowering agency (Bruzina 1982: 170)? The potter, working with bare hands, can feel the clay as he shapes it, but this is no less true of the woodcarver who – though he perforce must use a tool such as a knife or chisel – feels the wood through its contact with the tool more than he does the tool through its contact with the hand. It is not difficult, moreover, to think of examples where the technically effective gesture remains closely coupled to sensory perception, even though the application of force is indirect. The sailor, hauling a rope through a pulley block, still feels the wind in the sails. But the hurdy-gurdy player differs from the violinist in that, whereas the latter feels the resistance offered to the bow by the vibrating string (rather than that offered to his hand by the chock of the bow), the former feels only the resistance of the handle of the wooden wheel that, as it is turned, rubs against the strings and causes them to vibrate.

It is perhaps no accident, then, that most examples of devices in which a man acts, in Marx's words, only as 'a simple motor force', work by rotary motion. It would seem that, in operating a crank, the intimate link between hand and tool – by virtue of which the latter is experienced by the operator as an extension of the former – is severed. More generally, the conversion of reciprocating to rotary motion through a transmitting mechanism decouples action from perception, divorcing technically effective operations from their context in the immediate sensory experience of practitioners. It is no longer possible, as the exercise of skilled constraint requires, to feel or to respond to the work of the tool upon the material. Indeed the device may be operated just as well, if not better, by foot as by hand, as in the the case of the aforementioned potter's wheel. For while it lacks the dominant hand's dexterity, the foot is probably a more efficient deliverer of sustained muscle-power.

That the transition from hand-tools to man-powered machines generally involved a conversion of reciprocating to rotary motion is also indicated by the modifications entailed in their working parts. For example, oars give way to rotating paddles, the straight saw becomes circular, and the rectangular surface of the whetstone gives way to the cylindrical surface of the grinding stone. Where, on the other hand, mechanisation involves the substitution of machine power for manpower, as in the development of so-called machine tools, the mechanism of transmission often has quite the opposite function: not of converting the reciprocating movement of the body into the rotary movement of the working part, but of converting the rotary movement of the mechanical motor into a reciprocating movement that *imitates* the original movement of the body in its operation of a working part which remains unchanged in form (if not in scale). One example is the mechanised pile-driver; another is the electric toothbrush.

THE COMPLETE MACHINE

Up to now we have kept within Poncelet's conception, endorsed by Marx, of the complete machine as a combination of motor, transmitter and working parts or tools. Though at first glance this makes a good deal of sense, it will not withstand closer scrutiny, as was shown by Reuleaux in his classic work of 1876, *The Kinematics of Machinery*. Considering first the nature of the tool, Reuleaux observes that there is a large class of machines from which the tool is completely absent, namely those used for altering the positions of things, or 'place-changing machines'. An example is the crane. It might be supposed that the rope is the transmitter and the hook the tool. But we could, if need be, reject the hook and lift a load by tying a loop in the rope. Do we say, then, that the loop has become the tool? What if the load is discarded and we wish to wind up the empty rope? The tool has apparently disappeared, while what we had thought to be the transmitter of motion (the rope) has now become the object moved. Yet the crane functions entirely as before. If the functioning of the machine is indifferent to the presence or absence of the tool, the latter cannot be essential to its completeness.

Those machines that are equipped with tools, Reuleaux argued, have as their common object the alteration in form of some material: they are 'form-changing machines'. Looking more closely at the relation, in such machines, between the tool and the object worked upon (the work-piece), Reuleaux comes to a rather remarkable conclusion: that the work-piece is in fact an integral part of the machine, regarded as a 'closed kinematic chain'. The interface between tool and work-piece is just one of any number of points through which the chain continues without interruption. Indeed it is not always possible to draw the line at all between work-piece, tool and transmitter. In a spinning machine, for example, the thread is not only what is worked upon but also a transmitter of force, while every fibre of the thread acts as a tool for twisting each and every other. This same observation resolves the paradox of the crane, where the rope may be regarded interchangeably as a transmitter, a lifting device and an object lifted. In all these capacities both the rope and anything that may be attached to it are simply parts of the whole machine.

If the machine 'ends' in the work-piece rather than the tool, it likewise begins with the 'prime-mover' rather than with the receptor of that motion. The prime-mover, or driver, could be a machine such as a steam-engine, or a living agent (human or animal). Reuleaux's discussion of the mechanical employment of human muscle-power is especially revealing. Reproduced in Figure 15.4 is his diagram of a man operating a treadle grindstone. It shows that in operation, 'the body of the worker becomes kinematically chained with the machine' (1876: 500) – in other words the worker is as much a part of the machine as is the work-piece. Now if we disregard what the man is doing with his hands and arms, and the object he holds, the stone itself could be treated as the work-piece, and the whole machine as a place-changer designed to secure the rotation of the stone. From the diagram it can be seen that the machine operates through the kinematic conjunction of two lever cranks. One crank is formed by the links a, b and c, secured at points 1 and 4 by the fixed frame d. The other crank, which drives the first, is formed by the links a', b' and c', secured at points 1' and 4 by the fixed frame d'. There is no difference, in principle, between the artifical coupler b and the shinbone b', nor between the frame d, built into the structure of the device, and the frame d', formed through the posture of the man. As this example demonstrates, the machine is not external to the worker, 'receiving' from him its motive force, for in reality 'the worker makes a portion of his own body into a mechanism, which he brings into combination, that is chains kinematic-ally, with the mechanism to be driven' (1876: 501).

The definition of the machine that Reuleaux proposes (having discussed a whole catalogue of contemporary alter-natives, see his footnote 7, pp. 587–90) runs as follows: 'A machine is a com-bination of resistant bodies so arranged that by their means the mechanical forces of nature can be compelled to do work accompanied by certain deter-minate motions' (1876: 35, 503). Mumford's criticism (1946: 9) that this definition 'leaves out the large class of machines operated by manpower' is quite unfounded, since as we have seen, Reuleaux devotes some attention to the consideration of such machines, concluding that – insofar as the body delivers a purely physical effort – it is a 'force of nature' like any other, that can be harnessed to drive a kinematic chain. 'So far ... as machines driven by muscular power are themselves closed kinematic chains, they may be

Figure 15.4   Man working a treadle grindstone

From F. Reuleaux, *The kinematics of machinery*, published by Macmillan, 1876, p. 501.

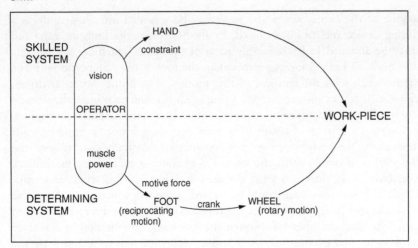

Figure 15.5 Skilled and determining systems.

regarded as complete machines, and do not themselves differ from machines driven by any other than muscular force' (Reuleaux 1876: 508). However, Reuleaux does recognise that the employment of humans and animals to drive machinery introduces a 'special complication' in that the movements of links in the organic part of the kinematic chain are necessarily constrained 'by the action of forces commanded by the will' (1876: 508). Returning to the man in the diagram (Figure 15.4), to the extent that the work performed by the lower part of his body is 'purely physical . . . and not intellectual', this complication may be safely ignored. But if we consider the upper part of the body, then it is apparent that he is linked into the machine in a quite different way: holding the work-piece in skilled hands, he is constantly adjusting its position and pressure against the stone, under a close and watchful gaze.

Like the potter in our earlier example, we may say of the grinder – with Reuleaux – that he 'is doubly connected to the machine at which he works', or that 'human agency has a twofold action in it' (1876: 509). In both machines, potter's wheel and grindstone, the work-piece stands at the point of intersection between the two systems: the one imparting 'determinate motions', the other skilled constraint. The fact that in the one case the work-piece is affixed to the rotating wheel while worked upon by the hand, whereas in the other it is held in the hand while worked upon by the rotating stone, is immaterial. The important point is that by the twofold action of the human operator, skill has been dissociated from motive force, even though both are delivered by the same agent. In Figure 15.5 this point is illustrated diagrammatically. In the determining system, operated through the foot, all possible motions are fixed in advance by the structure of the machine; in the skilled system, operating through the hand, motions may be varied at will, and the intended result is achieved through a continuous process of modification and adjustment, requiring constant visual attention (cf. Pye 1964: 54).

MACHINES AND ANIMALS

Before pursuing further the implications of this distinction between skilled and determining systems, I should like to make a brief detour to consider the human employment of domestic animals. I have noted in passing that human muscle power may be replaced by the power not only of inanimate machines, but also of non-human animals. How, then, does the use of domestic animals differ from the use of tools and machinery? And to what extent can the relation between the animal and its human master (or mistress) be compared to man's mastery over the machine?

Marx, at one point, is quite prepared to treat domestic animals as 'instruments of labour', taking their place alongside the established repertoire of simple hand tools: 'From the dawn of human history, man, in addition to making use of elaborated stones, pieces of wood, bones and shells, turned to account the services of domesticated animals as instruments of labour – these beasts, tamed, modified, bred by human labour, being among the chief of the primitive instruments of labour' (1930: 171–2). But to regard the animal as a mere tool is to deny its capacity for autonomous movement (Reed 1988a); tools cannot 'act back' or literally *interact* with their users, they only conduct the users' action on the environment (Cohen 1978: 43–4). Evidently, therefore, the human 'handling' of animals is quite different from the handling of tools. If anything, it can be compared to the craftsman's handling of raw material; but whereas the craftsman's aim is to realise a particular form, the trainer aims to establish a particular pattern of skilled behavioural responses.

In fact, animal domestication very often does involve the use of manual tools, but of a kind we have not so far encountered. They are tools of coercion, such as the whip or spur, designed to inflict physical force and very often acute pain (see Chapter Four, p. 73). Another class of tools consists of those attached to the animals themselves and operated as part of their performance. Thus the 'handling' of animals is really a two-stage operation in which the human master, through the use of the instruments of coercion, aims to control the skilled tool-using performance of his charges. Indeed there is an immediate and obvious parallel here with slave-driving: like human slaves, similarly compelled to work through the infliction of pain, animals constitute labour itself rather than its instruments (Ingold 1980: 88). Both humans and animals can, however, be virtually

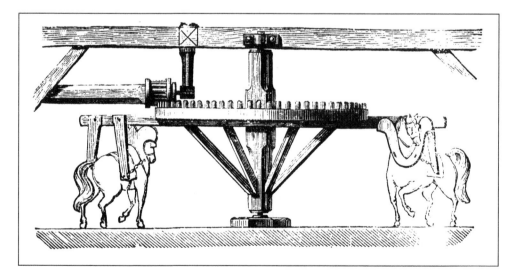

Figure 15.6 Gin-horses.

From F. Reuleaux, *The kinematics of machinery*, published by Macmillan, 1876, p. 501.

reduced to a machine existence through the systematic repression of their powers of autonomous action. Thus, Mumford dates the 'first complex, high-powered machines' to some five thousand years ago; they were composed of thousands of human bodies regimented in 'corpselike obedience' to an absolute despotic authority. Such was the 'megamachine' that constructed the Egyptian pyramids (Mumford 1966: 312). Moreover, there is little difference in principle between the oarsmen of the Roman slave-galley, chained to their benches so that they have no other possibility of movement, and the gin-horses depicted in Figure 15.6 (from Reuleaux 1876: 509).

Reuleaux writes: 'the locomotive has often been called a steam-horse – we may reverse the comparison and call the gin-horse . . . the locomotive of the machine which it drives' (1876: 508). Perhaps in no other employment has an animal come closer to being converted into a pure machine, functioning simply as a prime-mover. Harnessed to the apparatus, the horses have become parts of a closed kinematic chain, whose motions – just like those of the grindstone in Figure 15.4 – are precisely predetermined. Yet if the beasts really were machines as Cartesian philosophy would have us believe, converting oats into tractive effort, it would not be necessary to shield them from extraneous sensory inputs, for example by covering their eyes with blinkers. After all, the difference between the horse and the locomotive is that, barring mechanical failure, locomotives do not bolt, take fright, or simply decide to stop. As Marx shrewdly notes, the great disadvantage of horses as a motive force for industry, quite apart from the high costs of maintenance, lies in the fact that 'a horse has a head of its own' (1930: 397). In short, the essential difference between the human mastery over animals and over machines is that although both – in terms of Reuleaux's definition – 'can be compelled to do work', the machine is compelled by the very nature of its construction whereas the animal is compelled by the external imposition of coercive force. The Cartesian equation of animals and machines may have served to justify their use as mechanical prime movers, but is belied by the repressive techniques that had to be applied in fitting them to this role.

MANUFACTURE AND MACHINOFACTURE

We have seen how, in man- or animal-powered machines, the living body becomes an integral part of a complete determining system. Turning now to systems in which the prime-mover is an artificial motor mechanism, such as a steam-engine, what role is left to the human operator? Does he become, in Marx's phrase (1930: 408,451), no more than a 'living appendage' of the machine? Not quite, for it is a fact that the best-constructed system of automatic machinofacture, even if provided with a continuous supply of fuel and raw materials, would soon grind to a standstill without human attention. This is simply because machines, unlike living organisms, are not self-maintaining systems, and are incapable of making up themselves for the effects of wear and tear. As Marx himself admits, machine repair and maintenance call for skilled craftsmanship, but the mechanics and engineers who ply this craft 'comprise a superior class of workmen', having a higher status (and higher pay) than the mass of the factory workforce whose principal task is to keep the machines supplied. Considering the latter alone Marx notes how – at the time he was writing, in the middle of the nineteenth century – machinofacture had led both to a prolongation of the working day and to the homogenisation of the workforce. The former was possible because, excepting breakdowns, machine power can be kept going indefinitely, whereas man must have his food and rest. The latter was a result of the replacement of human skills by the determining motions of the machine. Moreover, once human motive force was dispensable, women and children – whose muscle power and endurance were deemed inferior to men's – became equally employable.

With regard to the relation between machines and their operators, it is vital to distinguish the influence of capitalist relations of production from the effects of mechanisation and automisation. Consider the following statements, which appear on the same page of *Capital* and which – on the face of it – seem directly contradictory:

1   In manufacture and in handicrafts, the worker uses a tool; in the factory he serves a machine;
2   In [all kinds of capitalist production] the worker does not use the instruments of labour, but the instruments of labour use the worker. However, it is only in machine production that this inversion acquires a technical and palpable reality.

(Marx 1930: 451)

By 'manufacture' Marx is referring to the largely pre-industrial phase of capitalist production, stretching roughly from the middle of the sixteenth century to the end of the eighteenth. The characteristic feature of such manufacture was the assembly, within a single workshop, of a large number of highly specialised, skilled artisans performing complementary tasks within a rigidly prescribed division of labour. These artisans, however, did not co-operate of their own accord, for their association was a result not of relations among themselves but of each having contracted to the same employer who commanded the sum total of their labour-power. In effect it was he who 'co-operated' the working capacities of his employees, much as in a later period, the factory-owner would 'co-operate' the working machines that eventually took over each of the functions originally performed by hand (Marx 1930: 400–1).

In this sense of co-operation, which appears equally applicable to both labour-power and machinery, we also find the sense in which, according to statement 2 above, instruments 'use' their operators. What is meant is that the will or purpose that the instrument serves to realise is not that of the worker but that of the employer. The worker who operates the instrument acts under a form of compulsion, ultimately backed by the threat of withdrawal of the means of subsistence. From the employer's point of view, tools are not made to be used by workers, rather workers are made to use tools. Moreover this 'making' does not only exist in the element of compulsion. For unlike the craftsmen of earlier ages, who might apply their skills to a range of tasks or commissions, the detail worker of capitalist manufacture is rigidly trained to the performance of one limited operation within the overall production system. Through its endless repetition, he 'converts his whole body into the automatic specialized instrument of that operation' (Marx 1930: 356). Given that these bodily aptitudes are largely acquired by long and enforced training on the job, it might reasonably be said that instruments not only use their operators, but make them as well. Combined together on the workshop floor, the aggregate of technically specialised bodies constitutes what Marx calls 'the living mechanism' of manufacture. Naturally, it invites comparison with the 'lifeless mechanism' of machinofacture, constituted by the assemblage of machines in the industrial factory (1930: 356, 451).

In this comparison, presented schematically in Figure 15.7, we regain the sense in which – according to the first of the two statements cited above – the detail worker nevertheless *uses* his tool. In the employment of hand tools, 'the movements of the instrument of labour proceed from the worker' (Marx 1930: 451); the tool does not itself prescribe the envelope of it movement. Yet it is this envelope that determines the form of the product

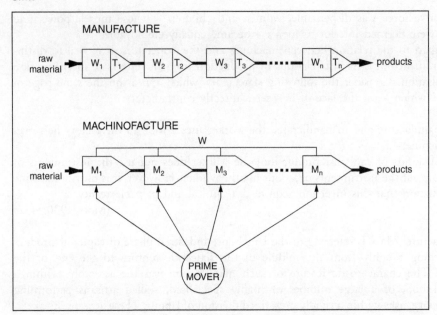

Figure 15.7 The organisations of manufacture and machinofacture.

$W_1 - W_n$ detail workers
$T_1 - T_n$ manual tools
$M_1 - M_n$ detail machines

that will be passed on, as material, to the next worker down the line. Thus the worker must already have some conscious idea of the form he sets out to reproduce, and must be able to translate that idea – through acquired sensorimotor skills – into the movements of hand and tool. In machinofacture, however, the situation is quite otherwise, for the shape of the product is already 'written in' to the machine, the movements of which are predetermined. The consciousness of the machine operative is, so to speak, short-circuited. Though the worker probably knows, if only from prior observation, what the product will look like, he does not actually need to know, and the product's materialisation is not at all dependent on such knowledge.

The organisation of the labour-process in manufacture is thus an organisation at once of specialised bodies and of trained minds, and rests on technical knowledge and skills possessed by the workers themselves. As this knowledge and these skills are replaced by the machine, the co-operation of workers – no longer differentiated in their tasks and therefore freely interchangeable among successive stages of production – is reduced from a complex to a simple form. In 'serving' the machine, factory workers are made to feel their subordination to capital in a way that the detail worker of the manufacturing period did not. For whereas the productive organism in manufacture, composed of sentient and intelligent human beings, has an essential subjective component, this 'no longer exists in the case of machine production. Here the whole process becomes objective, is considered in and by itself, analysed into its constituent phases; and the problem of carrying out each detail process, and of combining the various partial processes, is solved by the technical application of mechanics, chemistry, etc.' (Marx 1930: 402). That is to say, technique has been replaced by technology, 'rule-of-thumb methods by the purposive application of natural science' (1930: 408).

Marx's point that mechanisation transforms the organisation of production from the 'purely subjective' to the 'purely objective', thereby transferring human agency from the centre to the periphery of the fabricative process, brings us back to the question with which I began. Do machines make history?

CONCLUSION

The answer must surely be that they do not. The suggestion that they might derives from a particular reading of Marx's theory of history, encapsulated in his summary statement that 'in the social production of their existence, men inevitably enter into definite relations, which are independent of their will, namely relations of production appropriate to a given stage in the development of their material forces of production' (1970: 20). Whether he actually meant by this, and other similar statements, 'that the basic trajectory of human history is explained by the advance of the productive forces' (Shaw 1979: 171) is a moot point, but let us suppose for the sake of argument that this was his intention. What he certainly did not intend was the equation of productive forces with machinery, even allowing for the inclusion within the complete machine of human motive force and the raw material on which it operates. As Shaw points out, 'the forces of production are, for Marx, thoroughly human' (1979: 158), in the sense that they include not just muscle-power but every aspect of man's capacity to work. In handicrafts and manufacture this capacity is founded, as we have seen, in the knowledge, skill and experience of human subjects. Thus, the forces of production, as Marx himself wrote, may be 'subjective, appearing as qualities of individuals, as well as objective' (1973: 495). And later he refers to the 'degree of development of the material (and hence also the intellectual) forces of production' (1973: 502). It is unlikely that he meant to *exclude* 'intellectual' forces from 'material' ones', since his concept of the material was constituted by its opposition to the social rather than to the mental (Cohen 1978: 47).

Once human consciousness is admitted as a force of production, we have to conclude that 'people, as much as or more than the machine . . . make history' (MacKenzie 1984: 477). Indeed the burden of Marx's argument is that this history has involved a progressive *objectification* and *externalisation* of the productive forces, reaching its apotheosis in the industrial automaton. As the outcome of this process, machines have not so much made as been made *by* history, one in which human beings, to an ever increasing extent, have become the authors of their own dehumanisation.

Chapter Sixteen

Society, nature and the concept of technology

INTRODUCTION: TECHNOLOGY AND SOCIETY

For many centuries, Western thought has been dominated by the idea that the mission of mankind is to achieve mastery over nature. The world of nature is commonly characterised by its opposition to the essential condition of humanity, whose purest expression is taken to be civil society. My starting point in this chapter is the observation that the meaning of 'technology', as currently understood in the West, is firmly fixed within this polarity of society and nature. It is important to recognise from the outset, however, that terms such as society, nature and technology are far from mere labels, in themselves harbouring no moral, political or evaluative commitment. Of the concept of society, it has been observed that to use it is not to denote a thing but to make a claim (Wolf 1988: 757). Similarly, if we want to know what words like nature and technology mean, then rather than seeking some delimited set of phenomena in the world – as though one could point to them and say 'There, that's nature!' or 'that's technology!' – we should be trying to discover what sorts of claims are being made with these words, and whether they are justified. In the history of modern thought these claims have been concerned, above all, with the ultimate supremacy of human reason. Thus society is considered to be the mode of association of rational beings, nature the external world of things as it appears to the reasoning subject, and technology the means by which a rational understanding of that external world is turned to account for the benefit of society.

Now to the evolutionary anthropologists of the eighteenth and nineteenth centuries it appeared self-evident that societies differed in the degree of cultivation of their powers of reason, in the scope of their understanding of the natural world, and hence also in the extent to which they were able to bend the forces of nature to their own will. The more 'civilised' the society, and the more complex its technology, the more complete was thought to be its mastery or control over nature; conversely in 'primitive' societies, with simple technologies, control over nature was thought to be weak or non-existent. The most primitive societies of all, of course, were those of so-called 'savages', hunter-gatherers who had yet to achieve that basic level of control marked by the domestication of animals and plants. Such people were supposed to live wholly at the mercy of the vicissitudes of nature, and thus to represent the absolute antithesis of Western industrial man who, through the rational application of scientific knowledge, had at last subjugated nature to his sovereign will. And for those who saw technology as the driving force of social development, the simplicity of technology among primitive hunter-gatherers accounted for the rudimentary nature of their social organisation, just as the advanced industrial technology of the West was supposed to underwrite a complex social structure.

In contemporary anthropology, we have become used to treating such arguments with suspicion. We cite examples of societies in which an apparently simple technology is found side by side with systems of kinship and ritual of the utmost complexity. There is, we say, no single measure of social advancement; a society may score highly on one criterion but low on another. Technology is a Western preoccupation, but Australian Aborigines are preoccupied with kinship: neither kinship nor technology furnishes a universal scale of complexity. If Westerners belittle Aborigines on account of the simplicity of their technology, Aborigines are equally entitled to belittle Westerners on account of their primitive notions of kinship. As Franz Boas wrote long ago, 'we have simple industries and complex organisation', as well as 'diverse industries and simple organisation' (1940: 266–7). This denial of any necessary link between technology and society or culture has since become enshrined in the dominant relativistic credo of modern cultural anthropology (Pfaffenberger 1988: 243).

Yet despite the anthropological critique of the evolutionist doctrine of technologically-driven progress, no-one seems to doubt that there is a sphere of capability in every human society that can be identified by the concept of technology, and that in primitive societies (and above all in societies of hunters and gatherers) it may be characterised by its relative simplicity. Indeed in their self-conscious and often contrived attempts to avoid the derogatory connotations of the notion of primitiveness, anthropologists are inclined to qualify their references to 'simple societies' with the rider that 'simple' denotes *technological* simplicity, and carries no immediate implications as regards social organisation and culture. Thus we are told that hunting and gathering is essentially a technological regime, and that we are not entitled to draw conclusions from the rudimentary nature of this technology about the form or elaboration of the social relations in which its practitioners are engaged. It is meaningless, it is said, even to speak of 'hunting and gathering societies' as a class, since these societies have nothing more in common than the purely contingent fact that their members hunt and gather for their subsistence, possessing neither domestic herds nor crops.

Two views that are diametrically opposed often turn out to be so because they are based on common premises, and this is certainly the case with the opposition between evolutionism and relativism that I have sketched out above. On one side, in brief, are those who claim that the essential institutional forms of society are dictated by the requirements of operating a technological system of some given degree of complexity, and therefore that social change is driven by – and depends upon – technological change.[1] On the other side are those who hold that technology exerts no influence upon the form of a society, beyond setting outer limits on the scope of human action. Within those limits, society and culture are said to follow their own historical course, irrespective of the nature or complexity of the technological system. Not only, however, do both sides suppose that technology can be scaled in terms of degrees of complexity; they also share the assumption that technology comprises an objective system of relations among things, that is wholly *exterior* to the social domain of relations among persons. The impact of technology on society may be affirmative or neutral, its formulae prescriptive or permissive, but in itself technology has no part in society: it is simply given as an independent, external factor.

Having thus been placed outside of society and culture, technology could – so far as most anthropologists were concerned – be safely ignored. It was considered to be just one of those things, like climate or ecology, that may or may not be a determining factor in human affairs, but whose study can be safely left to others. As climate is for meteorologists and ecology for ecologists, so technology is for engineers. The study of technological processes was not seen as an integral part of the study of social relations, or of the study of those systems of meaning that go by the name of culture, and indeed anthropology lacked any framework of concepts or theoretical ideas in which to handle such processes. The result is that until very recently, insofar as technology appeared in anthropological accounts at all, it generally did so in the form of lists or inventories, catalogues of tools and techniques which – however valuable in themselves as documentary records – bore a purely descriptive purpose. Even today, and despite an upsurge of interest fuelled by the revolution in computing and telecommunications, the study of technology remains one of the least developed aspects of anthropological scholarship (a view shared, *inter alia*, by Lemmonier 1986, Pfaffenberger 1988, 1992, and Hornborg 1992).

Now it is precisely the notion that society and technology are external to one another that I wish to challenge. In my view, far from being a timeless datum of the human condition, this externality is a product of history, and a relatively recent one at that. It has emerged in the West, in the last few centuries, hand in hand with what could be called a 'machine-theoretical' cosmology. We cannot, I think, retroject into history or prehistory the modern separation of society and technology, nor can we impose it on non-Western societies, without seriously distorting our understanding of them. My thesis, in a nutshell, is that in the societies we study – perhaps even including our own – technical relations are embedded in social relations, and can only be understood within this relational matrix, as one aspect of human sociality. Two further claims follow: first, that what is usually represented as a process of complexification, a development of technology from the simple to the complex, would be better seen as a process of externalisation or of disembedding – that is, a progressive cutting out of technical from social relations. Secondly, the modern concept of technology, set up as it is in opposition to society, is a product of this historical process. If that is so, we cannot expect to find a separate sphere of human endeavour corresponding to 'technology' wherever we choose to look.

To put my case in the strongest possible terms: *there is no such thing as technology in pre-modern societies.* Let me add at once that I do not mean that people in such societies lack tools or technical skills. My point is that the concept of technology, at least in its contemporary Western usage, sets out to establish the epistemological conditions for society's control over nature by maximising the distance between them. Focusing in particular on societies of hunters and gatherers, I shall show that through their tools and techniques hunter-gatherers strive to *minimise* this distance, drawing nature into the nexus of social relations, or 'humanising' it. This 'drawing in' has as its object to establish the conditions not of control but of a kind of mutualism. In this, the tool delivers a force that is personal rather than mechanical. Hence technical relations, far from being set apart from social relations, are embedded in them.

Before proceeding further, I should perhaps add that the critical strategy I am adopting is a well-tried one in anthropology. Substitute the term 'economy' for 'technology', and everything I have said would be well in tune with most recent thinking in economic anthropology. Over the last two or three decades, anthropologists have been at pains to show how 'economy' and 'society' became institutionally separated in the history of Western capitalism, how the category of the economic is itself a product of this history, how in pre-capitalist societies economic relations are embedded in social relations, and how – with the development of market-oriented capitalism – economic life was progressively disembedded from social life (Polanyi 1957, Sahlins 1969, Godelier 1972: 92–103, Dumont 1986: 104–12). All that I am doing is to extend the same kind of argument to the concept of technology, which up to now has escaped the critical attention that has been devoted to the concept of economy. I believe this critical work is an essential first step in building a coherent and theoretically informed anthropology of technology, one that takes us beyond the mere cataloguing of tools and techniques from cultures around the world.

TOOLS, TECHNIQUES AND TECHNOLOGY

In the last chapter, I distinguished between technique and technology in terms of whether human powers of perception and action are either immanent in, or detached from, the processes by which things get made. In line with this distinction, in what follows I shall take technique to refer to *skills*, regarded as the capabilities of particular human subjects (see Layton 1974:3–4), and technology to mean a corpus of generalised, objective knowledge, insofar as it is capable of practical application. Both technique and technology must, of course, be distinguished from *tools*. A tool, in the most general sense, is an object that extends the capacity of an agent to operate within a given environment. But you do not necessarily have to use a tool to implement a technique. It is a fundamental mistake, as Marcel Mauss (1979; 104) recognised, to think that 'there is technique only when there is an instrument'. In the hands of a hunter or warrior the spear may be a tool for bringing down game or wounding an adversary, but in the hands of the athlete the flight of the javelin becomes an end in itself. He uses no instrument to augment his throw, yet he still has his technique.

Why is it, then, that in both specialised anthropological and popular Western discourse, it tends to be assumed that technical activity is *ipso facto* tool-using activity? Consider, for example, Roy Ellen's definition of subsistence technique: 'a combination of material artefacts (tools and machines) and the knowledge required to make and use them' (1982: 128). Here, technique is regarded not as a property of skilled subjects, but as an inventory of instrumental objects together with their operational requirements. This view, I believe, results from a conflation of the technical with the mechanical, a conflation that lies at the very core of the modern concept of technology. For as we saw in the last chapter, what this concept does, in effect, is to treat the workman as an *operative*, putting into effect a set of mechanical principles that are both embodied in the construction of the instruments he uses, and entirely indifferent to his own subjective aptitudes and sensibilities. In other words, productive work is divorced from human agency and assigned to the functioning of a device. Thus, technique appears to be 'given' in the operational principles of the tools themselves, quite independently of the experience of their users. If all technical activity is tool-using activity, it is because the technique is seen to reside, outside the user, in the tool, and to come 'packaged' – like the instruction manual for a piece of modern machinery – along with the tool itself.

My contention, to the contrary, is that technique is embedded in, and inseparable from, the experience of particular subjects in the shaping of particular things. In this respect it stands in sharp contrast to technology, which consists in a knowledge of objective principles of mechanical functioning, whose validity is completely independent both of the subjective identity of its human carriers and of the specific contexts of its application. Technique thus places the subject at the centre of activity, whereas technology affirms the independence of production from human subjectivity. Drawing out the contrast, Carl Mitcham notes that

> . . . tools or hand instruments tend to engender techniques, machines technologies . . .
> Technique is more involved with the training of the human body and mind . . . , whereas

technology is concerned with exterior things and their rational manipulation . . . Techniques rely a lot on intuition, not so much on discursive thought. Technologies, on the other hand, are more tightly associated with the conscious articulation of rules and principles . . . At the core of technology there seems to be a desire to transform the heuristics of technique into algorithms of practice.

(1978: 252)

Now it is commonly supposed that where there are techniques there must be technology, for if skill lies in the effective application of knowledge, there must be knowledge to apply (Layton 1974). I believe this view to be mistaken. For acting in the world is the skilled practitioner's way of knowing it. It is in the direct contact with materials, whether or not mediated by tools – in the attentive touching, feeling, handling, looking and listening that is entailed in the very process of creative work – that technical knowledge is gained as well as applied. No separate corpus of rules and representations is required to organise perceptual data or to formulate instructions for action. Thus, skill is at once a form of knowledge and a form of practice, or – if you will – it is both practical knowledge and knowledgeable practice. Moreover as a form of knowledge, skill (or technique) is different in kind from technology. The former is tacit, subjective, context-dependent, practical 'knowledge how', typically acquired through observation and imitation rather than formal verbal instruction. It does not therefore have to be articulated in systems of rules and symbols. Technological knowledge, by contrast, is explicit rather than tacit, objective rather than subjective, context-independent rather than context-dependent, discursive rather than practical, 'knowledge that' rather than 'knowledge how'. It is, besides, encoded in words or artificial symbols, and can be transmitted by teaching in contexts *outside* those of its practical application.

Historically, as the skilled manipulation of tools has given way to the operation of mechanically determined systems, knowledge of the first kind has been gradually devalued, whilst knowledge of the second kind has come to be regarded as increasingly indispensable. Far from complementing technique by providing it with a foundation in knowledge, technology has forced a division between knowledge and practice, elevating the former from the practical to the discursive, and reducing the latter from creative doing or making to mere execution. To see this, one has only to compare the classical, Aristotelian notion of *tekhnē*, with its connotation of skilled craftsmanship, with the modern idiom in which to say of practice that it is 'purely technical' is to intimate that it is merely mechanical. In the dichotomy between discursive knowledge and executive practice, no space remains for the practical knowledge (or knowledgeable practice) of the craftsman. Technology, in short, appears to erase technique, rather than to back it up.

Moreover the transition from technique to technology, on the level of knowledge, has its precise counterpart, on the level of material instruments, in the transition from the tool to the machine. Recall that in the classical conception, *tekhnē* referred to the skilled making of the craftsman, while *mēkhanē* referred to the manually operated devices that assisted its application. But now, just as technology has been removed from the sphere of practitioners' personal knowledge and experience, so the machine has come to signify the independence of technical operations from human sensibility. Overall, then, the evolution from the classical dualism of *tekhnē/mēkhanē* to the modern dualism of technology/machine has been one in which the human subject – both as an agent and as a repository of experience – has been drawn from the centre to the periphery of the labour process. In other words, as I have tried to show schematically in Figure 16.1, it has been a movement from the personal to the impersonal. I now intend to demonstrate that this movement is tantamount to a dis-embedding of technical relations from their matrix in human sociality, leading to the modern opposition between technology and society.

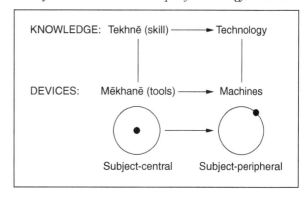

THE TECHNICAL AND THE SOCIAL

It is commonplace in anthropology to draw an absolute distinction between the domains of technical and social phenomena. This doubtless owes much to the influence of Emile Durkheim. The earliest anthropolog-ical reference to the distinction that I know is to be found in a tantalising footnote to the conclusion of Durkheim and Mauss's essay of 1903 on *Primitive Classification*,

Figure 16.1 The transition in knowledge and devices from the personal to the impersonal, associated with the substitu-tion of the modern dichotomy of technology/machine for the classical dichotomy of *tekhnē/mēkhanē*.

where they write of what they call 'technological classifications' as vague and unsystem-atic constellations of ideas, quite unlike the systematically interconnected categories of scientific classification which are grounded in the structure of social groups. Scientific clas-sifications, Durkheim and Mauss write,

> are very clearly distinguished from what might be called technological classifications. It is probable that man has always classified, more or less clearly, the things on which he lived, according to the means he used to get them: for example animals living in the water, or in the air or on the ground. But at first such groups were not connected with each other or systematized. They were divisions, distinctions of ideas, not schemes of classification. Moreover, it is evident that these distinctions are closely linked to prac-tical concerns, of which they merely express certain aspects.
>
> (1963: 81–2, fn. 1)[2]

What is important for my present argument is the way technological classification is linked here to the experience of individuals in practical activity, as opposed to the structuring force of society. From the start, technology was placed firmly on the individual side of a pervasive dichotomy between individual and society, while science was set apart on the social side.

In the subsequent elaboration of the Durkheimian paradigm, the distinction between technology and science was referred back to that between magic and religion, the former issuing from the individual and pragmatic in intent, the latter issuing from society and fundamentally expressive. The same distinction was later taken up by Edmund Leach, in a series of attempts to force a division between *technical* and *ritual* types or aspects of behaviour. Leach defines technical behaviour in purely pragmatic, means–ends terms: it 'produces observable results in a strictly mechanical way'. Ritual behaviour, by contrast, is essentially communicative, and serves to convey information, in a symbolic code, about group membership or social identity (Leach 1966: 403: cf. 1954: 12, 1976: 9). The divi-sion, then, is between a mechanics of technical systems and a semiotics of social systems. All practical action is 'fully mechanical' in the sense that its effects are entirely predictable from its initial conditions (1976: 23), whereas all social action, since it is designed to communicate a state of affairs but not to change it, is inherently non-practical.

To illustrate the effects of applying this conceptual framework across the board of human societies, let me return to the case of hunters and gatherers. It comes as no surprise that the usual anthropological characterisation of the activities of hunting and gathering as 'purely technical' carries the implications that they are not only 'fully mechanical' but also residually *non*-social. Thus the work of subsistence production is effectively removed from the sphere of social action, becoming merely a 'need-satisfying process of individual behaviour' (Sahlins 1972: 186 fn. 1). When human beings hunt and gather, even when they do so in co-operation, they can act only in their 'natural' capacity as individuals, rather than as social persons. 'Given such a distinction', as Gísli Pálsson has shown, 'production must take place in nature. The appropriation of nature only becomes social when the resources extracted from nature enter relations of sharing or exchange among groups' (Palsson 1991: 8). If, as Durkheim maintained, there are two parts to a man, the individual and the social being, it is apparently the individual who hunts and gathers, and the social being (as a member of a more inclusive group) who shares (Ingold 1988a: 275, cf. Durkheim 1976: 16). In Leach's terms, every act of hunting and gathering would be a mechanical event, and every act of sharing a communicative or semiotic event.

This view of the separation of production and distribution has been reinforced by a peculiarly Durkheimian reading of the distinction, taken from Marx, between social relations and technical forces of production, according to which these constitute mutually exclusive domains. Representing a widely held position in Marxist anthropology, Jonathan Friedman has written that 'the social relations of production are not, nor can they be, technical relations' (1974: 447). Included in the latter are the forces mechanically exerted by human bodies, when set to work, whether singly or in conjunction. Relations of co-operation in the tasks of hunting and gathering are thus built into the operation of the technical system – they are *technical* relations, part of the organisation of work, as distinct from the *social* relations activated in the distributive practices of sharing. Yet as Marx surely recognised, the externalisation of the forces of production was a historical consequence of the development of the machine. Where, as in hunting and gathering, food production depends on the skilled handling of tools, and indeed of one's own person, the productive forces appear as the embodied qualities of human subjects – as their technical skills. Such qualities cannot be generalised: whereas a technology is indifferent to the personhood of its operators, techniques are active ingredients of personal and social identity. Thus the very practice of a technique is itself a statement about identity; there can be no separation of communicative from technical behaviour.

Our conclusion must be that in hunting and gathering societies, the forces of production are deeply embedded in the matrix of social relations. That is to say, the 'correspondence' between technical forces and social relations is not external but internal, or in other words, the technical is one *aspect* of the social. The modern semantic shift from technique to technology, associated with the ascendance of the machine, is itself symptomatic of the disembedding of the forces of production from their social matrix, transforming the correspondence between forces and relations of production from the internal to the external, and setting up the now familiar opposition between technology and society. For as I have already shown, the concept of technology signifies the withdrawal of the person from production, which is consequently reduced to the operation of a quasi-mechanical system comprising human bodies, instruments and raw materials. If persons, human subjects, are external to production, then the sphere of social relations (between persons) must be external to the sphere of technical relations which, if they involve human beings at all, involve them as the bearers of natural and not personal powers (on this distinction, see Shotter 1974: 225).

The danger is that we are inclined to read back into history the modern separation of technology and society, identifying the forces of production with all that is external to the human subject. Hence we imagine the primitive precursors of the machine to have been such items of material culture as the hand-axe, spear and digging-stick. And this, in turn, leads us to view technical evolution as a process of complexification, accompanied perhaps by a simplification in the social spheres of kinship and ritual. However the machine is not simply a more advanced substitute for a tool, nor were hand-tools the original forces of production. For the development of the forces has transformed the entire system of relations between worker, tool and raw material, replacing subject-centred knowledge and skills with objective principles of mechanical functioning. In short, and to reiterate the conclusion of my argument from the last chapter, technical evolution describes a process not of complexification but of *objectification* of the productive forces.

This result suggests a radical recasting of the relation between technology and kinship. Instead of seeing an evolution in parallel, in which the former becomes ever more dominant and elaborate as the latter declines in significance, the view I have proposed suggests that the technical forces of production were originally *consubstantial* with the social relations of kinship. Only subsequently, as kinship was disengaged from the organisation of production, did the forces 'split off' and acquire separate institutional identity as a technology. At the same time the objectives of production were themselves transformed from the constitution of persons to the manufacture of things. In short, to find the antecedents of technology, we should look to the sphere of artifice, contained in social relations, rather than to the artefacts of material culture (Ridington 1982: 470).

WHAT TOOLS ARE FOR

The next step in my argument is to show how this view of the embeddedness of technical in social relations affects our understanding of the nature and use of the tool. In itself, of course, the tool is nothing (Sigaut 1993: 383). 'Being a tool' is not at all the same as, say, 'being a stone' or 'being a piece of wood'. For whereas the latter refers to intrinsic properties of the object itself, the former refers to what it affords for a user. An object – it could be a stone or a piece of wood – *becomes* a tool through becoming conjoined to a technique, and techniques, as we have seen, are the properties of skilled subjects. The presence of such a subject is already presupposed in our description of the object as a tool of a certain kind. Thus the tool is not a mere mechanical adjunct to the body, serving to deliver a set of commands issued to it by the mind; rather it extends the whole person. Indeed there is a certain parallel between the use of tools in production and the giving and receiving of gifts in exchange. The tool has an impact on raw material, as the gift has an impact on its recipient, only so long as it is animated by an *intention* that issues from the person of the user or donor. Divorced from the context of production, the tool reverts to its original condition as an inert object; likewise the gift is inert outside the social context of exchange (Mauss 1954[1925]: 10). Both tool and gift mediate an active, purposive engagement between persons and their environments.

Returning to hunters and gatherers, we can ask how this mediation is effected in the context of their relations with their environments. As Robin Ridington (1982: 471) has pointed out, hunter-gatherers 'typically view their world as imbued with human qualities of will and purpose'. From their perspective, tools are like words: they mediate relations between human subjects and the equally purposive non-human agencies with which they perceive themselves to be surrounded. Thus the tool, as I showed in Chapter Four (p. 72), is a link in a chain of personal rather than mechanical causation, which serves to deliver intentional action and not merely physical or bodily force. Moreover, unlike herdsmen and farmers, whose tools are used to establish some degree of domination over their environments, hunters and gatherers do not regard their tools as instruments of control. Thus in hunting, it is commonly supposed that the animal gives itself to be killed by the hunter who, as a recipient, occupies the subordinate position in the transaction. The spear, arrow or trap serves here as a vehicle for opening or consummating a relationship. If the arrow misses its mark, or if the trap remains empty, it is inferred that the animal does not as yet intend to enter into a relationship with the hunter by allowing itself to be taken. In that way, the instruments of hunting serve a similar purpose to the tools of divination, revealing the otherwise hidden intentions of non-human agents in a world saturated with personal powers of one kind and another. In short, whereas for farmers and herdsmen, the tool is an instrument of control, for hunters and gatherers it would better be regarded as an instrument of revelation.

This understanding that hunters and gatherers have of their relations with non-human components of their environments is fundamentally at odds with that basic premise of Western thought with which I began, that the destiny of humankind is to achieve domination over nature. 'In our traditional ways of thinking', as Winner writes, 'the concept of mastery and the master–slave metaphor are the dominant ways of describing man's relationship to nature, as well as to the implements of technology' (1977: 20). Viewed from this perspective, hunters and gatherers appear to be engaged in a struggle for existence which, on account of the simplicity of their material equipment, is not yet won. For them, nature remains untamed. Yet herein lies a paradox. For if technology implies the human control over nature, and if the condition of hunter-gatherers – or more generally of 'primitive man' – is the absence of such control, how can there be such a thing as 'primitive technology'?

Though the paradox is never stated so explicitly in the literature, the solution comes through clearly enough. It is to assume that hunter-gatherers are engaged in the operation of a system of forces which is none other than nature herself, viewed – characteristically, in Western eyes – as a vast, all-encompassing mechanism. Tied to the workings of this mechanism, they are regarded as subservient to nature in much the same way that, in the modern era, industrial workers are subservient to the artificially engineered machines of the factory. It follows that hunter-gatherer technology is seen to be grounded in the properties of the natural world just as Western technology is embodied in the artificial machine. Both delimit a set of production possibilities that are given prior to, and independently of, the persons of the producers. It is for this reason that the forces the hunter-gatherer operates are commonly denoted by the hybrid 'techno-environmental'. Where for everyone else, technology is supposed to be on the side of Man against Nature, for hunters and gatherers it appears to be on the side of Nature against Man, revealing in its application the hegemony of natural law rather than the dominance of human society and its interests. This, incidentally, is a view shared equally by both advocates and opponents of so-called 'techno-environmental determinism'. Advocates argue that technology and environment together determine social form, opponents argue that social form is independent of techno-environmental constraint, but both take it for granted that 'techno' is something that is intrinsically linked to environmental conditions, rather than an imposition of society.

My solution to the problem of whether technology lies on the side of nature or human society is simply to dispense with the dichotomy, and with it the concept of technology that is predicated on this dichotomy. The paradox then promptly disappears. What we have in reality are human beings, living and working in environments that include other humans as well as a variety of non-human agencies and entities. Through their experiences of dealing with these various components of the environment, persons develop with specific aptitudes and sensibilities, that is as bearers of techniques. Reciprocally, through the deployment of their technical skills, people actively constitute their environments. But in this mutually constitutive interrelation between persons and environment there is no absolute dichotomy between human and non-human components. There are techniques for engaging with fellow humans just as there are techniques for engaging with the animals and plants on which life depends, or with materials such as wood, clay or stone in the making of equipment. Any or all of these techniques may involve the use of tools. However these tools, as I have shown, are intended not to control but to reveal. And they are used not in a failed attempt to achieve emancipation from an alien world of nature, but in a successful attempt to draw the inhabitants of that world into an unbounded sphere of intimate sociality.

CONCLUSION

Hunters and gatherers have secured their place in Western thought as the bearers of a simple technology, as representatives of the original baseline from which a gradual process of complexification eventually culminated in the advanced technologies of the modern world. I have argued, to the contrary, that the concept of technology is itself a product of a modern machine-theoretical cosmology. One is inclined to see, in its indiscriminate extension to society at large, a particular instance of the more general anthropological fetishisation of culture, another Western concept which we have turned upon others as a mirror of our own superiority. People in 'primitive' or 'traditional' societies are made to appear as though their practical activities were entirely bound to the operation of technology, as their thought to the precepts of their culture, the one providing material support for the other. Technology and culture, twin pillars of the modern ideals of progress and enlightenment, confine the rest of humanity to the monotonous execution of determining systems: as technology determines practice, so culture determines thought.

Once the concept of technology is unpacked it is evident that its application distorts our understanding – above all of hunting and gathering societies – in the following ways:

1   Technique is detached from the practical experience of human subjects and ascribed to the properties of an instrumental apparatus, of which people are but mechanical operators.
2   Technical activity is partitioned off from social activity, and likewise production is separated from distribution as issuing from individuals and social persons respectively.
3   Technical forces are grounded in an environment conceived as 'nature', an alien and dehumanised presence that seems to dictate the terms of accommodation.

The principal conclusions of my argument are really two-fold. The first, reinforcing my thesis in Chapter Fifteen, is that technical evolution has to be seen as a process not of complexification but of objectification and externalisation of the forces of production. The second, related conclusion is that in the course of this evolution, technical relations have become progressively disembedded from social relations, leading eventually to the modern institutional separation of technology and society. The implications for anthropology are that we can no longer follow the Durkheimian precedent of taking this separation for granted, nor can the concept of technology remain immune from critical scrutiny. It is high time to restore technique to its rightful place alongside economy, politics, religion and kinship as a proper object of social anthropological inquiry.

Chapter Seventeen

Work, time and industry

Much anthropological discussion is couched in terms of a pervasive opposition between 'Westerners' and other, 'non-Western' people. Amongst other things, it is argued that Westerners have a specific attitude to time and work that is not shared by people in non-Western societies. I want to propose here that while the concepts of time and work have indeed acquired specific meanings through their implication in such key historical transitions as the rise of capitalism and the growth of industrial manufacture, there is nevertheless a sense in which none of us are Westerners, and that the challenge that non-Western perspectives present to Western modes of apprehension exists at the very heart of our *own* society, in the mismatch between our shared experience of dwelling in the lived-in world and the demands placed on us by external structures of production and control that seem to leave only a residual space, divorced from culture and social life, where we can truly be ourselves.

I shall proceed as follows. First, I consider the attitudes to work and time of people in 'traditional' or pre-industrial societies who still retain a large measure of control over the rhythms of their working lives. For such people, I suggest, time is intrinsic to the array of specific tasks that make up the pattern of quotidian activity of a community. I go on to show how the formal logic of capitalist production undermines this task-orientation by establishing an absolute division, in principle, between the domains of work and social life. This division, however, does not naturally conform to experience but is rather enforced, to varying degrees, against a resistance founded in the inevitability of people's mutual involvement in the concrete settings of practical activity. The very instruments – above all the industrial machine and the clock – that in theory serve to disengage the time and work of production from the current of social life, are in practice reappropriated by their operators in the process of production, not of commodities for the market, but of their own personal and social identities. To exemplify this point, I shall draw on some studies of one particular category of industrial workers, namely locomotive drivers. In conclusion, I argue that if we find the time-awareness of people in societies other than our own hard to grasp, this is not because it is strange to our experience, but rather because the political, economic and ideological apparatus of the 'West', with its peculiar conjunction of individual freedom and clockwork necessity, has made us, in a sense, strangers to ourselves.

TASK-ORIENTATION

Speaking of people in so-called primitive societies, Cato Wadel has observed that what is characteristic of these societies 'is not that activities we term as work are not conceptualised, but that these activities are conceptualised *in association with* social relations' (Wadel

1979: 380). Or as Sahlins puts it, 'a man works, produces, in his capacity as a social person, as a husband and father, brother and lineage mate, member of a clan, a village' (1968: 80). To see an activity as thus embedded in a social relation is to regard it as what I shall call a *task*. And of all the manifold tasks that make up the total current of activity in a community, there are none that can be set aside as belonging to a separate category of 'work', nor is there any separate status of being a 'worker'. For work is life, and any distinctions one might make within the course of life would be not between work and non-work, but between different fields of activity, such as farming, cooking, child-minding, weaving, and so on.

The same point applies quite generally in the pre-industrial world (Godelier 1980). In Ancient Greece, for example, 'we do not find the idea of one great human function, work, encompassing all the trades, but rather that of a plurality of different ones, each consti-tuting a particular type of action with its own particular product' (Vernant 1983: 272). Every artisan trade – with its specific instruments, raw materials and products, its tech-nical operations and the qualities required of its practitioners – was a separate system rather than part of an all-embracing division of labour. If there was any overarching divi-sion, it was not between work and leisure, but rather between the spheres of making and doing, *poiesis* and *praxis*, a division that subordinated the crafts of manufacture to the activities – including farming and warfare – of those who used the implements made.

What holds for the generalised category of work holds also for that of time. It is commonly observed, in ethnographic accounts of non-industrial societies, that the people described lack any concept that would correspond exactly to the idea of time current in the West. Here, for example, is Evans-Pritchard, writing in a justly celebrated passage about Nuer pastoralists of southern Sudan:

> The Nuer have no expression equivalent to 'time' in our language, and they cannot, therefore, speak of time as though it were something which passes, can be wasted, saved, and so forth. I do not think that they ever experience the same feeling of fighting against time or of having to co-ordinate activities with an abstract passage of time, because their points of reference are mainly the activities themselves, which are of a leisurely character. Events follow a logical order, but they are not controlled by an abstract system, there being no autonomous points of reference to which activities have to conform with precision. Nuer are fortunate.
>
> (Evans-Pritchard 1940: 103)

Among the Nuer, then, as much more generally in the pre-industrial world, time is insep-arable from the everyday round of activities. It is not something objective and external, *against* which tasks may be measured or *on* which they can be located, since it has no existence apart from the tasks themselves. Thus for the Nuer, 'the daily timepiece is the cattle clock, the round of pastoral tasks, and the time of day and the passage of time through a day are to a Nuer primarily the succession of these tasks and their relation to one another' (pp. 101–2).

We may speak, then, of a *task-orientation* in such societies, an orientation in which both work and time are intrinsic to the conduct of life itself, and cannot be separated or abstracted from it. If you want to say *when* something happened, you do so by relating it to another regular activity that took place concurrently – for example, 'so-and-so arrived in the camp at milking time'. And if you want to say *how long* it took for something to happen, you do so by comparing it with how long something else takes. In a pioneering though now rather dated work on primitive time-reckoning, the Swedish anthropologist Martin Nilsson wrote that

> To indicate the duration of time, primitive peoples make use of other means, *derived from their daily business*, . . . in Madagascar, 'rice-cooking' often means half an hour, 'the frying of a locust', a moment. The Cross River natives say: 'The man died in less than the time in which maize is not yet completely roasted', i.e. less than about fifteen minutes; 'the time in which one can cook a handful of vegetables'.
>
> (Nilsson 1920: 42)

Likewise in a classic paper about which I shall have more to say presently, the historian E. P. Thompson notes that in Medieval England, duration could be expressed by how long it took to cook an egg, say a prayer, or (apparently) to have a pee – though this latter time-span, known as 'pissing while', does seem 'a somewhat arbitrary measurement' (Thompson 1967: 58).

I have spoken of tasks as socially embedded activities, but should pause to explain more precisely what I mean. First and foremost, tasks are activities carried out by persons, calling for greater or lesser degrees of technical skill. Machines do not perform tasks, but people do. Thus with a task-orientation the human subject, equipped with a competence acquired through practising alongside more experienced hands, is situated right at the centre of productive activity. Secondly, tasks are defined primarily in terms of their objectives, without necessarily entailing any explicit codification of the rules and procedures to be followed in realising them. And these objectives, far from being independently prescribed in the form of exercises in problem-solving (as in the entirely artificial tasks of 'testing' in the school or psychological laboratory), themselves arise through the agent's involvement within the current of social life. Thirdly, the particular kinds of tasks that a person performs are an index of his or her personal and social identity: the tasks you do depend on who you are, and in a sense the performance of certain tasks *makes* you the person who you are. And finally, tasks are never accomplished in isolation, but always within a setting that is itself constituted by the co-presence of others whose own performances necessarily have a bearing on one's own. In other words, every task exists as part of what I have called a *taskscape*, understood as the totality of tasks making up the pattern of activity of a community (for an elaboration of this concept, see Chapter Eleven).

Now if, in traditional societies, time is intrinsic to tasks, and if tasks are the technically skilled activities of particular persons with particular social identities, then it must follow that there can be no real distinction between work and social life, and moreover that time is the movement or flow that inheres equally in both. What kind of time is this, that is thus inherent in the taskscape? Sociologists Pitrim Sorokin and Robert K. Merton, in a landmark paper dating from 1937, called it *social time*. I have already introduced this concept in Chapter Eleven (pp. 195–7), and will not elaborate further here save to stress again its inherent rhythmicity and its embeddedness in activities that are indexical of a person's belonging to locality and community (Sorokin and Merton 1937: 628). It is important to emphasise, too, that the rhythmic structure of social time emerges not only from the interweaving and mutual responsiveness of human movements, but also from the way these movements resonate to the cycles of the non-human environment. Traditionally, people had to *fall in* with the rhythms of their environment: with the winds, the tides, the needs of domestic animals, the alternations of day and night, of the seasons, and so on, in accordance with what the environment afforded for the conduct of their daily tasks. As a song of the Kabyle peasant farmers of Algeria puts it: 'It is useless to pursue the world, no-one ever overtakes it' (Bourdieu 1963). Similarly in Ancient Greece, the work of farming was regarded as a form of participation in an order at once natural and divine, and the artisan who supplied the farmer with his tools worked to a design that was inscribed within this order, and that was revealed in the raw material rather than artificially superimposed upon it (Vernant 1983: 248–63). In short, the world *opens itself out* to the traditional artisan or farmer, in both its form and its temporal rhythms, through his or her action in it.

The idea that human industry can run ahead of nature, and in so doing, transform it, belongs to the modern era of Western thought (Godelier 1980: 834). For the goal of modern technology has been to override the constraints of the natural world, to bring its forces under control, so that the rhythms of society can be brought into conformity with an imposed, artificially contrived schedule. Activities can now go on – as we say – 'around the clock'. Developments in the fields of transport and communications have had a decisive impact in this regard, though probably no single innovation has been of greater consequence than the electric light. The effect was to instal a new kind of time as the dominant regulator of human activity. Corresponding to what Sorokin and Merton (1937: 621) called astronomical or *sidereal* time, it is the time spun by the orbital motions of the planets, or by a perfectly functioning mechanical clock. As I shall now show, there is an intimate logical connection between this form of time and the estimation of work in terms of the generalised concept of labour.

THE TEMPORAL LOGIC OF CAPITALIST PRODUCTION

In 1967, E. P. Thompson published what has become a classic study of the effects of industrial capitalism on people's attitudes to time and work. After reviewing a great deal of evidence, he concluded that 'Mature industrial societies of all varieties are marked . . . by a clear demarcation between "work" and "life"' (1967: 93). Of course he does not mean that workers are not alive when they work. The distinction being drawn here between living and working is really one between what *we* do, and what we are *caused* to do; between action that issues from ourselves as responsible social agents, and action that stems from the pressing of various trained capacities into the service of a project that is not ours but is subject to the dictates of an alien will. It is a corollary of this view that life in an industrial society is lived in the activities of consumption rather than production, in the ways in which people take possession of, and use, the goods acquired with the money they earn. This implies that to understand the processes of social life in such a society we have to focus above all on what people are doing in those periods of each day when they are *not* under contract to an employer – that is, 'after business hours' (Sahlins 1968: 80).

The separation between the domains of 'work' and 'social life' is, in fact, a formal entailment of the logic of capitalist production. The defining principle of capitalism is the alienation of labour-power – the need for a certain class of people, lacking direct access to the means to procure a livelihood, to sell or rent out their very capacity to work to an employer, who owns the means of production, in return for a money wage with which they can purchase the wherewithal for their subsistence. People who have thus sold their capacity to work, their labour-power, are conventionally identified (within this context of capitalist class relations) as 'workers', and the activities in which they engage during that period when their labour-power is under the command of an employer who has appropriated it are likewise identified as 'work'. In this situation, labour-power has become a commodity that, like other commodities, can be bought and sold. Moreover the worker, in person, is in principle divorced from the activity of production, since in that very activity his capacity to work is under the command not of himself but of an employer. It follows that the domain of work relations, in which the labour-powers of several workers are combined in the factory or on the shop floor, is quite distinct from the domain of social life, in which workers may relate to one another as *persons*: as members of communities and as occupants of social roles. This is not to say that there are no social relations in the workplace, or to deny that they may exist side by side with co-operation in the labour process. It is to claim, however, that social relations are not themselves *constituted* by such co-operation.

How, following this formal logic, are we to understand the meanings of work and time in the context of industrial capitalism? Following the example of Marx (1930: 10–11), we might compare the work of the tailor with that of the weaver. Not only do they produce qualitatively different things (coats and linen), but also tailoring and weaving are activities of quite unlike kinds, calling for different skills, tools and materials. Yet as exchangeable commodities, we might nevertheless find that one coat is 'worth', say, twenty yards of linen. The value in which this worth consists cannot be in any way particular to coats, linen or anything else. It is rather value-in-general, a kind of worth that is common to all commodities but peculiar to none. Conventionally such value is expressed in terms of money, for money is a special kind of commodity that has no other use than as a medium of exchange. But by the same token, it should in principle be possible to compare tailoring and weaving, not as qualitatively different *kinds* of activity, but as varying *amounts* of 'activity-in-general'. So what is this activity: the lowest common denominator of all productive tasks that is nevertheless particular to none?

Marx, rather misleadingly, called it 'abstract social labour'. That labour is an abstraction, of the same order as value-in-general, is not in doubt. Yet what are relegated in the abstraction are precisely those situationally specific features of the practical contexts of engagement, with persons and materials, in which skills are acquired and deployed. The work of the tailor can be considered substitutable for that of the weaver only by cutting it out from the matrix of social relations within which it takes on its specific form. That specific, socially embedded form is what I have called a task. Now I have already observed that tasks do not exist in isolation but only as part of an interlocking array, a taskscape. Like the array of useful things (or use-values) that ordinarily clutter any inhabited environment, the taskscape is qualitative and heterogeneous (see Chapter Eleven, pp. 194–5). Labour, by contrast, like value-in-general, is quantitative and homogeneous. And in the reduction of the one to the other, effected by the logic of capitalist relations, the sociality of work is dissolved.

What, then, is the common measure by which different tasks may be reckoned to represent equivalent amounts of labour? The answer, of course, is *time*; but it is time of a particular sort – sidereal rather than social, to recall Sorokin and Merton's (1937) distinction. Now a certain task, say in weaving, will lead to the production of a particular object or use-value, say a length of linen. But if the work of the weaver is regarded not as a specific kind of task but as a determinate amount of labour, it will be represented in hours. And likewise, if the linen is regarded not as a specific kind of object but as a determinate amount of value, it will be represented in currency. Consequently, a certain time of labour has produced a certain moneysworth of goods. Or in short, time is money.

The phrase 'time is money', with its implication that time is something that can be spent or saved, used profitably or wastefully, hoarded or squandered, is a product, then, of the commodification of labour that accompanied the rise of industrial capitalism (for some of its metaphorical ramifications, see Lakoff and Johnson 1980: 7–9). Among the first to use the phrase was Benjamin Franklin, himself one of the major architects of the view of man as *Homo faber*, or nature-transformer. In 1751 he related the following story:

> Since our Time is reduced to a Standard, and the Bullion of the Day is minted out into Hours, the Industrious know how to employ every piece of Time to a real Advantage in their different Professions. And he that is prodigal of his Hours, is, in effect, a squanderer of Money. I remember a notable Woman, who was fully sensible of the intrinsic Value of *Time*. Her husband was a shoemaker, and an excellent Craftsman, but never minded how the Minutes passed. In vain did she inculcate to him, *That Time is Money.* He had too much Wit to apprehend her, and it prov'd his ruin. When in the Alehouse among his idle Companions, if one remark'd that the Clock struck Eleven, *What is that*, says he, *among us all?* If she sent him Word by the Boy, that it had struck Twelve; *Tell her to be easy, it can never be more.* If, that it had struck One, *Bid her be comforted, for it can never be less.*
>
> (cited in Thompson 1967: 89)

Let me recapitulate the argument in brief. With industrial capitalism, labour becomes a commodity measured out in units of time, goods become commodities measured out in units of money; since labour produces goods, so much time yields so much money, and time spent in idleness is equivalent to so much money lost. The result is not only a demarcation between work (time that yields money) and leisure (time that uses it up), but also a characteristic attitude to time as something to be *husbanded*. Thompson calls this attitude 'time-thrift' (1967: 83–4).

TASKS, LABOUR AND LEISURE

Thompson's thesis is that with the rise and maturation of industrial capitalist society, the task-oriented time of pre-industrial rural and urban life was gradually replaced by a regulation of production governed by the clock. In Sorokin and Merton's terms, this represents a transition from 'social time' (equivalent to Thompson's task-oriented time) to 'sidereal time' (equivalent to Thompson's clock time).

Task-orientation, as I have already mentioned, is person-centred, so that the experience of time is intrinsic to the performance of skilled activity. But with the rise of capitalist industry, so the theory goes, the person is withdrawn from the core to the margins of the labour process, and hence also the time inherent in personal experience and social life is *disembedded* from the time of work or production. This latter kind of time thus appears objective and impersonal, *extrinsic* to social relations, and governed by laws of mechanical functioning that have no regard for human feeling. It is, of course, the time of the *clock*. For just that reason, Lewis Mumford famously claimed that the clock was the archetypal machine, and that it was the clock rather than the steam engine that heralded the birth of the machine age (Mumford 1967: 286). For the aim of the industrial employer, having appropriated the labour-power or capacities to work of his employees (for a given number of hours each day), is to put together these capacities – on the factory floor or assembly line – into an efficient, working mechanism. And he does so by subjecting their operations to a precise and impersonal clockwork regimen. In many industries, such regimens of work were in place long before the advent of machine automation.

But the identification of the sphere of production with the ascendancy of clock time generates the expectation that the alternate sphere of consumption should be identified with a quite different kind of time, precisely opposed to clock time as individual freedom is opposed to mechanical constraint. This is what is colloquially called 'free time', and it is the time associated with what we call 'leisure' when this is defined by its *contrast* to work. Free time is the time we experience (or rather, think we experience) when we turn inwards on ourselves in the hedonistic pursuit of purely individual satisfactions: it is the time of that archetypal creature of neoclassical economics, the isolated consumer. In reality, of course, this creature is a figment of the imagination, for no-one consumes in isolation. For the same reason, free time is not so much something we actually experience as a category by which our experience is discursively represented, in contexts where we wish to draw attention to the space of our own private and subjective selfhood as against the regulative structures of public life whose temporality is epitomised by the clock.

The individual, in this discourse, is supposedly caught in a perpetual oscillation between work in the public domain of production and leisure in the private domain of consumption. Regulated by clock time in the former,

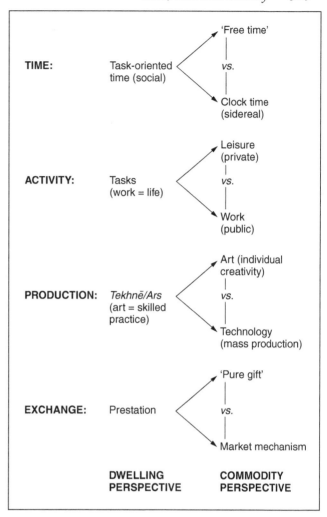

Figure 17.1 The opposition between the dwelling perspective and the commodity perspective in the spheres of time, activity, production and exchange.

he or she retreats into the sanctuary of free time in the latter. In a society dominated by the impersonal structures of the machine and the market, the sphere of leisure seems to offer a residual space for the spontaneous and purely individual expression of selfhood. Moreover the oppositions between work and leisure, and between clock time and free time, have exact homologues in other fields. There is a close connection, for example, between the ideally spontaneous expression of selfhood and the modern Western notion of artistic creativity, which is likewise opposed to the industrial technology of mass production as novelty is opposed to replication. And in the field of exchange, the privacy and spontaneity of the self is closely linked to the ideology of the 'pure gift', as an expression of individual feeling, by contrast to the impersonal 'market mechanism' regulating the exchange of commodities. Thus gifts are to commodities as art is to technology, as leisure is to work, as free time is to clock time. This series of oppositions is depicted in the right hand column of Figure 17.1.

What, then, has been the fate of task-oriented time in industrial society? Has it given way to an exhaustive division between free time and clock time? Before beginning to answer this question, we should note that the task-orientation of traditional societies also has its homologues in other fields. Thus in the field of production, the traditional notion of art as socially situated skilled practice, epitomised by the classical Greek *tekhnē*, and by its Latin equivalent *ars*, preceded the subsequent bifurcation into the opposed notions of art and technology, just as the classification of activities by task preceded the division between leisure and work. And the prestations of traditional societies, about which Mauss wrote so eloquently in his *Essay on the Gift* (1990[1950]), are neither spontaneous expressions of individual generosity nor market-regulated contracts but have as their objective the production of social relations in community. It is possible, therefore, to argue for an evolutionary progression, from a traditional state of affairs in which work is inseparable from life, and characterised by task-orientation with its attendant socially situated skills and prestations, to a modern condition in which every aspect of human life is split by a master dichotomy between freedom and necessity, to yield the series of oppositions spelled out above. Figure 17.1 summarises this argument.

I propose here to argue to the contrary. I do not believe that task-orientation has disappeared with the transition to industry: it persists, perhaps especially in those contexts in which we claim to be 'at home'. Indeed, one way of delineating the meaning of 'home' in our society might be as a domain in which activities are thought of primarily in terms of tasks. But the very ambiguity of this concept suggests two possible approaches to the continuing significance of task-orientation in industrial society. On the one hand, home may be thought of as a domain of activity that has remained relatively impervious to capitalist relations of production – a relic of the householding economy of the pre-industrial era kept alive by capitalism for the purposes of reproducing the labour force. On the other hand, home may represent a certain perspective on the world, which I have called the perspective of *dwelling*. Its focus is on the process whereby features of the environment take on specific local meanings through their incorporation into the pattern of everyday activity of its inhabitants. Home, in this sense, is that zone of familiarity which people know intimately, and in which they, too, are intimately known. As such, it encompasses all the settings of everyday life: whether the house, street, neighbourhood, or place of work.

Of the two approaches suggested by these alternative meanings of 'home', one entails a qualification of the evolutionary argument, the other a more radical critique. I shall start with the first and then move on to the second, with which I identify my own position.

TIME AND EXPERIENCE IN THE HOUSEHOLD AND THE WORKPLACE

The domain of householding, although by no means confined within the four walls of the house or dwelling, was until quite recently (though less so today) centred upon the figure of the housewife, who certainly used to enjoy no division between work and leisure. For her, work was indeed life, and consisted in a multitude of tasks of child-rearing and domestic maintenance. Moreover unlike the industrial worker, the housewife remained formally in command of her own working capacity: although her work was necessary and unavoidable, often punishing in its demands of energy and endurance, it was *not* done under external imposition. Thus the housewife and her sense of time, as Thompson

recognises, hold out as exceptions to his general thesis, which correlates the rise of industrial capitalism with a one-way transition from task-oriented to clock time:

> Despite schooltimes and television times, the rhythms of women's work in the home
> are not wholly attuned to the measurement of the clock. The mother of young chil-
> dren has an imperfect sense of time and attends to other human tides. She has not yet
> altogether moved out of the conventions of 'pre-industrial' society.
>
> (1967: 79)

Here, then, is the qualification: notwithstanding industrialisation, task-orientation continues to thrive in the domestic domain, as a kind of survival from the pre-industrial age,
albeit one that is destined to disappear in due course.

If this qualification is accepted, then so long as the household continues to be a focus
for social reproduction, we need to consider the dialectical interplay *between* the task-
oriented time of the home and the clock time of activities in the workplace. There are
two points about this that we can note immediately. First, the distinction falls – or at
least used to fall – to some extent along lines of gender and generation, with women and
children more committed to task-oriented time and men more committed to clock time.
In the past, an obvious indication of this was that men, and not women and children,
carried clocks or watches. If a woman or child wanted to know what the time was by
the clock, they had to ask a man. Secondly, there can be scheduling conflicts between the
two kinds of time which can cause quite severe disruptions within the household. The
routine of domestic and community tasks has to fall in with local environmental conditions, whereas industries and bureaucracies run to a universal clock time which can
co-ordinate production, transport and commerce on a national or even international scale,
but only at the expense of riding roughshod over local variations. Below, I shall present
an example of the problems that can arise in this connection, concerning the family life
of locomotive drivers.

Is the incongruence between task-oriented and clock time, as the qualified evolutionary
argument outlined above suggests, confined to the household – or, more broadly, to the
local community? Has task-orientation been banished by the inexorable logic of the capitalist mode of production from the workplace? Is it really so, as theory dictates, that
workers lose touch with the rhythms of their own bodies as soon as their physical powers,
placed in the service of capital, are subordinated to the imposed, mechanical regimen of
the production line? In his discussion of the alienation of labour under capitalism, included
in the *Economic and Philosophic Manuscripts of 1844*, Marx protested with all the rhetorical force he could muster that this is indeed the case. Having surrendered his capacity
to work to an employer, the worker 'only feels himself outside his work, and in his work
feels outside himself. He is at home when he is not working, and when he is working he
is not at home' (1964: 110). Now by 'home', Marx clearly meant something more than
a person's place of abode. Setting off to work in the morning, a man not only leaves his
dwelling but also, in a much stronger sense, *ceases to dwell*. He is not himself: as his
activity no longer belongs to him, so too he is a stranger to the world whose forms and
meanings are created through this activity.

Viewed from the perspective of the factory owner, workers may indeed appear as no
more than extensions of the total apparatus of production, and their activity as the mere
operation of a set of mechanical principles – that is, a technology – embodied in the
construction of the machinery employed. This, as we saw in Chapter Fifteen, was the

image that Marx invoked when he spoke of operatives as being treated like 'living appendages' of the 'lifeless mechanism' of the factory (Marx 1930: 451). The experience of the workers themselves, however, is a different one. For in their concrete presence, machines are substantial components of the immediate environment, and engaging with them is an inevitable part of the business of everyday coping in the world. Thus rather than simply operating a technology, the activity of industrial workers consists in *coping with machines*. And viewed in this light, such activity not only belongs to them, but also calls for a good measure of skill, of a kind that can only be acquired through experience on the job. Moreover it is through the development of skills of coping that workers are able to resist the impositions of a regime of command and control that would seek to reduce their activity to nothing more than the operation of an external system of productive forces. It is true that the machinery that workers are required to operate may – on account of its noise, heat, vibration or whatever – strain the human body to its limits of tolerance. However, despite Marx's claim to the contrary, the worker does not cease to dwell in the workplace. He is 'at home' there. But home is often a profoundly uncomfortable place to be.

I have already observed that machines do not perform tasks; only people do. The operation of technology, with or without inputs of human labour-power, is a machine performance. Coping with machines, on the other hand, entails a multitude of tasks, calling for specific aptitudes and sensibilities, which occupy the attention of workers on the shop floor. It is as persons, not as units of labour-power, that they engage with the industrial equipment around them, and the meanings that this equipment holds for them arise within the context of that engagement. Here, then, we rediscover task-orientation at the very heart of industrial production, in the workplace. For this discovery, I am indebted to François Sigaut, who has pointed out that as fast as machines have been contrived to do what had previously been done by skilled hands, different skills have sprung up for handling the machines themselves. He calls this the 'law of the irreducibility of skills', in the light of which 'the entire history of technics . . . might be interpreted as a constantly renewed attempt to build skills into machines by means of algorithms, an attempt constantly foiled because other skills always tend to develop around the new machines' (Sigaut 1994: 446). For precisely the same reason, task-orientation is indestructible. And everything I have said about tasks in general applies more specifically to the skilled handling of industrial machines in the process of coping. It is person-centred, it follows implicit 'rules of thumb' rather than explicitly codified procedures, its objectives are set within the current of activity among all those involved in the work situation rather than following directives laid down from above, it is continually responsive to the other activities that are going on around it, and – most importantly – it is constitutive of personal and social identity.

In short, whereas the operation of technology produces commodities for the owner of capital, coping with machines is part of the process of producing the worker as a skilled social agent. The same activity may be viewed from both perspectives, but it is the latter, grounded in the lived experience of engagement with the material paraphernalia of industry, that is the perspective of dwelling. And in the incongruence between these perspectives, of dwelling and commodity production, lies also the tension between the time of tasks and of the clock. We are inclined to speak of workers on an assembly line as being subjected to the regimen of clock time, while forgetting that the mechanism of the clock drives only the hands on its face, not the hands of the workers whose routine it allegedly controls. The ability to co-ordinate one's movements with the passage of time as measured by the clock is an acquired skill, and the co-ordination is itself a task that is carried on alongside all the other tasks of social life. Clocks are a ubiquitous feature of the environment of people in industrial society, who have to learn to cope with them, just as they must cope with other kinds of machines. But the time intrinsic to the experience of coping with clocks is not itself clock time. We may seek to attune our activity so that it resonates with the repetitions of the clock, or to gain an intuitive 'feel' for hours, minutes and seconds, but that does not turn our bodies into pieces of clockwork.

Having recognised that task-orientation is no mere survival from the pre-industrial age, but that it flourishes at the core of industrial production in workers' activities of coping with machines, the way is open for an analysis of industrial society couched in terms of the concepts listed in the left hand column of Figure 17.1. In particular, we can note that exchanges in the workplace, involving mutual assistance or co-operation in the tasks of coping, are conducted between persons, and that as such – like the customary prestations of traditional societies – they are constitutive of social relations instead of distinct from them. One might even argue, following the lead of Mauss rather than Marx, that the relations among factory workers resemble those of gift exchange:

> When such employees transact with one another as part of their work, they are morally obligated to do so and are transacting not as individuals but as parts of a social web that identifies them and their relationships and obligations to one another. Furthermore, the objects and services that employees transact with one another remain linked with the employees, because workers and what they transact have identities based on their places within the encompassing firm.
>
> (Carrier 1992: 202–3)

The implication of my argument, however, is that the dynamic of industrial society can be understood neither from the dwelling perspective represented by the left-hand column of Figure 17.1, nor from the commodity perspective represented by the right-hand column. It lies instead in the dialectical relation between these two perspectives.

In terms of the geometry of the figure, people in industrial society are caught in a 'horizontal' oscillation, not in a 'vertical' one, but it is an oscillation that incorporates the whole series of dichotomies in the right-hand column as one of its poles. From one perspective there is free time and clock time, from the other all time is task-oriented. From one perspective there is work and leisure, from the other all life consists of tasks. From one there is creative art and the operation of technology, from the other, skilled practices. And from one there are pure gifts and market contracts, from the other, socially situated prestations. But the move from left to right does not represent an evolutionary transition from tradition to modernity. The dwelling perspective has not been *replaced* by the commodity perspective. Indeed the whole thrust of my argument is to the contrary – namely that task orientation, with its attendant socially situated skills and prestations, is the primary condition of our being at home in the world. As such, it constitutes the baseline of sociality upon which the order of modernity has been built, and from which we have now to come to terms with it.

THE LIFE AND TIMES OF LOCOMOTIVE DRIVERS

I should like to exemplify some of the points made above by referring briefly to studies of one particular category of industrial workers – namely, locomotive drivers. They were the subject of a classic paper by the American sociologist W. F. Cottrell, published in 1939 under the title 'Of time and the railroader'. Cottrell paints a vivid picture of how the railroader is a slave to time. The railway system is, in effect, an extension of the assembly line of the factory; for example in automobile manufacture the various components may have to be brought from widely dispersed parts of the country, and if any one of these supply lines breaks down the entire operation founders. The stakes, then, are high, and everything depends on precise timing. Though at the time when Cottrell was writing, United States law stipulated that every engineer should have 8 hours' rest out of every 24, for the remaining 16 hours of each day he was constantly on call. Wherever he went he carried a watch, which was required to be checked for accuracy twice a year. The result, Cottrell writes, was an 'intense time-consciousness that marks the railroader in all his social relationships' (1939: 195).

But this very commitment made it difficult for the railroader to engage in *any* social relationships beyond those of the immediate family. Being constantly on call, he could not time-plan for other relationships. Frederick Gamst, in a more recent study of American railroad engineers ('hogheads') that confirms many of Cottrell's findings, vividly depicts the uncertainties of one of his informants, Slim Rogers, about participation even in family events. Would he be able to watch his son in a crucial baseball game?

> As usual, the hoghead promised nothing but said he would have to see how close he would be to his call, if he were not already on the road . . . Regrettably he had already missed his oldest son's graduation from junior high; maybe he would be able to make it for the graduation of the younger one. The only thing Slim could depend on was attending his own funeral, as he was once told by an old hoghead at the top of the seniority list. 'Then you'll have all the time in the world, Sonny,' the old head remarked.
> (Gamst 1980: 113)

By and large, then, the railroader's leisure activities were limited to solitary, individual recreations that called for no collaboration with others. But precisely because the field of his social relations was perforce so limited, the significance of close family ties was for him exceptionally great, so that his home life – when he *was* at home – was lived with a peculiar intensity.

Relations with the local community, partially mediated by the children of the family, were conducted almost entirely by the railroader's wife. For her, the family represented not a domain of retreat into privacy and solitude, but a point of entry into a wider network of community ties. But she would frequently experience scheduling conflicts between the demands of the children and of community affairs on the one hand, and her obligations towards her husband on the other. They might, for example, call for quite different mealtimes.

It would seem, in this example, that the railroader is oscillating between work and leisure, between the public clock time which regulates the railway system and the free time experienced in the privacy of his home or in the solitude of individual recreation. The housewife, on the other hand, perceives time as task-oriented and founded in the social relations of household and community. And the demands of the community do not necessarily coincide with those of the clock. All of this conforms rather neatly with the qualified evolutionary model, as elaborated in the previous section. The reality, however, may not be that simple. Two more recent studies of railway workers offer some clues as to why this should be so.

The first is by L. S. Kemnitzer, who speaks from his own experience as a railroad conductor in the mid-sixties, some 35 years after Cottrell was writing. He found that, by then, railroad workers no longer identified so closely with the temporal values of the work. That is, the importance of time-keeping for the operation of the railroad system was not matched by an 'intense time-consciousness' of the kind Cottrell had described. The reason for this lay in a general loss of identification with the job, resulting from rationalisation and automation – including the use of diesel engines, computer programming and radio communication. Thus while the accuracy of timing continued to be as important as ever, most personnel were no longer required to carry watches, and these were less regularly checked. However Kemnitzer goes on to emphasise the continuing importance of quite another sense of time, one tied closely to specific tasks and the embodied skills necessary to carry them out. This, so-called 'switching time' lies in the 'ability to integrate time, distance, and subjective estimates about weight, slope and speed in making decisions about the movement of cars and engines in switching' (Kemnitzer 1977: 27). Birgitta Edelman's study of shunters in a Swedish railway yard similarly stresses the importance of skilful estimations and perfect timing in allowing the work to 'flow' without accident (Edelman 1993). But here, rationalisation had proceeded still further. According to a new and controversial regime, the engines themselves were to be operated by remote control by a shunter standing beside the tracks!

Now the kind of timing to which Kemnitzer and Edelman refer is clearly integral to the railway workers' acquired skill of coping with heavy and potentially dangerous vehicles. Indeed 'switching time' sounds surprisingly similar to the Ancient Greek concept of *kairos*, the moment that must be seized, in the skilled work of the artisan, when 'human action meets a natural process developing according to its own rhythm' (Vernant 1983: 291). According to Vernant:

> In intervening with his tools, the artisan must recognize and wait for the moment when the time is ripe and be able to adapt himself entirely to circumstances. He must never desert his post, . . . for if he does the *kairos* might pass and the work be spoiled.
>
> (1983: 291–2)

Thus switching time, like the *kairos*, belongs to a task-orientation – we could almost say that it is part of the *tekhnē* of shunting. And as Edelman's study reveals, it is threatened by the relentless march of automation. Yet according to Kemnitzer, the process of automation had already brought about the demise of the 'intense time consciousness' described by Cottrell. Was not this time consciousness, too, part of a task-orientation, part of the railroader's ability to cope with the demands of his work?

I believe we misunderstand the railroader's sense of time if we equate it with the subjection of his movements, while on the job, to the mechanical determination of the clock. Were they so determined, he would have no need to carry a watch. What distinguished the experienced railroader was his practised ability to co-ordinate his movements with the indications of his timepiece. He had to be able to catch the right moment to accelerate or apply the brakes, or to judge his speed on a stretch of track, so as to arrive or depart safely and precisely on schedule. This was an acquired skill, and one moreover that was highly valued. The railroader's peculiar capacity to 'keep time' with a precision unmatched by practitioners of other trades conferred on him an identity that, as Cottrell notes, singled him out in all his relationships, both within and beyond the field of his employment. And the watch, as the symbol of this identity, was an object of lavish care and attention

(Cottrell 1939: 190). In the eyes of management, to be sure, the railroad system was conceived as a total technology which, in principle, should run with the predictability of clockwork, and employees were treated merely as means towards that end. But in the experience of the railroader, the watch and its temporal intervals were incorporated and accorded significance within an essentially task-oriented approach to the practical business of driving trains. Time consciousness belonged to the railroader's *tekhnē*.

TIME AND THE OTHER IN INDUSTRIAL SOCIETY

There exists, in the Western anthropological imagination, a specific category which is reserved for people whose form of life is considered to be most perfectly opposed to that of the inhabitants of modern industrial societies. This is the category of 'hunter-gatherers'. According to one rather Arcadian vision of hunter-gatherer society, recently introduced into anthropology under the rubric of 'the original affluent society' (Sahlins 1972: 1–39), their wants are few, and can be satisfied with little work, leaving ample time for leisure, rest and sleep. People work erratically, and on average for no more than three or four hours each day. Lacking foresight or any care for the future, hunters and gatherers consume whatever they have to hand, without trying to ration, save or store. They have, it would appear, made an institution out of indolence.

Now Sahlins's account of hunters and gatherers echoes, almost word for word, the sentiments of the English gentry, in the early days of capitalism, towards the labouring classes – likewise notorious for their alleged indolence and profligacy, their irregular hours, and their propensity to spend whatever they had on instant merriment, gambling or drunkenness. What these two cases have in common – the twentieth-century American anthropologist regarding the hunter-gatherer and the eighteenth-century English gentleman regarding the labourer – is that in both, a way of life is being evaluated in terms of a standard that measures work in hours, and that imposes a clearcut division between work and leisure. On these criteria it is found to be wanting. Indeed to people who are accustomed, as many of us are, to labour timed by the clock, the attitudes to work and time of allegedly traditional or 'primitive' folk, who are not, are almost bound to appear 'wasteful and lacking in urgency' (Thompson 1967: 60).

Yet contemporary captains of industry are still inclined to make surprisingly similar allegations about the incorrigible laziness and inefficiency of working people. To give just one illustration, I return to the ethnography of railway workers, in this case from Britain. I refer to Ken Starkey's (1988) analysis of an industrial dispute between British Rail and ASLEF (the Association of Locomotive Engineers and Firemen). The dispute, which concerned flexible rostering, was not about the duration of the working day – for in this regard there was no further scope for reduction – but about the intensity of work while on the job. The problem was that the Union was committed, by a time-honoured agreement, to the idea of a fixed eight-hour day. British Rail, however, wanted to introduce some flexibility in the length of the working day so that a man might be working more than eight hours on some days, less than eight on others – though with no more and probably fewer hours overall. The rationale for the proposed change was to try to reduce the 'porosity' of the working day, that is, the length of time during which a man might not, in fact, be doing anything but waiting around for the next train. Thus under existing arrangements, the average actual working time for an 8-hour shift was only 3 hours 20 minutes. Flexible rostering would increase the proportion of working time to waiting time within a shift, and by thus reducing the porosity of the working day would raise productivity. Why, then, did ASLEF object?

Quite apart from the fact that it would increase the intensity of work, ASLEF's main objection was that flexible rostering would leave men with much less control than before over the *scheduling* of their personal and social lives. Like the drivers described by Cottrell, who worked to a 16-hour limit but were liable to be called up at any time, ASLEF feared that flexible rostering would undermine railwaymen's ability to time-plan their own relationships outside work, and so would make their social life intolerable. At issue, then, was not the *amount* of time outside work, but control over the *timing* of this time.

In effect, the dispute focused on two ways of looking at time which are by now familiar from my previous discussion. These are the dwelling and commodity perspectives. In the commodity perspective, epitomised by the phrase 'time is money' and represented by the right-hand column of Figure 17.1, time is seen as a quantity to be budgeted, with a clearcut demarcation between work and leisure. Not only did British Rail management hold to this view themselves, they also attributed it to their Union opponents, assuming that their strategy was devised to produce a deal which would give them either more leisure for the same pay, or more pay for the same number of hours of work. For ASLEF, to the contrary, what mattered was the qualitative aspect of time and its significance for social life. Thus ASLEF's objections to the intensification of time use rested more on moral than on economic criteria. On the one hand they perceived the attempt to increase the intensity of time use during the working day as a threat to the traditional conception of locomotive driving as a skilled, almost craft-like activity which, by its very nature, involves a quality of time that is not uniform or homogeneous. On the other hand, they saw the attempt to introduce flexible rostering as a threat to their own social and community lives. In short, theirs was an approach firmly located in the dwelling perspective, represented by the left-hand column of Figure 17.1.

It would perhaps be a little far-fetched to conclude that ASLEF demonstrated a typically hunter-gatherer approach to work and time. Nevertheless, there is more than a passing similarity between Sahlins's portrayal of the intermittent, stop-go pattern of work in hunter-gatherer communities, and British Rail's view of its drivers, as spending the greater part of the working day waiting (chatting, resting, playing cards, drinking cups of tea) between trains. In terms of the actual number of hours worked – if any meaning can be given to such measurements – there is not much difference. It would seem, then, that the opposition between the 'West' and the 'Other' has its source rather closer to home than we might have imagined, and that we do not even have to leave the bounds of our own society in order to discover the challenge presented by supposedly non-Western perspectives to the dominant categories of Western thought. It would be fair to identify these latter categories – including the dichotomies between freedom and necessity, leisure and work, art and technology, the pure gift and the market mechanism, and free time and clock time – with the commodity perspective. However it would be quite wrong, as I have already shown, to conclude that life in modern industrial societies is confined to an oscillation between the poles of these dichotomies – that is, to the right-hand column of Figure 17.1.

An indication of this lies in our response to Evans-Pritchard's depiction of Nuer time, which I cited at the outset. When he tells us that for Nuer, time inheres in the round of daily tasks and their relations to one another, we do not find this strange or exotic. To the contrary, I am sure his words strike in most readers a deep chord of familiarity. We know exactly what he is talking about, because we have all experienced it ourselves, embedded in our memories of childhood, family, home and community. It is not only the basis of our sense of belonging, but also something we value very highly. 'Nuer are fortunate', says Evans-Pritchard, and we are quick to agree, wishing that we, too, were not harried by the regimen of the clock. In a sense, clock time is as alien to us as it is to the Nuer; the only difference is that we have to contend with it. If we differ from the Nuer, then, it is not because they have a task-orientation and we do not. The difference is rather that we are forced to accommodate this orientation – so fundamental to our personal and social identity, to our knowledge of place and people, and to the practice of our everyday skills – within the straitjacket of a 'Western' or commodity-based institutional and ideological framework that seeks at every turn to deny the reality of situated social experience. We are not Westerners, nor are we really non-Westerners; rather, we are human beings whose lives are caught up in the painful process of negotiation between these extremes, between the dwelling and commodity perspectives. In this process lies the temporal dynamic of industrial society, a dynamic which we – including anthropologists, in their writings – have merely displaced onto the relation between our society and the rest of the world.

Chapter Eighteen

On weaving a basket

Artefacts are made, organisms grow: at first glance the distinction seems obvious enough. But behind the distinction, as I aim to show in this chapter, lie a series of highly problematic assumptions concerning mind and nature, interiority and exteriority, and the genesis of form. We have only to consider the artefactual status of such an everyday object as a basket to realise that the difference between making and growing is by no means as obvious as we might have thought. I shall begin this chapter by showing that the reasons why the basket confounds our expectations of the nature of the artefact stem from the fact that it is woven. If the basket is an artefact, and if artefacts are made, then weaving must be a modality of making. I want to suggest, to the contrary, that we should understand making as a modality of weaving. This switch of emphasis, I believe, could open up a new perspective not just on basketry in particular, but on all kinds of skilled, form-generating practices. But it would also have the effect of softening the distinction between artefacts and living things which, as it turns out, are not so very different after all.

MAKING AND GROWING

What is implied about artefacts by their characterisation as things that are made rather than things that grow? First of all, a division is assumed between form and substance, that is between the design specifications of the object and the raw materials of which it is composed. In the case of living things, it is supposed that the information specifying the design of an organism is carried in the materials of heredity, the genes, and thus that every new life-cycle is inaugurated with the injection of this specification into a physical medium. But with artefacts, this relation between form and substance is inverted. Form is said to be applied from without, rather than unveiled from within. The very distinction between a within and a without of things, however, implies the existence of a *surface*, where solid substance meets the space of action of those forces that impinge upon it. Thus the world of substance – of brute matter – must present itself to the maker of artefacts as a surface to be transformed.

In commonsense, practical terms, this is not hard to imagine. Many of our most familiar artefacts are (or were, before the days of synthetic materials) made of more or less solid stuff such as stone, metal, wood or clay. The very usefulness of these objects depends on their being relatively resistant to deformation. We ourselves, however, inhabit a gaseous medium – air – which, offering no such resistance, not only allows complete freedom of movement, but also transmits both light and sound. Quite apart from the obvious fact that we need air to breathe, and thus simply to stay alive, the possibilities of movement and perception (visual and aural) that air affords are crucial for any artefact-producing activity. There is, then, a pretty clear distinction between the gaseous medium that surrounds us and the solid objects that clutter our environment; moreover the patterns of reflected light off the surfaces of these objects enable us to see them for what they are (Gibson 1979: 16–22).

These practical considerations, however, all too easily become confused in our thinking with speculations of a more metaphysical kind. To show why this is so, consider the case of the beehive. Is this an artefact or not? Surely, hives don't grow. Insofar as it results from the application of exterior force to raw material, the hive would appear to be as much 'bee-made' as the human house is 'man-made'. Or is it? Musing on this question, Karl Marx famously came to the conclusion that 'what from the very first distinguishes the most incompetent architect from the best of bees, is that the architect has built a cell in his head before he constructs it in wax'. In other words, the criterion by which the house is truly artificial – and by comparison the beehive only figuratively so – is that it issues from a representation or 'mental model' which has been fashioned in the imagination of the practitioner prior to its execution in the material. We may assume that bees, by contrast, lack the powers of imagination, and have no more conception of their hives than they do of their own bodies, both of which are formed under genetic control (Ingold 1983, cf. Marx 1930: 169–70)

Here, the exteriority of the forces that shape artefacts is understood in quite another sense, in terms not of the physical separation of gaseous medium and solid substance but of the *meta*physical separation of mind and nature. Unlike the forms of animals and plants, established through the evolutionary mechanism of natural selection and installed genetically at the heart of the organisms themselves (in the nucleus of every cell), the forms of artefacts are supposed to have their source within the human mind, as preconceived, intellectual solutions to particular design problems. And whereas organic growth is envisaged as a process that goes on *within* nature, and that serves to reveal its inbuilt architecture, in the making of artefacts the mind is understood to place its ideal forms *upon* nature. If making thus means the imposition of conceptual form on inert matter, then the surface of the artefact comes to represent much more than an interface between solid substance and gaseous medium; rather it becomes the very surface of the material world of nature as it confronts the creative human mind.

This is precisely the kind of view that lies at the back of the minds of anthropologists and archaeologists when they speak of artefacts as items of so-called 'material culture'. The last thing they mean to suggest, in resorting to this phrase, is that in the manufactured object the domains of culture and materiality somehow overlap or intermingle. For nothing about their substantive composition *per se* qualifies artefacts for inclusion within culture. The materials from which they are made – wood, stone, clay or whatever – are in any case generally available in nature. Even with objects manufactured from synthetic materials for which no naturally occurring counterparts exist, their status as items of material culture is in no way conditional upon their 'unnatural' composition. A child's toy made of plastic is no more cultural, on that account, than its wooden equivalent. It is the form of the artefact, not its substance, that is attributed to culture. This is why, in the extensive archaeological and anthropological literature on material culture, so little attention is paid to actual materials and their properties. The emphasis is almost entirely on issues of meaning and form – that is, on culture *as opposed* to materiality. Understood as a realm of discourse, meaning and value inhabiting the collective consciousness, culture is conceived to hover over the material world but not to permeate it. In this view, in short, culture and materials do not mix; rather, culture wraps itself around the universe of material things, shaping and transforming their outward surfaces without ever penetrating their interiority. Thus the particular surface of every artefact participates in the impenetrable surface of materiality itself as it is enveloped by the cultural imagination.

SURFACE, FORCE AND THE GENERATION OF FORM

Let us consider the most ordinary of everyday objects, one that crops up in a surprising range and variety of cultural settings around the world: a coiled basket. Has the basket been created through working on the surface of some raw material? Have the forces impacting on this surface been applied from without? Did they serve to impress onto the material a pre-existent, conceptual design? In every case, as I show below, the answer is 'Not exactly'. Thus the basket is not 'made' in the sense in which we normally understand the term. Nor, evidently, has it grown of its own accord. Thus neither of the available alternatives seem to work for the basket. It does not fit our stereotype of the artefact, and it is not a life-form. Let us start instead from the simple observation that constructing a basket is a process of weaving. In what follows, I shall consider what weaving entails, respectively, with regard to the topology of *surface*, the application of *force* and the generation of *form*.

We have seen that making, in what for convenience I shall henceforth call the 'standard view', implies the prior presence of a surface to be transformed. Thus the flint knapper chips away at the surface of stone, the carpenter carves and chisels the surface of wood, the blacksmith hammers on the surface of molten metal, and the potter applies manual pressure to the surface of clay. But once it has been cut and prepared for weaving, the basket-maker does nothing to the surface of her fibrous material. In the process of weaving, the surface of the basket is not so much transformed as built up. Moreover, there is no simple or straightforward correspondence between the surface of the basket and the surfaces of its constituent fibres. For example, the two outer surfaces of the transverse wrapping fibres that stitch successive loops of the coil are alternately 'outside' and 'inside' so far as the surface of the basket is concerned (see Figure 18.1). Indeed it is in the nature of weaving, as a technique, that it produces a peculiar kind of surface that does not, strictly speaking, have an inside and an outside at all.

In the special case of coiled basketry, there is a limited parallel with the technique of coil-building in pottery. Here the clay is first

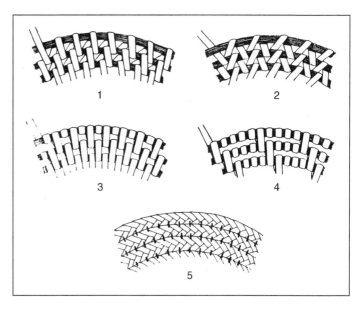

Figure 18.1 Patterns of wrapping in coiled basketry: (1) plain; (2) figure-of-eight ('Navajo'); (3) long and short ('lazy squaw'); (4) Peruvian coil; (5) sewn coil.

From H. Hodges, *Artifacts: an introduction to early materials and technology*, published by Duckworth, 1964, p. 131.

rolled out into long, thin, worm-like strips, rather analogous to the lengths of bundled fibres making up the basketry coil. These strips are then wound around and around to form the base and sides of the vessel. In this case too, a surface is built up. In the process, however, the original surfaces of the coiled strips congeal into a single mass, and the final smoothing leaves no trace of the original mode of construction. But there is another difference, equally critical, which brings me to the issue of force. The potter may have to contend with the force of gravity (his material, being both heavy and pliable, is inclined to sag). But the clay does not exert any independent force. This is not the case with basketry, however, which involves the bending and interweaving of fibres that may exert a considerable resistance of their own. Indeed the basket holds together, and assumes a rigid form, precisely because of its tensile structure.[1] In short, the form of the basket is the result of a play of forces, both internal and external to the material that makes it up. One could say that the form unfolds within a kind of force field, in which the weaver is caught up in a reciprocal and quite muscular dialogue with the material.

This point leads me to the final question concerning the generation of form. According to the standard view, the form pre-exists in the maker's mind, and is simply impressed upon the material. Now I do not deny that the basket-maker may begin work with a pretty clear idea of the form she wishes to create. The actual, concrete form of the basket, however, does not issue from the idea. It rather comes into being through the gradual unfolding of that field of forces set up through the active and sensuous engagement of practitioner and material. This field is neither internal to the material nor internal to the practitioner (hence external to the material); rather, it cuts across the emergent interface between them. Effectively, the form of the basket emerges through a pattern of *skilled movement*, and it is the rhythmic repetition of that movement that gives rise to the regularity of form. This point was made long ago by Franz Boas, in his classic work on *Primitive Art*.

> The basketmaker who manufactures a coiled basket, handles the fibres composing the coil in such a way that the greatest evenness of coil diameter results . . . In making her stitches the automatic control of the left hand that lays down the coil, and of the right that pulls the binding stitches over the coil brings it about that the distances between the stitches and the strength of the pull are absolutely even so that the surface will be smooth and evenly rounded and that the stitches show a perfectly regular pattern.
>
> (Boas 1955 [1927]: 20)

SPIRALS IN NATURE AND ART

Boas illustrates the point with a drawing, which I reproduce here (Figure 18.2A). Opposite, I have placed another drawing, this time taken from the work of the great biologist D'Arcy Wentworth Thompson, *On Growth and Form* (Figure 18.2B). It depicts the shell of a certain kind of gastropod. Although both the coiled basket and the shell have a characteristic spiral form, they are spirals of different kinds: the first is an equable spiral, the second logarithmic (that is, the radius of each successive whorl increases arithmetically in the one instance, and geometrically in the other). The equable spiral, as Thompson explains, is characteristic of artificial forms that have been produced by mechanically bending, coiling or rolling up a given length of material, whereas the logarithmic spiral is commonly produced in nature as a result of growth by deposition, where the material is cumulatively laid down at one end whilst maintaining an overall constancy of proportion

(Thompson 1961 [1917]: 178–9). Either way, however, the form appears to emerge with a certain logical inevitability from the process itself, of rolling up in the former case and laying down in the latter.

Now it is very often assumed, in the study of both organisms and artefacts, that to ask about the form of things is, in itself, to pose a question about *design*, as though the design contained a complete specification that has only to be 'written out' in the material. This assumption is central to the standard view which, as we have already seen, distinguishes between living and artificial things on the criterion of the interiority or exteriority of the design specification governing their production without questioning the premise that the resultant forms are indeed specified independently and in advance of the processes of growth or

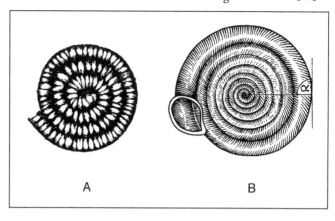

Figure 18.2 Artefactual and natural spirals: (A) Coiled basketry.

From F. Boas, *Primitive art*, published by Dover Publications, 1955 [1927], p. 20.

(B) Gastropod shell. The angle α is known as the 'spiral angle', which in this case is large.

From D. W. Thompson, *On growth and form*, published by Cambridge University Press, 1961 [1917], p. 192.

manufacture wherein they are realised. Thus it is supposed that the basic architecture of the organism is already established, as a genetic 'blueprint', from the very moment of conception; likewise the artefact is supposed to pre-exist, fully represented as a 'virtual object' in the mind, even before a finger has been lifted in its construction. In both cases the actualisation of the form is reduced to a simple matter of mechanical transcription: all the *creative* work has already been done in advance, whether by natural selection or human reason.[2]

How then, starting from this premise, might we set about accounting for the formation of spirals in nature and in art, in the shell of the gastropod and the coil of the basket? The account would likely run along the following lines: the form of the shell is internally specified in the gastropod's genetic inheritance, and revealed in its growth; the form of the basket is externally specified in the mind of the weaver, as part of a received cultural heritage, and revealed in its manufacture. Now natural selection, according to Darwinian orthodoxy, designs organisms to be adapted to their particular conditions of life, and as many scholars have suggested, a somewhat analogous process of blind variation and selective retention, operating in the arena of cultural ideas, could do likewise in designing artefacts that are well suited to their purpose. The fact that we come across spirals in the growth of living things (as in gastropods) as well as in the making of artefacts (as in basketry) may be purely fortuitous, or it may be the outcome of some kind of adaptive convergence – of natural selection and the human intellect, operating quite independently, arriving at parallel solutions to what might be, in essence, a rather similar problem of engineering design. If, to be more precise, the solution calls for a spiral of the equable type, or alternatively of the logarithmic type, then this is what we will find in the resultant forms, regardless of whether the design itself is encoded genetically or culturally. Hence by this account, the distinction between equable and logarithmic spirals would not, in itself, be relevant as an index of the organic or artefactual status of the objects concerned.

THE LIMITS OF DESIGN

According to the standard view, as outlined above, form is fully explicable in terms of the design that gives rise to it. Once you have accounted for the genesis of the design you have, to all intents and purposes, explained the form. Or have you? Would it be possible, even in theory, for any design to specify the form of an organism or artefact *completely*? In his fascinating study of the design principles embodied in the construction of living organisms and manufactured artefacts, originally written as a textbook for students of engineering, Michael French (1988: 266–7) speculates on the question of just how much information would be needed to specify every aspect of the form of an organism. His conclusion is that the amount would be unimaginably large, far beyond what could be coded in the DNA of any known life-form. Nor is the situation any different with artefacts. True, even the greatest achievements of human engineering are no match for the most commonplace of organisms: thus the steam locomotive, as French wryly observes, 'is simplicity itself compared with the intricacies of the buttercup' (1988: 1). But then, no human design could approach the DNA of the genome in its informational content. Once again, complete specification would apparently lie beyond the realms of possibility. In short, the forms of both organisms and artefacts seem to be significantly underdetermined by their underlying blueprints. That being the case, French suggests, we may have to recognise that a great many features of organisms and artefacts are merely accidental, due to chance, revealing not the designs themselves but their limitations.

Though intended to shore up the argument from design against the objection that no specification can be exhaustive, this appeal to chance is a *reductio ad absurdum* that does more to highlight the poverty of the argument itself. To show why, let me turn to another example of spiral formation: the vortex of bathwater as it runs out of the plug-hole. Is the form of the vortex a matter of chance? It is certainly not dictated by the specifications of any design. You can determine whether the spiral runs clockwise or anticlockwise by setting up a current through the water with your hand; beyond that, however, the spiral appears to form of its own accord. But its formation is anything but an accident. It can, in fact, be explained in terms of well-established principles of fluid dynamics.

The example of the vortex is not my own; it is taken from the work of the biologist Brian Goodwin (1982), who uses it to say something very important about the generation of spiral forms in living organisms. In a certain species of snail, the majority of individuals have shells with a right-handed, logarithmic spiral, but in some the spiral is left-handed. It has been shown that the direction of the spiral is controlled by the products of a particular gene, just as the direction of the spiral vortex in bathwater is controlled by the intentional movement of your hand. But – and this is the crucial point – the *form* of the shell is no more the product of a genetic programme than is the form of the vortex the product of a design in your mind. There is, in short, no design for the spiral of the gastropod shell. Rather, the form arises through a process of growth within what is known technically as the 'morphogenetic field' – that is, the total system of relations set up by virtue of the presence of the developing organism in its environment. And the role of genes in the morphogenetic process is not to specify the form, even incompletely, but to set the parameters – such as handedness and spiral angle (see Figure 18.2B) – within which it unfolds (Goodwin 1982: 111).

ON THE GROWTH OF ARTEFACTS

Returning from the growth of organisms to the manufacture of artefacts, a parallel argument applies. Just as organic form is generated in the unfolding of the morphogenetic field, so the form of the artefact evolves within what I have called a field of forces. Both kinds of field cut across the developing interface between the object (organism or artefact) and an environment which, in the case of the artefact, critically includes its 'maker'. Where the organism engages its environment in the process of ontogenetic development, the artefact engages its maker in a pattern of skilled activity. These are truly creative engagements, in the sense that they actually *give rise* to the real-world artefactual and organic forms that we encounter, rather than serving – as the standard view would claim – to transcribe pre-existent form onto raw material. Moreover as a moment's reflection on the example of the vortex in bathwater will show, the properties of materials are directly implicated in the form-generating process. It is therefore no longer possible to sustain the distinction between form and substance that, as we have seen, is so central to the standard view of making things. Finally, the templates, measures and rules of thumb of the artisan or craftsman no more add up to a design for the artefacts he produces than do genes constitute a blueprint for the organism. Like genes, they set the parameters of the process but do not prefigure the form.[3]

All these points apply to the making of a coiled basket. Thus the equable form of the spiral base of the basket does not follow the dictates of any design; it is not imposed upon the material but arises through the work itself. Indeed the developing form acts as its own template, since each turn of the spiral is made by laying the longitudinal fibres along the edge formed by the preceding one. Now D'Arcy Thompson was of course right to point out that there is a difference between *bending* material into shape, as in basketry, and an organism's *growing* into it, as with the shell of the gastropod, and that this can lead to forms with contrasting mathematical properties. Nevertheless, if the unfolding of the morphogenetic field is described as a process of growth, would it not be fair to suggest that there is a sense in which artefacts, whose forms likewise evolve within a field of forces, 'grow' too – albeit according to different principles?

We could describe that growth as a process of *autopoiesis*, that is, the self-transformation over time of the system of relations within which an organism or artefact comes into being. Since the artisan is involved in the same system as the material with which he works, so his activity does not transform that system but is – like the growth of plants and animals – part and parcel of the system's transformation of itself. Through this autopoietic process, the temporal rhythms of life are gradually built into the structural properties of things – or as Boas put it, with regard to artefacts:

> The rhythm of time appears here translated into space. In the flaking, adzing, hammering, in the regular turning and pressing required in the making of coiled pottery, in weaving, regularity of form and rhythmic repetition of the same movement are necessarily connected.
>
> (Boas 1955 [1927]: 40)

The artefact, in short, is the crystallisation of activity within a relational field, its regularities of form embodying the regularities of movement that gave rise to it.

I would like to conclude this comparison of the coiled basket and the gastropod shell by commenting on the reasons for the remarkable durability of their respective forms.

According to the standard view, since form emanates from design, the persistence of form can only be explained in terms of the stability of the underlying design specifications. In the case of the organism these specifications are genetic, in the case of the artefact they are cultural. The constancy of form is thus a function of the fidelity with which genetic or cultural information is copied from one generation to the next, combined with the effects of natural selection – or its analogue in the realm of cultural ideas – in weeding out less well-adapted variants.

The argument I have proposed here, however, is just the opposite. If forms are the outcomes of dynamic, morphogenetic processes, then their stability can be understood in terms of the generative principles embedded in the material conditions of their production. For the shell the principle is one of invariant proportion; for the basket it is the principle that every increment of longitudinal extension is coupled to what has gone before by transverse attachment. Whereas the first principle, through simple iteration, will always and everywhere generate a logarithmic spiral, the second will just as reliably generate an equable one. It is these generative principles, and not the fidelity of genetic or cultural copying, that underwrite the constancy of the respective forms, and explain their persistence over immense spans of both historical and evolutionary time.

MAKING AS A WAY OF WEAVING

I now return to my earlier suggestion, that we reverse our normal order of priorities and regard making as a modality of weaving, rather than the other way around. One intriguing observation points us in this direction. Our word 'loom' comes from Middle English *lome*, which originally referred to a tool or utensil of any kind. Does this not suggest that to our predecessors, at least, the surface-building activity of weaving, rather than any of those activities involving the application of force to pre-existing surfaces, somehow epitomised technical processes in general?

The notion of making, of course, defines an activity purely in terms of its capacity to yield a certain object, whereas weaving focuses on the character of the process by which that object comes into existence. To emphasise making is to regard the object as the expression of an idea; to emphasise weaving is to regard it as the embodiment of a rhythmic movement. Therefore to invert making and weaving is also to invert idea and movement, to see the movement as truly generative of the object rather than merely revelatory of an object that is already present, in an ideal, conceptual or virtual form, in advance of the process that discloses it. The more that objects are removed from the contexts of life-activity in which they are produced and used – the more they appear as static objects of disinterested contemplation (as in museums and galleries) – the more, too, the process disappears or is hidden behind the product, the finished object. Thus we are inclined to look for the meaning of the object in the idea it expresses rather than in the current of activity to which it properly and originally belongs. It is precisely this contemplative attitude that leads to the redesignation of the ordinary objects of the quotidian environment as items of 'material culture' whose significance lies not so much in their incorporation into a habitual pattern of use as in their symbolic function. In suggesting that the relation between making and weaving be overturned, my purpose is to bring these products of human activity back to life, to restore them to the processes in which they, along with their users, are absorbed.[4]

In what way, then, does weaving epitomise human technical activity? What sense does it make to say that the blacksmith in his forge, or the carpenter at his bench, in transforming the surfaces of metal and wood respectively, is actually weaving? Of course, to adopt this idiom is to interpret the notion of weaving more broadly than is customary. It does however help to draw attention to three points about skill which are exemplified in basketry but which are nevertheless common to the practice of any craft. First, the practitioner operates within a field of forces set up through his or her engagement with the material; secondly, the work does not merely involve the mechanical application of external force but calls for care, judgement and dexterity; and thirdly, the action has a narrative quality, in the sense that every movement, like every line in a story, grows rhythmically out of the one before and lays the groundwork for the next. In the following chapter, I shall explore these dimensions of skill at greater length.

This broad interpretation of weaving, though it may sound strange to modern, Western ears, is fully in accord with the understandings of the Yekuana, a native people of southern Venezuela. In his study of Yekuana baskets and basketry, David Guss observes that the master craftsman in this society, a person accredited with exceptional wisdom, 'not only weaves the world when making a basket, but *in everything he does*' (1989: 170, my emphasis). Yet this creative process of world-weaving, Guss shows, is not limited to the experts. It rather engages all Yekuana people throughout their lives – albeit at a lower level of perfection – in their manufacture of the essential equipment of traditional livelihood. In every case, from building houses and canoes to fabricating manioc graters and baskets, making is regarded as a way of weaving.

Paradoxically, however, in translating the indigenous term by which such locally produced items are distinguished from imported, commercially manufactured 'stuff' (such as tin cans and plastic buckets), Guss renders them as things not woven but *made*. Moreover the essence of making, in his view, lies in loading the object with metaphorical significance or semiotic content, such that artefacts become a mirror in which people can see reflected the fundamentals of their own culture. The symbolic capacity of artefacts, Guss insists, 'far outweighs their functional value' (1989: 70). Weaving the world, then, turns out to be a matter of 'making culture', of submitting the disorder of nature to the guidelines of traditional design.

Now the epistemology by which Guss converts the manifold products of world-weaving back into 'things made', instances of the cultural transformation of nature (1989: 161), is one that I reject. It is, as I have shown, an epistemology that takes as given the separation of the cultural imagination from the material world, and thus presupposes the existence, at their interface, of a surface to be transformed. According to what I have called the standard view, the human mind is supposed to inscribe its designs upon this surface through the mechanical application of bodily force – augmented, as appropriate, by technology. I mean to suggest, to the contrary, that the forms of objects are not imposed from above but grow from the mutual involvement of people and materials in an environment. The surface of nature is thus an illusion: the blacksmith, carpenter or potter – just as much as the basket-maker – works from within the world, not upon it. There are surfaces of course, but these divide states of matter, not matter from mind (see Chapter Thirteen, pp. 240–1, for further discussion of this point). And they emerge within the form-generating process, rather than pre-existing as a condition for it.

The philosopher Martin Heidegger expressed the very same point through an exploration of the notions of building and dwelling (see Chapter Ten, pp. 185–6). Opposing the modernist convention that dwelling is an activity that goes on within, and is structured by, an environment that is already built, Heidegger argued that we cannot engage in any kind of building activity unless we already dwell within our surroundings. 'Only if we are capable of dwelling', he declared, 'only then can we build' (1971: 160). Now dwelling is to building, in Heidegger's terms, as weaving is to making in mine. Where making (like building) comes to an end with the completion of a work in its final form, weaving (like dwelling) continues for as long as life goes on – punctuated but not terminated by the appearance of the pieces that it successively brings into being.[5] Dwelling in the world, in short, is tantamount to the ongoing, temporal interweaving of our lives with one another and with the manifold constituents of our environment.

The world of our experience is, indeed, continually and endlessly coming into being around us as we weave. If it has a surface, it is like the surface of the basket: it has no 'inside' or 'outside'. Mind is not above, nor nature below; rather, if we ask where mind is, it is in the weave of the surface itself. And it is within this weave that our projects of making, whatever they may be, are formulated and come to fruition. Only if we are capable of weaving, only then can we make.

Chapter Nineteen

Of string bags and birds' nests
Skill and the construction of artefacts

BEYOND ART AND TECHNOLOGY

'Art' and 'technology' are mere words. And as with all words, their meanings are not fixed but have changed significantly in the course of their history. They are still changing. But I believe it remains true of modern – if not post-modern – thought, that the meanings of art and technology are held to be somehow opposed, as though drawn from fields of human endeavour that are in certain respects antithetical. This opposition, however, is scarcely more than a century old, and would have seemed strange to Anglophone ears as late as the seventeenth century, when artists were still considered no different from artisans, when the methods of working in any particular branch of art could be described as 'technical', and when the term 'technology' had just been coined to denote the scientific study of these methods (Williams 1976: 33–4). Etymologically, 'art' is derived from the Latin *artem* or *ars*, while 'technology' was formed upon the stem of the classical Greek *tekhnē*. Originally, *tekhnē* and *ars* meant much the same thing, namely *skill* of the kind associated with craftsmanship (see Chapter Fifteen). The words were used, respectively in Greek and Roman society, to describe every kind of activity involving the manufacture of durable objects by people who depended on such work for a living, from the painter to the cobbler, from the temple architect to the builder of pigsties. This is not to say that customers failed to distinguish between aesthetic and utilitarian criteria in their estimations of the objects produced. But in every case, it was the craft skill of the practitioner that was supposed to ensure a successful outcome (Burford 1972: 13–14).

The connotation of skill is preserved in many words derived from the same roots and that remain in common currency today. On the one hand we have 'technics' and 'technique'; on the other hand such terms as 'artless' – meaning clumsy or lacking in skill – and, of course, 'artefact'. Yet the apparent continuity masks an important shift, towards abstracting the components of intelligence, sensibility and expression that are essential to the accomplishment of any craft from the actual bodily movement of the practitioner in his or her environment. Thus the technique of the pianist comes to refer to the practised ability of his fingers to find their way around the keyboard and to hit the desired notes, as distinct from the inherent musicality of the performance. 'A player may be perfect in technique', wrote Sir Charles Grove, 'and yet have neither soul nor intelligence'. Likewise, we have come a long way from the days when, as in the year 1610, it was possible to eulogise a certain composer as 'the most artificial and famous Alfonso Ferrabosco' (Rooley 1990: 5). As David Lowenthal has observed, 'time has reversed the meaning of artificial from "full of deep skill and art" to "shallow, contrived and almost worthless"' (1996: 209). By the same token, the artefact is regarded no longer as the original outcome of a skilled, sensuous engagement between the craftsman and his raw material, but as a copy run off mechanically from a pre-established template or design. This debasement of craft to the 'merely technical' or mechanical execution of predetermined operational sequences went hand in hand with the elevation of art to embrace the creative exercise of the imagination (Gell 1992b: 56). As a result, the artist came to be radically distinguished from the artisan, and the art-work from the artefact (Coleman 1988: 7).

The decisive break, according to Raymond Williams, came in the England of the late eighteenth century, with the exclusion of engravers from the newly formed Royal Academy, which was reserved for practitioners of the 'fine' arts of painting, drawing, and sculpture (Williams 1976: 33). It was, of course, symptomatic of a general tendency to distinguish intellectual from manual labour, along the common axis of a more fundamental series of oppositions between mind and body, creativity and repetition, and freedom and determination. But the more that 'art' came to be associated with the allegedly higher human faculties of creativity and imagination, the more its residual connotations of useful but nevertheless habitual bodily skills were swallowed up by the notion of technology. For by the beginning of the twentieth century this term, too, had undergone a crucial shift of meaning. Where once it had referred to the framework of concepts and theory informing the scientific study of productive practices, technology came to be regarded as a corpus of rules and principles installed at the heart of the apparatus of production itself, whence it was understood to generate practice as a programme generates an output. Technology, now, did not discipline the scholar in his study of techniques, but rather the practitioner in his application of them. He became, in effect, an operative, bound to the mechanical implementation of an objective and impersonal system of productive forces.[1]

Here, then, lies the source of the now familiar division between the respective fields of art and technology. An object or performance could be a work of art, rather than a mere artefact, to the extent that it escapes or transcends the determinations of the technological system. And its creator could be an artist, rather than a mere artisan, insofar as the work is understood to be an expression of his or her own subjective being. Where technological operations are predetermined, art is spontaneous; where the manufacture of artefacts is a process of mechanical replication, art is the creative production of novelty. These distinctions can be multiplied almost indefinitely, but they are all driven by the same logic, which is one that carves out a space for human freedom and subjectivity in a world governed by objective necessity. As I have shown in Chapter Seventeen (pp. 329–30), it is a logic that operates as much in the field of exchange as in that of production. Thus the modern distinction between the true work of art and the replicated artefact has its parallel in that between the 'pure gift' and the market commodity: the former given spontaneously and motivated (at least in theory) by personal feeling; the latter exchanged in line with impersonal calculations of supply and demand. But in both fields the distinctions are recent, and closely tied to the rise of a peculiarly modern conception of the human subject.

The division between art and technology, as it has come to be institutionalised in modern society, has affected anthropology as much as any other field of inquiry. Until fairly recently, the literatures in the anthropology of art and in the anthropology of technology remained almost completely isolated from one another. Technology was located within the sphere of ecological adaptation, mediating the material relations between human populations and their environments. For assorted cultural ecologists, cultural materialists, and Marxists, the conjunction of environment and technology – if not actually determinant of cultural form – constitutes the foundation upon which the house of culture is built. Art, by contrast, along with such forms as myth and ritual, is supposed to comprise the patterns on the walls, the world of sensory experience as it is refracted through the filters and lenses of the cultural imagination. It mediates a dialogue, not between human beings and nature, but among persons in society. Like language, it encodes meanings. Thus technology works; art signifies: technical action is aimed to produce results in a mechanically determined way, whereas the purpose of art is to communicate ideas. In short, art has been split from technology along the lines of an opposition between the mental and the material, and between semiotics and mechanics (see Chapter Sixteen, pp. 317–18).

Despite the apparent symmetry of this opposition, the respective trajectories of the anthropologies of art and technology have been decidedly asymmetrical. Having been placed beyond the pale of culture and society, as a quasi-autonomous system of productive forces, technology was largely neglected as a subject of anthropological inquiry. Only very recently has the anthropology of technology, as a subfield, begun to acquire a significant momentum of its own. The anthropology of art, by contrast, has long held a secure place in the discipline. But the very reasons that have led to the inclusion of art as an object of study for anthropologists – namely, that it is clearly positioned within a social context and embodies cultural meaning – have also given rise to persistent doubts about the cross-cultural validity of the concept of art itself. How can a concept that carries such strong evaluative overtones, and whose meaning is so closely bound up with widely held ideas about the ascendancy of Western civilisation, possibly be applied without courting accusations of ethnocentrism? Not for the first time, the very credentials that make a phenomenon eminently worthy of anthropological study have cast a pall of uncertainty over whether the phenomenon exists 'as such' at all. It happened with the study of kinship, it happened with the study of art, and now that anthropologists are at last beginning to recognise the social embeddedness of technological systems, it is happening to the study of technology too. No sooner is technology reclaimed for anthropological inquiry, than we cease to know, for sure, what we are dealing with.

The source of the problem, in my view, lies not in the concept of art, nor in that of technology, but in the dichotomy between them. It is this, along with the idea that art floats in an ethereal realm of symbolic meaning, above the physical world over which technology seeks control, that is tainted by its association with modernity. The idea would have made no sense to the craftsmen of Ancient Greece or Rome. They knew what they meant by *tekhnē* or *ars*, and it was a matter neither of mechanical functioning nor of symbolic expression, but of skilled practice. It is my contention that by going back to the original connotations of *ars* and *tekhnē* as skill, we can overcome the deep divisions that currently separate the anthropologies of art and technology, and develop a far more satisfactory account of the socially and environmentally situated practices of real human agents. In what follows I shall pursue three aspects of this task. First, I explain in more depth what I mean by skill. Secondly, I show how the continuity of tradition in skilled practice is a function not of the transmission of rules and representations but of the coordination of perception and action. Thirdly, I show how a focus on skill explodes the conventional dichotomy between innate and acquired abilities, forcing a radical reappraisal of the ways we think about what is 'cultural' and 'biological' in humans. I shall illustrate my argument by way of two examples: Maureen MacKenzie's (1991) study of the looping skills involved in making string bags (*bilum*) among Telefol people of Central New Guinea, and the study by N. E. and E. C. Collias (1984) of the nest building skills of the male weaverbird.

FIVE DIMENSIONS OF SKILL

I begin by drawing attention to five points which I believe are crucial to a proper appreciation of technical skills. The first concerns what it means to say that practice is a form of *use*, of tools and of the body. In one of his dialogues, Plato has Socrates debate with a character called Alcibiades on precisely this question. 'What are we to say of the shoemaker?', asks Socrates, 'Does he cut with his tools only, or with his hands as well?' Alcibiades is forced to concede that he does indeed cut with his hands, and moreover that he uses not just his hands but his eyes – and by extension his whole body – to accomplish the work. Yet he had already agreed, with Socrates, that there is a fundamental difference between the user and the things he uses. So who is this user? If it be man, counters Socrates, it cannot be his body, which is used. Only one possibility remains, it must be the soul. 'So', he concludes, 'do you require some yet clearer proof that the soul is man?' Alcibiades is convinced (in Flew 1964: 35–7).

There is no reason, however, why we should have to follow suit. 'It would be wrong to assume', as Roger Coleman caustically remarks, 'that because Plato was a Greek he knew what he was talking about'. He was no craftsman, and had no practical experience whatever of shoemaking or any other trade. Plato's objective, in forcing a division between the controlling mind and subservient body, was to establish the supremacy of abstract, contemplative reason over menial work, or of theoretical knowledge over practical application, and thereby to justify the institution of slavery (Coleman 1988: 11–12). Resurrected in the Renaissance, Plato's division anticipated the debasement of craft that, as we have seen, came to be one of the hallmarks of modernity. To recover the essence of skill we need a different concept of use from the one invoked by Plato. Instead of thinking of use as what happens when we put two, initially separate things together – an agent with certain purposes or designs, and an instrument with certain functions – we can take it as the primary condition of involvement of the craftsman, with his tools and raw materials, in an environment. In this sense the hands and eyes of the shoemaker, as well as his cutting tools, are not so much used as *brought into use*, through their incorporation into an accustomed (that is usual) pattern of dextrous activity. Intentionality and functionality, then, are not pre-existing properties of the user and the used, but rather immanent in the activity itself, in the gestural synergy of human being, tool and raw material.

My second point follows from this. It is that skill cannot be regarded simply as a technique of the body. This was the position advocated in a now classic essay by Marcel Mauss (1979[1934]). Taking his cue explicitly from Plato, Mauss observed that technique does not, in itself, depend upon the use of tools. Song and dance are obvious examples. The dancer, according to Mauss, uses his own body as an instrument; indeed so do we all, he declares, for the body is surely 'man's first and most natural technical object, and at the same time technical means'. Moreover in the deployment of these means, the human agent experiences the resulting bodily movements as 'of a mechanical, physical or physico-chemical order' (p. 104). This reduction of the technical to the mechanical is an inevitable consequence of the isolation of the body as a natural or physical object, both from the (disembodied) agency that puts it to work and from the environment in which it operates. To understand the true nature of skill we must move in the opposite direction, that is, to restore the human organism to the original context of its active engagement with the constituents of its surroundings. As Gregory Bateson argued, by way of his example of the skilled woodsman notching with an axe the trunk of a tree he is felling, to explain what is going on we need to consider the dynamics of the entire man–axe–tree system

(1973: 433). The system is, indeed, as much mental as physical or physiological, for these are, in truth, but alternative descriptions of one and the same thing. Skill, in short, is a property not of the individual human body as a biophysical entity, a thing-in-itself, but of the total field of relations constituted by the presence of the organism-person, indissolubly body and mind, in a richly structured environment. That is why the study of skill, in my view, not only benefits from, but *demands* an ecological approach.

Granted that the foundations of skill lie in the irreducible condition of the practitioner's embeddedness in an environment, it follows – and this is my third point – that skilled practice is not just the application of mechanical force to exterior objects, but entails qualities of care, judgment and dexterity (Pye 1968: 22). Critically, this implies that whatever practitioners do *to* things is grounded in an attentive, perceptual involvement *with* them, or in other words, that they watch and feel as they work. As the Russian neuroscientist Nicholai Bernstein argued some fifty years ago, the essence of dexterity lies not in bodily movements themselves, but in the responsiveness of these movements to surrounding conditions that are never the same from one moment to the next (Bernstein 1996). Given the freedom of movement of the limbs as well as the elasticity of the muscles, Bernstein had observed, it is just not possible to control the movements of the body in the same way as one might the workings of a machine made up of rigid, interconnecting parts. From a close study of the movements of a skilled blacksmith, hitting the iron on the anvil over and over again with a hammer, Bernstein found that while the trajectory of the tip of the hammer was highly reproducible, the trajectories of individual arm joints varied from stroke to stroke. At first glance the situation appears paradoxical: how can it be that the motion of the hammer rather than that of the limbs is reliably reproduced, when it is only by way of the limbs that the hammer is made to move (cf. Latash 1996: 286)? Clearly, the smith's movements cannot be understood as the output of a fixed motor programme, nor are they arrived at through the application of a formula. The secret of control, Bernstein concluded, lies in 'sensory corrections', that is in the continual adjustment or 'tuning' of movement in response to an ongoing perceptual monitoring of the emergent task.

All this has implications for the way skills are learned, which brings me to my fourth point. If, as Bernstein contended, skilled practice cannot be reduced to a formula, then it cannot be through the transmission of formulae that skills are passed from generation to generation. Traditional models of social learning separate the intergenerational transmission of information specifying particular techniques from the application of this information in practice. First, a generative schema or programme is established in the novice's mind from his observations of the movements of already accomplished practitioners; secondly, the novice imitates these movements by running off exemplars of the technique in question from the schema. Now I do not deny that the learning of skills involves both observation and imitation. But the former is no more a matter of forming internal, mental representations of observed behaviour than is the latter a matter of converting these representations into manifest practice. For the novice's observation of accomplished practitioners is not detached from, but grounded in, his own active, perceptual engagement with his surroundings. And the key to imitation lies in the intimate coordination of the movement of the novice's attention to others with his own bodily movement in the world. Through repeated practical trials, and guided by his observations, he gradually gets the 'feel' of things for himself – that is, he learns to fine-tune his own movements so as to achieve the rhythmic fluency of the accomplished practitioner (for an example, see Gatewood 1985). And in this process, each generation contributes to the next not by handing on a corpus of representations, or information in the strict sense, but rather by introducing novices into contexts which afford selected opportunities for perception and action, and by providing the scaffolding that enables them to make use of these affordances. This is what James Gibson (1979: 254) called an 'education of attention'.

It is because practitioners' engagement with the material with which they work is an attentive engagement, rather than a mere mechanical coupling, that skilled activity carries its own intrinsic intentionality, quite apart from any designs or plans that it may be supposed to implement (see Chapter Twenty-three, p. 415). My fifth point follows from this, and has to do with what we mean by making things. Let me return for a moment to the example of Socrates and the shoemaker. Socrates had asked what it means to say of the shoemaker that he uses tools. The other side of the question is to ask what it means to say that he makes shoes. If use, as Socrates maintained, is what happens when you put an agent having a certain purpose together with objects having certain functions, then the purpose must precede the use through which it is realised. In these terms, to refer to an action as one of making is to refer back to the prior intention that motivates it. It is as though the form of the manufactured object were already prefigured, as a design, in the mind of its maker, such that the activity of making issued directly from the design and served only to transcribe it onto the material. The assumption that every form is the outward expression of design is, as we saw in the last chapter, as prevalent in biology as it is in technology. Thus the form of an organism is said to be given in an evolved design specification, the genotype, in advance of its phenotypic 'expression' in an environment. And in modern architecture the form of a construction is supposed exist in miniature, in models, drawings and plans, before any building work begins (Coleman 1988: 16). To take this view, however, is to deny the creativity of the very process of environmentally situated and perceptually engaged activity, that is of *use*, through which real forms emerge and are held in place. It is the activity itself – of regular, controlled movement – that generates the form, not the design that precedes it. Making, in short, arises within the process of use, rather than use disclosing what is, ideally if not materially, ready-made.

HOW TO MAKE A STRING BAG

Among the Telefol people of central New Guinea, and indeed throughout this region, one of the most ubiquitous and multifunctional accessories to everyday life is the string bag or *bilum*. It is made by means of a looping technique from two-ply string spun from plant fibres. Children are introduced to the techniques of *bilum* making from a very early age. All young Telefol children, both boys and girls, help their mothers and elder sisters in preparing fibres for spinning. 'From the age of about two onwards they begin to experiment with roving, rolling the shredded fibres down their thigh to make a single ply, and progress to experiments with spinning. It is not uncommon to see very young girls, mere toddlers, diligently attempting to loop the string they have made into bilum fabric' (MacKenzie 1991: 101). Boys, as they grow older, do not go on to master fully the skills of looping, for the simple reason that they are soon removed, by the conventions of their society, from the sphere of women's activities. Men have no need to make their own bags, as these are willingly supplied for them by women, who thus maintain an effective monopoly on *bilum* making. Girls, by contrast, remain close to their mothers and other female relatives, and continue to develop their skills, quietly and unobtrusively following in their mothers' footsteps.

All the points I have made about skill, in the previous section, apply to the making of string bags. Apart from the maker's body – and especially her fingers – the only tools used are the mesh gauge (*ding*), made from a strip of leaf, to maintain the constancy of the mesh in an open weave (see Figure 19.1), and the needle (*siil*), made of bone, which is needed for making tightly looped baskets without the use of the gauge (MacKenzie 1991: 73). But in use the needle or the gauge, along with the fingers that hold it, are as much a part of the user as they are used. Moreover the accomplished *bilum*-maker does not experience the movements of her body as being of a mechanical nature. Far from answering to commands issued from a higher source, they carry their own intentionality, unfolding in a continual dialogue with the material. Telefol people liken this movement to the flowing water of a river. Thus the body-in-use is not moved, like a rigid object,

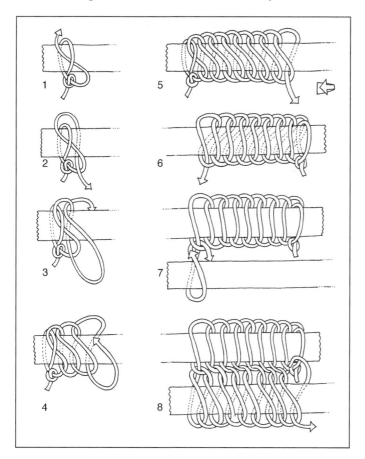

Figure 19.1   The step-by-step procedure for looping a flat strip of 'open, spaced' *bilum* fabric, as practised by Telefol people of central New Guinea. Steps 1–4 show how the first row of loops is constructed around the mesh gauge (*ding*), in a series of figure-of-eight loops with each loop connecting into the preceding one. By stage 5 the first row of loops is completed to the desired width. On completion of each row the work must be turned over so that the working thread is always on the left-hand side. In step 6 the work is thus reversed. Step 7 illustrates how a new strip of *ding* is inserted at the beginning of each successive row. This linear way of working, with each row connecting into the loops of the preceding one, is then repeated (step 8).

From MacKenzie, *Androgynous Objects: string bags and gender in central New Guinea*, published by Harwood Academic, 1991, pp. 86–7.

but rather becomes one with the flow (p. 102). However, in order to maintain the evenness of the string, in spinning, or of the weave, in looping, it is necessary to make continual adjustments in the course of the movement itself. 'By adolescence', MacKenzie writes, 'all girls have mastered the technique of spinning, gaining visual acuity in selecting equal assemblages of filaments during the roving process; and a sensitivity or balance in the amount of pressure applied between palm and thigh during the rhythmic plying motion' (p. 76). As this passage clearly reveals, dexterity in spinning depends on the fine-tuning of visual as well as haptic perception. And it is equally clear that the form of the *bilum* is an emergent outcome of rhythmically repeated, controlled movement in the processes of spinning and looping.

The issue on which I want to focus here, however, concerns how *bilum*-making skills are passed from generation to generation. MacKenzie herself describes this in terms of a fairly conventional model of social learning, according to which 'observation is followed by internalisation and then mimesis' (p. 100). Thus by watching the activity of her mother, a young girl absorbs and assimilates the 'intrinsic rules' of the craft. Once these are firmly implanted in her mind, she can proceed to execute them in the production of her own work. The fact that 'each daughter follows exactly the motor habits and bodily motions of her mother' leads to a remarkable cultural conformity from one generation to the next (p. 103). There is much in MacKenzie's own account, however, to suggest that conformity to tradition is *not* a consequence of the intergenerational transmission of rules or formulae, however intrinsic, but rather the result of a process of guided rediscovery in which the role of experienced *bilum*-makers is to set up the contexts within which novices are enabled to gain in proficiency for themselves, or in other words to 'grow into' the skills of spinning and looping.

First of all, it is clear that to advance in these skills it is not enough for the novice to know how their constituent movements look 'from the outside'; she has also to know how they feel 'from the inside' (cf. Bernstein 1996: 184–5). One young woman, recalling how she learned to loop as a child, told of how she had once tried to carry on with an unfinished *bilum* that her mother had left in the rafters of the house before leaving to work in the garden. She had been carefully watching the way her mother's hands moved as she looped the *bilum*. But on trying it out herself, the result was a disaster. When her mother returned, it took her hours to undo the mess. At first she was angry, but then she lectured her daughter with the following words of wisdom:

> You must practise to get the proper feel of looping. When you've made your first bilum it will be cranky but then we'll throw it in the river. The river will carry your wonky bilum away, and it will wash away your heavy handedness. Then your hands will be good at making bilums, your hands will move easily like running water.
>
> (from MacKenzie 1991: 102)

What does it mean to get the 'feel' of looping? It could mean that the observation on which learning depends is as much tactile as visual, or that the skill is embodied as a rhythmic pattern of movement rather than a static schema, or that the key to fluent performance lies in the ability to co-ordinate perception and action. All three are undoubtedly important, but none more so than the third. For it is this, as MacKenzie herself observes, that makes the difference between clumsiness and dexterity, between having heavy hands and hands that flow. 'Clumsiness, *iluum t'eb'e su* [to be heavy handed], is deemed natural at first, and must be practically worked through' (p. 103).

It seems, then, that progress from clumsiness to dexterity in the craft of *bilum*-making is brought about not by way of an internalisation of rules and representations, but through the gradual attunement of movement and perception. As in any craft, the skilled maker who has a feel for what she is doing is one whose movement is continually and subtly responsive to the modulations of her relation with the material. Conversely, the clumsy practitioner is precisely one who implements mechanically a fixed sequence of instructions, while remaining insensitive to the evolving conditions of the task as it unfolds. The hand that is heavy is experienced as a resistance to be overcome, and has to be moved from position to position in ways that seem contrary to its nature. The light hand, by contrast, finds its way of its own accord. The heavy-handed novice does not, of course, move in exactly the same way as her light-handed mother, nor can she be expected to produce such satisfactory results. This is precisely where the standard model of the social learning of technical skills goes wrong. For in attributing the intergenerational conformity of movements to rules that are transmitted and internalised *in advance* of their practical application in mimesis, the model assumes that practice is a matter of executing identical, rule-governed movements over and over again, leading to gains in speed, efficiency and automation. But a little girl, making her first *bilum*, is quite unable to produce these movements. Rather than repeatedly carrying out the same movements, generated from an already internalised schema, she is repeatedly set the same *task*, generated within the social context of mother–daughter relations. The ability to reproduce her mother's movements with precision, depending as it does on subtle sensory attunement, is not a natural foundation for enskilment but its consequence (cf. Reed and Bril 1996: 438).

Telefol women, according to MacKenzie, place great value on the standardisation of their looping techniques, since this is a way of confirming tribal identity (1991: 103). But I would contend that this standardisation is not brought about, as MacKenzie claims, by conformity to rules. Indeed there appear to be no rules, beyond general exhortations of the kind delivered by the mother to her daughter in the case described above, or vague 'rules of thumb' that help prepare the practitioner for her impending activity but in no way determine its course (Suchman 1987: 52). Like most commonplace practical skills, such as tying shoelaces in Western society, looping resists codification in the form of generative rules or algorithms (Dreyfus and Dreyfus 1987). One becomes aware of this simply by looking at the elaborate diagrams, accompanied by written commentary, by means of which MacKenzie attempts to explain the step-by-step procedure for open-spaced looping (pp. 83–99, and for an example, see Figure 19.1). Though these diagrams are admirable for their intended purpose, of ethnographic description, any attempt by the untutored reader to follow them in practice would likely lead to the same kind of tangle that the inexperienced Telefol girl produces, on secretly attempting to carry on with her mother's work. It would be quite mistaken to suppose that anything remotely equivalent exists in the native mind. But if standardisation does not follow from the application of rules, how are we to account for the persistence of technique from one generation to the next?

Partly in an attempt to answer this question, a group of us in the Department of Social Anthropology at the University of Manchester resolved to experiment with different ways of making knots. One of our experiments was to try making a completely unfamiliar and rather complicated knot, guided only by a manual which provided detailed verbal instructions and step by step diagrams. It turned out to be an immensely difficult and frustrating task. The problem we all experienced lay in converting each instruction, whether verbal or graphic, into actual bodily movement. For while the instruction was supposed to tell you how to move, one could only make sense of it once the movement had been accomplished. We seemed, almost literally, to be caught in a double bind, from which the only escape was patient trial and error. Of course we had resort to the instructions, but far from directing our movements, what they provided was a set of landmarks along the way, a means of checking that we were still on track. If we were not – if the tangle of string in front of us did not match the corresponding graph (and that, in itself, was not easy to discern) – there was no alternative but to unravel the whole thing and start again!

Our experiments seemed to lend strong empirical support for the view that the practices of knotting – which are, after all, among the most common and widely distributed in human societies – cannot be understood as the output of any kind of programme. They cannot, then, be learned by taking any such programme 'on board', as part of an acquired tradition, as if all you needed to know to make knots could be handed down as a package of rules and representations, independently and in advance of their practical application. In our experiments, despite having a manual to consult, we had to develop the necessary know-how from scratch. Generally speaking, of course, this is not a problem that novices face in real life. They are shown what to do by more experienced hands, as we have already seen in the case of the acquisition of looping skills by Telefol *bilum*-makers. But in seeking to emulate the work of the tutor, the novice is guided by the latter's *movements*, not by formal instructions that have somehow been already copied into his or her head. As Merleau-Ponty put it, citing the pioneering work of Paul Guillaume on imitation in children, 'we do not at first imitate others but rather the actions of others, and . . . find others at the point of origin of these actions' (1964b: 117, see also Bourdieu 1977: 87). It follows that the reproduction of movement patterns is a function not of the fidelity with which information specifying these patterns is copied from one generation to the next, but of the co-ordination of perception and action that lies at the heart of practical mimesis.

DISSOLVING THE DISTINCTION BETWEEN INNATE AND ACQUIRED SKILLS

It is obvious that Telefol girls have to learn to make string bags. It is not a skill that they are, in any sense, 'born with'. As MacKenzie notes, 'talent in bilum making, that is, having hands which flow, is [defined as] a physically acquired attribute rather than an inherent pre-disposition in the sense that westerners think of ability and talent' (1991: 103). My concern now is to look more closely at what it means to say that a particular skill is acquired rather than innate. I shall do so by way of another example, this time taken from the animal kingdom. For while we are used to thinking of human skills as belonging to this or that cultural tradition, the skills of non-human animals are commonly regarded as properties of their genetically encoded, species-specific nature. What are we to make, then, of the male weaverbird, which carries out the most intricate knotting and looping with its beak in the construction of its nest? The nest building of weaverbirds has been investigated in a remarkable series of studies by ornithologists N. E. and E. C. Collias, and in what follows I draw on their report (Collias and Collias 1984).

The nest is made from long strips torn from the leaves of grasses, which are intertwined in a regular lattice formed by passing successive strips over and under, and in a direction orthogonal to, strips already laid. It is held together, and attached to the substrate, by a variety of stitches and fastenings, some of which are illustrated in Figure 19.2. The bird uses its beak rather like a needle in sewing or darning; in this the trickiest part lies in threading the strip it is holding under another, transverse one so that it can then be passed over the next. The strip has to be pushed under, and through, just far enough to enable the bird to let go with its beak in order to shift its hold and pull it up on the other side. If the free end is left too short, the strip may spring back; pushed too far, it could fall to the ground. Mastering this operation calls for a good deal of practice. From an early age, weaverbirds spend much of their time manipulating all kinds of objects with their beaks, and seem to have a particular interest in poking and pulling pieces of grass leaves and similar materials through holes. In females this interest declines after about the tenth week from hatching, whereas in males it continues to increase. Experiments showed that birds deprived of opportunities to practise and denied access to suitable materials are subsequently unable to build adequate nests, or even to build at all. Indeed, fiddling about with potential nest material appears to be just as essential for the bird, in preparing itself for future building, as are the first experiments of Telefolmin toddlers in roving and spinning shredded fibres for their future *bilum* making (Collias and Collias 1984: 201, 206–7, 212, 215–20).

It is evident from the Collias' account that all the five qualities of skill which, as I have shown, are exemplified in the making of string bags by people of central New Guinea, are also manifest in the nest building of weaverbirds. Though the needle of the *bilum*-maker is detachable from the body whereas the bird's beak is not, in use both are not so much moved as incorporated into a habitual pattern of movement. The abilities of the weaverbird, just like those of the human maker of string bags, are developed through an active exploration of the possibilities afforded by the environment, in the choice of materials and structural supports, and of bodily capacities of movement, posture, and prehension. Furthermore, the key to successful nest building lies not so much in the movements themselves as in the bird's ability to adjust its movements with exquisite precision in relation to the evolving form of its construction. As Collias and Collias report:

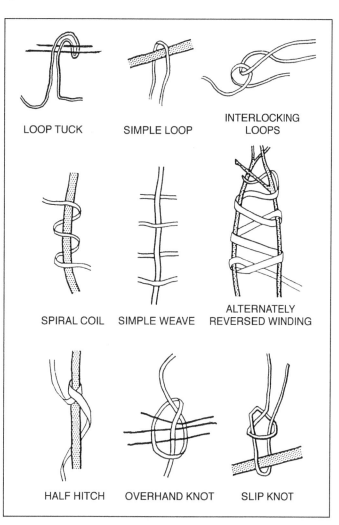

Figure 19.2 Various common stitches and fastenings used by male weaverbirds in constructing their nests.

From N. E. Collias and E. C. Collias, *Nest Building and Bird Behavior*, © 1984 by Princeton University Press, reprinted by permission of Princeton University Press.

In watching the numerous attempts of young male weavers to fasten initial strips of nest materials and their gradual improvement in weaving ability, it seemed to us that what every young male weaver has to learn is what in subjective terminology one would call 'judgement'.

(1984: 219)

One can sense the reluctance with which these hardnosed empirical observers find themselves having to resort to a notion of this kind. But the evidence leaves them with no alternative. It is clearly judgement, rather than a programme of instructions or a set of design specifications to be mechanically applied, that the bird acquires through mimetic practice. Finally, the form of the nest results from the iteration of a small number of basic movements, and from the fact that the bird stands throughout on the same spot while it weaves all around – above, below and in front – pushing out the developing shell of the main chamber as far as its beak will reach, and then tilting gradually backwards to complete the antechamber and entrance (1984: 193, 209–10).

Given that weaverbirds, in their nest building, exhibit the same properties of skill as are manifested in the looping techniques of the Telefolmin and their neighbours, wherein lies the difference? The conventional answer is to claim that the human *bilum*-maker follows the dictates of an acquired cultural tradition, while the bird works to a template that is genetically transmitted and thus innate. But if, as our experiments with knot-making suggested, there can be no programme for such tasks as knotting, looping, and weaving that is not immanent in the activity itself, then it makes no more sense to inter-pret the weaverbird's behaviour as the output of a genetic programme than it does to interpret the *bilum*-maker's as the output of a cultural one. In all likelihood the human maker of string bags has an idea in mind of the final form of the construction, whereas the weaverbird almost certainly does not. Yet in both cases it is the pattern of regular movement, not some prespecified design, that generates the form. And the fluency and dexterity of this movement is a function of skills that are developmentally incorporated into the *modus operandi* of the organism – whether avian or human – through practice and experience in an environment.

This last point is absolutely critical. Recall that Telefol girls develop their looping skills at a time of life when their bodies are also undergoing rapid growth. These skills, then, far from being added on to a preformed body, actually grow with it. In that regard they are fully part and parcel of the human organism, of its neurology, musculature, even anatomy, and so are as much biological as cultural. After all, a human being, with its particular aptitudes and dispositions, is a product of neither genes nor culture, nor of both together, but is rather formed within a lifelong process of ontogenetic development. To be sure, the skills of looping are acquired, in the sense that at whatever stage in the life-cycle they may be identified, a history of development already lies behind them. But the same would have to be said of the knotting and looping skills of the weaverbird, and indeed of *any* skill, human or non-human. Moreover one could just as well claim that such skills are innate, in the sense that so long as the necessary environmental conditions are in place (including the presence and activity of already skilled practitioners) they are more or less bound to develop. All Telefol girls learn to make string bags, just as they all learn to walk or to speak. All male weaverbirds learn to make nests, unless opportunities for practice are artificially removed. Conversely, Telefol boys and female weaverbirds never develop full-blown looping and weaving skills, since their respective activities and concerns take them too soon into other fields of practice. In short, whatever the difference between the two sets of skills, avian and human, it cannot be aligned on the axis of a distinction between the innate and the acquired.

This conclusion, however, leaves us with our earlier question unanswered. How, exactly, *do* human skills, such as those exemplified in the making of string bags, differ from those of animals such as the weaverbird? To be frank, I do not pretend to know. I remain perplexed by the question, and have yet to find an answer that is wholly convincing. Once again, however, MacKenzie's study of the Telefol offers a possible clue. It lies in the observation, to which I have already alluded, that Telefol people liken the dextrous manual movements of the fluent *bilum*-maker to running water (MacKenzie 1991: 136). For these inhabitants of intermontane valleys, the current of water in a river or stream is as familiar a part of experience as is the motion of the hands in looping. Now it seems reasonable to suppose, likewise, that the weaverbird has as much of a 'feel' for air currents, while on the wing, as it has for nest materials in building with its beak. However what the bird does not do, so far as we know, is to tie these different strands of perception and action together. If birds were human, they would say that the good weaver is one whose beak seems to 'fly', just as Telefol say that the skilled looper is one whose hands 'flow'. But they do not do this. Human beings, it seems, differ from other animals in that they are peculiarly able to treat the manifold threads of experience as material for further acts of weaving and looping, thereby creating intricate patterns of metaphorical connection. This interweaving of experience is generally conducted in the idioms of speech, as in story-telling, and the patterns to which it gives rise are equivalent to what anthropologists are accustomed to calling 'culture'.

However, culture thus conceived cannot be understood to comprise a system of intrinsic rules or schemata by means of which the mind constructs representations of the external world from the data of bodily sensation, nor can speech be regarded simply as a vehicle for the articulation of these mental representations. Speakers no more 'use' their voice, as Plato would have had it, as the mere instrument of a language-based intelligence, than they 'make' sense by superimposing their pre-existing designs upon the raw material of experience. Rather, in speech, the voice is incorporated into a current of sensuous activity – namely, narrative performance – from which, as it unfolds, form and meaning are continually generated. For speaking is itself a form of skilled practice, and as such, exhibits all the generic properties of skill to which I have already drawn attention. Like any other skill, speech develops along with the growth of the organism, is continually responsive to perturbations in the perceived environment, and is learned through repeated practical trials in socially scaffolded contexts. Above all, it cannot be reduced to the mechanical execution of a rule-governed system, or 'grammar'. Yet speech is no ordinary skill. Weaving together, in narrative, the multiple strands of action and perception specific to diverse tasks and situations, it serves, if you will, as the *Skill of skills*. And if one were to ask where culture lies, the answer would not be in some shadowy domain of symbolic meaning, hovering aloof from the 'hands on' business of practical life, but in the very texture and pattern of the weave itself.

Chapter Twenty

The dynamics of technical change

There is a wonderful footnote in Marx's *Capital* that sets a whole agenda for research. It runs as follows:

> Darwin has aroused our interest in the history of natural technology, that is to say in the origin of the organs of plants and animals as productive instruments utilised for the life purposes of these creatures. Does not the history of the origin of the productive organs of men in society, the organs which form the material basis of every kind of social organisation, deserve equal attention? Since, as Vico says, the essence of the distinction between human history and natural history is that the former is the work of man and the latter is not, would not the history of human technology be easier to write than the history of natural technology?[1]
>
> (1930: 392–3, fn. 2)

This passage suggests three crucial questions. First, what exactly is the difference between the 'history of natural technology' and the 'history of human technology'? In modern usage, we have grown accustomed to referring to the former as a process of evolution while reserving the concept of history for the latter. The question then becomes: how, if at all, can we distinguish between evolutionary and historical change in the field of technical phenomena? Secondly, Darwin was greatly perplexed by the issue of whether there is anything inherently progressive about the process he called 'descent with modification'. His considered conclusion was that progress, of a kind, *has* occurred, but that there is nothing in the theory of variation under natural selection that stipulates that it *must* occur. Is this also the case with technology? Finally, are the mechanisms of technical change comparable to, or quite different from, those that Darwin adduced for the adaptive modification of organic species? In other words, can we account for technical change in terms of a principle of variation under selection? In this chapter, I shall deal with each of these questions in turn.

THE EVOLUTION OF TECHNOLOGY AND ITS HISTORY

Comparing what students of animal behaviour on the one hand, and social and cultural anthropologists, on the other, have to say about technical change, one cannot help noting a curious discrepancy. Looking for the causes of such change, animal behaviourists typically attribute it to the evolution under natural selection of the animal species itself. Tools and tool-using behaviour are regarded as part of the phenotypic expression of an underlying genotype, and they change as the genotype changes – that is, as the species evolves.

Explaining the evolution of animal tool behaviour is thus no different, in principle, from explaining the evolution of those functional attachments – the finch's beak, the crab's pincers, the lion's claws – that remain joined to the body. Anthropologists, by contrast, often treat technology as an aspect of a cultural system that has a dynamic of its own, undergoing progressive development without entailing any further change in the basic biology of the species. It is as if, to all intents and purposes, technical change in humans were fully decoupled from the process of evolution, for the designs that underwrite the making process are supposed to lie in the minds of the makers, not in their genes, and to be encoded in cultural symbols rather than in strands of DNA (Wynn 1994: 137–45).

This seems like a neat way of distinguishing between the history of technicity and its evolution. But it poses a problem that has particularly exercised prehistorians, for it implies that at some point or other, history must have 'started up'. A threshold had to be crossed; our ancestors had to step beyond the old world of nature into a new world of culturally constructed meaning. This image of stone-age hunter-gatherers standing at the dawn of history sounds suspiciously like an imposition onto the Palaeolithic of a decidedly modern political rhetoric. And it has set prehistorians on a frantic and much publicised search for the point of origin of what they nowadays call 'modern humans'. I shall reserve my critique of this notion for the next chapter, and merely note at this juncture the implication that once the breakthrough to culture had been made, the history of technology must have truly taken off, leading from the earliest tools to modern machinery, without entailing any further change in the species-specific form of the human organism. History, as psychologists David and Anne James Premack maintain, consists in 'a sequence of changes through which a species passes while remaining biologically stable', and of all species in the world, only humans have it (1994: 350).

If we are to take this view, however, then we have also to admit that the artefactual products of technological culture cannot be taken as reliable indicators of the fundamental cognitive and biomechanical capabilities of their makers. A prehistorian of the future, surveying the material remains of Western industrial civilisation, would be making a serious error were he to infer that its people were considerably more advanced in their evolved capacities than were their predecessors of earlier millennia. As the linguist Philip Lieberman warns, 'who would think that we had essentially the same biological endowment as the human populations that lived 30,000 or 20,000 or 500 years ago if all he had to go on were the preserved artefacts – stone tools versus the ruins of great cities, dams, interlocking highways, etc.?' (1985: 628).

But the same argument cuts the other way. Who would think that the common human biological endowment was significantly different from that of chimpanzees on the evidence of the striking similarity between the toolkits of contemporary free-ranging chimpanzee populations and those of certain ethnographically recorded populations of human hunter-gatherers? In his controversially entitled book *Chimpanzee Material Culture*, Bill McGrew – one of the most experienced observers of chimpanzees in their natural habitat – attempts a systematic comparison of the subsistence technology of chimpanzee populations inhabiting a number of study areas in western Tanzania with that of the Aboriginal people of Tasmania, as documented in the early years of the nineteenth century. The Tasmanian Aborigines are notorious in anthropological literature for allegedly having had the simplest material culture ever recorded (Jones 1977: 197, see Figure 20.1). I shall not go into the details here of how the comparison was made, though one could have serious reservations about the selection of items for comparison and the terms in which they were rendered commensurable. I merely wish to highlight McGrew's principal conclusion, which is that

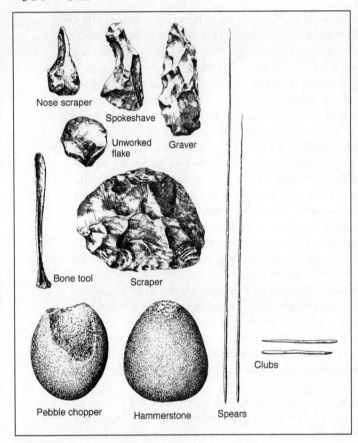

Nose scraper

Spokeshave

Unworked flake

Graver

Bone tool

Scraper

Clubs

Pebble chopper

Hammerstone

Spears

Figure 20.1 The Tasmanian toolkit.

From J. Clark, *The Aboriginal People of Tasmania*, published by Tasmanian Museum and Art Gallery, 1983, p. 22.

if we confine our attention to the respective toolkits, although the human hunter-gatherer toolkit is indeed more complicated than that of the ape, 'the difference is far from wide, and the gap between hominid and pongid is bridgeable' (1992: 144).

Not surprisingly, when McGrew first presented his findings, at a conference devoted to the anthropology of hunter-gatherer societies held in London in 1986, they drew a storm of protest. Was he really trying to tell us that Tasmanian hunter-gatherers had scarcely advanced beyond the apes, that they were stuck in an evolutionary time-warp? In his defence, his intention was no more than to suggest the possibility of an intermediate level of technology in the transition from our ape-like ancestors to the earliest hominid forms. Yet in taking nineteenth-century Tasmanian Aborigines as exemplars of early hominids, McGrew comes close to returning to the overt racism of an earlier era of anthropology, when it was quite usual to regard the 'savage' as representing an earlier stage in human biological evolution, and thus as occupying a half-way stage in the transition from apes to 'civilised' (that is, modern European) humans.

In fact the simplicity of the Tasmanian toolkit, even when compared with that of Aboriginal hunter-gatherers on the Australian mainland, presents an enigma that has never been adequately solved – though it may have something to do with Tasmania's prolonged and total isolation since rising sea-levels cut it off from the mainland some 11,000 years ago (Jones 1977). What does seem incontrovertible, however, is that a Tasmanian Aborigine, transported to the twentieth century and raised in an affluent part of the world, would have no particular difficulty in becoming, say, an airline pilot or a software engineer. But I would not, for my money, take a plane piloted by a chimpanzee! Indeed we are drawn almost irresistibly to the conclusion that behind the apparent similarity of chimpanzee and human hunter-gatherer toolkits there lies a fundamental difference of capacity, a difference that is manifested, above all, in the progression of human technology from the axe, spear and digging stick to the airplane and the computer. Thus while we might reasonably attribute the failure of chimpanzees to operate a complex technology to innate incapacity, we can only attribute the failure of Tasmanian Aborigines to do the same to unfulfilled historical conditions.

Now the development of human technology is very commonly presented as though it could be arrayed on a continuum from the earliest stone tools to modern machinery and electronics. Figure 20.2 is an example of such a figure. Yet if the conclusion we reached in the last paragraph is accepted, to posit such a direct line of continuity from the Oldowan chopper to the space shuttle would be quite absurd. Comparing the finely flaked blades of Upper Palaeolithic hunter-gatherers, dating from around 30–40,000 years ago, with the crude pebble tools used by *Homo habilis* at Olduvai Gorge in East Africa two million years ago, it is hard to deny that the differences reflect real changes in intellectual and manipulative abilities – changes that are also reflected in the increasing size of the brain and structural modifications to the hand. *Homo habilis* was, after all, a very different kind of creature than *Homo sapiens*, in

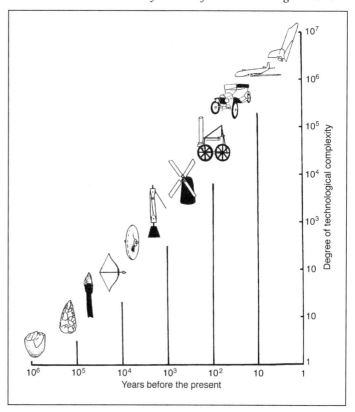

Figure 20.2 The development of material culture.

From B. Cotterell and J. Kamminga, *Mechanisms of Pre-industrial Technology*, published by Cambridge University Press, 1990, p. 9.

many ways much closer to an ape than a human being. On the other hand, it would appear that once a recognisably human level of competence had been achieved, all subsequent technological change – from Palaeolithic hunting and gathering to modern industry – could take place without any significant further change in the basic biological endowment of the species.

In short, it appears that whereas the change from Lower to Upper Palaeolithic tools is a chapter in the story of human evolution, the change from the latter to modern industrial technologies is a chapter of history. When we speak of evolution, it is assumed that changes in tools depend on – and can therefore be taken as indices of – changes in the forms and capacities of the creatures that use them. When we speak of history, by contrast, it is as though technology had broken free from the bonds of genetic constraint, and could henceforth undergo unlimited development without entailing any enhancement of innate human capacities. At what point, then, does the evolution of technology become the history of technology? How can we draw a dividing line between these two processes? Is it possible even in principle, let alone in practice, to distinguish those actions and events that carried forward the movement of human history from those that set it in motion in the first place? We are very far from resolving these questions, but I would like to conclude my discussion of this theme with the suggestion that the processes of evolution and history may not be so distinct after all.

The notion of capacity seems to imply a certain view of human nature, as comprising a set of universal structures or compartments, fully formed in the life of every individual from the start, and waiting to be filled up with all manner of particular cultural content. Thus the capacities are said to be innate, the products of an evolutionary process; the content acquired, changing through history. However my discussion of skill in the last chapter led me to conclude that the capabilities of action of both human beings and non-human animals are neither innate nor acquired but emergent properties of the total developmental system constituted by the presence of the agent (human or non-human) in its environment. In the case of humans, this is as true of the most widely distributed skills such as walking and speaking as it is of those of more restricted distribution such as swimming and writing.

We cannot, then, place universals on the side of evolution and particulars on the side of history. Rather, if history be understood as the process wherein people, through their activities, establish the conditions under which succeeding generations lead their lives, developing as they do the skills appropriate to these various forms of life, then it cannot differ in principle from the process in which organisms, quite generally, establish by their own presence and actions the context of development for their successors. That process is one of evolution. To understand evolution in this sense, however, is to make a clean break with the conventions of modern biology, and with the neo-Darwinian paradigm upon which they are founded. For it is to attribute the changing forms and capacities of living creatures not to changes in an internal programme, design or building plan (the genotype), but to transformations in the whole field of relationships within which they come into being. To take this idea further would be beyond the scope of the present chapter. It is, however, my subject for the next.

MEASURING TECHNOLOGICAL COMPLEXITY

Is there, then, anything progressive about technical change? It is remarkable that although the majority of anthropologists are deeply suspicious of the idea that there is any inherently progressive tendency in the history of human culture, they are inclined to make an exception of technology, and are quite content to talk about peoples with 'simple' and with 'complex' technologies. Precisely how the simplicity or complexity of a technology is to be gauged, however, has remained far from clear. One of the few attempts to construct such a measure has been made by Wendell Oswalt (1976). Oswalt defined the complexity of a tool by the number of 'technounits' that make it up. A technounit is a physically distinct part that makes a particular contribution to the overall implement. It was in these terms that McGrew compared the relative complexity of chimpanzee and human hunter-gatherer technologies. He found that none of the tools used by chimpanzees in the procurement of subsistence comprised more that one technounit, whereas the mean number of technounits (1.2) for the Tasmanian Aboriginal repertoire was very slightly greater. In fact, no Tasmanian implement was of more than one technounit; the raised mean is fully accounted for by two kinds of fixed facility used in hunting, involving two and four technounits respectively (McGrew 1992: 138, 144). By contrast, the Inuit (Eskimo) sealing harpoon shown in Figure 20.3 has no fewer than 26 structurally distinct components.

On the basis of a comparative survey of the toolkits of hunter-gatherers, farmers and herdsmen, Oswalt was able to refute the common assumption that hunters and gatherers have simpler tools than any other human groups. In fact the most complex tools were found among specialised hunters, especially hunters – like the Inuit – of large aquatic mammals, who have to use considerable ingenuity to obtain inaccessible or potentially dangerous prey. The herdsman, who has ready access to comparatively docile animals, faces nothing like the same technical challenges, and his toolkit is correspondingly simpler: thus the lasso, the principal instrument by which the reindeer herdsman catches hold of his animals, is no more than a length of rope tied to a sliding toggle (Ingold 1993b). The equipment of the gatherer tends to be simpler than that of the hunter (plants do not attempt to escape those who 'hunt' them, nor do they have to be outwitted or outmanoeuvred), but again, the tools of the farmer are no more complex. For both gatherer and farmer, the essentials may consist of just an axe or adze, digging stick, and some form of carrying device for transporting harvested produce.

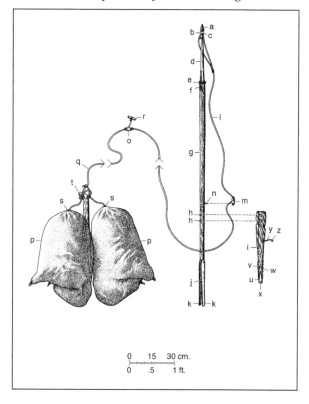

Figure 20.3 Inuit (Angmagsalik) toggle-headed 'feather' harpoon and throwing board for hunting large seals from a kayak.

Drawing by Patrick Finnerty, from W. H. Oswalt, *An Anthropological Analysis of Food-Getting Technology*, published by John Wiley & Sons, 1976, p. 100.

But comparisons based on the structural properties of the tools themselves can be misleading. Returning the objects to the contexts of their use reveals a different picture. The Inuit harpoon is a rather specialised piece of equipment, which is used *only* for sealing. The reindeer herdsman's lasso, by contrast, can be put to use in all manner of different ways. I have seen herdsmen use their lassos for setting traps, for tying animals to sledges for transport home, and for countless other purposes. Likewise among hunter-gatherers with an apparently simple inventory of tool types (including Tasmanian Aborigines), it is common to find that each kind of object is turned to an account for an astonishing variety of different tasks.

Among the Aboriginal people of the Australian Western Desert there is a clear division between men's tools (principally the spear and spear-thrower) and women's tools (principally digging sticks and wooden bowls). The spear-thrower, in the context of hunting, is designed to enhance the flight of the spear by imparting extra angular momentum to the throw. But it has numerous other uses: as a friction stick in making fire, a woodworking tool (with the addition of a hafted stone adze-flake), a mixing tray for pigments or tobacco, a percussion instrument in songs and dances, a device for clearing an area of thorns and pebbles when preparing a campsite, and (when embellished with decorative markings) a mnemonic for recalling the sequence and locations of waterholes and other features of the landscape (Gould 1970: 22, Figure 20.4). The woman's digging stick is similarly multifunctional. It can be used to obtain burrowing animals as well as plants, as a weapon in

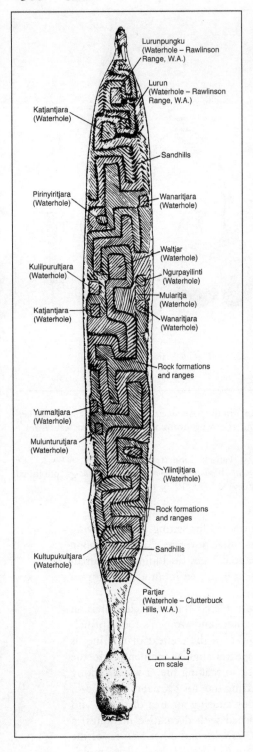

Lurunpungku
(Waterhole – Rawlinson Range, W.A.)

Lurun
(Waterhole – Rawlinson Range, W.A.)

Katjantjara
(Waterhole)

Sandhills

Pirinyiritjara
(Waterhole)

Wanaritjara
(Waterhole)

Waltjar
(Waterhole)

Kulilpurultjara
(Waterhole)

Ngurpayilinti
(Waterhole)

Mularitja
(Waterhole)

Katjantjara
(Waterhole)

Wanaritjara
(Waterhole)

Rock formations
and ranges

Yurmaltjara
(Waterhole)

Mulunturutjara
(Waterhole)

Yilintjitjara
(Waterhole)

Rock formations
and ranges

Sandhills

Kultupukultjara
(Waterhole)

Partjar
(Waterhole – Clutterbuck Hills, W.A.)

0   5
cm scale

small-game hunting and in self-defence. Small wooden bowls can be used to carry produce, but also to shovel away soil when digging. Large bowls can be used to carry both infants and drinking water (Hamilton 1980: 7).

Comparing Australian Aboriginal and Inuit toolkits, it might seem at first glance that the first is extremely simple and the second rather complex. But a more significant difference is between the economy and versatility of the Australian toolkit and the diversity and specialisation of the Inuit one. Australian Aboriginal people have few tools, but use them in whatever way they come in handy, for manifold purposes that we might never come to think of when we classify the objects by function – for example, as spear-throwers or digging-sticks. Inuit have many tools, some of them – like the harpoon – of great complexity and ingenuity, but each is used for a prescribed purpose which governs, at least to some extent, the manner of its construction. It is only because of a peculiar bias that leads us to look for technical operations in the properties of the tools themselves, rather than in the know-how of their users, that we are led to conclude that Inuit are somehow more 'advanced', in the technical sphere, than Australian Aborigines. As I have already shown (Chapter Sixteen, p. 315), the source of this bias lies in the concept of technology itself.

These observations all point towards a single conclusion: that to comprehend the technical accomplishments of hunter-gatherers, or of any other people for that matter, it is not sufficient just to look at their tools. We have to understand their *knowledge*. Tools are of no use if you don't know how to work with them; moreover up to a point, the simpler the tool, the more knowledgeable and skilled you have to be to be able to work it effectively. The reindeerman's lasso is a simple tool, but it requires immense skill to

Figure 20.4 Decorated spear thrower from the Nyatunyara people of the Australian Western Desert. Designs depict waterholes and landmarks along the track of a totemic snake.

From R. A. Gould, Spears and spear-throwers of the Western Desert Aborigines of Australia, *American Museum Novitates*, 1970, p. 28. Courtesy of the American Museum of Natural History use it effectively. The same could be said of an axe, digging stick, spear or boomerang. The food processor on my kitchen table is, by contrast, an extremely complex tool, with hundreds of interconnected parts. But it took only a few minutes to learn to use it.

As Robin Ridington has put it (1982: 470), understanding technical know-how means focusing on *artifice* rather than *artefacts*, on tool-use as skilled practice rather the mechanical operation of exterior devices. But by artifice we do not mean the kind of objective, generalisable, scientific knowledge which, in its application, might be covered by the modern concept of technology. It is rather knowledge of a very personal kind, partly intuitive, largely implicit, and deeply embedded in the particularities of experience. One grows into such knowledge much as one learns one's country or one's kinship system. It is knowledge that both enables a person to find his or her way in a world of human and non-human others, and that endows them with a specific identity. Thus, as we saw in Chapter Sixteen, it is indistinguishably social and technical.

THE ORGANIC ANALOGY

The idea that in the history of human technology, tools and machines have evolved according to principles similar to those governing the evolution of organic species is an attractive one that has had numerous adherents, from Marx, Butler and Pitt-Rivers in the nineteenth century to contemporary advocates of 'evolutionary archaeology' who argue that mechanisms of variation, differential replication and retrospective selection will account just as well for artefactual as for organic change.[2] All the necessary conditions seem to be present, in the technological domain, to support the analogy. There is *diversity*, which, if anything, is greater than that of species. George Basalla, for example, notes that the number of patents issued in the United States since 1790 (4.7 million) is more than three times the number of species of flora and fauna yet identified (Basalla 1988: 2). There is *continuity*, in the sense that technical change, by and large, seems to be gradual, amassed from a very large number of minor variations rather than punctuated by momentous steps of absolute invention. There is *novelty*, insofar as all making activity, however closely it strives to copy an existing model, is bound to diverge from it to some degree. Replication, in practice, can never be perfect. And finally, there is *selection*, albeit artificial rather than natural, in that it is guided by human intention in rather the same way as in the practice of animal or plant breeding. In other words, the context for the differential replication of technical variants is human, and therefore social and historical (Basalla 1988: 25).

Arguments for the analogy between organic evolution and technical change, though they vary in detail, generally run roughly as follows. In the replication of existing technical designs, innovations of one kind and another inevitably creep in. Some of these may be entirely accidental, and in that respect resemble genetic mutations. Others are clearly stimulated by the particular conditions in which the object or technique in question is to be applied: to the extent that this is the case, the evolutionary process is often said to be more 'Lamarckian' than 'Darwinian'. Another way of putting this would be to define Darwinian evolution as the special case in which the degree of coupling between a novel variation and its environmental conditions of selection is reduced to zero (Ingold 1996b: 196–7). Whether accidental or premeditated, the majority of innovations will probably turn out in practice to be useless or even detrimental. A small proportion, however, bring evident benefits. Variants that work well in the particular conditions prevailing in the environment will tend to 'catch on', through extensive replication, while others will dwindle and disappear. Thus in the long run, the more successful technical designs will undergo a kind of adaptive radiation, splitting into diverse forms suited to specific contexts of use, while others may become effectively extinct.

One of the virtues of the organic analogy is that it suggests a way of explaining how the majority of extant techniques and artefacts have come to be so admirably adapted to current requirements, without our having to suppose that they appeared from nowhere, dreamt up in a moment of inspiration by a designer who was somehow able to see the totality of every problem and conceive its solution in a vacuum. It is no more possible in the history of artefacts than in the evolution of species for new forms to appear out of thin air. Every object, and every technique, comes with a history attached, or as Basalla puts it, 'every novel artifact has an antecedent' (1988: 208–9). True, in the history of artefacts the selection involved carries a component of intentionality: human beings may be able to author their own designs in a way that other animals cannot. What they cannot do, however, is stand outside of history and treat the world as though it were a blank slate. Every designer is a creature of his or her own time, and the objects and practices with which each is surrounded, bequeathed through the activities of predecessors, form a necessary resource for the design process itself. That is why, as Reuleaux pointed out in his *Kinematics of machinery* of 1876, most of what goes for invention in the technical sphere consists in hitting on new uses for old things.

'The first machinal arrangements', Reuleaux argued, 'were of a kind which we may designate as make-shifts'. Cobbled together for one purpose, these arrangements were pressed into service for others, coming up against new demands for improvement which were met by further rearrangements, and so on.

> Very gradually each invention came to be used for more purposes than those for which it was originally intended, and the standard by which its excellence and usefulness were judged was gradually raised. An external necessity thus demanded its improvement, and from this cause machinal ideas slowly crystallised themselves out, and gradually assumed forms so distinct that men could use them designedly in the solution of new problems. These attempts resulted in further improvements, and these in their turn led once more to new applications and more extended use.
>
> (Reuleaux 1876: 231)

Only a few years previously, in his treatise of 1862 *On the various contrivances by which British and foreign orchids are fertilised by insects*, Darwin had advanced a precisely analogous argument to account for the evolution of mechanisms in nature. In order to facilitate the transfer of pollen, Darwin showed, the orchid uses whatever parts happen to be available, parts that may have arisen as adaptations to quite different functions.

> Although an organ may have been originally formed for some special purpose, if it now serves for this end, we are justified in saying that it is especially contrived for it. On the same principle if a man were to make a machine for some special purpose, but were to use old wheels, springs and pulleys, only slightly altered, the whole machine, with all its parts, might be said to be specially contrived for that purpose. Thus throughout nature almost every part of each living being has probably served, in a slightly modified condition, for diverse purposes, and has acted in the living machinery of many ancient and distinct specific forms.
>
> (Darwin 1862: 348)

As Darwin showed, natural selection, in adapting organisms to their conditions of life, continually puts old structures to work in new ways, having no other materials on which to work. More than a century later we find the same idea echoed in the work of the distinguished biologist, François Jacob. The process of organic adaptation under natural selection, for Jacob, is akin to 'tinkering'. The mammalian ear, for example, is derived from a part of the jaw of the fish, and birds' feathers, with their aerodynamic properties, are derived from hairs once designed for insulation (Jacob 1977).

As with organisms so with artefacts, every novelty is but an expedient solution to a very specific, context-bound, local difficulty: it is a matter of getting by with what is already available rather than producing the absolutely new. Thus it is an illusion to suppose that anything is ever perfectly fit for the purpose to which it is used. 'Every thing we design and make', writes David Pye, 'is an improvisation, a lash-up, something inept and provisional. We live like castaways ...' (1964: 10). More often than not, the stock of materials available to the maker consists of previously made things, constructed for other purposes but now co-opted for the project in hand. This is the kind of making that Claude Lévi-Strauss famously likened to *bricolage*. The *bricoleur* is someone who delights in making novel contraptions out of the bits and pieces of old ones. The inventory of tools and materials he has to work with, as Lévi-Strauss explains, 'bears no relation to the current project, or indeed to any particular project, but is the contingent result of all the occasions there have been to renew or enrich the stock or to maintain it with the remains of previous constructions or destructions' (1966b: 17). In the history of human technology, perhaps the outstanding example of *bricolage* lies in the so-called 'invention' of writing. Let me pause to say a few words about it.

The nameless inventors of the earliest scripts – and there seem to have been several, who arrived at the same idea quite independently – did not first conceive in the abstract, and then proceed to construct, full-blown, purpose-built writing systems. They did not even imagine the possibility of writing as we think of it now. What they did was simply to hit on the idea that a graph or diagram depicting a thing could be used instead to represent the sound of the word for that thing – a sound which could be homophonous with words or parts of words for other things. This, the so-called rebus principle, has been hailed as 'one of the greatest inventions of human history' (DeFrancis 1989: 50). Yet its significance has been hugely exaggerated by indirect and largely fortuitous consequences of which its originators can have known nothing. All they were doing was pressing into service, on an *ad hoc* basis, well-known and easily identifiable icons for the new purpose of representing speech sounds, in order to solve such limited problems as keeping accounts, recording proper names or divining fortunes. What modern historians rather grandly call 'writing systems' undoubtedly developed as accumulations of expediences of this kind. DeFrancis is right to describe them as 'jerry-built structures' that 'bear less resemblance to carefully constructed schemes for representing spoken languages than they do a hodgepodge of mnemonic clues that adept readers can use to arrive at coherent messages' (1989: 262). In short, they are more like Rube Goldberg devices than the exemplary instances of engineering design that the popular notion of writing as a technology of language would lead us to expect.[3]

Now organisms, it would appear, have evolved in rather the same way as writing systems. Jacob, it will be recalled, likened natural selection to a tinker, and a similar image is invoked by another leading contemporary exponent of Darwinian thinking, Michael Ghiselin: 'organic mechanisms may be shown ... to have been haphazardly thrown together, out of whatever materials the moment happened to supply' (Ghiselin 1969: 153).

In one respect, however, this kind of image is seriously misleading. For real, living organisms are not pieced together out of ready-made components, however fragmentary, heterogeneous and diverse in origin. Rather, they undergo growth and development in an environment. Thus to be more precise, the tinkering – if such it is – must occur not in ontogeny but in phylogeny, that is in the assemblage, by natural selection, of a *design* or construction blueprint for the organism. This design is what is generally known as the genotype. And if the same argument is to be applied by analogy to the construction of artefacts, we would have to conclude that what is fashioned, through a process of variation under selection, is likewise a design for the tool or machine in question rather than the object itself.

My discussion in Chapter Eighteen, however, led me to question the very idea that the making of artefacts consists of a simple transcription of a prior design onto raw material. I argued, to the contrary, that the forms of artefacts *emerge* through the unfolding of a system of relations comprised by the presence of the artisan in a richly structured environment that could include other persons, other examples of artefacts of the kind that it is desired to make, a selection of materials, and a range of tools and supporting surfaces. Should we conclude, then, that the analogy does not hold; that the processes that give rise to organisms and artefacts are profoundly dissimilar? Could it be, in complete reversal of commonsense understanding, that whereas organisms are built, artefacts grow?

I think not. The analogy is indeed sound. It is, in short, not that organisms are built like artefacts, knocked together out of bits and pieces as the Darwinian model suggests, but rather that artefacts grow like organisms, within the equivalent of a morphogenetic field. Where plans or blueprints exist, as they often do in the fields of architecture and engineering, they are generated within the same, environmentally situated process from which also emerge the forms they are said to specify. But they may not exist at all. Thus where apparently identical objects are made, generation after generation, this is not because each is a replica run off from a template that has been somehow transmitted from ancestors to descendants, independently and in advance of the construction process. It is rather, as we saw in the case of the making of string bags described in Chapter Nineteen, that form-making involves a precise co-ordination of perception and action that is learned through copying the movements of experienced practitioners in socially scaffolded contexts. Making, in other words, *is* copying; it is not the realisation of a design that has already been copied. The same point could be alternatively expressed in terms of a contrast between *reproduction* and *replication*: every artefact, formed as it is within the process of production, is an original, not a replica. And whatever variations may be introduced in the process lie in the dynamics of making, not in errors of transmission.

Now I believe that precisely the same argument may be applied to the growth of organisms. The transgenerational stability of organic form is due to the dynamics of reproduction, not to the mechanics of replication. In each generation the form emerges anew, in the course of ontogenetic development; it is not run off from a pre-existing design specification. Indeed for organisms, there is no such specification. The genotype, conceived as a programme or blueprint for the growth of the organism, does not exist. To recall my conclusion from the first part of this chapter, the forms and capacities of organisms are attributable not to genes but to the properties of developmental systems (of which the genes are, of course, an integral part). An exploration of the radical implications of this conclusion for evolutionary theory is my subject for the next chapter.

Chapter Twenty-one

'People like us'

The concept of the anatomically modern human

INTRODUCTION: THE ORTHODOX VIEW

Let me begin with a rather facetious question. Why did Cro-Magnon Man not ride a bicycle? I shall first elaborate on the answer that will surely seem obvious: it is not that he lacked the basic anatomical prerequisites to perform such a feat, but simply that he lived in an era long before anything as ingenious and complex as a bicycle had been developed. And even if it had, given the nature of the terrain and the prevailing mode of subsistence, a bicycle would probably have been of little use to him. In other words, although biologically prepared to take to the saddle, the cultural conditions that would make cycling a practicable option were not yet in place. I intend to show, however, that this answer is seriously flawed, and that the search for a more satisfactory alternative forces a fundamental revision of our most basic notions of evolution, of history and indeed of humanity itself. In particular, I shall argue that the idea of the 'anatomically modern human', the pivot around which all these other notions revolve, is an analytic fiction whose principal function is to cover up a contradiction at the heart of modern evolutionary biology.

Cro-Magnon Man, unearthed by Louis Lartet in the village of Les Eyzies, France, in 1868, has of course acquired the mantle of the prototypical 'modern', albeit by no means the earliest representative of its type in the fossil record. Compared with its predecessors – the 'archaic' Neanderthals and, before that, *Homo erectus* – this type was recognisably different: a kind of man, as William Howells wrote, 'who was entirely like ourselves' (1967: 240). In contemporary palaeoanthropology, the Cro-Magnons are included, along with all subsequent and present-day human populations, within the single sub-specific taxon *Homo sapiens sapiens*. And the implication of such categorisation is that, at least so far as their biological endowment was concerned, these Upper Palaeolithic people fell well within the existing range of variation of the sub-species. Had they been born in our own time, and grown up in a society like our own, they would undoubtedly have been able to do all the things we can: read and write, play the piano, drive cars, ride bicycles, and so on. That is, they had the *potential* to do all these things, a potential that nonetheless remained unrealised in their own lifetimes.

Now I should like to return to Howells's characterisation of the Cro-Magnons, as people 'entirely like ourselves', bearing in mind that at this stage of the argument my purpose is to spell out what I believe to be the orthodox position in current anthropology. Somebody might object that they were not like us at all. They did not, after all, live in cities, read books, write scientific monographs, play the piano or drive cars. To this kind of objection, two responses are immediately forthcoming. One is to point out that the objection rests on a narrow and ethnocentric view of who 'we' are, a view that would exclude a large proportion even of contemporary humanity. In comparing Upper Palaeolithic people to ourselves, the reference is to humankind in its global distribution, irrespective of cultural variation. The other response is to qualify the sense in which the people are said to have been 'modern'. This should not be confused with conventional usage in social and cultural anthropology, in which modernity has generally been linked to some notion of Western urban-industrial society. The Cro-Magnons were modern in an *anatomical*, not in a socio-cultural sense. They were 'like us' biologically, but not culturally.

What separates the anatomically modern humans of thirty thousand years ago (and earlier) from their contemporary descendants, according to orthodox theory, is a process not of evolution but of history – or as some would have it, of cultural rather than biological evolution. This is not to suggest that with the advent of the 'moderns', the evolution of our species literally stopped. There have been continuing changes, but these have been relatively minor, and pale into insignificance beside the truly colossal transformations in ways of life that have occurred – apparently at an escalating rate – throughout the course of human history. Whether, or in what sense, these transformations can be considered progressive has been hotly debated: nevertheless it seems to be generally agreed that the history of culture has been marked by a cumulative increase in the scale and complexity of its technological component. Not only, however, was the historical process of complex-ification in the technological sphere of culture made possible by a biological endowment that was already established by the Upper Palaeolithic; it also left that endowment unaf-fected. The motor car is a modern invention, but the man behind the wheel remains a creature biologically equipped for life in the Stone Age!

Thus so far as their basic biology is concerned, cyclists are no different from walkers, and the walkers of today are no different from their predecessors of the Upper Palaeolithic. It is generally accepted that bipedal locomotion is a universal human characteristic, whose evolution entailed a distinctive suite of anatomical adjustments (Lovejoy 1988). Cycling, by contrast, is an acquired skill which has appeared relatively lately in some, but not all human populations. Though its advent was conditional upon a long chain of prior circum-stances of invention and diffusion (from the discovery of the wheel to the manufacture of steel tubing), as well as of environmental modification (the construction of roads and tracks), it entailed no reconfiguration of human anatomy. In its structure and propor-tions, after all, the bicycle was designed to 'fit' a human body that had already evolved for walking, and its essential mechanical function is to convert bipedal into rotary motion.

This brings us back to the conventional answer to the question with which I began. The reason why Cro-Magnon Man did not ride a bicycle has nothing whatever to do with biology. That is, the reason is historical rather than evolutionary. The same distinc-tion, as we saw in the last chapter, is generally invoked to explain why the toolmakers of the Upper Palaeolithic worked with flaked stone rather than complex mechanical or elec-tronic equipment. And if it is absurd to posit a direct line of continuity from the very earliest stone tools to modern machinery, then it is equally absurd to posit a similar progression from quadrupedal to bicyclic locomotion. For whereas the transition from walking on four feet to walking on two belongs to evolution, the transition – if you will – from two feet to two wheels belongs to history.

WALKING AND CYCLING

I trust it will be agreed that this is a fair representation of the orthodox view. I shall now go on to show why I think it is wrong. Let me begin by taking a fresh look at the contrast between walking and cycling. It is commonly supposed that walking is something we are 'born with' whereas cycling is a product of enculturation; in other words the former is presumed to be innate, the latter acquired. Yet the fact is that new-born infants cannot walk. They have to *learn* to walk, and the help of older persons, already competent in the art, is invariably enlisted in the enterprise. In brief, walking is a skill that emerges for every individual in the course of a process of development, through the active involvement of an agent – the child – within an environment that includes skilled caregivers, along with a variety of supporting objects and a certain terrain (Ingold 1991: 370). How, then, can we continue to maintain that it comes, as it were, 'pre-packaged' in the human biogram? True, the vast majority of human infants do learn to walk, moreover they do so within a fairly narrowly defined period. Thus while the baby does not exactly land in the world on two feet, it comes with a built-in developmental schedule which ensures that it will eventually walk upright provided, however, that certain conditions are present in its environment.

This last proviso is absolutely critical. Infants deprived of contact with older caregivers will not learn to walk – indeed they would not even survive, which is why all surviving children *do* walk, unless crippled by accident or disease. One could imagine a future scenario in which human locomotive needs were met entirely by wheeled vehicles, or of life under conditions of weightlessness in outer space, where walking would disappear. Such scenarios are admittedly fantastic, but to imagine them serves to reinforce my point, which is that the capacity for bipedal locomotion can only be said to be innate by presupposing the presence of the necessary environmental conditions for its development. Strictly speaking, therefore, bipedalism cannot be attributed to the human organism unless the environmental context enters into the specification of what that organism is.

With this point in mind, let me turn from walking to cycling. Children can only become proficient in cycling, as in walking, through a process of learning in which adult assistance is generally required. Compared with walking, however, the conditions for the development of cycling are a good deal more stringent. Obviously, no-one can learn to cycle who does not have a bike to ride, and the environment must also include roads or tracks that are negotiable on two wheels. In contemporary industrial societies these conditions are so ubiquitously present that we tend to think it as natural that children beyond a certain age should be able to cycle as it is that they can walk. In other societies, by contrast, bicycles may be rare or absent altogether, or the terrain may be quite unsuited to their use. And so the skills of cycling are of far more limited distribution than those of walking.

This is a difference, however, of extent rather than principle. If walking is innate in the sense – and only in the sense – that *given certain conditions*, it is bound to emerge in the course of development, then the same applies to cycling. And if cycling is acquired in the sense that its emergence depends on a process of learning that is embedded in contexts of social interaction, then the same applies to walking. In other words, it is as wrong to suppose that cycling is 'given' exogenously (independently of the human organism) as it is to suppose that walking is 'given' endogenously (independently of the environment). Both walking and cycling are skills that emerge in the relational contexts of the child's involvement in its surroundings, and are therefore properties of the developmental system constituted by these relations.

Moreover these skills are literally *embodied*, in the sense that their development entails specific modifications in neurology, musculature, and even in basic features of anatomy. Though children generally learn to walk before they learn to ride, the modifications entailed in cycling are not simply inscribed upon an anatomy that comes, as it were, 'ready-made' for walking. For the human body is not ready-made for anything, but undergoes continuous change throughout the life-cycle as it is pressed into the performance of diverse tasks. Indeed the recurrent stresses and strains of everyday life do not just affect the relative development of different muscles; they also leave their mark on the skeleton itself. Thus carrying loads on the head affects the bones of the upper spine; squatting puts a strain on the knee, resulting in a notched kneecap, and no doubt cycling, too, leaves tell-tale signs.[1] It is of course true that the bicycle is designed for a creature already accustomed to bipedal locomotion, so that cycling calls for no *major* overhaul of human anatomy. Cyclists can still walk, and it is doubtful whether even the most percipient observer could distinguish a cyclist from a non-cyclist, save by putting them to the test. However the facts that no novice has succeeded in sustaining balance and co-ordination on a first attempt, and that the knack of riding a bicycle, once learned, is never lost, indicate that the exercise of the requisite sensory and motor skills leaves an indelible anatomical impression, if only in the normally invisible architecture of the brain. Indeed, this conclusion is supported by recent neurological research which shows, as Kandel and Hawkins report, that 'our brains are constantly changing anatomically', even as we learn (1992: 60).

In the light of these considerations, it is perhaps not so absurd, after all, to situate the emergence, respectively, of walking and cycling within the same overall process of evolution – an evolution, that is, of the developmental systems which underwrite these capacities. For once we introduce the environmental context of development into our specification of what an organism is, it must follow that a human-being-in-environment-A cannot be the same kind of organism as a human-being-in-environment-B. Thus Cro-Magnon Man was indeed a rather different kind of creature from the cycling or car-driving urban dweller of today. He was not 'like us' – not even biologically. He may have resembled us *genetically*, but that is another matter. How it was that biology came to be identified with genetics is a problem in the history of ideas to which I return below; suffice it to say at this juncture that such identification is already implicit in the notion that every individual receives his or her biological constitution, at the moment of conception, in the form of an *endowment*. Before examining this notion more closely, I should first like to review an area in which very similar issues arise to those raised in my comparison of walking and cycling, but which has been the site of far more serious controversy: namely, the evolution of language.

SPEECH AND WRITING

It is generally recognised that Cro-Magnon Man, as a paragon of anatomical modernity, had a fully-fledged capacity for language. He could speak just as well as you or I. But he could neither read nor write. I begin with the comparison between speech and literacy, since it bears the most obvious parallel with that between walking and cycling. Thus according to the orthodox view, the capacity for language is a human universal, something that we all receive as part of a common biological endowment that was in place by the Upper Palaeolithic, if not earlier (I am not here concerned with the arguments over dating). Literacy, by contrast, is a technology of language that arose independently in various parts of the world as a result of specific events of invention and diffusion, and which – even today – is by no means universally shared. The capacity for language, then, is a product of evolution; the capacity to read and write a product of history. The former is said to be innate, the latter acquired. Cro-Magnon's failure to read and write, like his failure to ride a bicycle, had nothing to do with his biology. It was rather that, in the epoch during which he was living, the cultural developments that culminated in the invention of writing systems had yet to run their course.

I believe this view is wrong, for reasons that I have already spelled out. Human babies are not born talking, any more than they are born walking. Their capacity for language *develops*, through a series of fairly well-defined stages. The support of speaking caregivers, and the presence in the environment of a rich and highly structured array of significant features, are essential for normal language development. Since these conditions are almost invariably fulfilled, the overwhelming majority of children learn to speak without difficulty, and the exceptions are those whose development is impeded by some other handicap. The conditions that have to be fulfilled if a child is to learn successfully to read and write are, of course, far more restricted. Indeed, just what these conditions are is a matter of vigorous debate, especially in educational circles. Since literacy skills and practices are in fact exceedingly diverse, having no more in common than the representation of words in a graphic medium, the conditions necessary for their acquisition are, in all probability, equally variable (Street 1984). But this does not affect my main point, namely that literacy is not 'added on', through enculturation, to a human constitution that is biologically ready-made for speech. Rather, the abilities both to speak and to read and write emerge within a continuous process of bodily modification, involving a 'fine-tuning' of vocal-auditory and manual-visual skills together with corresponding anatomical changes in the brain, and taking place within the contexts of the learner's engagement with other persons and diverse objects in his or her environment. Both capacities, in short, are the properties of developmental systems.

Without prejudging the vexed issue of whether the so-called 'archaic' humans, typified by Neanderthal Man, could speak, there is considerable agreement among contemporary palaeoanthropologists that this capacity – at least in its fully-fledged form – was not shared by earlier, pre-human hominids such as *Homo erectus* and *Homo habilis*. The question we need to ask, however, is this: in what way, if at all, did the failure of these early hominids to speak differ from the failure of Upper Palaeolithic hunter-gatherers to read and write? To recall a distinction I introduced in the last chapter (pp. 364–5), in the context of a comparison of the technical capabilities of chimpanzees and human hunter-gatherers, how can we justify the attribution of the former to innate incapacity, when the latter is attributed to unfulfilled historical conditions? If Cro-Magnon Man, had he been brought up in the twentieth century, could have mastered the skills of literacy, why should not *Homo erectus*, had he been brought up in the Upper Palaeolithic, have mastered language?

A somewhat comparable question arises in the context of research into the linguistic capacities of great apes, especially chimpanzees. Reared under 'natural' conditions – that is, without significant contact with humans – chimpanzees do not learn to speak. Yet recent research shows fairly convincingly that chimpanzees reared in a human environment with speaking caregivers are capable of the spontaneous acquisition of linguistic syntax and semantics of a complexity equivalent to that used by small children (Savage-Rumbaugh and Rumbaugh 1993). Does this prove that contrary to expectations, chimpanzees – and by analogy, early hominids – do or did have a capacity for language, albeit of a limited sort? Are we to believe that thanks to the legacy of their common ancestry with humans, such a capacity is pre-installed, as an hereditary endowment, in the mind of every individual chimpanzee, merely awaiting propitious environmental circumstances for it to be 'brought out'?

I think not, for the question itself rests on a false premise, namely that the capacity for language is something whose presence or absence may be attributed to individuals of a species, irrespective of the environmental contexts of their development. Indeed it makes no sense to ask whether chimpanzees or hominids 'have' or 'had' language, as though it were programmed into them from the start. The biological definition of species depends upon the possibility of a context-independent specification: thus a chimpanzee is a chimpanzee, *Pan troglodytes*, whether reared among other chimpanzees or among humans, whether in the forest or in the laboratory. Yet the chimpanzee-in-an-environment-of-other-chimpanzees is not at all the same kind of animal as the chimpanzee-in-an-environment-of-humans: the latter may be credited with a rudimentary capacity for language which the former lacks. This capacity, as Dominique Lestel has pointed out, is the outcome of a process of development situated in the peculiar context of the hybrid human–animal community set up for the purposes of ape-language research (Lestel 1998: 13). And while this context may seem rather exceptional, it is nevertheless true of any process of development that it must involve an organism in relationships that cross-cut the boundaries of conventional taxonomic groupings. It follows that if a capacity – like language – can be shown to arise as an emergent property of the developmental system comprised by these relationships, then it cannot be attributed to a species. (Conversely, to attribute language to species is automatically to have resort to an innatist view that involves some kind of neural 'hard-wiring' that comes miraculously ready-made.)

The notion of the 'capacity for language' is itself deeply problematic. The orthodox account, which attributes this capacity to 'anatomically modern humans', requires that it be clearly distinguished, as a human universal, from the capacity to speak *this* language rather than *that*. Competence in one's particular mother-tongue is supposed to be a product of enculturation rather than given as part of one's biological endowment as a member of the human species. But human children are not 'born with' an innate programme (a language acquisition device) for assimilating an acquired one (in the form of the rules of syntax for a particular language). For whatever devices may be deployed in the process of language acquisition have themselves to undergo formation within a developmental context which is the very same as that within which the child learns the language of his or her community. There are not, in other words, two distinct and successive processes – the first 'wiring up' the brain for language, the second providing specific syntactic and semantic content – for it is in learning to speak in the manner of the people in his or her surroundings, and with their active assistance and support, that the neurological connections underwriting the child's linguistic competence are forged. Consequently, speakers of different languages, exposed at critical stages of development to different patterns of acoustic stimulation in different environments, will also differ in those aspects of their neural organisation that are involved in the production and interpretation of vocal utterances.[2]

In short, it is only by artificially separating out the more general from the more particular aspects of the total developmental system within which the skills of speaking emerge that 'language' can be identified as a universal capacity as against the speaking of one language rather than another. And in this respect, speaking is much like walking. There are, indeed, as many different ways of walking as there are ways of speaking. But as Esther Thelen and her colleagues have shown, in a series of studies of infant motor development, there is no 'essence' of walking that can be isolated from the real-time performance of the action itself (Thelen 1995: 83). Thus to refer to 'bipedal locomotion' or to 'language' as a universal attribute, distinct from the manifold skills of walking or speaking as these are actually deployed in the everyday life of human communities, is to reify what is, at best, a convenient analytic abstraction. Moreover speaking, like walking, is an achievement of the whole human organism, it is not merely the behavioural output of a cognitive mechanism installed within the organism, and for which it serves as a vehicle. Thus both walking and speaking are, in Mauss's phrase, 'techniques of the body' (1979 [1934]: 97–123). We carry these techniques with us in the ways that our bodies have been formed in and through the developmental process.

The corollary of this conclusion, however, is quite radical. It is to overturn, once and for all, the deep-seated presumption that those differences in language, body posture and so on that we are inclined to call *cultural* are superimposed upon a pre-constituted substrate of human biological universals. We can no longer remain content with the facile notion that all human beings start out (biologically) much the same and end up (culturally) very different. Consider, for example, this formulation from Geertz: 'One of the most significant facts about us may finally be that we all begin with the natural equipment to live a thousand kinds of life but end in the end having lived only one' (1973: 45). My point, *contra* Geertz, is that human beings are not naturally pre-equipped for any kind of life; rather, such equipment as they have comes into existence as they live their lives, through a process of development. And this process is none other than that by which they acquire the skills appropriate to the particular kind of life they lead. What each of us begins with, then, is a developmental system. It follows that cultural differences – since they emerge within the process of development of the human organism in its environment – *are themselves biological*. Before examining the implications of this result, I must take a step back, to show how it was that biology and culture came to be separated in the first place. With this, I return to a reconsideration of the notion of 'biological endowment'.

THE GENOME AND THE GENOTYPE

As I have already indicated, anatomically modern humans are supposed to be biologically endowed not only with bipedalism but also with a host of other attributes from language to advanced cognitive and manipulative abilities, all of which are often lumped together under the general rubric of the capacity for culture. Let me remind you of Lieberman's comment, which I cited in the last chapter, that despite all the monuments to human technological advance which litter the landscape, present-day people have 'essentially the same biological endowment' as their predecessors of 30,000 years ago. That endowment, then, must be bequeathed to individuals in every successive generation, independently of the diverse environmental contexts in which they grow up as walkers or cyclists, as stone toolmakers or machine tool operators, as hunter-gatherers or city dwellers, and so on. In other words, it amounts to a context-independent specification of the human organism, given to each and every member of the species at the point of conception.

In modern biology, the technical term for such a context-independent specification is *genotype*. By contrast, to characterise the organism in the form in which it actually appears – in terms of its outward morphology and behaviour as revealed within any particular environmental context – is to specify its *phenotype*. A fundamental premise of evolutionary theory, in its current neo-Darwinian guise, is that only the characteristics of the genotype, and not those of the phenotype, are carried across generations. On this principle rests the conventional division between ontogeny and phylogeny, or between development and evolution. Whereas development refers to the process whereby, in the life-history of the individual, the initial genotype is 'realised' in the concrete form of an environmentally

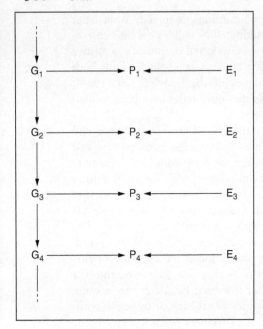

Figure 21.1 Schematic representation of the orthodox distinction between evolution and development. $G_1 - G_4$ are successive genotypes linked in an ancestor-descendant sequence. $P_1 - P_4$ are the respective phenotypes generated under environmental conditions $E_1 - E_4$. The vertical arrows depict an intergenerational phylogenetic pathway, the horizontal arrows depict ontogenetic processes confined within each generation.

specific phenotype, evolution refers to the gradual change, over a large number of successive generations, in the genotype itself (Figure 21.1). More exactly, it is the frequency of the constituent elements of the genotype, in populations of individuals, that is supposed to undergo evolutionary change, through a process of variation under natural selection.

To make this theory work, some vehicle is required that would serve to carry elements of the formal specification of the organism – namely genetic traits – from one site of development to another, heralding the initiation of a new life-cycle. With the discovery of DNA, it was thought that such a vehicle, long predicted, had at last been found. The DNA molecule comprises a very long string of nucleotide bases (some three billion in humans, contained within the twenty-three chromosomes of every cell in the body), each of which is one of only four possible kinds. This molecule has two critical properties. First, it binds with a complementary string which, rather like a photographic negative, provides a template in a chemical copying process that results in the synthesis of further strands of DNA with precisely the same sequence of bases as in the original. Secondly, segments of the molecule, of the order of ten thousand bases in length, guide the synthesis of specific proteins – the composition of each protein being determined by the linear sequence of bases in the corresponding segment. These proteins, in turn, are the fundamental constituents of the living organism. Thus the total complement of DNA in the cell, otherwise known as the genome, is supposed to encode in its base sequence a complete specification of the organism to which the cell belongs.

To explain this encoding, geneticists often resort to the language of information theory (Medawar 1967: 56–7). The genome, they say, carries a message which, roughly translated, means 'build an organism of such-and-such a kind' – that is, according to the formal specifications of the genotype. Now in fact, the theory of information, as it was developed in the 1940s by Norbert Wiener, John von Neumann and Claude Shannon, took up the notion of information in a specialised sense which had little to do with how the term was generally understood – namely to refer to the semantic content of messages passing between senders and recipients. Information for these theorists had no semantic value whatever; it did not *mean* anything. In their terms, a random string of letters could have the same informational content as a Shakespeare sonnet (Kay 1998: 507). This point, however, was entirely lost on the molecular biologists who, having realised that the DNA molecule could be regarded as a form of digital information in the technical, information-theoretic sense, immediately jumped to the conclusion that it therefore qualified as a *code* with a specific semantic content. The point was not lost on the information theorists themselves, however, who repeatedly warned against the conflation of the technical sense of information with its generic counter-part, and looked on in dismay as the scriptural metaphors of message, language, text and so forth became entrenched in a biology that had become seemingly intoxicated with the idea of DNA as a 'book of life'.[3]

The upshot of this conflation was that the information theoretic model, as it came to be reincarnated in the context of biological science, was all about messages and their transmission. It is a requirement of the model, thus conceived, that the message to be transmitted be first broken down into its minimal constituents of meaning, each of which is then represented, in coded form, in an appropriate physical medium. In verbal communication, for example, concepts are said to be represented by distinctive combinations of sounds (in the case of

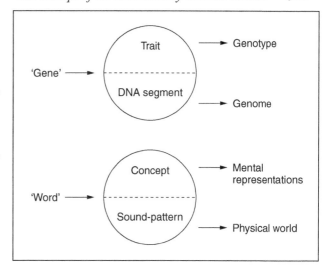

Figure 21.2 A schematic representation of the analogy between genes and words as signs.

speech) or graphic traces (in the case of writing). In this physical guise they are picked up by a receiver who, through a reverse process of decoding, recovers the original meanings and puts them together to reconstitute the message. In the case of genetic transmission, the minimal constituents of meaning were supposed to correspond to characters or traits, each represented by a DNA segment with a distinctive base sequence. Just as the linguistic sign is understood to unite a particular concept with a particular sound pattern, so the gene came to be conceived as the union of a particular trait with its corresponding segment of the DNA molecule (Figure 21.2).

I shall defer until later the question of whether this model of information transmission provides an adequate account of what goes on even in ordinary verbal discourse. Suffice it to say at this point that the model is premised upon an ontological separation of mind and world. Indeed this separation is intrinsic to the very notion of information in its original sense – to the idea that form is *brought in* to real-world contexts of inter-action. The message or instruction to be conveyed is thus supposed to pre-exist in the mind of the sender, and to be translated into a physical medium by means of a set of encoding rules that are themselves entirely independent of the contexts in which it is sent and received. How a message, once received, will be interpreted may of course depend upon the situation, but the message itself must be unambiguously specified. Likewise, if we are to suppose that the genome is a carrier of coded information from one context of development to another, then the 'message' – that is, the genotypic specification – must pre-exist its representation in the DNA, and be linked to it by context-independent encoding rules. In other words, it must be possible to 'read off' each element of the genotype – each trait – from its corresponding DNA segment, regardless of local conditions of development. However, just as a received message may be interpreted differently in different circumstances, so also the genotype will be 'realised' in different ways depending upon the environmental context, leading to observed variations in phenotypic form (Figure 21.3).

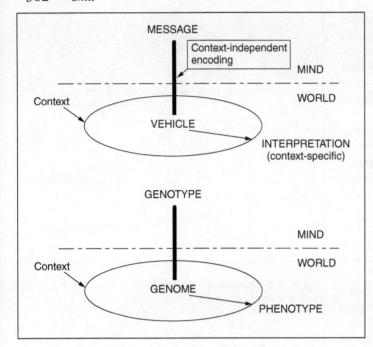

Figure 21.3 The relation between message, vehicle and interpretation (above), and its analogue in the biological domain (below).

The problem inherent in this kind of account may be posed in terms of a simple question: where is the genotype? Where, in other words, is the formal specification that – according to the model – is said to be imported with the genome into the inaugural context of a new life-cycle, as a 'biological endowment'? We may grant that the newly conceived organism comes into being with its complement of DNA; taken on its own, however, the DNA 'specifies' nothing. It is, after all, just a molecule, and a remarkably inert one at that. But in reality, DNA never exists on its own, except when artificially isolated in the laboratory. It exists within cells, which are the parts of organisms, themselves situated within wider environments. And it is only by virtue of their incorporation into the living machinery of the cell that molecules of DNA have the effects they do. They do not, unaided, make copies of themselves or construct proteins, let alone build entire organisms (see Lewontin 1992: 33, for an exceptionally lucid exposition of this point). Thus the DNA is not an agent but a reactant, and the particular reactions it sets in train depend upon the total organismic context in which it is situated. Only by presuming such a context can we ever say what any particular gene is 'for' (Ingold 1991: 368). To put it another way, it is the cellular machinery that 'reads' the DNA, and that reading is part and parcel of the very development of the organism in its environment. Hence there is no 'decoding' of the genome that is not itself a process of development; no attributes of form that do not themselves originate within that process; no specification of the organism that is independent of the developmental context.

So to return to my earlier question, 'where is the genotype?', there can be only one possible answer: 'in the mind of the biologist'. The genotype, I would argue, is the outcome of biologists' attempts to write a programme or algorithm for the development of the organism, in the form of a coherent system of epigenetic rules. These rules are derived by abstraction from the organism's observed characteristics, in a manner analogous to the way in which a linguist would derive the rules of syntax by abstraction from a sample of recorded utterances – an analogy that receives explicit acknowledgement in the notion of the 'biogram'. Moreover the same trick is then applied: as Bourdieu (1977: 96) puts it, by transferring onto the object of study the exteriority of the observer's relation to it, that object appears as the mere vehicle for an interiorised system of rational principles, a kind of 'intelligence' installed at the heart of the organism and directing its activity from within. Just as the linguist regards speaking as the application of syntactic structures located inside speakers' heads, so the biologist regards the development and behaviour of the organism as having its generative source in an innate biogram. In both cases aspects of form, abstracted from the contexts in which they arise, are converted into the elements of a programme that is said to precede and govern the processes of their production. As an explanation for the genesis of form, the circularity of this argument needs no further elaboration.

Nothing better illustrates the transferral, onto the organism, of the principles of the observer's external relation to it, than the fate of the concept of biology itself. Referring initially to the procedures involved in the scientific study of organic forms, 'biology' has come to be seen as a framework of rational principles – literally a *bio-logos* – supposedly residing in the organisms themselves, and orchestrating their construction. For any particular organism, this bio-logos is, of course, its genotype. Herein, then, lies the explanation for the identification, noted above, of 'biology' with genetics. In the final analysis, this identification betrays a logocentrism that biology shares with the entire enterprise of Western natural science: the assumption that the manifest phenomena of the physical world are underwritten by the work of reason. But the reason that science sees at work there is its own, reflected in the mirror of nature.

FORM AND DEVELOPMENT

If organisms do not receive their form, with the genome, as a 'biological endowment', then how are we to explain the stability of form across generations? The answer lies in the observation that the life of any organism is inaugurated with far more than its complement of DNA. For one thing, as Lewontin points out, the DNA is contained within an egg which, even before fertilisation, is equipped through its own development with the essential prerequisites for launching future growth. 'We inherit not only genes made of DNA but an intricate structure of cellular machinery made up of proteins' (Lewontin 1992: 33). For another thing, that egg exists not in a vacuum but in an already structured environment. Life begins, then, with DNA, in an egg, in an environment. Or as Oyama succinctly puts it, 'what is quite literally passed on or made available in reproduction is a genome *and a segment of the world*' (1985: 43, my emphasis). Together, these constitute a developmental system, and it is in the dynamic functioning of this system – in the complex interactions among components both internal to the organism (including the genome) and beyond its boundaries – that form is generated and maintained (Ho 1991: 346–7).

It follows that no one component – such as the DNA – can be privileged as 'holding' the form, which the others 'bring out', since the form itself is an emergent property of the total system consisting in the relations between them. Change in any component of the system, whether in the genome or in some aspect of the intra- or extra-organismic environment, insofar as it alters the parameters of development, may bring about significant change in form; however the possibilities for change are not unlimited but are constrained within the range of forms that can be generated by the system's properties of dynamic organisation. Thus the explanation for the intergenerational stability of form is to be found not in the fidelity of DNA copying, but in the self-organising potentials of the entire field of relations within which development occurs (Goodwin 1988, see also Chapter Eighteen, pp. 345–6).

It is important to be precise about how this conclusion differs from what is generally accepted in evolutionary biology. The issue of whether organisms are determined by their nature or their nurture, by innate endowment or environmental conditioning, has long been declared obsolete, having given way to an interactionist perspective according to which every organism, at any moment of its life-cycle, is the product of a complex and ongoing interplay between genetic and environmental factors. Naturally, it is argued, organisms take on different appearances in different environments. It is nevertheless assumed that these environmentally induced differences merely reveal the potential for variation of what is essentially the *same* organism, and that only those differences attributable to genetic modification attest to evolutionary change in the organism itself. And it is on precisely this assumption, with its implicit privileging of the genome as the true bearer of organic form, that the conventional distinctions between genotype and phenotype, and between evolution and development, have been allowed to rest.

For orthodox theory, these distinctions are quite critical. Evolution, as we have seen, is taken to refer to intergenerational changes in the genotype; development to the translation, within each generation, from genotype to phenotype (see Figure 21.1). This is not to say that these processes are thought to be unrelated. Thus it is recognised, on the one hand, that the circumstances of development – insofar as they have a bearing on genetic replication – may exert an influence on evolution, and on the other hand that it is the evolved genotype that establishes the schedule for development (Hinde 1991: 585). But the theory rules out any possibility that the life-history of the organism may itself form an intrinsic part of the evolutionary process. From an evolutionary perspective, it is not what organisms do but the reproductive consequences of their activity that are significant. Considerations of agency and intentionality have no place in evolutionary explanation: these are assigned to the proximate mechanisms involved in the realisation of strategies whose ultimate rationale is already established by natural selection. For this reason, it is customary to speak of organisms as the sites *where* evolution occurs, but not as agents of evolutionary change. Thus changes are said to take place *in*, but not to be brought about *by*, populations of organisms.

But if form, as I have argued here, is a property not of genes but of developmental systems, then to account for the evolution of form we need to understand how these systems are constituted and reconstituted over time. We have seen that what an organism initially receives from its predecessors includes, besides its complement of genetic material, the environment wherein this material is placed. This placement sets up specific relations that are enfolded in the developing form. Yet as it develops, the organism also contributes by way of its actions to the environmental conditions not just for its own further development but for the development of other organisms – of its own and of different kinds – to which it relates. It may do so either directly, insofar as it has an immediate presence in the other's environment, or indirectly, insofar as its actions sustain, modify or transform the environment of another's experience. For example, the human child may grow up surrounded by parents and siblings, in a house constructed long ago by predecessors whom she will never meet. Yet all these people, and doubtless many more besides, play or have played their part in establishing the conditions for that child's development. Conversely, as she grows older and her powers of agency expand, she in turn will contribute to the conditions of development for her own contemporaries and successors.

Speaking of human beings, it is usual to refer to this process, wherein the people of each generation furnish through their life-activities the contexts within which their successors grow to maturity, as *history*. My point, however, is that human history is but one part of a process that is going on throughout the organic world (see Ingold 1990: 224). In this process, organisms figure not as the passive products of a mechanism – variation under natural selection – that stands outside of time and change, but as active and creative agents, producers as well as products of their own evolution (Ho 1991: 338). For every organism not only undergoes development within a wider field of relationships, but also contributes through its activity to the perpetuation and transformation of that field. Thus what it does, in its life, is not expended in the reproduction of its genes but is incorporated into the developmental potentials of its successors. There can, then, be no separation between ontogeny and phylogeny, development and evolution. Ontogenesis, far from being accessory to evolutionary change, is the very fount from which the evolutionary process unfolds.

To forestall any possible misunderstanding, let me be quite clear about what I am claiming. I do not deny the existence of the genome or its importance as a regulator of developmental processes. Nor do I deny that changes can and do occur in the composition of the genome, as a result of the mutation, recombination and differential replication of its constituent segments across generations. I *do* deny, however, that the genome contains a specification of the essential form of the organism, or of its capacities for action, and therefore that a record of genetic change is in any sense tantamount to an account of its evolution. Much genetic change occurs without any corollary on the level of form or behaviour; conversely, significant morphological or behavioural transformation may occur without any corresponding changes in the genome. We have seen that since organisms, in their activities, can modify the conditions of development for successor generations, developmental systems – and the capacities specified therein – can go on evolving without requiring any genetic change at all. Nowhere is this more evident than in the evolution of our own kind. In order to explain how change can occur in the absence of significant genetic modification, orthodox evolutionary theory has had to conceive of a 'second track', of culture history, superimposed upon the baseline of an evolved genotypic heritage. Once it is realised, however, that capacities are constituted within developmental systems, rather than carried with the genes as a biological endowment, we can begin to see how the dichotomies between biology and culture, and between evolution and history, can be dispensed with. This is a matter to which I now turn.

BIOLOGY AND CULTURE

Let me begin by returning to the comparison between walking and cycling. Bipedal locomotion, according to orthodox theory, is part of the human biological endowment – that is, it is included as a property of the 'anatomically modern' genotype. Now we have seen that the genotype is the product of biologists' attempts to attribute the capacities of the organism to an interior programme, consisting of a set of rules or algorithms capable of generating appropriate responses under any given environmental circumstances. Thus if the capacity to walk belongs with the genotype, then it must be possible to comprehend walking as the output of a programme of this kind, designed by natural selection and imported with the genome into diverse contexts of development. What, then, are we to make of the capacity to ride a bicycle? It is doubtful whether much could be learned about the origins and development of this capacity through an examination of changing gene frequencies in the cycling public! By common consent, it forms no part of the human genotype, and for that reason is not generally considered to have evolved in the biological sense. Yet clearly, cycling is a skill that, in some sense, is passed on from one generation to the next. It cannot therefore be ascribed to the phenotype, since phenotypic characters are not supposed to be transmitted across generations.

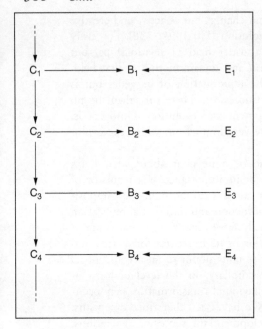

Figure 21.4 Individual and social learning. The vertical arrows depict the intergenerational transmission of cultural information through social learning in the ancestor-descendant sequence C_1 – C_4. The horizontal arrows depict the processes of individual learning through which, in each generation, the received cultural schemata are translated into overt behaviour (B_1 – B_4) under given environmental conditions (E_1 – E_4). Compare Figure 21.1.

To accommodate the kind of non-genetic transmission that is apparently at work here, it has often been proposed that in human populations, a second mode of inheritance operates in parallel with the genetic one. 'Human beings', as Durham puts it, 'are possessed of *two* major information systems, one genetic, one cultural' (1991: 9). The capacity to ride a bicycle, then, is included in a cultural analogue of the genotype – a 'culture-type' (Richerson and Boyd 1978: 128) – whose constituent elements or traits are likewise encoded in a symbolic medium. This model of enculturation rests on precisely the same assumptions that I have already spelled out in connection with genetic transmission. It presupposes that the cultural 'message' that the individual receives from its conspecifics pre-exists its symbolic representation, that the message can be 'read off' from the representation by means of context-independent decoding rules, and that this reading precedes the application of the received cultural knowledge in the settings of practice. Thus a clear distinction has to be drawn between the intergenerational transmission of cultural information and its expression in the career of each individual, exactly parallel to the distinction that orthodox theory in evolutionary biology draws between the transmission of the elements making up the genotype and the latter's realisation, within the life of every organism, in the guise of the phenotype. The former distinction has conventionally been made by means of a contrast between 'individual' and 'social' learning (Figure 21.4).

Individual learning, here, refers to the way in which behaviour, just as much as morphology, is 'acquired' through the environmental steering of development culminating in the mature phenotype. In this each organism learns for itself, through experience, and the process of learning is coterminous with its own lifespan. Social learning, on the other hand, refers to the transmission, across generations, of a body of cultural knowledge in the form of a tradition. This tradition consists not in behaviour itself, but in a system of schemata – 'plans, recipes, rules, instructions' (Geertz 1973: 44) – for generating it. In the case of bicycle riding, for example, what an individual acquires from his or her seniors are the elements of a programme, analogous to the genetically encoded programme that supposedly underwites the skills of walking, which is then 'realised' through practice and experience in an environment. Notice how this division between the social and the individual components of learning effectively divorces the sphere of the learner's involvement with others from the contexts of his or her practical engagement in the world. It assumes that what is passed on, in learning, is a context-independent specification for behaviour, and that such a specification is available for transmission, in coded form, outside the situations of its application. Accordingly, the inter-generational stability of cultural form is seen to lie in the fidelity with which this information is copied from mind to mind.

As an account of what goes on in learning to ride a bicycle, or for that matter in the acquisition of any other practical skill, this is highly artificial. For one thing, the art of cycling – as indeed that of walking – defies codification in terms of any formal system of rules and representations. Even if it were possible to devise a programme for bicycle riding, it is doubtful whether a creature endowed with such a programme, and equipped with a machine to ride, would ever be able to achieve the fluency of the skilled practitioner. For another thing, where adult assistance is required it is above all to provide demonstration and support – that is, to set up situations in which the novice is afforded the possibility of getting the feel of things for him- or herself. The same is true in language learning, aptly described as a process of 'guided reinvention' (Lock 1980), in which the contribution of adults in the infant's environment is to provide contextually specific interpretations of the infant's vocal utterances that lead it to the discovery of how words can be used to convey meaning. What each generation contributes to the next, then, are not rules and schemata for the production of appropriate behaviour, but rather the specific conditions of development under which successors, growing up in a social world, acquire their own embodied skills and dispositions.

Words and deeds, of course, are full of meaning, and in any situation of learning the novice will listen to what people say and watch what they do. Yet there is no 'reading' of words or deeds that is not part of the novice's own practical orientation to his or her environment. Spoken words, for example, taken in themselves, are no more *for* anything than are genes. They do not carry meaning *into* contexts of interaction, as the orthodox model of information transmission requires. Rather, again like genes, they gather their meanings from the contexts of activities and relationships in which they are in play (I return to this point in Chapter Twenty-three, p. 409). Thus culture, as a body of context-independent, traditionally transmitted knowledge, encoded in words or other symbolic media, can exist nowhere except in the mind of the anthropological observer. It is derived by abstraction from observed behaviour, in just the same way that the biologist derives the genotype by abstraction from the observed characteristics of the organism, and the linguist derives a grammar from the record of utterances. And by the same trick that we have already noted in the fields of linguistics and biology, this abstraction is imagined to be implanted within the minds of the actors themselves, as the generative source of their behaviour.

I have argued, to the contrary, that whether our concern be with walking or cycling, talking or writing, making tools or operating machines, what people do cannot be understood as the behavioural output of an inner programme but only as the intentional activity of the whole human organism in its environment. Thus to reiterate my earlier conclusion, we have no grounds for distinguishing between those capacities for action due to 'biology' and those due to 'culture'. True, there are things that human beings can do which are apparently impossible for any other creature, even if raised in a human environment. And it is reasonable to suppose that these potentials would not have emerged were it not for certain changes in the genome that could, in principle, be traced in ancestral populations. But the genome, on its own, does not specify a capacity of any kind. Thus we will search in vain for a capacity for culture, whose evolutionary emergence might have marked what is sometimes called the 'human revolution'. For there is no such thing, apart from the diverse capacities of human beings growing up in different surroundings. These differences of developmental experience, as I have shown, are incorporated anatomically so as to make of each of us an organism of a different kind.

EVOLUTION AND HISTORY

Where does all this leave the Cro-Magnons? Did their arrival on the scene really mark the appearance of people 'entirely like ourselves'? We are not, of course, by any means perfect; nevertheless – Howells remarks – 'it is not unfair to say that *Homo sapiens* seems to have finished up all the unfinished business of human progress in the Pleistocene' (1967: 242). Yet in another sense, human progress had scarcely begun. These two senses of progress correspond, as we have seen, to what are customarily distinguished as evolution and history. Now this is not a distinction that would generally be made for any other species. It is assumed, in other words, that there can be no cumulative or progressive changes in the behavioural capacities of non-human kinds that are not tied to evolutionary changes in their essential, species-specific forms. For this reason, no-one finds it necessary to speak, for example, of 'anatomically modern chimpanzees' or 'anatomically modern elephants'. What the concept of anatomical modernity does, in effect, is to recognise an alternative sense in which people can be 'modern', only to place it out of bounds, as of no concern to the student of human biological evolution. Yet this second sense of modernity, founded as it is upon a commitment to the supremacy of reason, is built into the very project of contemporary science and underwrites its claim to be able to deliver an authoritative account of the workings of nature. Here, then, lies the contradiction to which I referred at the outset. For the historical process, which purports to raise humanity onto a level of existence above the purely biophysical, is presupposed by science as providing the platform from which its practitioners – who are of course humans too – can launch their declarations to the effect that the human is just another species of nature (Foley 1987).

The roots of the contradiction considerably antedate the rise of evolutionary theory in its modern Darwinian form, and may be traced back to a basic dualism in eighteenth-century thinking between nature and reason. In his *Systema Naturae* of 1735, Linnaeus recognised the status of man as a species within the animal kingdom, under the designation *Homo*. Yet unlike all other animal species, it was not by his physical characteristics that he was to be known. Indeed, Linnaeus declared himself hard-pressed to find *any* definitive criterion whereby human beings could be distinguished anatomically from the apes. Rather, he chose to identify the human distinction by means of a word of advice: *Nosce te ipsum* ('know for yourself'). It is in his wisdom, Linnaeus thought, not in his bodily form, that man differs essentially from the apes. Through our unique possession of the intellectual faculty of reason, we are the only beings who can seek to know, through our own powers of observation and analysis, what kinds of beings we are. There are no scientists among the animals.

The great nineteenth-century theorists of social and cultural evolution – men like Edward Tylor and Lewis Henry Morgan – placed their scenarios of human progress within a similarly dualistic framework. While all animal species were ranked, according to their physical form, in a chain of being culminating in humankind, the latter was supposed to have been uniquely endowed by the Creator with an incorporeal consciousness which, through history, has undergone progressive advance under laws of development of its own, within the bounds of an unchanging body (Ingold 1986b: 58–60). Thus all human beings were deemed to be alike in their essential nature and developmental potentials, but populations were supposed to differ in the degree to which these potentials were realised in the passage from savagery to civilisation. With the publication, in 1871, of Darwin's *The descent of man*, the doctrine of common human potential – or, as it was then known, of the 'psychic unity of mankind' – was brought into contention, challenged by the view that inter-population differences on the scale of civilisation could be attributed to anatomical variation, above all in the size and complexity of the brain. Thomas Huxley went so far as to declare that the superiority of the European over the allegedly small-brained savage was no different, in principle, from that of the savage over the even smaller-brained ape. There ensued a period of quite rampant racism from which anthropology did not begin to recover until the second decade of the twentieth century. It did so by reasserting the universality of human nature, and by insisting that whatever differences of biological endowment may exist between populations are of no consequence for history and cultural development.

Indeed so long as it is assumed that the biological constitution of human organisms is given as a genetic endowment, there can be no escape from racism save by disconnecting cultural from biological variation. Clearly there is no foundation in fact for the raciological belief that cultural differences have a genetic basis. My point, however, is that in turning its back on racist dogma, subsequent theorising about human evolution has reconstituted the eighteenth-century view in all its essentials. Once again human beings figure in a dual capacity, on the one hand as a species of nature, on the other as creatures who – uniquely among animals – have achieved such emancipation from the world of nature as to make it the object of their consciousness. It is true that unlike Linnaeus, contemporary students of human evolution are able to point with some precision to a whole cluster of anatomical features by which human beings may be distinguished not only from extant, non-human primates but also from their pre-human, hominid forbears. These are the diagnostic features for the recognition of anatomical modernity. But humans of this recognisably 'modern' type did not evolve as scientists, let alone with a ready-made theory of evolution. Science and its theories are widely understood to be the products of a cultural or civilisational process quite separate from the process of biological evolution: a cumulative growth of knowledge that has left our basic natures unaffected.

We thus have two distinct continua, one evolutionary, leading from ancestral pongid and hominid forms to 'anatomically modern' *Homo sapiens sapiens*, the other historical, leading from our presumed hunter-gatherer past to modern science and civilisation (Ingold 1998: 89–93). And it is the intersection of these continua that sets up a point of origin, without parallel in the history of life, at which our ancestors stood on the threshold of culture and, for the first time, came face to face with meaning (Figure 21.5). This point is believed to mark the emergence of what is sometimes called 'true humanity' (see, for example, Botscharow 1990: 64), or the arrival, in Howells's words, of 'the new kind – our kind – of man' (1967: 242). This kind of man, equipped anatomically for life as a hunter-gatherer, was possessed of a mind that would eventually enable him to reason like a scientist. Cro-Magnon Man, it seems, had all the biological potential necessary to make him into a scientist: his brain was as big, and as complex, as Einstein's. But the time was not ripe, in his era, for this potential to be brought out. Stretched between the poles of nature and reason, epitomised respectively by the contrasting figures of the hunter-gatherer and the scientist, lies the entire history of human culture, a history that has unfolded within the parameters of an essentially stable bodily form. And that form, which all human beings are supposed to receive as a common biological endowment, irrespective of cultural or historical circumstance, is of course none other than the 'modern human' genotype.

Just as in the eighteenth-century doctrine of psychic unity, the human genotype – albeit installed by natural selection rather than divine intervention – is said to establish a universal baseline for cultural development. As an ideal representation of the essential form of

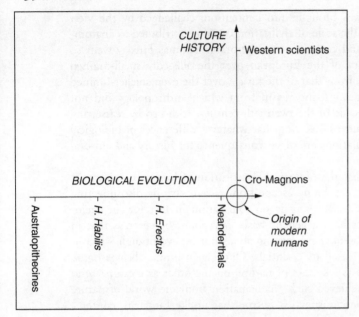

Figure 21.5 The origin of 'true humanity', conceived as lying at the intersection between the continuum of biological evolution leading from ancestral pongid and hominid forms to anatomically modern humans, and the continuum of culture history leading from Palaeolithic hunting and gathering to modern science and civilisation.

humanity, the 'modern human' is itself a creature of modern Western thought. He (or she) is conceived as the epitome of everything a human being possibly could be, a compendium of universal capacities abstracted from the manifold forms of life that have actually appeared in history, and retrojected onto the Palaeolithic past as a set of genetically inscribed, developmental potentials underwriting their realisation.[4] Thus the course of history reappears as the progressive unfolding of the latent capacities of our ancestors, biologically fixed in evolution even before history began. There is a certain irony here. Biologists, who long ago co-opted the notion of evolution to describe the process that Darwin had originally called 'descent with modification', have been scathing in their criticism of social scientists who have continued to use the notion, with reference to human history, in its original sense of progressive development. Yet just such a view of human history, as the developmental realisation of innate potentials, is implied by their own theory!

I have argued that the distinction between evolution and history, as set out in the orthodox view, cannot be sustained. Regarded as a process whereby people, in their activities, shape the contexts of development for their successors, history reappears as the continuation, by another name, of a process of evolution that is going on throughout the organic world. In the *Eighteenth Brumaire*, Marx wrote that 'men make their own history, but they do not make it just as they please, they do not make it under circumstances chosen by themselves, but under circumstances directly encountered, given and transmitted from the past' (Marx 1963 [1869]: 15). In just the same way do organisms in general make their own evolution. There is, then, no point of origin when history began; no moment of emergence of 'true humanity'. Thus we do not need one theory to explain how apes became human, and another to explain how (some) humans became scientists. For the business of human evolution was not finished with the arrival of the Cro-Magnons, but has carried on into the present – though we call it history now. I have attempted to show that the various forms and capacities that have emerged within this process are neither given in advance as a genetic endowment, nor transmitted as components of a separate body of cultural information, but are rather generated in and through the dynamic functioning of the developmental systems constituted by virtue of the involvement of human beings in their diverse environments.

For human as for any other organisms, such involvement is an inescapable condition of existence. I believe we need to recast the whole way we think about evolution, taking this condition of involvement as our point of departure. Orthodox theory, which attributes evolutionary change to underlying modifications in the genotype, requires that human beings be completely specifiable, independently of the relational contexts of their development. But such a specification, as I have shown, exists only in the mind of the observer, and therefore introjects a division between mind and world, or between reason and nature, as an ontological *a priori*. There is, in truth, no species-specific, essential form of humanity, no way of saying what an 'anatomically modern human' *is* apart from the manifold ways in which humans actually *become* (Ingold 1991: 359). These variations of developmental circumstance, not of genetic inheritance, make us organisms of different kinds. Thus my conclusion, that the differences we call cultural are indeed biological, carries no racist connotations whatever. By refocusing on the human-being-in-its-environment, we can dispense with the need for a species-specific characterisation of humankind, and so also with the opposition between species and culture. People inhabit one world, not because their differences are underwritten by universals of human nature, but because they are caught up – along with other creatures – in a continuous field of relations, in the unfolding of which all difference is generated.

Speech, writing and the modern origins of 'language origins'

As Horne Tooke, one of the founders of the noble science of philology, observes, language is an art, like brewing or baking; but writing would have been a better simile. It certainly is not a true instinct, for every language has to be learnt. It differs, however, widely from all ordinary arts, for man has an instinctive tendency to speak, as we see in the babble of our young children; whilst no child has an instinctive tendency to brew, bake or write.

Charles Darwin, *The descent of man* (1871: 131)

THE LANGUAGE CAPACITY: ORIGINS OF AN ILLUSION

All theorising about the origins and evolution of language rests on a distinction that, by and large, is regarded as so obvious that it virtually goes without saying. It is that by 'language', in this context, is meant not any particular language, as spoken presently or in the past by members of some human community, but a *capacity* that is manifestly common to all human beings, and that is surely one of the hallmarks of our species. One could of course examine the changes over time that have given rise to the immense proliferation of languages spoken around the world, but that is a problem for philologists or historians of language. Does not the very possibility of this history, however, rest on the fact that all of us, including our ancestors up to a certain critical point, share (or shared) the capacity to speak? If so, then explaining how, when and why this capacity arose is a problem not of history but of evolution. The twin distinctions, between particular languages spoken and the capacity for language, and between history and evolution, do indeed seem intuitively reasonable. For my part, however, I am convinced that they are unsustainable, and in this chapter I shall try to show why.

I contend that there is no essence of language, no way of saying what language *is*, apart from the manifold ways in which people actually speak. But if there is no such thing as language *as such*, what is the point of seeking its origins? I do in fact take the view that it is futile to inquire into the origins of language, not for the reason that is usually offered – namely, that such inquiry calls for empirical evidence about the behaviour of our earliest ancestors that is simply not available – but because the very idea of an origin is a fiction that serves more to confer legitimacy on the present than to illuminate the past. I shall argue that Charles Darwin, and Horne Tooke before him, were right to compare language to an art like brewing or baking, though it might have been more appropriate to select different examples, such as singing, dancing or playing a musical instrument, which do not involve the procurement and processing of raw materials. But no more than these other arts did language evolve at some point, as a built-in property of the human make-up. Rather, it inheres in the very practice of the art, in the activities of speaking themselves. These activities, in their unfolding, *constitute* a process of evolution. Thus there is, in reality, no point of origin, since the evolutionary process continues even as we speak.

Although my thesis as regards the question of origin is a negative one, I would not want what I have to say to be construed in an entirely negative light. It may make no sense to seek the point where language began, but it makes a good deal of sense to inquire into the evolution of speech. To do this, however, it will be necessary to drop two assumptions that lie at the heart of most contemporary theorising on the subject. First, we must cease to regard speech as the derivative output of something else – that is, 'language' – which is supposed to pre-exist as a generative potential or capacity independently of human activity in the world. And secondly, we must not assume that what evolves is some kind of context-independent specification of the essential form of humanity.

Closely bound up with the argument I have just introduced is another one, about the relation between speech and writing. Reflecting on the parallel between language and other practical arts, Darwin came to the conclusion that the latter could be better compared to writing than to speech, and that spoken language was – after all – a rather special case. I propose to argue, somewhat to the contrary, that language looks special to us only because we view it from a perspective that has been conditioned through our familiarity with certain practices of writing. I contend that these practices have had a decisive impact in shaping our modern view of language as an objective system of rules and meanings – as something that people *have*, and can *use*. According to my argument, it is only thanks to the reification of speech which writing makes possible, that the idea of language as a thing, and hence of language origins, becomes even conceivable. If language, in a certain formal sense, is a consequence of writing, then to seek the evolutionary origins of language in this same sense, as a precondition for writing, is manifestly circular.[1]

I shall conclude, however, by suggesting that besides considering the effects of writing on our view of what language is, we need to attend to the possible bias in our view of what *writing* is, a bias that stems from the frequently asserted notion that writing is a technology of the word. It is not, then, writing *per se*, but rather a *technologised* conception of writing, associated with the rise of modern print literacy, that leads to the objectification of speech as language, and thence to the problematic of language origins.

THE STANDARD MODEL: GENETIC BASES OF CULTURAL TRANSMISSION

That, stripped to its bare essentials, is what I have to say. In what follows I shall elaborate on, and seek to demonstrate, the various claims I have made. I begin, however, by returning to what I shall henceforth call the 'standard model' of the relation between language as a universal human capacity, and the manifold languages of particular communities. This holds that the former is a product of evolution under natural selection, and is transmitted genetically, thereby establishing the cognitive foundations, in successive generations, for the acquisition of the latter through a parallel process of cultural transmission.

I have summarised the standard model in Figure 22.1, and shall devote a few moments to spelling out three of its key features. The first is that every particular language may be fully described as a system of acquired rules and representations – comprising its syntax and lexicon – inscribed in the minds of its speakers and transmissible as a body of information, from one generation to the next, independently of its instantiation in those acts

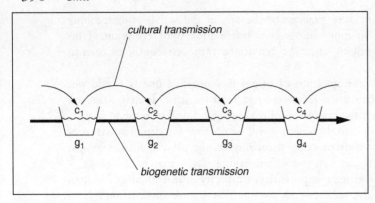

Figure 22.1 The orthodox view of the relation between biogenetic and cultural transmission. The letters g_{1-4} refer to the genetic specifications, in successive generations, of an innate acquisition device; the letters c_{1-4} refer to the content, again in successive generations, of acquired culture.

of speaking and listening for which it is prerequisite. The second is that this transmission is possible only thanks to the presence, in the mind of each and every human being, of a ready-made acquisition device that allows the novice to derive the specifications of his or her language from the input of otherwise unintelligible speech sounds. And the third is that the relation between the acquisition device and the acquired information is one of container to content. The novice starts life with a certain capacity already in place, which is then gradually filled up with the informational content upon which his or her linguistic competence is based.

Now I believe that in each of these respects the standard model is wrong. Let me begin with the second. It is perfectly true that *if* the essence of linguistic competence lies in acquired rules and representations, then the mind must be pre-equipped with cognitive devices of some kind that allow the relevant information to be reconstructed through a processing of the raw input of sensory data. Consider, for example, the following definition of learning, from one of the leading exponents of cognitive science, Philip Johnson-Laird. Learning, he writes, amounts to 'the construction of new programs out of elements of experience'. But if you need programmes to *process* the data of experience, how can they be constructed *from* such data? There is only one possible answer, and that is by means of programmes that are already in place. Thus, if you are to learn anything, you must be pre-equipped with a programme governing the construction process. Perhaps this latter programme was constructed in the same way, through the processing of experiential input according to yet another programme. 'You can learn to learn', Johnson-Laird continues, 'but then that learning would depend on another program, and so on. Ultimately, learning must depend on *innate* programs that make programs' (Johnson-Laird 1988: 133, my emphasis).

Following this line of reasoning, what applies to learning in general must also apply to language acquisition in particular. Maybe there are rules or algorithms governing the acquisition of language that are themselves acquired. But then there must be processing devices in place that make possible *their* construction in the mind of the learner. So where do these come from? Whence comes the information that specifies the construction of the *innate* devices, without which no learning would be possible at all?

By and large, in the literature of cognitive science, the postulation of innate structures is taken to require no more justification than vague references to genetics and natural selection. It is assumed that the problem of where they come from has already been solved, at least in general terms, by evolutionary biology. Unfortunately this is not the case. For one thing, most biologists claim that they have long since discarded the distinction between innate and acquired structures. According to what is often called the 'first law of biology', the actual characteristics of organisms are neither innate nor acquired, but are products of the interaction, throughout the life cycle, between endogenous, genetic causes and exogenous, environmental ones. Thus interactionism has long since replaced innatism as the dominant creed within biological science. In fact, however, a doctrine of genetic preformation still lurks beneath the surface of orthodox interactionism, since it is built into biology's own master theory – the theory of evolution under natural selection. To see how this is so, we need to focus on the account that is offered, within the framework of Darwinian evolutionary biology, of the process of ontogenetic development. This calls for a brief detour into the realms of biological theory.

THE EVOLUTION OF FORM: GENOTYPES AND DEVELOPMENTAL SYSTEMS

Interactionism describes development as an unfolding relation between genes and environment. In this relation, however, it is the genes that are supposed to hold the essence of form, whereas the environment is conceived merely to furnish the material conditions for its realisation. Each gene is taken to represent a unit of pure, digital information, encoded in the molecular structure of DNA. Put together, these units make up a formal specification of the organism-to-be (the genotype) which, by definition, is given independently and in advance of any real-world context of development. At the commencement of every new life-cycle, this genotypic specification is introduced, by way of the DNA of the germ cells, into a particular environmental context. In development, the information carried in the genes is then said to be outwardly expressed in the phenotypic form of the resultant organism. But whereas the elements of the genotype are transmitted across generations, the characteristics of the phenotype are not. Over many generations within a population, through accidents of mutation and recombination coupled with the effects of differential reproduction, the informational content of the genotype changes. These changes, it is claimed, add up to a process of evolution.

This is all very neat, save for one problem. To be sure, every organism starts life with its complement of DNA. But if genes are to be understood, as the theory requires, as the carriers of a formal design specification, shaped up through natural selection, from one locus of development to another, then there must be some systematic correspondence between the elements of this specification and the actual DNA of the genome that is *independent* of any developmental process. Such a correspondence has been generally assumed, but has never been demonstrated (see Cohen and Stewart 1994: 293–4). What happens in practice, as I showed in the last chapter (pp. 382–3), is that biologists seek to redescribe the observed phenotypic characteristics of organisms as the outputs of a formal system of epigenetic rules. These are then 'read in' to the genome, so that development can be seen as the 'reading off' of a programme or specification that is already there, and that is imported with the genome into the site of inauguration of a new life-cycle. In short, as an account of the evolution of form, Darwinian theory rests on a simple circularity. That is one reason, of course, why it has proved so hard to refute.

At root, the issue comes down to one about copying. The orthodox account has it that the formal design features of the incipient organism are copied along with the DNA, in advance of its interaction with the environment, so that they can then 'interact' with the environment to produce the organism. I would argue to the contrary, and as illustrated schematically in Figure 22.2, that copying is itself a process that goes on within the context of organism-environment interaction. In other words, the 'missing link' between the

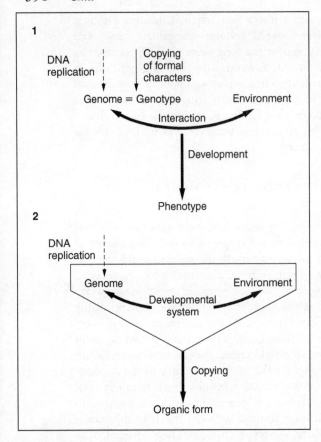

Figure 22.2 Two theories of copying: (1) in the orthodox, Darwinian account, a design for the organism is copied with the DNA of the genome, which is then 'brought out' in the course of development within an environmental context; (2) in the 'developmental systems approach' proposed here, the process of copying is equivalent to that of the organism's development in its environment.

genome and the formal characteristics of the organism is none other than the developmental process itself. There is, then, no design for the organism, no genotype – except, of course, as this might be constructed by the observing biologist. Organic form, in short, is *generated*, not expressed, in development, and arises as an emergent property of the total system of relations set up by virtue of the presence of the organism in its environment. Hence the evolution of form, as Susan Oyama has put it, is tantamount to 'the derivational history of developmental systems' (Oyama 1989: 5).

THE ARCHITECTURE OF THE MIND: ITS CONSTRUCTION AND FURNISHING

Let me now return to the question I left hanging a moment ago. From where are we to conjure up the innate devices that are supposed to make possible the acquisition of language? It is generally assumed that having been fashioned by natural selection, these devices must have a genetic basis. Thus the information that specifies their construction must form one component of the human genotype. Yet here, psycholinguistics runs into the very same dilemma that, as we have seen, derails Darwinian theory – in an even more acute form. It is more acute because the cognitive devices in question must already exist, not merely in the virtual guise of a design, but in the concrete hardwiring of human brains. Somehow or other, in order to kick-start the process of ontogenetic development, strands of DNA have miraculously to transform themselves into information processing mechanisms. This is rather like supposing that merely by replicating the design of an aircraft, whether on the drawing board or on the computer screen, one is all prepared for take-off.

Attempts in the literature to resolve this problem, insofar as it is even recognised, are confused and contradictory. To cut a rather long and tangled story short, they boil down to two distinct claims. One is that the concrete mechanisms making up what has been called the 'evolved architecture' of the human mind are reliably constructed under all normal environmental circumstances. The other is that these universal mechanisms proceed to work on 'variable environmental inputs' to produce the diversity of manifest competencies and behaviours that we actually observe (Tooby and Cosmides 1992: 45).

Let me unpack these claims, illustrated schematically in Figure 22.3, with specific reference to language acquisition. Here the alleged universal mechanism is the 'language acquisition device' (LAD). During a well-defined stage of infancy, this device is said to be activated, operating upon the input of speech sounds from the environment so as to establish, in the infant's mind, the grammar and lexicon of the particular language (or languages) spoken in his or her community. An infant reared in social isolation, and thus deprived of relevant environmental input, would not learn a language, but would still possess a fully formed LAD. It would thus appear that language acquisition is a two-stage process: in the first, the LAD is constructed; in the second it is furnished with specific syntactic and semantic content. That, at least, is the theory, but is it borne out in practice? Is there any basis in reality for separating out the construction of innate psychological mechanisms from the transmission of acquired cultural information, as shown in Figure 22.4, or is the division into these two stages merely an artefact of our own analytic procedures? In what follows, I shall argue that the latter is the case.

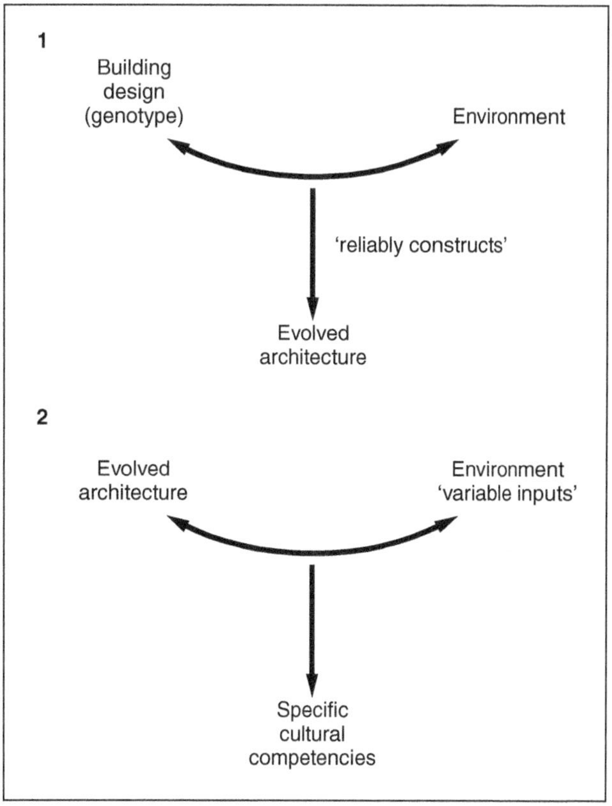

THE MYTH OF THE LANGUAGE ACQUISITION DEVICE

The first point to note is that the mechanisms (if we can call them that) underwriting the child's ability to speak

Figure 22.3 Two claims for the construction of mind, following the model presented by Tooby and Cosmides (1992). (1) A universal building design (one component of the genotype) interacts with the environment to 'reliably construct' the 'evolved architecture' consisting of a number of cognitive mechanisms including, for example, the 'language acquisition device'. (2) The architecture (presumed universal) interacts selectively with the environment, accepting information specifying diverse cultural competencies such as, for example, the ability to speak English, Japanese or Swahili.

are not constructed in a vacuum, but rather emerge in the context of his or her sensory involvement in a richly structured environment. Recent research has shown that from well before birth, infants are sensitive to the surrounding ambience of sound, and above all to the mother's voice (De Casper and Spence 1986). Thus the human baby comes into the world already attuned to certain environmentally specific sound patterns. From birth onwards, it is surrounded by an entourage of speakers who provide support in the form both of contextually grounded interpretations of the infant's vocal utterances and of demonstrations, or 'attention-directing gestures' (Zukow-Goldring 1997: 221–3), to accompany their own. This environment, then, is not a source of variable input for pre-constructed mechanisms, but rather furnishes the variable conditions for the self-assembly, in the course of early development, of the mechanisms themselves. And as the conditions

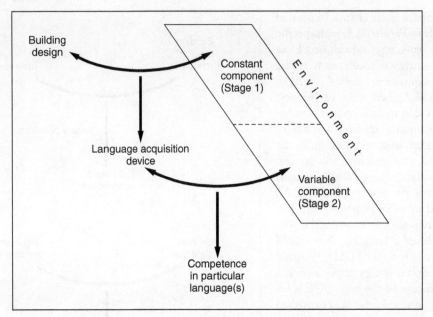

Figure 22.4 Putting the two claims of Figure 22.3 together yields a two-stage model of cognitive development. Note, however, that this model depends on factoring out those features of the environment that are constant, or 'reliably present' in every conceivable developmental context, from those that represent a source of 'variable input' from one context to another. Only the former are relevant in the first stage (the construction of innate mechanisms such as the 'language acquisition device'); only the latter are relevant in the second (the acquisition of specific cultural competencies such as the ability to speak a particular language or languages).

vary, so the resulting mechanisms will take manifold forms, each differentially tuned both to specific sound patterns and to other features of local contexts of utterance. These variably attuned mechanisms, and the competencies they establish, are of course the neurophysiological correlates of what appear to us observers as the diverse languages of the world.

In short, language – in the sense of the child's capacity to speak in the manner of his or her community – *is not acquired*. Rather, it is an ability that is continually being generated and regenerated in the developmental contexts of children's involvement in worlds of speech (Lock 1980).[2] And if language is not acquired, then there can be no such thing as an innate language acquisition device (Dent 1990).

This conclusion puts paid to the last of the three features of the standard model that I outlined earlier: that learning a language is like filling a universal, genetically specified container with particular cultural content. Of course, people raised in different environments learn to speak in different ways. But these differences, far from being received into the prefabricated compartments of a universal psychology, are immanent in those very fields of relations wherein human beings undergo the organic processes of growth and maturation, and in which their powers of speech are developed and sustained. Bearing this in mind, we can now return to the first feature of the standard model, that each particular language is transmissible as a corpus of context-independent rules and representations from one generation to the next. This cannot be true, for the simple reason that it rests, as we have seen, on the impossible precondition of a ready-made cognitive architecture. For the theory of language learning as information transmission to work, lengths of DNA would have magically to transform themselves into concrete brain mechanisms, ready and prepared to process relevant environmental input. In reality, as Dent has pointed out (1990: 694), there can be no mechanisms in advance of experience, since no matter at what point in development the mechanisms are identified, the individual at that point already has a history of interaction with the environment.

Lest this argument be misunderstood, let me emphasise that my purpose in questioning the real existence of innate mechanisms is not to argue for the priority of nurture over nature, or to substitute for innatism a doctrine of the environmental determination of human capacities. These are not the only theoretical alternatives, and indeed both are fallacious for the same reason, most succinctly expressed by Oyama, namely that the information specifying the capacities in question – whether its source be supposed to lie inside the organism or outside in the environment – must be presumed to 'pre-exist the processes that give rise to it' (Oyama 1985: 13). My point is that these capacities are neither internally prespecified nor externally imposed, but arise within processes of development, as properties of dynamic self-organisation of the total field of relationships in which a person's life unfolds.

WRITING, PRINT LITERACY AND THE MODERN CONCEPTION OF LANGUAGE

What is the source of the peculiar conception of language enshrined in the standard model? Consider the following three implications of the notion that language is fully describable as an objective system of rules and representations for generating well-formed and meaningful utterances. First, every verbal composition must exist initially as an entity in its own right – a mental construction – independently of the contexts of its enunciation and interpretation in the real world of other persons and relationships. Secondly, performance is a matter of placing this composition 'on line' for mechanical execution by the physical apparatus of the body. Thirdly, the particular qualities of performance – such as tone of voice, facial expression, and so on – may be considered superfluous to linguistic competence and therefore disregarded.

Now in ordinary speech, these conditions *never* obtain, although linguists often write as though they do. That is to say, in real life verbal composition is inseparable from performance, and performance is an intentional and finely nuanced activity that draws its meaning from the situational contexts of its enactment. In modern literate societies, however, there is one domain of activity where the conditions outlined above *approximately* obtain – and this is the activity of writing. There is a sense in which the written verbal composition does exist as an entity in its own right, moreover with modern print technology the writing itself does seem like the mechanical replication of a preconstructed design, while words printed on paper are, in themselves, expressionless, and are silent to the work and feeling that went into their production.

Thus we are brought at length to writing, or more precisely to the rise of modern print literacy, as the source of the conception of language that underpins what I have called the standard model. It would be no exaggeration to claim, with Roy Harris (1980: 6), that no other historical development has had such a profound impact on the concept of what a language is. It is from systems of writing, as David Olson has convincingly shown, that the concepts and categories have been drawn for thinking about the structure of spoken language, rather than the other way around. Moreover it is our experience of reading written texts that leads us to regard the spoken utterance as 'composed of words related by means of a syntax' (Olson 1994: 68–78). As units of linguistic analysis, the phoneme, the word and the sentence are all artefacts of writing that, far from being intrinsic to speech, have latterly been imposed upon it (Coulmas 1989: 39).[3] In most modern, literate societies, grammarians and lexicographers have worked hard to rationalise and standardise the forms of speech so as to bring them into line with these artificial, scribal conventions, setting up canons of correctness against which actual utterances may be judged more or less well-formed, and which citizens are encouraged (or sometimes forced) to emulate. In these societies, language has become an institution.

It is hardly surprising, then, that linguists working from within this institutional context imagine that in learning, language is copied into the minds of practitioners in much the same way that, in their own analyses, it is reproduced on the printed page. It is this scriptist bias that leads many linguists naïvely to assume that the 'languages' of non-literate communities exist, each complete with grammar and lexicon, implanted in the unconscious minds of their speakers, simply waiting to be discovered and written down. The idea, however, that writing is simply the transcription of speech – or that, in the words of Jonathan Rée, 'everything that is linguistic must in principle be writable as well' (1999: 320) – is an illusion. For what is not writable, and therefore lost in the transcription, is everything that gives the spoken utterance its 'illocutionary force' (Austin 1962: 100), that is its power to launch intentions and produce effects, including intonation, voice quality, accompanying manual or facial gesture, and so on. Much of the history of literacy may be understood as a struggle to compensate for this limitation, largely through an elaboration of the lexicon to convey subtleties of intention and interpretation that are normally expressed non-lexically in speech (Olson 1994: 109–10). Thus in its rendering as the output of a language that is fully writable, speech is not so much transcribed as transformed.

Such is the power of writing on the way we both conceive and practice speech that it takes quite an effort of imagination to think ourselves back into the condition of what Walter Ong (1982) calls 'primary orality', in which speech had the power to move people, as song does still, by virtue of its immediate impact on the senses. To get a perspective on this, we could do worse than adopt the advice of Giambattista Vico, offered in his *New Science* of 1725. For a genuine understanding of the origins of civilisation, Vico wrote, 'we must reckon as if there were no books in the world' (1948 §330). That, presumably, was the state of affairs in prehistory. How, says Vico, can we have a theory of the origins of civilisation in prehistory if our very concept of civilisation presupposes the existence of the book? How likewise, we could ask, can we have a theory of language origins whose very notion of what language is presupposes print literacy? As John Shotter puts it, commenting on Vico's counsel, 'if we are to grasp the nature of the beginnings of language, and reckon as if there were no books in the world, ... we must grasp the nature of a form of communication which does not consist in a sequential occurrence of events or things, nor in a series of products or of component meanings, but which rather "subsists" in the continuous flow of sensuous, "moving" activity between people' (Shotter 1991: 385).

IF SPEAKING IS A SKILL, IS WRITING A TECHNOLOGY?

This is the point at which to return to my initial claim that speaking is akin to the practice of an art like singing or dancing. I do not mean art in its modern sense, a sense that has come to be opposed to technology as the spontaneous creation of novelty to the mechanical replication of pre-existing design (see Chapter Nineteen, pp. 349–50). I have in mind, rather, the traditional meaning of art as *skill*, of the kind we associate with craftsmanship – a sense preserved in such words as 'artisan' and 'artefact'.

Before proceeding further, it is necessary to reiterate three general points about skill. I have already introduced and discussed these points at length in Chapter Nineteen (pp. 352–4), and will summarise them only briefly here. First, skills are not techniques of the body considered, objectively and in isolation, as an instrument in the service of culture. They are rather properties of the whole system of relations constituted by the presence of the practitioner in his or her environment. Secondly, skilled practice is not just the mechanical application of external force but is continually responsive both to changing environmental conditions and to the nuances of the practitioner's relation to the material as the task unfolds. Thirdly, skills are refractory to codification in the programmatic form of rules and representations. Thus it is not through the transmission of any such programmes that skills are learned, but rather through a mixture of improvisation and imitation in the settings of practice. Now all these points, which apply to skills in general, also apply to speaking in particular. Speaking is not a discharge of representations in the mind but an achievement of the whole organism-person in an environment; it is closely attuned and continually responsive to the gestures of others, and speakers are forever improvising on the basis of past practice in their efforts to make themselves understood in a world which is never quite the same from one moment to the next.

What, then, of the difference between speaking and writing? Earlier, I drew attention to certain properties of writing, specifically of the kind associated with modern print literacy, that may be responsible for the conception of language enshrined in the standard model. These properties – that writing divorces the author from the immediate context of sensuous engagement with his or her surroundings, that it involves the more or less mechanical execution of a preconceived verbal composition, and that it is fully analysable in terms of an objective system of rules and representations – are the precise opposites of the three general properties of skill outlined above. Viewed in these terms, it would seem that the key difference between speaking and writing is that the latter is not a skilled practice at all, not an art in that sense, but the operation of a *technology*.

The idea of writing as a technology of language enjoys widespread currency in the literature (Sampson 1985: 17, Coulmas 1989: 9–11). A leading proponent of the idea has been Walter Ong. One of the things that makes writing technological, according to Ong, is that it involves the use of tools and other equipment (Ong 1982: 81). For us the tool that immediately comes to mind is, of course the pen or pencil, or perhaps the typewriter. But it is worth remembering, in passing, that the writer's equipment may involve far more than that. For example the tools of the medieval English scribe, according to Michael Clanchy, included: a knife or razor for scraping parchment, a pumice for smoothing it, a boar's tooth for polishing the surface, a ruler, plumbline and awl for ruling the lines, and, for the writing itself, quill pens and a penknife, inkhorn and inks of various colours. This is not to mention the furniture, lamp-lighting and other paraphernalia of the study (Clanchy 1979: 116). Where writing is pressed on wet clay, as in Sumerian cuneiform, or engraved in stone, stamped on metal or embroidered in tapestry, the tools would have been quite different, and often of a kind that we would not immediately associate with writing at all. My concern, however, is not with what kinds of tools are used, or even with whether tools are necessarily used at all (think of writing in the air, or with a finger in the sand), but whether the use of tools in writing is tantamount to operating a technology.

Ong thinks it is, and to demonstrate his point he invites us to compare writing with playing the violin. The violinist, in Ong's characterisation, is an operative whose task is to induce vibrations in the strings of her instrument, according to its principles of acoustic functioning, in order to render a pre-prepared musical composition in the concrete medium of sound. Let me cite the relevant passage in full:

> A violin is an instrument, which is to say a tool. An organ is a huge machine, with sources of power ... totally outside its operator ... What do you think the sounds of an organ come out of? Or the sounds of a violin or even a whistle? The fact is that by using a mechanical contrivance, a violinist or an organist can express something poignantly human that cannot be expressed without the mechanical contrivance. To achieve such expression of course the violinist or organist has to have interiorized the technology, made the tool or machine a second nature, a psychological part of himself or herself.
>
> (Ong 1982: 83)

Just as the violinist has to interiorise a technology, Ong goes on to argue, so also must the writer, in order to be able to use his tools to inscribe linguistic forms upon a material surface.

Now whatever one may think of the organ, to describe the violin as a 'mechanical contrivance' seems a little odd, and certainly contrary to the experience of any practising musician. It is evident that in this passage, Ong has fallen prey to the fallacy, already discussed in Chapter Sixteen, that where tools or instruments are being used there must exist a technology (p. 316). For what the concept of technology does, as we have seen, is to recast the skilled activity of artisans as the behavioural or mechanical output of a formal system of rules and principles, a *logos* of *tekhnē*, that is embodied in the construction of the tools of the trade, and that practitioners are bound to put into effect, regardless of their personal experience and sensibilities. There is far more to playing the violin, however, than the mechanical execution of a pre-prepared series of instructions. And if there is a certain analogy between violin-playing and writing, it must point to a conclusion that is the very converse of the one that Ong draws from it: namely, that the activity of the writer, like that of the violinist, is an *art in itself*.

THE ART OF WRITING

To learn to play the violin, the novice has to practise with her instrument, over and over again, and often from a young age while her body is still rapidly growing, until her movements and the sounds that flow from them gain the fluency and responsiveness of the accomplished performer. Precisely the same is true, as we saw in Chapter Nineteen (pp. 356–7), of learning to make string bags in Central New Guinea. And in just the same way, too, the young apprentice scribe learns the craft of writing. This is not a matter, as Ong would have it, of interiorising a technology, but rather one of developing a skill. As with any skill, the art of handwriting emerges through a continuous process of bodily modification within the contexts of novices' engagement with other persons and diverse objects in their environments. That writing is not merely added on, as a cultural supplement, to a body that is naturally ready-made for speech is apparent as soon as we pause to consider the demands, both postural and gestural, that it places on the developing human organism.

The postures routinely adopted in writing are in fact very variable, depending in part on tools, raw materials and furniture, and in part on status etiquette. For example the postural change adopted by Sumerian scribes when they started writing on large rectangular clay tablets rather than small square ones was probably responsible for the 90° rotation of all the originally pictographic signs of the cuneiform script (Powell 1981, Coulmas 1989: 74–5). Ancient Egyptian scribes adopted a variety of positions from cross-legged or kneeling to standing upright. Japanese and Chinese calligraphers knelt on the floor with the paper spread before them, while the Medieval European scribe settled into a solid wooden chair with a table or desk to support his work. Despite his relative immobility, however, he considered his writing to be an act of endurance 'in which', as one scribe mournfully wrote, 'the whole body labours' (Clanchy 1979: 116). And at least one contemporary professor of linguistics would agree. It is no more true, observes Roy Harris, to say that writing consists simply in the movements of the hand in holding a pen (or other instrument) than it is to say that speech consists only in the movements of the vocal tract. For 'we speak and write with our whole body', including the head, eyes, facial musculature, hands, arms, and general posture (Harris 1980: 99).

Jack Goody has characterised writing as a 'technology of the intellect' (1977: 151), but from the examples cited above it would seem equally appropriate to follow the lead of Marcel Mauss (1979 [1934]), and regard it as a technique of the body. For the regular practice of writing, like that of any other skill, leaves an indelible anatomical impression, whether in the visible form of the scholar's rounded shoulders or in the normally invisible architecture of the brain. Writing, as Paul Connerton has observed, is an *incorporating* as well as an *inscribing* practice: that is, it has an 'irreducible bodily component', not just in the controlled movement of the hand but in the way in which the hand together with the tool it holds is brought into a certain angular relation with the surface of the material to be inscribed, which in turn affects the writer's entire comportment (Connerton 1989: 76–7). Without diminishing the importance of the inscriptional aspect of writing, we should not forget that there can be no inscription without incorporation – without, in other words, the building of habitual patterns of posture and gesture into the bodily *modus operandi* of the skilled practitioner. Just like speech, in short, writing is an achievement of the whole human organism-person in his or her environment.

To view writing as an art is to think of it, in the first place, as a kind of dextrous movement, and to think of the text (recalling a distinction introduced in Chapter Eighteen (pp. 346–8)) as something woven rather than made. That is to say, the patterning or weave of the text emerges as the crystallisation of this movement, and is not prefigured as a mental construction which the writing hand merely serves to transcribe onto a surface. This is what André Leroi-Gourhan had in mind when he referred to prehistoric inscriptions as instances of 'graphism', whose meaning was drawn from contexts of oral narrative now irretrievably lost. Graphism, as Leroi-Gourhan insisted, is not representational but the congelation, as an enduring trace, of those rhythmic bodily movements that are intrinsic to preliterate speech (Leroi-Gourhan 1993: 190). Regarded as an instance of graphism, writing, just like mapping (see Chapter Thirteen, pp. 231–5), is *in*scriptive, not *trans*-criptive. Indeed the idea that its forms and patterns are woven into the surface rather than impressed upon it is supported by the derivation of the word 'text' from the Latin *texere*, meaning 'to weave' (Carruthers 1990: 12). Comparably, the word for writing among the Quiché Maya of Guatemala (*tz'ib*) comes from the stem -*tz'iba*, which refers to actions involving 'the creation of designs by means of weaving' (Tedlock and Tedlock 1985: 124–6).

In sum, far from being conceived as the operation of a technology, writing would be better understood as a graphic counterpart to speech. Since we speak, to recall Harris's point, with the whole body, and not just with the voice, the relation between speech and writing is not so much between a sonic reality and its visual representation as it is between the communicative bodily gesture and its graphic inscription.

HISTORY AS AN EVOLUTIONARY PROCESS: THE ILLUSION OF ORIGINS

With this point I return, at length, to Darwin, and to his idea that writing is comparable to brewing or baking, conceived as a skilled practical activity rather than a technology to be applied. Now for Darwin, it will be recalled, writing differed from speaking only insofar as it is not grounded, as is speaking, in an 'instinctive tendency'. In the last chapter, however, I set out to demonstrate that speaking is no more or less 'instinctive' than writing. As varieties of skilled practice, both speaking and writing emerge quite naturally in the course of development, so long as the necessary support structure or 'scaffolding' is present in the environment. Now if, as I have suggested, writing is an inscriptive counterpart to speech, it must follow that any account of the evolution of speech, in the sense I have proposed here, must at one and the same time be an account of the evolution of writing. Hence, contrary to conventional wisdom (Sampson 1985: 13, Coulmas 1989: 3), speech and writing are not separated on opposite sides of a dichotomy between human biological evolution and the history of technology, but are mutually implicated in a single evolutionary process.

It is this dichotomy between evolution and history, as I showed in the last chapter, that sets up a point of origin at their intersection. This is where scholars have conventionally placed the genesis of language, art, technology, religion, and all the other capacities that are supposed to mark our distinctive humanity. Yet not only has the conception of language enshrined in this origin story been profoundly influenced by writing, but also our conception of writing has been equally profoundly shaped by the idea of technology. It is, I suggest, the inherent 'logocentrism' of modern Western thought, its understanding of practice as rule-governed execution, that renders writing as a technological system. Hence it is this, too, and not writing *per se*, that is ultimately responsible for the reification of speech as language, and thus for the establishment of the whole problematic of language origins. To that extent, the problematic itself has its origins in modernity. I have argued here, to the contrary, that there is no point at which language could be said to have originated. For language exists only in the activities of speaking and writing themselves. These activities, and the skills in which they are based, emerge through what Harvey Whitehouse (1996: 113) has aptly called 'the labours of maturation', within fields of practice constituted by the activities of predecessors. And as each generation, through its activities, contributes to the conditions of maturation of the next, they continue to evolve.

It is, to conclude, fundamentally wrong to populate the past with people like ourselves, equipped with the capacities or potentials to do everything we do today, such that history becomes nothing more than the teleological process of their progressive realisation. The notion of an origin, defined as the point at which these capacities became established, awaiting their historical fulfilment, is part of an elaborate ideological justification for the present order of things and, as such, an aspect of the pervasive presentism of modern thought. I have shown that the capacity to speak (or write) is inseparable from the capacity to speak (or write) in this way or that. We would not say, I think, that all human beings have evolved with the innate capacity to play musical instruments, and that this is distinct from the capacity to play the violin, the trumpet or the oboe. Likewise, it makes no sense to distinguish a universal capacity for language or speech from the ability to speak English, Japanese or Swahili. Speech is a dynamic phenomenon, and its forms change through history. As it does so, capacities evolve. They are still evolving. Language has not originated yet, and it never will.

Chapter Twenty-three

The poetics of tool use

From technology, language and intelligence to craft, song and imagination

INTRODUCTION

In recent years, neo-Darwinian biology, cognitive science and psycholinguists have conspired to produce an extremely powerful approach to understanding the relations, in human evolution, between technology, language and intelligence. It is argued that linguistic and intellectual capacities, common to all human beings, are built-in properties of a mind whose basic architecture has evolved through a process of variation under natural selection. Remaining issues for debate concern whether the selective pressures guiding the evolution of these capacities lay in the social domain of the relations among conspecifics or in the technical domain of adaptation to the non-human environment, and whether – or at what point in either ontogeny or phylogeny – technical capacities are dissociated from linguistic ones. What is the difference, it is asked, between the kinds of mental constructional tasks involved in toolmaking and tool-using, on the one hand, and speaking, on the other? To what extent does the performance of these tasks call upon similar or even identical neurophysiological mechanisms?

As a social anthropologist, perched precariously on a narrow ledge while buffeted by contrary winds from the humanities and the natural sciences, I view these debates with increasing unease. I am disturbed by their apparent disregard of the intellectual ferment that has accompanied the contemporary critique of modernism, by the commitment of those involved to a version of 'normal science' that brooks no challenge to fundamental paradigmatic assumptions, and by their readiness to frame their various, competing accounts – of the entire career of humanity from earliest origins to the present day – in terms of concepts that, like the disciplines to which they belong, are recent products of a very specific history in the Western world. These concepts, as we have already seen (Chapter Sixteen, p. 312), are grounded in a general claim to the supremacy of human reason – a claim that is perhaps the defining feature of the discourse of modernity. Thus intelligence is the faculty of reason, language its vehicle, and technology the means by which a rational understanding of the external world is turned to account for human benefit.

I would like to propose a radically alternative claim: namely, that there is no such thing as technology, or language, or intelligence, at least in pre-modern or non-Western societies. By that I do not for one moment mean to suggest that people in such societies do not make common use of tools in their everyday activities, that they do not engage with one another in the verbal idioms of speech, or that these and other activities do not represent creative ways of coping in the world. My concern is rather to focus attention on what it means to say that everyday tool-using is a behavioural instantiation of technology, or that spoken dialogue is the instantiation of language, or that creative activity is the instantiation of intelligence. Even in our own society, in which these propositions form a part of received wisdom, they are not immediately or obviously borne out in experience.[1]

For example, I am presently writing with a pen, I am wearing spectacles which help me to see, I carry on my wrist a watch which tells me the time, a chair and table provide supports respectively for my body and my work, and I am surrounded by innumerable other bits and pieces that come in handy for one thing and another. I incorporate these diverse objects into the current of my activity without attending to them *as such*: I concentrate on my writing, not the pen; I see the time, not my watch. Indeed it could be said that these and other instruments become truly available to me, as things I can use without difficulty or interruption, at the point at which they effectively vanish as objects of my attention. And if anything links them together, it is only that they are brought into the same current, that of my work. Drawing an explicit parallel with tool-use, Wittgenstein made much the same point about the use of words in speech (1953, §11): different words have different uses, just as do the pen, watch and spectacles; one normally attends not to the words themselves but to what the speaker is telling us with them, and they are bound together solely by virtue of the fact that the various situations of use are all embedded within a total pattern of verbal and non-verbal activity, a form of life.

There are, then, words, and activities that people do with words (i.e. speaking). And there are tools, and activities that people do with tools (i.e. tool-using). But is there language? Or technology? What is entailed in the assumption that for people to speak they must first 'have' language, or for people to use tools they must first 'have' technology – or indeed for people to engage in intelligent activities of any kind they must first 'have' intelligence? If, on the other hand, we drop the assumption, what further need do we have of these concepts? Suppose, to pursue my alternative claim, that we set ourselves the task of examining the relation, in human evolution, not between technology, language and intelligence, but between craftsmanship, song and imagination. The resulting account, I suspect, would be very different. Without prejudging the issue of which is the better conceptual frame, I shall attempt in what follows to indicate where some of the differences might lie. I begin with language and song.

LANGUAGE, MUSIC AND SONG

In the voice, human beings are equipped with a wonderfully expressive and versatile instrument. We use it to speak, and we use it to sing. But how, if at all, can we distinguish speaking from singing? In the modern conception the answer is simple: speaking is essentially linguistic, singing is essentially musical. Of course, speech may be present *in* the song, in the words that accompany the music – thus the song may be conceived as it is written on paper, in two registers proceeding in parallel: the musical sequence written as a series of notes, and the linguistic sequence as a concurrent series of words. So what is the difference between these two sequences, between the melodic line and the syntagmatic chain? One possible answer, to which I have already alluded in Chapter Fourteen (pp. 247–8), is that the former is immanent in the stream of sound, whereas the latter lies in some sense *behind* the sound. To listen to music is to dwell in a world of sound, which permeates our entire awareness. When we listen to speech, however, it is as though our awareness reaches through the sound to a world of words beyond – a world that is as silent as the book, where there are no sounds as such but only *images* of sound. What happens, then, when we listen to song?

'When words and music come together in song', writes Susanne Langer, 'music swallows words' (1953: 152). Her point is that the sounds of speech, to the extent that they are incorporated into a total musical phenomenon, cease to draw the listener's attention to meanings beyond themselves – meanings that, in speech, the sounds had served only to convey or deliver up to the listener rather than actually to embody. For Langer, sound that does not convey meaning in this sense is no longer *verbal* sound. Thus what essentially distinguishes verbal sound is that its significance can be extracted from the sound itself. Musical sound, by contrast, delineates its own meaning: it is meaningful not because of what it represents, but simply because of its affective *presence* in the listener's environment. If this were so, then speech is what you would be left with if you took the music out of song, and music is what you would be left with if the verbal component of song were swallowed up in its entirety, while poetry lies ambiguously, somewhere in between: more verbal than song, and yet more musical than speech. Thus in poetry we stretch words beyond the limits of normal utterance so that, in their sounding, they become expressive in themselves.

The very idea of a 'coming together' of words and music, however, presupposes their original separation. To produce a song, it seems, we have to *combine* two things that are initially distinct, music and language. But on what grounds do we assume this distinction? Could we not, equally well, put the argument in reverse, and suggest that music and language, as separate symbolic registers, are the products of a movement of analytic *decomposition* of what was once an indivisible expressive totality, namely song? To support such a reverse argument, we would need to be able to demonstrate that the difference between speech and melodic gesture is one of degree rather than kind, that to speak is indeed – in a sense – to sing, and hence that no absolute line can be drawn between them.[2]

The issue here largely hinges on the question of how words acquire meaning. The orthodox view has it that words refer to concepts. And concepts are the building blocks of comprehensive mental representations. At once there is presupposed a division between a subject, in whose mind these representations are to be found, and an objective world 'out there'. Meaning is in the mind, not in the world – it is *assigned* to the world by the subject. As I move around physically in the world, and advance through time, I carry my concepts with me – rather as I might carry a map in navigating the landscape (see Chapter Thirteen pp. 223–4). In different times and places I experience different sensations, but like the map, the system of concepts which organizes these sensations into meaningful patterns remains the same, regardless of where I stand. But if the world exists for me only as I have thus constructed it from the data of perception, how can it be shared? How can subjects inhabit a common world of meaning?

Again, the orthodox account argues that meanings are shared through verbal communication. Thus, my pre-prepared thought or belief has to be 'encoded' in words, which are then 'sent' in the medium of sound, writing or gesture to a recipient who, having performed a reverse operation of decoding, finishes up with the original thought successfully transplanted into his mind. Of course every act of communication takes place in a context, involving a particular speaker and a particular listener (or listeners) in a given environmental setting. But since words refer to abstract concepts rather than real-world objects, the relation of signification (between word and concept) is itself context-independent. The logic of this account therefore entails that signs can achieve the status of words, that is they become properly 'linguistic', only at the end point of a process of decontextualisation. At this point, the sign severs all connection with the external world, such that the relation between sign and meaning is wholly interior to the subject.

Not only must this relation of signification be context-free, it must also be conventional. Agreement on the conventional meanings of words is clearly a condition for the faithful transcription of ideas from one mind to another, according to the model of communication presented above. Such conventions, moreover, are presumed to be arbitrary – again on the grounds of the severing of iconic links between verbal signs and the properties of the exterior world. Linguists are fond of reminding us, naïve speakers all, that one word is as good as another for signifying the same concept, so long as the pattern of phonemic contrast that serves to set each word off from each and every other in the language is retained. To me it may seem that a quality of hardness is presented in the very utterance of the word 'hard', just as it is presented in a passage of music played staccato. And likewise, the word 'smooth' *sounds* smooth, as does the same passage played legato. But that, says the linguist, is an illusion born of the frequent association, in experience, of words and their 'real-world' denotata. To clinch the argument, he points to the sheer diversity of natural languages, to the fact that the different words – say – for 'dog', in these different languages, may bear not the slightest resemblance to one another, nor indeed to the real-world animal of that name.

Perhaps it is time for naïve speakers to put linguists in their place. For what the former can provide, which the latter cannot, is the perspective of a being who, quite unlike the dislocated, closed-in subject confronting an external reality, is wholly immersed, from the start, in the relational context of dwelling in a world. For such a being, this world is already laden with significance: meaning inheres in the *relations* between the dweller and the constituents of the dwelt-in world. And to the extent that people dwell in the same world, and are caught up together in the same currents of activity, they can share in the same meanings. Such communion of experience, the awareness of living in a common world of meaningful relations, establishes a foundational level of sociality which exists – in Pierre Bourdieu's (1977: 2) phrase – 'on the hither side of words and concepts', and that constitutes the baseline on which all attempts at verbal communication must subsequently build. For although it is indisputable that verbal conventions are deployed in speech, *such conventions do not come ready made.* They are forever being built up over time, through a cumulative history of past usage: each is a hard-won product of the hazardous efforts of generations of predecessors to make themselves understood. When we speak of the conventional meaning of a word, that history is simply presupposed or, as it were, 'put in brackets', taken as read. And so we are inclined to think of use as founded on convention when, in reality, convention can only be established and held in place through use. Thus to understand how words acquire meaning we have to place them back into that original current of sociality, into the specific contexts of activities and relations in which they are used and to which they contribute. We then realize that, far from deriving their meanings from their attachment to mental concepts which are imposed upon a meaningless world of entities and events 'out there', *words gather their meanings from the relational properties of the world itself.* Every word is a compressed and compacted history.[3]

Armed with this 'dwelling perspective', how should we view the difference between the spoken word and the musical gesture? It is no longer possible to argue that the former carries a conventional meaning that can be detached from the sound whereas the latter embodies its meaning in itself. We should rather argue that in words, the process of sedimentation and compression of past usage which contributes to the determination of their current sense has advanced to an exceedingly high degree, whereas in melody it is still incipient. But this is a difference of degree rather than kind, one that has perhaps been stretched to its maximal extent in the West by virtue of a cultural emphasis on the novelty of music as against the conventionality of language. One cannot expect the difference to be everywhere, and at all times, to be so clearcut. For all music, viewed in this light, is on its way to becoming speech, and there is no Rubicon beyond which we can say that it is unequivocally one thing rather than the other. Conversely, all speech has its origins in vocal music, that is in song. As Merleau-Ponty put it, once we put speech back into the current of intercourse from which it necessarily springs, 'it would then be found that the words, vowels and phonemes are so many ways of "singing" the world' (1962: 187) – not, it should be stressed, in the naïve sense of producing an onomatopoeic resemblance between particular sounds and particular aspects of the world, but in the sense of entering intentionally and expressively into it, of 'living' it.

EMOTION AND REASON

The decomposition of song into the two 'compartments' of language and music has come about, I believe, through the assimilation of vocal gesture to a particular view of the human constitution, one that has long held a central place in Western thought, and that reached its apotheosis in the rationalism of Descartes. According to this view, every human being is a composite creature made up of body and mind, susceptible, on the one hand, to emotions and feelings (bodily sensations), but capable, on the other, of rational deliberation (mental operations). Thus the musical phrase is envisaged as a feeling shaped in sound, the verbal utterance as the representation of a thought. One is visceral, the other cerebral; one is experienced directly, the other presupposes a mental processing of received sound to extract the 'message'. In music (and more obviously still in dance) the body *resonates* with the world, in language one mind *communicates* with another. Music, assumed to be devoid of propositional content, is placed on the 'purely expressive' side of human existence; language is placed on the 'purely rational' side – all expressive aspects of speech being removed from language itself and assigned to contingent aspects of performance. Moreover, the rational is normally ranked above the expressive, as an index of 'higher' cognitive faculties that enable their possessors to step outside the world and – from this decentred vantage point – to take a cool, dispassionate view of it.

Such, of course, is the professed aim of natural science. Since the ascendancy of reason over emotion is implicated in science's claim to deliver an objective account of the natural world, it comes as no surprise to find the same principle of ranking at the basis of scientific accounts of the evolution of language – for it is surely language that enables humans to be scientists. Early formulations of the gestural theory of language origins, for example, rested on claims that the vocalisations of non-human primates (and by imputation, those of early hominids) were purely emotional or affective, and were therefore unlikely candidates as precursors for linguistic communication, whose key property was taken to be the conveyance of propositional information. Neurophysiologists, for their part, claimed to find empirical proof of the existence of a dichotomy between volitional and emotional behaviours and body movements, and proceeded to map these onto different regions of the brain (Myers 1976). Language was unequivocally ascribed to the former category of behaviour: thus Ronald Myers could assert that 'the use of words in verbal communications is clearly volitional'. What, then, are we to make of those words that are uttered without deliberate, prior intent? Myers is at least dimly aware of the problem. He continues:

> The existence of a second type of use of the voice, i.e. in emotional expression, remains uncertain, and its neurology poorly defined. Indeed the neurologist, when confronted

with the proposition of an emotional use of the voice, inevitably thinks of curse words or interjections.

(1976: 746)

The implication is that what are rather primly called 'curse words' do not really merit inclusion within the domain of language at all! Language proper comes to be marked out, through the exclusion of all vocal expression of emotion, as a realm of propositional statements delivered completely free from emotional or affective overtones. Gordon Hewes suggests an example: 'The message "the house is on fire" can, if need be, be conveyed with no more excitement than the information that Paris is a city in France' (Hewes 1976: 490).

This may be so. Yet in practice, anyone who says 'the house is on fire' does so in a context, and in a tone of voice that may vary from a level monotone to a high-pitched shout. In the context of utterance the former tone is as expressive of indifference as is the latter of urgency or anguish, and each is liable to evoke a quite different response on the part of the audience, from a detached contemplation of the conflagration to a rush to evacuate the building. How, then, can these possibly be regarded as alternative renderings of the same proposition? Only by abstracting the verbal phrase from its context, by treating it as though – like words printed, as they appear here, on paper – it had a separate existence of its own. In reality, regardless of whether I utter the words with excitement or indifference, or of whether or not I have already rehearsed my speech beforehand in thought, my speaking is an intentional act which can only artificially be broken down into propositional and expressive components. And the same, of course, goes for the utterance of a swearword, which may indeed be no more premeditated than my cry, 'the house is on fire', but which nevertheless launches my intention into the world and carries it forward towards its goal.

In short, whether I speak, swear, shout, cry or sing, I do so with feeling, but feeling – as the tactile metaphor implies – is a mode of active and responsive engagement in the world, it is not a passive, interior reaction of the organism to external disturbance (see Chapter One, pp. 23–4). We 'feel' each other's presence in verbal discourse as the craftsman feels, with his tools, the material on which he works; and as with the craftsman's handling of tools, so is our handling of words sensitive to the nuances of our relationships with the felt environment. Thus, far from characterising mutually exclusive categories of behaviour – namely 'volitional' and 'emotional' – intentionality and feeling are two sides of the same coin, that of our practical involvement in the dwelt-in world. Only by imagining the human organism to be an isolated, preconstituted entity, given in advance of its external relations, do we come to regard feeling as an inner, affective state that is 'triggered' by incoming sensations. And by the same token, we are led to recover the intentional (or 'volitional') character of speech by supposing that what makes it so is that it does *not* arise in reaction to external stimulus but is rather caused by an internal mental representation – by a thought, belief or proposition pressing to make itself heard (Chomsky 1968: 10–11).

What, then, is language? Or more precisely, how do we come to have the idea that such a thing as language exists, and that it therefore has an evolution that we can attempt to describe and explain? One answer might be that the idea is a by-product of the process of 'interiorisation' of personhood that has marked the emergence of the modern Western concept of the individual (Mauss 1985, Dumont 1986). It is this concept that leads us to look within the human being, rather than to the sphere of its involvement in a wider field of relations, to discover the ultimate, generative source of purposive action. Thus every individual, as we saw in the last chapter, is supposed to come independently equipped with a 'built-in' language capacity (or at least a device for its acquisition), located somewhere inside the brain, which is the generative source of speech. Another possible answer, related to the first, is that the idea of language is necessarily entailed by a rationalism that is unable to conceive of action except as the mechanical replication, in a physical medium, of assemblies already constructed in thought. To language, then, is accorded the responsibility for constructing those assemblies, namely sentences, which are merely *executed* in speech. Yet a third answer might be that the idea of language is a 'fetish of linguists' (Goodman 1971: 34) who have sought to model the activities of speaking as the application of a coherent system of syntactic and semantic rules, derived by abstraction from observed behaviour. To be able to do this, they have to stand back from the current of discourse, focusing on speech *as* speech whilst the rest of us concentrate on what other people are telling us *in* their speech. But they have gone on to transfer, onto the speakers themselves, their own external relationship to the object of study, imagining the abstractions derived from this 'view from the outside' to be implanted within the speakers' minds and to constitute the essence of their competence. Hence, speaking is seen to consist in the implementation of linguistic rules. Inside the head of every speaker there appears a miniature linguist.[4]

Irrespective of which of the three answers presented above we might favour, the idea of language is a relatively recent one in the annals of human history. Yet it has had a profound impact, not only on the way we interpret our own activities of speaking, but also on those activities themselves. I have already shown, in the previous chapter, how the explicit codification of lexical conventions and grammatical rules sets standards of correctness which may – to varying degrees – be emulated or enforced. This institutionalisation of language is reflected in systems of education. Children not only learn to speak, as they have always and everywhere done, through immersion in an environment of vocally accomplished caregivers, they also receive formal schooling in the principles of language, as formulated by those appointed by society to act as its guardians – the grammarians and dictionary-makers. Above all, they are taught *to write*. The influence of writing on modern ideas and practices of language cannot be overestimated (Harris 1980: 6). For writing is not simply the equivalent of speech in an alternative medium. It is rather a kind of reconstructed, *as if* speech: as if the verbal utterance were fully amenable to systematic analysis in terms of syntactical rules; as if the tone of voice and pronunciation were entirely dispensable to meaning; as if the utterance had an autonomous existence, independently of the context of its production.

None of these things are actually true of speech, except perhaps for some kinds of 'reading aloud'. Yet modern linguistics has operated largely on the assumption that they are. Thus it turns out that the prototypical instance of the linguistic utterance, a rule-governed, context-independent proposition delivered without expression or affect, is that artefact so familiar to us but unknown to non-literate societies: the sentence of writing. Every theory of language evolution that holds up this prototype as its point of culmination, as the exemplar of a fully evolved language capacity, has an inbuilt 'scriptist' bias, treating speech that emulates or imitates writing as more perfect than speech that does not, and regarding the latter's deviations from the ideal as imperfections or errors. It is no wonder that in modern society, where the practices of speech have come to be modelled on writing and where speakers are taught to observe a rationalised system of rules and conventions (that is, to apply language), it has fallen to a specialised branch of verbal craft, namely poetry, to attempt to make up for the resulting expressive and aesthetic impoverishment by producing forms which – whilst approaching the rhythmic and tonal patterns of music – are lexically and syntactically aberrant. But as Alfred Gell has argued, in a brilliant analysis of the vocal artistry of the Umeda, a society of Papua New Guinea, for a non-literate people whose speech has retained its expressive, song-like quality, unexpurgated by the rationalizations of the language-makers, all speaking is inherently poetic. 'What need of poets then?' (Gell 1979: 61).[5]

TECHNOLOGY, ART AND CRAFTSMANSHIP

I have argued that song, far from being put together from separate linguistic and musical components, is rather an expressive unity that is decomposed into these components through the imposition of a concept of language of recent, Western origin. Exactly the same argument can be made for the kind of skilled, technical artistry that I denote by the term 'craftsmanship'. For the concept of technology recasts the technical skills of the craftsman in terms of an objective system of rational principles, a *logos*, in just the same way that the idea of language recasts the verbal art of speaking in terms of the rules of grammar (see Chapter Fifteen, pp. 294–5). And as practice comes to be seen as the mechanical application of technological rules, so its expressive, aesthetic aspects are consigned to a separate domain of 'art' – a concept once synonymous with technical skill but whose meaning is now constituted by its *opposition* to technology on precisely the same grounds that music, in the modern conception, is constituted by its opposition to language (see Chapter Nineteen, pp. 349–51).

In a technologically literate society, tool-using is assimilated to the operation of artificial systems, much as speaking is assimilated to writing. Hence the prototypical tool appears as the mechanical gadget which embodies in its own construction the principles of its operation. As an antidote to the scriptist bias of formal linguistics, I have suggested (following Merleau-Ponty) that we regard speech as a species of song. To follow up this suggestion into the analogous field of tool-use, I propose that we consider, as a prototypical instance, the kind of tool-using that comes closest of all to song – that is, playing a musical instrument. For if to speak is to sing, then surely to use a tool is to play. Since, as every anthropologist knows, it is helpful to be able to draw on first-hand experience, I shall consider the example of playing the 'cello. As a reasonably proficient 'cellist, my experience is that when I sit down to play everything falls naturally into place – the bow in my hand, the body of the instrument between my knees – so that I can launch myself directly, and with the whole of my being, into the music. I dive in, like a swimmer into water, and lose myself in the surrounding ambience of sound.

This is not to say that I cease to be aware, or that my playing becomes simply mechanical or automatic: quite the contrary, I experience a heightened sense of awareness, but that awareness is not *of* my playing, it *is* my playing. Just as with speech or song, the performance embodies both intentionality and feeling. But the intention is carried forward in the activity itself, it does not consist in an internal mental representation formed in advance and lined up for instrumentally assisted, bodily execution. And the feeling, likewise, is not an index of some inner, emotional state, for it inheres in my very gestures, in the pressure of my bow against the strings, in the vibrato of my left hand. In short, to play is itself to feel, so that in playing, I put feeling *into* the music. It makes no more sense, then, to split off a rational-technical component from the (residually) expressive component of playing a musical instrument than it does to split off a propositional component from the expressive component of speech or song.

I do not claim, of course, that all of what I have described above happens spontaneously, without preparation or rehearsal. A great deal of practice is required, and there are puzzles to be solved. To get around awkward passages, complex configurations of fingering and hand position have to be worked out in advance, and bowing movements have to be planned so that at the end of one phrase the bow is in the right place on the strings for the beginning of the next. At such times, as also when something goes wrong in the performance, one becomes painfully aware both of oneself and of the instrument, and of the distance that separates them. The instrument is felt to be obdurate or resistant; it sticks. My point, however, is that this opposition between player and instrument is collapsed in the instant when the former begins actually to *play*. In that instant, the boundaries between the player, the instrument and the acoustic environment appear to dissolve.

Lest my choice of example may seem to force the issue – for in playing a musical instrument one does not achieve any direct, practical effect beyond the rapidly fading tapestry of sound – let me suggest another instance of tool-use, again drawn from my own experience, this time of anthropological fieldwork among reindeer herdsmen in northern Finland. The tool I have in mind is the lasso, and the herdsman uses it to capture selected deer from the throng of animals circulating in the round-up enclosure (Ingold 1993b). In construction, the lasso is extremely simple: no more than a length of rope with a sliding toggle. When not in use it hangs limply in a coil from the hand, or trails loose on the ground. Yet in the moment of being cast, it assumes the lively form of a flying noose, a form which never stands still even for a single instant. Like the musical phrase shaped in sound, the form hangs suspended in the current of action. Thus, working a lasso, like playing a musical instrument, is pure movement or flow, and everything that I have said applies to the latter applies to the former as well. It involves an embodied skill, acquired through much practice. It carries forward an intention, but at the same time is continually responsive to an ever-changing situation. Just as, with the orchestral 'cellist, the processes of his visual attention to the conductor and his manual handling of the instrument are indissociable aspects of one ongoing process of action, so also the herdsman's handling of the lasso is inseparable from his attention to the movements of the herd in the enclosure. The attentive quality of the action is equivalent to what, in relation to musical performance, I have called 'feeling': to play is to feel; to act is to attend. The agent's attention, in other words, is fully absorbed in the action. Yet things can go wrong in the roundup, as they can in performance: the lasso can miss its mark, ropes can become entangled, the efforts of other herdsmen working in the enclosure may be disrupted, animals can even be injured. The frustrated herdsman then becomes an object of embarrassed self-regard, not to mention abuse from his fellows (I speak from experience). The flow is broken, and one has to begin all over again.

COGNITION AND PRACTICE

So much for the view of the naïve, yet reasonably skilled practitioner. Enter now the cognitive scientist, who claims that where tools are used, there must be a technology – a theory of how the tools are to be operated – lodged, albeit unbeknown to its possessors, inside their heads. The claim is, of course, parallel to that of the linguist who assumes that the 'languages' of non-literate peoples exist fully-formed in the minds of speakers, merely awaiting explicit formulation. One wonders, then, what such a *logos* of 'cello-playing or lasso-throwing would look like. It would consist, presumably, in a set of formal rules or algorithms capable of combining elementary motor schemata into complex, patterned sequences which, precisely executed, should produce instrumental gestures appropriate to any given context. The task of representing the technique of 'cello-playing or lasso-throwing in such formal terms would likely be an infinite one, but even supposing it were possible, would an imaginary creature, programmed with this knowledge, and provided with the requisite material equipment, be able to function remotely like a skilled practitioner?

The answer, I believe, is that it would not. It would produce, rather, a sort of 'as if' action, as if what in reality is a continuous flow could be reconstructed in the form of countless steps, each the mechanical execution of a pre-established plan or assembly – analogous to the sentence of language (Bourdieu 1977: 73, Ingold 1986b: 209–10). It is as though the quality of attention that, as we have seen, inheres in the skilled practitioner's conduct were to be withdrawn from the conduct itself and concentrated in the operation of a mental constructional device (an 'intelligence'), which, on the basis of a processing of sensory inputs, is supposed to generate plans and place them 'on line' for execution. Thus thought becomes active, action passive. In essence, the 'as if' actor and the skilled practitioner employ different kinds of intentionality. The first is the kind entailed in orthodox Cartesian accounts of volitional behaviour, in which to have an intention is to prefix that behaviour with a thought, plan or mental representation which it serves to deliver. The second is a kind of intentionality that is launched and carried forward in the action itself, and corresponds to the attentive quality of that action. It is the intentionality not of an isolated mind, of the cogitating subject confronting an exterior world of things, but rather that of a being wholly immersed in the relational nexus of its instrumental 'coping' in the world.

There is a certain (though as we shall see, inexact) parallel between the 'as if' actor and the inexperienced novice, and they fail for the same reason. Every act has to be thought out in advance, and once embarked upon, it cannot be changed without further deliberation which, in turn, interrupts the action. Attention *precedes* response, introducing a time lag which would make anything like orchestral playing or capturing reindeer with lassos completely impossible. The skilled practitioner, by contrast, is able continually to attune his movements to perturbations in the perceived environment without ever interrupting the flow of action, since that action is itself a process of attention. Skilled practice cannot, therefore, be understood as the application of objective knowledge in the form of an 'expert system', as though it followed the steps of (say) a 'cello-playing or lasso-throwing programme. This is not to deny that complex neurophysiological processes are involved, which operate on sensory inputs and yield appropriate motor responses. But it is to suggest that whatever goes on in the brain of the practitioner cannot be modelled as entailing anything analogous to mental rules and representations (Dreyfus 1991: 219). It is, of course, entirely tautologous to model neurological processes in this way and then, inverting the relation between model and reality, to claim that neurology provides independent confirmation for the existence of mental representations.

The novice becomes skilled not through the acquisition of rules and representations, but at the point where he or she is able to dispense with them. They are like the map of an unfamiliar territory, which can be discarded once you have learned to attend to features of the landscape, and can place yourself in relation to them. The map can be a help in beginning to know the country, but the aim is to learn the country, not the map. Similarly, the 'cello-teacher may place marks on the fingerboard to show the novice where to put his fingers in order to obtain different notes. The novice is thereby enabled to feel for himself the particular muscular tensions in the left hand, and to hear the resulting intervals of pitch. Having learned to attend to these things, his fingers will find their own place (he can now play in tune), and the marks, which serve no further purpose, can be removed. The same applies to any other branch of apprenticeship in which the learner is placed, with the requisite equipment, in a practical situation, and is told to pay attention to how 'this' feels, or how 'that' looks or sounds – to *notice* those subtleties of texture that are all-important to good judgement and the successful practice of a craft. That one learns to touch, to see and to hear is obvious to any craftsman or musician. As Gibson succinctly put it, learning is an 'education of attention' (1979: 254).

This kind of learning exemplifies what Lave (1990: 310) has called 'understanding in practice', to which she counterposes 'the culture of acquisition'. The latter phrase denotes the theory of learning long favoured by cognitive science (and by Western educational institutions), according to which effective action in the world depends on the practitioner's first having acquired a body of knowledge in the form of rules and schemata for *constructing* it. Learning, the process of acquisition, is thus separated from doing, the application of acquired knowledge. It is implied, moreover, that a body of context-free, propositional knowledge – namely a technology or, more generally, a culture – actually *exists* as such and is available for transmission by teaching outside the context of use. Learning, in this view, entails an internalisation of collective representations or, in a word, *enculturation*. 'Understanding in practice', by contrast, is a process of *enskilment*, in which learning is inseparable from doing, and in which both are embedded in the context of a practical engagement in the world – that is, in dwelling. According to this theory of learning, the kind of know-how thus gained, 'constituted in the settings of practice, based on rich expectations generated over time about its shape, is the site of the most powerful knowledgeability of people in the lived-in world' (Lave 1990: 323).

By and large, discussions of the relationship between tool-using and speech have adopted the unequivocally 'logocentric' perspective of cognitive science and structural linguistics, whose ontological baseline postulates a rational subject positioned *vis-à-vis* an objective world. The aim has then been to demonstrate a parallel, overlap or even identity between cognitive structures involved in generating representations, on the one hand, of object assemblies (for execution as tool-using behaviour), and on the other, of word assemblies (for execution as speech). The former are glossed as 'technology', the latter as 'language'. The argument sketched above, however, suggests the possibility of a diametrically opposed approach, which takes as its ontological starting point the inescapable condition of human beings' engagement in the world, and that foregrounds the performative and poetic aspects of speech and tool-use that have been marginalised by rationalism. From the vantage point of this approach, the relationship between tool-using and speech, far from being the surface manifestation of a more fundamental deep-structural connection between technology and language, is really one between the vocal artistry of speech and song, and the technical artistry of craftsmanship. Moreover, I have found no absolute line of demarcation between speech and song, nor between singing with the voice and 'singing' with an instrument (as, for example, in 'cello-playing), nor between the latter and other forms of tool-assisted, skilled artistry even of a thoroughly practical, subsistence-oriented kind. One thinks, for example, of the harvester at work (see Chapter Eleven, p. 207), swinging his scythe in a constant, rhythmic, dancelike movement and singing as he does so: that, to my mind, is the archetypal situation of human tool-use, not the puzzle-solving scenarios beloved of cognitive psychologists.

INTELLIGENCE AND IMAGINATION

Human beings do, of course, solve puzzles: witness the chess-player devising a strategy of future moves, or the 'cellist working out the fingering for a difficult passage. How, from the point of view of a dwelling perspective, is this kind of puzzle-solving to be understood? And how would our account differ from the rationalist argument that regards every solution as the output of a cognitive device, an intelligence, located somewhere within the organism? This latter argument, as we have seen, sets out from the postulate of an original detachment of the intelligent subject, who has then to construct (or reconstruct) the world in his or her mind, prior to bodily engagement with it. The direction in which we proceed is precisely the reverse: postulating an original condition of engagement, of being-in-the-world, we suppose that the practitioner has then to *detach* himself from the current of his activity in order to reflect upon it. Only having achieved such a stance of contemplative detachment can he begin to ask such questions as (of an object) 'What can this be for?' or (of a word) 'What might this mean?' In answering them, he may suppose himself to be contributing meaning or value to an external world that, in itself, is devoid of significance, that is merely *there* for people to do with it what they will. There are, after all, many things you can do with a stone, and if, in response to my own or another's query, I say of that stone that it is a 'missile', am I not contributing my own subjective meaning to an otherwise meaningless, occurrent object?

A being who is dwelling in the world, however, does not encounter stones. He encounters missiles, anvils, axes or whatever, depending on the project in which he is currently engaged. They are available for him to use in much the same way as are the mouth, hands and feet. In the game of football, we use the feet for running and kicking; we do not, however, consider feet *as* feet (that is, as occurrent anatomical structures) and wonder what to do with them. Such may be the view of the cobbler or chiropodist, but he is playing a different game! As I have already shown in discussing the issue of how words acquire significance, meaning already inheres in the relational properties of the dwelt-in world. In order to release or 'free up' the qualities of objects in themselves, this original meaning has to be stripped away, reducing the 'available' to the 'occurrent'.[6] This is done by distancing ourselves from, or stepping outside, the activities in which the usefulness of these objects resides. Only by virtue of such dissociation do we come to confront the spectre of a meaningless environment, the kind of objective world 'out there' that, in the discourse of Western science, goes by the name of nature. Taking nature as a datum of existence, we may then see ourselves as dealing with it by appropriating it symbolically, by attaching cultural significance to its occurrent properties. In so doing, we attempt to recover the meaning that is initially lost through our disengagement from the current of practical action.

What, then, are we doing when we step outside of this current? Or to rephrase the question: what kind of activity does *not* involve a palpable engagement in the world? The answer is that it is activity of the special kind we call *imagining*. This is what the chess-player is up to when, sitting apparently immobile and without touching the pieces on the board, he nevertheless proceeds to work out a strategy. Now there are three points I wish to make about this kind of activity. The first is that imagining *is* an activity: it is something people *do*. And as an activity it carries forward an intentionality, a quality of attention that is embodied in the activity itself. Were it otherwise, were every instance of planning supposed to be prefixed by a prior intention in the form of a plan, we would at once be led into the absurdity of an infinite regress (Ingold 1986b: 312–13). We have already seen that skilled practice cannot be understood as the mechanical execution of prefigured design; it is now clear that the same applies to the design process itself. Where this process of imagination differs from other forms of activity, and what makes it so special, is that attention is turned inwards on the self: in other words, it becomes reflexive. I dwell, in my imagination, in a virtual world populated by the products of my own imagining.

The second point, which follows from the first, is that whatever we call these products – whether plans, strategies or representations – their forms are generated and held in place only within the current of imaginative activity. The same, moreover, is true of material forms generated in the practical activity of craftsmanship. It is said colloquially, yet with good reason, that the craftsman *casts* the material into its projected form: the form, that is, arises out of a practical movement depicted metaphorically as a 'throw' (though in the case of the herdsman casting his lasso, this is quite literally true). Thus, as the musician casts sound into the form of a phrase, so likewise the potter casts clay into the form of a vessel. Yet unlike sound, clay congeals, and as it does so the form, generated in movement, is 'frozen' in the shape of a static artefact that endures beyond the context of its production. It is this, perhaps, that inclines us to think that in the making of artefacts, forms pre-existing as images in the mind are simply transcribed onto the material, as though the movement issued directly from the form and served only to disclose it (see Chapter Eighteen, pp. 343–6, for a critique of this view). The reality is more complex, since both the image of the projected form and the material artefact in which it subsequently comes to be embodied are independently generated and 'caught' within their respective intentional movements, of imagination and practice. The problem, then, is to understand the relationship between these two generative movements, a relationship that might be characterised, provisionally, as *rehearsal*. One may, in imagination, 'go over' the same movement as a preparation or pre-run for its practical enactment. But the enactment no more issues from the image than does the latter from an image for imagining.

The third point is that imagining is the activity of a being who nevertheless dwells in an actual world. However much he may be 'wrapped up' in his own thoughts, the thinker is situated in a time and place and therefore in a relational context. The scientist may indeed think himself to be an isolated, rational subject confronting the world as a spectacle, yet were he in reality so removed from worldly existence he could not think the thoughts he does. 'We do not have to think the world in order to live in it, but we *do* have to live in the world in order to think it' (Ingold 1996a: 118). This is why, as I mentioned earlier, the parallel between the novice practitioner, who has to work out his movements in advance, and the 'as if' actor whose behaviour is the output of a mental constructional device, is an inexact one. The 'as if' actor is the (fictitious) pure subject, possessed of a rational intelligence that delivers thoughts for execution. Such a subject can only dwell within a space circumscribed by the intellectual puzzles it sets out to solve (as against the objective world in which its solutions are applied). The novice, by contrast, though one step removed from the uninterrupted engagement of the skilled practitioner, nevertheless carries on his deliberations 'against a background of involved activity' (Dreyfus 1991: 74). He continues to dwell in a world that provides, above all in the presence of other persons, a generous source of support for his deliberations. The same is true of the scientist, who confronts nature in rather the same questioning way that the novice player confronts his instrument, as a domain of occurrent phenomena whose workings one is out to understand.

Here, then, we have the final, essential difference between intelligence and imagination. The former is the capacity of a being whose existence is wrapped up within a world of puzzles, the latter is the activity of a being whose puzzle-solving is carried on within the context of involvement in a real world of persons, objects and relations. And of all the historical products of the human imagination, perhaps the most decisive and far-reaching has been the idea that there exists such a thing as an 'intelligence', installed in the heads of each and every one of us, and that is ultimately responsible for our activities.

Notes

CHAPTER ONE   CULTURE, NATURE, ENVIRONMENT

1   For detailed ethnographic description of Cree attitudes to animals, see Feit (1973), Tanner (1979), Scott (1989) and Brightman (1993). I return to the idea of animals offering themselves to human hunters in Chapter Four (p. 67).

2   I return in the concluding section to the reasons why this point of observation cannot, in practice, be attained.

3   The occasion was the Nineteenth Annual Korzybski Memorial Lecture, presented in New York in January 1970, and the text was originally published in the *General Semantics Bulletin* of that year (volume 37).

4   This was the Gildersleeve Lecture, delivered at Barnard College, New York, in March 1972. The text first appeared in *Barnard Alumnae*, Spring 1972, and is reprinted as Lévi-Strauss (1974).

5   Bateson developed this idea in his last work, *Mind and Nature* (1980: 107). There are striking parallels here with ideas developed by two other major writers on the philosophy and psychology of perception, Maurice Merleau-Ponty and James Gibson (see Chapter Fourteen). Merleau-Ponty, in his essay on 'Eye and mind' (1964: 159–90), insisted on the 'intertwining of vision and [eye] movement', neither of which could occur without the other (p. 162). Gibson, for his part, placed movement at the heart of his ecological theory of visual perception, regarded as 'a process of *information pickup* involving the exploratory activity of looking around, getting around, and looking at things' (1979: 147). All three authors stressed the primacy of the perceiver's total sensory engagement with the environment. The convergences are striking, especially bearing in mind that they came from such different intellectual backgrounds. There is no evidence that Bateson ever read or took the slightest note of the work of either Gibson or Merleau-Ponty. A comparison of their respective ideas is, however, long overdue.

6   The Pintupi, whose country borders that of the Walbiri to the southwest, adopt a rather similar procedure. When young men are to be initiated, 'fathers, older brothers and other close relatives take them to sacred sites and show them rituals. They are "introduced" (*nintinu*) to the place. This visiting and seeing the site, learning about it, become important in laying claim to control or share in the control of a site' (Myers 1986: 151). The acquisition of knowledge through initiation, whereby it passes from 'outside' to 'inside', is described as 'giving (*yunginpa*) knowledge to young people, as revealing (*yutininpa*) it, or as teaching (*nintininpa*) it' (pp. 242, 68). I return to the Pintupi ethnography in Chapter Three (pp. 52–4).

7   Howard Morphy appears to invoke the notion of the key in just this sense, in his account of the interpretation of so-called 'geometric' designs in the paintings of the Yolngu, an Aboriginal people of Northeast Arnhem Land. He invites us to consider a simple (and very common) motif: a circle with a line running into it. The first clue links the design with a familiar waterhole (the circle) into which there drains a creek (the line). The next links it to old man kangaroo, who made the waterhole by digging a well (the circle), using his tail as a digging stick (the line). And the next links it to the old man's penis (the line) emerging from the waterhole to penetrate the vagina (the circle) of a lady kangaroo who was bending over to drink. Through these successive revelations, the experiences of topography, subsistence activity and sexual relations are all drawn together in an ongoing process of discovery (Morphy 1991: 169). Morphy, however, confuses the clue with the cipher, and proceeds to describe these revelations as decodings which gradually empty the formal design of its semantic content.

8   These examples are taken from *Janáček's Uncollected Essays on Music*, edited by Mirka Zemanová (1989: 106, 117, 195, 224). In letters to the great love of his life, Kamila Stösslová, Janáček jotted down the snort of his favourite domestic pig, but confessed to having some difficulty with notating the 'strange melody' of the cock that woke him every morning (Tyrrell 1994: 22, 77).

CHAPTER TWO   THE OPTIMAL FORAGER

1   These lines were written prior to the publication, in 1998, of an article by James L. Boone and Eric Alden Smith. Ostensibly a critique of 'evolutionary archaeology', an approach that seeks to explain change in the archaeological record as a result of the direct action of natural selection on variation in artefacts and behaviour, the article in fact sets out to restate the contrasting position of human evolutionary ecology. What this restatement offers, however, is an almost total retraction of the earlier claim of evolutionary ecology to account for locally adapted foraging strategies as the outputs of algorithms shaped by the operation of natural selection on culturally transmitted information. These strategies, Smith and Boone now argue, are not attributable to natural selection at all, but to the operation of capacities of rational choice and decision-making that all humans have in common and that owe their formation to 'earlier evolutionary processes extending back thousands or millions of years' (1998: S145). This, they go on to declare, 'is the fundamental tenet of evolutionary ecology' (p. S156). If so, then evolutionary ecology has effectively capitulated to evolutionary psychology, and the difference between them is merely one of emphasis: on the phenotypic plasticity of adaptive responses to particular environmental circumstances, as against the universal, genotypic hardwiring of evolved human problem-solving capacities. Thus evolutionary ecology, in its new guise, remains committed to an ecological perspective only in its insistence that the adaptive strategies it seeks to explain *have not evolved*!

CHAPTER THREE   HUNTING AND GATHERING

1   Subsequent ethnographic work among the Mbuti has, it should be noted, cast considerable doubt on the authenticity of Turnbull's somewhat 'romantic' account. Thus, Grinker (1992) fails to find indigenous conceptions that would correspond to the feeling for the forest that Turnbull imputes to the Mbuti. And Ichikawa (1992) observes that Mbuti attitudes towards the forest are, in reality, decidedly ambivalent: the forest is held to be the home of destructive as well as benevolent powers. But such ambivalence is equally characteristic of intimate relations in the human domain, which also have their undercurrent of negativity. However by addressing the forest as 'Father', Ichikawa states, Mbuti 'are appealing to it for the benevolence normally expected from a parent' (1992: 41).
2   In responding to the criticisms of Abramson (1992) and myself (Ingold 1992b), Bird-David significantly softens this contrast. Following Gudeman (1992), she stresses the pragmatic – as against the cognitive – aspect of modelling, regarding it in the first place as a kind of activity or performance. Through performance, the model is actualised as lived experience. Considering the example 'a dog is a friend', she points out that by bestowing the affection due to a human familiar upon her dog – to which the dog evidently responds by showing every sign of affection for her – it actually *becomes* a friend, and is not merely 'thought of' as such (Bird-David 1992a: 44). To refer to the dog as her friend is thus to draw attention to an underlying quality of relationship that can subsist just as well in gestures towards non-human as towards human familiars. This argument, though it comes close to agreement with that advanced in this chapter, by the same token departs significantly from the approach of Lakoff and Johnson (1980).
3   As Bird-David puts it, in connection with the friendliness of her dog (see note 2, above), the dog is not merely 'like' a friend, 'it *is* a friend' (1992a: 44).
4   This contradiction has also been noted by Edward Casey. 'Whom are we to believe?', he asks, 'The theorizing anthropologist, the arsenal of his natural attitude bristling with explanatory projectiles that go off into space? Or the aborigine on the ground who finds this ground itself to be a coherent collection of pre-given places – pre-given at once in his experience and in the Dreaming that sanctions this experience?' (Casey 1996: 15).

CHAPTER FOUR   FROM TRUST TO DOMINATION

1   For more detailed reviews and analysis of the 'savage' in literature, see Street (1975), Berkhofer (1979) and Barnard (1989).

2   I return to this comparison, and to some of the pitfalls that it harbours, in Chapter Twenty (pp. 363–5).

3   In the opinion of Sir John Lubbock, writing in 1865, the comparison of savages to children 'is not only correct but also highly instructive . . . The life of each individual is the epitome of the history of the race, and the gradual development of the child illustrates that of the species . . . Savages, like children, have no steadiness of purpose' (1865: 570).

4   Just what 'being alive' entails is a matter I explore in greater depth in Chapter Six (pp. 95–8).

5   For examples, see Marshall (1961) on Kalahari Bushmen, Turnbull (1978) on the Mbuti Pygmies, Dentan (1968) and Robarchek (1989) on the Semai, Briggs (1970) on the Inuit and Howell (1989) on the Chewong.

6   See, for example, Fienup-Riordan (1990: Ch. 8) on the Yup'ik Eskimos.

7   I should stress that the contrast I am drawing here is between hunting and pastoralism as ways of relating to animals, not between hunting and pastoral *societies*. It is perfectly possible for the same people in the same society to relate concurrently to different animals in quite different ways. The Blackfoot Indians of the North American Plains, for example, were hunters in relation to the buffalo, but herdsmen in relation to the horse (Ewers 1955).

8   Pernille Gooch's recent study of the Van Gujjars, nomadic buffalo pastoralists inhabiting the forested foothills of the Indian Himalayas, presents a fascinating exception to this argument, in three respects. First, the Van Gujjars relate to their buffaloes in the same way that they relate to other animals native to the forest: thus if the latter are classed as 'wildlife', then buffaloes are wildlife too, despite their evident tameness and familiarity with humans. All are 'at home' in the forest world. Secondly, the principle of this relationship, according to Gooch, is one not of domination but of trust. Thirdly, the forest – along with its animal inhabitants – is likened not to a parent but to a child. Thus people provide the environment of nurture in which trees and buffaloes grow and thrive, rather than vice versa (Gooch 1998: 186–7, 192, 209). The key to understanding this case lies in the fact that the Van Gujjar do not hunt, nor do they ever kill or eat their buffaloes – the animals are kept exclusively for their milk, and eventually die of old age. On the one hand, this makes it possible for Van Gujjar to extend the pastoral attitude of parental care from their buffaloes in particular to the forest and its creatures in general; on the other hand, it divests the caring relationship of its more coercive, authoritarian aspects. Though more cared for than caring, buffaloes retain a measure of control over their destiny.

9   In an influential article, Nicholas Humphrey takes the idea that one could share with animals to be an example of the 'fallacious reasoning', commonly branded as magic, in which 'primitive and not so primitive peoples' are said to indulge. Their mistake, Humphrey tells us, is to suppose that you can transact with non-human entities just as you can with human partners. In this, you are bound to be disappointed, since 'nature will not transact with man, she goes her own way regardless' (Humphrey 1976: 313). But it is surely Humphrey's reasoning, not that of the primitive, that is fallacious. For it assumes, from the start, a separation of nature and humanity that is in reality the consequence of transactional failure, not its cause.

CHAPTER FIVE   THINGS, PLANTS, ANIMALS AND CHILDREN

1   Deleuze and Guattari (1988: 18) contrast the agricultural practice of sowing seeds derived from an ancestral stock in fields carved out from the forest, with the horticultural practice of successive planting, unearthing and replanting of cuttings or offshoots. They link the former to a peculiarly Western ontology of transcendence, and to a genealogical model of relatedness: every seed is an individual entity whose nature is fixed by descent and revealed in its growth. The latter however, which is characteristic of Hagen practice, is seen to instantiate a non-Western ontology of immanence. For every cutting or offshoot is itself a section of a path of growth, one of the reticulate network of paths comprising the garden as a whole. Every strand of this network, which Deleuze and Guattari liken to a rhizome, is the embodiment of a relationship. I return to the contrast between genealogical and relational models in Chapter Eight.

2   The use of the idiom of parental nurture to talk about the growth of tuberous plants is widely reported in Melanesian ethnography. Sabarl gardeners, for example, 'think of their growing food as being like children, and see themselves in the role of parents who by giving nurture now will be nurtured by their offspring' (Battaglia 1990: 94). And Matayans refer to their yam seed tubers, once harvested and lifted from the ground, as sons (Gross 1998: 264).

3   Japanese upland foresters, according to John Knight, would see it both ways. Every tree, they say, has two lives. In its first life, the tree is grown in the ground. 'Foresters', Knight reports, 'liken tree-growing to child-rearing. The raising of the young tree saplings is characterised as parental nurturance. According to one local expression, the forester should "treat the mountain as though you are bringing up a child"' (Knight 1998: 199). Upon being felled, however, the tree enters its second life, when it 'goes to work' as a house timber. The incorporation of the tree into the building, after felling, is compared to the incorporation of a woman into the household after marriage. Now it is the tree that brings up the human inhabitants of the household, just as a mother nurtures her children. Despite having been cut down, the tree is still alive, it 'breathes' (1998: 205, 213).

4   In a review of the book in which an earlier version of this chapter appeared (Harris 1996), Peter Rowley-Conwy picks up the phrase 'continuous field of relationships', but takes it to mean something entirely different from what I intended – namely, a *continuum of variation* between the poles of foraging and farming. Accordingly, he portrays me as an advocate of the view that the transition from one pole to the other was gradual, progressive and wide-ranging. This view, as he correctly observes, was propounded by Eric Higgs and his associates some three decades ago (Higgs and Jarman 1969), but has been increasingly called into question by studies which point to a more irregular pattern of multiple, short-term and local transitions (Rowley-Conwy 1998: 218–19). There is nothing, however, in the notion of a relational field encompassing plants, animals and humans to suggest that it cannot undergo rapid transformation in particular regions.

Chapter Six   A circumpolar night's dream

1   Hallowell's work was carried out in the decade 1930–40 among the people of the Berens River band, numbering about nine hundred. These people were often known as the Saulteaux (derived from *Saulteurs*, a name given them by French traders which translates as 'people of the rapids'). In much of his earlier work, Hallowell himself referred to them by this name (Hallowell 1955); moreover it is customarily used as a term of self-identification by the people themselves. Many other authors refer to the people inclusively as Ojibway. An alternative designation, officially adopted by the Bureau of American Ethnology, was Chippewa (*ibid*.: 115). However Wub-e-ke-niew (1995: xviii), who refers to his people of Red Lake as Ahnishinahbæeó'jibway (literally 'Ojibway people'), claims that 'Chippewa' was an entirely artificial category that the US Government created by lumping them together with French Métis people in the region involved in the fur trade. Steinberg (1981) provides a useful summary account of the history, distribution, organisation and nomenclature of the Ojibwa/Saulteaux bands around Lake Winnipeg. For the sake of simplicity and consistency with Hallowell's later usage, I will continue to refer to them as Ojibwa.

2   All the ethnographic material in this chapter, unless stated to the contrary, is drawn either from this article, or from the earlier collection of Hallowell's essays, *Culture and Experience* (1955). Page references will be provided only for direct quotations from these sources, or where I cite very specific points. 'Ojibwa ontology, behavior and world view' will be abbreviated throughout as OO, and *Culture and Experience* as CE.

3   From my (so far) very limited and superficial reading of the ethnography on native Amazonian societies, I have been startled by the recurrence of just the same themes here too. The parallels are extraordinary, and warrant further investigation (see, especially, Descola 1992, 1996, and Viveiros de Castro 1998).

4   This is the assumption that John Kennedy (1992) makes, in branding as anthropomorphic any attempt to attribute to animals such things as mental states, motivations, intentions and feelings. For Kennedy, any attribution of this sort is a 'definite mistake', a dereliction of scientific reason, or worse still, 'a throw-back to primitive animism' (1992: 9, 32). But in criticising what he sees as the anthropo*morphic* bias in studies of animal behaviour, he fails to address, or even to notice, the anthropo*centric* bias in his own thinking, which equates the condition of humanity with the power of rational intelligence to overcome the determinations of nature. This bias has no empirical justification whatever *in* science; it is, however, a crucial part of the ideological justification *for* science.

On the distinction between anthropomorphism and anthropocentrism, see Viveiros de Castro (1998: 484–5, fn.11).

5   This is a wonderful example of what Viveiros de Castro (1998) calls 'perspectivism', namely the conception 'according to which the world is inhabited by different sorts of subjects or persons, human or non-human, which apprehend reality from distinct points of view' (1998: 469). These apprehensions are not alternative points of view of the same world, as orthodox cultural relativism would have it, but rather result from a carrying over of the same point of view into alternative realities. Thus to be a person is to assume a particular subject-position, and every person, respectively in their own sphere, will perceive the world in the same way – in the way that persons generally do. But *what* they see will be different, depending on the form of life they have taken up. Thus if beaver are food for human persons, then they are food for non-human persons also, such as for the Thunder Bird and the 'masters' of the hawks. But what are 'beaver' for the birds are batrachians and reptiles from the perspective of humans.

6   Significantly, while spirits of the dead and grandfathers have the same dual structure, of inner essence and outward form, only the former can appear as ghosts, since the latter never die (CE, pp. 179–80).

7   Nurit Bird-David makes an almost identical point in her analysis of the notion of *devaru* among the Nayaka, hunter-gatherers of South India. A certain stone may reveal itself to be *devaru* if it comes towards a person or, as in one reported instance, jumps up onto her lap. Whether it is *devaru*, or just another stone, will depend on whether it engages in any kind of relationship with Nayaka people. Thus 'devaru are not limited to certain *classes* of things. They are certain things-in-situations of whatever class or, better, certain situations' (Bird-David 1999: S74–5).

8   The Cree people, neighbours of the Ojibwa who speak a closely related Algonkian language, have a virtually identical word meaning 'life', *pimaatisiiwin*. Colin Scott (1989: 195) reports that one Cree man translated the word as 'continuous birth' (see Chapter Three, p. 51). This translation seems to resonate perfectly with Ojibwa notions.

9   In a discussion of the attribution of animacy to stones, J. Baird Callicott suggests that it is just as reasonable to assume that all corporeal things, including animals, plants, and even stones, have an 'associated consciousness', as it is to assume that none do (with the singular exception of human beings). He identifies the former assumption with the 'Indian attitude', and the latter with the attitude of Europeans and Euro-Americans. But in setting up this contrast, Callicott remains imprisoned within his Western preconception that 'to be "alive", i.e., conscious, aware or possessed of spirit' is a property intrinsic to things as such, rather than thinking of life as the generative movement wherein they come into being through the unfolding of wider fields of relationship (Callicott 1982: 301–2).

10   In his chapter on 'language', Wub-e-ke-niew explains that in his native Ahnishinahbæó'jibway, 'rather than acting upon the world . . . one acts in concert with the other beings with whom one shares Grandmother Earth . . . A person harmoniously "meets the Lake", rather than "going to get water"' (Wub-e-ke-niew 1995: 218).

11   Since the Ojibwa have no concept of the natural, Hallowell maintains, they also lack any notion of the supernatural. It would therefore be quite wrong to interpret Ojibwa ideas, for example, about the animacy of certain stones or the power of other-than-human persons within the framework of a natural–supernatural dichotomy (OO, p.28). Åke Hultkrantz (1982) disagrees. The distinction between a natural and supernatural reality, in his view, is a universal foundation for human religious experience. It is not, he writes, 'a distinction in a philosophical sense, between two absolutely separate worlds, but a more practical distinction between an everyday reality and a reality of another order to which spirits and miracles belong' (Hultkrantz 1982: 179). However, Hallowell's point, if I understand him right, is that the experience of other-than-human persons is one of superior power, rather than one of a reality that is superior to nature. Such experience amounts to an intensification rather than a transcendence of everyday reality. Smith (1998: 423–4) makes a similar point in a recent essay on the ontology of the Chipewyan.

12   As this example shows, the very openness of the Ojibwa self to the world, especially in dreams, has its downside. For it renders the self peculiarly vulnerable to the potentially hostile intent of other persons. This accounts for people's chronic anxiety, vividly documented by Hallowell (CE, pp. 250–90), about falling victim to sorcery and other kinds of covert attack, for the mutual suspicion that lurks beneath the placid surface of interpersonal life, and for what – to the outsider – looks like an exaggerated concern to avoid causing offence to others (OO, pp. 40, 47).

13   The so-called 'shaking tent ceremony' is common to both the Ojibwa and their neighbours, the Cree. For detailed descriptions of the Cree ceremony, see Feit (1994) and Brightman (1993: 170–6).

The multilingual character of the ceremony is especially clear from Brightman's account: thus the spirit voices issuing from the tent may speak in Cree, English, French, Saulteaux, Chipewyan, or unknown spirit languages. Since members of the audience differ in their knowledge of these languages, spirits may be intelligible to some listeners and not to others. Animal beings are recognisable from their intonations: 'bears speak in a low and rumbling voice, lynxes in a hissing voice, and fish with a gurgling intonation as if from underwater' (Brightman 1993: 174).

14 A further clue to the interchangeability of hearing and vision lies in the prevalence of metaphors of vision and sight in relation to the auditory experience of other-than-human persons in performances of the shaking tent ceremony (Hallowell 1942: 9–10). Moreover among the Cree, as Feit notes (1994: 292), the name of the ceremony, *koaspskikan*, contains a linguistic root which has been identified as meaning 'see, vision', along with 'try'.

15 In other words, it drops the anthropocentric assumption that automatically renders as anthropomorphic any attribution of intentions and feelings to non-human beings (see footnote 4).

CHAPTER SEVEN   TOTEMISM, ANIMISM AND ANIMALS

1 The idea of comparing totemic systems and animic systems was proposed some years ago by Philippe Descola (1992: 113–15), who illustrates his argument with ethnography from Amazonian Indian societies. Following the classic studies of Lévi-Strauss (1964, 1966b), Descola conceives of totemism as a classificatory project that seeks to model social distinctions on the basis of given discontinuities between species in nature. This conception, however, is of limited value in the ethnographic context of Aboriginal Australia, where totemism is fundamentally about people's connections with the land.

2 Here, and in what follows, I draw extensively on Luke Taylor's (1996) superb study of bark painting in Western Arnhem Land. See also Carroll (1977) and Taylor (1989). I am most grateful to the National Museum of Australia, and to Luke Taylor in particular, for advice and assistance in relation to the two Kunwinjku paintings reproduced here (Figures 7.2 and 7.3).

3 Morphy (1992) has discussed this point in relation to the rather similar painting tradition of the Yolngu, whose homeland lies to the east of that of the Kunwinjku.

4 The classic account of this kind of depiction is Nancy Munn's *Walbiri iconography* (1973b). On more recent developments, see Crocker (1983) and Layton (1992a).

5 I draw here on the studies of Crawford (1977) and Layton (1985: 441–8). For an overview, see Layton (1992b).

6 Heonik Kwon notes that the 'perilous interchangeability' of the roles of predator and prey is a theme of common concern among indigenous hunters throughout the circumpolar north. In Siberia as in northern North America, 'the position of the human hunter is insecure. As soon as he succeeds in a predatory act, the hunter falls into the position of prey' (Kwon 1998: 119).

7 I am most grateful for John MacDonald, of the Igloolik Research Centre, for assistance with translating the Inuit text accompanying the drawings reproduced here as Figures 7.4 and 7.5, and for explaining the significance of *nasaittuq*. My thanks also to Michael Bravo for information on this point.

8 In Chapter Six, I discuss in detail the nature of this division as it figures in Hallowell's (1960) account of the ontology of the Ojibwa.

9 For more on this, see Ray (1967), Lévi-Strauss (1983), Fienup-Riordan (1987) and Oosten (1992).

10 Among the Ojibwa, whose ontology I discussed in Chapter Six, the spirits of animals and other non-human persons are not generally seen but are rather heard. Their presence may be invoked in the midst of the human community, as in the ceremony of the 'shaking tent', through the intonation of their distinctive voices. If the mask, for the Inuit and Yup'ik, is the *look* of other-than-human being, then likewise the spirit-voice is the *sound* of such being for the Ojibwa. And so what applies to masks in the one case applies to voices in the other. The true voice of the animal is its spirit-voice, which may bear little resemblance to the sounds or calls it 'naturally' makes. And when this voice is rendered audible through the efforts of a human performer, whether in ceremony or in the recital of myth, it does not disguise but displaces the performer's voice.

11 I am indebted to Eduardo Viveiros de Castro for this idea.

12 I return to this theme in Chapter Twenty-one.

CHAPTER EIGHT   ANCESTRY, GENERATION, SUBSTANCE

1 See Paine (1991) for a discussion of these issues in relation to the case of Norwegians and Saami, and Lane (1998) for comparable remarks on the status of Basarwa *vis-à-vis* Bantu-speaking populations in Botswana.

2 The source for this definition is the ILO Convention of 1989 on 'Indigenous and tribal peoples in independent countries'. According to Article 1.b of the Convention, people 'are regarded as indigenous on account of their descent from populations which inhabited the country, or geographical region to which the country belongs, at the time of conquest or colonisation or the establishment of present state boundaries . . .' (ILO 1989, Art 1.b).

3 John Barnes succinctly defines the genealogy as the 'account of one's descent from an ancestor or ancestors by enumeration of the intermediate persons' (1967: 101).

4 The distinction here, between a person's positioning as an abstract figure on a genealogical chart and their positioning as a living being in an inhabited world, corresponds to Bourdieu's (1977: 37–8) between 'official' and 'practical' kinship, the first conceived in exclusively genealogical terms, the second as relationships 'continuously practised, kept up, cultivated'. Bourdieu himself likens the contrast to that between routes marked on a map, and paths in the landscape kept open by regular use.

5 This is a paraphrase by Quinn and Holland (1987: 4) of an influential definition offered some thirty years previously by Ward Goodenough. In much the same vein, Clifford Geertz wrote that the information provided by culture closes the gap 'between what our body tells us and what we have to know in order to function' (1973: 50). See Chapter Nine (pp. 159–60).

6 The difficulties arise in part because rates of change along different lines of descent are not necessarily constant, and in part because of the possibilities of adaptive convergence. For these reasons, genealogical proximity cannot automatically be inferred from taxonomic likeness. These problems are discussed with regard to approaches to human diversity in historical linguistics and molecular genetics by Renfrew (1992: 447–8).

7 It is not. The source of the metaphor may lie in Gregory Bateson's classic, *Naven*, where he compares Iatmul and Australian Aboriginal kinship systems. In the Australian system people are divided into a fixed number of closed, bounded groups. The Iatmul community, however, comprises 'an infinitely proliferating and ramifying stock . . . which continually divides and sends out offspring "like the rhizome of a lotus"' (Bateson 1958: 248–9). I have suggested elsewhere (Ingold n.d.) that a better image than the rhizome might be that of the fungal mycelium. In an argument that parallels my own, the mycologist Alan Rayner has asked what biological science would look like had the fungus, with its underground network of mycelial fibres, rather than the animal, as a discrete self-contained entity bounded by the skin, been taken as the paradigmatic instance of a life-form (Rayner 1997). For my present purposes I shall stay with the image of the rhizome, since it enables me to incorporate into my discussion some (though by no means all) of the ideas of Deleuze and Guattari. My use of this image, however, departs significantly from theirs, and perhaps comes closer to Bateson's original conception. For while their aim is to liberate our thinking from the constraints of linear and hierarchical reasoning, mine is to return it to the contexts of lived experience.

8 Bird-David actually distinguishes the idiom of parentage adopted by the Nayaka and other gatherer-hunters from that of ancestry which, she argues, prevails among peoples whose livelihood is based on the cultivation of crops. Whereas parents give unconditionally, relations with ancestors are based on conditional reciprocity (1990: 190–1). Though significant in the context of Bird-David's argument, this distinction has no bearing on the appropriateness of the genealogical model, and need not concern us here.

9 Notice that Kroeber's tree of human culture, reproduced in Figure 8.1, is already straining in that direction: it retains its arboreal form, as it were, against the odds. Ralph Linton took this even further in choosing *The tree of culture* as the title for his massive survey of the world's civilisations, first published in 1955. In a posthumous preface to the book, Adelin Linton explains that the title refers 'not to the familiar evolutionary tree with a single trunk and spreading branches, but to the banyan tree of the tropics. The branches of the banyan tree cross and fuse and send down adventitious roots, which turn into supporting trunks' (Linton 1955: v). Commenting on this passage, James Fernandez argues that 'the banyan tree suggests a circularity, if not a tensile netlike interconnectedness of parts, in human affairs, . . . that the normal tree metaphor either conceals or cannot manage to convey' (Fernandez 1998: 99). Thus arboreal imagery, contrary to what Deleuze

and Guattari seem to think, does not *have* to be linear and hierarchical. It all depends on the form of what you take to be the prototypical tree.

10 The significance of the distinction between 'entity' and 'site' for understanding person and self has been recently, and most lucidly explored by Rom Harré (1998).

11 Elsewhere, I have elaborated on this point in relation to the Darwinian paradigm of evolutionary biology, which of course rests squarely on the genealogical model (Ingold 1986b: 105–6).

12 For help in the formulation of these ideas, I am indebted to James Leach. See also Leach (1997: 34–5) and Ingold (1999: 407–8).

13 Bird-David (1994: 596–7) likens the person in a hunter-gatherer community to a drop of oil floating on the surface of a pool of water. When these drops come together, they coalesce into a larger drop. But drops can also split up into smaller ones that may then coalesce with others.

14 This leaves us with the question of how the information specifying the linguistic code can be acquired in the first place. The only solution is to suppose that all human beings are innately endowed, from the start, with some kind of inbuilt decoding device. Indeed the genealogical model of cultural transmission inevitably has recourse to the positing of one or several such devices. For a critique, see Chapter Twenty-two (pp. 397–9).

15 A particularly clear example of the transformation wrought by the genealogical model on hunter-gatherer self-perceptions lies in the changing meaning of the Eskimo term *inuit* (the plural form of *inuk*, meaning 'person'). In the past to be a person, an *inuk*, meant to be alive, to inhabit a certain place, and to undergo growth and development within a nexus of social relations. The plural form, *inuit*, referred to 'existence', or 'the state of being animate'. It was not, as Henry Stewart points out, 'a classificatory noun, and most certainly not a collective designation for all original inhabitants of the Far North' (Stewart n.d.: 3). Since the early 1970s, however, *inuit* has been explicitly adopted as an ethnonym to be applied on the basis of common descent from a putatively aboriginal population. To be an *inuk*, then, is no longer to occupy a particular subject position *vis-à-vis* others, but to belong as a member of a more inclusive genealogically defined category.

CHAPTER NINE   CULTURE, PERCEPTION AND COGNITION

1 Geertz included his article of 1966 in a volume of selected essays, *The interpretation of cultures*, published seven years later. But he introduced the volume with a chapter in which, among other things, he denounces Goodenough's aforementioned definition of culture as 'the main source of theoretical muddlement in contemporary anthropology'. It has become, he complains, the *locus classicus* for a 'school of thought [which] holds that culture is composed of psychological structures by means of which individuals or groups of individuals guide their behavior' (1973: 11). Sensing that his readers may have some difficulty in distinguishing this view from his own, which is indeed expressed in almost identical terms, Geertz invites us to consider a Beethoven quartet. No-one, he declares, would equate the quartet with the score (comprising a set of instructions for the performers), or with any particular performance of it. For the quartet is neither of these things, but the music itself – 'a temporally developed tonal structure, a coherent sequence of modeled sound'. Whatever this might mean (and no-one, least of all Geertz himself, has been able to figure this out), it is clear that if culture is analogous to music in this sense, it is nothing like the 'instructions . . . for the governing of behavior' of the 1966 article. Rather than facing up to a blatant contradiction in his thinking, Geertz prefers, as Bradd Shore puts it, 'to write his way out of it' (Shore 1996: 34). It would not be unreasonable to conclude that if anyone has been a source of theoretical muddlement in anthropology, it is Geertz himself (see Strauss 1992: 5–7, Shore 1996: 32–5, 50–1).

2 The concept of *habitus* is not original to Bourdieu. It was introduced to anthropology by Marcel Mauss in his study, dating from 1934, of techniques of the body, to refer to the repertoire of culturally patterned postures and gestures to be found in any particular society (Mauss 1979: 101).

3 Claudia Strauss completely misunderstands what Bourdieu means by *habitus* when she describes it as just another species of cultural model, comprising a set of mental structures, unconsciously extracted from practice, internalised through informal learning, and applied in novel situations. She fails to realise that in placing the *habitus* at the centre of his theoretical project, Bourdieu's purpose is to demolish the oppositions between mind and world, and between knowledge and practice, upon which the whole programme of cognitive anthropology is founded (1992: 9). The same error is reproduced by D'Andrade (1995: 147–8).

4 In Chapter Two (pp. 37–8) we established this point with regard to the practice of hunting.

5 The contrasting terms are drawn, by analogy, from 'phonetics' and 'phonemics' in linguistics. See also Chapter Three, p. 41.

6 Gibson was by no means consistent on this point, and it has been a continuing source of dispute among his followers. The following passage, however, appears unequivocal:

> The observer may or may not perceive or attend to the affordance, according to his needs, but the affordance, being invariant, is always there to be perceived. An affordance is not bestowed upon an object by a need of an observer and his act of perceiving it. The object offers what it does because of what it is.
>
> (Gibson 1979: 139)

A critique of this view, from a more phenomenologically inspired standpoint, is presented by Varela, Thompson and Rosch (1991: 203–4). In their approach to cognition as 'embodied action', the environment of the perceiver exists only as it is enacted in and through a history of 'structural coupling', in which person and environment are strictly co-determined.

7 The affinity, here, between the approaches to perception and action of Merleau-Ponty and Gibson is striking – all the more so because they came from such different intellectual backgrounds. They were one in insisting upon the centrality of movement to visual perception. This convergence is further explored in Chapter Fourteen. Gibson never referred to Merleau-Ponty's work, but there is anecdotal evidence that he had read the *Phenomenology of perception*, and that he approved of it (Heij and Tamboer n.d.).

CHAPTER TEN BUILDING, DWELLING, LIVING

1 Approaches from ecological psychology and phenomenology are reviewed in Chapter Nine. For the developmentalist challenge to neo-Darwinism, see Chapter Twenty-one.

2 Characterising human beings, by contrast to apes, as 'thing users', Francis Evans notes how the human capacity to use things in diverse ways calls for an ability not only to abstract the qualities of objects – such as hardness, heaviness and shape – from the objects themselves, but also to relate these qualities to a certain project. 'A stick becomes different things according to desire: digger, pointer, walking aid, club – it is our perception, not the stick that changes. *Thing user . . .* has to make a mental pattern, akin to a gestalt perception, of what it wants to do' (Evans 1998: 195).

3 I return to this parallel between the dynamics of organic and technical change in Chapter Twenty (pp. 369–72).

4 Animal behaviourists do not, of course, rule out the possibility that conduct may be intentionally motivated. But they argue that intentions are but proximate causes of acts whose ultimate cause lies in tendencies or dispositions established through natural selection.

5 For a discussion of the implications of Heidegger's concept of dwelling for architecture, see Norberg-Schulz (1985).

6 In Chapter Twenty-two I show that on the same grounds, it is equally illusory to seek the origins of language.

7 I return to this point in the next chapter (pp. 206–7).

CHAPTER ELEVEN THE TEMPORALITY OF THE LANDSCAPE

1 Heonik Kwon (pers. comm.) makes the important point that unlike native dwellers, archaeologists do not incorporate into their own practice the modes of environmental engagement of the characters of whom they tell. That is to say, the peoples of the past whose lives are revealed through excavation were not themselves excavators. On remembering as a way of perceiving the environment, see Chapter Eight (pp. 147–8).

2 I am referring to land, here, in the specific sense entailed in the genealogical model (see Chapter Eight). In the alternative sense entailed in the relational model, land and landscape are much closer in meaning.

3 This contrast is further explored in Chapter Fourteen, where it is linked to a distinction between *wayfinding* (journeying from place to place in a region) and *navigation* (plotting a course from one location to another in space).

4 For an exemplary analysis of 'the rhythmic structures of economic life', see Guyer (1988).

5 For further confirmation of this point, again with reference to Australian Aboriginal ethnography, see Chapter Seven (p. 128).

6 Barbara Adam proposes a rather similar project, arguing that the kind of knowing entailed in what she calls the 'landscape perspective' needs to be extended through an attention to 'timescape', requiring us 'to develop an analogous receptiveness to temporal interdependencies and absences, and to grasp environmental phenomena as complex temporal, contextually specific wholes' (Adam 1998: 54).

7 David Lowenthal contrasts the perception, respectively, of works of art and of landscapes in similar terms. 'Works of art . . . are detached from the observer, framed in space and time, quite distinct from their milieux. But landscapes surround the observer, merging continuously with other land-scapes to the horizon; the absence of a set frame challenges the viewer to create his own perspectives' (Lowenthal 1978: 375). This, of course, begs the question of how the perception of the landscape is reproduced in the art of painting. Indeed in seeking to represent, on canvas, the experience of dwelling, the landscape painter has to cultivate much the same duplicity as the ethnographer whose medium is the written word. Both are required to reflect, from a position of studied detachment, upon their own experience of engagement in the world (Ingold 1997).

8 In this regard, trees may be said to have a social life. However a recent volume, entitled *The social life of trees*, paradoxically took as its starting point a question that would deny to trees any such life. Contributors to the volume were asked to consider: 'To which symbolic ends have trees been used?' (Rival 1998: xiii). This is to suppose that the social life being symbolised is human, and that trees have no part in it.

9 Note that the distinction between coevalness and duration, represented by the corn and the tree, is not at all the same as the classic Saussurian dichotomy between synchrony and diachrony: the former belongs to the perspective of the A-series rather than the B-series, to the temporality of the landscape, not to its chronology (Ingold 1986b: 151).

10 On the idea of the key to meaning, as a clue rather than a cipher, see Chapter One (p. 22).

Chapter Twelve   Globes and spheres

1 The alleged opposition between visual and aural perception is the subject of Chapter Fourteen.

2 The artist Paul Klee wrote, in his notebooks, of 'our faltering existence on the outer crust of the earth' (Klee 1961: 5). Yet Klee's perspective was anything but a global one. His concern was rather to show how tenuous and superficial is the conceit that we could ever arrest the movement of the world or subordinate it to our own purposes.

3 I return to this conception of the earth's surface in the next chapter, where I show that it depends upon the specialised mode of apprehension of the cartographer or navigator (Chapter Thirteen, pp. 240–1).

4 Cooper distinguishes these two senses of environment by using capital letters for the former and lower case letters for the latter. Thus 'The Environment' is the object of modern scientific and geopolitical discourse, whereas 'the environment' comprises my familiar surroundings. The first is something that every living creature is *in*, the second is something that every creature *has* (1992: 167–9).

Chapter Thirteen   Maps, wayfinding and navigation

1 In the literature, it is more usual to bring traditional Micronesian seafaring skills under the general rubric of 'navigation'. I wish to avoid this, for reasons that will become clear later. In brief, I shall show that unlike their modern Western counterparts, Micronesian mariners were engaged in wayfinding as *opposed* to navigation.

2 Pandya suggests that people in Western societies generally proceed in the reverse order, first marking places at their respective locations, and then drawing in the connecting lines (Pandya 1990: 784). As I shall show, this contrast is probably exaggerated. Asked to draw an informal sketch map, for example to indicate the route to a friend's house, the Westerner may well proceed in the same order as the Ongee, starting with movements, despite his or her familiarity with the cartographic princi-ples embodied in the modern, topographic map.

3 André Leroi-Gourhan (1993: 190) brings the production of traces of this kind under the general rubric of *graphism*. As he shows, graphism is deeply embedded within contexts of oral narrative, and may be as old as the accompaniment of speech by gesture – long antedating the advent of writing proper.

4 This has been taken one step further, as Thomas Widlok notes, with the development of the so-called 'Global Positioning System' (GPS), a satellite-supported device that enables the user to obtain, at any moment, a precise locational fix according to a universal set of coordinates. 'Both a map and a GPS depend on a history of human-environment interactions (observations, measurements, triangulations) from which the experiential aspects of the humans involved have been systematically eliminated to leave nothing but formalized, de-personalized procedures' (Widlok 1997: 326).

5 It is probably for this reason, as Benjamin Orlove (1993: 29–30) points out, that historians of cartography have focused on how people draw maps, almost to the exclusion of any concern with how people draw *on* maps. This bias has weighty political implications. Precisely because the topographic map renders invisible the movements, or ways of life, of the native inhabitants of a country, it can be a potent instrument of colonial expropriation.

6 This is not to deny that in their use of instruments, European navigators may rely just as much on *ad hoc* improvisation, based on current perception and past experience, as do Micronesian mariners in their handling of the boat itself (Suchman 1987: viii-ix).

7 I return to this issue of the status of material surfaces in Chapter Eighteen (pp. 339–41), in relation to the making of artefacts.

Chapter Fourteen   Stop, look and listen

1 For an excellent discussion of this point, see Rée (1999: 42–5). He concludes that it is precisely in its inhabiting a world of ephemeral sounds rather than solid objects that hearing parts company from seeing: 'you do not hear things in the sound as you see them in the light' (p.43).

2 The same appears to be true of the apprehension of birds among the Kaluli of Papua New Guinea, who inhabit a densely forested environment. During his fieldwork among the Kaluli, Steven Feld found that their avian taxonomy was, first and foremost, a classification of sounds rather than living things. To Feld's persistent inquiries, his Kaluli companion, Jubi, retorted: 'Listen – to you they are birds, to me they are voices in the forest'. Reflecting on this comment, Feld observes that 'birds are "voices" because Kaluli recognise and acknowledge their existence primarily through sound' (Feld 1982: 45).

3 One of the leading advocates of this view of visual perception has been Richard Gregory. 'There seems to be no sudden break', Gregory writes, 'between *perceiving* an object and *guessing* an object. If all perceiving of objects requires some guessing, we may think of sensory stimulation as providing *data* for *hypotheses* concerning the state of the external world. The selected hypotheses, following this view, are perceptions' (1973: 61–3). And by the same token, '*illusions are failed hypotheses*' (p. 74, original emphases).

4 Heidegger, in particular, strove to regain this sense of belonging by replaying dominant visual metaphors in aural terms, and frequently invoked the kinship, in the German language, between *Hören*, *Horchen* and *Gehören* – hearing, harkening and belonging (Caputo 1985: 255).

5 In his essay on 'the notion of person, the notion of "self"', Marcel Mauss discusses the etymology of the Latin *persona*, and suggests that it may have been of Etruscan origin, perhaps originally borrowed from Greek. The idea of its derivation from *personare*, he thinks, was a retrospective invention (Mauss 1979: 78–9).

6 An intriguing variation on the same idea comes from the Japanese philosopher Yanagida Kunio (1875–1962), the acknowledged founder of Japanese folklore studies. According to Kunio, 'both speech and writing exist as means for expressing one's thoughts, but, at present, writing is not so close to thought as speech is. If speech is able to express eight thoughts out of ten, writing is only able to express six' (cited in Ivy 1995: 7).

7 The inspiration for this move comes from the philosophy of Merleau-Ponty, especially his essay 'Eye and mind' (Merleau-Ponty 1964a, see Stoller 1989: 37–40). I discuss Merleau-Ponty's ideas at much greater length later on in this chapter.

8 For helpful reviews of this philosophical lineage, see Jay (1993a: 21–82) and Synnott (1993: 128–55).

9 Descartes does qualify the analogy in one respect. You cannot direct light rays towards objects in the environment exactly as the blind man can direct his stick. This is possible, Descartes thought,

only for creatures such as cats, which can see in the dark by illuminating objects with rays shining from their own eyes (1988: 59). The idea that cats' eyes are like twin torches in the head was all that was left, by Descartes' day, of the once widely accepted notion – originally propounded by Euclid in his *Optica* (c. 300 BC) – that in all vision, rays of light are emitted from the eyes rather than reflected into them (Hagen 1986: 300–4).

10 Rorty is therefore wrong to claim that 'in the Cartesian model, the intellect *inspects* entities modeled on retinal images' (Rorty, 1980: 45). Descartes was very explicit that the job of the intellect was not to inspect but to construct, that this construction did not depend on any resemblance between the data on which it operates and the retinal image, and that any representations in the mind are products, not precursors, of its constructive activity. On this point, see Houlgate (1993: 102).

11 As Judovitz points out, 'Descartes's paradoxical reappropriation of vision by reason . . . corresponds to an act of denunciation of its phenomenal and experiential character' (1993: 78).

12 The following definition of intuition, from Descartes' 'Rules for the direction of our native intelligence' of 1628, may serve as an example of this usage: 'intuition is the indubitable conception of a clear and attentive mind which proceeds solely from the light of reason' (1988: 3).

13 Gibson has a particular problem with the sun and moon, along with other celestial bodies. For as he elsewhere concedes, the information that would specify their form and composition is just not available to the technologically unaided, terrestrial observer, who cannot move around them. As objects, therefore, they are not visible to the eye (1979: 259). Nor can sunlight or moonlight be seen 'as such'. How, then, can the sun or moon be seen at all?

14 On this point, Gibson chooses to take issue with Ronchi, whose views I have reviewed above. While he agrees with Ronchi that optics, as a science of vision, must be anchored on the eye, he holds that light depends on the presence of the eye not for its existence, but for its *relevance*. Its existence is a physical datum, its relevance is an ecological one (Gibson 1966: 222).

15 According to Cohen and Stewart (1994: 154–6), the illusion of vision is precisely that of supposing that you are 'looking out of your head through a window', or 'out of holes in your head where your eyes should be'. The brain, they say, has to work very hard to create this illusion. But it is certainly not an illusion that I have ever experienced, nor has anyone else to my knowledge.

16 Thus as Jay points out, Merleau-Ponty did not accept, as an ontological *a priori*, the radical cleavage between the 'real light' (*lumen*) of the physicists and the 'phenomenal light' (*lux*) of naive consciousness. For in his view, physical science 'grew out of natural perception, rather than being its antithesis or corrective' (Jay 1993b: 163).

17 Another way of putting this is to say that we should rediscover the seer that is in all of us, and that lies concealed behind our assumed role as spectators. The seer's way of seeing, as David Levin writes, 'is more primordial than our everyday way: its ecstatic openness, . . . though not understood, and not consciously practised, by more "ordinary" mortals, in fact underlies *all* human perception' (1988: 462).

18 Paul Klee, to whose art Merleau-Ponty makes frequent reference, encapsulated these points in his 'Creative Credo' of 1920. 'Art does not reproduce the visible but makes visible . . . The pictorial work springs from movement, it is itself fixated movement, and it is grasped in movement (eye muscles)' (Klee 1961: 76, 78).

19 Oliver Sacks documents a modern-day example of this phenomenon. It concerns a patient, Virgil, who after being blind for forty-five years, underwent an operation to restore his sight. Some time after the operation, he told Sacks that at the first moment, when his bandages were removed, 'he had no idea what he was seeing. There was light, there was movement, there was color, all mixed up, all meaningless, a blur'. Commenting on this, Sacks notes that 'when we open our eyes each morning, it is upon a world we have spent a lifetime *learning* to see. We are not given the world: we make it through incessant experience, categorization, memory, reconnection. But when Virgil opened his eyes . . . there was no world of experience and meaning awaiting him. He saw, but what he saw had no coherence' (Sacks 1993: 61).

20 Levin makes a similar point, in somewhat more elaborate terms: 'the seer is seen and sees himself as seen, seen through what he sees. The seer can feel his seeing as it is felt, or received, by the other, the one who sees' (1988: 333).

21 Juhani Pallasmaa elaborates on this point with regard to the acoustic properties of architecture:

> One can . . . recall the acoustic harshness of an uninhabited and unfurnished house as compared to the affability of a lived-in home, in which sound is refracted and softened by the numerous surfaces of the objects of personal life. Every building or space has its characteristic sound of

intimacy or monumentality, invitation or rejection, hospitality or hostility. A space is conceived and appreciated through its echo as much as through its visual shape, but the acoustic percept usually remains an unconscious background experience.

(Pallasmaa 1996: 35)

22 As an example of this prejudice, Armstrong, Stokoe and Wilcox cite an influential textbook in linguistics by John Lyons, in which it is claimed that 'sign language', 'body language' or 'the language of bees' would be considered by most people as a metaphorical use of the word 'language' (Lyons 1981: 2, see Armstrong, Stokoe and Wilcox 1995: 65). Brenda Farnell (1995: 31–8) has shown how the denigration of gesture, its association with humanity in its primitive or animal state, is a concomitant of the very same evolutionary bias that has led generations of Western scholars to take writing as the measure of civilisation. The resulting exclusion of sign languages from linguistics, as she points out, has severely impeded the proper recognition of the signed languages of the deaf, and research into their structure.

23 'Par exemple, dans une forêt, j'ai senti à plusieurs reprises que ce n'était pas moi qui regardais la forêt. J'ai senti, certains jours, que c'étaient les arbres qui me regardaient, qui me parlaient. Moi, j'étais là . . . écoutant' (Charbonnier 1959: 143). This passage is cited by Merleau-Ponty in his 'Eye and mind', but is introduced with the words: 'As André Marchand says, after Klee . . .' (Merleau-Ponty 1964a: 167). Presumably, Merleau-Ponty meant that Marchand's words echoed the sentiments that Klee had often expressed, though in other terms. However the passage from Charbonnier's interview with Marchand is reproduced once again in Paul Stoller's essay, 'Eye, mind and world in anthropology' (Stoller 1989: 38), where it is attributed directly to Klee (cited by Marchand, in Charbonnier, cited by Merleau-Ponty)!

24 This point is established, with specific reference to Yup'ik and Inuit masks, in Chapter Seven (pp. 123–4).

25 For example it is well established, according to Sacks, 'that in blind people who read Braille the reading finger has an exceptionally large representation in the tactile parts of the cerebral cortex' (1993: 70). In a representation of the sensory homunculus, therefore, this finger would appear grossly enlarged.

26 The idea that it is possible to enumerate the senses has been cogently criticised by Seremetakis. 'Enumerated sensory capacities and the corresponding segmentation of material experience into specialized semantic domains', she writes, 'may freeze the actual fluidity of sensory crossing and mutual metaphorization of one sense by another . . . Enumeration thus imposes an objectifying grid that distorts or effaces the manner in which a culture senses the senses'. Moreover, the notion that in any specific culture, a certain balance or ratio may be struck between the senses implies that each may be reduced to a common denominator which is itself 'natural' or 'pre-cultural' (Seremetakis 1994: 126).

27 Levin spells out this view in a passage of incomparable verbosity. 'In fact', he writes, 'the field of visibility yields itself much more readily than do all the other fields of sense to the kind of structuring process which wilfully *re-presents* whatever presents itself, so that every presence manifesting in the field of vision is essentially reduced to the ontology of a mere thing' (Levin 1988: 65).

CHAPTER SIXTEEN   SOCIETY, NATURE AND TECHNOLOGY

1 Leslie White (1959: 18–28) offers a classic statement of this position; see also Harris (1968: 232).
2 This idea of technical classification seems, in many ways, to anticipate the notion of the 'constellation of knowledge' subsequently developed, *inter alia*, by Wynn (1993: 396–403) and Keller and Keller (1996: 89–107). The constellation is an idiosyncratic collection of various bits and pieces of knowledge – aesthetic, stylistic, functional, procedural, financial – peculiar to each individual artisan (rather than shared) and assembled specifically for the task at hand (rather than forming part of an enduring tradition).

CHAPTER EIGHTEEN   ON WEAVING A BASKET

1 To adopt an architectural term, the coherence of the basket is based upon the principle of *tensegrity*, according to which a system can stabilise itself mechanically by distributing and balancing

counteracting forces of compression and tension throughout the structure. Significantly, tensegrity structures are common to both artefacts and living organisms, and are encountered in the latter at every level from the cytoskeletal architecture of the cell to the bones, muscles, tendons and ligaments of the whole body (Ingber 1998).

2 This prioritisation of design over execution betrays a ranking of intellectual over physical labour that, as we saw in Chapter Sixteen, is one of the hallmarks of Western modernity. It divides the scientist from the technician, the engineer from the operative, the architect from the builder, and the author from the secretary.

3 In a wonderful article on the building of the great cathedral of Chartres, in the thirteenth century, David Turnbull (1993b) shows that this most magnificent of human artefacts was preceded by no plan whatsoever. The building took shape gradually, over a considerable period of time, through the labour of many groups of workers with diverse skills, whose activities were loosely co-ordinated by the use of templates, string and constructive geometry.

4 I do not intend by this to reinstate the time-worn opposition between practical utility and symbolic meaning. The notion of utility implied by this opposition is an impoverished one that sets up a radical division between the acting subject and the object used, and reduces skilled practice to purely mechanical relations of cause and effect. In speaking of the *absorption* of artefacts into the life-activity of their users my aim is to emphasise, to the contrary, the inseparability of persons and objects in real-life contexts of accustomed (that is, usual) practice. The usefulness of an object, then, lies not in its possession of utility but in its partaking of the *habituality* of everyday life (Gosden 1994: 11).

5 Among the Bunu, a Yoruba-speaking people of central Nigeria, this idea is expressed in their weaving of lengths of white cloth:

> Cloths are often removed [from the loom] without cutting, accentuating the endless quality of these pieces. When eventually the unwoven warp is cut in order to use the cloth, the fringes are left, again suggesting continuity rather than the finiteness of cut and hemmed edges.
>
> (Renne 1991: 715)

CHAPTER NINETEEN   OF STRING BAGS AND BIRDS' NESTS

1 This shift in the meaning of technology, from a systematic mode of inquiry to the generative logic of practice, remained more or less confined to the Anglophone world. In France, technology continues to this day to mean 'the study of techniques'. For this reason, the word technique has retained its connotation of skilled craftsmanship. And French scholars have taken the lead in developing an anthropological approach to craft skills (Sigaut 1985).

CHAPTER TWENTY   THE DYNAMICS OF TECHNICAL CHANGE

1 Marx is referring, in this passage, to the principle thesis of Giambattista Vico, in his *New Science* of 1725. Vico had berated philosophers for having wasted so much effort in studying the world of nature which, having been made by God, ultimately lies beyond human comprehension, at the expense of the study of things which owe their origination to the human mind and which philosophers – being human too – could hope to understand.

2 For a review of the contributions of Butler and Pitt-Rivers, see Basalla (1988: 15–21). On evolutionary archaeology, which is but one of several recent approaches that have sought to apply Darwinian principles in the explanation of technical change, see O'Brien (1996). For a critique, see Boone and Smith (1998).

3 This general conclusion even applies to the 'invention' of the alphabet, often described as the most perfect system ever devised for representing the sounds of speech, and as the goal towards which the evolution of writing has naturally progressed. David Olson, however, has shown that the development of the alphabet was a contingent consequence of attempts to put a script adapted for use in one language – namely Semitic, in which vocalic differences were relatively insignificant – to use in another – namely Greek, where they were highly significant (Olson 1994: 84).

CHAPTER TWENTY-ONE 'PEOPLE LIKE US'

1 From her studies of skeletal remains from the Neolithic village of Abu Hureyra, in what is now northern Syria, Theya Molleson was able to deduce that the village's female inhabitants had spent long hours kneeling on the ground while grinding grain on a saddle quern. Patterns of wear on the big toes and knees, and bulges in the bones of the upper arm and forearm at the points of attachment of what would have been strongly developed muscles, are entirely consistent with this interpretation. It is tempting to regard these marks of activity upon the skeleton as deformities or abnormalities (Molleson 1994: 62–3). Yet the bones of the skeleton can grow and take shape only within a body that is active in the world; hence one can define the 'normal' skeleton only in relation to 'normal' activities. Why should the notched kneecap that comes from prolonged squatting be regarded as abnormal when, for the great majority of the human population, this is the usual position of rest? It is only perceived by us as an abnormality since, having been brought up in a society in which it is usual to sit on chairs, we find having to squat for any length of time acutely stressful. There can, then, be no such thing as the standard form of the human skeleton.

2 I develop this argument further in the following chapter (pp. 397–8).

3 The story of this confusion, which – if anything – is still more prevalent today than in those heady days when the structure of DNA was first unravelled, is superbly documented by Lily Kay (1998), and I have drawn on her account here.

4 One of the most bizarre examples of this kind of thinking comes from a recent book, widely hailed as a masterpiece in evolutionary psychological circles, by Donald E. Brown. Entitled *Human universals*, the book offers a comprehensive description of what Brown calls 'Universal People' (UP). The UP are characterised by a compendium of traits that 'all people, all societies, all cultures, and all languages have in common' (Brown 1991: 130). These traits are said to add up to what is popularly known as human nature, whose evolution is confidently attributed to natural selection, and whose ultimate foundation lies in the genes. Since no human population has ever existed that remotely resembles the UP, it is difficult to see how they could have evolved. In fact what Brown presents, in the guise of a suite of universal characteristics, is a thinly veiled version of the Western model of the person.

CHAPTER TWENTY-TWO SPEECH, WRITING AND 'LANGUAGE ORIGINS'

1 This is the kind of circularity that Jacques Derrida is getting at when he asks what a science of writing would be like, given that the very ideas of science and scientific objectivity depend on writing. 'The science of writing should . . . look for its object at the roots of scientificity. The history of writing should turn back toward the origin of historicity'. But can there be a 'science of the possibility of science', or a 'history of the possibility of history'? (Derrida 1974: 27).

2 This conclusion was anticipated by V. N. Vološinov in his remarkable study *Marxism and the philosophy of language*, first published in Russian in 1929. Language, Vološinov argued, is not tossed like a ball from generation to generation, but moves together with, and is indeed inseparable from, the actual current of speech:

> Language cannot properly be said to be handed down – it endures, but it endures as a continuous process of becoming. Individuals do not receive a ready-made language at all, rather, they enter upon the stream of verbal communication; indeed, only in this stream does their consciousness first begin to operate. . . . People do not 'accept' their native language – it is in their native language that they first reach awareness.
>
> (Vološinov 1973: 81)

3 Intriguingly, in the languages of the Gonja and LoDagaa, both non-literate societies of northern Ghana, there is no word for 'word' (Goody 1977: 115).

CHAPTER TWENTY-THREE THE POETICS OF TOOL USE

1 Whether the people of any known society have ever been 'modern', in the strict sense, is rather doubtful (Latour 1993). We may therefore have to admit that 'modern society' is a fiction of the same order as the economists' 'economic man' or the 'rational individual' of political science.

2   One issue arising from this concerns the nature of the difference between writing and musical nota-tion. It seems reasonable to suppose that this difference reflects the way in which the distinction is conventionally drawn between speech and song. Thus musical notation leads us to a realm of sound, writing to the words behind the sound. But if speech and song are fundamentally indistinguish-able, then the same must be true of writing and notation. While a discussion of this issue is beyond the scope of the present chapter, it does have important implications as regards the history of writing. For if the distinction between writing and musical notation, like that between speech and song, has arisen in the course of history, we cannot assume that it has been there from the start. Any history of writing, therefore, must be a history of notation as well.

3   I take this idea from the linguistic philosophy of Maurice Merleau-Ponty. 'Strictly speaking', Merleau-Ponty writes, 'there are no conventional signs, . . . there are only words into which the history of a whole language has been compressed, and which effect communication with no absolute guar-antee, dogged as they are by incredible linguistic hazards' (1962: 188). We find in the writings of Emile Durkheim an apparent precedent for this appreciation of the way word meanings are freighted with the sedimentations of the past. In their making, Durkheim argued, 'a multitude of minds have associated, united and combined their ideas and sentiments; for them, long generations have accu-mulated their experience and their knowledge' (1976[1915]: 16). Yet despite the superficial similarity, these thinkers were poles apart in their conclusions. What for Merleau-Ponty is hazardous and uncertain had, for Durkheim, all the certainty of pre-established and unquestioned tradition. The history that Merleau-Ponty identifies with the ongoing current of speech itself was reified, in Durkheim's conception, as an object – an already completed past – that weighs down upon the individual in the name of society.

4   See Bourdieu (1977: 94) and Ingold (1986b: 94) for closely comparable arguments regarding the anthropological derivation of 'culture' from observations of practice, and Chapter Twenty-one (pp. 382–3) for the parallel derivation, in biology, of the genotype.

5   Edmund Carpenter makes a similar point in a study of the relation between speaking, thinking and carving among the Aivilik Eskimo (Inuit) of Southampton Island. There is, in Eskimo speech, no separation of prose and poetry: 'all Eskimo speech has a musical quality and for heightened emotional expressions the speaker moves easily into song' (Carpenter 1966: 212).

6   The terms are Heidegger's; for an excellent discussion of how he uses them, see Dreyfus (1991: Ch. 4); see also Chapter Nine (pp. 168–9).

References

Abramson, A. 1992. Comment on Nurit Bird-David, 'Beyond "The Original Affluent Society"'. *Current Anthropology* 33(1): 34–5.

Adam, B. 1998. *Timescapes of modernity: the environment and invisible hazards.* London: Routledge.

Adams, F. D. 1938. *The birth and death of the geological sciences.* London: Billière, Tindall and Cox.

Adams, R. McC. 1996. *Paths of fire: an anthropologist's inquiry into Western technology.* Princeton, N.J.: Princeton University Press.

Adorno, T. 1981. *In search of Wagner,* trans. R. Livingstone. London: New Left Books.

Alexander, C. 1964. *Notes on the synthesis of form.* Cambridge, Mass.: Harvard University Press.

Alpers, S. 1983. *The art of describing: Dutch art in the seventeenth century.* London: Penguin.

Anderson, D. 2000. *Identity and ecology in Arctic Siberia.* Oxford: Oxford University Press.

Aristotle 1938. *De Interpretatione,* trans. H. P. Cook. London: Loeb Classical Library.

Armstrong, D. F., W. C. Stokoe and S. E. Wilcox 1995. *Gesture and the nature of language.* Cambridge: Cambridge University Press.

Atran, S. 1990. *Cognitive foundations of natural history: towards an anthropology of science.* Cambridge: Cambridge University Press.

Austin, J. L. 1962. *How to do things with words.* Cambridge, Mass.: Harvard University Press.

Bachelard, G. 1964. *The poetics of space.* Boston: Beacon Press.

Bacon, F. 1965. *Francis Bacon: a selection of his works,* ed. S. Warhaft. Toronto: Macmillan.

Bakhtin, M. M. 1981. *The dialogic imagination: four essays,* trans. C. Emerson and M. Holquist, ed. M. Holquist. Austin: University of Texas Press.

Barkow, J. H., L. Cosmides and J. Tooby (eds) 1992. *The adapted mind: evolutionary psychology and the generation of culture.* New York: Oxford University Press.

Barnard, A. 1989. The lost world of Laurens van der Post? *Current Anthropology* 30: 104–14.

Barnes, J. A. 1967. Genealogies. In *The craft of social anthropology,* ed. A. L. Epstein. London: Tavistock.

Basalla, G. 1988. *The evolution of technology.* Cambridge: Cambridge University Press.

Basso, K. 1984. 'Stalking with stories': names, places, and moral narratives among the Western Apache. In *Text, play and story: the construction and reconstruction of self and society,* ed. E. M. Bruner. Washington, D.C.: American Ethnological Society, pp. 19–55.

Bateson, G. 1958. *Naven: a survey of the problems suggested by a composite picture of the culture of a New Guinea tribe drawn from three points of view* (second edition). Stanford, Calif.: Stanford University Press (original edition, 1936).

—— 1973. *Steps to an ecology of mind.* London: Fontana.

—— 1980. *Mind and nature: a necessary unity.* London: Fontana/Collins.

Battaglia, D. 1990. *On the bones of the serpent: person, memory, and mortality in Sabarl Island society.* Chicago: University of Chicago Press.

Belyea, B. 1996. Inland journeys, native maps. *Cartographica* 33: 1–16.

Benveniste, E. 1969. *Le vocabulaire de institutions indo-européennes,* Vol. 1. Paris: Editions de Minuit.

Berger, J. 1972. *Ways of seeing.* London: BBC and Penguin Books.

Bergson, H. 1911. *Creative evolution,* trans. A. Mitchell. London: Macmillan.

Berkhofer, R. F. Jr. 1979. *The White Man's Indian: images of the American Indian from Columbus to the present.* New York: Vintage.

Bernstein, N. A. 1996. On dexterity and its development. In *Dexterity and its development,* eds M. Latash and M. T. Turvey. Mahwah, N.J.: Lawrence Erlbaum Associates, pp. 3–244.

Béteille, A. 1998. The idea of indigenous people. *Current Anthropology* 39: 187–91.

Bettinger, R. L. 1991. *Hunter-gatherers: archaeological and evolutionary theory.* New York: Plenum Press.

Binford, L. R. 1983. *Working at archaeology.* London: Academic Press.

Bird-David, N. 1990. The giving environment: another perspective on the economic system of gatherer-hunters. *Current Anthropology* 31: 189–96.

—— 1992a. Beyond 'The Original Affluent Society': a culturalist reformulation. *Current Anthropology* 33: 25–47.

—— 1992b Beyond 'the hunting and gathering mode of subsistence': culture-sensitive observations on the Nayaka and other modern hunter-gatherers. *Man* (N.S.) 27: 19–44.

—— 1994. Sociality and immediacy: or, past and present conversations on bands. *Man* (N.S.) 29: 583–603.

—— 1999. 'Animism' revisited: personhood, environment, and relational epistemology. *Current Anthropology* 40 (Supplement): S67–S91.

Bjerkli, B. 1996. Land use, traditionalism and rights. *Acta Borealia* 1: 3–21.

Black, M. B. 1977a. Ojibwa taxonomy and percept ambiguity. *Ethos* 5: 90–118.

—— 1977b. Ojibwa power belief system. In *The anthropology of power: ethnographic studies from Asia, Oceania, and the New World*, eds R. D. Fogelson and R. N. Adams. New York: Academic Press, pp. 141–51.

Blier, S. P. 1987. *The anatomy of architecture.* Cambridge: Cambridge University Press.

Bloch, M. 1991. Language, anthropology and cognitive science. *Man* (N.S.) 26: 183–98.

Bloomfield, L. 1933. *Language.* New York: Holt.

Boas, F. 1940. *Race, language and culture.* New York: Macmillan.

—— 1955. *Primitive art.* New York: Dover Publications (original 1927).

Bock, K. 1980. *Human nature and history.* New York: Columbia University Press.

Bohm, D. 1980. *Wholeness and the implicate order.* London: Routledge and Kegan Paul.

Bökönyi, S. 1969. Archaeological problems and methods of recognising animal domestication. In *The domestication and exploitation of plants and animals*, eds P. J. Ucko and G. W. Dimbleby. London: Duckworth, pp. 219–29.

—— 1989. Definitions of animal domestication. In *The walking larder: patterns of domestication, pastoralism and predation*, ed. J. Clutton-Brock. London: Unwin Hyman, pp. 22–7.

Boone, J. L. and E. A. Smith 1998. Is it evolution yet? A critique of evolutionary archaeology. *Current Anthropology* 39 (Supplement): S141–S173.

Botscharow, L. J. 1990. Paleolithic semiotics: behavioral analogs to speech in Acheulean sites. In *The life of symbols*, eds M. L. Foster and L. J. Botscharow. Boulder, Colorado: Westview Press.

Bouquet, M. 1993. *Reclaiming English kinship.* Manchester: Manchester University Press.

—— 1995. Exhibiting knowledge: the trees of Dubois, Haeckel, Jesse and Rivers at the Pithecanthropus centennial exhibition. In *Shifting contexts: transformations in anthropological knowledge*, ed. M. Strathern. London: Routledge, pp. 31–55.

—— 1996. Family trees and their affinities: the visual imperative of the genealogical diagram. *Journal of the Royal Anthropological Institute* (N.S.) 2: 43–66.

Bourdieu, P. 1963. The attitude of the Algerian peasant toward time. In *Mediterranean countrymen*, ed. J. Pitt-Rivers. Paris: Mouton.

—— 1977. *Outline of a theory of practice*, trans. R. Nice. Cambridge: Cambridge University Press.

—— 1990. *The logic of practice.* Oxford: Polity Press.

Bourgeois, A. P. (ed.) 1994. *Ojibwa narratives of Charles and Charlotte Kawbawgam and Jacques LePique, 1893–1895* (recorded with notes by H. H. Kidder). Detroit: Wayne State University Press.

Braidwood, R. J. 1957 *Prehistoric men*, 3rd edition. Chicago Natural History Museum Popular Series, Anthropology, **37**.

Briggs, J. 1970. *Never in anger: portrait of an Eskimo family.* Cambridge, Mass.: Harvard University Press.

Brightman, R. 1993. *Grateful prey: Rock Cree human–animal relationships.* Berkeley: University of California Press.

Brookfield, H. C. 1969. On the environment as perceived. *Progress in Geography* 1: 53–80.

Brown, D. E. 1991. *Human universals.* New York: McGraw Hill.

Bruzina, R. 1982. Art and architecture, ancient and modern. *Research in Philosophy and Technology* 5: 163–87.

Burford, A. 1972. *Craftsmen in Greek and Roman society.* Ithaca: Cornell University Press.

Burns, T. 1964. Technology. In *A dictionary of the social sciences*, eds. J. Gould and W. L. Kolb. London: Tavistock.

Callicott, J. B. 1982. Traditional American Indian and Western European attitudes toward nature: an overview. *Environmental Ethics* 4: 293–318.

Caputo, J. D. 1985. The thought of being and the conversation of mankind: the case of Heidegger and Rorty. In *Hermeneutics and praxis*, ed. R. Hollinger. Notre Dame, Ind.: University of Notre Dame Press.

Cardwell, D. S. L. 1973. Technology. In *A dictionary of the history of ideas*, ed. P. P. Wiener. New York: Scribner's.

Carpenter, E. 1966. Image making in arctic art. In *Sign, image and symbol*, ed. G. Kepes. London: Studio Vista, pp. 206–25.

—— 1973. *Eskimo realities*. New York: Holt, Rinehart and Winston.

Carpenter, E. and M. McLuhan 1960. Acoustic space. In *Explorations in communication: an anthology*, eds E. Carpenter and M. McLuhan. London: Beacon Press, pp. 65–70.

Carrier, J. 1992. Occidentalism: the world turned upside down. *American Ethnologist* 19: 195–212.

Carroll, P. J. 1977. Mimi from Western Arnhem Land. In *Form in indigenous art: schematisation in the art of Aboriginal Australia and prehistoric Europe*, ed. P. J. Ucko. Canberra: Australian Institute of Aboriginal Studies, pp. 119–30.

Carruthers, M. 1990. *The book of memory: a study of memory in medieval culture*. Cambridge: Cambridge University Press.

Casey, E. S. 1996. How to get from space to place in a fairly short stretch of time: phenomenological prolegomena. In *Senses of place*, eds S. Feld and K. H. Basso. Santa Fe, N.Mex.: School of American Research Press.

Certeau, M. de 1984. *The practice of everyday life*. Berkeley, Calif.: University of California Press.

Chapman, D. 1991. *Vision, instruction and action*. Cambridge, Mass.: MIT Press.

Charbonnier, G. 1959. *Le monologue du peintre*. Paris: René Julliard.

Chaussonnet, V. 1988. Needles and animals: women's magic. In *Crossroads of continents: cultures of Siberia and Alaska*, eds W. W. Fitzhugh and A. Crowell. Washington, DC: Smithsonian Institution Press, pp. 209–26.

Childe, V. G. 1942. *What happened in history*. Harmondsworth: Penguin.

Chomsky, N. 1968. *Language and mind*. New York: Harcourt Brace Jovanovich.

Clanchy, M. T. 1979. *From memory to written record: England 1066–1307*. London: Edwin Arnold.

Clark, A. 1997. *Being there: putting brain, body and the world together again*. Cambridge, Mass.: MIT Press.

Clark, J. 1983. *The Aboriginal people of Tasmania*. Hobart: Tasmanian Museum and Art Gallery.

Classen, C. 1993. *Worlds of sense: exploring the senses in history and across cultures*. London: Routledge.

—— 1997. Foundations for an anthropology of the senses. *International Social Science Journal* 153: 401–12.

Clutton-Brock, J. 1994. The unnatural world: behavioural aspects of humans and animals in the process of domestication. In *Animals and human society: changing perspectives*, eds A. Manning and J. Serpell. London: Routledge, pp. 23–35.

Cohen, G. A. 1978. *Karl Marx's theory of history: a defence*. Oxford: Clarendon Press.

Cohen, J. and I. Stewart 1994. *The collapse of chaos: discovering simplicity in a complex world*. Harmondsworth: Viking.

Coleman, R. 1988. *The art of work: an epitaph to skill*. London: Pluto Press.

Collias, N. E. and E. C. Collias 1984. *Nest building and bird behavior*. Princeton, N.J.: Princeton University Press.

Collins, S. 1985. Categories, concepts or predicaments? Remarks on Mauss's use of philosophical terminology. In *The category of the person: anthropology, philosophy, history*, eds M. Carruthers, S. Collins and S. Lukes, pp. 46–82. Cambridge: Cambridge University Press.

Connerton, P. 1989. *How societies remember*. Cambridge: Cambridge University Press.

Cooper, D. E. 1992. The idea of environment. In *The environment in question: ethics and global issues*, eds D. E. Cooper and J. A. Palmer. London: Routledge, pp. 165–80.

Cosgrove, D. 1989. Geography is everywhere: culture and symbolism in human landscapes. In *Horizons in human geography*, eds D. Gregory and R. Walford. Basingstoke: Macmillan, pp. 118–35.

Cotterell, B. and J. Kamminga 1990. *Mechanisms of pre-industrial technology: an introduction to the mechanics of ancient and traditional material culture*. Cambridge: Cambridge University Press.

Cottrell, W. F. 1939. Of time and the railroader. *American Sociological Review* 4: 190–8.

Coulmas, F. 1989. *The writing systems of the world*. Oxford: Blackwell.

Crawford, I. M. The relationship of Bradshaw and Wandjina art in north-west Kimberley. In *Form in indigenous art: schematisation in the art of Aboriginal Australia and prehistoric Europe*, ed. P. J. Ucko. Canberra: Australian Institute of Aboriginal Studies.

Cribb, R. 1991. *Nomads in archaeology*. Cambridge: Cambridge University Press.

Crocker, A. (ed.) 1983. *Papunya: Aboriginal paintings from the Central Australian Desert*. Alice Springs: Aboriginal Artists Agency Ltd and Papunya Tula Artists Pty Ltd.

Csordas, T. 1990. Embodiment as a paradigm for anthropology. *Ethos* 18: 5–47.

Daes, E.-I. 1997. *Protection of the heritage of indigenous people* (Human Rights Study Series 10). New York and Geneva: United Nations.

D'Andrade, R. G. 1981. The cultural part of cognition. *Cognitive Science* 5: 179–95.

—— 1984. Cultural meaning systems. In *Culture theory: essays on mind, self and emotion*, eds R. A. Shweder and R. A. LeVine. Cambridge: Cambridge University Press, pp. 88–119.

—— 1990. Some propositions about the relations between culture and human cognition. In *Cultural psychology: essays on comparative human development*, eds J. W. Stigler, R. A. Shweder and G. Herdt. Cambridge: Cambridge University Press, pp. 65–129.

—— 1992. Schemas and motivation. In *Human motives and cultural models*, eds R. G. D'Andrade and C. Strauss. Cambridge: Cambridge University Press, pp. 23–44.

—— 1995. *The development of cognitive anthropology*. Cambridge: Cambridge University Press.

Daniels, S. and D. Cosgrove 1988. Introduction: iconography and landscape. In *The iconography of landscape*, eds D. Cosgrove and S. Daniels. Cambridge: Cambridge University Press, pp. 1–10.

Darwin, C. 1860. *Journal of researches during the voyage of HMS 'Beagle'*, 2nd edition. London: Collins.

—— 1862. *On the various contrivances by which British and foreign orchids are fertilised by insects*. London: John Murray.

—— 1871. *The descent of man, and selection in relation to sex*. London: John Murray.

—— 1875. *The variation of animals and plants under domestication*, 2nd edition. London: John Murray.

Davies, D. 1988. The evocative symbolism of trees. In *The iconography of landscape*, eds D. Cosgrove and S. Daniels. Cambridge: Cambridge University Press, pp. 32–42.

Dawkins, R. 1982. *The extended phenotype*. San Francisco: Freeman.

De Casper, A. and M. Spence 1986. Prenatal maternal speech influences newborns' perception of speech sounds. *Infant Behavior and Development* 9: 13–50.

DeFrancis, J. 1989. *Visible speech: the diverse oneness of writing systems*. Honolulu: University of Hawaii Press.

Deleuze, G. and F. Guattari 1988. *A thousand plateaus: capitalism and schizophrenia* (trans. B. Massumi). London: Athlone Press.

Dent, C. H. 1990. An ecological approach to language development: an alternative functionalism. *Developmental Psychobiology* 23: 679–703.

Dentan, R. K. 1968. *The Semai: a nonviolent people of Malaya*. New York: Holt, Rinehart and Winston.

Derrida, J. 1974. *Of grammatology*, trans. G. C. Spivak. Baltimore, Md: Johns Hopkins University Press.

Descartes, R. 1988. *Descartes: selected philosophical writings*, trans. J. Cottingham, R. Stoothoff and D. Murdoch. Cambridge: Cambridge University Press.

Descola, P. 1992. Societies of nature and the nature of society. In *Conceptualizing society*, ed. A. Kuper. London: Routledge, pp. 107–26.

—— 1994. *In the society of nature: a native ecology in Amazonia*, trans. N. Scott. Cambridge: Cambridge University Press.

—— 1996a. Constructing natures: symbolic ecology and social practice. In *Nature and society: anthropological perspectives*, eds P. Descola and G. Pálsson. London: Routledge, pp. 82–102.

—— 1996b. *The spears of twilight: life and death in the Amazon jungle*, trans. J. Lloyd. London: Harper Collins.

Douglas, M. 1966. *Purity and danger*. London: Routledge and Kegan Paul.

—— 1970. *Natural symbols: explorations in cosmology*. Harmondsworth: Penguin.

Dreyfus, H. L. 1991. *Being-in-the-world: a commentary on Heidegger's 'Being and Time, Division I'*. Cambridge, Mass.: MIT Press.

Dreyfus, H. L. 1992. Introduction to the MIT Press edition. In *What computers still can't do*. Cambridge, Mass.: MIT Press, pp. ix–lii.

Dreyfus, H. L. and S. E. Dreyfus 1986. *Mind over machine*. New York: Free Press.

—— 1987. The mistaken psychological assumptions underlying the belief in expert systems. In *Cognitive psychology in question*, eds A. Costall and A. Still. Brighton: Harvester Press, pp. 17–31.

Drucker, P. F. 1970. *Technology, management and society*. London: Heinemann.

Ducos, P. 1978. 'Domestication' defined and methodological approaches to its recognition in faunal assemblages. In *Approaches to faunal analysis in the Middle East*, eds R. H. Meadow and M. A. Zeder. Harvard University: Peabody Museum Bulletin 2, pp. 53–6.

—— 1989. Defining domestication: a clarification. In *The walking larder: patterns of domestication, pastoralism and predation*, ed. J Clutton-Brock. London: Unwin Hyman, pp. 28–30.

Dumont, L. 1986. *Essays on individualism: modern ideology in anthropological perspective*. Chicago: University of Chicago Press.

Dunbar, R. 1987. Darwinizing man: a commentary. In *Human reproductive behavior: a Darwinian perspective*, eds L. L. Betzig, M. Borgerhoff Mulder and P. Turke. New York: Cambridge University Press, pp. 161–9.

Durham, W. H. 1991. *Coevolution: genes, culture and human diversity*. Stanford: Stanford University Press.

Durkheim, E. 1976 [1915]. *The elementary forms of the religious life*, trans J. W. Swain, 2nd edn. London: Allen and Unwin.

Durkheim, E. 1982 [1895]. *The rules of sociological method and selected texts on sociology and its method*, ed. S. Lukes, trans. W. D. Halls. London: Macmillan.

Durkheim, E. amd M. Mauss 1963 [1903]. *Primitive classification*. London: Routledge & Kegan Paul.

Edelman, B. 1993. Acting cool and being safe: the definition of skill in a Swedish railway yard. In *Beyond boundaries: understanding, translation and anthropological discourse*, ed. G. Pálsson. Oxford: Berg.

Edney, M. 1993. Cartography without 'progress': reinterpreting the nature and historical development of mapmaking. *Cartographica* 30: 54–68.

Ellen, R. F. 1982. *Environment, subsistence and system: the ecology of small-scale social formations*. Cambridge: Cambridge University Press.

Endicott, K. 1979. *Batek Negrito religion*. Oxford: Clarendon Press.

Engels, F. 1934. *Dialectics of nature*, trans. C. Dutton. Moscow: Progress.

Evans, F. T. 1998. Two legs, thing using and talking: the origins of the creative engineering mind. *Artificial Intelligence and Society* 12: 185–213.

Evans-Pritchard, E. E. 1940. *The Nuer*. Oxford: Oxford University Press.

Ewers, J. C. 1955. *The horse in Blackfoot Indian culture*. Smithsonian Institution Bureau of American Ethnology, Bulletin 159. Washington, D.C.: US Government Printing Office.

Fabian, J. 1983. *Time and the other: how anthropology makes its object*. New York: Columbia University Press.

Farnell, B. 1995. *Do you see what I mean? Plains Indian sign talk and the embodiment of action*. Austin, Tex: University of Texas Press.

Feibleman, J. K. 1966. Technology and skills. *Technology and Culture* 7: 318–28.

Feit, H. 1973. The ethnoecology of the Waswanipi Cree: or how hunters can manage their resources. In *Cultural ecology: readings on the Canadian Indians and Eskimos*, ed. B. Cox. Toronto: McClelland and Stewart, pp. 115–25.

—— 1994. Dreaming of animals: the Waswanipi Cree shaking tent ceremony in relation to environment, hunting and missionisation. In *Circumpolar religion and ecology: an anthropology of the North*, eds T. Irimoto and T. Yamada. Tokyo: University of Tokyo Press, pp. 289–316.

Feld, S. 1982. *Sound and sentiment: birds, weeping, poetics and song in Kaluli expression*. Philadelphia: University of Pennsylvania Press.

—— 1996. Waterfalls of song: an acoustemology of place resounding in Bosavi, Papua New Guinea. In *Senses of place*, eds S. Feld and K. H. Basso. Santa Fe, N.Mex.: School of American Research, pp. 91–135.

Fernandez, J. W. 1998. Trees of knowledge of self and other in culture: on models for the moral imagination. In *The social life of trees: anthropological perspectives on tree symbolism*, ed. L. Rival. Oxford: Berg.

Fienup-Riordan, A. 1987. The mask: the eye of the dance. *Arctic Anthropology* 24: 40–55.

—— 1990. *Eskimo essays: Yup'ik lives and how we see them*. New Brunswick: Rutgers University Press.

—— 1994. *Boundaries and passages: rule and ritual in Yup'ik Eskimo oral tradition*. Norman, Okla.: University of Oklahoma Press.

Firth, R. 1939. *Primitive Polynesian economy*. London: Routledge & Kegan Paul.

—— 1964. Capital, saving and credit in peasant societies: a viewpoint from economic anthropology. In *Capital, savings and credit in peasant societies*, eds R. Firth and B. S. Yamey. London: Allen & Unwin, pp. 15–34.

Fitzhugh, W. W. 1988. Comparative art of the North Pacific rim. In *Crossroads of continents: cultures of Siberia and Alaska*, eds W. W. Fitzhugh and A. Crowell. Washington, D.C.: Smithsonian Institution Press, pp. 294–312.

Flew, A. (ed.) 1964. *Body, mind, and death*. London: Crowell-Collier.

Foley, R. 1985. Optimality theory in anthropology. *Man* (N.S.) 20: 222–42.

—— 1987. *Another unique species: patterns in human evolutionary ecology*. London: Longman.

French, M. J. 1988. *Invention and evolution: design in nature and engineering*. Cambridge: Cambridge University Press.

Friedman, J. 1974. Marxism, structuralism and vulgar materialism. *Man* (N.S.)9: 444–69.

Frisch, K. von 1975. *Animal architecture*. London: Hutchinson.

Gambetta, D. (ed.) 1988. *Trust: making and breaking co-operative relations*. Oxford: Blackwell.

Gamst, F. C. 1980. *The hoghead: an industrial ethnology of the locomotive engineer*. New York: Holt, Rinehart and Winston.

Gatewood, J. B. 1985. Actions speak louder than words. In *Directions in cognitive anthropology*, ed. J. W. Dougherty. Urbana and Chicago: University of Illinois Press, pp. 199–219.

Gebhart-Sayer, A. 1985. The geometric designs of the Shipibo-Conibo in ritual context. *Journal of Latin American Lore* 11: 143–75.

Geertz, C. 1964. The transition to humanity. In *Horizons of anthropology*, ed. S. Tax. Chicago: Aldine.

—— 1973. *The interpretation of cultures*. New York: Basic Books.

—— 1984. 'From the native's point of view': on the nature of anthropological understanding. In *Culture theory: essays on mind, self and emotion*, eds R. A. Shweder and R. A. LeVine. Cambridge: Cambridge University Press, pp. 123–36.

Gell, A. 1979. The Umeda language-poem. *Canberra Anthropology* 2(1): 44–62.

—— 1985. How to read a map: remarks on the practical logic of navigation. *Man* (N.S.)20: 271–86.

—— 1992a. *The anthropology of time: cultural constructions of temporal maps amd images*. Oxford: Berg.

—— 1992b. The technology of enchantment and the enchantment of technology. In *Anthropology, art and aesthetics*, eds J. Coote and A. Shelton. Oxford: Clarendon, pp. 40–63.

—— 1995. The language of the forest: landscape and phonological iconism in Umeda. In *The anthropology of landscape: perspectives on place and space*, eds E. Hirsch and M. O'Hanlon. Oxford: Clarendon, pp. 232–54.

Ghiselin, M. T. 1969. *The triumph of the Darwinian method*. Berkeley: University of California Press.

Gibson, J. J. 1966. *The senses considered as perceptual systems*. Boston: Houghton Mifflin.

—— 1979. *The ecological approach to visual perception*. Boston: Houghton Mifflin.

—— 1982. *Reasons for realism: selected essays of James J. Gibson*, eds E. Reed and R. Jones. Hillsdale, New Jersey: Lawrence Erlbaum.

Gibson, T. 1985. The sharing of substance versus the sharing of activity among the Buid. *Man* (N.S.) 20: 391–411.

Gibson, W. S. 1977. *Bruegel*. London: Thames and Hudson.

Glacken, C. J. 1967. *Traces on the Rhodian shore*. Berkeley: University of California Press.

Gladwin, T. 1964. Culture and logical process. In *Explorations in cultural anthropology*, ed. W. H. Goodenough. New York: McGraw-Hill, pp. 167–77.

Godelier, M. 1972. *Rationality and irrationality in economics*. London: New Left Books.

—— 1980. Aide-mémoire for a survey of work and its representations. *Current Anthropology* 21: 832–5.

—— 1986. *The mental and the material*, trans. M. Thom. London: Verso.

Gooch, P. 1998. *At the tail of the buffalo: Van Gujjar pastoralists between the forest and the world arena*. Lund: Lund Monographs in Social Anthropology 6.

Goodman, N. 1978. *Ways of worldmaking*. Brighton: Harvester Press.

Goodman, P. 1971. *Speaking and language: defence of poetry*. London: Wildwood House.

Goodwin, B. C. 1982. Biology without Darwinian spectacles. *Biologist* 29: 108–12.

—— 1988. Organisms and minds: the dialectics of the animal–human interface in biology. In *What is an animal?*, ed. T. Ingold. London: Unwin Hyman.

Goody, J. 1977. *The domestication of the savage mind*. Cambridge: Cambridge University Press.

Gosden, C. 1994. *Social being and time*. Oxford: Blackwell.

Gould, J. L. and C. G. Gould 1988. *The honey bee*. New York: W. H. Freeman.

Gould, P. and R. White 1974. *Mental maps*. Harmondsworth: Penguin.

Gould, R. A. 1970. Spears and spear-throwers of the Western Desert Aborigines of Australia. *American Museum Novitates* 2403: 1–42.

Gould, S. J. and E. S. Vrba 1982. Exaptation – a missing term in the science of form. *Palaeobiology* 8: 4–15.

Gow, P. 1990. Could Sangama read? The origin of writing among the Piro of Eastern Peru. *History and Anthropology* 5: 87–103.

Gregory, R. 1973. The confounded eye. In *Illusion in nature and art*, eds R. L. Gregory and E. H. Gombrich. New York: Scribners, pp. 49–95.

Griffin, D. R. 1976. *The question of animal awareness*. New York: Rockefeller University Press.

Griffin, D. R. 1984. *Animal thinking*. Cambridge, Mass.: Harvard University Press.

Grinker, R. R. 1992. Comment on Nurit Bird-David, 'Beyond "The Original Affluent Society"'. *Current Anthropology* 33(1): 39.

Gross, C. 1998. *Following traces, creating remains: relatedness and temporality in the upper Awara, Papua New Guinea*. Unpublished doctoral dissertation, University of Manchester.

Groves, C. P. and J. Sabater Pi 1985. From ape's nest to human fix point. *Man* (N.S.) 20: 22–47.

Gudeman, S. 1986. *Economics as culture: models and metaphors of livelihood*. London: Routledge & Kegan Paul.

—— 1992. Comment on Nurit Bird-David, 'Beyond "The Original Affluent Society"'. *Current Anthropology* 33(1): 39–40.

Gudeman, S. and A. Rivera 1990. *Conversations in Colombia: the domestic economy in life and text*. Cambridge: Cambridge University Press.

Guss, D. M. 1989. *To weave and sing: art, symbol and narrative in the South American rain forest*. Berkeley, Calif.: University of California Press.

Guyer, J. 1988. The multiplication of labor: gender and agricultural change in modern Africa. *Current Anthropology* 29: 247–72.

Hagen, M. A. 1986. *Varieties of realism: geometries of representational art*. Cambridge: Cambridge University Press.

Hallowell, A. I. 1942. *The role of conjuring in Saulteaux society*. Philadelphia: University of Pennsylvania Press.

—— 1955. *Culture and experience*. Philadelphia: University of Pennsylvania Press.

—— 1960. Ojibwa ontology, behavior and world view. In *Culture in history: essays in honor of Paul Radin*, ed. S. Diamond. New York: Columbia University Press, pp. 19–52.

—— 1976. The role of dreams in Ojibwa culture (1966). In *Contributions to anthropology: selected papers of A. Irving Hallowell*, eds R. D. Fogelson, F. Eggan, M. E. Spiro, G. W. Stocking, A. F. C. Wallace and W. E. Washburn. Chicago: University of Chicago Press, pp. 449–74.

Hallyn, F. 1993. *The poetic structure of the world: Copernicus and Kepler*, trans. D. M. Leslie. New York: Zone.

Hamilton, A. 1980. Dual social systems: technology, labour and women's secret rites in the eastern Western Desert of Australia. *Oceania* 51: 4–19.

Harley, J. B. 1989. Deconstructing the map. *Cartographica* 26: 1–20.

Harré, R. 1998. *The singular self: an introduction to the psychology of personhood*. London: Sage.

Harris, D. R. (ed.) 1996. *The origins and spread of agriculture and pastoralism*. London: UCL Press.

Harris, M. 1968. *The rise of anthropological theory*. New York: Crowell.

Harris, R. 1980. *The language-makers*. London: Duckworth.

Hastrup, K. 1989. Nature as historical space. *Folk* 31: 5–20.

Hediger, H. 1977. Nest and home. *Folia Primatologica* 28: 170–87.

Heft, H. 1996.The ecological approach to wayfinding: a Gibsonian perspective. In *The construction of cognitive maps*, ed. J. Portugali. Dordrecht: Kluwer Academic, pp. 105–32.

Heidegger, M. 1971. *Poetry, language, thought*, trans A. Hofstadter. New York: Harper and Row.

Heij, P. and J. Tamboer n.d. Embodied intentionality: the significance of Merleau-Ponty's embodied intentionality for the foundations of Gibson's ecological psychology. Paper presented at the Workshop on Situated Action, International Society for Ecological Psychology, Manchester, UK, 23–24 September 1991.

Heilbroner, R. L. 1967. Do machines make history? *Technology and Culture* 8: 335–45.

Hewes, G. W. 1976. The current status of the gestural theory of language origins. In *The origins and evolution of language and speech*, eds S. R. Harnad, H. D. Steklis and J. Lancaster. Annals of the New York Academy of Sciences, Vol. 280, pp. 482–504.

Higgs, E. and H. Jarman 1969. The origins of agriculture: a reconsideration. *Antiquity* 43: 31–41.

Hill, M. H. 1985. Bound to the environment: towards a phenomenology of sightlessness. In *Dwelling, place and environment*, eds D. Seamon and R. Mugerauer. New York: Columbia University Press, pp. 99–111.

Hinde, R. A. 1991. A biologist looks at anthropology. *Man* (N.S.) 25: 583–608.

Ho, M-W. 1989. Reanimating nature: the integration of science with human experience. *Beshara* 8: 16–25.

—— 1991. The role of action in evolution: evolution by process and the ecological approach to perception. *Cultural Dynamics* 4(3): 336–54.

Ho, M-W. and P. T. Saunders (eds) 1984. *Beyond neo-Darwinism: introduction to the new evolutionary paradigm.* London: Academic Press.

Hodges, H. 1964. *Artefacts: an introduction to early materials and technology.* London: John Baker.

Hornborg, A. 1992. Machine fetishism, value, and the image of unlimited good: towards a thermodynamics of imperialism. *Man* (N.S.) 27: 1–16.

Houlgate, S. 1993. Vision, reflection and openness: the 'hegemony of vision' from a Hegelian point of view. In *Modernity and the hegemony of vision,* ed. D. M. Levin. Berkeley, Calif.: University of California Press, pp. 87–123.

Howell, S. 1989. 'To be angry is not to be human, but to be fearful is': Chewong concepts of human nature. In *Societies at peace: anthropological perspectives,* eds. S. Howell and R. Willis. London: Routledge, pp. 45–59.

—— 1996. Nature in culture or culture in nature? Chewong ideas of 'humans' and other species. In *Nature and society: anthropological perspectives,* eds P. Descola and G. Pálsson. London: Routledge.

Howells, W. 1967. *Mankind in the making: the story of human evolution.* Harmondsworth: Penguin.

Howes, D. 1991a. Introduction: 'to summon all the senses'. In *The varieties of sensory experience: a sourcebook in the anthropology of the senses,* ed. D. Howes. Toronto: University of Toronto Press, pp. 3–21.

—— 1991b. Sensorial anthropology. In *The varieties of sensory experience: a sourcebook in the anthropology of the senses,* ed. D. Howes. Toronto: University of Toronto Press, pp. 167–91.

Hull, J. 1997. *On sight and insight: a journey into the world of blindness.* Oxford: Oneworld Publications.

Hultkrantz, Å. 1982. Religion and experience of nature among North American hunting Indians. In *The hunters: their culture and way of life,* eds Å. Hultkrantz and Ø. Vorren (Tromsø Museum Skrifter, Vol. XVIII). Tromsø, Oslo, Bergen: Universitetsforlaget, pp. 163–86.

Humphrey, N. 1976. The social function of intellect. In *Growing points in ethology,* eds P. Bateson and R. A. Hinde. Cambridge: Cambridge University Press, pp. 303–17.

Hutchins, E. 1995. *Cognition in the wild.* Cambridge, Mass.: MIT Press.

Ichikawa, M. 1992. Comment on Nurit Bird-David, 'Beyond "The Original Affluent Society"'. *Current Anthropology* 33(1): 40–41.

Ihde, D. 1976. *Listening and voice: a phenomenology of sound.* Athens, Ohio: Ohio University Press.

Ingber, D. E. 1998. The architecture of life. *Scientific American* 278(1): 30–39.

Inglis, F. 1977. Nation and community: a landscape and its morality. *Sociological Review* 25: 489–514.

Ingold, T. 1980. *Hunters, pastoralists and ranchers: reindeer economies and their transformations.* Cambridge: Cambridge University Press.

—— 1983. The architect and the bee: reflections on the work of animals and men. *Man* (N.S.) 18: 1–20.

—— 1986a. *The appropriation of nature: essays on human ecology and social relations.* Manchester: Manchester University Press.

—— 1986b. *Evolution and social life.* Cambridge: Cambridge University Press.

—— 1988a. Notes on the foraging mode of production. In *Hunters and gatherers I: history, evolution and social change,* eds T. Ingold, D. Riches and J. Woodburn. Oxford: Berg.

—— 1988b. The animal in the study of humanity. In *What is an animal?,* ed. T. Ingold. London: Unwin Hyman.

—— 1988c. Introduction. In *What is an animal?,* ed. T. Ingold. London: Unwin Hyman.

—— 1989. The social and environmental relations of human beings and other animals. In *Comparative socioecology,* eds V. Standen and R. A. Foley. Oxford: Blackwell Scientific.

—— 1990. An anthropologist looks at biology. *Man* (N.S.) 25: 208–29.

—— 1991. Becoming persons: consciousness and sociality in human evolution. *Cultural Dynamics* 4: 355–78.

—— 1992a. Culture and the perception of the environment. In *Bush base: forest farm. Culture, environment and development,* eds E. Croll and D. Parkin. London: Routledge, pp. 39–56.

—— 1992b. Comment on Nurit Bird-David, 'Beyond "The Original Affluent Society"'. *Current Anthropology* 33(1): 41–2.

—— 1992c. Foraging for data, camping with theories: hunter-gatherers and nomadic pastoralists in archaeology and anthropology. *Antiquity* 66: 790–803.

—— 1993a. The art of translation in a continuous world. In *Beyond boundaries: understanding, translation and anthropological discourse,* ed. G. Pálsson. Oxford: Berg, pp. 210–30.

—— 1993b. The reindeerman's lasso. In *Technological choices: transformation in material cultures since the Neolithic,* ed. P Lemmonier. London: Routledge, pp. 108–25.

—— 1996a. Human worlds are culturally constructed: against the motion (I). In *Key debates in anthropology*, ed. T. Ingold. London: Routledge, pp. 112–18.

—— 1996b. Social relations, human ecology and the evolution of culture: an exploration of concepts and definitions. In *Handbook of human symbolic evolution*, eds A. Lock and C. R. Peters. Oxford: Clarendon Press, pp. 178–203.

—— 1997. The painting is not the terrain: maps, pictures and the dwelt-in world (comment on T. Lemaire, 'Archaeology between the invention and the destruction of the landscape'). *Archaeological Dialogues* 4(1): 29–31.

—— 1998. Evolution of society. In *Evolution: society, science and the universe*, ed. A. C. Fabian. Cambridge: Cambridge University Press, pp. 79–99.

—— 1999. On the social relations of the hunter-gatherer band. In *The Cambridge encyclopedia of hunters and gatherers*, eds R. B. Lee and R. Daly. Cambridge: Cambridge University Press, pp. 399–410.

—— n.d. Two reflections on ecological knowledge. Unpublished paper presented at the conference on 'Nature Knowledge', Instituto Veneto di Scienze, Lettere ed Arti, Venice, December 1997.

International Labour Organisation 1989. Indigenous and tribal peoples in independent countries. Convention 169. Geneva: ILO.

Ivy, M. 1995. *Discourses of the vanishing: modernity, phantasm, Japan.* Chicago: University of Chicago Press.

Jackson, M. 1983. Thinking through the body: an essay on understanding metaphor. *Social Analysis* 14: 127–48.

—— 1989. *Paths toward a clearing: radical empiricism and ethnographic inquiry.* Bloomington, Ind.: Indiana University Press.

Jacob, F. 1977. Evolution and tinkering. *Science* 196: 1161–6.

James, W. 1892. *Psychology.* New York: Henry Holt.

Janáček, L. 1989. *Janáček's uncollected essays on music*, trans. and ed. M. Zemanová. London: Marion Boyars.

Jarman, H. N. 1972. The origins of wheat and barley cultivation. In *Papers in economic prehistory*, ed. E. S. Higgs. Cambridge: Cambridge University Press.

Jay, M. 1993a. *Downcast eyes: the denigration of vision in twentieth-century French thought.* Berkeley, CA: University of California Press.

—— 1993b. Sartre, Merleau-Ponty, and the search for a new ontology of sight. In *Modernity and the hegemony of vision*, ed. D. M. Levin. Berkeley, Calif.: University of California Press, pp. 143–85.

Jenks, C. 1995. The centrality of the eye in Western culture: an introduction. In *Visual culture*, ed. C. Jenks. London: Routledge, pp. 1–25.

Johnson-Laird, D. N. 1988. *The computer and the mind: an introduction to cognitive science.* London: Fontana.

Jonas, H. 1966. *The phenomenon of life.* Chicago: University of Chicago Press.

Jones, R. 1977. The Tasmanian paradox. In *Stone tools as cultural markers*, ed. R. V. S. Wright. Canberra: Australian Institute of Aboriginal Studies, pp. 189–204.

Judovitz, D. 1993. Vision, representation, and the technology of Descartes. In *Modernity and the hegemony of vision*, ed. D. M. Levin. Berkeley, Calif.: University of California Press, pp. 63–86.

Kandel, E. R. and R. D. Hawkins 1992. The biological basis of learning and individuality. *Scientific American* 267: 53–60.

Kant, I. 1933. *Immanuel Kant's critique of pure reason*, trans. N. K. Smith. London: Macmillan.

Kaplan, H. and K. Hill 1992. The evolutionary ecology of food acquisition. In *Evolutionary ecology and human behavior*, eds E. A. Smith and B. Winterhalder. New York: Aldine de Gruyter, pp. 167–201.

Kay, L. E. 1998. A book of life? How the genome became an information system and DNA a language. *Perspectives in Biology and Medicine* 41: 504–28.

Keller, C. M. and J. D. Keller 1996. *Cognition and tool use: the blacksmith at work.* Cambridge: Cambridge University Press.

Kemnitzer, L. S. 1977. Another view of time and the railroader. *Anthropological Quarterly* 50: 25–9.

Kennedy, J. S. 1992. *The new anthropomorphism.* Cambridge: Cambridge University Press.

Klee, P. 1961. *Notebooks, Volume 1: the thinking eye.* London: Lund Humphries.

Kluckhohn, C. 1949. *Mirror for man.* New York: McGraw Hill.

Knight, J. 1998. The second life of trees: family forestry in upland Japan. In *The social life of trees: anthropological perspectives on tree symbolism*, ed. L. Rival. Oxford: Berg, pp. 197–218.

Kroeber, A. L. 1948. *Anthropology* (revised edition). New York: Harcourt Brace Jovanovich.

—— 1952 [1917]. *The nature of culture.* Chicago: University of Chicago Press.

Kroeber, A. L. and C. Kluckhohn 1952. *Culture: a critical review of concepts and definitions*. Papers of the Peabody Museum of American Archaeology and Ethnology, Harvard University, vol. XLVII, no. 1. Cambridge, Mass.

Kubler, G. 1962. *The shape of time: remarks on the history of things*. New Haven, Conn.: Yale University Press.

Kwon, H. 1998. The saddle and the sledge: hunting as comparative narrative in Siberia and beyond. *Journal of the Royal Anthropological Institute* (N.S.)4: 115–27.

Lakoff, G. and M. Johnson 1980. *Metaphors we live by*. Chicago: University of Chicago Press.

Lane, P. J. 1998. Indigenous or autochthonous? Establishing a role for archaeology in the negotiation of Basarwa identity. In *Indigenous peoples in modern nation-states*, ed. S. Saugestad. University of Tromso, Faculty of Social Science, Occasional Papers Series A, 90.

Langer, S. K. 1953. *Feeling and form: a theory of art*. London: Routledge and Kegan Paul.

—— 1957. *Philosophy in a new key*. Cambridge, Mass.: Harvard University Press.

Latash, M. 1996. The Bernstein problem: how does the central nervous system make its choices? In *Dexterity and its development*, eds M. Latash and M. T. Turvey, pp. 277–303. Mahwah, NJ: Lawrence Erlbaum Associates.

Latour, B. 1993. *We have never been modern*, trans. C. Porter. New York: Harvester Wheatsheaf.

Lave, J. 1988. *Cognition in practice*. Cambridge: Cambridge University Press.

—— 1990. The culture of acquisition and the practice of understanding. In *Cultural psychology: essays on comparative human development*, eds J. W. Stigler, R. A. Shweder and G. Herdt. Cambridge: Cambridge University Press, pp. 309–27.

Lawrence, D. L. and S. M. Low 1990. The built environment and spatial form. *Annual Review of Anthropology* 19: 453–505.

Lawrence, R. J. 1987. What makes a house a home? *Environment and Behavior* 19: 154–68.

Layton, E. T. 1974. Technology as knowledge. *Technology and culture* 15: 31–41.

Layton, R. 1985. The cultural context of hunter-gatherer rock art. *Man* (N.S.) 20: 434–53.

—— 1992a. Traditional and contemporary art of Aboriginal Australia: two case studies. In *Anthropology, art and aesthetics*, eds J. Coote and A. Shelton. Oxford: Clarendon Press, pp. 137–59.

—— 1992b. *Australian rock art: a new synthesis*. Cambridge: Cambridge University Press.

Leach, E. R. 1954. *Political systems of highland Burma*. London: Athlone.

—— 1964. Anthropological aspects of language: animal categories and verbal abuse. In *New directions in the study of language*, ed. E. H. Lennenberg. Cambridge, Mass.: MIT Press, pp. 23–63.

—— 1966. Ritualization in man. *Philosophical Transactions of the Royal Society of London*, Series B, vol. 251: 403–8.

—— 1976. *Culture and communication: the logic by which symbols are connected*. Cambridge: Cambridge University Press.

Leach, J. 1997. *The creative land: kinship and landscape in Madang Province, Papua New Guinea*. Unpublished doctoral dissertation, University of Manchester.

Leakey, M. D. 1971. *Olduvai Gorge*, vol. 3. Cambridge: Cambridge University Press.

Lemonnier, P. 1986. The study of material culture today: towards an anthropology of technical systems. *Journal of Anthropological Archaeology* 5: 147–86.

Leroi-Gourhan, A. 1993. *Gesture and Speech*, trans. A. Bostock Berger, intr. R. White. Cambridge, Mass. and London: MIT Press.

Lestel, D. 1998. How chimpanzees have domesticated humans: towards an anthropology of human–animal communication. *Anthropology Today* 14(3): 12–15.

Levin, D. M. 1988. *The opening of vision: nihilism and the postmodern situation*. London: Routledge.

—— 1993. Introduction. In *Modernity and the hegemony of vision*, ed. D. M. Levin. Berkeley, Calif: University of California Press, pp. 1–29.

Lévi-Strauss, C. 1964. *Totemism*, trans. R. Needham. London: Merlin Press.

—— 1966a. Overture to 'Le cru et le cuit'. *Yale French Studies* 36/7: 41–65.

—— 1966b. *The savage mind*. London: Weidenfeld & Nicolson.

—— 1974. Structuralism and ecology. *Social Science Information* 12(1): 7–23.

—— 1983. *The way of the masks*, trans. S. Modelski. London: Jonathan Cape.

Lewis, G. M. 1993. Metrics, geometries, signs, and language: sources of cartographic miscommunication between native and Euro-American cultures in North America. *Cartographica* 30: 98–106.

Lewontin, R. C. 1982. Organism and environment. In *Learning, development and culture*, ed. H. C. Plotkin. Chichester: Wiley, pp. 151–70.

—— 1983. Gene, organism and environment. In *Evolution from molecules to men*, ed. D. S. Bendall. Cambridge: Cambridge University Press.

—— 1992. The dream of the human genome. *The New York Review*, May 28th 1992, pp. 31–40.

Lieberman, P. 1985. Comment on S. T. Parker, 'A socio-technical model for the evolution of language'. *Current Anthropology* 26: 628.

Linton, A. 1955. Preface. In R. Linton, *The tree of culture*. New York: Knopf, pp. v-viii.

Lock, A. J. 1980. *The guided reinvention of language*. London: Academic Press.

Lovejoy, C. O. 1988. Evolution of human walking. *Scientific American* 259: 82–9.

Lovelock, J. E. 1979. *Gaia: a new look at life on earth*. Oxford: Oxford University Press.

Lowenthal, D. 1978. Finding valued landscapes. *Progress in Human Geography* 2: 373–418.

—— 1996. The past is a foreign country: for the motion (1). In *Key debates in anthropology*, ed. T. Ingold. London: Routledge, pp. 206–12.

Lubbock, J. 1865. *Prehistoric times as illustrated by ancient remains and the manners and customs of modern savages*. London: Williams and Norgate.

Luhmann, N. 1979. *Trust and power*. Chichester: Wiley.

Luhmann, N. 1988. Familiarity, confidence, trust: problems and alternatives. In *Trust: making and breaking co-operative relations*, ed. D. Gambetta. Oxford: Blackwell, pp. 94–107.

Lye, T.-P. 1997. *Knowledge, forest, and hunter-gatherer movement: the Batek of Pahang, Malaysia*. Unpublished doctoral dissertation, University of Hawai'i.

Lyons, J. 1981. *Language and linguistics: an introduction*. Cambridge: Cambridge University Press.

MacArthur, R. H. and E. R. Pianka 1966. On optimal use of a patchy environment. *American Naturalist* 100: 603–9.

MacCormack, C. 1980. Nature, culture and gender: a critique. In *Nature, culture and gender*, eds C. MacCormack and M. Strathern. Cambridge: Cambridge University Press.

MacKenzie, D. 1984. Marx and the machine. *Technology and Culture* 25: 473–502.

MacKenzie, M. 1991. *Androgynous objects: string bags and gender in central New Guinea*. Chur: Harwood Academic.

Malinowski, B. 1922. *Argonauts of the Western Pacific*. London: Routledge & Kegan Paul.

Margolis, J. 1978. Culture and technology. *Research in Philosophy and Technology* 1: 23–37.

Marshall, L. 1961. Sharing, talking and giving: relief of social tensions among !Kung Bushmen. *Africa* 31: 231–49.

Marx, K. 1930 [1867]. *Capital*, vol. I, trans. E. and C. Paul from 4th German edition of *Das Kapital* (1890). London: Dent.

—— 1963 [1869]. *Eighteenth Brumaire of Louis Bonaparte*. New York: International Publishers.

—— 1964. *Pre-capitalist economic formations*, trans. J. Cohen, ed. E. J. Hobsbawm. London: Lawrence and Wishart.

—— 1964. *The economic and political manuscripts of 1884*, trans. M. Milligan, ed. D. J. Struik. New York: International Publishers.

—— 1970 [1859]. *A contribution to the critique of political economy*. Moscow: Progress.

—— 1973. *Grundrisse*, trans. M. Nicolaus. Harmondsworth: Penguin.

Mauss, M. 1954 [1925]. *The gift*, trans. I. Cunnison. London: Routledge & Kegan Paul.

—— 1979. *Sociology and psychology: essays*. London: Routledge & Kegan Paul.

—— 1985. A category of the human mind: the notion of person; the notion of self, trans. W. D. Halls. In *The category of the person: anthropology, philosophy, history*, eds M. Carruthers, S. Collins and S. Lukes. Cambridge: Cambridge University Press, pp. 1–25.

—— 1990 [1950] *The gift*, trans. W. D. Halls. London: Routledge.

Mauss, M. and H. Beuchat 1979. *Seasonal variations of the Eskimo*, trans. James J. Fox. London: Routledge & Kegan Paul (first published, 1904–5).

Mayr, E. 1976 [1961]. Cause and effect in biology. In *Evolution and the diversity of life: selected essays*. Cambridge, Mass.: Belknap Press of Harvard University Press, pp. 359–71.

McGinn, R. E. 1978. What is technology? *Research in Philosophy and Technology* 1: 179–97.

McGrew, W. C. 1992. *Chimpanzee material culture: implications for human evolution*. Cambridge: Cambridge University Press.

McLuhan, M. 1962. *The Gutenberg Galaxy: the making of typographic man*. Toronto: University of Toronto Press.

Mead, G. H. 1977 [1938]. The process of mind in nature. In *George Herbert Mead on Social Psychology*, ed. A. Strauss. Chicago: University of Chicago Press, pp. 85–111.

Mech, L. D. 1970. *The wolf*. Garden City: Natural History Press.

Medawar, P. 1967. *The art of the soluble*. London: Methuen.

Meggitt, M. J. 1962. *Desert people: a study of the Walbiri Aborigines of Central Australia.* Sydney: Angus & Robertson.

Mellaart, J. 1975. *The Neolithic of the Near East.* London: Thames and Hudson.

Meillassoux, C. 1972. From reproduction to production. *Economy and Society* 1: 93–105.

Meinig, D. W. 1979a. The beholding eye: ten versions of the same scene. In *The interpretation of ordinary landscapes*, ed. D. W. Meinig. Oxford: Oxford University Press, pp. 33–48.

—— 1979b. Introduction. In *The interpretation of ordinary landscapes*, ed. D. W. Meinig. Oxford: Oxford University Press, pp. 1–7.

Merleau-Ponty, M. 1962. *Phenomenology of perception*, trans. C. Smith. London: Routledge & Kegan Paul.

—— 1964a. Eye and mind, trans. C. Dallery. In *The primacy of perception, and other essays on phenomenological psychology, the philosophy of art, history and politics*, ed. J. M. Edie. Evanston, Ill.: Northwestern University Press, pp. 159–90.

—— 1964b. The child's relations with others, trans. W. Cobb. In *The primacy of perception, and other essays on phenomenological psychology, the philosophy of art, history and politics*, ed. J. M. Edie. Evanston, Ill: Northwestern University Press, pp. 96–155.

Merrill, R. S. 1968. The study of technology. In *International encyclopaedia of the social sciences*, ed. D. L. Sills. New York: Crowell Collier Macmillan, Vol. 15, pp. 576–89.

Michaels, C. F. and C. Carello 1981. *Direct perception.* Englewood Cliffs, NJ: Prentice-Hall.

Mitcham, C. 1978. Types of technology. *Research in Philosophy and Technology* 1: 229–94.

—— 1979. Philosophy and the history of technology. In *The history and philosophy of technology*, eds G. Bugliarello and D. B. Doner. Urbana: University of Illinois Press.

Molleson, T. 1994. The eloquent bones of Abu Hureyra. *Scientific American* 271: 60–65.

Monmonier, M. 1991. *How to lie with maps.* Chicago: University of Chicago Press.

Monod, J. 1972. *Chance and necessity*, trans. A. Wainhouse. London: Collins.

Morgan, L. H. 1868. *The American beaver and his works.* New York: Burt Franklin.

Morphy, H. 1991. *Ancestral connections: art and an Aboriginal system of knowledge.* Chicago: University of Chicago Press.

—— 1992. From dull to brilliant: the aesthetics of spiritual power among the Yolngu. In *Anthropology, art and aesthetics*, eds J. Coote and A. Shelton. Oxford: Clarendon Press, pp. 181–208.

Morris, B. 1995. Woodland and village: reflections on the 'animal estate' in rural Malawi. *Journal of the Royal Anthropological Institute* (N.S.) 1: 301–15.

Morton, J. 1995. The organic remains: remarks on the constitution and development of people. In *Persons, bodies, selves, emotions*, eds J. Morton and M. Macintyre. Special issue of *Social Analysis*, No. 37. Department of Anthropology, University of Adelaide, pp. 101–18.

Mumford, L. 1946. *Technics and civilization.* London: Routledge.

—— 1966. Technics and the nature of man. *Technology and Culture* 7: 303–17.

—— 1967. *The myth of the machine: technics and human development.* London: Secker and Warburg.

Munn, N. 1970. The transformation of subjects into objects in Walbiri and Pitjantjatjara myth. In *Australian Aboriginal anthropology: modern studies in the social anthropology of the Australian Aborigines*, ed. R. M. Berndt. Perth: University of Western Australia Press.

—— 1973a. The spatial presentation of cosmic order in Walbiri iconography. In *Primitive art and society*, ed. J. A. W. Forge. Oxford: Oxford University Press, pp. 193–220.

—— 1973b. *Walbiri iconography: graphic representation and cultural symbolism in a Central Australian society.* Ithaca, N.Y.: Cornell University Press.

Myers, F. R. 1986. *Pintupi country, Pintupi self: sentiment, place, and politics among Western Desert Aborigines.* Washington: Smithsonian Institution Press.

Myers, R. E. 1976. Comparative neurology of vocalization and speech: proof of a dichotomy. In *Origins and evolution of language and speech*, eds S. R. Harnad, H. D. Steklis and J. Lancaster. Annals of the New York Academy of Sciences, Vol. 280, pp. 745–57.

Nelson, E. W. 1983. *The Eskimo about Bering Strait.* Washington, D.C.: Smithsonian Institution Press. [Originally published as pp. 3–518 in the 18th Annual Report of the Bureau of American Ethnology, 1896–97, Washington, D.C.: Government Printing Office]

Nelson, R. K. 1983. *Make prayers to the raven: a Koyukon view of the northern forest.* Chicago, Ill: University of Chicago Press.

Nilsson, M. P. 1920. *Primitive time reckoning.* Oxford: Oxford University Press.

Norberg-Schulz, C. 1985. *The concept of dwelling: on the way to figurative architecture.* New York: Rizzoli International.

Oatley, K. G. 1977. Inference, navigation and cognitive maps. In *Thinking: readings in cognitive science*, eds P. N. Johnson-Laird and P. C. Wason. Cambridge: Cambridge University Press, pp. 537–47.

O'Brien, M. J. (ed.) 1996. *Evolutionary archaeology: theory and application*. Salt Lake City: University of Utah Press.

Olson, D. R. 1994. *The world on paper: the conceptual and cognitive implications of writing and reading*. Cambridge: Cambridge University Press.

Ong, W. 1982. *Orality and literacy: the technologizing of the word*. London: Methuen.

Oosten, J. 1992. Representing the spirits: the masks of the Alaskan Inuit. In *Anthropology, art and aesthetics*, eds J. Coote and A. Shelton. Oxford: Clarendon Press, pp. 113–34.

Orlove, B. 1993. The ethnography of maps: the cultural and social contexts of cartographic representation in Peru. *Cartographica* 30: 29–46.

Oswalt, W. H. 1976. *An anthropological analysis of food-getting technology*. New York: John Wiley.

Oyama, S. 1985. *The ontogeny of information: developmental systems and evolution*. Cambridge: Cambridge University Press.

——— 1989. Ontogeny and the central dogma: do we need the concept of genetic programming in order to have an evolutionary perspective? In *Systems in development: the Minnesota Symposia on child psychology*, Vol. 22, eds M. Gunnar and E. Thelen. Hillsdale, N.J.: Erlbaum.

Paine, R. 1991. The claim of aboriginality: Saami in Norway. In *The ecology of choice and symbol: essays in honour of Fredrik Barth*, eds R. Gronhaug, G. Haaland and G. Henriksen. Bergen: Alma Mater.

Pallasmaa, J. 1996. *The eyes of the skin: architecture and the senses*. London: Academy Editions.

Pálsson, G. 1991. *Coastal economies, cultural accounts: human ecology and Icelandic discourse*. Manchester: Manchester University Press.

——— 1994. Enskilment at sea. *Man* (N.S.) 29: 901–27.

Pandya, V. 1990. Movement and space: Andamanese cartography. *American Ethnologist* 17: 775–97.

Pearson, M. P. and C. Richards 1994. Ordering the world: perceptions of architecture, space and time. In *Architecture and order: approaches to social space*, eds M. P. Pearson and C. Richards. London: Routledge, pp. 1–37.

Pfaffenberger, B. 1988. Fetishised objects and humanised nature: towards an anthropology of technology. *Man* (N.S.)23: 236–52.

——— 1992. Social anthropology of technology. *Annual Review of Anthropology* 21: 491–516.

Pittendrigh, C. S. 1958. Adaptation, natural selection and behavior. In *Behavior and evolution*, eds A. Roe and G. G. Simpson. New Haven, Conn.: Yale University Press, pp. 390–416.

Plato 1973. *Phaedrus and Letters VII and VIII*, trans. W. Hamilton. Harmondsworth: Penguin.

Polanyi, K. 1957. The economy as an instituted process. In *Trade and markets in the early empires*, eds K. Polanyi, C. Arensberg and H. Pearson. Glencoe: The Free Press, pp. 243–70.

Poncelet, J-V. 1844. *Traité de mécanique industrielle*. Liége: A. Leroux.

Powell, M. A. 1981. Three problems in the history of cuneiform writing: origins, direction of the script, literacy. *Visible Language* 15: 419–40.

Premack, D. and A. J. Premack 1994. Why animals have neither culture nor history. In *Companion encyclopedia of anthropology: humanity, culture and social life*, ed. T. Ingold. London: Routledge, pp. 350–65.

Price, J. A. 1975. Sharing: the integration of intimate economies. *Anthropologica* 17: 3–27.

Putnam, W. C. 1964. *Geology*. New York: Oxford University Press.

Pye, D. 1964. *The nature of design*. London: Studio Vista.

——— 1968. *The nature and art of workmanship*. Cambridge: Cambridge University Press.

Quinn, N. and D. Holland 1987. Culture and cognition. In *Cultural models in language and thought*, eds D. Holland and N. Quinn. Cambridge: Cambridge University Press, pp. 3–40.

Rapoport, A. 1994. Spatial organisation and the built environment. In *Companion encyclopedia of anthropology: humanity, culture and social life*, ed. T. Ingold. London: Routledge, pp. 460–502.

Rappaport, R. A. 1968. *Pigs for the ancestors*. New Haven: Yale University Press.

Ray, D. J. 1967. *Eskimo masks: art and ceremony* (with photographs by A. A. Blaker). Seattle: University of Washington Press.

Rayner, A. 1997. *Degrees of freedom: living in dynamic boundaries*. London: Imperial College Press.

Reason, D. 1987. A hard singing of country. In *The unpainted landscape*, with contributions by S. Cutts *et al.* London: Coracle Press, pp. 24–87.

Rée, J. 1999. *I see a voice: a philosophical history of language, deafness and the senses*. London: Harper Collins.

Reed, E. 1987. James Gibson's ecological approach to cognition. In *Cognitive psychology in question*, eds A. Costall and A. Still. Brighton: Harvester Press, pp. 142–73.

—— 1988a. The affordances of the animate environment: social science from the ecological point of view. In *What is an animal?*, ed. T. Ingold. London: Unwin Hyman, pp. 110–26.

—— 1988b. *James J. Gibson and the psychology of perception*. New Haven: Yale University Press.

Reed, E. S. and B. Bril 1996. The primacy of action in development. In *Dexterity and its development*, ed. M. Latash and M. T. Turvey. Mahwah, N.J.: Lawrence Erlbaum Associates, pp. 431–51.

Renfrew, C. 1992. Archaeology, genetics and linguistic diversity. *Man* (N.S.) 27: 445–78.

Renne, E. P. 1991. Water, spirits and plain white cloth. *Man* (N.S.) 26: 709–22.

Reuleaux, F. 1876. *The kinematics of machinery: outlines of a theory of machines*. London: Macmillan.

Reynolds, P. C. 1993. The complementation theory of language and tool use. In *Tools, language and cognition in human evolution*, eds K. R. Gibson and T. Ingold. Cambridge: Cambridge University Press, pp. 407–28.

Richards, P. 1974. Kant's geography and mental maps. *Transactions of the Institute of British Geographers* (N.S.) 11: 1–16.

—— 1996. Human worlds are culturally constructed: against the motion (2). In *Key debates in anthropology*, ed. T. Ingold. London: Routledge.

Richerson, P. J. and R. Boyd 1978. A dual inheritance model of the human evolutionary process, I: Basic postulates and a simple model. *Journal of Social and Biological Structures* 1: 127–54.

—— 1992. Cultural inheritance and evolutionary ecology. In *Evolutionary ecology and human behavior*, eds E. A. Smith and B. Winterhalder. New York: Aldine de Gruyter, pp. 61–92.

Ridington, R. 1982. Technology, world view and adaptive strategy in a northern hunting society. *Canadian Review of Sociology and Anthropology* 19: 469–81.

Rival, L. 1993. The growth of family trees: understanding Huaorani perceptions of the forest. *Man* (N.S.) 28: 635–52.

—— (ed.) 1998. *The social life of trees: anthropological perspectives on tree symbolism*. Oxford: Berg.

Robarchek, C. A. 1989. Hobbesian and Rousseauan images of man: autonomy and individualism in a peaceful society. In *Societies at peace: anthropological perspectives*, eds S. Howell and R. Willis. London: Routledge, pp. 31–44.

Robinson, A. H. and B. B. Petchenik 1976. *The nature of maps: essays towards understanding maps and mapping*. Chicago: University of Chicago Press.

Rodaway, P. 1994. *Sensuous geographies: body, sense and place*. London: Routledge.

Romanyshyn, R. D. 1989. *Technology as symptom and dream*. London: Routledge.

Ronchi, V. 1957. *Optics: the science of vision*, trans. E. Rosen. New York: Dover.

Rooley, A. 1990. *Performance: revealing the Orpheus within*. Shaftesbury, Dorset: Element Books.

Rorty, R. 1980. *Philosophy and the mirror of nature*. Oxford: Blackwell.

Rouse, J. 1987. *Knowledge and power: toward a political philosophy of science*. Ithaca, N.Y.: Cornell University Press.

Rousselot, J.-L., W. W. Fitzhugh and A. Crowell 1988. Maritime economies of the North Pacific rim. In *Crossroads of continents: cultures of Siberia and Alaska*, eds. W. W. Fitzhugh and A. Crowell. Washington, D.C.: Smithsonian Institution Press, pp. 151–72.

Rowley-Conwy, P. 1998. The origins and spread of agriculture and pastoralism – are the grey horses dead? *International Journal of Osteoarchaeology* 8: 218–24.

Rubin, D. 1988. Go for the skill. In *Remembering reconsidered: ecological and traditional approaches to the study of memory*, eds U. Neisser and E. Winograd. Cambridge: Cambridge University Press, pp. 374–82.

Rundstrom, R. A. 1990. A cultural interpretation of Inuit map accuracy. *Geographical Review* 80: 155–68.

—— 1993. The role of ethics, mapping, and the meaning of place in relations between Indians and Whites in the United States. *Cartographica* 30: 21–8.

Rykwert, J. 1972. *On Adam's House in Paradise: the idea of the primitive hut in architectural history*. New York: Museum of Modern Art.

—— 1991. House and home. *Social Research* 58: 51–62.

Sacks, O. 1993. To see and not to see. *The New Yorker*, May 10, 1993: 59–73.

Sahlins, M. D. 1968. *Tribesmen*. Englewood Cliffs, NJ: Prentice Hall.

—— 1969. Economic anthropology and anthropological economics. *Social Science Information* 8: 13–33.

—— 1972. *Stone age economics*. London: Tavistock.

—— 1976. *Culture and practical reason*. Chicago: University of Chicago Press.

Saladin d'Anglure, B. 1979. *Inuit and caribou* (Inuit texts and illustrations concerning caribou, collected by B. Saladin d'Anglure). Inuksiutiit Allaniagait 2, Association Inuksiutiit Katimajiit, Département d'Anthropologie, Université Laval, Quebec, Canada.

—— 1990. Nanook, super-male: the polar bear in the imaginary space and social time of the Inuit of the Canadian Arctic. In *Signifying animals: human meaning in the natural world*, ed. R. Wills. London: Unwin Hyman, pp. 178–95.

Sampson, G. 1985. *Writing systems: a linguistic introduction.* London: Hutchinson.

Saugestad, S. 1998. *The inconvenient indigenous: remote area development in Botswana, donor assistance, and the First People of the Kalahari.* University of Tromsø, Faculty of Social Sciences.

Saussure, F. de 1959. *Course in general linguistics*, eds C. Bally and A. Sechehaye, trans. W. Baskin. New York: The Philosophical Library.

Savage-Rumbaugh, E. S. and D. M. Rumbaugh 1993. The emergence of language. In *Tools, language and cognition in human evolution*, eds K. R. Gibson and T. Ingold. Cambridge: Cambridge University Press.

Schafer, R. M. 1985. Acoustic space. In *Dwelling, place and environment*, eds D. Seamon and R. Mugerauer. New York: Columbia University Press, pp. 87–98.

Schneider, D. M. 1968. *American kinship: a cultural account.* Chicago: University of Chicago Press.

Schneider, H. K. 1974. *Economic Man.* New York: Free Press.

Schutz, A. 1951. Making music together: a study in social relationship. *Social Research* 18: 76–97.

—— 1970. *On phenomenology and social relations*, ed. H. R. Wagner. Chicago: University of Chicago Press.

Scott, C. 1989. Knowledge construction among Cree hunters: metaphors and literal understanding. *Journal de la Société des Américanistes* 75: 193–208.

—— 1996. Science for the West, myth for the rest? The case of James Bay Cree knowledge construction. In *Naked science: anthropological inquiry into boundaries, power, and knowledge*, ed. L. Nader. London: Routledge.

Seeger, A. 1975. The meaning of body ornaments: a Suya example. *Ethnology* 14: 211–24.

—— 1987. *Why Suyá sing: a musical anthropology of an Amazonian people.* Cambridge: Cambridge University Press.

Seremetakis, C. N. 1994. Implications. In *The senses still: perception and memory as material culture in modernity.* Boulder, Colo.: Westview Press, pp. 123–45.

Shaw, W. H. 1979. 'The handmill gives you the feudal lord': Marx's technological determinism. *History and Theory* 18: 155–76.

Shore, B. 1996. *Culture in mind: cognition, culture and the problem of meaning.* New York: Oxford University Press.

Shotter, J. 1974 The development of personal powers. In *The integration of the child into a social world*, ed. M. P. M. Richards. Cambridge: Cambridge University Press.

—— 1991. A poetics of relational forms: the sociality of everyday social life. *Cultural Dynamics* 4: 379–96.

Shweder, R. 1990. Cultural psychology – what is it? In *Cultural psychology: essays on comparative human development*, eds J. W. Stigler, R. A. Shweder and G. Herdt. Cambridge: Cambridge University Press.

Sigaut, F. 1985. More (and enough!) on technology. *History and Technology* 2: 115–32.

—— 1993. How can we analyse and describe technical actions? In *The use of tools by humans and non-human primates*, eds A. Berthelet and J. Chavaillon. Oxford: Clarendon Press, pp. 381–97.

—— 1994. Technology. In *Companion encyclopedia of anthropology: humanity, culture and social life*, ed. T. Ingold. London: Routledge.

Singer, C., E. J. Holmyard and A. R. Hall (eds) 1954–58. *A history of technology.* Oxford: Clarendon.

Smith, D. M. 1998. An Athapaskan way of knowing: Chipewyan ontology. *American Ethnologist* 25: 412–32.

Smith, E. A. and B. Winterhalder 1992. Natural selection and decision making: some fundamental principles. In *Evolutionary ecology and human behavior*, eds E. A. Smith and B. Winterhalder. New York: Aldine de Gruyter, pp. 25–60.

Smith, E. Baldwin 1950. *The dome: a study in the history of ideas.* Princeton, N.J.: Princeton University Press.

Sorokin, P. A. and R. K. Merton 1937. Social time: a methodological and functional analysis. *American Journal of Sociology* 42: 615–29.

Sperber, D. 1985. *On anthropological knowledge.* Cambridge: Cambridge University Press.

—— 1996. *Explaining culture: a naturalistic approach.* Oxford: Blackwell.

Stanner, W. E. H. 1965. The dreaming. In *Reader in comparative religion*, eds W. A. Lessa and E. Z. Vogt. New York: Harper & Row.

Starkey, K. 1988. Time and work organisation: a theoretical and empirical analysis. In *The rhythms of society*, eds M. Young and T. Schuller. London: Routledge.

Steinberg, J. H. 1981. Saulteaux of Lake Winnipeg. In *Handbook of North American Indians, Vol. 6, Subarctic*, ed. J. Helm, pp. 244–55. Washington, D.C.: Smithsonian Institution.

Stewart, H. n.d. Ethnonyms and images: genesis of the 'Inuit' and image manipulation. Unpublished paper, presented at the Eighth International Conference on Hunting and Gathering Societies, Osaka, Japan, October 1998.

Stoller, P. 1989. *The taste of ethnographic things: the senses in anthropology*. Philadelphia: University of Pennsylvania Press.

Strathern, A. and M. Strathern 1971. *Self-decoration in Mount Hagen*, London: Duckworth.

Strathern, M. 1980. No nature, no culture: the Hagen case. In *Nature, culture and gender*, eds C. MacCormack and M. Strathern. Cambridge: Cambridge University Press.

Strauss, C. 1992. Models and motives. In *Human motives and cultural models*, eds R. G. D'Andrade and C. Strauss. Cambridge: Cambridge University Press, pp. 1–20.

Stravinsky, I. 1936. *An autobiography*. New York: Simon and Schuster.

Street, B. V. 1975. *The savage in the literature: representations of 'primitive' society in English fiction, 1858–1920*. London: Routledge & Kegan Paul.

—— 1984. *Literacy in theory and practice*. Cambridge: Cambridge University Press.

Suchman, L. 1987. *Plans and situated actions: the problem of human–machine communication*. Cambridge: Cambridge University Press.

Sullivan, T. and D. Gill 1975. *If you could see what I hear*. New York: Harper & Row,

Symons, D. 1992. On the use and misuse of Darwinism in the study of human behavior. In *The adapted mind: evolutionary psychology and the generation of culture*, eds J. H. Barkow, L. Cosmides and J. Tooby. New York: Oxford University Press, pp. 137–59.

Synnott, A. 1993. *The body social: symbolism, self and society*. London: Routledge.

Tani, Y. 1996. Domestic animal as serf: ideologies of nature in the Mediterranean and the Middle East. In *Redefining nature: ecology, culture and domestication*, eds R. Ellen and K. Fukui. Oxford: Berg, pp. 387–415.

Tanner, A. 1979. *Bringing home animals: religious ideology and mode of production of the Mistassini Cree hunters*. New York: St Martin's Press; London: Hurst.

Tapper, R. 1988. Animality, humanity, morality, society. In *What is an animal?*, ed. T Ingold. London: Unwin Hyman, pp. 47–62.

Taylor, L. 1989. Seeing the 'inside': Kunwinjku paintings and the symbol of the divided body. In *Animals into art*, ed. H. Morphy. London: Unwin Hyman, pp. 371–89.

—— 1996. *Seeing the inside: bark painting in Western Arnhem Land*. Oxford: Clarendon Press.

Tedlock, B. and D. Tedlock 1985. Text and textile: language and technology in the arts of the Quiché Maya. *Journal of Anthropological Research* 41: 121–46.

Thelen, E. 1995. Motor development: a new synthesis. *American Psychologist* 50: 79–95.

Thomas, W. L., C. O. Sauer, M. Bates and L. Mumford (eds) 1956. *Man's role in changing the face of the earth*. Chicago: University of Chicago Press.

Thompson, D. W. 1961. *On growth and form*, abridged edition, ed. J. T. Bonner. Cambridge: Cambridge University Press (original 1917).

Thompson, E. P. 1967. Time, work-discipline and industrial capitalism. *Past and Present* 38: 56–97.

Tolman, E. C. 1948. Cognitive maps in mice and men. *The Psychological Review* 55: 189–208.

Tolman, E. C., B. F. Ritchie and D. Kalish 1946. Studies in spatial learning, I: Orientation and the short-cut. *Journal of Experimental Psychology* 36.

Tooby, J and L. Cosmides 1992. The psychological foundations of culture. In *The adapted mind: evolutionary psychology and the generation of culture*, eds J. H. Barkow, L. Cosmides and J. Tooby. New York: Oxford University Press, pp. 19–136.

Toulmin, S. 1981. Human adaptation. In *The Philosophy of Evolution*, eds U. Jensen and R. Harré. Brighton: Harvester Press, pp. 176–95.

Trevarthen, C. and K. Logotheti 1989. Child in society, society in children: the nature of basic trust. In *Societies at peace*, eds S. Howell and R. Willis. London: Routledge.

Tuan, Y-F. 1979. Thought and landscape: the eye and the mind's eye. In *The interpretation of ordinary landscapes*, ed. D. W. Meinig. Oxford: Oxford University Press, pp. 89–102.

Turnbull, C. M. 1965. *Wayward servants: the two worlds of the African Pygmies*. London: Eyre & Spottiswoode.

—— 1978. The politics of non-aggression (Zaire). In *Learning non-aggression: the experience of non-literate societies*, ed. A. Montagu. Oxford: Oxford University Press.

Turnbull, D. 1989. *Maps are territories: science is an atlas*. Geelong: Deakin University Press.

—— 1991. *Mapping the world in the mind: an investigation of the unwritten knowledge of Micronesian navigators*. Geelong: Deakin University Press.

—— 1993a. Local knowledge and comparative scientific traditions. *Knowledge and Policy* 6: 29–54.

—— 1993b. The ad hoc collective work of building Gothic cathedrals with templates, string and geometry. *Science, Technology and Human Values* 18: 315–40.

—— 1996. Constructing knowledge spaces and locating sites of resistance in the modern cartographic transformation. In *Social cartography: mapping ways of seeing social and educational change*, ed. R. G. Paulston. New York: Garland, pp. 53–79.

Turner, L. M. 1979. *Ethnology of the Ungava Distrist, Hudson Bay Territory: Indians and Eskimos in the Quebec-Labrador Peninsula*. Québec, Canada: Presses Coméditex. [Originally published as pp. 165–350 in the 11th Annual Report of the Bureau of American Ethnology, 1889–90, Washington, D.C.: Government Printing Office]

Tyler, S. A. 1969. Introduction. In *Cognitive anthropology*, ed. S. A. Tyler. New York: Holt, Rinehart and Winston, pp. 1–23.

Tylor, E. B. 1871. *Primitive culture*. London: John Murray.

Tyrrell, J. 1994. *Intimate letters: Leoš Janáček to Kamila Stösslová*, ed. and trans. J. Tyrrell. London: Faber & Faber.

Uexküll, J. von 1957. A stroll through the worlds of animals and men: a picture book of invisible worlds. In *Instinctive behavior: the development of a modern concept*, ed. C. H. Schiller. New York: International Universities Press.

United Nations 1997. *The rights of indigenous peoples* (Human Rights Fact Sheet 9). New York and Geneva: United Nations.

van Beek, W. E. A. and P. M. Banga 1992. The Dogon and their trees. In *Bush base: forest farm. Culture, environment and development*, eds E. Croll and D. Parkin. London: Routledge.

Varela, F. J., E. Thompson and E. Rosch 1991. *The embodied mind: cognitive science and human experience*. Cambridge, Mass.: MIT Press.

Vernant, J. P. 1983. *Myth and thought among the Greeks*. London: Routledge & Kegan Paul.

Vico, G. 1948 [1744]. *The New Science of Giambattista Vico*, ed. and trans. T. G. Bergin and M. H. Fisch. Ithaca, N.Y.: Cornell University Press.

Viollet-le-Duc, E. 1990. *The architectural theory of Viollet-le-Duc: readings and commentary*, ed. M. F. Hearn. Cambridge, Mass.: MIT Press.

Viveiros de Castro, E. 1998. Cosmological deixis and Amerindian perspectivism. *Journal of the Royal Anthropological Institute* (N.S.)4: 469–88.

Vološinov, V. N. 1973. *Marxism and the philosophy of language*, trans. L. Matejka and I. R. Titunik. Cambridge, Mass.: Harvard University Press.

von Bertalanffy, L. 1955. An essay on the relativity of categories. *Philosophy of Science* 22: 243–63.

Wadel, C. 1979. The hidden work of everyday life. In *Social anthropology of work*, ed. S. Wallman (ASA Monograph 19). London: Tavistock.

Wagner, R. 1986. *Symbols that stand for themselves*. Chicago: University of Chicago Press.

Walter, E. V. 1969. *Terror and resistance*. New York: Oxford University Press.

Weber, M. 1947. *The theory of social and economic organization*, trans. A. M. Henderson, ed. T. Parsons. New York: Oxford University Press.

Weiner, J. F. 1991. *The empty place: poetry, space and being among the Foi of Papua New Guinea*. Bloomington: Indiana University Press.

White, L. A. 1959. *The evolution of culture*. New York: McGraw Hill.

White, L. Jr. 1962. *Medieval technology and social change*. Oxford: Clarendon.

Whitehead, A. N. 1929. *Process and reality: an essay in cosmology*. Cambridge: Cambridge University Press.

Whitehead, A. N. 1938. *Science and the modern world*. Harmondsworth: Penguin.

Whitehouse, H. 1996. Jungles and computers: neuronal group selection and the epidemiology of representations. *Journal of the Royal Anthropological Institute* (N.S.) 2: 99–116.

Widlok, T. 1997. Orientation in the wild: the shared cognition of the Hai|om Bushpeople. *Journal of the Royal Anthropological Institute* (N.S.) 3: 317–22.

Wikan, U. 1992. Beyond words: the power of resonance. *American Ethnologist* 19: 460–82.

Williams, N. M. and E. S. Hunn (eds) 1982. *Resource managers: North American and Australian hunter-gatherers*. Boulder, Colo.: Westview Press.

Williams, R. 1972. Ideas of nature. In *Ecology, the shaping enquiry*, ed. J. Benthall. London: Longman.

—— 1976. *Keywords*. London: Fontana.

Willis, R. 1990. Introduction. In *Signifying animals: human meaning in the natural world*, ed. R. Willis. London: Unwin Hyman.

Wilson, P. J. 1988. *The domestication of the human species*. New Haven: Yale University Press.

Winner, L. 1977. *Autonomous technology: technics-out-of-control as a theme in political thought*. Cambridge, Mass.: MIT Press.

Winterhalder, B. 1981a. Foraging strategies in the boreal forest: an analysis of Cree hunting and gathering. In *Hunter-gatherer foraging strategies: ethnographic and archeological analyses*, eds B. Winterhalder and E. A. Smith. Chicago: University of Chicago Press, pp. 66–98.

—— 1981b. Optimal foraging strategies and hunter-gatherer research in anthropology: theory and models. In *Hunter-gatherer foraging strategies: ethnographic and archeological analyses*, eds B. Winterhalder and E. A. Smith. Chicago: University of Chicago Press, pp. 13–35.

Winterhalder, B. and E. A. Smith 1981. Preface. In *Hunter-gatherer foraging strategies: ethnographic and archeological analyses*, eds B. Winterhalder and E. A. Smith. Chicago: University of Chicago Press.

—— 1992. Evolutionary ecology and the social sciences. In *Evolutionary ecology and human behavior*, eds E. A. Smith and B. Winterhalder. New York: Aldine de Gruyter, pp. 3–23.

Wittgenstein, L. 1953. *Philosophical investigations*. Oxford: Blackwell.

Wolf, E. 1988. Inventing society. *American Ethnologist* 15: 752–61.

—— 1994. Perilous ideas: race, culture, people. *Current Anthropology* 35: 1–12.

Wood, D. 1992. *The power of maps*. New York: Guilford Press.

—— 1993a. The fine line between mapping and mapmaking. *Cartographica* 30: 50–60.

—— 1993b. What makes a map a map? *Cartographica* 30: 81–6.

Woodburn, J. 1980. Hunters and gatherers today and reconstruction of the past. In *Soviet and Western anthropology*, ed. E Gellner. London: Duckworth.

—— 1982. Egalitarian societies. *Man* (N.S.) 17: 431–51.

—— 1988. African hunter-gatherer social organisation: is it best understood as a product of encapsulation? In *Hunters and gatherers, I: history, evolution and social change*, eds T. Ingold, D. Riches and J. Woodburn. Oxford: Berg, pp. 31–64.

Wright, D. 1990. *Deafness: a personal account*, new edition. London: Faber and Faber.

Wub-e-ke-niew 1995. *We have the right to exist*. New York City: Black Thistle Press.

Wynn, T. 1993. Layers of thinking in tool behaviour. In *Tools, language and cognition in human evolution*, eds K. R. Gibson and T. Ingold. Cambridge: Cambridge University Press, pp. 389–406.

—— 1994. Tools and tool behaviour. In *Companion encyclopedia of anthropology: humanity, culture and social life*, ed. T. Ingold. London: Routledge, pp. 133–61.

Young, M. 1988. *The metronomic society: natural rhythms and human timetables*. London: Thames and Hudson.

Zuckerkandl, V. 1956. *Sound and symbol: music and the external world*, trans. W. R. Trask. Bollingen Series XLIV. Princeton, N.J.: Princeton University Press.

Zukow-Goldring, P. 1997. A social ecological realist approach to the emergence of the lexicon: educating attention to amodal invariants in gesture and speech. In *Evolving explanations of development: ecological approaches to organism-environment systems*, eds C. Dent-Read and P. Zukow-Goldring. Washington, D.C.: American Psychological Association.

Index